CULTURAL COMMUNICATION
AND INTERCULTURAL CONTACT

COMMUNICATION TEXTBOOK SERIES

Jennings Bryant — *Editor*

Intercultural Communication
W. Barnett Pearce — *Advisor*

CARBAUGH • Cultural Communication
and Intercultural Contact

CULTURAL COMMUNICATION AND INTERCULTURAL CONTACT

edited by
Donal Carbaugh
University of Massachusetts

LEA LAWRENCE ERLBAUM ASSOCIATES, PUBLISHERS
1990 Hillsdale, New Jersey   Hove and London

Lawrence Erlbaum Associates, Inc., Publishers
365 Broadway
Hillsdale, New Jersey 07642

Library of Congress Cataloging-in-Publication Data

Cultural communication and intercultural contact / edited by Donal
     Carbaugh
          p.   cm. -- (Communication textbook series. Intercultural
     communication)
     Includes bibliographical references (p.).
     ISBN 0-8058-0167-7. --ISBN 0-8058-0727-6 (pbk.)
     1. Communication and culture. 2. Intercultural communication.
     I. Carbaugh, Donal C. II. Series.
     P91.C85 1990
     306.4'4--dc20   89-29388
                                                              CIP

Printed in the United States of America
10 9 8 7 6 5 4 3

*For LuAnne,
Andrew, and Jonathan*

Contents

Acknowledgments

Several people are to be thanked for their assistance in preparing this book, especially the contributors who willingly and graciously offered their work, and if possible, wrote original epilogues to the pieces included here. Their high level of competence and generosity has made this project a delightful and rewarding one. Special thanks go to Gerry Philipsen whose support and scholarship has been seminal during the project, and similarly to Dell Hymes who agreed to "stand in" for the late Michelle Rosaldo and contribute an epilogue to her piece which is included in the third section of this book. I wish also to thank Jules Chametzky of the Institute for Advanced Study in the Humanities at the University of Massachusetts for providing the opportunity of a Junior Fellowship. The Fellowship enabled me to pursue a focused and intensive study of the chapters and ideas included here. As a part of the fellowship, a small faculty seminar convened on the topic, "cultural codes in communication," and as a result, I benefited from lively and pointed discussions with Ian Angus, Vernon Cronen, Jeffrey Eisemann, Denny Salzmann, and Linda Smith. Bill Gudykunst and Stella Ting-Toomey hosted a small conference at Arizona State University in April 1988 on Culture and Communication Theory, and were kind enough to include me. For the opportunity I thank them, and the other participants, Mary Jane Collier, Vern Cronen, Michael Hecht, Nemi Jain, Young Y. Kim, Felipe Korzenny, Gerry Philipsen, and John Wiemann. Just as rewarding is a kind of continuing communal conversation with others who share these interests, and for which I thank: Pua Aiu, Charles Braithwaite, Victoria Chen, James Cumming, Kristine Fitch, Brad Hall, Sally O. Hastings, Mike Huspek, Tamar Katriel, Myoung-Hye Kim, Gerry Philipsen, and George Ray. Similarly, the "Stockbridge circle" — Vern Cronen, Don Ellis, Barnett Pearce, Bob Sanders, and Stuart Sigman — has afforded continuing intellectual stimulation and challenges. To W. Barnett Pearce I owe a special thanks for encouraging this project early on, when it seemed a remote possibility, and for his continuing support and reactions I am indebted. I am thankful also to my colleagues and students at Amherst who heard, read and/or reacted to some of the readings included here. Special mention in this regard goes to Marissa Richardson of the University of New Hampshire. Debra Madigan, Elaine Stockwell, and April Tidlund kindly typed and retyped diagrams and manuscripts, responding more often than duty should rightfully call. Hollis Heimbouch, Robin Marks Weisberg, Art Lizza, and the staff at Lawrence Erlbaum Associates have helped immeasurably with the production process. To all I extend my fondest thanks. But most of all, I thank LuAnne for her unending support, encouragement, and understanding, and Andrew and Jonathan, twin pleasures, for deepening my senses of continuity, connectedness and commonality.

Donal Carbaugh

Some of the following chapters are reprints with permissions kindly granted as follows: Chapter one, Gerry Philipsen (1975), "Speaking like a man" in Teamsterville: Culture patterns of role enactment in an urban neighborhood, *Quarterly Journal of Speech, 61,* 13–22; Chapter three, Jack Daniel and Geneva Smitherman-Donaldson (1976), How I got over: Communication dynamics in the Black community, *Quarterly Journal of Speech, 62,* 26–39; and chapter seven, Tamar Katriel and Gerry Philipsen (1981), "What we need is communication": "Communication" as a cultural category in some American speech, *Communication Monographs, 48,* 301–317, all by the kind permission of the authors and the Speech Communication Association. Chapter nine, Tamar Katriel (1985), "Griping" as a verbal ritual in some Israeli discourse, in M. Dascal (Ed.), *Dialogue: An interdisciplinary approach* (pp. 367–381), Amsterdam: John J. Benjamins, by kind permission of the author and publisher. Chapter eleven, Donal Carbaugh (1987), Communication rules in *Donahue* discourse, *Research on Language and Social Interaction, 21,* 31–61, by permission of the author. Chapter 12, Kenneth Liberman (n.d.), Intercultural communication in central Australia, Sociolinguistic Working Paper number 104, in R. Bauman and J. Sherzer (Eds.), *Case studies in the ethnography of speaking,* Austin, TX: Southwest Eucational Development Laboratory, by kind permission of the author. Chapter 14, Thomas Kochman (1981), chapter eight from his *Black and White Styles in Conflict* (pp. 106–109), Chicago, IL: The University of Chicago Press, by kind permission of the author and publisher. Chapter 15, Thomas Kochman, selected excerpts from his Black and White cultural styles in pluralistic perspective, in B. Gifford (Ed.), *Education, Language, and Testing,* Boston, MA: Kluwer-Nijoff, by kind permission of the author. Chapter 16, Keith Chick (1985), The interactional accomplishment of discrimination in South Africa, *Language in Society, 14,* 299–326; chapter 22, Susan Philips (1976), Some sources of cultural variability in the regulation of talk, *Language in Society, 6,* 81–95; and chapter 24, John Searle (1976), A classification of illocutionary acts, *Language in Society, 5,* 1–23, all by kind permission of the authors and Cambridge University Press. Chapter 25, Michelle Rosaldo (1982), The things we do with words: Ilongot speech acts and speech act theory in philosophy, *Language in Society, 11,* 203–237, by kind permission of Renato S. Rosaldo, Jr. and Cambridge University Press. Chapter 18, Ronald Scollon and Suzanne Wong Scollon (1981), chapter two from their *Narrative, literacy, and face in interethnic communication* (pp. 11–37), Norwood, NJ: Ablex Publishing Corporation, by kind permission of the authors and publisher. Chapter 20, Keith Basso (1970), To give up on words: Silence in Western Apache culture, *Southwest Journal of Anthropology, 26,* 213–230, by kind permission of the author and the *Journal of Anthropological Research.*

Contributors

Keith Basso, Department of Anthropology, University of New Mexico, Albuquerque, New Mexico, 87131

Charles Braithwaite, Department of Communication, New Mexico State University, Las Cruces, New Mexico, 88003

Donal Carbaugh, Department of Communication, University of Massachusetts, Amherst, Massachusetts, 01003

Keith Chick, Department of General Linguistics and Communication, University of Natal, Durban, South Africa.

Jack Daniel, Department of Communication, University of Pittsburgh, Pittsburgh, Pennsylvania, 15260

Dell Hymes, Department of Anthropology, University of Virginia, Charlottesville, Virginia, 22903

Tamar Katriel, School of Education, University of Haifa, Haifa, Israel, 31999.

Thomas Kochman, Department of Communication and Theatre, University of Illinois-Chicago, Box 4348, Chicago, Illinois, 60680

Kenneth Liberman, Department of Sociology, University of Oregon, Eugene, Oregon, 97403-1291

Susan Urmston Philips, Department of Anthropology, University of Arizona, Tucson, Arizona, 85721

Gerry Philipsen, Department of Speech Communication, University of Washington, Seattle, Washington, 98195

Steven Pratt, Department of Oral Communication, Central State University, Edmond, Oklahoma, 73060

Ronald Scollon, P.O. Box 1149, Haines, Alaska, 99827

John Searle, Department of Philosophy, University of California, 2120 Oxford Street, Berkeley, California, 94720

Geneva Smitherman-Donaldson, Department of English, Michigan State University, East Lansing, Michigan, 48824

D. Lawrence Wieder, Department of Communication, University of Oklahoma, Norman, Oklahoma, 73019

Suzanne Wong-Scollon, P.O. Box 1149, Haines, Alaska, 99827

Introduction

DONAL CARBAUGH

This is a book about communication in cultural contexts, its meaningfulness to situated participants, the local forms it takes, and the moral orders created as participants interact socially. The chapters in the book explore how communication displays membership in communities, as well as the dynamics involved when persons from one community contact those from another. The book is also, and perhaps more subversively, about communication theory. It displays various conceptual lenses through which one can see culture(s) in communication and, in turn, communication in cultures.

Two problems that are basic both to the cultural practice and theory of communication run through the book. One is *shared identity,* the other is *common means and meanings.*

How is shared identity created in, yet influenced by communication? The authors demonstrate how participants in communities display shared identity in particular and revealing ways. Communication patterns are discovered and described with each getting done distinctly, and each associated with a particular group's sense of itself. The groups discussed in the book are diverse, namely, Teamsters, Blacks, Osage Indians, Anglos, and Americans broadly (as designating general patterns of a geographic and popular sort), Israelis, Aboriginal Australians, Zulus, Athabaskans, Western Apache, Warm Springs Indians, and the Ilongot. What the authors show are ways each group organizes their communication, at least on some occasions, and in so doing, demonstrates who they are, achieving what Philipsen (1989) has called, a communal function of "membering."

The second basic question could be posed: What common means and meanings of communication are associated with situations of communal life? Investigated are the ways communication is organized, the means available to people in contexts, and the meanings those patterns have for those who use them. Again, diverse resources are evident, both in local frames for speaking such as "calling" and "responding" among Blacks;

"razzing" among the Osage; or "griping" among Israelis; and in local patterns of general forces such as the Athabaskan, Zulu, and/or Anglo patterns of politeness. Each such means is also locally meaningful, for it holds a place symbolically and interactionally in the lives of those being studied. To know the places of communicative means and their meanings, and to develop general ways of knowing such things, is a second problem addressed in the chapters that follow.

That communication is everywhere "contexted," locally designed, situationally managed, and individually applied; that cultural identity, at some times on some occasions, has something to do with the nature of this patterning; that the meaningfulness of such patterns to participants is something always in need of discovery; and, that communication theory must provide adequate bases for describing (interpreting and explaining) such patterns, suggests some common grounds for many of the chapters in this book, especially as they explore the interactional coding of cultural identity through the available means and meanings of communication.

However, the contributors and contributions in the book represent a broad range of fields. Readers will recognize ideas from rhetorical theory and criticism, ethnomethodology, ethnography, conversation analysis, performance studies, linguistics, pragmatics, sociolinguistics, interactional sociolinguistics, and possibly many more. Each author priveleges some method, theoretical problem, and so on. Yet, at base, all of the contributions represent work by an author(s) who has expressed an affinity with, or whose work has appeared as a part of, the ethnography of communication. All, at some level, and at least in part, explore culturally distinctive patterns of communication. The only exception is the piece by John R. Searle on speech acts, included in the third part because of its fundamental importance to a type of cross-cultural analysis of communication.

The ethnography of speaking was begun in 1962 by Dell Hymes who called for studies that were ethnographic in scope and communication in design. The assumptions were and are (a) communication is systematically patterned and needs to be studied on its own and for its own sake; (b) the systematicity is intimately linked with social life and needs to be studied as such; and (c) the nature of communication itself is culture-specific, therefore cross-culturally diverse. To date, there is a corpus of well over 200 studies that lends empirical support to each assumption, suggesting — as do the readings that follow — features of communication that are culture specific, and their instantiation of patterns that are much more general (cf. Hymes, 1962, 1972; Philipsen & Carbaugh, 1986). The general ethnographic agenda thus includes, as evidenced in these studies, theory on the level both of specific practices of communication that are distinctive to a culture and community, and of general principles of communication that hold across cultures and communities. One sees twin goals: to particularize from general theory, and to generalize from the cultural particulars. One way of doing ethnography is to conduct field work and write reports within such an iterative process. Ethnographic study of communication thus covers broad theoretic and substantive, as well as geographic, grounds, but does so in a rather systematic and focused way.

By looking through the studies included here, one gets a sense of deep distinctiveness in the cultural patterning of communication. Looking across the studies, one senses as well some commonalities. The studies have been brought together, under one cover, with both ends in view. In addition to demonstrating the dual goals of particularity and generality, the volume has three further objectives, namely, (a) to display a relatively coherent ethnographic approach to communication; (b) more specifically, to bring some relevant ethnographies of communication to bear on questions of cultural communication and intercultural contact; and (c) to demonstrate the importance and productivity of focusing inquiry on actual practices of communication that are situated in social contexts. Because I selected studies with these aims in mind, most are empirically grounded, but none are merely descriptive. Each contributor thus works with varying methods and theoretical frameworks, but each also addresses questions of theory related to problems of culture, identities, communicative means, and meanings (cf. Collier & Thomas, 1988); each also uses data from naturally occurring communicative conduct. Taken together, one sees the fundamental role of culture in situated communication practices; one also sees its role in developing communication theory (cf. Carbaugh, in press; Pearce, 1989).

Plan of the Book

This book has three main parts, with each addressing questions at the forefront of cultural communication inquiry. The first part explores how some communication patterns give voice to culture through the construction, and evaluation, of cultural identites. Part II explores moments when culture patterns of communication contact one another, with special attention given to interactional sources of asynchrony. And, the third part is concerned with comparative study of cultural patterns, exploring how communication theory can achieve a cross-cultural utility without losing its cultural sensitivity.

The three parts of the book, however, are not independent, nor can they be. Any element of cultural communication invites, even requires, consideration of the others. Asking how communication gives voice to culture (Part I), involves inquiring about its use in intercultural encounters (Part II), and to know its distinctiveness involves its comparison with others (Part

III). Also, to develop theory that is culturally sensitive but with some degree of cross-cultural utility (Part III), one must grapple also with specific cultural practices (Part I), as well as with intercultural encounters (Part II). Each such concern is interwoven with the others, and hopefully, when taken together, gives some sort of holistic and general picture.

Each part of the book includes three main sections. First is a chapter that introduces the part. The introduction to each part identifies some common threads across readings in the part, previews the chapters in the part, and raises issues that the chapters address. The introduction to the part on intercultural communication is somewhat more involved, inducing as it does from the field literature three core elements in cultural and intercultural communication theory. The heart of each part includes readings that report original field work about communication patterns, by authors who have lived them. Including the original field work reports is an effort to maintain the integrity of the ethnographies, in a way that second-order interpretations about them cannot. Finally, and rather unusually, each part includes original epilogues to the field work reports that typically include reflections of the authors on their work, but sometimes includes commentary by another. This introduces a kind of dialogue on the works, affording reflections on and extensions of the original empirical work.

Part I is titled "Culture Talking About Itself." In it, a general cultural approach to communication is displayed. Chapters explore communication patterns that put culture on display, such as "being a man" in Teamsterville (Philipsen), calling and responding in Black churches (Daniel and Smitherman-Donaldson), performing as a "real Indian" (Wieder and Pratt), "griping" in Israel (Katriel), as well as ritual (Katriel and Philipsen) and rules (Carbaugh) for some "mainstream" (North) American communication. Addressed are questions about communication as it creates and affirms shared identity, common meanings, and discursive tensions. Various conceptual frameworks are used and developed, with special attention given to communication norms, forms, and codes. Each such study thus affords a view of culture in specific and situated communication practices.

Part II is titled "Intercultural Contact." In it, moments of intercultural communication are explored. Chapters investigate the dynamics yielded when cultural patterns of communication contact one another. The specific cases explore various sources of misunderstanding in intercultural communication as it occurs between Aboriginal and Anglo Australians (Liberman), Black and White (North) Americans (Kochman), Zulu and Anglo South Africans (Chick), and Athabaskan and English (North) Americans (Scollon and Wong-Scollon). Each chapter analyzes the intercultural encounters through specific conceptual concerns, such as prosodic cueing, indigenous frames for talk, or politeness formula. The introduction to Part II sketches a general, and tentative, theoretical framework, bringing together the main elements, and relations among such elements in the studies. Highlighted in the chapters is the concern for understanding both cultures in communication and their simultaneous use in specific interactional contexts.

Part III is titled "Cross-Cultural Comparisons of Communication Phenomena." In it, specific communication phenomena are explored in various cultural fields. The three phenomena of concern in these chapters are, respectively, the communicative uses of silence (Basso and Braithwaite), the regulation of talk (Philips), and speech acts (Searle, Rosaldo, Hymes). These are each explored on the basis of several culture patterns. So, for example, with regard to silence, we find its interactional uses and interpretations in Western Apache culture (Basso) converging in some very interesting ways with many others (Braithwaite). By juxtaposing culture patterns of communication, with regard to specific communication phenomena, comparative study helps clarify cultural distinctiveness in some communication phenomena, and lays ground for cross-cultural generalities, hopefully in a culturally sensitive way.

References

Carbaugh, D. (in press). Toward a perspective on cultural communication and intercultural contact. *Semiotica.*

Collier, M. J., & M. Thomas. (1988). Cultural identity: An interpetive perspective. *International and Intercultural Communication Annual, 12* 99–120.

Hymes, D. (1962). The ethnography of speaking. In T. Gladwin & W. Sturtevant (Eds.), *Anthropology and human behavior* (pp. 13–53). Washington, DC: Anthropological Society of Washington.

Hymes, D. (1972). Models of the interaction of language and social life. In J. Gumperz & D. Hymes (Eds.), *Directions in sociolinguistics: The ethnography of communication* (pp. 35–71). New York: Holt, Rinehart & Winston.

Pearce, W. B. (1989). *Communication and the human condition.* Carbondale, IL: Southern Illinois University Press.

Philipsen, G. (1989). Speech and the communal function in four cultures. *International and Intercultural Communication Annual, 13,* 79–92.

Philipsen, G., & Carbaugh, D. (1986). A bibliography of Fieldwork in the ethnography of communication. *Language in Society, 15,* 387–398.

I

Culture Talking About Itself

DONAL CARBAUGH

The chapters in Part I share at least three commitments for communication study. First, they focus attention on communication patterns that are culturally identifiable. Each explores a resource for communicating that the people under study could, and do, perform, identify, and discuss. The studies are thus grounded in patterns familiar to participants, and used by them. Second, the chapters in Part I take the notion of situation seriously, exploring how the communication pattern of study is situated socially. Where is the pattern used, by whom, toward what ends? The relationship among the pattern, and social situations, is significant generally because all situations support some sayings, while constraining others, with knowledge of the relationship between situations, and patterns of communication appropriate within them, being central to the practice and theory of communication.

Each chapter also demonstrates, in its distinctive way, a general point: There are situations and uses of communication where cultural identity is on display. With regard to the following chapters, the social situations described are quite diverse, including the street corner, the church, classrooms, the home, and television talk shows. The range of uses to which talk is put in such situations is also diverse including responding to insults by peers, discipling children, spiritual (and secular) "calling" and "responding," playfully insulting one's peers, solving personal problems including those of self-identity, griping with friends, and giving personal opinions. But in each situation, through historically grounded and socially constrained uses of speech, a more general outcome is getting done: A culture is being put on display as people symbolize a common identity. This is done of course in various ways, because every social context or community is grounded deeply with its own roots. But each such situation and community, through its unique patterns, situations, and uses of communication, says something about itself, displaying—what could be called—its cultural identity.

A Preview

The chapters in Part I describe patterns of communication in social situations by interpreting, at least in part, a culture, a symbolicly acted meaning system. Each chapter shows how parts of culture, or subsystems of meaning-making, are used by persons to conceive of and evaluate moments of everyday life, thus laying bases for a common identity.

Consider chapter 1 by Gerry Philipsen. We see in one community of Teamsters in Chicago how speaking is in some situations motivated by a common identity, being a man, with male performances sometimes aligned with that gender identity. But more than that, the standards for "manly" speech are applied by Teamsters generally, beyond situations where men are men and boys are boys, especially, and quite tellingly, to situations where the Teamster male must make sense of, and coordinate actions with, an outside male who acts in what is to Teamsters an "unmanly" way. On such occassions, standards for Teamsterville maleness are used in order to interpret and subsequently to evaluate the violation by the outsider of the local communication norms. Speaking "like a man" is thus both a reaffirmation of a shared identity (in situations where actions are aligned), and the creative use of the identity to meet the contingencies of daily life (when dealing with the less usual as with some outsiders). Communication—in such situations—thus displays a shared identity of a community, and its uses both to affirm that identity and to creatively interpret problematic moments in daily life. In this sense, the shared identity—like all situations in which cultural identity is creatively affirmed—displays a way of being, the sense of which provides common bases for meanings and actions that are invoked both when acting with those who share the identity, and when dealing with others who do not, as in intercultural contacts with outsiders.

In chapter 3, Daniel and Smitherman-Donaldson give a detailed interpretation of communication within the Black church. They provide a way of listening deeply to a cultural form, call/response, which is of special importance in the Black church. The call/response form evokes a whole historically grounded system of meanings that is in part constitutive of a Black cultural identity. The centrality of religion, the unity of the spiritual and the material within a hierarchy of beliefs, the harmony of person and spirit as when one is possessed by the spirit, the cyclical conception of rhythm and events, are all cultural premises ignited by and reaffirmed through the call/response form. By hearing this meaning system in the call/response performance, one gains a richer sense of this relatively intense and collective performance. Daniel and Smitherman-Donaldson also show how the form is used in secular contexts as well as in sacred ones, and how an understanding of this Black form and its meanings helps unravel some moments of intercultural communication, especially when this Black pattern confronts distinctive others. By enriching our sense of Black identity through this form of expression, Daniel and Smitherman-Donaldson lead us to see (and hear) more sharply not only some cultural bases of the identity, but also others which it exposes through cross-cultural juxtaposition.

Where Daniel and Smitherman-Donaldson demonstrate the importance of a religious situation, a call/response form, and its historical meanings to a cultural identity, Wieder and Pratt (chapter 5) explore various situations in order to identify how a "real" Osage Indian both cues and enables "real Indianness" with others. Wieder and Pratt, as do the Osage of which Pratt is a member, take cultural identity not as a given but as a problem that must be continually and convincingly performed. The importance of the performance was suggested to them by the prominence among the Osage of the question, "Who is an Indian?" Note that the question motivating their investigation is not just a "research question," but is moreover a culturally loaded question for the Osage at least in some social situations. In responding to this culturally located question, they show how Osage use norms to structure and evaluate communication, to engage each other in cultural forms such as "razzing" (including how this form is distinct from similar other cultural forms such as Black "ranking"), and to express meanings of harmony and modesty in the performance. The moment-by-moment use of these resources, they argue, is not merely a manifestation of some ascribed or achieved status, but is an essential constituent in the cultural "being" of "a real Osage Indian." In their epilogue, Wieder and Pratt discuss problems they confronted in coming to know a "native view," thus sensitizing readers to possible "discordances" between the cultural actors' and the ethnographers' meanings.

In chapters 7 and 9, the cultural form of ritual is used to demonstrate how rather routine moments of communication can attain great forcefulness in the construction of cultural identity. In chapter 7, Katriel and Philipsen describe a "communication ritual" that is discussed and practiced by some Americans. They interpret the ritual along dimensions of folk meanings and elaborate its sense with two metaphors, one indigenous (communication as industrious work) and another more analytic (communication as ritual). They describe a sequence of communicative acts that seeks the purposes of solving personal problems and celebrating the cultural identity of "self" and close "relations" among participants. In chapter 9, Katriel describes how Israeli "griping parties" follow a similar ritualized form, but its shape is more cyclical, and its purposes more public, celebrating a cultural identity not of self and uniqueness, but of commonality, with the "common feeling" less as an individual and more as a communal member who shares a fate and feelings of entrapment in a common community life. Because these two studies employ the same conceptual framework, the juxtaposition of them easily reveals what is distinct to each: A tone of seriousness in some American "communication" versus a playfully plaintive Israeli "griping," personal problems as topics for "communication" versus public problems for "griping," the culturally sensed goals of self-identity versus communal solidarity, and a linear versus a spiralling form, respectively. Noteworthy as well is the commonality to both ritual forms: They both provide ways for persons to discuss the problems of their common cultural life. Katriel's and Philipsen's work further shows how advantageous it can be to work in intercultural research teams, especially with similar analytical tools, for one is positioned better to identify what is distinctive in specific cultural performances, as well as what holds more generally across cultures.

The final chapter in Part I displays a system of communication norms and codes that is used during a popular American media event. The norms, like those reported for the "communication ritual," include the preference for self-presentation, but unlike the "communication ritual," they suggest ways for persons to address problems publicly, with the relevant tone being tolerance and respect, rather than closeness and intimacy. Note that resulting from the cultural performance is—at the level of topic—not agreement, but great dissonance. The cultural form for the discussion is, however, agreeable, and is unveiled by exploring a system of rules that persons use to orient and assess the propriety of their communication conduct. Complementing these normative rules are codes that suggest interpretations linking one level of discourse, such as the act of opinion-giving, to another, such as the cultural identity of "self." Examining mediated communication this way demonstrates how a cultural identity, when spoken, can produce interactional outcomes such as topical dissonance and a cultural personalization of standards. A system of mediated communication thus produces a public situation of topical dissonance through a communal standard of intimacy. A cultural identity, through a situation and uses of communication, is linked closely to intimacy and dissonance as well as to common and cultural norms.

As is shown in these chapters, the possibilities for, and consequences of cultural communication are quite varied. For example, cultural resources of communication can identify the conditions and constraints for proper communicative performance itself, how these resources are socially enacted and evaluated, their moment-by-moment use in the local management of sequences, and how some such resources even assume the status of ritual. Taken together, then, the chapters show how some situations and uses of communication display parts of a culture and, in turn, how various communication resources perform, coordinate, and evaluate cultural identities. As such, the chapters suggest ways to hear—in communication patterns, situations, and uses—a display of cultural identity, culture talking to and about itself.

Cultural Communication

The chapters presented in Part I can be conceived broadly as exercises in cultural communication, that is, each chapter shows how socially situated knowledge is necessary for interpreting the common meaningfulness of communication to its participants. Although the authors of these chapters do not label their contributions as "cultural communication studies," I treat them as such in order to highlight some of the issues that — taken together — the chapters raise, and note why such an exercise is fundamental for developing a cultural understanding of communication (the focus of Part I), and intercultural practices (the focus of Part II), which has some degree of cross-cultural utility (the focus of Part III).

The general approach addresses three fundamental problems. The first is a problem of *shared identity* or group membership: How does communication create, affirm, and develop a common identity? This problem in turn is based on three fundamental subissues: of symbolic meaning, the common sense of the identity; of symbolic form, the episodes in which the identity is creatively played out; and of social function, the union of people through some degree of identification. The second problem is the more general problem of shared, public, and *common meaning:* How does communication create, affirm, and develop common meanings? The third problem is the problem of *dialectical tensions* intrinsic to cultural communication itself: How does communication create yet reaffirm, individuate yet unify, stabilize yet change common meanings and members?

Respective to these problems, cultural communication can be conceived as the creation and affirmation of a shared identity, through specific domains, which mediates between basic discursive dialectics, such as autonomy and union, individual and community, powerful and powerless. I comment briefly on the three basic elements in this statement, shared identity, domains, and dialectics, with reference to the chapters in Part I.

Note that cultural communication, so conceived, includes, first, *a sense of shared identity* that is not only affirmed or reaffirmed, but also created in contexts. In this sense, the communication of culture involves not merely a reproduction of a historical and common sense, but also its fluid shaping and use to meet the various contingencies of everyday living. As Wieder and Pratt discuss the Osage communication of a "real Indian" identity, they show not just that the Osage have patterns that display a common identity, but moreover that these are variously pitched and combined to meet the contingencies of daily life. Exigencies for asking, "who is an Indian," ways for evaluating whether or not this is the right thing to ask, and when asked appropriately, ways for responding to the question, as well as criteria for evaluating responses, all such concerns vary, but they do so in a patterned way, according to the culture system used, and the social situations in which participants find themselves. Consequently, Osage who find themselves in classrooms with other Osage may avert eyes, be silent or defer to others, but when with peers elsewhere, may engage in a kind of raucous verbal dueling. Both performances—in their proper places—are constitutive of "real Indianness." But it is not only that cultural identity suggests patterns of variability across situations in one community's life, but also that such patterns are invoked sometimes to meet the contingencies of life outside one's community, as when Philipsen early on used academic patterns to guide his communication with Teamsters, rendering his performances ineffectual to them, just as Teamsters used their local patterns to interact with and evaluate him. Cultural communication is not just a simple playing out of broad common patterns; it is the variable and moment-by-moment use of these inside and out—to produce one's actions as a kind of person and to hear other's actions so produced—to guide the senses, performances, and evaluations of communication, within and across social worlds.

Note that cultural identity is being proposed here as a broad communicational and cultural concept, entitling a system of practices that spans many types of *persona,* each of course embedded within the broader discursive formations of social life. The intent is to exclude none. The concept thus includes identities based on various criteria including gender and occupation (Teamsterville male), race (Black), ethnicity generally (Osage), and some more broadly geographic and national in scope (Israeli, American). The theoretical point is an organization of particular discursive practices as they position identities, as they situate the communication of personhood, within an identifiable context or sociocultural (including political, economic, and historical) field.

Note also how various *cultural domains* can serve as bases for identity displays. The identity(ies) of a culture may revolve around one substantive area more than others involving claims in an idiom of persons, or communication, or may be grounded in others such as religion, politics, history, society, nature, or some creative combination of these. For example, the call/response form occurs within and elaborates a domain of religion that itself, in some situations, becomes a marker of Black cultural identity—expressing in a social situation a cultural identity through a religious domain—just as the domains of public problems for Israelis, or personal problems for some Americans, become socially situated markers of cultural identity. For any given people in a place, some domains are elaborated, and some are not; and, for every people, the domains used, are developed in local and particular ways. So tailored, they become markers of cultural identity.

Third, notice how cultural communication is heard as a *dialectically elastic process,* including tensions between creation and affirmation, the individual and communal, closeness and distance, equal and unequal, resource endowed or deprived, the social goals of autonomy and union, or between personal and social orders. One goal in such study is interpreting, in culturally situated practices, whether and if such tensions operate, their local conception and power, their role in shaping patterns of interaction, as well as the possible means available for their resolution. Cultural communication may thus range from moments of integrative and ritualized recreation, as in some Black churches, to hotly contested, creative, and discordant battles, as on "Donahue." Displayed across such moments, as shown in the following chapters, are the tensional bases of communication performance and their role in motivating, affirming, and transforming cultural identities.

Norms, Forms, and Codes

By viewing communication as the creation and affirmation of cultural identities in social situations, several theoretical issues are highlighted, such as problems of common identity, symbolic meanings, forms, social functions, common meanings, and dialectical tensions, among others. Here I suggest three such problems that — among others — the chapters in this first part address.

The three problems can be posed as questions, with each responded to by positing local patterns of situation and use. The questions are:

1. Questions of norms: How does communication create senses of moral order, and in turn, how do moral orders influence communication?;
2. Questions of forms: What interactional shapes are used to coordinate, conceptualize, and evaluate social life?; and, more generally,
3. Questions of cultural codes: What range of common meanings are used by participants to render their ways mutually intelligible?

Each author responds to one or more of these questions — and of course to others — as they unravel a situated use of communication. One way to characterize these chapters is by seeing how the authors posit, as responses to the above questions, norms, forms, and codes, respectively.

Some of the authors, including Wieder and Pratt and Philipsen, respond to the question of local moral orders by positing a normative system, "ought" statements, or standards for proper conduct, which persons make in their routine interactions, such as the rules for speaking properly in Teamsterville, among Osage, or on "Donahue." By exploring how persons discursively describe "what is proper" in their performances, and especially how they evaluate moments of impropriety, these authors demonstrate the use of *norms* in communicative action. For example, consider the following norm: When in the presence of one's peers, a Teamsterville male, if he is to be judged "manly," should respond nonverbally to an outsider's insult about his wife, such as by physical fighting. On the basis of this norm, one cannot of course predict that a male will fight. One can however predict a moral and discursive standard to which a Teamster male's public performance can be held accountable. Such a claim of maleness is granted legitimacy as a moral claim in this community. Note that the concept, norm, is being used in this way to identify stateable imperatives, which can be used by participants to instruct, regulate, and evaluate their communication conduct. This use of norm is distinct from others who claim to identify a behavioral regularity, or a typical actional sequence. What is being identified, through a more discursive conception of norm, is a *communication* of morals, a system of ought statements that participants can use as bases for instructing, regulating, and evaluating social action. Moral systems, so conceived, are situational and contingent, contestable, variously organized, and speak of various cultural identities including those more generationally and positionally based such as the Osage and Teamsters, and those more personally based such as the Anglo-American. By positing systems of communication norms, these authors describe particular moments when moral standards are verbally invoked, and thus provide bases for coordinating conduct. In such moments, one can hear standards for acting properly being displayed.

The question of interactional shapes is responded to by positing *forms* of expression such as the Black call/response, the Osage "razzing," the ritual for some Americans of "communication," or the Israeli ritual of "griping." One might conceive of discursive forms, following Kenneth Burke, as the interactional creation and satisfaction of appetencies. For example, the call in the Black church creates an expectation for a response as a next communicational move; razzing, when initiated among Osage peers, creates expectations for mutual insults; the initiation of the ritual forms of "communication" and "griping" anticipates further talk about problems. Each such sequence creates expectations which are then subsequently met, or if unmet, become noticeably and "officially absent." By using this general notion of form, the following chapters describe various shapes, spanning linear, spiralling, and circular sequences, with each identifiable by participants as a more or less-bounded episode, marked by its own peculiar topics and rhythms, and used for its own particular purposes. Part of the intrigue in studying forms in communication is the increased sensitivity to the various shapes given interaction, especially as they enable the coordination of movements and rhythms in sequences, around specific topics and purposes. As becomes apparent in the second part of the book, some intercultural misunderstandings are grounded in one person's use of one form, a cyclical form, as others—in positions of power—speak more linearly.

The question of meaning is responded to generally by positing a *code,* a semantic system-in-use that renders communal ways intelligible. The communication system, so coded, enables one to infer patterns in the variablitity of performances within a situation or society, as well as to infer broader themes in variable performances across situations and societies. As is shown through the premises of the Black and Osage cultures, or with dimensions and metaphors of "communication," cultural identities and communication performances can be interpreted as deeply coded, as activating in communication patterns some archetypical radiants of meanings while constraining others. By positing such a code, one is thus able to identify the range of meanings that cohere a great variety of performances, the domains of coherence that are treated elaborately, the systems of oppositions that give communication a dramatic cultural force, and the mediating concepts that may resolve disparities, all lending a kind of regnant resonance to communication performance. In this general sense, it is codable meaning systems that suggest, and bring coherence to, culture in communication.

By exploring the cultural bases and the situated uses of norms, forms, and codes, the authors help us not only hear particular cultures in communication, but also suggest issues for study and general strategies for listening. Such an approach is warranted for communication theory and practice, for we must sensitize ourselves to cultures in communication, the diverse norms, forms, and codes that pattern social lives. On this base, we can understand better the nature of communication during intercultural contacts, for it is here where the unquestionables of different cultural worlds are thrown into stark relief. And further, by exploring cultures in communication, alone and together, we can come to understand both what are the important bases for comparison, and the contexts—cultural and intellectual—in which such comparisons inevitably take place. On such a base, by listening to culture speaking about itself, and with others, we may understand better the practice and theory of communication.

1

Speaking "Like a Man" in Teamsterville: Culture Patterns of Role Enactment in an Urban Neighborhood

GERRY PHILIPSEN

TALK is not everywhere valued equally; nor is it anywhere valued equally in all social contexts. Speaking is an object of a high degree of interest, elaboration, and positive evaluation in some cultures, such as those of the Burundi[1] and St. Vincentians[2] but is relatively deemphasized in other cultures, such as those of the Paliyans[3] and La Have Islanders.[4] Cultures are not only varied but are also internally diverse in the emphasis they place on the value of talk; in all communities there are some situations in which "silence is golden" and some in which talk is the most valued mode of social behavior.[5] Each community has its own cultural values about speaking and these are linked to judgments of situational appropriateness.

"Teamsterville," which is located on the near south side of Chicago, is a neighborhood of blue-collar, low-income whites who share a cultural outlook on communication.[6] Teamsterville's cultural (i.e., shared, tacit) understandings about the value of speaking are sharply defined and susceptible of discovery, although they are not written down in native treatises on effective communication, nor can native informants necessarily verbalize them. One manifestation of cultural outlook is the local view of the appropriateness of speaking versus other actional strategies (such as silence, violence, or non-verbal threats) in male role enactment or self-presentation. Whether and how well a man performs in a manly way is a principal criterion in Teamsterville for judging whether his behavior is appropriate and proper to

[1] Ethel M. Albert, "Culture Patterning of Speech Behavior in Burundi," in *Directions in Sociolinguistics: The Ethnography of Communication,* eds. John J. Gumperz and Dell Hymes (New York: Holt, Rinehart, and Winston, 1972), pp. 72-105.

[2] Roger Abrahams and Richard Bauman, "Sense and Nonsense in St. Vincent: Speech Behavior and Decorum in a Caribbean Community," *American Anthropologist,* 73 (1971), 762-772.

[3] Peter Gardner, "Symmetric Respect and Memorate Knowledge: The Structure and Ecology of Individualistic Culture," *Southwestern Journal of Anthropology,* 22 (1966), 389-415.

[4] Richard Bauman, "The La Have Island General Store: Sociability and Verbal Art in a Nova Scotia Community," *Journal of American Folklore,* 85 (1972), 330-343.

[5] Two ethnographies of communication

which verify and illustrate the culture patterning of silence behavior are Keith H. Basso, "'To Give up on Words': Silence in Western Apache Culture," *Southwestern Journal of Anthropology,* 26 (1970), 213-230 (also ch. 20 this volume); Susan U. Phillips, "Acquisition of Rules for Appropriate Speech Usage," *Georgetown University Monograph Series on Languages and Linguistics,* 21 (1970), 77-94.

[6] "Teamsterville" is a fictitious name. Description of the physical setting and the economic and political characteristics of the neighborhood are presented in Gerry Frank Philipsen, *Communication in Teamsterville: A Sociolinguistic Study of Speech Behavior in an Urban Neighborhood,* Diss. Northwestern University, 1972, 102-114.

the social identity, "male." Manliness is a theme of much neighborhood talk about self and others and a Teamsterville man is aware that his social performances will be judged frequently as to their manliness. To know how to perform, or present oneself, "like a man" in Teamsterville as elsewhere is to be privy to implicit understandings shared by members of the speech community, i.e., it is to have access to the culture. It is because the male role is highly important in the culture that description of the place of speaking in male role enactment reveals much in general about the community's valuation of talk, and cultural interpretations of the value of speaking in male role enactment are the special concern of this report.

COLLECTION AND ANALYSIS OF DATA

I had two periods of contact with Teamsterville. The first was a twenty-one month period during 1969 and 1970 spent as a social group worker in the neighborhood. The second, which began after a twelve month absence from the neighborhood, was for nine months in 1971 and 1972 devoted exclusively to field work research.

Participant observation and interviewing were used as techniques of data collection and data were analyzed using an ethnography of communication model.[7] All available data, including field records of speech behavior, informants' statements (spontaneous and elicited), and tape-recorded verbal interaction provided the evidence from which the culture pattern was inferred, and against which it was tested. Thus, multiple

sources of data were used in constructing descriptions and verifying hypotheses relevant to the inferred culture pattern.[8]

One research technique was particularly useful in constructing the culture pattern. The two episodes analyzed in this paper draw attention to role enactments which were judged ineffective by Teamsterville residents. Native reactions to out-of-role behavior are instructive because they bring into sharp focus role expectations which have been violated.[9] While exclusive use of this technique could produce a distorted view of the culture pattern,[10] it is useful as one source of clues to discovery of a pattern. The episodes reported below were clues to discovery and provide concrete instances of a pattern which was verified systematically through ethnographic research.

THE CULTURE PATTERN

A Teamsterville native shares tacit understandings about the situational appropriateness of speech behavior—specifically, that in some situations speech is appropriate in male role enactment, but that in others it is not and its use casts doubt on the speaker's manliness. Three classes of situation can be discerned: those which are marked in the culture for a relatively great amount of talk by men, those marked for minimal

---

7 My use of the term "situation" and my reference to "an ethnography of communication model" are based on the programmatic essays of Dell Hymes, particularly "The Ethnography of Speaking," in *Anthropology and Human Behavior*, eds. T. Gladwin and W. C. Sturtevant (Washington, D.C.: Anthropological Society of Washington, 1962), pp. 15-53.

8 This is an adaptation of a procedural technique suggested in Eugene J. Webb, Donald T. Campbell, Richard D. Schwartz, and Lee Sechrest, *Unobtrusive Measures: Nonreactive Research in the Social Sciences* (Chicago: Rand McNally, 1966), pp. 1-5.

9 Cf. Erving Goffman, *The Presentation of Self in Everyday Life* (Garden City, New York: Doubleday Anchor 1959), chapter five.

10 Raoul Naroll cautions against selecting field data which are conspicuous because exotic, thereby overlooking other field data which are inconspicuous because familiar to the ethnographer. "Data Quality Control in Cross-Cultural Surveys," in *A Handbook of Method in Cultural Anthropology*, eds. Raoul Naroll and Ronald Cohen (Garden City, New York: The Natural History Press 1970), p. 928.

talk by men, and those in which an emphasis of the verbal channel is proscribed for effective male self-presentation and for which other means of expression are required. Following are brief analyses of the first two of these classes of situation and a more extensive analysis of the third.

When the social identity relationship of the participants in a situation is symmetrical, the situation can appropriately realize a great amount of talking by a Teamsterville man. Specifically, the participants in a speaking situation should be matched on such identity attributes as age, sex, ethnicity, occupational status, and location of residence and the participants should be long-time friends. Speaking is a dominant focus of all-male social interaction in corner groups and corner bars. For boys the street corner and for men the corner bar is the principal setting for sociability, and speaking is a dominant activity in these settings. Typically, small groups of boys "hang" on their own corner and groups of men have their own corner bar, a public drinking establishment which has been claimed by them as their "turf," a territory to which outsiders are not invited or welcomed. Teamsterville men seek out other men of like identity, in well-established locations, and these are the situations in which it is most appropriate and proper for a man to produce a great quantity of talk.

A high quantity of speaking is considered inappropriate in situations in which the participants' identity relationship is asymmetrical. Such relationships are, for the adult man in Teamsterville, those with a wife, child, boss, outsider to the neighborhood, or a man of different ethnicity. Certainly, Teamsterville men do speak to their wives, girlfriends, children, and employers but these are not contexts of relationship which call for a high quantity of speaking nor are these

the "natural" situations in which to engage others in a state of talk. Thus one criterion in Teamsterville for marking a "speech situation" for men is the variable, the social identity relationship of the interlocutors; in speech situations the relationship is symmetrical on relevant identity attributes, in non-speech situations the relationship is asymmetrical.

For some situations the question is not so much whether there should be a great quantity or frequency of talk but rather what mode of action is to be emphasized in male self-presentation, and it is this kind of situation which I have selected for more detailed analysis. Specifically, an analysis of the Teamsterville data produces the generalization that when a man must assert power over or influence another person, speaking is disapproved as a dominant means of self-presentation and in such situations other means of expression are preferred, sometimes required, if the actor's male role enactment is to be credible to those who witness it. Three instances of this class of situation have particular relevance for a Teamsterville man: when he responds to insult, an insult directed either at him or at his female relative or girlfriend, when he seeks to influence the behavior of a status inferior, such as a child, and when he asserts himself in politics or economics. These instances of the class of situation are analyzed and illustrated below.

It is not uncommon that a Teamsterville man must respond to insults directed at him or at the reputation of a woman relative or girlfriend. An episode illustrates the Teamsterville view that an emphasis of the verbal channel is not appropriate for men in such situations. A settlement house group worker took a group of Teamsterville boys (thirteen and fourteen years of age) on a trip to Old Town, an entertainment area in

Chicago. On the drive from Teamsterville to Old Town, conversation turned to the topic of defending the honor of women. The question was put to the group worker, who was not a native of Teamsterville: "What would you do if a guy insulted your wife?" The group worker responded that he did not know, that it would depend on the situation. The answer did not satisfy the boys, who pressed the question by asking, "But you'd hit him, wouldn't you?" The worker answered that he did not know, that he probably would not hit him, or fight, but would instead probably try to talk to him, or persuade him to leave. The boys, however, pressed the point, and became increasingly nervous and upset, to the point that their moving vehicle was shaking from the activity. They were, as I recorded it at the time, visibly agitated. As the group drove off Lake Shore Drive, a main highway in Chicago, into the Old Town area, all of the boys, who were usually enthusiastic about Old Town visits, clamored to go home, saying they did not want to go to Old Town after all.

How can the Teamsterville boys' apparently sudden decision to go home be explained? In spite of their fondness for Old Town, the boys were—on this and previous occasions—uneasy about many of the people they expected to meet there, and they freely verbalized their apprehensions of blacks, "hippies," and "pot-smokers." On a typical walk with the boys on Wells Street—Old Town's main street—some of the boys would always be close to the side of their adult group worker. At the start of the trip in question, the boys apparently assumed they would be in the company of a normal man who protects those in his care in their culturally prescribed way, for example, by fighting for them as he would for the honor of female relatives. When the boys learned, through the dis-

cussion in the car, that their adult companion of the evening was not the kind of man who protects those dependent upon him in what is for Teamsterville the culturally prescribed way they became frightened. The boys' definition of the situation had been radically altered by the conversation in the car. The closer they got to Old Town (where, they would reason, they might need an adult for security), the uneasier they became. To the boys, given their assumptions, the situation was threatening. The boys faced a problem of trying to deal with an alien situation, created by a man who said he would choose silence or talk when fighting is, to the boys, the proper and appropriate response.

A second episode is about the Teamsterville reaction to a man who did not know—or who for some other reason did not act in conformity to—a local conception of appropriate role enactment. Again, the outsider's out-of-role behavior was the choice of speech over fighting as the preferred mode of self-presentation in an exigent situation, one which required a man to influence the behavior of his status inferiors. The episode, which took place over a period of days, was prompted by the trouble a Teamsterville settlement house had with teenage boys in its youth program—the boys were undisciplined, rude, and defiant of authority. The director of the program approached the problem in what he thought was a constructive and sympathetic way, by trying to reason with the boys, to involve them in decision-making, to understand their feelings, etc. These were techniques which had, in other settings, proved effective for the director. The strategy was not effective in Teamsterville; the boys became more rebellious and increasingly verbally abusive and disrespectful of adult staff members.

John, a long-time resident of the

neighborhood, embodied the local norms of the strong, physically aggressive male. John, who witnessed much of what went on during teen program hours, had to face, as I now interpret it, a dilemma. On the one hand, the director of the program had a position of high status in the community and he was a married, adult man. On the other hand, the director did not physically subdue the boys, as John thought he should. John's dilemma can be phrased as the resolution of conflicting information: either the director was not a normal male or the role expectation of corporal punishment and the speech proscription for men in such situations was not applicable.

John dealt with the dilemma in three stages. He apparently ruled out the possibility that the director belonged in the non-normal category.[11] At first he hinted, and eventually stated outright, that the director ought to "beat the hell out of these kids." He even expressed his willingness to help and reassured the adult that he could obtain the boys' parents' permission for such action. John's suggestion was reinforced by his explanation to the non-native that Teamsterville boys interpreted the verbal strategies as a sign of homosexuality, a point which I verified repeatedly in other observations and through elicitation of role expectations from informants.

Having failed to change his interlocutor's behavior to conform to Teamsterville expectations, John adopted a second strategy, shifting from persuasion to an attempt at rationalizing the be-

havior. Since the director failed to live up to the social-moral code, John sought to interpret the behavior in light of another code—it was illegal, he reasoned, for someone in the position of director to hit minors: "I know you'd like to hit these kids, but someone in your job can't do it, it's against the law, but I know that you'd like to hit them." It appears that John was beginning actively to reevaluate the alien behavior. However, recourse to "higher authority" as an explanation apparently did not satisfy him for long.

John's third and final strategy can also be described from a moral perspective. The director was not immoral (homosexual), or guided by an extralocal morality (legally bound not to hit minors), but was now, in John's eyes, so proper that he was able to transcend the expectations which apply to mere mortals; John said to the director: "You know what you are, all the trouble you get from these kids, I don't know how you can keep from belting em' one; you're a saint, that's what you are." The director's speaking strategy had been interpreted and rationalized. John applied several levels of the Teamsterville moral code to account for the alien behavior, to preserve the director's role enactment as appropriate, proper, and convincing. The preference of a verbal to a physical role enactment was itself a message in the community, but John had to search for a meaning to that message with which he could comfortably live, a meaning that was at each stage of his interpretation a moral one.

In both of the above situations—an insult by a stranger and rude behavior by boys—the Teamsterville man discerns a threat to the credibility of his role enactment as male. The challenge requires a response, a self-presentation which answers the challenge. What resources for self-presentation are appro-

11 One reason why it would be hard for John to assign the director to the category, non-normal, is that the director was married and in Teamsterville marriage is automatically accepted as proof that a man is not a homosexual. An illustration of this is that in a group discussion at the Teamsterville settlement house someone interpreted my wearing of colored socks as a sign that I was a homosexual; the assertion was quickly disputed when someone else said, "He can't be a queer, he's married."

priately available to him? Speech is the currency of social interaction when participants have similar social identities, including membership in a close-knit friendship group; speech purchases an expression of solidarity or assertion of status symmetry. Therefore a response in which speaking is the dominant mode of self-presentation has little value as a counter to the threat—indeed, the threat itself might be an inappropriate assertion of status symmetry. A speech surrogate as the dominant means of self-presentation purchases an assertion of distance, difference, or status asymmetry, and may therefore appropriately be used to counter the threat. The man must respond in such situations and the sanctioned resource for responding is something other than talk.

In Teamsterville speech is judged appropriate for male self-presentation in assertions of solidarity but not in assertions of power over another person. "Responding to insults" provides a neat illustration of this two-point theme. First, when an outsider to his group insults a boy's girlfriend or mother, to take a speaking "part" is to run the risk of having one's performance judged to be ineffective. By not defending his girlfriend physically the boy invites further attacks on himself, inferiority feelings for himself, and possible future attacks on the girl. After all, the Teamsterville boy would reason, who will protect her if her boyfriend is not "man enough" to defend her? I am here describing, as a construction from relevant data, the Teamsterville boys' own conceptualization. As in any study of norms, so in this, rules do not necessarily predict behavior. Speech, at least as a dominant mode of response, is *judged* ineffective as role enactment when dealing with an insult to a woman under a man's protection when the offender is an outsider. However, if a boy insults a peer's mother

or girlfriend (e.g., the mother or girlfriend of a member of his own corner group), speech is judged an effective, appropriate means for neutralizing the attack. Preferred is a verbal put-down which in effect humiliates or defeats the attacker, but a simple appeal to stop is also appropriate. Speech is, in the situation defined, a sanctioned resource for acting to respond to the exigence of the situation. It should be emphasized that speech is efficatious for an expression of power only in the context of a previously established, continuing relationship which is based primarily on a solidarity tie. The strength of the tie supports the verbal appeal, and a verbal strategy but serves to activate the solidarity ties which are themselves persuasive resources.

Teamsterville residents not only believe that speech is inappropriate and improper in dealing with a threat from an outsider, but that its use will bring negative consequences to the boy such as future attacks on himself and his friends. So too, when a Teamsterville adult man wants to affirm or assert power over or influence the behavior of a child, the use of speech is not only ineffective but may also entail damaging consequences for the man's reputation. The operation of the principle is seen in the failure of a man to respond to verbal abuse from a child by a show of physical power. For the child to challenge the man with speech, particularly brash speech, is an initiation of status symmetry, a challenge which, if met only with talk by the adult, is not met at all. The use of speech by the child signals to the other a comment about the relationship, an implicit announcement that the speaker is in a solidarity relationship to the hearer. And in Teamsterville, as elsewhere, assertions of solidarity are judged to be the prerogative of the high-power

member of a pair.[12] For the man to restore the relationship to its properly
asymmetrical state requires the use of an
effective cultural resource for that situation, and such an effective resource is
physical fighting or nonverbal threat, not
talk. One informant summarized the
Teamsterville view when he responded
to my question of how a man would be
judged if he *talked* to an erring child
before spanking him: "I don't know of
that ever happening. That just wouldn't
be natural for a man to do."

In Teamsterville, speech is proper
and functional in asserting male solidarity, but not in asserting power and influence in interpersonal situations. In
critical symbolic ways, as protector and
as master of a house, the Teamsterville
man disvalues speech as a resource for
male role enactment. In another critical way, as breadwinner, speech is not
an integral part of earning a living or
of other aspects of economic life. A list
of Teamsterville occupations, prepared
from my survey data and corroborated
by government census figures,[13] suggests
that the Teamsterville man requires relatively little verbal interaction in connection with his employment. And yet,
when the Teamsterville man needs a job,
or must deal with the civil authorities,
or must plead a case, what means of
persuasion are properly available to
him? I would coin the phrase a "rhetoric
of connections" as the answer to the
question, meaning that connections with
a political leader, a prospective employer, or other kinds of officials, are
personal resources which may be morally
and effectively marshalled in times of
personal need. Whereas speech is not a
resource critical to male role enactment
in exigent situations, connections have
a very real value. When I raised the subject of connections with my male informants, each of them smiled broadly.
Apparently they were pleased by mention of the subject and enjoyed discussing it. Each emphasized the personal importance of connections and told how he
himself had used connections successfully in some situations requiring effective action. "The more connections a
man has, the more he is a man," is how
one informant explained it.

For the Teamsterville man, minimal
emphasis of talk in work settings is one
part of a pattern of minimal talk with
outsiders to the neighborhood, with persons in positions of authority who are
not long-time associates, and with white-
collar persons, with whom there is a perceived status difference. Most of the
Teamsterville man's necessary contacts
with "outsiders" are mediated through
a local precinct captain, Catholic parish
priest, or union steward. The politician
—a precinct captain or his block assistant
—serves as an intermediary in matters of
employment, law, politics, and social welfare, and various other matters, thus minimizing the resident's direct dealings
with the outside world. This is an extension of a widespread European pattern that extends from minor secular
situations to religion. In the European
countries of origin of Teamsterville residents, not only in politics are dealings
with authority normally conducted by
means of an intermediary, but also in
the sacred realm, where the resident does
not directly address the deity but relies
upon such intermediaries as ministers,
priests, or holy figures to whom he prays.

12 Roger Brown and A. Gilman, "The Pro
nouns of Power and Solidarity" in *Style in
Language*, ed. T. A. Sebeok (Cambridge, Mass.:
M.I.T. Press, 1960) pp. 253-276. Brown and
Gilman state: "The suggestion that solidarity
be recognized comes more gracefully from the
elder than from the younger, from the richer
than from the poorer, from the employer than
from the employee, from the noble than from
the commoner, from the female than from the
male."

13 Evelyn Kitagawa and Karl Taeuber, *Local
Community Fact Book, 1960* (Chicago: University of Chicago, 1963).

It should be noted that the intermediary principal redefines situations requiring assertion of influence from the use of speech by the supplant to the use of solidarity or locality ties with the intermediary, who is eventually to state the case for the resident. Speaking is easy and appropriate for the intermediary in virtue of his higher social status and his demands for convincing role enactment as an intermediary.

The concept of the intermediary was confirmed in conversations with informants, who verified the "rule" of access to outsiders through an intermediary. In addition, the concept proved useful in explicating what I had, previous to formulation of the principle, viewed as inexplicable behavior. Throughout my years as employee-participant and as ethnographer-participant observer at a Teamsterville settlement house, I had occasion to observe on numerous occasions the following illustration of the intermediary principle in action. The settlement house required that any teenage boy wishing to join the group work program in the middle of the school year come to the office to register and speak to the director. Whenever a teenage boy came to register, however, he always brought a friend, someone who was already a member of the program, who stated the newcomer's case, while the applicant stood by as if mute, although he might later prove to be capable of loud and frequent talk. My uninformed response, borne of being socialized to a very different culture, was skepticism about a teenage boy who could not come on his own and speak "as a man." In Teamsterville, however, I discovered that many of these applicants were speechless only in situations of their choosing. To speak "like a man" in Teamsterville required knowing when and under what circumstances to speak at all.

Teamsterville residents do not think in terms of organized action for community improvement, nor do they think in terms of using a verbal strategy for self-assertion. I asked one block politician, who praised the connections system for satisfying the needs of individuals and families, whether a community group would be able to secure some needed improvement through a persuasive campaign. I tried phrasing the question in several different ways, but my interlocutor would or could answer my question only by pointing to the ways in which individuals secured personal favors through the effectiveness of an intermediary in the social or political system. The connections system—and the local conceptualization of its efficacy—is based on personal ties to intermediaries. My interviews of long-time residents and my own experience produced only two instances of a community group that organized a persuasive campaign for community improvement. Both instances were described by respondents as following this pattern: first, the groups tried to promote a cause through a group-organized persuasive campaign, including appeals through news media, but the groups did not have connections and the campaigns failed; then, someone in the neighborhood who had connections noticed the campaign and acted to secure the needed action. The importance is not the actual, but the reported, result of using personal connections in attaining the desired end. In Teamsterville, speech and group action are not regarded as effective methods for attaining difficult goals, and sometimes speech is thought to be counter-productive.

In summary, speech in Teamsterville is not an effective means for the display of a manly role before one who is not a peer. If an assertion of power is necessary, custom sanctions other means of expression. Naturally, the means vary with the nature of the situation. If one's addressee is of lower status—a child, a woman, a member of another Teamsterville ethnic group—the power assertion may rely on nonverbal threat or physical combat. When one's addressee is of higher status—a boss, an outsider from a more prosperous neighborhood, a government official—male power assertion may properly employ personal connections with an intermediary who states the resident's case for him. When speech is used in asserting influence among peers or in securing the services of an intermediary, the role enactment is effective because of the strength provided by the established solidarity tie rather than the style or content of the verbal message. Just as the woman who has learned her roles in the speech community knows her place is in the home, so a man who has learned his roles in Teamsterville knows his "place" when it comes to speech behavior. He asserts himself in civil or economic affairs through an intermediary, and is neither so bold as to engage in talk with those far above him on the social scale nor so lacking in self-esteem that he must use speech to deal with those below him. To be able systematically to render a convincing performance of the male role in Teamsterville requires control of the culture, particularly that part of the culture which specifies the efficacy of speaking in appropriate, proper, and convincing role enactment.

CONCLUSIONS

The statement that talk is not everywhere valued equally is well established by ethnographic research. There is now a small but growing list of empirical studies which, taken together, verify Dell Hymes' statement that ". . . speaking may carry different functional loads within the communicative economies of differ-

ent societies."[14] The Teamsterville study, as a descriptive datum, is further verification of that statement and also prompts me to speculate about cultural diversity of communication patterns in America. In Teamsterville, talk is negatively valued in many of the very situations for which other American communities most highly prize speaking strategies. Speaking is a culturally prized resource for male role enactment by black Americans in urban ghettos; the black man who *speaks* as a strategy for dealing with outsiders or females is enacting the male role appropriately according to the standards of his speech community.[15] The white collar man who can "talk things through" with his wife, child, or boss is using speech in culturally sanctioned ways.

The statement that talk is not anywhere valued equally in all social contexts suggests a research strategy for discovering and describing cultural or subcultural differences in the value of speaking. Speaking is one among other symbolic resources which are allocated and distributed in social situations according to distinctive culture patterns. In Teamsterville, for example, talk is negatively valued in some situations, positively valued in others, and where it is negatively valued other modes of action are prescribed. To describe Teamsterville men as linguistically deprived, taciturn, or uncommunicative (all of which they are, by the standards of the black ghetto or of middle class suburbia) would be to obscure the nature of the subcultural differences. What should be described, and eventually compared, is the subcultural allocation and distribu-

14 "Models of the Interaction of Language and Social Setting" *Journal of Social Issues* 22 (1967), 10.
15 Cf. Ulf Hannerz "Streetcorner Mythmaking," *Soulside: Inquiries into Ghetto Culture and Community* (New York: Columbia University Press, 1969), pp. 105-117.

tion of communicative resources. What such a perspective implies is not only that communities value speaking differently, but that speaking is a different part, albeit an important one, of the total culture pattern of communication. Fundamental to analysis of the place of speech in communication and social life is the discovery of where and when speech is used, and for what ends it is sanctioned.

Teamsterville is one of many American communities whose members share a distinctive cultural outlook on the value of speaking. If America is the home of diverse views about the value of speaking, then when Americans from diverse communities—or with diverse regional, class, or ethnic backgrounds—try to communicate with each other they bring to the communication encounter different underlying values about what is appropriate and proper communicative conduct. This suggests the importance of understanding the diversity of cultural outlooks on speaking in contemporary America. We have barely any information on what groups in the United States view speaking as an effective means of social influence and what alternatives they envision. Such a deficit in the fund of information should be remedied by descriptive and comparative studies of American speech communities. This study is intended as one contribution to the fund.

2

Reflections on Speaking "Like a Man" in Teamsterville

GERRY PHILIPSEN

Speaking "like a man" in Teamsterville was, for me, initially a practical problem. For 21 of the 30 months in which I participated in Teamsterville-spoken life I was a group worker and the director of a group work program in Teamsterville. These positions required that I enact roles whose convincing performance demanded the display of authority and competence. My acquired speech ways, learned in the academic study of communication and practiced successfully in other professional contexts working with youth, were confusing and troubling to the Teamstervillers, so much so that my persona as a man was fundamentally problematic for them, and thus for me. For an adult male not to be seen and heard as "a man" in Teamsterville rendered him incredible and ineffective in his interpersonal relations. And yet, my professional tasks required that I work effectively, daily, among the Teamstervillers. This problematic of daily life was the crucible in which I learned how to speak "like a man" in Teamsterville.

Learning about Teamsterville speech ways was not, of course, merely a matter of trial and error and it was not, for me, only a practical matter. My practical learning coincided with academic study in the ethnography of communication. It was heavily dependent on the use of the model set forth in Hymes (1962), the rich background represented by the papers included in Hymes (1964), and such early exemplars as Albert (1964), Abrahams and Bauman (1971), Bauman (1970), Basso (1970, and ch. 20, this volume), and Philips (1970). The theoretical and empirical work of Bernstein (1964) and its anthropological reformulation in Douglas (1970) were of fundamental importance as descriptive–analytic resources. Goffman (1959) provided a precedent for studying everyday performances *in situ* and a way to think about performances as constituted by and constitutive of situations. And several works of urban ethnography were of great importance in helping to understand Teamsterville ways of speaking (including, but not limited to, Gans, 1962; Suttles, 1968; Whyte, 1943).

These learnings, practical and academic, local and theoretical, helped to form in me a view or hearing of human communication as deeply situated and deeply cultured. They provided or suggested ways to observe, describe, and interpret communicative practices that, on first experience, were alien to me. They also helped to suggest a larger project of inquiry.

During the Teamsterville experience, and in the course of informally contrasting Teamsterville speech ways with those of other speech communities, I decided to study two ways of speaking, one that finds its expression in the set of social circumstances identified by Bernstein (1964) as hospitable to an emphasis on a "public" code. It was my intent to discover, in Teamsterville communicative practices, a code, if there is one there, pertaining to persons, society, and communication. "Speaking 'Like a Man' " is one in a series of studies in which aspects of an indigenous code are revealed through analysis and interpretation of particular themes. The emphasis on male role enactment articulates with and illustrates a code in which *social* or *positional* (rather than *personal* or *psychological*) attributes are seen (heard?) as pivotal to self-presentation. The later paper on *place* in Teamsterville (Philipsen, 1976a) and the paper on Mayor Daley's council speech (1986), which introduces the formulation of a *code of honor,* continue the formulation of this cultural communicative code.

The code developed in Philipsen (1975, 1976a, 1986) can be juxtaposed to the code developed in Philipsen (1976b), Katriel and Philipsen (this volume), Philipsen (1984, 1987). This is a code of dignity, which emphasizes the personal, the intimate, and the individual, rather than the social, the public, and the cultural, as sources of meaning and motivation in human conduct. Such a code, like the code of honor, is a code pertaining to persons, society, and communication. My move in developing these two codes has been to use each of them heuristically as a resource for explaining and interpreting communicative conduct in the speech communities in which they have force. And I have used the two, juxtaposed to each other, as a heuristic strategy in formulating and applying the codes.

The point never was to posit just two codes but rather to infer from the existence of these two codes the possibility of variety, across speech communities, in communicative codes. With the benefit of the ethnography of communication literature of the past 15 years, it is now possible to see the force of this possibility, as other codes have been proposed that can be comparatively analyzed (see Hymes, 1972, pp. 47–48; Katriel, 1986; Philipsen, 1989).

The various responses to this chapter in the literature of communication studies have been gratifying and instructive to me. I had intended it to be read as a localized theory and not simply as a descriptive report. Reviews of it in Cushman and Sanders (1981); Sanders and Cushman (1984); Cronen, Pearce, and Harris (1979); and Pearce, Cronen, Johnson, Jones, and

Raymond (1980), have all shown ways to treat the chapter as constituting a communication theory and a way of explaining communicative conduct as culturally situated (also see Walter, 1976). Several authors, including those just cited, have helped me to clarify my own thinking about the way the chapter provides a model for illustrating the operation of normative force in shaping communicative conduct (Hart, 1986; Shimanoff, 1980). Uses of it in Braithwaite (1982) and Philipsen (1989) have illustrated how this, and other ethnographic data, taken together, can be used comparatively in building and testing communication theories. And the chapter has been proposed as a resource in teaching communication (see Trenholm, 1986; Trenholm & Jensen, 1988; Cronen et al., 1979; Deetz & Stevenson, 1986) and as containing data useful for thinking about research in communication education (Gorden, 1982; Wiemann, 1978).

A retrospective criticism I would make is that there is very little quoted material presented in this chapter. Were I to re-do the study, I would try to develop a larger corpus than I had of Teamsterville utterances about communication, including a list of terms used to talk about talk (contextualized within utterance and situation). Hymes (1962, p. 110) suggested the usefulness of eliciting terms for speech events and speech acts and Abrahams and Bauman (1971) illustrated a way to use such materials. Later authors provide other useful models of description and analysis (see especially selections in Bauman & Sherzer, 1974) and had I appreciated more fully the utility of such materials and the moves that can be made with them, I would have made a greater effort to collect more. The same can be said of spontaneous comments, made in the flow of social interaction, about communicative activity. Such material, it has been abundantly demonstrated in the literature on the ethnography of communication, is an important resource in discovering ways of speaking.

Of course, Teamsterville was a difficult community in which to elicit talk about talk. It was not a place of which it could be said, as Albert (1972) could say of Burundi, "sensitivity to the variety and complexity of speech behavior is evident in a rich vocabulary for its description and evaluation and in a constant flow of speech about speech" (p. 74). Interviews, even paid interviews, with Teamsterville residents, sometimes ended in considerable frustration for me. I had hoped to elicit talk about talk as well as general background information in the interviews, but in many instances my respondents said very little. As frustrating as this was at the moment, eventually these "failures" were transformed into "data," as instances suggesting that, in some situational contexts, speech is inappropriate as a social activity. In particular, in situations in which a male stranger talks to a woman about her life, reticence for the woman is prescribed. Difficulties notwithstanding, increased efforts to elicit talk about talk would have strengthened the study.

A closely related point is the use of audio and visual recording of communicative activity. Although I did collect several audiotape recordings of Teamsterville speech events, and although some of these are used in the published studies, I would now try to gather more of this kind of material. Where it is feasible, any ethnography of communication should be based substantially on the collection, transcription, detailed analysis, and public display of recorded materials. The experience of listening repeatedly to a segment of conversation and of working extensively at transcribing the communicative activity of such a segment cannot help but impress upon investigators the inadequacies of field notes jotted down after the event. The repeated hearing and painstaking effort to transcribe faithfully some segment of speech helps to bring culturally significant phenomena to the investigator's attention in a way that would not have been possible without the detailed inspection that repeated viewings/hearings provide. And the public display of communicative activity makes these materials available for re-analysis by the original investigator and by others. These points are illustrated in part by comparing the chapter reprinted in this volume with Philipsen (1986), in which a transcription of a Teamsterville-related speech event is presented and analyzed. For the data on male role enactment, audio- and videotaped instances that could be made public and subjected to critical analysis would have strengthened substantially the research report. Moerman (1988) provided an important rationale, perspective, and resource for such work and suggests, I think, a general direction that such studies should take in the future.

References

Abrahams, R., & Bauman, R. (1971). Sense and nonsense in St. Vincent: Speech behavior and decorum in a Caribbean community. *American Anthropologist, 73,* 762–772.

Albert, E. (1964). "Rhetoric," "logic," and "poetics" in Burundi: Culture patterning of speech behavior. In J. J. Gumperz & D. Hymes (Eds.), The ethnography of communication. *American Anthropologist, 66,* pt. 2(6), 35–54.

Basso, K. (1970). "To give up on words": Silence in Western Apache culture. *Southwestern Journal of Anthropology, 26,* 213–230.

Bauman, R. (1970). Aspects of 17th century Quaker rhetoric. *Quarterly Journal of Speech, 56,* 67–74.

Bauman, R., & Sherzer, J. (1974). *Explorations in the ethnography of speaking.* Cambridge: Cambridge University Press.

Bernstein, B. (1964). Elaborated and restricted codes: Their social origins and some consequences. *American Anthropologist, 66,* (6), 55–69.

Braithwaite, C. A. (1982). *Cultural uses and interpretations of silence.* Unpublished master's thesis, University of Washington, Seattle, WA.

Cronen, V. E., Pearce, W. B., & Harris, L. M. (1979). The logic of the coordinated management of meaning: A rules-based approach to the first course in interpersonal communication. *Communication Education, 28,* 22–38.

Cushman, D. P., & Sanders, R. E. (1981). Rules theories of human communication processes: The structural and functional perspectives. In B. Dervin & M. Voigt (Eds.), *Progress in communication sciences* (pp. 71–78). Norwood, NJ: Ablex.

Deetz, S. A., & Stevenson, S. L. (1986). *Managing interpersonal communication.* New York: Harper & Row.

Douglas, M. (1970). *Natural symbols.* New York: Pantheon Books.

Gans, H. I. (1962). *The urban villagers: Group and class in the life of Italian-Americans.* New York: The Free Press.

Goffman, E. (1959). *The presentation of self in everyday life.* New York: Doubleday.

Gorden, W. I. (1982). Narratives of life in work organizations. *Communication Education, 31.*

Hart, R. P. (1986). Contemporary scholarship in public address: A research editorial. *Western Journal of Speech Communication, 50,* 283–295.

Hymes, D. (1962). The ethnography of speaking. In T. Gladwin & W. C. Sturtevant (Eds.), *Anthropology and human behavior* (pp. 13–53). Washington, DC: Anthropological Society of Washington.

Hymes, D. (Ed.). (1964). *Language in culture and society.* New York: Harper & Row.

Hymes, D. (1972). Models of the interaction of language and social life. In J. J. Gumperz & D. Hymes (Eds.), *Directions in sociolinguistics: The ethnography of communication* (pp. 35–71). New York: Holt, Rinehart & Winston.

Katriel, T. (1986). *Talking straight: "Dugri" speech in Israeli Sabra culture.* Cambridge: Cambridge University Press.

Moerman, M. (1988). *Talking culture: Ethnography and conversation analysis.* Philadelphia: University of Pennsylvania Press.

Pearce, W. B., Cronen, V. E., Johnson, K., Jones, G., & Raymond, R. (1980). The structure of communication rules and the form of conversation. *Western Journal of Speech Communication, 44,* 20–34.

Philips, S. U. (1970). Acquisition of rules for appropriate speech usage. *Georgetown University Monograph Series on Languages and Linguistics, 21,* 77–94.

Philipsen, G. (1975). Speaking "like a man" in Teamsterville: Culture patterns of role enactment in an urban neighborhood. *Quarterly Journal of Speech, 61,* 13–22.

Philipsen, G. (1976a). Places for speaking in Teamsterville. *Quarterly Journal of Speech, 62,* 15–25.

Philipsen, G. (1976b). *Speaking as a cultural resource.* Paper presented at the annual convention of the Speech Communication Association, Chicago, IL.

Philipsen, G. (1984). *Joanna Kramer's identity crisis and the myth of dignity.* Paper presented at the annual convention of the Speech Communication Association, Chicago, IL.

Philipsen, G. (1986). Mayor Daley's council speech: A cultural analysis. *Quarterly Journal of Speech, 72,* 247–260.

Philipsen, G. (1987). The prospect for cultural communication. In D. Kinckaid (Ed.), *Communication theory from Eastern and Western perspectives* (pp. 245–254). New York: Academic Press.

Philipsen, G. (1989). Speech and the communal function in four cultures. *International and Intercultural Communication Annual.*

Sanders, R. E., & Cushman, D. P. (1984). Rules, constraints, and strategies in human communication. In C. C. Arnold & J. W. Bowers (Eds.), *Handbook of rhetorical and communication theory* (pp. 230–269). Newton, MA: Allyn & Bacon.

Shimanoff, S. B. (1980). *Communication rules: Theory and research.* Beverly Hills: Sage.

Suttles, G. D. (1968). *The social order of the slum: Ethnicity and territory in the inner city.*

Chicago: University of Chicago Press.

Trenholm, S. (1986). *Human communication theory.* Englewood Cliffs, NJ: Prentice-Hall.

Trenholm, S. & Jensen, A. (1988). *Interpersonal communication.* Belmont, CA: Wadsworth.

Walter, O. M. (1976). *Speaking intelligently: Communication for problem-solving.* New York: Macmillan.

Whyte, W. F. (1943). *Street corner society: The social structure of an Italian slum.* Chicago: University of Chicago Press.

Wiemann, J. M. (1978). Needed research and training in speaking and listening literacy, *Communication Education, 27,* 310-315.

3

How I Got Over: Communication Dynamics in the Black Community

JACK L. DANIEL
GENEVA SMITHERMAN

THIS study is an analysis of the sacred and secular dynamics of the African-American communications system . . . *My soul look back and wonder . . .* which has served to extrapolate, ritualize, and thus preserve the African essence of Afro-American life . . . *how I got over.* We seek to develop a theoretical and conceptual framework for defining Black communication by explicating the cosmology of traditional Africa and demonstrating its continuity in both sacred and secular Black[1] life. Of necessity we have centered our search on the Traditional Black Church[2] because of its crucial and long-standing historical role in sustaining the culture and communication process of African-Americans.

In seeking to clarify the communication patterns of superficially different Black Americans, we take as our text what many a "street man" has told "young-bloods": "Beauty is only skin deep but love is to the bone." This text calls attention to the existence of two levels of reality which will be referred to here as "surface" and "deep" structures. In this context, beauty is a surface structure and love is something that resides within the deep structure—"love is to the bone."

Surface and deep structures have unique but complementary natures. Surface structures are objective, empirical, subject to relatively rapid change, constrained by time and space, and non-generative in nature. Deep structures are intangible, subjective, archetypal, not culturally bound, and generative in nature. Consider the nature of surface and deep structures from the structuralist viewpoint: "The reality sought by structural analysis . . . is not empirical reality but reality at the level of abstract pattern, in terms of certain diagnostic features of empirical phenomena. We seek in the observed phenomena evidence of a regularity that inheres at some other level. . . . It is the set of rules—'knit one, purl two,' and so on—that is the structuralist reality, not the ribbing on Susie's new cardigan."[3] Here we are concerned with apprehending the "knit ones, purl twos" of Black communication. The Black communications network is actualized in different specific ways, contingent upon the socio-cultural context

---

[1] Throughout the paper, we will use the terms Black, Afro-American, and African-American interchangeably to refer to Americans of African descent.

[2] This paper is anchored in the life-long experiences of Jack L. Daniel at Mt. Sinai Baptist Church, Johnstown, Pennsylvania, and Geneva Smitherman at Tennessee Baptist Church, Detroit, Michigan. Both are Traditional Black Churches. For a detailed analysis of the Traditional Black Church, see Melvin D. Williams, *Community in Black Pentecostal Church: An Anthropological Study* (Pittsburgh: Univ. of Pittsburgh Press, 1974), and Henry Mitchell, *Black Preaching* (New York: J. B. Lippincott, 1970).

[3] Eugene A. Hammel, "The Myth of Structural Analysis: Levi-Strauss and the Three Bears," Addison-Wesley Module in Anthropology (Module XXV, 1972), p. 3.

(e.g., "street" vs. "church"), but its basic underlying structures, being grounded in the Traditional African World View, are essentially similar. We bear witness to the cultural continuities between such seemingly disparate groups as preachers and poets, bluesmen and Gospel-ettes, testifiers and toast-tellers, reverends and revolutionaries.

Among these variations, the Traditional Black Church is an exemplary form of Black communication. To speak of the "traditional" Black Church is to speak of the holy-rolling, bench-walking, spirit-getting, tongue-speaking, vision-receiving, intuitive-directing, Amen-saying, sing-song preaching, holy-dancing and God-sending Church. Put another way, this Church may be defined as that in which the cognitive content has been borrowed from Western Judaeo-Christian tradition, and the communication of that content—the affective process—has remained essentially African. This specific convergence of Judaeo-Christian content and African process is found in Protestant denominations, such as Baptist, Methodist, Holiness, and Sanctified, where the worship patterns are characterized by spontaneous preacher-congregation calls and responses, hollers and shouts, intensely emotional singing, spirit possession, and extemporaneous testimonials to the power of the Holy Spirit.

The Traditional Black Church is peopled by lower socio-economic, working class Blacks—domestics, factory workers, janitors, unskilled laborers, etc. While today there is an ever increasing number of high school graduates, most "pillars of the Church" have less than a high school education. It is within the Traditional Black Church that traditional Black folk (Blacks who haven't been assimilated into the elusive American mainstream) create much of their reality. The Traditional Black Church is both a sacred and secular community whose special character, according to Joseph R. Washington, is: ". . . not its content but its intent, for the cult is a synthesis of Western Christianity beliefs, practices, ceremonies, rituals, and theologies, with the African tradition of religion as permeating all dimensions of life, without final distinction between the sacred and the secular. The intent of the Black cult is that of traditional African religions—the seeking of the power of the spirit of God in all times, places, and things because without that power man is powerless."[4] Given these kinds of demographics, the Traditional Black Church becomes "more than a church. It is more than a community. It is a human phenomenon responding to social and economic upheavals."[5]

The essential nature of communication in that Church is an interacting, spontaneous process which has been referred to as "call-response." Briefly defined, this African-derived process is the verbal and nonverbal interaction between speaker and listener in which each of the speaker's statements (or "calls") is punctuated by expressions ("responses") from the listener. As a fundamental aspect of the Black communications system, call-response spans the sacred-secular continuum in Black Culture. In the Church, it is often referred to as the congregation's way of "talking back" to the preacher, the most well-known example of which is "A-men." But Traditional Black Church members also call and respond between themselves as well as the preacher, and Church musicians frequently will "get a thang goin" betwen themselves and their instruments. More than an observed ritual in Church services, call-response is an organizing principle of Black Cultural Reality which enables

---

4 Joseph R. Washington, *Black Sects and Cults* (New York: Doubleday, 1973), p. 20.
5 Williams, p. 183.

traditional Black folk to achieve the unified state of balance or harmony which is essential to the Traditional African World View.

In contrast to those historians, such as E. Franklin Frazier, who have held that American enslavement obliterated for the slaves "the habits and customs as well as the hopes and fears that characterized the life of their forebears in Africa . . . ,"[6] our argument is that the residue of an African heritage persists, undiminished and intact, in the call-response pattern of Black communication. A heritage that may indeed have been amputated in substance yet survives in form.

We have postulated the following two hypotheses to be dealt with in this paper:

(1) There are similarities in the world views of geographically disparate Africans which we refer to as the "Traditional African World View." This View, though possibly not distinctive to Africans, is nevertheless significant for understanding patterns of Black communication in the United States.

(2) The call-response pattern, exhibited most clearly in traditional Black worship service, is reflective of the Traditional African World View. Upon close examination, we find that it is pervasive in secular dimensions of Black Culture and communication and that it reveals not simply a surface difference between white and Black Americans, but a more profound "deep structure" difference rooted in the Traditional African World View.

TRADITIONAL AFRICAN WORLD VIEW

Our hypotheses, of course, rest on the conviction that there *is* a Traditional African World View. While there are

differences in the many tribes, languages, customs, physiognomies, spirits, and deities that exist throughout the African continent, these seeming "diversities" are surface variations on the basic themes acknowledged by traditional Africans. Focusing on such surface differences as tribal customs or politically defined African boundaries may only serve to obscure the existence of the deep structure that is shared by all traditional African people.

Of importance here is the fact that basic underlying thought patterns do exist amid the unending diversity of African people, and thus it is appropriate to speak of traditional African thought as a single entity—albeit with complex and diverse manifestations. Robert F. Thompson conducted field studies of African art in nine different African cultures, and was able to identify common canons of form pervading them all.[7] Similarly, Daryll Forde's studies of African social values in various tribal cultures brought him to remark that: "One is impressed, not only by the great diversity of ritual forms and expressions of beliefs, but also by substantial underlying similarities in religious outlook and moral injunction."[8]

To be sure, students of African culture have yet to detail *all* of the salient features that transcend tribal differences and constitute what we are calling the "Traditional African World View." Yet sufficient patterns of commonality have emerged from research findings and field studies to suggest an interlocking network of cultural and philosophical syn-

---

[6] E. Franklin Frazier, *The Negro Family in the United States* (Chicago: Univ. of Chicago Press, 1966), p. 21.

[7] Robert Farris Thompson, *African Art in Motion* (Los Angeles: Univ. of California Press, 1974), pp. 5-45.

[8] Daryll Forde, ed., *African Worlds: Studies in the Cosmological Ideas and Social Values of African Peoples* (New York: Oxford Univ. Press, 1954), p. x.

onymity in Africa.[9] We turn now to consider some of these common patterns.

UNITY BETWEEN SPIRITUAL AND MATERIAL

A fundamental tenet of the Traditional African World View is what Daryll Forde considers as the African formulation about the workings of the universe,[10] and what E. G. Parrinder referred to as the traditional Africans' perception of a "spiritual universe."[11] The conception is that of a dynamic, hierarchical unity between the spiritual and material aspects of life. Specifically, there is a unity between God, man, and nature, with God serving as the head of the hierarchy. God is followed by lesser deities, spirits, man, other forms of life, and things. Man resides in the middle of the hierarchy, and as such, he is composed of both a spiritual and material self, with, as K. A. Busia noted,[12] the fundamental sense of causation being spiritual. Fela Sowande also speaks to this basic assumption: "Here there is no room for the clear-cut separation of spirit and matter as opposites; spirit is matter at its most rarefied, while matter is spirit at its most congealed. Thus, it is that man has both a 'lower mind,' his heritance from the visible world of nature, and also a 'higher mind' equally his inheritance, but from the invisible world of spirit."[13]

John Mbiti notes the existence of a hierarchy with spiritual and intellectual determinants. He presents the following categories of traditional African religious ontology.

1. "Gods" as the ultimate explanation of the genesis and sustenance of both man and all things.
2. "Spirits" being made up of superhuman beings and the spirits of men who died a long time ago.
3. "Man" including human beings who are alive and those about to be born.
4. "Animals and plants" or the remainder of biological life.
5. "Phenomena and objects without biological life."[14]

As this hierarchy is presented by Mbiti, there are divinities ranging from God through lesser deities who number up to the one thousand and seven hundred "orisha" found among the Yoruba. Closer to man, there are the spirits of the ancestors who continue to have influence over their descendants.

The traditional African world is alive with Gods, spirits, the living dead (persons who recently died), people, animals, plants, and objects without biological life. God is omnipresent, and as Balandier and Maquet indicate, "from the supreme God to the recent dead, there stretches a hierarchy of divine or semi-divine figures who possess the vital force preeminently and whose cooperation must be sought."[15] Spirits dwell in animate and inanimate objects, and man, upon completing his development, transubstantiates into the spiritual realm. That is, the Traditional African World View assumes that man's ultimate destiny is to move on to the "higher ground" of the spiritual world. Both Sowande, a West African, and Mbiti, an East African, emphasize the common be-

[9] For a good summary of the underlying similarity of thought found among diverse African people, see George Balander and Jacques Maquet, *Dictionary of Black African Civilization* (New York: Leon Amiel, 1974), pp. 276-78.

[10] Forde, p. x.

[11] E. G. Parrinder, *African Traditional Religion* (London: Hutchinson House, 1954), pp. 20-28.

[12] K. A. Busia, "The African World View," in Jacob Draker, ed. *African Heritage* (New York: Crowell-Collur, 1963), pp. 146-51.

[13] Fela Sowande, "The Quest of an African World View: The Utilization of African Discourse," in Jack L. Daniel, ed., *Black Communication: Dimensions of Research and Instruction* (New York: Speech Communication Association, 1974), p. 76.

[14] John S. Mbiti, *African Religions and Philosophies* (New York: Doubleday, 1969), p. 20.

[15] Balander and Maquet, p. 277.

lief in the importance of man's spiritual self in the material-spiritual hierarchy. Sowande goes even further to note that when the connection to man's higher self is disrupted, man slips down to a lower level of the hierarchy—i.e., he becomes an animal. "But the senior partner must be his 'higher mind' for this is his one and only link with the world of reality, the invisible world of spirit. It is the disruption or negation of this link that results in that subtle change of attitude by which a world view degenerates into an opportunistic, hypocritical, callously inhuman view of the world, which turns man from a god-in-the-making into a hairless predatory male animal on two legs, no matter what his human pretensions may be socially, academically, or otherwise."[16]

CENTRALITY OF RELIGION

Concomitant with the African emphasis on spirituality is the centrality of religion as a pervasive, dominating force in the life of man. Throughout Africa (and the African diaspora as well), there is no dichotomy between sacred and secular life. Mbiti indicates that there are "no irreligious people" in traditional African society for to be "without religion amounts to a self-excommunication from the entire life of society . . . African people do not know how to exist without religion."[17] Religion permeates all aspects of life since every phase of life in some way relates to man's journey to the spirit world.

Traditional African people are, as Joseph R. Washington wrote, "a people for whom religion was as common as daily bread."[18] "Religion is not a sometime affair. It is a daily, minute involvement of the total person in a community

and its concerns. Indeed, the spirit will not come forth with power apart from the community emptying itself (and thus the priest), so that the power can reign without interference. . . . The heart of traditional African religions is the emotional experience of being filled with the power of the spiritual."[19] Religious beings engaged in the drama of life in a spiritual universe constitute a basic concept of the traditional African "religious configuration."[20]

And among many Blacks in America, religion plays the same active role in life. C. Eric Lincoln maintained that religion was an inextricable dimension on all levels of Black existence in America: "The black man's pilgrimage in America was made less onerous because of his religion. His religion was the organizing principle around which his life was structured. His church was his school, his forum, his political arena, his social club, his art gallery, his conservatory of music. It was lyceum and gymnasium as well as sanctum sanctorum. His religion was his fellowship with man, his audience with God. It was the peculiar sustaining force which gave him the strength to endure when endurance gave no promise, and the courage to be creative in the face of his own dehumanization."[21] Thus, religion, as a fundamental construct of the Traditional African World View, became (to borrow a term from Melville J. Herskovits[22]) the "cultural focus" of Afro-Americans.

HARMONY IN NATURE AND THE UNIVERSE

In traditional African thought, it is believed that the laws governing one's

16 Sowande, p. 76.
17 Mbiti, p. 3.
18 Washington, p. 31.

19 Ibid., p. 30.
20 Adolf E. Jensen, *Myth and Cult Among Primitive People* (Chicago: Univ. of Chicago Press, 1951), p. 9.
21 C. Eric Lincoln, "Foreword," in Leonard E. Barrett, *Soul-Force* (New York: Anchor Books, 1974), p. viii.
22 Melville J. Herskovits, *The New World Negro* (New York: Minerva Press, 1969), p. 13.

self and the laws governing the universe are one and the same. But one cannot simply hold this belief, he must be it and act it. Thus the African World View is manifested in any given individual only when he has become truly a "living witness." One becomes a "living witness" when he aligns himself with the forces of nature, and instead of being a proselytized "true believer," strives to live in harmony with the universe. That is, adherents of the Traditional African World View live as if they are microcosms of a universe that is maintained by the synergic functioning of its spiritual and material essences. Living in harmony with the nature of the universe means, as Sowande indicates, that this World View is not simply a tool for operating in and on the world. Rather, the "world view" emerges "only when the individual has lived himself into what these elements stand for; he must breed into himself the attitudes that they represent; he must turn into the laws of his own being. . . ."[23] For the traditional African, then, the universe is not an intellectual concept, but a "force field with all things interacting" in balance and harmony.[24]

In *Childhood and Cosmos: The Social Psychology of the Black African Child*, Pierre Erny presents an African perspective on childhood that is based, in part, on the propositions being set forth here. Erny indicated that an understanding of who the Black child is must be premised on the deeper understanding of the African Cosmos. "In the traditional African World View, being is identical with life. A vital force similar to that of man animates each object: from god to the least grain of sand the African universe is a seamless cosmos. Each living force is in necessary union with other forces if it wants to increase rather than dwindle. It is inserted in a dynamic hierarchy in which everything is interdependent. Thus, we are introduced into a universe of correspondences, analogies, harmonies, interactions. Man and cosmos constitute one single network of forces; to grasp one intellectually is to grasp the other."[25]

The complementarity of all things in the force field of the universe provides the paradigm for resolving seeming opposites in life. Just as the traditional African finds unity in the sacred and secular aspects of life, he does not dichotomize day and night, good and bad, life and death, or beginning and end. Instead of a perception of opposites, there is a perception of complementary, interdependent, interacting forces, each of which constitutes the beginning and end of the other. The two given forces are synergic in nature, and together they produce a "beat" or rhythm such as the beat of the heart. The universe moves by the many rhythms that are created by the various, complementary, interdependent forces. Thus, traditional African religious ontology constitutes a unity in which "one mode of existence presupposes all others and a balance must be maintained so that these modes neither drift too far apart from one another nor get too close to one another."[26] Put another way, "there is a time and place for everything."

AFRICAN SOCIETY PATTERNED AFTER NATURAL RHYTHMS

In traditional Africa, people pattern their social interactions after the presumed existence of natural rhythms. A traditional African community is itself a rhythm based on the synergic functioning of "I" and "We." Such a com-

23 Sowande, pp. 67-88.
24 Barrett, p. 17.

25 Pierre Erny, *Childhood and Cosmos: The Social Psychology of the Black African Child* (Rockville, Md.: Media Intellectic, 1973), p. 15.
26 Mbiti, p. 20.

munity survives on the rhythm of "I am, because we are; and since we are, therefore, I am."[27] What happens to one in some way affects the entire community, and what happens to the entire community necessarily affects all individuals within that community. Neither "I" nor "We" have meaning apart from the other. As an example of the impact of this rhythmic functioning of "I" and "We," consider the traditional attitude toward marriage.

For African people, marriage is the focus of existence. It is the point where all the members of a given community meet: the departed, the living and those yet to be born. All the dimensions of time meet here, and the whole drama of history is repeated, renewed, and revitalized. Marriage is a drama in which everyone becomes an actor or actress and not just a spectator. Therefore, marriage is a duty, a requirement from the corporate society, and rhythm of life in which everyone must participate. Otherwise, he is a rebel and a lawbreaker, he is not only abnormal but 'underhuman.' Failure to get married under normal circumstances means that the person concerned has rejected society and society rejects him in turn.[28]

Throughout the rhythm of life there are many special events that require the participation of every member of the community. Participation is always individual and corporate, i.e., "I" and "We." There are to be no chains broken nor any rhythms stopped.

TIME AS PARTICIPATION IN EVENTS

Community participation is such a crucial element of the Traditional African World View that the African concept of time is defined in terms of participation in experienced events rather than fixed, abstract points. According to Pierre Erny, "African temporality is not lineal, going from a beginning to-

wards an end."[29] On the other hand, as Erny states: ". . . It's not purely circular either. At each return, something remains behind, and something new is added. It is more precise, therefore, to speak of time as a 'spiral.' The peasant and traditional African has a very strong consciousness of being in a world where everything takes place in cycles, where a single life disappears only to better reappear, in a world where there is nothing new under the sun, where a fundamental continuity underlies all changes that can be perceived, where past, present, and future answer one another endlessly."[30]

In discussing the World View with regard to the concept of time, we will employ the term "phase" to steer us away from the notion of numerically fixed points so common to Western world ontology. As a conceptual term, "phase" should suggest the traditional African predisposition towards recurring, harmonic cycles, and towards series of events which occur in relation to each other. . . . "What goes around comes around. . . ." African phase is related to natural rhythms such as the seasons of the year; it is rhythmical and cyclical rather than linear, in nature. What matters is not the exact, abstract time of the month or day, but one's participation in a wedding or harvest during a given period of the year or season. Being on time has to do with participating in the fulfillment of an activity that is vital to the sustenance of a basic rhythm, rather than with appearing on the scene at, say "twelve o'clock sharp." The key is not to be "on time" but "in time."[31]

27 Ibid., p. 141.
28 Ibid., p. 174.

29 Erny, p. 149.
30 Ibid., p. 149.
31 For a detailed discussion of African and Black American temporality, see Dorothy Pennington, *Temporality Among Black Americans: Implications for Intercultural Communication,* Diss. Univ. of Kansas 1974.

Traditional African phase focuses on present and past experiences rather than on the future which has not been experienced. Since the World View conceptualizes a universe which is cyclical in nature, the "future" is perceived as the past recurring in a different form. Hence there is considerable importance attached to the present and its relation to the past as opposed to the "future." Phase thus is said to be "backward looking," as the traditional African is firmly rooted in the past experiences of elders and the living dead.

From our foregoing discussion of the Traditional African World View, several salient features emerge:

1. There is a fundamental unity between the spiritual and the material aspects of existence. Though both the material and the spiritual are necessary for existence, the spiritual domain assumes priority.

2. While the universe is hierarchical in nature, all modes of existence are necessary for the sustenance of its balance and rhythm. Harmony in nature and the universe is provided by the complementary, interdependent, synergic interaction between the spiritual and the material. Thus we have a paradigm for the way in which "opposites" function. Specifically, "opposites" constitute interdependent, interacting forces which are necessary for producing a given reality.

3. Communities are modeled after the interdependent rhythms of the universe. Individual participation is necessary for individual survival. Balance in the community, as in the universe, consists of maintaining these interdependent relationships.

4. The universe moves in a rhythmical and cyclical fashion as opposed to a linear progression. "Progression," as such, occurs only into the past world of

the spirit. Thus the "future" is the past. In the community, then, one's sense of "time" is based on participation in and observation of nature's rhythms and community events.

5. Since participatory experiences are key to one's sense of "time," the fundamental pedagogy in the school of life becomes experience, and age serves as a fundamental basis for hierarchical social arrangements.

CALL-RESPONSE

Recall that the Traditional African World View conceptualizes a cosmos which is an interacting, interdependent balanced force field. Further, the society is based on such an assumption, and accordingly, the communications system takes on an interactive, interdependent nature. As Oliver Jackson succinctly states it:

The moral sanctity of . . . life [in African society] derives from the idea that all is spiritual and that the Supreme Power embodies the totality of the cosmos in one spiritual unity . . . the African continuum is essentially harmonious. Men, in building their societies, endeavor to reproduce this 'divine or cosmic harmony.' This is the basis of all ethical and moral behavior in community life. This human microcosm must reaffirm the harmonious modality of the cosmic macrocosm.[32]

As a basic communications tactic, call-response seeks to synthesize "speakers" and "listeners" in a unified movement. It permeates all communication, and in the Traditional Black Church it is the basis of all other communicative strategies. Call-response reaffirms the "modality of the cosmic macrocosm."

We are talking, then, about an interactive network in which the fundamental requirement is active participation of all individuals. In this kind of com-

[32] Oliver Jackson, "Preface". *Kuntu Drama*. ed. Paul Harison (New York: Grove, 1974). pp. ix-xiii.

munications system, "there is no sharp line between performers or communicators and the audience, for virtually everyone is performing and everyone is listening."[33] The process requires that one must give if one is to receive, and receiving is actively acknowledging another. Robert Farris Thompson refers to the antiphonal nature of Black communication as "perfected social interaction." He elaborates on this concept as follows:

The arrogant dancer, no matter how gifted or imaginative, may find that he dances to drums and handclaps of decreasing strength and fervor. He may find, and this is damaging to his reputation, that the chorus will crystallize around another person, as in the telling of tales among the Tiv of northern Nigeria. There, we are told by Laura Bohannan, the poor devil who starts a tale without proper preparation or refinement will find the choral answering to his songs becomes progressively weaker until they ultimately reform about a man with stronger themes and better aesthetic organization He is soon singing to himself. The terror of losing one's grip on the chorus is a real one in some African societies, a poignant dimension of social interaction that for some reason is not mentioned in discourse on singing in African music . . .
Thus call-and-response and solo-and-circle, far from solely constituting matters of structure, are in actuality levels of perfected social interaction. The canon is a danced judgment of qualities of social integration and cohesion . . . .[34]

The power potential and fundamental essence of this interactive system is such that Thompson conceives of it as the "politics of perfection."

Call-response or "perfected social interaction" embodies communality rather than individuality. Emphasis is on group cohesiveness and cooperation; the collective common good and spiritual regeneration is reinforced by the visita-

tion of the Spirit, and the efforts of all are needed to bring this about. The preacher says "Y'all ain wid me today, the church is dead," therein acknowledging that he can't make it by himself. But the existence of the "call," which is issued by a single individual in the Group, underscores the importance of individual roles within the Group. The individual is challenged to do what he can within the traditional mold, and he is reaffirmed by the infinite possibilities for unique responses. Centuries-old group norms are balanced by individualized, improvisational emphases. By taking advantage of process, movement, creativity of the moment, and emotional, intuitive, and spiritual guidance, the individual can exercise his sense of Self by virtue of his unique contribution to the Group.

The musical tradition of Black singing groups (sacred and secular) well exemplifies the call-response tradition. Characteristically, a group is comprised of a lead singer ("caller") and his background ("responders"). The leader opens the song and sets the initial mood, but from that point on, the direction and execution of the song depend on the mutual forces of the leader in spiritual combination with his background. For instance, note the opening of the well-known Gospel "How I Got Over":

Leader (Call):	How—
Background (Response):	How I got over.
Leader (call repeated with emphatic feeling):	I said how—
Background (response building with the lead):	How I got over.
Leader:	My soul—
Background:	My soul look back and wonder—
Leader:	How—
Background:	How I got over.

The next verse usually repeats the words of this opening but with greater feeling and emotional intensity, there-

[33] Leonard Doob, *Communication in Africa* (New Haven: Yale Univ. Press, 1961), p. 79.
[34] Thompson, p. 27.

by taking the song to another spiritual level. The total performance of the group is gauged by their skill in manipulating this musical interplay to move their listeners to get the "spirit in the dark."

We find the same musical tradition in the secular world of Black singing groups (who became the model for contemporary mainstream white groups). For example, note the opening lines to "Don't You Know I Love You So," a popular song from the early 1950s and the beginnings of Black "rock n' roll soul music." The song was recorded by the Clovers, a Black group that has perhaps long since been forgotten.

Leader (call):	Oh, don't you know—
Background (Response):	I love you, love you so.
Leader (call repeated):	Oh, don't you know—
Background (Response):	I love you, love you so.
Background (taking over call):	Oh, don't you know I love you, love you so—
Leader (responding):	And I'll never, never let you go—
Leader and Background together:	Ooo-dee — ooo-duu — do-wah — I love you so.

CALL-RESPONSE IN THE TRADITIONAL BLACK CHURCH

The Traditional Black Church, it may be recalled, is that church where Blacks use drums, pianos, organs, guitars, tambourines, other musical instruments, their hands, feet, and voices for producing rhythms, guiding holy dancing, and facilitating spirit possession. In such churches, spirit possession is fundamental to the worship of Jesus Christ (who, at times, appears to be a functional substitute for an African deity). Communication in these church-es involves an interactive, interdependent, spontaneous process for achieving a sense of unity in which members of the congregation obtain a feeling of satisfaction within themselves, between

themselves and others, and between themselves and spiritual forces. Call-response is a fundamental communications strategy designed to bring about this sense of satisfaction.

Much of what is accomplished by call-response can be witnessed by moving through the hierarchy of the Traditional Black Church. That hierarchy is outlined below:

God (The Father, Spirit, and the Holy Ghost)
Minister, Reverend, Elder (God sent men)
Mother of the Church
Old Folk—Elders
Deacons (Spiritual men who assist the Church Head)
Trustees (Lower in hierarchy because of their fiscal concerns)
Saved Adults
Adult Ushers and Nurses
Saved Young Folk
Unsaved Adults and Children
Backsliders (Former Saved people who have resorted to sin)
Sinners

God must send the man who is to lead, and, subsequently, God tells the man what to say and inspires him to say it. From the outset, Church communication takes on a degree of spontaneity since the leader must "wait on the Lord." Simultaneously, it is the beginnings of process, i.e., the *call* by God and the man's *response* by taking up the ministry. Once one acknowledges God's call and one affirmatively responds (many, to their detriment, have tried to ignore God's call), one must still await God's guidance in the daily conduct of one's affairs. Thus, process and spontaneity are maintained by the calls-and-responses between God and the man.

Service in the Traditional Black Church begins with the recognition of the need for God's entrance at the outset. Because it is necessary for God to enter the service, the initial part of the service consists of everyone's making simultaneous calls-and-responses to invoke the spirit. The deacons pray, and, as they pray, the minister, the deaconesses, and elders of the church facilitate their efforts.

Deacon:	Come by here today Lord, come by here
Minister:	Yes Lord, come by here
Deaconesses:	Please Lord, Please Lord
Deacon:	Won't you enter our hearts this morning
Adult:	Here I am Lord, help me, please

The order varies in terms of who's calling and who's responding at any given moment. In addition to the above involvements, the elders are usually singing or humming, and musicians are also helping to bring God into the service.

Following this "warming up" period of invoking the spirit, and other intermediate parts of the service, the preacher gets into his sermon by issuing his initial call: "My theme for today is Waiting on the Lord." The congregation responds with "Take your time," "Fix it up, Reb.," "Come on up, now," or simply "Preach, Reb." When the preacher's calls get stronger and more emotional, you can see the Spirit moving over there in the Amen Corner, and hear the congregation urging him on with "Go 'head, now!" "Yessuh!" "Watch yo-self, now!" and such nonverbal responses as nodding of heads, clapping of hands, stomping feet, jumping up and down, jerking the body, holy dancing, "shouting." While the preacher is moving his congregation through the Power of the Word, the congregation's verbal and body responses are also moving him to a higher level of emotional feeling and understanding of the Magic of the Word. Many's the time the Black preacher has been heard to say, "I sho was gon take it easy today, but the folks made me preach."

In the following example of a funeral sermon from Richard Wright's novel, *The Long Dream,* note the congregation's various insistent and emotional responses which the preacher plays off of as he concretely drives home the abstract notion of death.

'Tell it! Tell it!'
'Look down on us, Lawd!'
'Mercy, mercy, have mercy, Jesus!'
'Who dares,' the reverend asked in a wild cry, 'say "No!" when that old Angel of Death calls? You can be in your grocery store ringing up a hundred-dollar sale on the cash register and Death'll call and you'll have to drop the sale and go! You can be a-riding around in your big Buick and Death'll call and you have to go! You about to git out of your bed to go to your job and old Death'll call and you'll have to go! Mebbe you building a house and done called in the mason and the carpenter and then old Death calls and you have to go! 'Cause Death's asking you to come into your *last* home! Mebbe you planning on gitting married and your wonderful bride's a-waiting at the altar and you on your way and old Death calls: "Young man, I got another bride for you! Your *last* bride!"'
'Lawd, it's true!'
'Gawd's Master!'
'Be with us, Lawd!' . . .
[The Reverend demanded:] '. . . Who understands the Divine Plan of Justice? On the Fourth of July, Gawd reared back and said:
           "Death, come here!"'
'Wonderful Jesus!'
           '"Death, go down to that place called *America!"*'
'Lissen to the Lawd!'
           '"Death find that state they call Mississippi!"'
'Gawd's a-talking!'
           '"Death, go to a town called *Clintonville!"*'
'Lawd, Lawd, Lawd!'
           '"Death, I want you to tell Tyree Tucker that I want to see 'im!"'
'Have mercy, Jesus!'

A black woman gave a prolonged scream and began leaping about; ushers rushed to her and led her bounding body out of the church.

' "Death, tell Tyree that I don't care *what* he's doing, he's got to come home!" '35

As the process gets more and more involved, spiritual forces "take over." Shouting breaks out all over the church. Older saved people and children with "special gifts" start speaking in tongues. The preacher moves on up to his climax, and the congregation suddenly breaks out in song. Now Reverend can't quit. The Spirit won't let him stop. He runs down out of the pulpit. Nurses are fanning those shouters who have passed out. The musicians and the choir begin to take over as the Spirit has driven the physical bodies to exhaustion. "My, my, my!" . . . "My, my, my!" . . . "Yes! yes!" . . . "oo-koo-Koomaba-sigh!" . . . "ak-baba-hunda!". . . . Thus, community is achieved. God has moved from the minister through the elders, and with the involvement of the saved, the "doors of the church are opened" to the unsaved.

CALL-RESPONSE IN SECULAR LIFE

As we have noted throughout this paper, traditional views distinguish but seek a unity between sacred and secular life. Thus not only is call-response necessary in the Traditional Black Church, it is also a basic communication strategy permeating Black secular life.

In secular style, call-response takes the form of a back-and-forth banter between the rapper (rhetor) and various members of his group, in which, for instance, group members might raise points to see how skillfully the rapper deals with them. Or the group will spur the rhetor on to greater heights of verbal accomplishment by expressions of approval, like "Oh, you mean, nigger" (said with affinity), "get down, man," or "get back, baby," and with nonverbal

35 Richard Wright, *The Long Dream* (New York: Ace Books 1958), pp. 295-97.

behavior like laughter, giving skin, hitting on the wall or backs of chairs, and rich body movements, like rocking back and forth on the heels, circular movements approximating a kind of short dance step. In the secular world, too, there is a kind of hierarchy (though not as rigidly stratified with distinct roles, as in the Church). The secular hierarchy is headed by the heroic man of words in the form of poolroom, barbershop, or street corner rapper; sharp-witted player of the Dozens; or creative narrator of Toasts and other Black folk stories.

In addition to the plain, everyday conversational sets where this pattern comes into play, it is interesting to observe it in operation in more "formal" secular settings, such as at Black political rallies and poetry performances. Just as in Church, the speaker's initial call will be punctuated by expressive responses, (secularized, of course). Instead of "Preach, reverend," we hear "Teach, brother." "Amen" is replaced by "Do it, baby." And we hear many *tell the truth's, shonuff's,* and *yeah! yeah's!,* just as in the Church. There are gestures such as the giving of the Black Power sign (raised clenched fist), which replaces the church gesture of waving one's hand in the air ("I couldn't say nothing, I just waved my hand"). When it really gets good, and the speaker is shonuff tellin it like it T.I.IS., folk begin to holler, jump up and down in their seats (i.e., "shouting" as in church), and stomp their feet. Like the preacher and everyday Black people, poets and political rhetor-rappers thrive on audience involvement— they need to know that their audience is moved by their rap and gauge its power by the degree and extent of their responses.

Calling-responding; stating and counter-stating; acting and re-acting; testing your performance as you go—it is such a natural, habitual dynamic in Black communication that Blacks do it quite unconsciously when rapping to other Blacks. But call-response can be disconcerting to both parties in Black-white communication, presenting a real case of cross-cultural communication interference. When the Black person is speaking, the white person, because call-response is not in his cultural heritage, obviously does not engage in the response process, remaining relatively passive, perhaps voicing an occasional, subdued "mmmm-hhm." Judging from the white individual's seeming lack of involvement in the communication, the Black communicator gets the feeling that the white isn't listening to him, and may repeatedly punctuate his "calls" with questions, such as "Are you listening to me?" "Did you hear me?" etc. In an extended conversation, such questions become annoying to the white, and he may exclaim, "Yes, I'm listening, of course, I'm listening, I'm standing right here!" Then when the white communicator takes over the "call," the Black person, as is customary, begins to get all into it, responding with verbal expressions, like "Dig it!" "Tell it," "I hear you," "Go head, run it down," and moving and dancing around when he hears something that he thinks is really dynamite. Judging from all this apparent "communication interference," the white person gets the feeling that the Black person isn't listening because he "keeps interrupting and turning his back on me." (There is also the possibility that the Black person will not be his natural self and respond at all; hence also preventing maximum communication.)

In the excerpt below, from Ralph Ellison's short story, "Mister Toussan," Buster and Riley exemplify a secular version of call-response. Buster is narrating the story of the Haitian General, Toussaint L'Ouverture, who, in 1791, led the only successful slave revolt in his-

tory. Note how Riley punctuates and reinforces each line of the story (i.e., Buster's "call") with varied "A-men" type responses, occasionally, as he probably does in Church, repeating the exact words of the "call," other times issuing forth with exclamatory *Jesuses* and *Yeah's!*, and sometimes adding the completer to Buster's "call" statements.

Riley looked hard at Buster and seeing the seriousness of the face felt the excitement of a story rise up within him.

'Buster, I'll bet a fat man you lyin'. What'd that teacher say?'

'Really, man, she said that Toussan and his men got up on one of them African mountains and shot down them peckerwood soldiers fass as they'd try to come up. . . .'

'Why good-God-a-mighty!' yelled Riley.

'Oh boy, they shot 'em down!' chanted Buster.

'Tell me about it, man!'

'And they throwed 'em off the mountain. . . .'

'. . . Goool-leee! . . .'

'. . . And Toussan drove 'em cross the sand. . . .'

'. . . Yeah! And what was they wearing, Buster? . . .'

'Man, they had on red uniforms and blue hats all trimmed with gold, and they had some swords all shining what they called sweet blades of Damascus. . . .'

'Sweet blades of Damascus! . . .'

'. . . They really had 'em,' chanted Buster.

'And what kinda guns?'

'Big, black cannon!'

'And where did ole what-you-call-'im run them guys? . . .'

'His name was Toussan.'

'Toussan! Just like Tarzan. . . .'.

'Not *Taar-zan*, dummy, *Toou-zan!*'

'Toussan! And where'd ole Toussan run 'em?'

'Down to the water, man. . . .'

'. . . To the river water. . . .'

'. . . Where some great big ole boats was waiting for 'em. . . .'

'. . . Go on, Buster!'

'An' Toussan shot into them boats. . . .'

'. . . He shot into em. . . .'

'. . . Shot into them boats. . . .'

'Jesus!! . . .'

'With his great big cannons. . . .'

'. . . Yeah! . . .'

'. . . Made a-brass. . . .'

'. . . Brass. . . .'

'. . . An' his big black cannon balls started

killin' them peckerwoods. . . .'

'. . . Lawd, Lawd. . . .'

'. . . Boy. till them peckerwoods hollowed *Please, Please Mister Toussan, we'll be good!'*

'An' what'd Toussan tell em, Buster?'

'Boy, he said in his big deep voice, *I oughta drown all a-you bastards.'*

'An' what'd the peckerwoods say?'

'They said, Please Please, *Please,* Mister *Toussan.* . . .'

'. . . We'll be good,' broke in Riley.

'Thass right, man,' said Buster excitedly. He clapped his hands and kicked his heels against the earth, his black face glowing in a burst of rhythmic joy.

'Boy!'

'And what'd ole Toussan say then?'

'He said in his big deep voice: *You all peck- erwoods better be good, 'cause this is sweet Papa Toussan talking and my nigguhs is crazy 'bout white meat!'*

'Ho, ho, ho!' Riley bent double with laugh- ter. The rhythm still throbbed within him and he wanted the story to go on and on. . . .[36]

At this point, Riley has become uncon- trollably ecstatic about the story and superconfident that he knows how to "put the right stuff" to story-telling. So they switch roles, Riley becoming the "caller," Buster the "responder," and thus the moving rhythm of this story within a story is sustained to its climax.

As a communicative strategy, then, call-response is the manifestation of the cultural dynamic which finds audience and listener or leader and background to be a unified whole. Shot through with action and interaction, Black communi- cative performance is concentric in qual- ity—the "audience" becoming both ob- servers and participants in the speech event. As Black American Culture stresses communality and group experi-

36 Ralph Ellison, "Mister Toussan," in *Black American Literature: Fiction*, ed. Darwin Turner (Columbus: Charles E. Merrill, 1969), pp. 98-99.

entiality, the audience's linguistic and paralinguistic responses are necessary to co-sign the power of the speaker's rap or call. They let him know if he's on the right case. A particular individual's lin- guistic virtuosity is rewarded with a mul- tiplicity of fervent and intense responses. Thus despite the cultural constraints im- posed on individuality, skillful sacred and secular rappers can actualize their Selfhood within the community setting. Finally, as with other rhetorical strate- gies in Black communication, call- response is universally imbedded in the Traditional African World View, the "deep structure" of Black Culture, and we find this structure surfacing in con- crete reality by witnessing the various ways individuals manipulate the strategy or deal within the ritual.

CONCLUSION

We contend that the Traditional Afri- can World View constitutes the basis, the source, the "deep structure" and in- deed, the fountainhead, of Black com- munication in America. We find that View most carefully preserved and re- tained in the Traditional Black Church. Recognizing that one cannot duplicate in America *precisely* what would have existed in traditional African society, we have been concerned with demonstrating communicative *patterns*—"knit ones and purl twos"—which clearly reveal the ap- propriation and transformation of the Traditional African World View for the complex social situations that obtain in America. And these tasks have led us to conclude that call-response is a basic communicative strategy necessary to the social and cultural life-blood of Black America.

4

How I Got Over and Continue to Do So in Our Mothers' Churches

JACK L. DANIEL
GENEVA SMITHERMAN-DONALDSON

Testifying about the congregations to whom she has preached, Reverend Renita J. Weems (1988) affirmed that the dynamics of the traditional Black Church are still operative, although there were some Black militants of the 1960s who "shook their fists at the church and resolved to shoot their way into the promised land" (p. 64). Very perceptively, Reverend Weems also noted that, "Here in our mothers' church we also learn what it means to hold fast to visions others cannot see" (p. 64). We here bear witness to the truth of this statement, and in so doing, reaffirm our long-held view about the central role of the Traditional Black Church in preserving the culture and communication of African Americans.

It has now been over a decade since we wrote "How I Got Over: Communication Dynamics in the Black Community." Many considered it a pioneering article at that time, and it came to be widely cited in studies of Black rhetoric and culture. Then, as now, we thought it to be of critical importance to demonstrate the linkages between *colleged* (to borrow a term from Langston Hughes' Jess B. Simple) and noncolleged Blacks, between sacred and secular essences, and between the spiritual and material realms of Black life. For those who needed "hard data," we presented communication patterns from diverse Black sources demonstrating the continuity of the Traditional African World View in people seemingly as variant as rappers and reverends.

Although we focused our earlier attention on the Traditional Black Church as the place where the continuity of culture, communication, and community were most evident, in a profound sense, we were not advocating organized religion, per se, nor proselytizing for any particular Black Church. At bottom, we were bearing witness to the power of vision, faith, and collective Spirit found in the Black Church that had enabled African Americans to "make a way outa no way" for nearly 4 centuries.

The present historical moment is characterized by crack and crime running rampant in the "Chocolate Cities" of the Nation. Seemingly undaunted by the social deterioration in their midst, for many young Blacks, *def*[1] is the order of the day. "Buppies" (the Black upwardly mobile) are on the run from the Black underclass, and Black leadership is divided and immobilized by factors such as Reagan Era policies.

During the decade since we wrote the original article, Blacks have undergone increased rates of "being in the world" (i.e., not living in accordance with the "Word," as rendered in the Traditional Black Church). Some of the new higher education degree-holders have kneeled to the modern Baals of high technology and high information. In this midnight hour, we believe more strongly than a decade ago that the African American community needs to "go back to the Old Landmark."

With the changing ethnography of the Black community, modern rappers such as Run DMC, the Fat Boys, Salt-n-Pepper, and a host of others have seized an aspect of the communicative baton. That is, the contemporary rap musicians have appropriated a number of Black communication dynamics (call/response, rhythmic discourse, signifying, indirection, and testifying) to preach secular sermons primarily to Black youth. As powerful as the rappers seem to be, however, we see no evidence that the rappers can substitute for the reverends. Notwithstanding, the sound moral and political content of some rap musicians, Los Angeles Black gang violence, and Black-on-Black homicide throughout the Nation are sufficient testimony to the inadequacy of manipulating the Word without spiritual roots.

The Traditional Black Church, our ages-old landmark, is still a place where weary souls are fortified, where a sense of secular and sacred community is affirmed, where joyful ceremonies take place, and where the cultural life-blood of the Black community is purified and enriched by the Spirit. It is still a place where call/response is the communicative well-spring of collective catharsis, and where visions of Black survival and advancement are seen in the mind's eye.

These are the visions that informed both the 1984 and the 1988 Presidential quests of Reverend Jesse Jackson. Both his political rhetoric and the cultural context that gives rise to it are rooted in the Traditional Black Church, which is to say, as we have shown, rooted in the traditional African world view. In fact, it was precisely Jackson's Black communication (read: Black Church) style that bonded him to African Americans, who are rooted in these dynamics, and simultaneously helped distance him from White Americans, to most of whom, despite some linguistic cross-over

---

[1]*Def,* widely used among Black teens and young adults, a positive superlative applied to even greatly diverse realities (i.e., "her rap was def," as well as "it was a def funeral").

(though mostly surface), these Black communication dynamics remain alien.

We illustrate with Jackson here not only because he has become virtually a household word, but also to set the stage for a significant point of departure in our current research on Black communication dynamics. We have turned our attention to the language and culture of African American women, long neglected in both our own work and that of other scholars. The "womanist" (Walker, 1983) tradition of Black women has been vital in nurturing and maintaining the traditional African world view in the culture and communication of the Traditional Black Church. Writing with two other scholars, we have taken note of the sexism that leads to an excessive focus on the Black male preacher as stimulus in Church dynamics (Daniel, Daniel, Poag-Rhodes, & Smitherman-Donaldson, 1987). Therefore, we have called for a reversal of the "figure and ground" and the need to focus on the roles of Black church women. Our position is as follows:

> Black women have been the key to maintaining the institutional structure of the traditional Black church as well as the critical cultural products emanating from that church . . .
>
> . . . Black women . . . carefully structure the environment. Hugs and kisses flow freely as they greet Black women and others. Dyadic and small group conversations are sprinkled throughout the pews. Smiles, head nods, and other body language are used to conduct conversations across the aisles . . . As Evangeline Grant Redding put it, "Without the black woman, and the support and communication she so fervently and tirelessly renders, the oldest, most entrenched, richest, and most influential institution and government of black humanity might sink into hopeless oblivion." (1987, p. 39)

Where do we go from here? African American women, particularly those in the Black Church, are key to answering this question. Assuming leadership in the current national Black crisis, they can take us back to the old landmark of communication and community. The current Black community crisis, as many have noted, involves massive social and economic dislocation, "babies having babies," high rates of functional illiteracy and school drop-outs, high rates of alcohol and other substance abuse, spiritual malaise, and abandonment of Black community and culture among those with "degrees and do."

In looking to African American women, we are not proceeding from a naive optimism about their power nor an illusory celebration of their potential role in healing the Black community. Indeed, the tradition of our Black foremothers in Black liberation, in general, and in religion, in particular, speaks for itself, from the reigns of the Ethiopian Makeda, known as the Queen of Sheba, to Hatshepsut and Nefertiti of Egypt, the latter noted by John Henrik Clarke (1978) for having "almost singlehandedly keeping alive the new religion that he [King Akhenaton] had founded" (p. v). Just as Queen Nzingha led the 16th-century resistance to the Portuguese pursuit of slaves, we are reminded of "hard-line" freedom fighters like Harriet Tubman, who escaped from slavery in Maryland, leaving behind her husband who had threatened to report her to "ole massa," and who went on to rescue more than 300 slaves, and the Black-English-speaking orator, Sojourner Truth, one of the first Black women preachers, who fought for both Black and women's rights.

Historically, African American women, as well as bold Black women of today, are anchored in the Traditional Black Church. In fact, most Black Church congregations are approximately 80% female. It is Black Church women, with communication symbols rooted in the sacred-secular traditional African world view, who can impose the abstract reality of "He never failed me yet" on the concrete case of the crack addict. Whereas their "worldly" Brothers only speak of "on T./on time" in reference to the NBA, Black Church women apply the psychic power of the "Word" both to basketball and to the bread-winner, now unemployed, without enough money for basketball or bread ("He may not come when you want Him, but He's right on time").

The "womlich" (gloss: standard English womanly, i.e., as opposed to girlish) talk of Black women is a fruitful area of research not only for communication scholars but also for those committed to the healing of the Black community. For it is primarily Black women, those steady-on-the-case, "eyes-on-the-prize" Faithful, whose communication dynamics echo the ancient call of the traditional African world view, who can recreate the healing power of "Sweet Mother of Mine" in our mothers' churches as well as in our communities. If Black communication scholars make these Black women's communication their cynosure, then such scholars can make a major contribution to the maintenance of the Black community's historical lifeblood.

References

Daniel, J. L., Daniel, J. E., Poag-Rhodes, L., & Smitherman-Donaldson, G. (1987). The nurturing role of black church women. *The Griot, 6* (3), 33–43.

Clarke, J. H. (1978). New introduction. In C. A. Diop (Ed.), *The cultural unity of black Africa* (pp. i–xv). Chicago: Third World Press.

Walker, A. (1983). *In search of our mothers' gardens: Womanist prose.* New York: Harcourt, Brace.

Weems, R. J. (1988, September). Amen, Sister!. *Essence,* pp. 63–64, 132.

5

On Being a Recognizable Indian Among Indians

D. LAWRENCE WIEDER
STEVEN PRATT

In conducting their everyday affairs, persons unavoidably confront the problem of observing others and being observed by them.[1] Every course of action that in any way requires the cooperation of others, or that can be impeded by others, requires that the actor correctly recognize who the others are and requires that the actor make who he or she is and what he or she is doing visible and recognizable.[2]

Being a particular type of person and being engaged in a particular type of action covers a large territory — it includes such diverse matters as being one who is standing in line and being a true friend. However broad and diverse the territory, it is unified by some common features. These include the following:

1. By appropriately behaving or otherwise indicating that one is a person of a particular sort, a person obliges and/or induces others to treat him or her as that sort of person.[3] For example, by appropriately (visibly and recognizably) standing in line at the theater box office, one obliges others who wish a place in line to take their place behind oneself. By behaving and otherwise indicating that one is a friend, one obliges and induces the other to treat one as a friend.

2. The very action that indicates who one is requires the appropriate response of the other for its fulfillment and completion. To be a certain kind of person (e.g., a male, a student, a physician) requires

---

[1] See Sacks (1972), Goffman (1959), and Wieder (1984).
[2] That is, he must make himself and his action "account-able" in Garfinkel's (1967) sense.
[3] Compare Goffman (1959, p. 13).

that one elicit the enabling responses[4] of others that permit the enactment or performance of that persona.[5]

3. Those actions and other displays that make being that type of person visible and recognizable are not mere indicators or signs of being that type of person, as Goffman (1959) would have it, which can be divorced from actually being that type of person or doing what that type of person does. They are essential, organizing constituents of being that type of person. That is, the ways that persons make who they are (or what they are doing) visible and recognizable to others are essential and organizing constituents of living a life as that kind of person or of doing that kind of action.[6] Whatever it is that one does to make it evident to others that one is, for example, actually standing in line, that activity of making it evident is an essential constituent of standing in line itself. And that activity of "making evident" and its "method" is an organizing constituent of standing in line. It orders that activity for those who witness it, and it orders the activity from the standpoint of the person who does it or "undergoes" it. Similarly, however it is that one shows that one is a friend, that activity is an essential and organizing constituent of being a friend. However some persons make it evident (make it visible and recognizable) that they are a woman, the methods and activity of making it evident are essential organizing constituents of being a woman or living one's life as a woman.[7]

4. What one does in making it evident that one is a particular type of person is necessarily correlated with what others recognize in recognizing that particular type of person. Of course, who it is that stands as an audience makes a difference here.[8] In one important range of cases, the audience is also an incumbent of the category being recognized. It is very common that members of a category not

---

[4]See Wieder (1984, pp. 31–36) and Zaner (1981).

[5]If this is not inevitably so, it is surely characteristically so. Perhaps this is most vivid in the case of "being a leader." Without someone following, the claim of being a leader is empty.

[6]Compare Garfinkel (1967, pp. 1–34) and Wieder (1984).

[7]Perhaps, at some point, we will be in a position to say that the methods and activity of making it evident that one is some particular thing or is doing some particular thing *is* that thing, but, here, we only argue that these are essential, organizing constituents of that thing.

[8]For example, the methods that the police use to recognize probable criminals only overlap in part with the methods employed by criminals in recognizing their fellow criminals (cf. Sacks, 1972). The recognition here is complicated by the fact that criminals generally seek to avoid recognition by the police. Further, some audiences seek to recognize categories of persons that are unknown to the persons being categorized—psychiatrists and other staff in geriatric hospitals are in such a position. But cases with this form are located at one end of the diverse territory. They are worthy of analysis, but they are not considered here.

only seek to be recognized as members, but it is also the case that being a member of that category requires such recognition. Being one who stands in line is one such example. Being a recognizable American Indian among American Indians is another.[9] In these instances, the adequacy of one's recognition of other members of the category is itself a constituent feature of making oneself recognizable as a member. Thus, for example, properly recognizing other persons who are standing in line is one feature of "doing" "standing in line" in a visible and recognizable way. Recognizing other real Indians and only other real Indians as real Indians is one feature of being a recognizable real Indian for other real Indians.

In this chapter, we focus our attention on the question of how Indians determine the answer to the question, "Who is an Indian?" and the counterpart of that question, "How does a real Indian make himself or herself recognizable as a real Indian?" The problem of "recognition and being recognized" among Indians recommends itself as an especially useful example for investigation, because the matter is so consequential and problematic for Indians. It also illuminates the phenomenon of "leading one's life as an Indian." On frequent occasions, the issues of recognition become a matter of discussion and "folk analysis." That is, Indians discuss the obvious Indianness, or lack of it, of a candidate Indian. "Is he really an Indian?" is a question that they ask, and they know that it can be asked about them. They are, then, reflective in areas that most of us simply take for granted. In their reflectiveness, Indians make especially good informants on the problem of recognition and being recognized. In its being problematic, the matter is also open to direct observation as it emerges and is dealt with in gatherings of two or more Indians.

In our research, we capitalized on this reflectiveness and observability. Pratt, who collected most of the primary data, is an actively participating member of the Osage tribe. In becoming a participant observer of matters that he was already participating in, he did little to alter his usual activity, other than taking notes and becoming somewhat more focused in his attention. He also employed his family, friends, and others as informants, but his questions were questions that he might well have asked as part of his ordinary pursuits. Some of these conversations were tape-recorded, but that, too, was not extraordinary in a setting in which participants record

---

[9]An attractive possible claim here is that the activity and method of making oneself visible and recognizable as "standing in line" or as "being a real Indian" is correlated, point for point, with the "criteria" employed by others (who are "standing in line" or who are recognizable real Indians) in competently recognizing another as being one of them. The material we have in hand suggests such a claim, but does not warrant it.

each others' stories and songs. Some of the data comes directly from Pratt's own cultural expertise and recollected experiences. Some of these materials were elicited by Wieder's treating Pratt as an informant.

On the Question: "Who is an Indian?"

The question, "Who is an Indian?" is of critical importance to the Bureau of Indian Affairs (BIA), to the Indian Health Service, to the U.S. Census, to the Department of Labor, to those charged with certifying voters for tribal elections, and, crucially, for those persons who are regarded by others and by themselves as "really and truly" authentic Indians — persons who live their lives as Indians and who are facilitated in doing so by others who also live their lives as Indians — we call them *real Indians*.[10]

The question, the method whereby it is answered, and that which follows from an answer to it is clearly consequential. These considerations are consequential for the determination of who is entitled to BIA services, who is entitled to health care, who may vote in tribal elections, who controls BIA-recognized tribal politics, how many Indians there are, "officially speaking," and where they reside, how many are unemployed and, hence, which counties within states will receive federal grants for services to unemployed Indians, and so on, and, finally, who will be permitted or blocked, encouraged or discouraged, facilitated or left to their own devices in their desire and effort to be recognized as an Indian among Indians and to live their life as an Indian.

The variety of "interested parties," the variety of interests in the question, the variety of candidate Indians, and the variety of historically embedded methods of answering the question make the real Indian's version of the question particularly problematic. And in view of the real Indian's method of answering the question, this manifold of interests, interested parties, and interested candidates also makes the question especially consequential for the real Indian.

How the real Indian poses and answers the question and how he or she guarantees that others will arrive at the correct answer about him or her is the focus of our research. But, because the question is contexted by and complicated by the other modes of asking and answering the question, a short digression into an oversimplified and compacted version of American Indian history is unavoidable.

The question, "Who is an Indian?" may be traced in its complexity to

---

[10]Real Indians do use the expression "real Indian," but not with the regularity and standardization that our usage implies. They do, however, refer to persons who are "really Indian" in just those words with regularity and standardization.

sometime during the late 1700s and early 1800s. By then, intermarriages between Whites and Indians were of sufficient frequency that some full-fledged tribal members, and even tribal leaders, were of mixed blood. Some Whites married into Indian families just to be able to claim tribal status and eligibility for lands, while retaining White modes of life and White identities. When the U.S. government, through a variety of different actions, established and/or recognized tribal rolls around the turn of the century, the issue of identity was settled on a variety of practical grounds and was, at that point, further complicated by the assignment, to some tribes' rolls, of some White families living in the area occupied by that particular tribe. With continued intermarriage, loss of their tribal language by some tribes, the success of the BIA in forcing assimilation and migration off reservations and Indian territories to major American cities, and other parallel processes, "Who is an Indian?" became even more ambiguous.

Although tribal rolls and claims and demonstrations concerning so-called "blood quantum" serve as the grounds for answering the question by the Bureau of Indian Affairs and other governmental agencies, departments, and bureaus, these are neither especially helpful for nor relevant to answering the question as posed by real Indians. The government's methods cause to be included many who are not real Indians and exclude many persons who are real Indians. Thus, the real Indian, the embodiment and carrier of the tradition, is faced with many candidate colleagues, only some of whom qualify.[11]

Although this proposal is accurate, it is also misleading. From the standpoint of the U.S. government, through its agencies, one either is or is not an Indian in the same sense that one is or is not a male or is or is not 46 years old. Several considerations are involved here. The categories are finite and mutually exclusive. Assignment to the categories is ascribed at birth. If the assignment was correctly made, it is permanent. It describes an indelible property of the person. Finally, it is a property of the person — it is possessed independently of the person's contingent performances with others and independently of his or her being recognized by others.

From the standpoint of the practices of the real Indian, being a real Indian is not ascribed, nor is it even merely achieved.[12] Being a real Indian is not something one can simply be, but is something that one becomes

---

[11]Even here, we oversimplify. Many of those who are governmentally recognized as Indians have no desire to be so recognized. Some of those do desire to be recognized by the government, but not by Whites or by real Indians, and so forth.

[12]This is not to say that there are no ascriptive or achieved features of being a real Indian. One must be able to make some claims to kinship with others who are recognized as real Indians, and one must have learned how to behave as one. These are at most necessary, but not sufficient, grounds for being recognized as a real Indian by other real Indians, and, often, these issues of ascription and achievement do not emerge in the recognition.

and/or is, in and as "the doing" of being and becoming a real Indian. To be sure, one must learn how to "do" being and becoming a real Indian, but if one does not continue to "practice" what one knows, one ceases to be a real Indian.[13] Finally, "doing" being and becoming a real Indian is not something that can be done by oneself. In a multitude of ways, it requires the participation of other real Indians.

To put the point more directly, being a visible and recognizable (i.e., accountable, in Garfinkel's, 1967, sense) real Indian for other real Indians is a continuous, ongoing, contingent achievement involving both the doings of the person who would be a real Indian and the doings of those real Indians with whom he or she interacts. Properly conceived, being and becoming a real Indian, in and as "the doing" of being and becoming a real Indian, is not even a feature of the constituent actions of the recognizable real Indian. To adapt Goffman's (1959, p. 253) language, being a recognizable real Indian is an emergent dramatic effect that arises out of the interaction between and among real Indians. But herein lies part of the consequentiality of the very question, "Who is an Indian?" Not only is getting oneself recognized as an Indian crucial to the persistent and effective doing of being and becoming an Indian, the way that one makes the determination that someone else is or is not a real Indian is also a constituent part of doing being and becoming a real Indian. That is, incorrectly identifying someone as a real Indian when they are not, or not recognizing them when they are, places one's social being as a real Indian in jeopardy. Real Indians will take the misidentification as an indicator that one is not as real an Indian as had heretofore been supposed. But the matter does not end here. The misidentification is also consequential for the real Indianness of one's kin, and it entails the acceptance of costly obligations that, if accepted on behalf of one who is not a real Indian, impede the continuous achieving of "doing" being and becoming a real Indian.

Being a Recognizable Indian

How then does a real Indian identify another person as a full-fledged cultural colleague—as a real Indian like himself? Government certification or the claim that one is Indian hardly counts—indeed, such claims, if advanced as sole or primary grounds, would more likely lead toward disqualification. Physical appearance, although it is not disqualifying, cannot be relied on, because many have an Indian's appearance who are not real Indians. Costumes can be adopted by anyone who chooses to wear

---

[13]Here it should be noted that ceasing to practice law or medicine does not, thereby, mean that one is no longer an attorney or a physician.

them. The use of costumes is more likely to play a part in disqualification than it is to lead to qualifying one as a real Indian, for certain modes of costume are known to be adopted by those who would like to be accepted as a real Indian but who are not: for example, a male college student's routinely wearing his hair braided on campus. Open and active displays of knowledge of Indian lore are also likely disqualifiers. In brief, all the standard ways that White Americans use to identify themselves as this or that are quite likely, indeed in most cases are certain, to fail if applied to being recognized as a real Indian among Indians. To be recognized as a real Indian among Indians, one must, above all else, act like an Indian, comport and carry oneself as an Indian, and do what one does in the fashion that an Indian does what he does. Although there are important tribal differences and one cannot be a real Indian without tribal identification and linkage, "acting like a real Indian" crosses all tribal lines and also is employed in recognizing any real Indian, whatever his tribe or tribes.

Among the prominent modes of comporting oneself as a real Indian — modes of communicative behavior that are "criterial" in the identification of a real Indian — we discuss (a) reticence with regard to interaction with strangers, (b) the acceptance of obligations, (c) razzing, (d) attaining harmony in face-to-face relations, (e) modesty and "doing one's part," (f) taking on familial relations, (g) permissible and required silence, and (h) public speaking.

Reticence With Regard to Interaction With Strangers

Reticence is a peculiarly White American way of characterizing this form of communicative behavior. The real Indian pattern has no name within the experience of the real Indian and is the ground against which the distinctive figure of stereotypically White American chattiness, gregariousness, or free and idle talk stands out. To the real Indian, it appears that White Americans who are strangers to each other may freely engage in conversation in such public places as the supermarket check-out line. Commercial airlines provide an even more intense opportunity for easy conversation between strangers. Seatmates often disclose their life histories to each other. In the culture of real Indians, these are extraordinary and improper ways to behave, especially when both parties are real Indians. When real Indians who are strangers to one another pass each other in a public place, wait in line, occupy adjoining seats, and so forth, they take it that it is proper to remain silent and to not initiate conversation. Being silent at this point is a constituent part of the real Indian's mode of communicating with others, especially other Indians. Among other things, it communicates that the one who is silent is a real Indian.

Two of our informants, from different tribes, provided us with examples of this identifying form of conduct. One said:

> I passed this Indian girl on the way to class for two months, and we never spoke——She knew who I was, and I knew her name.

Another told us that:

> When I was at this conference, this other Indian girl and I never did talk to each other until the last night. There was one girl who was there and did come up and talk to me who said she was Indian, but I could tell she wasn't, because if she was, she probably wouldn't have come up and talked to me.

That is, a real Indian would not initiate an interaction so casually, abruptly, and idly, nor would they attempt to establish themselves as an Indian by simply saying that they were an Indian. We should also note that when our informant said that the brash girl was not an Indian, she was not speaking to issues of bloodline or tribal rolls. Instead, she was speaking exclusively about the girl's status as a real Indian, that is, one who is knowledgeable of and respectful of Indian ways and embodies them in their own action.

Knowing when to be silent and, by the White Man's standards, "passive" applies to many occasions beyond the initiation of conversation. But before these instances can be discussed, we must treat another feature of what appears to Whites as reticence in initiating conversation.

The Acceptance of Obligations

This other feature pertains to rights and obligations. Among Whites, initiating a conversation with a stranger does not establish rights and obligations that extend beyond that conversation, unless they are, in some fashion, agreed to within the conversation. And, even here, the conversation tends only to uncover rights and obligations that the parties would have already acknowledged had they previously known about them. For example, the parties might discover that they were fellow Masons, or fellow Heideggarians, or fellow students of Aron Gurwitsch. But most casual conversations with strangers do not entail such discoveries.

For real Indians, any conversation with a stranger who may turn out to be a real Indian will, in the discovery of the other's Indianness, establish substantial obligations between the conversants just through the mutual acknowledgment that they are Indians and that they are now no longer strangers to one another. Real Indians cannot be related to one another as "mere acquaintances," as the White man would put it. A real Indian who moves in the White man's world may have a relationship of "mere acquaintance" with a "White Indian," but that relationship is lived in the ways of Whites, not in the ways of Indians. And throughout this relationship, he neither acknowledges the other's potential real Indianness nor asserts his own.

Among the obligations that a real Indian incurs in conversing with another real Indian (wherein each acknowledges the other as a real Indian) is the obligation to engage in further interaction whenever the conversants' paths cross again. For students and businessmen, these obligations may be quite cumbersome, for they supersede other obligations, such as the meeting of a class or an appointment with a customer.

One student informant described her dealings with another Indian student in the following words:

> After we started talking, I had to stop and talk each time I saw her. We both usually wound up being late for class, but if I hadn't stopped to talk, she would have thought I was "acting-some-kind-of-way."

By "acting-some-kind-of-way," by not stopping to talk and to talk as long as the other wanted to talk, the Indian girl would have undermined her own claim to being a real Indian, not only in the eyes of the other Indian who wished to speak, but also in the eyes of other Indians who might learn about the episode.

The prospect of the encumbering obligation to interact once a single initial interaction has occurred, leads some Indian students, especially graduate students, to avoid direct contact with fellow Indians in their own classes. Pratt sometimes found himself in this fix when he was a student.

We defer further discussion of the treatment of obligations — an important feature of being a recognizable real Indian among Indians — in order to continue our focus on an initial interaction.

Razzing as a Distinct Mode of Indian Interaction

Let us suppose that a conversation between two real Indians has been initiated. In their search for the other's real Indianness and in their display of their own real Indianness, the parties frequently proceed to engage in a distinctive form of verbal sparring. By correctly responding to and correctly engaging in this sparring, which Indians call "razzing," each participant further establishes his cultural competency in the eyes of the other.

Razzing has a surface similarity to "doin' the dozens" and "ranking" that are done in Black street-corner society (Labov, 1972). All three of these practices involve humor, skillful verbal sparring, and a display of virtuosity at cultural form that exhibits cultural competency. However, in their details, the practices differ substantially.[14] Razzing is a typically extemporaneous form of communication about the ongoing events of a particular situation—razzing is dependent on the situation, evolves from it, is a feature of that situation that is done within that situation, and is about it. Furthermore, the same story may be repeated in future situations, with alterations and abbreviations, when something in that future situation "evokes" it. It is, therefore, a fully reflexive account, in the ethnomethodological sense (cf. Garfinkel, 1967; Wieder, 1974, 1977).

What Indians call a "shame story" illustrates the way in which razzing is dependent on and is a feature of the ongoing situation. If one participant in a situation were to violate some not-so-important social custom, the event would provide a culturally appropriate occasion for a "shame story" and would provide adequate social grounds for telling it. For example, a "shame story" can be based on "snagging a buffalo" (being seen with a rather large Indian woman) or "being painted up" (a common practice among younger Indians in which one Indian falls asleep in the presence of others and his or her face is painted in a bizarre fashion by the others present).

Pratt observed the way in which any occasion may provide grounds for razzing in an encounter between two Indians who were participating in a tribal dance. When one participant spied the other participant's former girlfriend, who had put on considerable weight, he remarked, "Check out the south side; there's your old babe—— In fact, she *is* the *whole* south side."

In response to the razz the other participant immediately responded, "She looks just as tiny as she always has." The recipient of the razzing, by making light of the situation, responded in the appropriate manner. If the recipient had responded in a negative or offended manner, he would have been viewed negatively by the others present. One who razzes another must also expect to be the recipient of razzing. One Indian was observed cautioning another, who had begun to bristle at a particular razz: "If you can dish it out, you've got to be able to take it."

Who may and, indeed, who should razz whom about what and in which situations is another matter that is defined by cultural convention. Razzing, in which both parties razz each other, is restricted to persons of the same age. Furthermore, certain topics, such as the recipient's family, personality

---

[14]Further, Blacks may face a different problem in establishing their being Black than do Indians in establishing Indianness. One would have to ask if an absolute inability to engage in "ranking" and/or knowing how to respond to it would disqualify a person as really being Black. Knowing how to "razz" and knowing how to respond to "razzing" is "criterial" for Indians. Although it is the case that being a virtuoso of "razzing" engenders the bestowal of stronger cultural competency by others present, not knowing how to engage in "razzing" and how to be its recipient are more crucial. Inappropriately "razzing" or inappropriately dealing with it leads to rejection as a candidate real Indian.

characteristics, and socioeconomic status, are generally prohibited. Razzing may occur in almost every situation except those that involve formalized speaker and audience roles. An attempt at razzing that did not conform to these conventions would be offensive and would undermine the credibility of the speaker as a real Indian.

Although Indians take delight in razzing and find it funny, they regard it as distinctively Indian humor, which is unintelligible to Whites. One Indian was observed by Pratt to say:

> They have amateur night over at this comedy club in Tulsa. We ought to put a table on the stage and let three Indian guys razz each other——They'd probably run all the White people out, because they wouldn't be able to understand what they were saying.

Attaining Harmony in Face-to-Face Relations

Gearing (1962) described the ethic of harmony in his account of the Cherokee, but the practices entailed in the ethic are general to all those who are recognized as Indians by real Indians.

> First, in the usual circumstances of everyday life, one must exercise foresight so as not to intrude. The harmony ethic is maintained by the recommendation that a good Cherokee must be a "quiet" man avoiding disharmonious situations. It is maintained by not giving offense, the unwillingness of the individual to thrust his ideas or personality in the limelight or to make decisions for or to speak for others. (p. 30)

The real Indian manages his face-to-face relations with others in such a way that he appears to be in agreement with them (or, at least, he does not overtly disagree), is respectful of them, is modest, and "fits in." He may well be in disagreement, but he does not openly show it. He may not respect others, but he shows respect. He may feel superior, but he does not assert his heartfelt superiority. He may have interests over and against those of the group, but in his visible relations with others, he accepts his obligations, and he maintains solidarity. He shows accord and harmony and is reserved about his own interests, skills, attainments, and position. He may engage in active conflict and competition, but not within the face-to-face encounter that includes himself and his antagonist or co-competitor. Each of these aimed-for appearances is a trap for one who would claim to be a real Indian.

An encounter between the members of three different tribes, in which Pratt was a participant, displays these aimed-for features of the real Indian, and shows how they are traps for the unwary and uninformed. At the onset of this particular encounter, which took place in the offices of the Native American Studies Center, "Mr. Osage" and "Mr. Kiowa" knew each other well and regarded each other as real Indians. They knew "Mr. Other Tribe" somewhat and were uncertain of his being a real Indian.

Mr. Kiowa: What's been going on?

Mr. Other Tribe: Been pretty busy——I've been commissioned by this rich White woman back East to make her a peyote fan—— She's paying me a lot of money to do it.

Mr. Kiowa: That sounds pretty good——There's always somebody who'll pay money.

After Mr. Other Tribe had left the room, Mr. Kiowa and Mr. Osage discussed what he had said and their responses to what he had said.

Mr. Osage: You knew Mr. Other Tribe was bullshitting about making that fan——Why didn't you say something?

Mr. Kiowa: Yeah, I knew he was bullshitting——He's probably never even *seen* a peyote fan. Besides, why didn't you say something?

Of course, both knew why they had not "said something," as they later told Wieder, for, as real Indians engaging in talk with a candidate real Indian, they knew that it was un-Indian to confront Mr. Other Tribe to his face. Similarly, it would have been inappropriate and un-Indian to have drawn attention to his un-Indian comportment, but it was quite proper to discuss it after he had left. Thus, Mr. Kiowa remarked: "I don't know why that guy tries to act like he's an Indian——[He] doesn't even know how."

Mr. Other Tribe betrayed himself in several ways. Although it is appropriate to know about peyote fans, it is not appropriate to "brag" about that fact. It is even less appropriate to attempt to elevate one's standing as an Indian by mentioning one's standing with a "rich White woman." Making a peyote fan should be done only by one who is truly qualified to do so. Mr. Other Tribe probably could have made a peyote fan, but he had no right to do so and no business doing so. Selling this piece of religious paraphernalia was a marginal practice at best. However, the thing Mr. Osage and Mr. Kiowa objected to most was the way that he talked about the fan—his backfiring attempt to elevate himself as a real Indian by intimating that he knew more than they did about peyote fans. Further, he did not see that their not challenging him was not, as he apparently thought, polite and quiet acceptance. That he treated their avoidance of conflict as acceptance was further grounds for rejecting him as not being a real Indian, for a real Indian would have known what Mr. Osage and Mr. Kiowa would and should do if they disagreed with him.

In his interactions with other real Indians, the real Indian is visible as a real Indian for other real Indians in his respectfulness, his avoidance of open, face-to-face conflict, his modesty, and his "doing his part." The latter two related features require further comment.

Modesty and "Doing One's Part"

In his relations with other real Indians, the real Indian shows that he is "just one of us" and "truly one of us." To outsiders, it often appears that the real Indian has no independent ambition, cannot be assertive, and permits others to make decisions for him. The real Indian understands his own behavior differently from that. Instead, he understands that he should not elevate himself over other real Indians. And he understands that the complex system of obligations he has to kin and other real Indians takes priority over those contractual obligations and pursuit of self-interest that Whites prize so highly.

In being appropriately modest or being "just one of us," the real Indian will not present himself as being more knowledgeable than other group members or boast about personal achievements. Rather, the norm is to remain silent about individual achievements and to refrain from expounding on the expertise an individual might possess in any given area, unless directly asked to do so.

When real Indians are asked to participate in discussion groups (e.g., on college campuses), they produce a remarkably standardized pattern. What happened in a course on the psychology of race and ethnic relations, which Pratt observed, illustrates the pattern. In placing all members of the same ethnic group together in the same discussion group, the instructor placed all self-identified Indians together. They were asked to discuss matters concerning their own cultural heritage. Despite the fact that the students were advanced undergraduate and graduate students, and despite the fact that they each knew a great deal about the topic, most did not participate, and those who did participate knew the least. Those who knew the most contributed remarks such as, "I don't know; what do you think?" and, "I guess so; that sounds all right to me."

Without realizing it, the instructor had asked the students to volunteer as experts on a matter that was important to them. The real Indians in the group found themselves in a bind. To have spoken on the matter, as far as they were concerned, would have been to put themselves forward as knowing more than the others did. To have done that would have been something hurtful and offensive to the others. Because most of them did not know each other, it also would have indicated to the real Indians who might have been present that he who spoke to the matter was not a real Indian.

Had the real Indians not been placed together, those real Indians who were knowledgeable of the "White man's" ways, and were not uncomfortable with his practices, would have participated. But in the actual situation in which they were placed, the one who spoke would have been "putting himself above the others," as one real Indian put it.

Even those who are recognized as real Indians must be constantly vigilant about this matter, because being a real Indian is not a static affair — it is a continuous achievement — one could always become not "just one of us," but a White man instead. When Indian graduate students go home, they must soften their own achievements in order to avoid being seen as offensive and/or White. When a student is told, "It's real nice that you are getting that degree," it is appropriate to answer, "I've gotten a lot of help," that is, it is appropriate to disclaim credit.

Also, it is inappropriate for a real Indian to place his own interests above the interests of his kin, his tribe, or his real Indian friends. Openly doing so undermines one's claim to being a real Indian. Pratt queried a friend about his brother and received the following reply:

> He's not one of us anymore——He thinks he's White. All he cares about is himself and not the rest of us anymore——He's not my brother.

There is a domain of offenses that can properly result in the proclamation, "You are not one of us anymore." This domain concerns doing one's part, participating in our activities, "chipping in" when appropriate, and helping out — it is a domain of familial and quasi-familial obligations. These obligations are especially articulated with respect to those recurrent gatherings in the community of real Indians that dramatize and celebrate the Indianness of those who participate. Planned-for dinners are the most frequent of these occasions that also include weddings, funerals, and religious and/or ceremonial dances and other gatherings. Depending on the type of occasion, it is the obligation of particular participants to properly extend invitations. Those who have been properly invited are obliged to be present. The range of appropriate excuses for nonattendance is much narrower than it is in White society. For most gatherings, all those who participate are expected to help with their labor and their money. Not meeting obligations such as these is not simply disapproved. It occasions serious questions about whether or not one is "truly one of us," and, in turn, whether or not one is really an Indian.

Taking on Familial Relations

Within the "community" of real Indians, there is a tendency for non-kin relationships to develop beyond what Whites might call simple friendship.

By mutual agreement, two men may call each other "brother," or a man may come to call a woman "sister" or "aunt" or "mother."[15] When one takes on such a relationship (e.g., "brother"), one takes on the same range of rights and obligations that one would have in a relationship with a brother as defined in strict genealogical terms. Furthermore, one takes the relation on not only for oneself, but also for one's kin. If I take you on as my brother, you are also the brother of my brothers and the son of my mother, and so on.

One who intimates that he is, or seeks to become recognized as, a real Indian need not be engaged in such relationships, although to be so engaged is validating of such an identity. And a real Indian must be knowledgeable of the existence of such relationships, their range of application, and their consequences. To betray one's ignorance of such matters betrays one's claim to be a real Indian. At a recent ceremonial dance, Pratt observed a middle-aged man addressing a middle-aged woman as "Sister." She replied, "I'm not your sister; I don't know who your people are." To Pratt, as both participant and observer, it was clear that the man had been misled into calling any woman "sister," because he could see that many nongenealogically defined kin were addressing each other with kin terms. No real Indian, however, would have made such an error.

Participation in quasi-kinship groups facilitates and activates the doing of being a real Indian among Indians, especially for persons who are not in physical proximity to their own tribe. Quasi-kinship groups may occur across tribes and commonly do so on college campuses. By holding dinners and other gatherings, the quasi-kinship group gives the real Indian the appropriate occasions within which to engage in distinctively Indian modes of comportment, such as "Indian public speaking" and "being present while silent."

Permissible and Required Silence

The real Indian further displays his Indianness in and through his acceptance of and participation in other characteristic modes of Indian interaction. He must be competent in "doing his part" in participating in conversations that begin with the participants' exchanging greetings and other amenities and then lapsing into extended periods of silence. He must know that neither he nor the others has an obligation to speak—that silence on the part of all conversants is permissible. The real Indian must be able to recognize these friendly, accepting silences—a way of being with others in silence—as differing from that silence of the other that is an avoidance of conflict and that means that the other disagrees or disapproves.

---

[15]These relations bear a surface similarity to those in Black street-corner life as described by Liebow (1967).

When silence is combined with those seating arrangements that are culturally preferred by Indians,[16] a scene is set that to Whites is distinctly odd and suggestive of peculiar, excessively close, and intimate relationships. In Indian communities, and in communities where Indians are a large minority, it is commonplace to see two male Indians, either both older or one younger and one older, seated side-by-side in silence. The real Indian recognizes such a scene for what it is and can participate in it with visible comfort.

When he is among Indians, the real Indian must also be able to perform in the roles of "student" and "teacher" and be able to recognize the behaviors appropriate to these roles. These roles are brought into play exclusively when the appropriate occasion arises for transmitting cultural knowledge (i.e., things pertinent to being a real Indian). Although White Americans find it proper to ask questions of someone who is instructing them, Indians regard questions in such a situation as being inattentive, rude, insolent, and so forth. The person who has taken the role of "student" shows that he is attentive by avoiding eye contact and by being silent. He does not interrupt nor does he ask direct questions, even at those points at which he could properly speak. For his part, one who takes on the role of "teacher" is to speak only when he is ready. The preparedness of the pupil to listen does not signal an obligation on the part of the teacher to speak. The teaching situation, then, as a witnessed or audienced monologue, lacks the dialogical features that characterize much of Western instruction.

The real Indian must know how to be instructed and how to instruct. He must not be impatient with his instructor and, if instructing, must recognize the attentiveness of his pupil or pupils. To not recognize and respect these cultural forms, undermines one's claim to competence as a real Indian. Clearly, it is also the case that the demands of the role of pupil in the White man's classroom are likely to be incongruous and a source of troubles for the real Indian in the classroom, for the very behaviors that indicate attentive listening in the Indian context indicate inattentiveness in the White context.[17] Furthermore, the White anthropologist who asks a question may appear to be asking for instruction. If he is taken as a pupil, he will be seen as rude and inattentive (if he attempts to learn through a series of questions), while his Indian instructor will be seen by him as uncooperative and as not really knowing what he is talking about, because he only speaks in apparently rote monologues.[18]

---

[16]The seating position "side-by-side" is atypical for White Americans, especially so for male–male interactions. (See Knapp, 1978.)

[17]A similar difficulty is apparently encountered by young Puerto Rican males in New York City schools as reported by Scheflin (1972).

[18]One further feature of the teaching situation demands attention, although it is not as clearly relevant to our main theme as are the other features. Many items of cultural knowledge

Public Speaking

A very wide variety of gatherings provides the occasion for public speaking. Large gatherings that are focused on some specific ceremony provide the occasion for prearranged speaking, as well as seemingly spontaneous, but formalized, public speaking. This seemingly spontaneous, but formalized, public speaking also occurs at dinners, parties, and other gatherings. By saying, "I have a few words to say," or, "My Brother has asked me to say something for him,"[19] the speaker can convert a loud, multiconversationed party into a quiet, formal, speaker–audience situation. The speaker may then proceed to speak at some length in an uninterrupted monologue. For example, a speaker might say:

> My Sister comes here at this time and has asked me to say a few words for her. She tells me that she feels good to be back here around our people, and she wants me to convey that to our people. She says that she has enjoyed the singing and the hospitality that has been extended to her by this family responsible for putting on this dinner. In appreciation for the kind words, good feelings, and hospitality that has been extended to her, she would like to give a gift to the family.

Or, in the midst of a party, one participant might say:

> I'd like your attention. [Pause.] My Nephew has asked me to say a few words for him. He tells me that it bothers him to see members of this family not getting along, and he would like to see the members not getting along to resolve their differences and to become brothers and sisters again. He wants to give a gift to the family members now in hopes that they will get over the hard feelings that they have been having.

We speak of such a talk as "seemingly spontaneous" to point to its feature of not having been pre-announced. Such a talk might have been prepared,

---

are taught only in the appropriate occasion. Although there may well be tribal variations on the particulars here, for any tribe, it will be the case that some things are to be taught when the occasion appropriate to them arises. One is taught, for example, how to wear ceremonial clothes when preparing for a ceremony. As a Navaho, one is taught Navaho astronomy at night when the stars are out. Other matters can be spoken of, and thereby taught, only in the appropriate season. To the extent that important cultural knowledge is so situated, great difficulties are posed for urban Indians who wish to retain or obtain an Indian identity.

[19]Two rather standard, but more elaborate, introductions have the following form:
> My nephew Frank has asked me to say a few words for him today. I really don't feel that I am qualified to express his wishes in the manner that he has expressed them to me, but I'm going to do the best that I can, so please bear with me.

And:
> My Mother has a few words that she wants me to express for her, so I want to address our people and try to convey her wishes as best I can.

and the occasion itself (e.g., a dinner) might have been organized to enable the speaking. Such preparation is regarded as legitimate and expectable in the community. On the other hand, some talks are not prepared, are done on the spur of the moment, and the giving of them does not motivate the organizing of the gathering. "Saying a few words" has the same form, whether it is prepared or not and whether it is pre-arranged or not. It demands that the others present drop what they are doing and take up the posture of an attentive audience, and it is regulated by well understood norms concerning who may speak.

Only elder males may speak for themselves as well as for others in the fashion of addressing the gathering. Younger males and all women must seek out an elder male who will "talk for" or "speak for them," if they have something they want to say. Violation of the prohibition against younger males and females' speaking is regarded as serious misconduct, requiring intervention, although not at the time that the speaking is going on. In a formal situation observed by Pratt, a young Indian woman spoke for herself. After she had spoken, her husband was chastised by the elder males who had been present. They found him to be at fault for ". . . not teaching his wife how to act——She's gone over her bounds."

Whereas a young woman is sanctioned through her husband, or, if unmarried, her father, a young man is sanctioned directly. Further, the offense is a different one—his offense is his failure to recognize that he is not yet old enough to speak. Pratt observed a 27-year-old male being chastised after having spoken. He was told by the elder males: "You're just a kid. You're not supposed to be speaking for yourself."

There is no fixed age at which one becomes an elder male. For tribal or district gatherings, one is typically accepted as an elder male in one's 40s, but only for speaking for someone else. To speak for oneself requires more seniority. For less formal and smaller gatherings, being an elder male is established by the relative ages of those present.

A real Indian knows how to deal with these occasions. He or she knows how and when to drop what they are doing and take up participation as a member of an audience. Those who may not speak for themselves know how to approach someone else to speak for them. If the real Indian is an elder male in the situation, he has learned how to speak for others and when to accept such a request. Like the other recurrent situations we have discussed, the public-speaking occasion prompts behaviors that show other real Indians that a candidate real Indian does or does not know how to conduct him or herself in the company of other Indians.

Concluding Remarks

Among all those persons who, by reason of ancestry, may claim to be Indians, real Indians recognize only those who "know" and "respect"

"Indian ways." "Knowing" those ways and "respecting" them is not demonstrated by reciting an account of those ways and speaking of one's respect for them, although real Indians, for the most part, can and do do those things. Demonstrating that one "knows" and "respects" Indian ways precisely parallels demonstrating one's competence as a member of a society—it is demonstrated in the visible and recognizable ways that one behaves and is implicated in every choice that one makes (cf. Garfinkel, 1967, esp. pp. 1–34).

Knowledge and respect is displayed in and through such witnessed courses of action as the following: the way in which one approaches strangers who may be Indians; the way in which one displays appropriate sociability in encounters with Indians whom one knows; the ways in which one engages in razzing others and being razzed by them, which is respectful of the appropriateness of the target "razzee," the appropriateness of the occasion, and the appropriateness of the topic; the ways in which one strives for and maintains harmony in face-to-face encounters by avoiding conflict and disagreement; the ways in which one displays appropriate modesty and does not visibly pursue one's own interests at the expense of the group; the ways in which one recognizes "one's part" and fulfills it; the way in which one recognizes the organization of quasi-kinship relationships and pays heed to them; the way in which one conducts conversational interaction according to distinctly Indian conventions; the way in which one recognizes and appropriately engages in "Indian public speaking;" and the way in which one engages in other patterns of conduct known to real Indians as "our ways," which have not been specified here. Further, the real Indian displays his Indianness through his use of these ways as "criteria" in judging the Indianness of others.

Being a real Indian is not a material thing that can be possessed and displayed. It consists of those patterns of appropriate conduct that are articulated in such a way that they are visible and recognizable to other Indians as specifically Indian ways of conducting oneself. In the performance of these visible patterns, being a real Indian is realized.[20]

We have spoken of being and becoming a real Indian to stress the never-ending processual character of realizing one's Indianness and of demonstrating that one is a real Indian. Not only are there strangers to be met who will silently question any Indian's Indianness, and, thus, the demonstration must begin once again from the beginning, but also the demonstration must continue for those, such as the members of one's own family, who have stood as one's witnesses for all of one's life.[21]

If we were to depict the becoming of a real Indian as movement through

---

[20]Here we paraphrase Goffman (1959, p. 79); see also Sartre (1956, p. 59) for this theme.

[21]It is instructive here to compare the circumstances of being a real Indian with that of Agnes, an inter-sexed woman, described by Garfinkel (1967, pp. 116–185, esp. pp. 172–185).

a sequence of steps through which the candidate Indian was progressively accepted as a real Indian, then we would have to allow for the fact that there is no stage at which that Indian's full acceptance would be finalized. But the imagery of a sequence of steps toward final acceptance is unsatisfactory on other grounds as well. It does not provide for the enabling part played by other Indians, whose status as real Indians is likewise unsecured. Only through engaging in concerted action with other Indians can any Indian be questioned, tested, supported, enabled, sustained, and realized in his becoming and becoming-being a real Indian.

References

Garfinkel, H. (1967). *Studies in ethnomethodology.* Englewood Cliffs, NJ: Prentice-Hall.

Gearing, F. (1962). Priest and warriors: Social structure for Cherokee politics in the eighteenth century. *American Anthropologist, 64,* 30–36.

Goffman, E. (1959). *The presentation of self in everyday life.* New York: Doubleday.

Knapp, M. (1978). *Nonverbal communication in human interaction.* New York: Holt, Rinehart & Winston.

Labov, W. (1972). Rules for ritual insults. In D. Sudnow (Ed.), *Studies in social interaction* (pp. 120–169). New York: The Free Press.

Liebow, E. (1967). *Talley's corner: A study of negro streetcorner men.* Boston, MA: Little Brown.

Sacks, H. (1972). Notes on police assessment of moral character. In D. Sudrow (Ed.), *Studies in social interaction* (pp. 280–293). New York: The Free Press.

Sartre, J.-P. (1956). *Being and nothingness* (Hazel Barnes, Trans.). New York: Philosophical Library.

Scheflin, A. (1972). *Body language and social order.* Englewood Cliffs, NJ: Prentice-Hall.

Wieder, D. L. (1974). *Language and social reality.* The Hague: Mouton.

Wieder, D. L. (1977). Ethnomethodology and ethnosociology. *Mid-America Review of Sociology, 2,* 1–18.

Wieder, D. L. (1984). Toward a general theory of the communicative situation: Reflections on signs, appearances, and reality in Goffman's *Presentation of self in everyday life.* Paper presented at the annual meeting of the International Communication Association, Honolulu, HI.

Zaner, R. (1981). *The context of self: A phenomenological inquiry using medicine as a clue.* Athens, OH: Ohio University Press.

6

On the Occasioned and Situated Character of Members' Questions and Answers: Reflections on the Question, "Is He or She a Real Indian?"

D. LAWRENCE WIEDER
STEVEN PRATT

We have taken the invitation to write this epilogue as an occasion to examine our original claims and to do so with the benefit of further ethnographic material and reflections stimulated by the recent ethnomethodological work of Garfinkel and his students.[1] While inspecting our claims, their grounds, the ways that we or others could and would extend them, and the modes of theorizing that generated them and that generate similar claims advanced by others, we encountered a collection of theorizing practices. When these practices are brought to light, they substantially effect the proper reading of our claims as well as the claims of many others who investigate naturally occurring native talk and/or who employ it as a point of departure for analyzing the world as known to and experienced by the natives.

In doing ethnography, it is tempting to treat naturally occurring members' questions and the answers they provoke as "stand-ins" for the theorist's questions. This procedure resembles the anthropological gloss in which the analyst creates a glossary of approximate translations of native terms. The glossary is employed in reporting what the natives said and what they referred to and meant. The approximate nature of the translation and the ways in which it is used, however, leave open and unspecified exactly what it is that the natives were saying and what they were talking about. As Garfinkel and Sacks (1986) described it, the analyst:

---

[1]Much of this material is reported in Pratt's (1985) doctoral dissertation. The ethnographic methods and an extended version of the findings on which our 1985 paper was based are also reported there. In ways difficult to specify, but nonetheless worth mentioning, this epilogue owes much to reflections on the recent writings of Garfinkel, Livingston, Lynch, MacBeth, and Robillard (1988) and M. D. Bacus (1986). Our use of the expressions "a generality," "administering" a procedure, and "situated logic" are adapted from these sources.

recommends to collegues that *he* will mean by *his* translations of natives' terms what the natives were really talking about, [and] that he will treat the natives and their practices as final authority [for what he, the analyst, means], although what . . . [that] might consist of beyond what he has written he cannot say and says so. The writer means what the native really means. (p. 186)

By inverting this gloss, the analyst (generally tacitly) asserts that what the native means by some remark is what the analyst means in his or her analysis. The analysis specifies what the native really, after all, and in the last analysis means. The inverted anthropological gloss (hereafter *inverted gloss*) has been a particular temptation of certain forms of ethnoscience, cognitive anthropology, or "new ethnography," given the relevance of naturally occurring members' or natives' questions and their answers to these enterprises.

When members' questions are treated as glosses for the theorist's questions, the logical properties that would obtain for the theorist's question and answers to it are attributed to the members' talk. Although the attribution of particular logical properties to the members' talk can be done reflectively, it characteristically is done by simply not noticing that there is a potential difference between the logic required by the theorist's analysis and the logical properties of some collection of naturally occurring expressions. To the extent that we engaged in the practice (and we believe that we did so primarily in our talk of "criteria" and in implications that we left unstated, but nonetheless invited), we know it as a tacit practice at the edge of our awareness that accompanies the theorist's zeal on spotting an interesting argument that can be made with the ethnographic material that is at hand.

The Practice of Mobilizing Indexical Expressions to Do the Work of Objective Ones

This associated practice supports the inverted gloss and many other theorizing practices. It permits the argument that the analysis is based on many observations, despite all the well-known difficulties in generalizing with indexical expressions. The indexical properties of naturally occurring expressions (that the same utterance means differently in different contexts and that these contexts do not admit of enumeration)[2] pose a practically solvable problem for the task of making a collection of instances of the same expression. If one wants to say, as we did, that one observed many

---

[2]For discussions of objective and indexical expressions and their treatment by social scientists, see Garfinkel (1967), Garfinkel and Sacks (1986), and Heritage (1984).

occasions in which the natives said, for example, "Is he (or she) a real Indian?" one needs to make such a collection. Even if it is not said in so many words, it is implied in any talk of a collection of observations, that each instance of the collection means the same as every other instance, despite differences in the context of the occurrence, the purposes of the speaker, the nature of the occasion, and so forth, and despite the fact that the meaning and reference of some instances of the expression-as-an-utterance-of-the-self-same-words does mean and refer differently from the instances that have been mobilized into the collection.

Mobilizing instances into the collection is achieved through the subsidiary practices of editing out any particular piece of talk that is not heard by the investigator as having the same core meaning as the other expressions in the collection being assembled. The editing out practice is not primarily a matter of throwing out data (with respect to our own practices, we know of no such cases) but happens instead in the initial hearing of a piece of talk. If it is not heard as expressing the thought intended through the other instances in the collection, it is not typically noted and recorded in the first place. For the especially diligent fieldworker and those engaged in certain kinds of sociolinguistic investigations, such a piece of talk is noted and recorded, but as an instance of something else (e.g., a joke or a sarcastic remark).

Another subsidiary practice involves collecting alternative ways of saying the same thing as instances of the same collection. For example, our collection of instances of the expression, "Is he (or she) a real Indian?" includes instances instantiated through such utterances as, "Is he one of us?" and, "Is she an apple?"

Quite clearly, we engaged in the practices of mobilizing indexical expressions to do the work of objective ones, and do so once again in this writing. To do otherwise, at least with ethnographic materials, would eliminate the possibility of referring to a collection of instances of the same expression.

Some Ways of Employing the Inverted Gloss and Employing It to Throw Into Relief Some Features of the Situated Logic of Naturally Occurring Questions and Answers

Faced with a collection of instances of the "same question" (treatable, for all practical purposes, as the same question) and the answers associated with each instance, the investigator as theorist may proceed to treat the answers as expressions of underlying criteria that define the object of the question (e.g., taking answers to, "Is this an X? If not, why not?" as expressions of the necessary and sufficient features of "X" for the natives whose culture as a cognitive map is under study).

If we were to treat our materials in this way, we would scrutinize answers to the question, "Is he (or she) a real Indian?" which went on to provide grounds for saying that a candidate was or was not a real Indian. We would treat these grounds as criteria in the form of the necessary and sufficient conditions for counting someone as a real Indian. We would claim that that specification was a definition of a real Indian in real Indian thought (i.e., that it was part of the real Indian's cognitive map).

We would be sorely tempted, in a bout of theorist's zeal, to extend our analysis by employing such a definition in further research in which we sorted candidate Indians into "real Indians" and "not real Indians." We would anticipate that our count of "real Indians" would differ substantially from the Bureau of Indian Affairs' count. We would count many as real Indians not counted by the government (e.g., some members of tribes that are not federally recognized). Some persons whose ancestry is entirely Indian, but multi-tribal—the BIA stipulates that only those and all of those of "one-fourth degree of Indian blood" of a federally recognized tribe are legally countable as Indians. They would count and do offer services to large numbers who do not regard themselves as real Indians and are not so regarded by real Indians. We would criticize the BIA for cultural insensitivity and various other forms of mischief.

Attractive as such an analysis would be as a "generality," there is no way to move from this exercise in imagination to a set of empirical procedures. No matter which direction we choose as a point of departure—whether it be by enumerating that collection of candidate Indians who have already been judged to be real Indians, or by attempting to catch the judging as it happens, or by attempting to rigorously formulate the criteria as procedures that we would then "administer" to candidate real Indians—we would find insurmountable roadblocks in the form of absurdities, paradoxical traps, and antinomies that would force us to conclude that there is no enumerate-able population of real Indians. That is, that there is no population that corresponds to their question as they ask it, in the situations in which they ask it, and in light of the contingencies and constraints under which they ask it. In turn, we would have to conclude (and do conclude here) that the actual ways that the naturally occurring question is employed, its embeddedness in the particular situations in which it occurs, and the circumstances that occasion its being asked are not consistent with its treatment as productive of logical defining criteria, with talk of necessary and sufficient conditions, or, in general, with its being the receptacle of logical properties attributed to it in an inverted gloss.

To be sure, there is a sense in which real Indians have an enumerate-able population "in mind" and, indeed, through their recognitions and judgings, do produce an enumerate-able population-of-sorts, although, as we will see, its logic is incomensurate with any that would be attributable to it through the inverted anthropological gloss. Real Indians have an enumerate-able population "in mind" when they ask, "Is this a real Indian?" or its alternative, "Is he (or she) one of us?" in the sense that an enumerate-able population of "us" or "real Indians" is horizonally posited in the question. But, like the elusive real rate of crime (in contrast to crimes reported to the police), it remains forever "on the horizon." Although clearly imaginable, it can neither be brought into view, nor can it be reproduced through procedures that are both independent of and duplicative of the recognition or judgment that "here is a crime" and "there is an Indian," as these are contingently achieved in their real and natural habitat.

The three ill-fated paths to disclosing an enumerate-able population provide us with a device for finding and displaying the contrast between the enthusiastic theorist's logic and the discoverable logic of (some) naturally occurring situated questions and answers. Let us begin by considering the inverted anthropological gloss in light of the enumerate-able population that it projects and then contrasting it to the "population" produced by real Indians making situated judgments.

The First Path.   The situationally transcendent logic accompanying an inverted gloss invites the theorist to regard "Indianness" as a stable property of individuals, whereas the judgment, "He (or she) is a real Indian," and the object of the judgment are both situated and contingent achievements. The situationally transcendent logic of the gloss requires that one cannot be both "A" and "not A" (i.e., both "real Indian" and "not real Indian").

If we turn to count real Indians as judged by real Indians, however, we must contend with the fact that real Indians (like strong students in our own academic departments) are recognized and judged only in actual situations, each with its own events and contingencies, and within each only by the available personnel and by those who hear a recounting of that situation's events. A simple enumeration of real Indians, identifiable as the objects of actual judgments concerning their Indianness, will produce an enumerated population consisting of candidates who are "not real Indians," candidates who are "real Indians," and candidates who are both "real Indians and not real Indians," a product not reconcilable with the projections of the inverted gloss.

This state of affairs, at least as it is instantiated in single instances, is not, however, irreconcilable within the situated logic of the naturally occurring question, embedded as it is in actual particular situations. We do not mean that "real Indian" and "not real Indian" are rendered in the same judgment. We do mean that the discovery of two contrastive judgments about the same person made in different situations by different parties, if learned about by one or both sets of parties, does not demand a revision of one's own judgment or a reassessment of one's regard for the parties making a judgment contrary to one's own. A revision may occur, but it is not obligatory.[3] The native as judge *appears* to have a grasp of his or her judgment—that it is embedded in a situation and finds its grounds in the contigencies of that situation—that is unimagined in the projections of the situated gloss. We say *appears* to have such a grasp, because we have no ethnographic material to directly support this claim beyond the "intuitions" of one native with respect to his or her own judgments—namely Pratt as real Indian. It is not even clear what supporting ethnographic material for this claim would look like.[4] It is nonetheless clear that two contrary judgments can be left standing. Although the conflict may be resolved "in the light of future evidence," the conflict may also be ignored or simply left standing until it fades in relevance and finally is effectively forgotten.

The Second Path.   If we attempt to find a path to an enumerate-able population of real Indians by attempting to observe the recognition and the judging as it happens, we must employ instances of the naturally occurring question as our evidence that recognition and judging is happening. Here we encounter a constraint on our procedure that cannot be squared with the aims of the inverted gloss. The theorist's question, "Is he (or she) a real Indian?" has any person whatsoever as its object; its range of use is unrestricted. The actual range of the natives' question, the range of contexts in which it occurs, and the range of possible objects of the question are restricted. For example, the question is not asked of or about those Indians whom Pratt (1985) has described under the title of "grass roots Indians," who reside in isolated reservation areas and who have little or no contact with members of other tribes or representatives of White society. Seldom venturing from their reservation, their primary contact with the outside

---

[3]The fact that discordencies do occur, that revisions may be motivated by such a finding, that the revisions can include one's own judgment of the "real Indianness" of the parties rendering a judgment contrary to one's own, that judgments concerning one's own "real Indianness" may also be made by parties rendering a judgment contrary to one's own are, from the standpoint of the well practiced real Indian, well known circumstances that may surround any judgment.

[4]The light of those ethnographic materials, whatever they might look like, might lead us to conclude that two contrary judgments were only superficially instances of one and the same judgment; that as judgments, they differ from one another in a fashion paralleling the differences between two expressions which *refer* to the same object but *mean* differently.

With respect to the management of discordant judgments (deep or superficial), the circumstance here has so many parallels to the circumstance of judgments concerning the excellence of a scholarly piece of work in the humanities and the human sciences that we invite the reader to consider all the practical devices for managing discordant judgments that exist within the academy.

world is through interactions with those "contact Indians" who have left the reservation and have returned for a visit or to resume residency. The "Indianness" of "grass roots Indians" is not questioned by themselves or by others.

The question is not simply not asked of or about the "grass roots Indian," *it is not askable.* That is, a replica of the question that we encountered in our research cannot be asked on the reservation about or of a "grass roots Indian." The utterance would be heard in some occasions as a questioning slur, whereas in others it would be heard as a remark about Indians. However it would be heard, it would not be heard as expressing the question that we have been treating.

The proponent of the reverse anthropological gloss and other analytic maneuvers might ask at this point, "Why can't we ask about the Indianness of the 'grass roots Indian'?" Our reply would be that it is their asking of their question that concerns us here, and their asking of their question has this odd quasi-logical constraint that it cannot be asked just anywhere about just anyone. Of course, real Indians *accept* the "grass roots Indian" as a real Indian, they simply do not employ the question, "Is he (or she) a real Indian?" and its answers to publicly pronounce the judgment. Consequently we could not find an occassion in which such a judgment was being made.

Other twists of sense would be encountered if the question, as the question that real Indians ask, were attempted about persons who were plainly and obviously White (e.g., a small, blue-eyed, blond and freckle-faced boy in imitation Indian garb on the front lawn of a suburban residence as observed by three real Indians in a passing car). Any talk about the boy's Indianness would not and could not be heard as a serious consideration of his possible status as a real Indian. The opportunities for razzing oneself or others in this situation are so prominent as to make a comment about the boy's "Indianness" quite likely.

The question's natural range of application is in situations involving real Indians in which some person is of doubtable real-Indian status – situations in which there are both grounds for considering and grounds for doubting someone's Indianness. The question can be asked without incongruity about anyone who has taken up White or Anglo ways of life – anyone who has his or her residence "off the reservation" or outside rural and primarily Indian communities, anyone who has taken up occupations that require adaptation to the White Man's ways, or anyone who has gone away to a "White school, college, or university," and so on.

The question thus arises in encounters between[5] what Pratt has referred to as "contact Indians," Indians who have frequent contact with Whites and

---

[5]A related form of the question may also be posed by a "grass roots Indian" about a "contact Indian," but we do not consider that here.

characteristically have contact with members of other tribes and who retain or at least intend to retain the identity of Indian.[6] "Contact Indians" are candidate real Indians and are the proper object of the question. Although the question can be asked within or following an isolated encounter between two individuals, the circumstances that prompt the question are fully incorporated into multiparty gatherings of persons who anticipate that most others present will be real Indians. Participation in such a gathering intimates that one is a real Indian, *and* that intimation motivates the question, even if more explicit claims are not advanced. We have in mind those formal affairs and intertribal activities such as pow-wows (which are social gatherings) and intertribal religious events, attendance at Indian churches and schools, meetings for Indian students at schools, colleges, and universities, meetings of Indian professionals, and so forth and such informal gatherings as parties and dinners primarily for Indians, such gatherings as occur on college and university campuses at offices of Native American Study Centers, at Native American Student Centers, outside the office of a Native American counselor, and so on, and those gatherings that occur in Indian bars and other local "hang-outs."

For one whose appearance is consistent with possibly being Indian, the tacit claim that accompanies one's mere presence in such a gathering provides the relevance of the question concerning one's Indianness. Although the question is intelligibly askable about all persons present (the location of the gathering betokens the "contact Indian," hence doubtable status of each participant), the question becomes obligatory—its absence would be notable—upon the occasion in which some participant behaves in a recognizably non-Indian manner (i.e., their behavior is inconsistent with those modes of communicative behavior that we have called "criterial" in the identification of real Indians and now call "criterial considerations" to dampen the implicit suggestion that they are, after all, counterparts of the theorist's conception of criteria and that they should be so treated).

The Third Path.   Some of the logical and quasi-logical properties of "criterial considerations" become apparent as we encounter obstacles on the third path to an enumerate-able population of real Indians by rigorously formulating these criteria as procedures that we could "administer" to candidate real Indians.

The "criterial considerations" are visible in answers to the question

---

[6]It almost goes without saying that if one seeks to retain an identity as Indian, the most straightforward way of achieving this is to stay on the reservation or in the home community and to engage only in those economic pursuits and other activities that members of one's own tribe see as entirely consistent with "our way of life." Alternatively, one can avoid the question by leaving home, never returning, and by ceasing to claim or intimate that one is Indian.

concerning someone's Indianness as grounds for saying that a candidate is or is not a real Indian. They refer to forms and features of interaction that are recurrently troublesome for those who identify themselves as Indians and, in that identification, desire and require the recognition of other Indians as one of them. This ensemble of recurrently troublesome forms and features of interaction points to events and circumstances in the developing mutual history of two or more parties that serve to strengthen or weaken the support for claims of Indianness that one party is willing to extend to the other. The temporality of the use of the "criterial considerations" contrasts with that of the ideal template of necessary and sufficient conditions that are projected in the inverted gloss: The template is "administered" "all at once" to each new case as it is encountered. The circumstances under which the criterial considerations are employed emerge over the course of a developing history. They are employed if and when the event or situation appropriate to them arises. How the other treats being razzed, for example, is likely to arise much sooner than an occasion in which the other attempts to "say a few words" or to have them said by someone else.

The ways in which the judgment, "He (or she) is (or is not) a real Indian," is embedded within situations that motivate it make such judgments intrinsically provisional. Those now recognized can spoil their acceptance or have it spoiled and those not now accepted can have another chance even when others do not want to extend it. Consider that the one judged "not a real Indian" in one situation may seek out another gathering of Indians of the sort that are open to anyone who attempts to attend. By attending such a gathering, he or she once more insinuates the claim to being a real Indian. Even if the gathering consists of the same parties who previously judged the candidate to be not a real Indian, the current encounter could lead them to judge that, "He's learning, he's more Indian than I thought."

Repeated failed attempts with the same crowd may occur with the candidate's encountering increasingly sharp and prolonged razzing focused on his or her shortcomings as an Indian, which may be interspersed with remarks that directly deny that the candidate knows what he or she is talking about. For the candidates who knew how to hear what was being said in these sessions, advice on how to correct their behavior could be found. Often, however, candidates who receive such treatment do not know enough to know how to interpret it and do not know that there are things to know that they do not know. Unless they confess their ignorance and ask for instruction, no real Indian will offer it.

A failing candidate who repeatedly attempts to participate with real Indians in those gatherings that are open to anyone who presents themselves may receive what is acknowledged in the candidate's absence as "torture" and "verbal abuse." Puzzling to real Indians, such a person can be around the fringes of their life for years, while making no headway toward acceptance. Open gatherings are accessible to them, but gatherings that require an invitation (e.g., a dinner party) would be closed. Building a reputation as a "hanger-on," they would endanger the reputation of any real Indian who sought out their company and, by being with them by choice, appeared to endorse their claim to being "one of us."

The fact that "criterial considerations" refer to contingencies that emerge over the course of a developing *mutual* history, when and if the occasion arises, and the fact that judgments based on them are intrinsically provisional, makes them extremely awkward objects for rigorous formulation as procedures that we might "administer." Giving in to the temptation to formulate them as "competencies" (which indeed could be procedurally formulated and administered) would generate an enumeration of a population of "real Indians" through procedures that were independent of the actual judgment of real Indians. It would, however, hardly duplicate those judgments. As a "once and for all" and "all at once" judgment, an administered formulation of "competencies" would miss the provisional and temporally extended and developing character of actual, naturally occurring judgments. As a judgment exclusively concerning the candidate being judged (a candidate freed from the fortunes of unpredictable situations and freed from the participation of chosen and unchosen companions), an administered formulation of "competencies" would purge the affair being judged of its situationally contingent and collaborative features.

The tacit and ignored theorist's practice of attributing to naturally occurring native talk those logical properties that his or her theorizing requires permits the theorist to claim that the natives' talk furnishes empirical grounds for the theorizing. Those practices can be productive of elegant theorizing, but they cannot treat and could never discover the logical and quasi-logical properties of naturally occurring questions and answers in the actual occasions in which they occur and in face of the actual contingencies that they manage. By treating the theorist's device of the inverted anthropological gloss as a foil, we have attempted to expose some of these properties as they pertain to the natives' question, "Is he (or she) a real Indian?" and to provide some of them with an initial description.

References

Bacus, M. D. (1986). Multipiece truck wheel accidents and their regulations. In H. Garfinkel (Ed.), *Ethnomethodological studies of work* (pp. 20–59). London: Routledge & Kegan Paul.

Garfinkel, H. (1967). *Studies in ethnomethodology.* Englewood Cliffs, NJ: Prentice-Hall.

Garfinkel, H., & Sacks, H. (1986). On formal structures of practical actions. In H. Garfinkel

(Ed.), *Ethnomethodological studies of work* (pp. 160–193). London: Routledge & Kegan Paul.

Garfinkel, H., Livingston, E., Lynch, M., MacBeth, D., & Robillard, A. (1988). *Respecifying the natural sciences as discovering sciences of practical action, I & II: Doing so ethnographically by administering a schedule of contingencies in discussions with laboratory scientists and by hanging around their laboratories.* Unpublished manuscript.

Heritage, J. (1984). *Garfinkel and ethnomethodology.* Cambridge, England: Polity Press.

Pratt, S. (1985). *Being an Indian among Indians.* Unpublished doctoral dissertation, University of Oklahoma, Norman, OK.

7

"What We Need is Communication": "Communication" as a Cultural Category in Some American Speech

TAMAR KATRIEL
GERRY PHILIPSEN

THE materials which provided both the stimulus and the data for this study suggest that in some American speech about interpersonal life, "communication" carries localized and highly poignant meanings. The pervasiveness of "communication" in such speech, but more importantly the systematicity of its occurrence, its "compelling facticity,"[1] and the moral freight it carries for its users, make it an important term in an American symbolic universe and vocabulary of motives. This study is an ethnographic exploration of that term and of the discursive field in which it finds a place.

Our basic purpose is to make problematic the meaning of "communication" in some American texts. We are interested, for example, in what is meant by "communication" in the statement made by a mother, who said in discussing her daughter, "She don't communicate with me anymore" (earlier in the conversation she said she and her daughter do exchange routine information through speech);[2] in an advertisement placed in a business magazine which includes the message that "if the listener doesn't show genuine interest and sensitivity to what's being said . . . the communication will fail" (the advertisement attests to the importance of communication both at work and in home-work);[3] or in the description of a play by its director as being about "contemporary humanity's failure to communicate to reach love."[4] Consideration of these and other statements, in which "communication" is naturally embedded, has led us to ask, What differentiates that potent term "communication" from "mere talk" when Americans use it to discuss the quality of interpersonal life?

Our claim about the meaning of

---

[1] The phrase is attributed to Clifford Geertz. See Hervé Varenne, *Americans Together: Structured Diversity in a Midwestern Town* (New York: Teachers College Press, 1977), p. 49.

[2] Anonymous caller, on the *Jennifer James Show*, KVI Radio, Seattle, Washington, March, 1981.

[3] An advertisement placed by Sperry in *Fortune*, 12 Jan. 1981, pp. 90–1.

[4] The statement is attributed to Bob Egan, Associate Artistic Director of the Seattle (Washington) Repertory Theatre, in reference to Tom Huey's *Wild Air*, in Jane Estes, "Playwright's *Wild Air* Study," *Seattle Post-Intelligencer*, 1 Feb. 1981, p. H6.

"communication" in some American speech is limited in two ways. First, we have not exhaustively surveyed American uses of "communication" but have described one field of discourse—interpersonal relationships—in which it has a localized sense; it has other senses in other fields of American discourse. Second, we do not claim that all Americans ever inhabit the field of discourse in which "communication" finds a place.[5] We have, rather, uncovered and described the meanings and premises which give credence to *a* recognizable way of speaking that is part of the workings of the society in which we have conducted our inquiry. It is that way of speaking itself, as a code or system of meanings, and not its social ecology, which holds our attention here.

In showing that a domain of everyday experience and its linguistic representation are cultural creations, we record and interpret a datum, an instance of humans creating and constituting a world of meaning in their own terms. That "communication" labels the academic discipline we practice is more or less incidental to the general point being made—that domains of everyday experience, such as communication, and the terms in which people make them intelligible to each other, such as "communication," are subject to human invention and coloration. Thus, in providing a glimpse into an American definition of

"communication" we hope to show the possibility for scientific and critical insight which the cultural perspective affords the student of speech behavior.[6]

METHOD

Data for the inquiry were gathered, by both of us, during the course of one year of collaborative field work, directed toward discovering a culturally patterned way of speaking in contemporary America. Our field work took many forms, including the construction of in-depth life studies of several people, the analysis of everyday events and scenes, the collection and interpretation of assorted texts, and the reading of commentaries on American life.

The core material for the project consists of case studies of communication in the lives of two women, each of whom was born and raised in the American Pacific Northwest. Each case study is treated as a text constructed on the basis of (1) transcripts from several unstructured interviews, (2) a log kept by each woman for three days, describing, along a given format, the communication events in which she took part during those days,[7] and (3) focused, *in-situ* observations of each woman's communication conduct. Many other texts were also examined, a few of which are interspersed throughout this report.

The principal case studies were given detailed interpretations with an eye to the role played by "communication" and related categories such as "self" and "relationship" in each informant's pre-

[5]By way of contrast, note that the study by Hart, *et al*, concludes with a section on "Toward a Sociology of Interpersonal Communication," whereas we delineate only a cultural perspective or ideology, not its sociological distribution. See Roderick P. Hart, Robert E. Carlson, and William F. Eadie, "Attitudes Toward Communication and the Assessment of Rhetorical Sensitivity," *Communication Monographs*, 47 (1980), 1–22. But also see Hawkins, *et al*, whose data suggest that at least part of the ideology we describe below plays well in one part of America's heartland, Marion County, Indiana. James L. Hawkins, Carol Weisberg, and Dixie W. Ray, "Spouse Differences in Communication Style: Preference, Perception, and Behavior," *Journal of Marriage and the Family*, 42 (1980), 585–93.

[6]For our use of the cultural approach, we are indebted to David M. Schneider, "Notes Toward a Theory of Culture," in *Meaning in Anthropology*, ed. Keith H. Basso and Henry A. Selby (Albuquerque, New Mexico: University of New Mexico Press, 1976), p. 208.
[7]The diary: diary-interview method is discussed in Don Zimmerman and D. Lawrence Wieder, "The Diary: Diary-Interview Method," *Urban Life*, 5 (1977), 479–98.

sentation of herself and her life. In their presentation below, we deliberately mixed our readings of the lives studied with readings of other texts which constitute part of the life-world which we and our informants inhabited, and with our readings of academic treatises.[8] We consciously used our experiencing of these texts, considered singly and in juxtaposition to each other, to develop a grounded theory of "communication" as a cultural category in the speech examined.

Once the primary analysis was, for the most part, completed, we examined another set of cultural texts, transcripts of The Phil Donahue Show, which is a popular program shown daily on American television and the inspiration of a recent best-selling book.[9] Each show selected dealt with the subject of interpersonal relationships, and each thematized "communication" as the remedy to all problems. These transcripts were examined for their general structure and content to test, and to articulate further, the theory initially grounded in life studies and anecdotal evidence.

A READING OF TWO LIVES AS AMERICAN TEXTS

Informant One

M is a 36-year old woman, divorced, the mother of two daughters, ages six and eight. She has a degree in social work but has not worked in that field and is presently not employed outside her home.

A key distinction in M's metalinguistic lexicon is that between "small talk,"

[8]Among the works consulted are Peter Berger, Hansfried Kellner, and Brigitte Berger, *The Homeless Mind: Modernization and Consciousness* (New York:Vintage Books, 1973); Francis L. K. Hsu, *Clan, Caste, and Club* (New York: Van Nostrand, 1963); Richard Sennett, *The Fall of Public Man* (New York: Alfred A. Knopf, 1976); Varenne.

[9]Phil Donahue and Company, *Donahue: My Own Story* (New York: Fawcett Crest, 1979).

the speech of acquaintances, and "real communication," which is to her the speech of close friends in an intimate context (either face-to-face or by telephone). She sees persons as occupying a "personal space" (a term she used many times) that may or may not be penetrated by another person. "Communication" is, in part, an act of interpenetration. The expression "close friend" reinforces M's essentially spatial metaphor for "communication" (the equivalent expression in Hebrew is "good friend"). "Close friends," people with whom M can talk about her problems, and who will listen sympathetically even if they disagree with her, are contrasted with other friends with whom she associates mainly by "doing things together." When M says about a friend that he or she is "close" enough to hurt her, she implies that intimacy involves the highest of rewards as well as of risks, and the tension between the two is a source of interpersonal problems that persist after initial differences are overcome.

Much of M's biographical speech with us reports her frustration in meeting her need for "real communication." She feels her parents punished her for expressing herself, and she said as a result she was an (emotionally) "abused" child. M described her relationship with her ex-husband in similar terms. Her husband constantly "put her down" verbally as "a lousy person" and criticized her because to him, as she said, "an o.k. person does not have problems." His refusal to discuss her problems, which he said were intrapersonal difficulties, was for M the major source of distress in the marriage. She saw her ex-husband's attitude as one step more extreme and destructive than that of her parents in terms of her sense of self-worth; with the parents it was the verbalization of a problem, with the husband the very experience of one, which was unacceptable.

Thus, "communication" was the substance of the major conflicts in M's life. In not being allowed to express herself in the way she felt she both needed and deserved to do, she felt she was disconfirmed as a person. The relationships M had with her parents and ex-husband lacked "supportiveness," the term she most often used to describe the nature of positively experienced forms of interaction.

Like many modern parents, M reports that much of her communication with her children stands in defiance of her own childhood experience. She tries to help her children "feel good about themselves"—she listens to them, answers all their questions, and provides detailed explanations and information about the world around them. A crucial function of parent-child communication, for M, is to help the child develop a "positive self-image." It is important to her not to have any "hassles" with her children in the morning before school, so that they do not spend the day feeling "what a no good person I am," which in turn makes them vulnerable to the inevitable "hassles" they encounter in dealing with others. To M the world is basically hostile, and one needs a "thick skin" to shield one from its troubles. She believes a "positive self-image" is such a shield, so that feeling good about oneself is a key to survival. A "positive self-image" can be achieved, according to M, only through "supportive communication."

The sense of problematicity that pervades M's experience of herself and of her world is in her view part of human experience in general. She inevitably attributes interpersonal problems to discrepant life experiences which resulted in irreconcilable personal differences. For example, she said her marriage could not have succeeded because she and her husband had different backgrounds; even if they had

had similar needs, she said, they needed to meet them in different ways.

In the view we are explicating, human uniqueness makes "communication" both vitally important and highly problematic. If people are unique, the kind of mutual disclosure and acknowledgment entailed in "communication" provide a necessary "bridge" from self to others. But if people are unique, they also lack the mutuality necessary for achieving interpersonal meaning and coordination.

The resolution to the dilemma posed by human uniqueness is found in M's belief that the individual has the capacity to change through "communication." One source for new definitions of self is the communication by others about oneself. The moral imperative which attends this possibility is to be "open" to the "feedback" which others can supply. For M, it is both natural and desirable that persons be continually exposed to and "open" to such a "rhetoric of conversion" in the interpersonal realm. Another source of materials for "personal growth" is the exercise of what is believed to be the innate capacity to choose what to be and become. We call the sense of moral obligation which attends this capacity "the imperative for self definition." According to M, if a person is unhappy with his or her self at a given time, then the person can and should change so as to maximize a sense of well-being. For example, she expressed strong disapproval of a man who would not quit a well-paying but personally unsatisfying job; she criticized him both because he would not change jobs and because he was not "open" to others' suggestions that he explore the possibility of change.

Thus, in the life and speech of M, "communication" derives its potency from the combined effect of the beliefs in personal uniqueness and personal malleability and from the normative injunctions to be "open" and to define one's self continually. These beliefs and norms are predicated on a view of the self as constantly changing and the concomitant experience of one's identity as shifting not only through time but also across roles and situations. With respect to the assumption of uniqueness, "communication" functions as the "how" of self, as the way to create and sustain a sense of personal identity by having it validated by another person. And, to the degree there is a tension between the demands imposed by the imperative to yield control for self-definition to others and the imperative continually to re-make one's self, "communication" is viewed as the dialectic of these opposing forces from which emerges a "negotiated self."

One of the fundamental tensions of that dialectic is the clash between the belief that persons constantly change with the belief that each person has a "core," a unique endowment. M reconciles those beliefs by claiming that life experiences affect persons crucially but mainly affect the external layers of "self." The core is affected only by a traumatic experience, or through the intervention of counseling, which M believes is the only way to solve difficult personal problems. She vacillates between an emphasis on either the fixed or fluctuating aspects of self in constructing an acceptable account of her life and world.

The belief that there is a personal core gives rise to a "rhetoric of naturalness." It was stated in so many words by the instructor in a workshop we observed on "Effective Oral Presentations." The instructor said to students preparing to give a speech: "Be yourself, be natural." And, in describing the experience of giving a stilted speech, the instructor warned: "You actually become somebody else, you're not relaxed." Thus, the

"work" of being oneself consists of shedding unnecessary impediments to the experience and of presenting one's "true self." It can also be the "work" involved in constructing a unified entity experienced (and presented) as one's self. For M, this must be done against the background of a diverse and changing world. Thus, she feels the need constantly to check her interpretations of events against the "feedback" derived from others through "communication." In this way she enhances her sense of reality: "Then I could deal with what was really happening and not what I imagined."

In conclusion, the study of "communication" in M's life became a study of the many ways she has tried, failed, and succeeded in building up a sense of "self," of the symbolic and interpretive code underlying this struggle, and of the way it has been played out in several crucial interpersonal relationships.

Informant Two [10]

K is a 25-year old woman. She is single, holds a degree in business administration, and works in a health food store during the day and in a tavern two nights a week.

K frequently used the term "communication" in talking about herself, others, and life in general. As with M, all of K's references to "communication" relate to its interpersonal function. This was of particular interest in that a great deal of K's talk referred to work settings, yet she made no reference to the instrumental function of communication.

K's self image is explicitly linked to her view of her own abilities as a

[10]We are indebted to Cheryl R. Marty-White, who collected the materials used in our study of informant two, and who allowed us to use her field materials. We are responsible for the analysis and interpretations given.

communicator, and she prides herself on her versatility as a communicator saying she can communicate equally well with "a bum on First Avenue and the president of a corporation." When she expressed self-doubts concerning her worth as a person, these took the form of misgivings concerning her abilities as a communicator: "It's very important to me to communicate well with people . . . sometimes you are taken aback . . . you realize you are not so good at that . . . then you kind of humble yourself and realize maybe you are not this open person you thought you were. . . ." Being a good communicator and being an "open" person are near-equivalents in K's parlance.

"Open communication" is the phrase K reserves for her preferred form of communication, which is on a par with "really talking" for M. The former phrase encompasses both the notion of full mobilization of inner resources, so as to be able "to totally experience what is happening to me," as well as the notion of full utilization of the interactional opportunities posed by a unique other person. Thus: "I'm usually very open to conversation with our customers. I take advantage of the unique, unusual people that may pass through the door by verbally communicating with them."

K conceives both the self and the other as resources, as potentialities to be exploited. "Communication" is the process by which this exploitation of resources is carried out. The industrial metaphor which underlies this way of speaking, whereby the person is seen as both the resource and the product of social life, is quite apparent. "Communication" thus becomes the production process, which in itself is both a resource and a product.

For K, the self constantly changes in and through "communication." She invariably conceptualizes such change positively—as development, improve-ment, or "growth." Lack of "communication" implies more than lack of growth, but rather a sense of running in place, of stagnation: "Communication allows me to grow . . . it scares me to be stagnant." Through "communication" the experience of self and other are merged and intensified: "The only way to get ultimate experiences is to experience other people through communication." Whereas M is concerned mainly with the supportive role of communication in validating self images, K is at least as much concerned with the prior stage of constructing a self through "communication," so that the self as "communicator" becomes the paramount role with which she identifies. It is the most neutral and universal of roles, as in one form or another it applies to all social situations. In thinking of herself in these terms, K seems to mitigate the experience of multiple realities, and the ominousness of an open-ended identity.

Our second informant uses "prison-house" imagery to describe the non-interacting self. She described how, as an adolescent, she felt inhibited in her social interaction although deep inside she knew she was "open" to "communication." She said she felt she had to "lock the extrovert inside this cage." Similarly functioning expressions are "outlet" and "escape into another," the latter describing "communication" as that process whereby one is emancipated from the prison-house of the non-interacting self. Of her family, K said: "Our family is not really an open family. You didn't just sit down and work out and talk about problems." She links this to a widespread shortcoming of people of her parents' generation, which consisted of "not communicating, not getting in touch with their children's feeling." K was able to "communicate" with her mother, who was her confidant. However-er, her father's unwillingness to engage in communication of the type she felt she needed, and thereby to legitimize it as the preferred way to conduct family affairs, had a detrimental effect on the way she experienced her communication with her family. Thus, she described her communication with her mother in terms of refuge rather than of liberation: "In communicating with my mother, she was great and she took refuge in me because she could communicate with me and she couldn't with my dad, and he was so closed and she needed the outlet."

Although K said she knew her parents loved her, she also said she was very unhappy during her adolescence. The source of her distress was the absence of a forum accepted by all family members in which to discuss feelings, air differences, and examine divergent orientations. The communicative climate, which was marked by a lack of "open" interpersonal communication among all members of the family, rendered their family, as an integrative unit, less than satisfactory to K. K predicted that she would repeat some of the mistakes her parents had made in raising her, but, she insisted, "there are things I have learned, and that is that communication is important."

"Communication" is so important to K that the highest level of communication she recognizes is talk about talk. In the log she kept, K described the most rewarding communicative experience she had ever had, which occurred in the initial phase of what was to become an intimate relationship: "We sat for two hours at breakfast discussing each person's ability and method of communicating. We spoke on levels far beyond normal chit-chat." The level of "normal chit-chat" seems to be the equivalent of the term "small talk" in the speech of M. Talking about one's communicative profile is, presumably, part of what M defined as "real talk." The purpose of this intense preoccupation with ways of communicating was to pre-illumine each person's mode of operation in the communicative sphere so as to be able to anticipate and thereby prevent possible "breakdowns" in "communication." As "communication" is the "how" of love, or the vehicle of intimacy, its inner workings should be studied and controlled.

In conclusion, the second informant conceives of persons much in the same way as the first: they inhabit a "personal space" which can be penetrated through the act of "communication"; each person is unique and this is a resource to be exploited for one's growth and development; lack-of-growth-through-"communication" equals stagnation, even the loss of identity. The self is experienced as an event or is not experienced at all; one's identity is closely tied to one's view of oneself as communicator, which seems to be the generalized role of the person in this orientational system. Thus, concern with self-definition and self-validation is expressed as concern over one's own quality as a communicator. Like M, K is extremely concerned with having control over life, which she interprets as control over her communicative encounters. She is cheerful and pleasant with everybody, assuming that thereby she will secure a similar response to herself, and she engages in metacommunicative discussion as a form of "preventive treatment" in the interpersonal domain.

THE SEMANTIC DIMENSIONS OF "COMMUNICATION"

In the speech of our informants, and in the other texts we have examined in the course of our inquiry, there is evidence of two distinctive clusters of terms referring to communication. One cluster includes such terms as "real communication," "really talking," "supportive communication," and "open communication." "Communication," without a modifier, can also be included in this cluster when the term appears in the context of discussing "self" and "relationships." The other cluster includes such terms as "small talk," "normal chit-chat," and "mere talk." It is probably the case that neither cluster is exhaustively delineated here, but the present assignment of terms is defensible in the light of our field materials.

"Communication" and "mere talk" are differentiated on several semantic dimensions. The dimensions discussed below were derived from our readings of the lives of M and K and of related texts in which "communication" was a key term. We tried to make sense of these various instances of the use of "communication" by submitting them to a kind of distinctive features analysis. The dimensions were thus derived inductively, based on scrutiny of the texts we collected and constructed.[11] M and K, and the producers of the other texts we examined, use the dimensions *close/ distant, supportive/neutral,* and *flexible/rigid* to differentiate "communication" from "mere talk." In what follows, these dimensions will be defined, analyzed into finer discriminations, and applied to "communication" and "mere talk."

The first dimension identified, *close/ distant,* suggests an essentially spatial metaphor. "Communication" is the medium for intercourse between those who are "close," such as "close friends" and intimates. Although the spatial metaphors of proximity and similarity are relevant here, perhaps of most relevance is the spatial metaphor of penetration. Specifically, "communication" is high on interpenetration of the interlocutors'

unique psychological worlds. To the degree that each interlocutor makes public what was previously private information about his or her unique self image, *closeness,* one feature of "communication," is manifested. This is intimate speech, speech which penetrates psychological boundaries and barriers. "Mere talk," by contrast, is talk in and through which one "keeps his distance" or "stays at arm's length" from another. The content of this latter kind of speech is "everyday chit-chat," a content which is independent of the unique self images of the speakers.

Supportive/neutral refers to the degree in which each interlocutor is committed to providing positive evaluations of the other's self. To engage in "communication," it is not necessary that one approve everything the other has *done*—the other's *actions*—but that one approve the other *qua* unique and precious individual. This is speech in which unconditional positive regard finds its natural home. The dimension does not contrast positive with negative evaluation, but the degree to which positive evaluation is relevant and salient. Thus, the polar opposite, manifested in "mere talk," is not negative evaluation, but rather is the absence of a commitment to, and the absence of the relevance of, positive evaluation.

A third dimension refers to the degree of *flexibility* manifested by the participants in the speech event. By flexibility is meant a willingness to listen to and acknowledge the other's presentation of self, to listen to and actively try to understand the other's evaluation of oneself, and to be willing to consider changing one's perception of self or other contingent upon the meanings which emerge in the speech event. This is the speech of emergent realities, of negotiated selves and the negotiated relationship. "Mere talk," by contrast is considered that talk which is governed by a set of conventions

[11]We follow closely here the suggestions and wording of Peter Seitel, "Haya Metaphors for Speech," *Language in Society,* 3 (1974), 51-67.

independent of those which have been forged between the two interlocutors.

The three dimensional contrasts made above are formalized here to make explicit our emergent hypothesis about the mapping of the semantic dimensions represented by the native terms "communication" and its opposite "mere talk." The analysis suggests that, for our informants, "communication" refers to *close, supportive,* and *flexible* speech between two or more people, and that it can be contrasted with "mere talk," which is relatively more *distant, neutral,* and *rigid.*

"Communication" as Interpersonal "Work"

Thus far we have defined "communication" by contrasting it with "mere talk." We further define it here by discussing its relationship to two other terms, which have emerged as salient for the interpersonal domain. An examination of "self," "relationship," and "communication," as they occur in our informants' speech, indicates that these terms label categories which together constitute a domain of meaning. In what follows we explore the key figure of speech which makes that domain of meaning intelligible, and we articulate the key interrelationships among these terms. The purpose of these explorations is to deepen understanding of "communication" as a cultural category by examining it as one term in a larger "code of talking."

Our field notes yield the following observations about the words used in some American speech: People "work" on their "relationship" or make their "relationship work"; they "work" on "themselves" and on their "communication" together; "nervous breakdowns" within the person's mental machinery have been supplanted by "breakdowns" in "relationships" and "breakdowns" in

"communication." Thus in the world of meaning constituted by the speech we have examined, "self," "relationship," and "communication" are things one can have and discuss, as well as take apart, examine, put together again, and make to "work."

The figure which lends coherence to these three terms is the "work" metaphor. This is manifested in the use of "self," "relationship," and "communication" as objects of the "work" people do, as things which can be "worked on." It is also manifested in the notion of "communication" as the "work" necessary to construct a "self" and develop a "relationship." Although most of the metaphorical expressions used invoke the notion of a machine, there is an extension of the metaphorical domain to include other, not necessarily machine-based, industries. For example, people are said to "invest" in each other, but mainly in their "relationships"; people "contribute" to a "relationship," give one thing to it and take another. This secondary metaphoric domain is based on more organismic images, so there is talk of the "relationship growing," of "communication" being "alive," and of the "self" being involved in a continuous process of "growth."

Metaphors, as James Fernandez has written, "take their subjects and move them along a dimension or set of dimensions."[12] In the way of speaking examined here, interpersonal life is made intelligible by moving it along the *work* dimension and thus increasingly derives its validation from its ethos of performance. This is epitomized by the notion of "competence" that is so naturally applied to the interpersonal domain. Interpersonal life, which in some ways of speaking is associated with home and

[12] James Fernandez, "Persuasions and Performances: Of the Beast in Every Body . . . and the Metaphors of Every Man," *Daedalus,* 101 (1972), p. 47.

subjectivity,[13] has in the speech of our informants been made an arena for work and technique. To the first informant, a person can be judged by the quality of their "relationships"; the second judges herself and others by the quality of their "communication." The "self," when it is discussed, is described in terms of its components; references are made to feelings, responses, and experiences, all of which can be "worked on," and not to the person as a whole. Both informants imply that interpersonal life is fundamentally an arena for work in which one's competence is the primary determinant of performance success.

People can be judged by many standards—their birth, blood, heroic deeds, or as intrinsically precious by virtue of being alive. The way of speaking we have examined is notable for the emphasis it places on the competence to perform interpersonal "work." In this speech, "communication" competence would be a person's capacity for *close, supportive, flexible* speech in the discussion of—and thus, in the "work" upon—one's self and one's relationships. Note that competence here is not an attainment, it is a capacity, and given the changing nature of persons and the moral imperative not to "stagnate," it is a capacity which is and should be continually put to new tests. Thus, interpersonal life, in the terms of this communication code, is a life of unrelenting work in which one's competence is ever newly applied and newly tested.

If the conceptualization of the interpersonal domain as an arena for "work" creates great demands for effective performance, it also provides a way to mitigate a sense of personal responsibil-

ity for one's interpersonal difficulties or failures. Our informants attributed family problems and divorces to the absence of "communication" and to the reluctance of people to "work" on their "relationship" or their "communication." If "the relationship" can be made responsible for some aspects of human conduct, then the burden of the "self" is eased. Thus, when "communication breaks down," and "the relationship" does not "work," both parties can still be "O.K." Such a way of speaking helps to mitigate the discomfort which attends difficulties or misconduct and thus enhances the state of "feeling good about oneself," which is the ultimate goal of interpersonal life as here conceived.

Given the importance of effective interpersonal work in the way of speaking formulated here, we could expect that highly routinized procedures have been developed for doing that work. Such procedures have been codified in our discussion of the "communication" ritual to which we turn next. Here we turn from a metaphor supplied by our informants, that of "communication" as "work," to one supplied by us, that of "communication" as "ritual."

THE "COMMUNICATION" RITUAL

Throughout this paper we have noted that the people we have studied do not consider all talk to be "communication." Nor is all interpersonally oriented talk experienced to be as satisfying and liberating as "communication" implies for the informants. A more specific set of expectations has evolved concerning the episodic sequence referred to by the native phrases "sit down and talk," "work out problems," or "discuss our relationship." We call such a sequence the "communication" ritual. It functions as ritual as it is the culturally preferred way to reaffirm the status of what the culture defines as a sacred object—the

[13]David S. Kemnitzer, "Sexuality as a Social Form: Performance and Anxiety in America," in *Symbolic Anthropology: A Reader in the Study of Symbols and Meanings*, ed. Janet L. Dolgin, David S. Kemnitzer, and David M. Schneider (New York: Columbia University Press, 1977), esp. pp. 297–8.

definition of "self" as experienced by any one of the participants, usually the one who initiates the sequence.

In what follows we outline the basic ingredients of the "communication" ritual in terms of several components of speech events as discussed by Hymes.[14] The purpose of this outline is to point to a general mold, not to provide a recipe for communicative encounters. Obviously, each enactment of the ritual, each token of the general type, will deviate from it one way or another, but this general account captures the essential ingredients of the ritual as we understand it. The following of Hymes' categories were used for the description: topic, purpose, participants, act sequence, setting, and norm of interaction.

Topic. The topic is problems arising in one's experience of one's "self" and one's world. Both "self" and world must be defined by each individual but these definitions must also be validated by others. The simultaneous awareness of personal uniqueness and the demand for intimacy and mutual validation is a continual source of problems, which are experienced as inter- rather than intrapersonal. Thus, their solution naturally calls for "communication," and this is not accompanied by a sense of imposition because the others will consider the problems their own, too. Turning inward and brooding over a problem is not considered a step toward its solution. Hamlet, if he were a member of this culture, would have tried to sit down and talk things over with his family or at least discuss his problem with Ophelia. "Communication" seems closely related to this sense of problematicity, and it seems that the term "fun" as in "having

lots of fun together" is reserved to the description of light-heartedness and well-being in the interpersonal domain (in which "communication" is not "fun" but "work").

Purpose. The purpose of the ritual is to resolve the sense of problematicity that one or more of the participants experiences, by affirming participants' identities and engendering intimacy. In a "talk show," which dealt with death, recently shown on American television, one of the participants said the purpose of the sequence she advocates is for "people to relate to each other in a positive way around a difficult issue." This captures much of the purpose of the "communication" ritual and indicates that it is not a problem solving session in the regular sense that participants have a specific problem that can be overcome and resolved. Rather, participants are expected to face whatever problem emerges in a dignified way, i.e., through talk of the supportive variety. The person who refuses to face problems by discussing them is felt to be "copping out," to be relinquishing control over life, and thereby that person becomes unwholesome.

Participants. Participants are (potentially) all the persons considered by the initiator of the ritual to be intimates who will not be imposed upon by discussion of the "problem" as they consider it, in part, their own. For a primary unit such as a family to be considered well-functioning, all its members have to be committed to the communication ritual on a symmetrical basis, so that the enactment of the ritual is surrounded by a climate of legitimacy.

Act sequence. There are constraints on the way the episodic sequence labelled the communication ritual can proceed.[15] The structural constraints

[14]Dell Hymes, "Models of the Interaction of Language and Social Life," in *Directions in Sociolinguistics: The Ethnography of Communication,* ed. John J. Gumperz and Dell Hymes (New York: Holt, Rinehart and Winston), pp. 35–71.

[15]This formulation is patterned after Goffman's description of the "remedial interchange." Erving

that seem to govern its unfolding are: (1) Initiation: a member of an intimate pair initiates the sequence by announcing the existence of a personal problem which can be "worked out" only through "communication" with other members of the primary group. The initiator suggests that they "sit down and talk about it." (2) Acknowledgment: The addressee(s) acknowledge the problem, its legitimacy as an interpersonal concern, and its relevance to the other members of the primary group by indicating their willingness to enact the sequence. They disengage themselves from other activity and make ready to render the discussion of the problem the focus of their attention. They "sit down to talk." (3) Negotiation: The problem is formulated, its ingredients examined from as many perspectives as possible, and its implications for the initiator and the other participants in the ritual are studied. The initiator does a great deal of the self-disclosing, and the other participant's behavior is marked by empathic listening, non-judgmental comments, and non-inquisitiveness. The initiator's attitude is that of openness both to feedback and to change. (4) Reaffirmation: The need for this phase seems to derive from the potential effect on the negotiation phase, in which discrepant positions, needs, and interpretations between committed individuals are brought into relief. At times a compromise on the substantive level is not possible, and at all times the discord is threatening on the relationship level. It is this threat that the reaffirmation phase seeks to mitigate.

Goffman, "On Face-Work: An Analysis of Ritual Elements in Social Interaction," *Interaction Ritual: Essays on Face-to-Face Behavior* (Garden City, New York: Anchor Books, 1967), esp. pp. 19–23. Our remarks here are also informed by Thomas S. Frentz and Thomas B. Farrell, "Language-Action: A Paradigm for Communication," *Quarterly Journal of Speech,* 62 (1976), 333–49.

Setting. The setting in which the ritual is appropriately enacted is one in which talk is accepted as the focal activity, in which interlocutors have privacy and can be fully immersed in each other.

Norm of interaction. When a person experiences a problem related to his or her sense of identity and/or to his or her functioning in the social world, the person should initiate the "communication" ritual. Conversely, a person who is approached by an intimate concerning a problem the latter experiences should reciprocate by helping him or her to enact the communication ritual. The norm calling for enactment of the sequence is very powerfully felt, to the extent that it loses its formative status of the "how" of love and the "how" of self and becomes the only indicator of their very existence. In this orientational system, not having a problem is interpreted as suppression or reluctance to face the problems one "must have" by virtue of being "alive" in the world today. A state of nothing in particular happening in one's life—no change—is experienced as dullness and deadening boredom, and long-term relationships are particularly vulnerable to it. As one of our informants put it, the comforts of a long-term marriage and its habitual structure prevent one from searching for a higher awareness of "self" and "relationship." This kind of probing is made possible and legitimate in enacting the ritual, so that for some people the absence of the ritual becomes the problem. This can be a tangled issue when partners disagree about their commitments to enact the ritual with each other. Unlike any other disagreement, this one cannot be remedied through "communication"—an attempt to do so would be a *de facto* enactment of the "communication" ritual. The gripping force the norm can have was indicated on two occasions when people with whom we discussed this project at length, a few days later in the context of discussing their lives, expressed the strong belief that "communication" is important, and that one should "sit down and talk." The ethnographic smile that lighted our faces did not jolt them into "hearing" what they were saying. When it was pointed out explicitly, they noticed and concurred.

Finally, we speculate that the intensity of the preoccupation with the kind of speech found in the "communication" ritual stands in sharp contrast to the communicative requirements of non-intimate encounters in this society, where the ruling injunction seems to be: "Thou shalt exude well-being." Our first informant commented on this bitterly, saying, "If I am mad I don't care who knows that I am mad," and she described herself as a social misfit in this regard. The second informant seemed rather compulsive in following this injunction, pointing out that she took care not to burden others with her problems and, by so doing, secured a similar behavior towards herself. This, it seems to us, puts an added burden on interpersonal relationships in primary groups or dyads. They become the only source of personal validation, given the strong proscription against self-exposure in non-intimate settings. The "communication" ritual, then, is so terribly important not only because it allows the expression of the "how" of love and the "how" of self, but also because it is the only place to find them.

Having defined "communication," situated it in a larger code of meaning about interpersonal work, and formulated the episodic sequence by which such a work is most naturally performed, we can make sense of "communication" (as it appears in some American speech) in a way we could not have done before. Thus, we conclude by turning to a brief examination of a communication event which has a prominent

place in American life. We turn now to an examination of a television show which is witnessed daily by a large number of Americans and in which "communication," as we have formulated it, is very naturally and poignantly spoken by the participants.

On Being "in Touch" With Phil Donahue

The Phil Donahue show practices and preaches the "communication" creed we have described. At the studio in Chicago, Phil Donahue and his guests "sit down and talk." They discuss interpersonal problems that many Americans would not talk about in the privacy of their homes, and the voice travels across America: "What you need is communication." Indeed, to be fully "in touch" with Phil Donahue, one must also be in touch with the "communication" ritual and the meanings to which it gives expression.[16]

Phil Donahue, it will be noted, does not deal with insoluble problems in his broadcasts, he deals with problems that *seem* insoluble to the people "out there" who are enmeshed in them. To his guests, these are problems they have solved. Underlying these shows is a rhetoric of conversion. It is not the person who beats his wife and cannot stop—it is the ex-wife batterer—who is invited to the show; it is not the person who is struggling with his sexual identity but the person who has come to terms with it that we see. It is they who have a message to convey, and the message is: "I could change, you can, too."

The Phil Donahue show marks off a world of talk where the "real stuff" is brought to light; emotions are thematized and simplified by being abstracted from conduct and experience ("today's

[16]Our analysis of the Phil Donahue Show is based on shows broadcast during June and July of 1980.

show deals with jealousy"). The climate is generally supportive (when it is not, Donahue chastises the audience); interlocutors openly "share" their feelings and views; the phenomena dealt with are provocative and problematic, such as children who "divorce" their parents, husbands who beat their wives, couples who agree to have extra-marital affairs, and so on. The specific topic is not of concern here, the point is that anything can be a problem if so perceived, and any problem can (and should) be overcome by enacting a version of the "communication" ritual. A statement to this effect by one of the participants in the show which dealt with parents' and children's rights was as follows:

Okay. Well, I think what Lee is talking about here is that she felt that she wasn't getting an adequate forum at home to discuss her problem. . . . This first woman that spoke was saying: "Well, we could have talked it out, and if the child didn't want to go that's fine." But many of these cases come up when there is just no communication at home. Now Cindy here went to court to have herself declared incorrigible and taken away from her parents. And she said there were long stretches of time when her parents just didn't talk to her at all, let alone have a basis for communication.

The excerpt, which is representative of many others taken from Donahue shows, illustrates the high value assigned to "communication" by Donahue participants, and implies awareness, and belief in the efficacy of the "communication" ritual. The healing value of communicating about problems is attested by the mother of a woman who, through her childhood, had been sexually abused by her father. Like many other people on the show, she feels her message to the public has a missionary value to it, and it involves a call for "communication": "I'm here to support our daughter and to offer help to people who have had the same thing happen to

them who will understand. But mostly, that things can be worked out, and as a family you can learn to communicate, you can learn to overcome what has happened." On another show, dealing with marital infidelity, a couple who had overcome the "problem" described their newly found intimacy. The wife said: "The communication we have now is so different. I trust his honesty, he'll answer any question, won't become vague . . . doesn't say, 'put it behind you, forget it.' "

In line with the view that problems are always to be solved in an interacting context, the guest whose problems are thematized often appear with some of their intimates, i.e., potential participants in the "communication" ritual. The clearest example we found was the above-mentioned show on incest in families, where the sexually abused daughter appeared on the show with both parents (who were in silhouettes). This appearance, like all others, was a post-conversion one, so that given the episodic structure of the ritual, the normative expectation is that by following the "communication" ritual in which they all had taken part (and to which they testified), their relationship could be fully reaffirmed. It was interesting, therefore, to note that the daughter, who appeared to us to be angry with her father, worked so hard to contain her anger; anger was out of place in the "script" implicit in the Donahue show, which presupposes a sequence which ends with a reaffirmation phase.

The special rhetorical effectiveness of the Donahue "communication" shows is due to the iconicity of its form and its content: Donahue does what he says, and he says what he does. He both embodies and calls for the possibility of personal conversion. He capitalizes on his standing as the arch-convert who has learned that women are persons, too, and that if you have a problem you must not keep it to yourself, but "sit down and talk about it."

In response to an obstinate caller who refused to see the light, Phil Donahue expressed the injunction that underlies his show and seems to underlie interpersonal ceremony in private life as well: "We are not asking you to change this culture, but we can ask you as an adult to step back and look at what you are saying." This seems very much like the ethnographer's task—to step back and look at what people are saying, Phil Donahue among them.

CONCLUSION

By interpreting several instances of American speech, we have constructed a way to hear the term "communication" which renders its use in that speech intelligible and illuminating. We have found that in the field of discourse in which "communication," "self," and "relationship" co-occur, "communication" refers to that speech which manifests mutual self disclosure, positive regard for the unique selves of the participants, and openness to emergent, negotiated definitions of self and other. Such *close, supportive,* and *flexible* speech is the artful "work" required to follow the contradictory cultural injunctions, "be yourself" and "be the self you want to be" while simultaneously conceding to others part of the control for self definition.

Thus, "communication" is a culturally distinctive solution to the universal problem of fusing the personal with the communal. In the ideology in which "communication" is a pivotal term, affirming oneself in and through a process of social interaction is the highest good. But this is always problematic. Each person is unique among persons, that is, different from all others due to differential life experiences, and each person is malleable, that is, subject to change due to personal will and changing definitions supplied by others. Given human uniqueness, the interpenetration of life worlds is always necessary for understanding another person, and thus validation of another's self image is always problematic. Given human malleability, such interpenetration holds the promise of the kind of interpersonal speech which fosters the favorable conditions of growth and change, and failure to expose oneself to such experiences is tantamount to denying one's full humanity. Thus, the achievement of commonality with others and the construction of a sense of self are always problematic, but "communication" is the process in which the problematicity is relieved, or at least "worked on." "Communication" is the solution to the problem of "relationship" (love) and of "self" (personhood). In terms of overcoming personal differences, "communication" functions as the "how of love," the primary vehicle and constituent of a "relationship"; in terms of constructing and validating a "self," "communication" is the "how of self."

Given the cultural meaning and ideational context of "communication," as delineated here, it should be no surprise to find that "communication" finds its quintessential place in the ritual we have described. Like other rituals, the "communication" ritual, by its very enactment, takes as its theme that which is problematic for its performers and constitutes, in its enactment, the solution to the problem. Just as prayer takes as its theme man's separation from God, and solves it through ritual acts of obeisance to a deity, so the "communication" ritual takes as its theme the reality of human separation and solves it through acts of obeisance to the co-construction of selves in and through "communication."

Thus, the "communication" ritual functions to reinforce the unspoken consensus underlying intimate life—an agreement to be *close, supportive,* and *flexible,* and its performance thereby implicates and insinuates the performers in a world of meaning and morality which gives credence and legitimacy to "the relationship." It is this constitutive power of the ritual which makes the fact or the possibility of its performance so poignant.

If various types of cultural performance, such as everyday and public dramas, are "dialectical dancing partners,"[17] then our readings of the everyday lives we have studied should help us to understand the meanings underlying some more public dramas. For example, for us, *The Phil Donahue Show* was made intelligible in the very terms and tropes which color the speech of M and K. Just as a reading of Phil Donahue's autobiography suggests a striking parallelism between the structure and the content of his program and of his life, so his show simultaneously reflects and provides "a rhetoric, a mode of emplotment, and a meaning"[18] which articulates with the ideals espoused by M and K. But the dramatic metaphor fails us here. It is more apt to say that Donahue and company communicate in evangelistic tones. Following a public display of "communication," they endorse it and preach it, apparently to a fervently appreciative audience. That we could find so prominent and so plausible a public use of the code we formulated suggests, not that it is universal in America but that discourse which uses it is *intelligible to* many Americans.

So, we have, as Donahue exhorted his viewer to do, stepped back and looked at what some of the people in this country were saying. We found that a "wholesome adult" in the ideology studied looked suspiciously familiar—he is his own ethnographer. The difference between the ethnographer and the reflective person who can deal with his problems through "communication" is further minimized if we accept Ricoeur's dictum that the aim of ethnography is to reach an understanding of the self via an understanding of the other.[19] Our study of American "communication" has led us to think of ethnography less as a journey into a foreign land or culture, and more as a journey into a no-man's land, which is neither the territory of the self nor of the other. As every Israeli child who was taken on that mandatory field-trip to the border knows, one cannot risk more than a few steps into unsettled territory. In doing so, however, one becomes aware not only of the existence of the other's territory, but of one's own, and of the concept of territory in general. The ethnographer, like the careful tourist, pays his or her tribute to the border at designated spots, but the border stretches and winds between these spots as well, and it is in this unmarked territory that the "person" searches for a sense of personal meaning. The "communication" ritual provides members of the social world we studied a context comparable in import to the ethnographic encounter for the ethnographer, but the sign, if any, would say "exchange station" rather than "border." Thus, despite the territorial metaphors, we hope this study does not read as an exercise in cartography. We

---

[17]Victor Turner, "Social Dramas and Stories about Them," *Critical Inquiry,* 7 (1980), 159.

[18]Turner, p. 153.

[19]Paul Ricoeur, "The Model of the Text: Meaningful Action Considered as a Text," in *Understanding and Social Inquiry,* ed. Fred R. Dallmayr and Thomas A. McCarthy (Notre Dame, Indiana: University of Notre Dame Press, 1977), p. 33.

hope we have not only delineated some of the scenery in that stretch of no-man's land, in that area of heightened consciousness in which our informants told their stories and we made our interpretations, but that we have conveyed as well a sense of possibility for ethnography as perspective and method in human communication.

8

Reflections on "Communication" as a Cultural Category in Some American Speech

GERRY PHILIPSEN

Like the Teamsterville research, the research on "communication" as a cultural category in some American speech was originally part of a plan to discover and comparatively analyze two culturally distinctive communicative codes. With regard to the "American" code, early influences were Schneider (1965) and Hsu (1963), two ethnographers who provided a way to think about American life as deeply cultured. The first concrete expression of this plan is found in Philipsen (1976), a paper heavily indebted to Bernstein (1964), in which I articulated several dimensions of contrast between Teamsterville and "Sunnyville," a designation for middle-class, college-educated Americans in southern California, whose communicative practices Mary Jo Rudd and I had studied through ethnographic fieldwork there. These practices were cast at the level of behavioral tendencies, beliefs, values, and indigenous speech situations. It was not until reading Varenne (1977) that the full implication of a cultural approach to American communication, such as Katriel and I took in the paper, became evident. Varenne, applying the ethnographic approaches of Geertz (1973) and Schneider (1976), showed a way to treat American culture as a system of symbols and meanings rather than as only a set of institutions and practices. Our research built on this foundation by treating "communication" as a cultural category.

Some reviewers of chapter 7 have misunderstood us slightly in describing the research as being based on two case studies, the cases of "M" and "K." Although we do present these two cases, and although they were important sources of data, they were among *many* sources of primary data. The life stories of M and K are narratives in which the cultural category "communication" is prominently used, by the tellers. In these stories, like many other observed instances of American speech, the cultural category and term were used. In the introduction to the chapter, we signal that our primary unit of analysis is not the life study but the episodic instance in which "communication" is used, although perhaps we should have made this more explicit.

At the empirical level, this research can be read as an effort to articulate a cultural communicative code, one important part of which is the term *communication* and its relation to such other terms as *self* and *relationship*. One goal was to draw attention to these as cultural terms, as part of a system of symbols and meanings, so as to help develop the available understanding of that cultural system that has been labeled *American,* after the term used to designate the nation in which the code has achieved greatest prominence. Our localized, case-driven study, although conducted quite independently of other, broader surveys, seems to corroborate and be corroborated by several other studies that were published at the same time (e.g., Veroff, Douvan, & Kulka, 1981; Yankelovich, 1981) and later (Bellah, Madsen, Sullivan, Swidler, & Tipton, 1985).

Another goal of ours was to implement an analytic-interpretive scheme. Although the chapter is presented primarily as an analysis and interpretation of data, some readers have detected in it a general stance toward the study of culturally situated communication (e.g., see Cushman & Cahn, 1985, chapter 8). Our working model, displayed in chapter 7, includes attention to the key terms from which culturally significant utterances are constructed, relations of contrast, substitutability, and co-occurrence among key terms, situational contexts of use of these terms, dimensions of meaning, metaphorical meanings, and the use of generic cultural forms as heuristic frames. With regard to the latter, in chapter 7 we pay particular attention to ritual, but our larger model gives equal weight to social drama and myth. This descriptive-analytic — comparative-interpretive frame has since been applied and extended in a series of published studies, including Philipsen (1986), Katriel (1986), and Carbaugh (1988), and has been explicated more fully in Philipsen (1987). Philipsen (1984) presents an application of myth to American cultural data in a paper that can be read as a companion to chapter 7. It is now possible to say that the 1981 paper has been productive of a considerable body of research, which is now available for assessment in terms of its theoretical contribution vis-à-vis the development of an interpretive model.

An important feature of chapter 7 is that it was truly collaborative. There are insights (hearings?) in it that could not have been gleaned by either author working alone. We believe this supports the case for the kind of unique collaboration represented here, specifically, two ethnographers, one socialized in the host culture, one alien to it. Our research method explicitly capitalized on this opportunity. It exemplifies the model in which the culture being analyzed is (a) analyzed by an insider and by an outsider and is (b) further analyzed by each ethnographer systematically examining the other examining the culture. In our case such a dialogic collaboration proved invaluable.

The idea of "communication" is, in 1990 as prominent in everyday life in the United States as it was in 1981. The term is used extensively as a God term and there is considerable work that can still be done in tracing out the nuances of its meaning and use, not only in intimate but in organizational, technical, and public contexts. Our 1981 paper is a beginning, but the full meaning and function of this category in American culture is yet to be delineated.

References

Bellah, R N., Madsen, R., Sullivan, W. M., Swidler, A., & Tipton, S. M. (1985). *Habits of the heart: Individualism and commitment in American life*. Berkeley, CA: University of California Press.

Bernstein, B. (1964). Elaborated and restricted codes: Their social origins and some consequences, *American Anthropologist, 66* (6), 55–69.

Carbaugh, D. (1988). *Talking American: Cultural discourses on "Donahue."* Norwood, NJ: Ablex.

Cushman, D. P., & Cahn, D. D., Jr. (1985). *Communication in interpersonal relationships*. Albany, NY: State University of New York Press.

Geertz, C. (1973). *The interpretation of cultures*. New York: Basic Books.

Hsu, F. L. K. (1963). *Clan, caste, & club:* New York: Van Nostrand.

Katriel, T. (1986). *Talking straight: Dugri speech in Israeli Sabra culture*. Cambridge: Cambridge University Press.

Philipsen, G (1976). *Speaking as a cultural resource*. Paper presented at the annual convention of the Speech Communication Association, Chicago, IL.

Philipsen, G. (1984). *Joanna Kramer's identity crisis and the myth of dignity*. Paper presented at the annual convention of the Speech Communication Association, Chicago, IL.

Philipsen, G. (1986). Mayor Daley's council speech: A cultural analysis, *Quarterly Journal of Speech, 72,* 247–260.

Philipsen, G. (1987). The prospect for cultural communication. In D. Kinkcaid (Ed.), *Communication theory from Eastern and Western perspectives*. (pp. 245–254). New York: Academic Press.

Schneider, D. M. (1965). American kin terms and terms for kinsmen: A critique of Goodenough's componential analysis of Yankee kinship terminology. *Formal Semantic Analysis, American Anthropologist, 67,* 288–308.

Schneider, D. M. (1976). Notes toward a theory of culture. In K. H. Basso & H. A. Selby (Eds.), *Meaning in anthropology* (pp. 197–220). Albuquerque, NM: University of New Mexico Press.

Varenne, H. (1977). *Americans together: Structured diversity in a midwestern town*. New York: Teachers College Press.

Veroff, J., Douvan, E. Kulka, R. A., (1981). *Mental health in America: Patterns of health seeking from 1957 to 1976*. New York: Basis Books.

Yankelovich, D. (1981). *New rules: Searching for self-fulfillment in a world turned upside down*. New York: Random House.

9

'Griping' as a Verbal Ritual in Some Israeli Discourse

TAMAR KATRIEL

> "The function of ritual, as I understand it, is
> to give form to human life, not in the way of
> a mere surface arrangement, but in depth."
> (Campbell 1972)

1. *Introduction*

This paper examines the speech mode known in colloquial Israeli Hebrew as *kiturim* or *kuterai*, whose closest English equivalent would be 'griping'. As many Israelis concede, and some lament, griping has become an ever-present speech activity in informal encounters among Israelis. So much so that Friday night gatherings in Israeli homes, which form the major context for middle-class Israelis to get together socially, have earned the label *mesibot kiturim,* that is, 'griping parties'.

The overall flavor of these parties is conveyed by the following lines from an article by a prominent Israeli journalist:

> "About a year ago a group of us were sitting at a friend's house and, as is the habit among Israelis, we were griping about the situation. The immediate pretext for this collective bathing in our national-frustration-puddle was a rumor which circulated at the time concerning some instance of corruption in an important government agency (and which, incidentally, later proved to be largely untrue) and some half-insane political act of a marginal group that manages to conquer the newspaper headlines from time to time". (*Ma'ariv*, Nov.29th, 1980; my translation)

A few months later, the same author talks about "the masochistic 'griping parties' held on Friday nights, which more than anything else reflects the attitudes of the public" (*Ma'ariv*, April 24th, 1981; my translation).

Thus, in contemporary middle-class Israeli society, the griping mode finds its primordial expression in the type of speech event known as a *Griping*

M. Dascal (ed.), *Dialogue*, 367-381.

Party; however, it is by no means restricted to this prototypical context. In what follows, I will delineate the structure and functions of griping in Israeli discourse, arguing that it constitutes a well-bounded and readily recognizable type of communicative event, both in its more and in its less paradigmatic forms. Moreover, I will not only argue that griping has evolved as an implicitly patterned interactional routine in Israeli social life, but also that its import and functions can be best understood by regarding it as a verbal ritual.

The term 'ritual' as used here refers to patterned symbolic action whose function it is to re-affirm the relationship of members to a culturally sanctioned 'sacred object' (or 'unquestionable', in the secularized language of contemporary anthropology (Moore and Meyerhoff 1977)). According to Firth (1973: 301), symbolic actions of this kind "are communicative, but the information they convey refers to the control and regularization of a social situation rather than to some descriptive fact."

In a previous paper (Ch. 7, this volume), a similar attempt has been made to apply the ritual metaphor to the description of the speech event we have dubbed the *Communication Ritual*, to which Americans refer by the locutions *sit down and talk* or *discuss our relationship*. This ritual pertains to the domain of intimate relationships and provides the major context for members of the culture to construct as well as validate personal identities and generate intimacy through the form of talk known as 'communication', which is culturally interpreted as 'supportive speech'. Comparisons will be drawn between the Communication and the Griping Rituals whenever this seems appropriate.

The observations contained in this paper are based both on my own intuitions as a 'native griper' and on discussions with over 50 informants of a predominantly middle-class background, of which I recorded spontaneously expressed attitudes towards griping, descriptions of actual griping, as well as elicited responses to various appropriate and inappropriate uses of the term *lekater* 'to gripe' and its morphologically related terms, such as *kuter* (which stands for an 'habitual griper') and *kuter mikzo'i* (which indicates a 'hopeless one'). This set of moves has provided the data base for the analytic description of griping as a distinct type of communicative event, and for the outline of the symbolic structuring involved in its ritualistic enacting.

The colloquial term *lekater* is explicated in the popular dictionary of Hebrew slang compiled by Dan Ben-Amotz and Netiva Ben-Yehuda (1972), where it is rendered as 'to complain' and illustrated with an example that can be roughly translated as 'Stop griping, nothing will come out of talk'. It is said to be a Yiddish borrowing, but its etymology is not specified. Several informants, however, were familiar with the word's history and noted that it has sprung from the Yiddish word *kuter*, which denotes a male cat who is whining even while mounting a female, thus giving expression to basically unwarranted plaintiveness. The cat's griping disposition and its metaphorical extension to the human domain were attributed to a generally defensive orientation, nourished by the belief that one should not appear overly contented so as not to attract the devil's attention (as happened, for example, to the Biblical figure of Job). People also tended to see the griping mode as an expression of a 'national character', counting evidence as ancient as the Children of Israel complaining on encountering their first difficulties after the exodus from Egypt. Thus, in its folkloristic roots, griping is viewed as part of the national ethos, constituting both a spontaneous expression of lack of faith and a culturally sanctioned form of 'preventive treatment'.

Most informants, it should be noted, were not aware that *kuter* was a borrowing from Yiddish and related the word either to the Hebrew word *katar* 'steam engine' or to the word *ktoret* 'incense'.[1] Both words conjure up the image of smoke and of the blowing out of surplus, waste material, which is quite in line with the way the griping mode is generally conceptualized. In sum, the family of words related morphologically and semantically to *lekater* is felt by many Israelis to be a colloquial form with native roots rather than a foreign-sounding borrowing. This is indicated both by the morphological productiveness of the root-stem and by the semantic motivation it is felt to have.

The slang dictionary rendering of *lekater* as 'to complain' is not upheld by native speakers of Hebrew, who draw a clear disctinction between the two words, indicating that, although both verbs denote plaintive speech acts, they cannot be used interchangeably. Some of the semantic differences between the Hebrew equivalents of 'to gripe' and 'to complain' will be brought out by the forthcoming analysis.

Despite the general recognition of the long-standing cultural roots of the griping mode, many informants pointed out that the family of terms related to *lekater* has gained currency in colloquial Hebrew mainly during the past decade or so (some confidently dated its emergence in the days following the 1967 war; two clearly remembered learning it as a new word on returning to Israel after a few years' absence at that time). Informants also noted that griping has become increasingly salient in recent years; some even referred to it as 'the trademark of Israeli society'.

This is corroborated by a passage from a recently published book by Ben-Yehuda (1981) which depicts the ethos of the *Palmach*, a major division of the pre-Independence mainstream army. The passage describes the wholehearted commitment and sense of unquestionable rightfulness that filled the lives of the youngsters who had volunteered to assume the role of the 'realizers', through whose deeds the Zionist dream for national revival would come true:

> "We sang with great enthusiasm, danced energetically, went out to camps, climbed mountains, prepared whole-heartedly to 'realize' ... and we were happy, content with what we had, pleased with our goals, at peace with everything ... Nobody complained or criticized, nobody slandered, or noticed anything negative. We didn't speak ill of ourselves. We did not speak ill of our leaders, and this was no mistake. We didn't comment on anything. The very notion of 'criticism' was a negative concept. Absolutely negative. Like throwing mud. Making filthy. Slander and griping (*kiturim*) — these concepts didn't even exist. In the state-to-become, among us, the ardent pioneers, there was not the slightest trace of these concepts". (Ben-Yehuda 1981: 131; my translation)

This description of 'then' is written against the background of the present. It is the prevalence of the griping mode in present-day Israel that hovers at the edges of this picture of enthusiastic, committed 'realizers' who are actively engaged in the pursuit of communal goals. Conversely, it is the memory of this wholehearted, 'gripeless' commitment and active participation in communal life that nourishes some of the frustration that give rise to griping. The above passage, then, suggests that the rise of the griping mode, indeed the very coinage of the term, has to do with an ideological crisis, some dimensions of which are due to the fact that, as Rubinstein (1977) puts it, social cohesiveness in Israel nowadays is predicated on a common *fate* rather than a common *faith*. It is this common fate and the problems surrounding it as a source of communal identification that — as we will argue — the Griping Ritual dramatizes.

The Griping Ritual and the Communication Ritual are, thus, functionally comparable in that they each provide a major context for members of their respective cultures to give expression to, and form an experience of, a central problem area in their culture. The topic of each is, accordingly, a problem; but while the Communication Ritual addresses a problem whose locus is the 'self' in an attempt to reaffirm its status as the culture's 'unquestionable', the Griping Ritual locates the problem in public life and in its members' participation in it, reaffirming the status of the 'public interest' or 'community' (*haklal*) as the culture's 'unquestionable'.

I will now turn to a description of the structure and functions of griping in Israeli discourse, in keeping with Geertz's (1973: 364) general formulation of the goal of anthropological inquiry as that of "describing and analyzing the meaningful structure of experience ... as it is apprehended by representative members of a particular society at a particular point in time — in a word, a scientific phenomenology of culture." As was done in the case of the Communication Ritual, I will employ a subset of Hymes' (1972) components of speech events to describe the 'structure of experience' a communicative event must manifest for middle-class Israelis to identify it as having involved griping rather than, say, complaining or chatting, for example.[2]

2.   The Griping Ritual

The speech components to be used in organizing the description of the Griping Ritual are the following: topic, purpose, channel, participants, setting, key, act sequence.

2.1.   Topic

One never gripes about something one feels good about: the topic of griping must always be a problem. As noted, the problem griped about has its locus in some aspect of that external reality Israelis refer to with the sweeping term *hamatzav* — the Situation writ large. The topic may be a more general one, such as the nation's economy or the public morale, or a more 'localized' one, such as teachers' low salaries and the quality of one's neighborhood school. Personal problems can become the topic of griping only insofar as they are incorporated into the discussion of some aspect of the current Situation (e.g. as 'an example of', or 'evidence for'), in which case these personal problems are dressed in a public language and presented, so to speak, in disguise.

Some informants consequently claimed that habitual gripers tend to project (and blame) their personal problems onto external factors rather than taking responsibility for their own lives. This is generally said in the anti-griping mode, which will be discussed later. Whether this accusation is warranted or not, we might at least argue that the Griping Ritual channels the expression of discontent, providing an established pattern for the structuring of plaintive talk in informal encounters among middle-class Israelis, so that feelings of frustration and dissatisfaction that might lead Americans to examine their personal lives through enactments of the Communication

Ritual would tend to be cast in the form of the Griping Ritual in informal encounters among Israelis.

Notably, not all aspects of the general Situation are proper candidates as the topic of griping: we are unlikely to say that the inhabitants of a border settlement are griping about the frequent shelling they are subjected to, although this is part of their Situation *par excellence*. Similarly, as one informant put it, when people who are reasonably well-off complain about inflation, we call it griping, but when a jobless father of twelve does so, we do not. On the other hand, the foreign policy of the U.S.A. might be subject to objections or criticism, but it is not likely to serve as the topic of griping. If it does, it will most likely be interpreted as an indirect comment on the inadequacy of Israeli foreign policy since griping, unlike complaining, is essentially interpreted as self-addressed. Gripers are basically consumers of their own talk.

The problem Israelis tend to gripe about, then, is a problem related to the domain of public life, and one which they feel they should have been able to deal with through some form of collective social effort. Israelis' disposition towards griping seems to be nourished by a deep sense of frustration related to their perceived inability to partake in social action and communal life in a way that would satisfy the high level of commitment and involvement which characterized the small community of 'realizers' as described in the excerpt from Ben-Yehuda's book. The prevalence of griping suggests an overwhelming, culturally sanctioned concern with the public domain, on the one hand, coupled with a marked absence of widely satisfying participation channels, on the other.

In sum, the topic of griping is constrained in a number of ways: it must be a problem related to the Situation, i.e. that shared fate around which Israeli communal life revolves and on which Israelis' sense of solidarity is most clearly predicated. However, not all aspects of the Situation can be properly griped about; griping is generally restricted to problems with the fabric of Israeli social life that 'somebody around here' should be able to do something about, not problems felt to be overwhelming thrusts of fate.

2.2. *Purpose*

Most informants noted that the function of griping is to relieve pent-up tensions and frustrations. This therapeutic orientation is similar to that of many Americans towards the Communication Ritual. In both cases, downplaying the sense of difficulty experienced by a fellow member of the culture — as expressed by an attempt to initiate either the Griping or the

Communication Ritual — would be interpreted as a rejection. Thus, responses of the form "I don't see what you mean; I'm quite pleased with the way the relationship is going" in the one case, or "People gripe about inflation but the standard of living is so much higher than it used to be" in the other, are not experienced as encouragements, but rather as refusals to validate the problem bearer, despite the face value encouraging content of the message.

There is, however, a difference between the kind of 'therapy' provided by 'communicating' among Americans and by 'griping' among Israelis. While 'communicating' is actually perceived as talk which constitutes the *solution* to the problem forming the topic of the ritual, 'griping' is perceived as an activity that constitutes an *anti-solution* to the problem griped about. Rather than being the preferred action strategy for dealing with the problem invoked, *talk* in the case of the Griping Ritual is seen as the dispreferred strategy: it is because gripers perceive the problem as beyond their power to solve, but cannot rid themselves of their overall concern with problems of this type, that they opt for the dispreferred channel of talk in dealing with it.

This cultural valuation of talk as counterproductive, as a dispreferred alternative to social action, is epitomized in the often heard injunction 'Stop talking, do something'. This injunction apparently lies behind recent institutionalized efforts to provide participation channels for the solution of communal problems, which have taken the form of highly dramatized fund-raising drives conducted through the mass media. The money was raised for causes which enjoy a high degree of consensus (the children of Cambodia, a special defense fund, disabled children). The economic need was recognized by all, but the impact and drama attending the drive was felt by many to go far beyond the monetary side of it. The donation was presented in terms of a rhetoric of participation. As a major 'character' in the drama — a TV personality — put it in countless previews of the event: "Let nobody find himself in the unpleasant position when he gets to work the morning after the fund-raising drive that he has to admit he is the only one who has not donated." Being in such a position would amount to being a non-participant in Israeli communal life. Donating was interpreted as partaking in the life of the community: attesting to one's commitment to the public interest through the form of social action provided by the occasion.

That one major such event was carried out on TV was particularly significant: this positively-oriented anti-griping ritual was brought right into the main setting of the griping ritual, the living room of the man-in-the-street, where he had spent many a Friday night 'sitting and griping', i.e. being socially useless. Also, the media, and TV in particular, are generally accused of being the enemies of the public morale — they are said to be digging up all the Negative, painting a picture of a world one can really do nothing about but gripe. In fact, news items are often employed as starters in a griping chain. Here, they have blessedly reversed their role.

In addition to its overt, ventilating function, the Griping Ritual has a less recognized integrative function on its hidden agenda. In probing their experience of griping as a communicative event, people mentioned the sense of *zavta* 'togetherness' that it engendered. The proposition that griping produces solidarity was never contradicted. Some informants maintained that this sense of *zavta* made griping 'a lot of fun' for them. This stands out particularly if we remember that griping is usually referred to in derogatory terms. Notably, griping was never relegated metaphorically to the domain of 'work'; in this, it is unlike 'communicating', which is conceptualized metaphorically as work-related (along with other concepts in the interpersonal domain; thus, you *work* on your *communication*, you *work* on your*self*, and you *work* on your *relationship*).

In fact, griping and joke telling are two major interactional resources for Israelis to reaffirm their common fate. In joke telling, Israelis often poke fun at themselves and their Situation. In times of crisis, such as war, both griping and joke telling disappear from the social scene, as cohesion is spontaneously achieved by virtue of the criticalness of the moment. Moreover, those topics which are too serious, or sacred, or delicate to be joked about will not be appropriate topics for the Griping Ritual either.

Griping and joke telling are the two major types of speech activities that give form and predictability to the domain of informal relationships among Israelis — they are the cornerstones of the everyday interpersonal task of socializing. Someone I can gripe with or joke with shares with me at least one dimension of social experience, this shared dimension being both reflected in and produced by the possibility of griping or exchanging a joke.

2.3. *Channel*

The Griping Ritual typically involves face-to-face oral engagements, although phone conversations and perhaps personal letters might qualify as well.

2.4. *Participants*

The Griping Ritual typically takes place among friends, casual acquaintances or even strangers, unlike the Communication Ritual which is typically enacted among potential intimates. The less familiar the participants are with each other, the more general the theme that functions as the topic of the ritual. A general griping comment about the Situation is a ready-to-hand opener for a conversation between unacquainted Israelis who thereby legitimate their entrance into a state of talk by invoking and affirming their shared communal bond.

Griping can proceed undisturbed as long as there are no outsiders, i.e. non-Israelis such as tourists or newcomers, around. The very same talk that would be considered incidental griping among Israelis turns into malicious slander, *hashmatza*, when uttered in the presence of an outsider. The reason for this is that Israelis know very well that griping should not be taken at face value, that it commands a special interpretive norm according to which the referential function of the talk is, as it were, suspended. Griping is not really an information-oriented speech activity. Although purporting to be a response to the Situation 'as it is', it is by no means a reflection of reality. Outsiders are unlikely to be familiar with this interpretive convention, and are likely to take the talk too literally, constructing for themselves a skewed picture of life in Israel.

A number of informants related anecdotes describing cases in which a group of loosely acquainted Israelis discovered that one of its members was a tourist or a prospective newcomer after griping had been underway for a while. This discovery generated a great deal of embarrassment as the 'outsider' took the talk to be informative, while the 'insiders' were aware of its non-informative, ritual functions.[3]

In a similar vein, griping is not considered a verbal activity to be encouraged in the presence of children who, like tourists and newcomers, have not been fully socialized into the adult griping mode, and may be vulnerable to the content of the talk. Some informants noted the cumulative effect of exposure to griping on children and youth: the picture of the Situation they are presented with is so exaggeratedly bleak, the borderline between informative and non-informative talk so fuzzy that they 'don't know what to think' — so goes the claim.

We might rephrase this by saying that many Israelis find themselves gearing their talk to the topical format that the structure of the Griping Ritual 'suggests'. Consequently, the Situation, as constructed through the talk about it, is perceived as more and more lamentable, i.e. more and more amenable to griping. This state of affairs generates a sense of discrepancy between reality and the talk about it, and griping thus becomes a problem in the collective perception of reality, to whose aggravation all Israelis unwittingly contribute as they 'sit and gripe'. In fact, the most immediate 'solution' to the problem of griping that is proposed by anti-gripers involves a change in perceptual emphasis rather than direct social action. It takes the form of a call to point out and talk about the 'great and beautiful things that have been accomplished in this country' and avoid a one-sided emphasis on the Negative.

A different type of constraint on participation in the Griping Ritual concerns more 'localized' problems: if, say, a group of office employees are sitting and griping about their working conditions, the approach of their boss is most likely to silence them. In the presence of the person(s) who may hold the solution to the problem griped about, the talk turns into complaining. This awareness of the potential change in the status of the talk lies behind many embarrassed shifts in such contexts.

2.5. *Setting*

As indicated, the typical settings for the enacting of the Griping Ritual are Friday night gatherings in private homes, but they are certainly not restricted to the latter. They must, however, be settings in which participants can make their talk a focal activity and in which people who are not potential participants are excluded.

2.6. *Key*

The key or tone that prevails in the Griping Ritual is that of plaintiveness and frustration, accompanied by a sense of entrapment and enmeshment in the event itself. Thus, informants said they felt themselves unwillingly 'sliding' into the griping mode, expressing bewilderment at their own participation in it, since they held a very low opinion of this speech mode.

One important aspect of griping as far as its 'key' is concerned is that participants in the ritual should achieve a synchronization of their emotive display in terms of the degree of frustration they express, so that the enacting of the ritual is felt to be reasonably well 'orchestrated'. An extreme example of lack of synchronization is observed when a member of a gathering engaged in griping does not take part in the ritual, consistently keeping his or her silence. His or her behavior is construed as a critical comment on the verbal conduct of the gripers in attendance and tends to give rise to discomfort, if not resentment (much like the case of the non-drinker in a drinking party).

Loss of such synchronization is often accompanied by a disruption of the Griping Party. As some of the informants said, there is that feeling that griping had 'gone too far': either the topics touched upon were considered too delicate or 'touchy' to be griped about, or the cumulative effect of the griping that had been going on became too oppressive for the participants in the ritual who felt they needed a change of 'key'.

The sense of 'togetherness' or solidarity forms a secondary strand in the 'key' of the Griping Ritual. Griping, unlike communicating in its role as supportive speech in interpersonal relations among Americans, is a speech activity deeply entrenched in the domain of casualness and triviality. This difference in the status of griping and communicating as speech activities is also detectable in bodily postures which accompany these two rituals, and their tolerance for side involvements à la Goffman (1967): one can slouch and gripe, but one can hardly slouch and 'communicate'; one can gripe while doing dishes, but one cannot accomplish the purposeful, concerted activity of 'communicating' under these circumstances. A similar difference is observed between 'complaining' and 'griping': plaintive speech produced while slouching is more likely to be interpreted as 'griping' than as 'complaining'. The same goes for plaintive speech produced while doing the dishes. For plaintive talk to be heard as a complaint it must be addressed to an agent who can act towards the solution of the problem referred to, and the talk must be interpreted as a concerted, purposeful speech activity commanding the speaker's full commitment.

2.7. Act sequence

While the unfolding of the Communication Ritual has been shown to follow a linear pattern, proceeding from one phase of the talk to the next, the sequential organization of the Griping Ritual can be said to follow a 'spiral' pattern, proceeding from one 'round' of talk to another. This may prove to be a more general distinction between communicative encounters oriented towards problem solving and those oriented towards the production of solidarity: the internal structure of the Griping Ritual is reminiscent of the case of joking or anecdotal exchanges which are similarly structured around a common theme, e.g. jokes about national characters, with each contribution linked to the others through the relation of 'more of the same'. Among strangers, the Griping Ritual tends to proceed in a centripetal pattern, from the more general to the more local theme; among well-acquainted people, the opposite pattern is possible, and often more natural: the talk proceeds in a centrifugal pattern, from a more local to a more general topic.

The overall structural differences between the sequential organization of the Griping and the Communication Ritual are brought out when we consider what it would take for a participant to join either type of ritual in mid-session: for this to be properly accomplished in the case of the Communication Ritual, the talk has to come to a halt and current participants will have to retrace and fill the newcomer in on what came before. In the case of the Griping Ritual, all a new arrival has to know is the general theme currently engaged in. Even if he or she repeats some of what came before, it would not be a great disaster, just another expression of shared ground.

The Griping Ritual, like the Communication Ritual, is usually initiated by a particular participant who voices a complaint of greater or lesser generality. This is the *initiation phase*. A typical 'opener' is a report or a comment on some news item which illustrates some unfavorable aspect of the Situation. A comment that elaborates on the 'opener', or suggests some comparable item, functions as an *acknowledgment phase*, indicating the participants' willingness to enact the ritual (or else the attempt to enact it would be aborted). This phase triggers a 'chain-effect' of individual contributions which are, by and large, 'more of the same'. The ritual often proceeds by progression from one sub-theme to the next, each sub-theme dominating a 'round' of talk; the rounds combine to form the aforementioned 'spiral structure'.

Typical forms for terminating the ritual[4] involve standardized ways of dramatizing the participants' 'shared fate' with such expressions as *That's life* or *It's no joke, things are getting worse all the time* or *The Situation is real lousy* (these are translated examples given by informants to illustrate terminations of the Griping Ritual). This would be the case of 'smooth' terminations. At other times the ritual is disrupted with the loss of emotive synchronization as described in the discussion of its 'key' (cf. section 2.6.).

2.8. Finally, let us briefly note that the Griping Ritual has given rise to two subsidiary verbal modes which have become increasingly salient on the Israeli social scene: I have dubbed one of them *kitur-al* 'meta-griping' and the other *al-kitur* 'anti-griping' (the rather fortunate rhyming effect is possible because /al/ is a homophone in Hebrew meaning 'about' and a form of negation, respectively. They are spelled differently and would, in fact, be also pronounced differently in some dialects of modern Hebrew).

Meta-griping is itself an instance of griping, often taking the form of griping about the low morale among Israelis, as manifested, of course, in their disposition to 'sit and gripe'. The increasing salience of meta-griping in public discourse seems to indicate a growing awareness of the griping mode's underlying ideological erosion that marks our time and age. The purpose of meta-griping is to help gripers extricate themselves from the griping mode by drawing attention to questions of morale and their social-communicative manifestations. Since it is itself still located within the griping province, this form of talk is not likely to be effective in achieving the persuasive goals it set for itself.

The anti-griping mode, which was briefly illustrated in relation to the fund-raising dramas staged through the local media, is similarly geared towards the containment of the griping activity and its counterproductive implications. Unlike 'meta-griping', it is optimistic in tone, and is epitomized in the already mentioned injunction to 'Stop griping and do something'; it may be said to represent a non-griping variant of meta-griping. This communicative mode is amply represented in public discourse as is exemplified by a huge advertisement or announcement issued by an independent group of citizens calling for "Renewal and Change" which appeared in the evening paper *Ma'ariv* (Feb. 1st, 1981). Its large-lettered title WE ARE TO BLAME is an attention-getter precisely because of its implied reference to the customary griping mode, and its proper interpretation is predicated on our familiarity with the Griping Ritual. It is interesting to note that the announcement sketches three alternatives faced by members of Israeli society:

(a)   to become stagnant;
(b)   to run away;
(c)   to act.

Obviously, readers are called upon to choose the third alternative, *viz.* social action, which is the generally acknowledged alternative to griping. Let me just mention that 'stagnation' and 'escapism' were the very terms used by my American informants to refer to the state of 'lack of communication'; here, the very same metaphors refer to the state of lack of social action, typically filled in by griping in Israeli society. Thus, from the point of view of anti-gripers, griping occupies a place comparable in import to the state of 'lack of communication' in some corners of American society.

3. Concluding remarks

This paper has provided a detailed examination of griping as a pervasive speech mode in contemporary middle-class Israeli society. It was argued that griping has evolved as a standardized communicative event and that, as such, it constitutes a readily available pattern for the structuring of plaintive talk in a considerable section of the community. It was pointed out that in the contexts around which griping resolves, talk is viewed as a dispreferred social strategy, as the antithesis to social action. One result of this is that any attempt by a rather dissatisfied group of people to clarify issues through discussions of problems pertaining to the social domain may be labeled as 'griping' and dismissed as such. A well-known manipulation of the format implicit in the Griping Ritual occurs in the military where commanders will often assemble their soldiers for what is known as *erev kuterai* 'griping evening': in such contexts any justified complaint addressed to the commanders themselves is pre-defined as a 'gripe', i.e. as unwarranted and self-addressed. The function of the event is strictly that of ventilation.

Throughout the paper, I have drawn comparisons between the Griping Ritual as studied here, and the Communication Ritual, which in a previous paper has been argued to be a central communicative event for many Americans nowadays. Both rituals share the task of dramatizing major cultural problems and providing a preferred social context for the crystallization of feelings of frustration, on the one hand, and a sense of (personal or communal) identity, on the other. The analysis has emphasized contextual constraints which govern the enacting of the rituals, while paying particular attention to the ritualistic, non-referential dimensions of the talk and the specialized interpretive norms they give rise to.

An important implication of the analysis presented here is that informal verbal rituals of this kind are both shaped by, and formative of the social experience of the individuals participating in them. For the researcher, they provide clues to the construction of the social reality of the participants, as well as intriguing illustrations of the many ways in which such verbal rituals can shape our communicative lives through their dynamics of form.

NOTES

1. The word *lekater* is, in fact, used in Biblical language to refer to the ritual act of using incense, but it is not part of the active vocabulary of colloquial Hebrew.

2. The social status of 'griping' as a verbal activity is somewhat reminiscent of that of 'self-talk' (Goffman 1978): neither of them is considered a proper engagement so that, like self-talk, griping tends to be disavowed. Thus, it would be highly incongruous for someone to say: "I'm sorry, I can't come now. We are sitting and griping."

3. The link between the role of the outsider and that of the non-griper is indicated in a journalist's (T. Avidar) humorous summing up of her homecoming experience after a prolonged stay abroad (in the States); one of the sources of alienation from one's surroundings, she says, is the fact that "one is not yet an active participant in Griping Parties. One still listens and finds it hard to believe the stories. One cannot yet grasp how come — if the country has it so bad — its citizens, who are griping all around us, seem to have it so good" (*Ma'ariv*, Aug. 5th, 1981).

4. I am grateful to Marcelo Dascal for suggesting that I consider postural differences, as well as terminating techniques associated with the enacting of the Griping Ritual. I am also grateful to Joseph Shimron and Perla Nesher for helpful comments on an earlier version of this paper.

REFERENCES

Ben-Amotz, D. and N. Ben-Yehuda
    1972   *The world dictionary of Hebrew slang.* Tel Aviv: Levin-Epstein.

Ben-Yehuda, N.
    1981   *1948 — Between calendars.* Jerusalem: Keter.

Campbell, J.
    1972   *Myths to live by.* New York: Bantam Books.

Firth, R.
    1973   "Verbal and bodily rituals of greeting and parting" In J. Sybil La Fontaine (ed.), *The interpretation of ritual.* London: Tavistock.

Geertz, C.
    1973   *The interpretation of culture.* New York: Basic Books.

Goffman, E.
    1967   *Interaction ritual.* New York: Doubleday.

    1978   "Response cries". *Language* 54:4.787-815.

Hymes, D.
    1972   "Models of the interaction of language and social life". In J. Gumperz and D. Hymes (eds.), *Directions in sociolinguistics: The ethnography of speaking.* New York: Holt, Rinehart, and Winston, 35-71.

Katriel, T. and G. Philipsen
    1981   "What we need is communication: 'communication' as a cultural category in some American talk". *Communication Monographs* 48.301-317.

Moore, S.F. and B. Myerhoff (eds.)
    1977   *Secular ritual.* Assen: Van Gorcum.

Rubinstein, A.
    1977   *To be a free people.* Tel Aviv: Schoken.

10
Reflections on the Israeli 'Griping' Ritual

TAMAR KATRIEL

The "griping" chapter was written shortly after the "communication" chapter, and its Hebrew version was published in 1982. Each of them, although in different ways, embodies my understanding of both American and Israeli cultural communication forms. Thus, although these studies are examples of "cultural communication," they are also the product of "cultures in contact." Moving back and forth between Israel and the United States has helped to heighten my sensitivity to my 'home scene' as well as to deepen my understanding of American cultural ways. Given my familiarity with both cultures, I have recently become interested in questions of cultural influence, or, as some Israeli commentators have put it, in communicative expressions of "the Americanization of Israel."

At the level of cultural meanings, the dominant theme for me has been the difference in cultural focus between an individualistic (American) and a collectivistic (Israeli) orientation as it relates to communicative phenomena. This should not be read as a claim that Israeli culture accords no place to the individual, or that Americans are not concerned with communal life. Rather, it is a question of identifying cultural forms (e.g., ritualized conduct) that attest to that which is "held sacred" in one cultural group as compared to the other. The comments on "communicating" found in the very influential book *Habits of the Heart* by Bellah, Madsen, Sullivan, Swidler, and Tipton (1985) and in Carbaugh's (1988) detailed analysis of the "Donahue" show, as well as many responses we have received to the paper itself, suggest that our analysis of "communication" as a cultural category was essentially correct. It seems to me that things have not changed drastically since our writing with respect to middle-class American orientations toward the "self." I have encountered largely similar orientations in a recent study of American scrapbooks as a cultural form of self-telling (Katriel & Farrell, in press).

As is well known, Israeli culture has become increasingly individualistic since the early nation-building days. Yet, in immersing myself in American culture, I came to realize, inter alia, how deeply collectivistic it has nevertheless remained. Taking account of the contours of change, including the impact of American culture, would yield a more complex (and more interesting) picture. I have tried to do some of that in later work, and much more needs to be done.

For the case at hand — ritualized expressions of "problematicity" in either "communicating" or "griping" — one notes that alongside the "griping" ritual still prevalent in Israeli discourse there has emerged a rather intense "therapeutic culture," which has made "communication" one of its God terms. The value of self-disclosive talk for one's emotional well-being is championed by one and all (although griping is still considered the unfortunate "national trait"). In other contexts, the individualistic coloring of "communication" has been subtly re-interpreted in truly Israeli fashion so as to underscore processes of group formation and the value of solidarity. For example, the educational goal of promoting cohesion (*gibush*) in Israeli school culture is nowadays accomplished, inter alia, by means of group activities that come under the rubric of "communication," and are clearly modeled on interpersonal communication training in the United States with its highly individualistic bend (cf. Katriel & Nesher 1986). Thus, despite surface linguistic similarities, and considerable cultural contact, I believe the notions of "individual" and "community" carry highly distinctive resonances in the two cultures between which I move. A more detailed study of the uses of "communication" on the contemporary Israeli scene would be a highly instructive case of cultural borrowing and change.

Both the "communication" and the "griping" paper seek to go beyond the goal of analytic description and offer a critical appraisal of a communicative form. This is, of course, more easily done when working in one's own culture, when one can claim the right of "voice" in a more straightforward way. In exploring American notions of "communication," we pointed out the pragmatic paradox encountered in cases where there is no agreement between interactional partners with respect to the enactment of the "communication" ritual: What do you do when your partner refuses to "sit down and talk"? Insist on sitting down to discuss his or her refusal? Would those who prize "open communication" be open enough to accept such a refusal? Or is "open communication" constrained by a rule of "openness"? We must ask these questions as we come to recognize what is entailed in considering "communication" as a cultural form, and cultural practices as essentially rule-governed activities. The cultural critique implied in the "griping" paper is perhaps more directly stated: It is precisely through its therapeutic function that the "griping" ritual works to perpetuate a state of disaffection and social malfunction. Indeed, its inherently paradoxical nature is not only an analyst's discernment but is sometimes explicitly recognized by informants.

Both papers were received with an "aha" response by cultural members. The Hebrew version of the "griping" paper that came out in a scholarly journal received considerable coverage in the popular press. I believe that my fellow gripers responded warmly to the paper for two reasons. First, for the usual sense of self-discovery that attends readings about one's own culture. Second, for its humorous tone. Joking, like griping, is a well-established Israeli mode of generating or affirming community. The self-distancing and self-critique that are implicit in the effort to analyze such a commonplace communicative phenomenon were thus comfortably framed for readers (and native-ethnographer), marking a balance of affirmation and critique that might very well have shifted were I to write the paper today.

References

Bellah, R., Madsen, R., Sullivan, W., Swidler, A., Tipton, S. (1985) *Habits of the heart.* Berkeley, CA: University of California Press.

Carbaugh, D. (1988). *Talking American.* Norwood, NJ: Ablex.

Katriel, T., & Nesher, N. (1986) *Gibush:* The rhetoric of cohesion in Israeli school culture. *Comparative Education Review, 30,* 216-231.

Katriel, T., & Farrell, T. (in press) Scrapbooks as cultural texts: An American art of memory. *Text and Performance Quarterly.*

11

Communication Rules in *Donahue* Discourse

DONAL CARBAUGH

In the past several years, analysts of communication have been using and developing a rules approach (e.g. Hymes, 1962, 1972; Cushman and Whiting, 1972; Sanders and Martin, 1975; Cushman and Pearce, 1977; Shimanoff, 1980; Sigman, 1980; Cronen, Pearce, and Harris, 1982; Cushman, Valentinsen, and Dietrich, 1982). And several research programs have emerged from this perspective (e.g. Ervin-Tripp, 1972; Philipsen, 1975, 1976; Pearce and Conklin, 1979; Cronen, Pearce and Snavely, 1979; Katriel and Philipsen, 1981; Enninger, 1984; Nofsinger, 1976; Hawes, 1976). At the same time, however, critics of the rules perspective have labeled the approach as "broad, grossly diffuse, and imprecisely articulated" (Delia, 1977, p. 54), as "devoid of specific theoretical substance" (Delia, 1977, p. 54) and as in dire need of "descriptive and interpretive work" (Hawes, 1977, p. 66). One way of responding to these charges is through empirical work that is theory driven. In what follows, I will present an ethnographic report of communication in a prominent American scene as a way of developing communication theory from a rules perspective.[1]

I begin by introducing two modes of analysis used herein as a way of contextualizing the inquiry. These perspectival "moves" suggest a way to unravel some of the general functions of communication through the use of distinctive theoretical models. The two general types of models can be called source models and analytical models (Harré, Clarke, and De Carlo, 1985). The inquiry that follows derives primarily from a *source model*, a way of viewing communication that uses a game metaphor, and searches the common conventions that are creatively played or employed (Harré, et al., 1985; Wittgenstein, 1958; Cushman, 1982; Stewart, 1983). As such, the focal concerns are the generative *agreements* that guide coordinated communication conduct. Such inquiry is well-adapted for questions of meanings and motives, e.g. what is the comon meaning of this activity? and, why do persons communicate in this fashion? The general goal served in using the source model is the explanation of human conduct through a formulation of communication rules (cf. Hymes, 1962).

The use of source models is distinct from, and complementary to the use of *analytical* models (Harré, Clark, and De Carlo, 1985). The latter treats communication as drama, as a flow of event and episodes that has identifiable shapes and functions (Burke, 1965, 1968; Hymes, 1972). As such, the focal concern is the flow of communication processes, of proper enactments that mold social action around common goals. This type of inquiry addresses questions of the sort: in what fashion do persons communicate? how are communicative acts performed? what gets accomplished socially when people speak? The general goal is the discovery, description, and interpretation of identifiable shapes and functions of communication conduct. Where analytical models highlight the appropriate forms and functions of speaking, source models highlight its generative meanings and motives.

Throughout the following, I am primarily abstracting communication rules that generate social conduct. It is a source model of rules that informs the primary analysis. Yet, I will also detail the flow of communication events that provides evidence for, and derives from, these rules. As such, the analytical model guides the description of social events negotiated through the rules. As discussed in the concluding section, I am investigating both constitutive motives for, and normative enactments of, communication.

The discussion proceeds as follows. After some very brief comments on methods and the *Donahue* scene, I will demonstrate four communication rules in *Donahue* discourse. I will then explore the functioning of the rules by examining some of their broader conversational and cultural features. In the final section, I will explicate more abstractly the two types of rules abstractions that inform the report. Through this type of analysis, I hope to increase theoretical precision through the workings of empirical study. The three major purposes that motivate the inquiry are: to demonstrate how a rules approach can point to common generative agreements among participants in communication scenes; second, to demonstrate some of the conversational and cultural functions of communication rules in public discourse; and finally, to develop communication theory by discussing the nature, function, and use of two types of rules.

Method

The following analyses are based on a three year viewing of over one hundred hours of the popular American "talk show" *Donahue*. The inquiry proceeded in three general phases. The first phase consisted of a general exploration of American communication rules that were relevant to the discourses used on *Donahue*. Data for this phase included the viewing of sixty hours of *Donahue* shows, textual analysis of transcripts from twenty-eight shows, several unstructured interviews with persons who watched, and appeared on, *Donahue*, field observations of persons watching and talking about *Donahue*, and a reading of several commentaries on American speech and life (Bellah, Madsen, Sullivan, Swidler, and Tipton, 1985; Davis, 1982; Sennett, 1978; Varenne, 1977; Veroff, Douvan, and Kulka, 1981; Yandelovich, 1981; Robertson, 1980; Heath, 1983; Tocqueville, 1835/1945), and Phil Donahue's best-selling autobiography (Donahue & Co., 1981).

The second phase of analysis focused on those communication rules that are central to this report, that is, those that occurred prominently on *Donahue*. Throughout this phase of analysis, a set of rules was evulted for its explanatory adequacy. In the final form, all of

the rules met the following criteria: 1) they were *reportable* by participants of *Donahue*, that is, participants invoked some fascimile
of the communication rules as a matter of routine communication
conduct; 2) they were *repeatable*, recurrent, patterns in the "talk"
of *Donahue* participants; 3) they were widely *intelligible* to partic-
pants as sensible guides for spoken action, i.e. no one questioned
the meaning of the rules nor their appropriateness in this context;
and 4) they were invoked as *repair mechanisms* in response to
problematic actions. Thus, each of the following communication rules
was reported, repeated and intelligible to participants, as well as used
in response to various untoward actions (cf. Hymes, 1981: 75-135;
Stokes and Hewitt, 1976; Philipsen, 1975).[2]

Finally, after carefully refining the rules, I collected additional
broadcasts of *Donahue* to test my formulations against new data. This
procedure was followed until the rules exhibited a high degree of
validity. Thus, the analytical procedure amounted to a form of
hypothesis generation and testing that triangulated among the data
and transcripts, field notes, and subsequent broadcasts of *Donahue*.[3]

Of course, not everyone on *Donahue* speaks in accordance with
the following rules, nor does everyone testify to their value and use.
Nonetheless, the following system of rules does summarize a set of
agreements that has a powerful practical force in *Donahue* discourse,
and it guides prominently the conversations that occur there.

The Scene

The *Donahue* scene is orchestrated by the very popular host of
the show, Phil Donahue.[4] The high profile of Phil Donahue was evident throughout the term of this research as he helped moderate a
presidential campaign debate, was featured in the popular American
television newsmagazine *60 Minutes*, and captured the attention of
national newspapers especially in the movement of his nationally syn-
dicated television show from Chicago to New York.

The *Donahue* television show is named of course after its host. Natives label the show a "talk show," a place where "talk" is shown and heard by about seven to eight million persons daily (Donahue staff, 1983; Robinson, 1982). The show recurs every weekday as the audience witnesses, what is advertised to be, "perhaps the most important television program of your day."[5]

Donahue occurs in a studio setting with guests seated on a slightly elevated stage. During the show, Donahue, microphone in hand, paces up and down the aisles giving audience members the opportunity to speak. In fact, it would be hard to dispute Donahue's claim that his show involves the audience more than any other on the air (Donahue & Co., 1981, p. 236). Further, the setting is designed for maximum audience contact. However, the participating audience is not limited to those in the studio. It also includes the caller, or those who call the show by telephone from the privacy of their home. Thus, the following rules display their practical force in discussions among Donahue, his guests, and callers, and other audience members regarding important, and often controversial issues of the day, e.g. nuclear armament, educational institutions, helping professions, atheism, parenting for peace, freeform marriage (among two men and one woman), underwater births, abortion, birth control, male go-go dancers, the coming matriarchy, dropping sperm count in men, etc.

Four communication rules

Rule # 1: In the conversations of *Donahue*, a) the presentation of "self" is the preferred communication activity, and b) statements of personal opinions count as proper "self" presentations.

The general question raised here is this: what prominent quality or qualities of persons are marked for display in public conversation? What are persons expected to display when they speak? In the *Donahue* scene, interlocutors are evaluated positively when they speak from their own personal experiences, and do so in a way that asserts their "self." The proper and preferred act for the person is "standing up and speaking your mind." Consider the following utterances made, at a rapid pace, by a young co-ed audience member during a heated discussion about fraternities:

Co-ed: I've been speaking to some people who are in fraternities and they told me that the values they learned from fraternities are violence, vandalism, racism, homophobia, and sexism. And I was told, this was from an ex-fraternity member, that it's not "boys will be boys" and "sowing wild oats," but that it's a training ground and this behavior goes on for the rest of their lives. There are often incidents of alumni coming back chasing women into dorm rooms and standing outside doors waiting for them to come out. And I have an interesting comment...

Donahue: (interrupting) Uh, now, wait a minute. Ah, I'm impressed with your... You seem to be ready for us. (audience delighted laughter) You are who from where, may I ask?

Co-ed: My name is Sharon Markeson and I'm from Brown University and I wanna talk about good works from fraternities. There was an interesting incident during spring week-end last year at Brown. A fraternity held a marathon, a foos ball-a-thon to benefit Sojourner House, a shelter for battered women. Now, in the course of this (sarcatically) "good work," they were rating women who walked by with a score card, from their foos ball-a-thon, y'know, one to ten; in the midst of raising money for a women's shelter! And I think this totally sums up the attitude. Good works are cosmetic. They're to justify their existence to the university administration, but they're totally superficial.

(one second pause)

Donahue: Well...(hearty applause as camera scans audience members' and Donahue's delighted smiles)

What has happened here? And why has it received a positive public evaluation, i.e. applause and smiles? In this scene, a young woman has spoken out; she has said what she wanted to say; and said it in a way that asserted her opinion. The form of this opinion is technically an argument with data, including an interview with fraternity alumni and observations of fraternity events, linked through a common vision of fraternities as animalistic, e.g. as portrayed in the *Animal House* movie, to the claim that their "good deeds" are "totally superficial." But not all opinions stated are in the form of an argument. Nor would it be proper, from the natives' view, to label such statements as "arguments." To these speakers, they are not engaged prominently in "argument," but in "communication," "being honest" and "sharing" (Katriel and Philipsen, 1981; Carbaugh, 1984, pp. 261-363). "Communication" like this from the co-ed, displays the proper enactment for "self" as a holder of opinions. Statements as these are evaluated positively for they strike a familiar chord with interlocutors who value such verbal presentations, as this one of "self."

In the context of *Donahue* conversation, "self" is a powerful symbol that signifies an independent center, somewhat bounded, that only individual acts can access, and make available to others. The assumption that persons have a "self" pervades American discourse (Varenne, 1977; Yankelovich, 1981; Lasch, 1979), and is assumed to inhere within persons as part of the discursive consensus. So conceived, the having of "self" is a taken-for-granted (Varenne, 1977; Hopper, 1981), and forms the common *social* center from which opinions are generated, and through which statements are publicly evaluated.

As a communicative construction, however, "self" is contained less in the dermatological membranes of human organisms, and more in the spoken symbols through which persons display and evaluate their living acts. As one comes to this scene, one can witness mass communication like that of this young co-ed, where presentations of "self" are something more than individual acts; they are also social enactments that are learned and played in social scenes, and subject to the public's appraisal — be it applause or boos, and both are used. Thus, as this co-ed's speaking demonstrates, there is a socially valued and applaudable form of public presentation. In this scene, it is the verbal presentation of "self."

Since "self" presentation is an assumed and valuable feature in this social conversation, the interlocutor who wants to participate verbally is faced with the task of making "self" available to other. In the *Donahue* situation, this is done prominently and preferrably through statements that display uniqueness. Having experiences that are unique to "self," is part of the unspoken consensus, is a taken-for-granted, and is assumed to be an intrinsic part of the person (cf. Varenne 1977). It is the public affirmation of this value that leads to the presentation of "self," sometimes in extreme forms such as gay atheists, absentee mothers (mothers who abandon their families), freeform marriages, male erotic dancers, punk rockers, etc.; i.e. persons with a unique "self" to display. Such display affirms publicly the importance of "being your own person," of expressing who "you are," and emphasizes the wide range of persons it is possible to be. So, to speak in the *Donahue* scene involves and invokes "self" as a unique speaker of opinions and experiences.

As "self" is successfully enacted, as by the co-ed above, a contribution is made not only to the topic at hand, in this case about fraternity life, but also to the proper form of public enactment, i.e. "self" presentation.[6] The creation and positive appraisal of such conversational accomplishments place unspoken burdens on the event as interlocutors search for something distinctive to say, attempt to then say it properly, and finally applaud the fact that such sayings have occurred and are indeed valuable. The first rule, then, when followed, 1) creates a communication scene in which persons should express "self," 2) through expressions of unique personal experiences and opinions.[7]

That such a communication pattern is distinctive to American society is evident from a brief look to the ethnographic literature. Other peoples, through their routine communicative enactments, construct a sense of the person less as a speaker of opinion, and more as silent thinker (Gardner, 1966; Lehtonen & Sajavaara, 1985), as a player of public roles in which individuality and uniqueness is foreign (Geertz, 1976), as a purveyor of harmonious relations in which "self" is downplayed or, if spoken, depreciated (Johnson & Johnson, 1975; Scollon & Scollon, 1981), and as a holder of social rank of which only one, or a very few, may speak publicly (Wieder & Pratt, this volume). That public expression, and thus models for speakers, are so variously conceived is a testament to human diversity, and helps highlight the sayings on *Donahue* as relatively individualistic, self-relexive, and loquacious (cf. Reisman, 1974).

Rule # 2: Interlocutors must grant speakers the moral "right" to present "self" through opinions.

Where the first rule highlights the importance of speaking as "self" from a personal point-of-view, the second rule assures that such speakings may occur as a guaranteed "right" and privilege to those who participate in this social scene. Such a rule is no mere extension of the first, but rather marks a transition from the communicative act deemed proper individually — one thread in the conversational fabric — to a common moral premise that enables these acts and others to indeed occur — an identifiable pattern in the cloth. Consider one problematic guest on *Donahue* who repeatedly interrupted others, accused Donahue of asking "all of the wrong questions," associated his fellow guests, policy chiefs and officers, with "the KGB... in Russia," and criticized a woman audience member saying, "that's for a different reason lady!" As the show went on, tensions among interlocutors mounted, and a woman told the man (and he happened to be a Black man) that he was "more prejudiced than anyone else in the room," to which the audience cheered and applauded cathartically. The guest replied: "You're right!" Donahue asked the audience: "Do you feel better!!?" And they replied in unison: "Yes!!" Donahue turned to his guest: "I don't think that you should be surprised that someone would call to your attention your rather negative personality. Which is still okay. This is America and you are allowed to have one." In so many words, the substance of the male guest's ribald opinions was deemed improper, but his "right" to speak them was rendered proper. As Donahue said, this is "America," where persons have the "right" to so speak, even if disagreeably.

Such a rule guarantees both the moral capacity of "Self" to speak, and the availability of a public forum for being heard. It enables the person to speak indeed on any topic, no matter what the opinion might be, and no matter how disagreeable the person might be in presenting it. Such a rule was invoked tellingly during one show when Donahue interviewed an unrepentant murderer of a college professor. Donahue was asked by an audience member how he felt about the murderer appearing on his show, and he responded that he "was not happy" about the act of murder, but felt the public had a right to be informed about it. The further reasoning is that, if the public is to be informed, there is no person better able to inform than the murderer (then released from prison), who has the renewed "right" to so speak.

Rule # 3: The presentation of "self" through opinions should be "respected," that is, tolerated as a rightful expression.

While rule # 2 prescribes an obligatory moral capacity for interlocutors, enabling their voice to be stated and heard publicly, what is suggested here is the preferred tone to be maintained during the conversation. The tone could be called one of *righteous tolerance*, creating a scene where it is right and proper to tolerate a variety of viewpoints. Consider the unpopular comment made by a male: "A woman's role is a woman's and a man's is a man's!" Upon hearing this, the audience reacted with a loud "Oooohhhh!" Donahue then stated the norm, using the educational metaphor: "Class, we will show respect to all of the members." Similarly, on another occasion an audience member accused a freeform triad, a female and two male guests who were "married" to each other, of "an immoral act," to which one of the guests immediately retorted: "There may be some differences in our views of morality. I respect your views of morality and I would expect you to respect mine." In each of these cases, and others, interlocutors are co-orienting to a cultural code of "respect," a code that suggests the proper tone for conversing with unique others.[8]

To enrich our understanding of the "respect" code as it is practiced here, it is necessary to examine several related discursive premises. First, "respecting" does not imply "accepting." Interlocutors can "respect" the person's "right" to speak without necessarily accepting who that person is, or the opinion he/she has just stated. Two examples of this common premise occur immediately above.

Second, speaking "respectfully" often involves an explicit lack of evaluation. Consider the mother, a guest on a show about sex and senior citizens, who said:

> In our family, we don't give advice. I don't try to run my kids' lives and they don't try to run mine. They want me to be happy. And if I'm happy having an affair, they're all for it.

An audience member added: "I think that's great and, after all, who are we to condemn you people (the guests)?" And another guest added: "Right!" To which the audience member responded: "We're not God." A male guest agreed: "That's correct." And the audience applauded. In this example, a mother has stated an opinion, presented her "self," which her children and present others do not judge, just as she does not "give advice" to them. Each has the "right" to his/her own personal opinions which are *explicitly not judged*. By speaking in this non-judgmental way, a proper "respect" is shown to others; a respect that preserves the "rights" of individuals to display any opinion or experience, while protecting "self" from judgment by this-world others.

Third, as diverse opinions are presented, interlocutors are asked to "tolerate" a range of views. This is often accomplished with prefatory comments like: "I'm not going to argue with anyone's morals, but..."; "If that's what you believe fine, but..."; "You're entitled to your opinion...(and here's mine)"; "You have a right to your feeling..."; and "You have no obligation to conform...." Through this manner of speaking, interlocutors explicitly tolerate a range of stated opinions on the current topic, many of which run counter to traditional codes of conduct, thus enacting a proper "respect" for fellow speakers.

In sum, "respect" can be heard as a communal code guiding the tone of conversation that dissociates it from agreement or acceptance, while associating it with non-judgment and tolerance. So enacted, conversants display "respect" through a tone of righteous tolerance, where it is right, and obligatory, to tolerate others' unique presentations.

Rule # 4: Asserting standards that are explicitly trans-individual, or societal, is dispreferred since such assertions are heard a) to unduly constrain the preferred presentations of "self," b) to infringe upon the "rights" of others, and c) to violate the code of proper "respect."

In a sense, this final rule adds a qualification to rule # 2. Specifically, while an interlocutor has the "right" to state any opinion, s/he should not state opinions that extend beyond "self" and potentially "impose" upon others. The rule is a practical realization of "negative face wants" in Brown and Levinson's scheme (1978): i.e. when stating an opinion, one should speak only for one's "self" and not "impose" one's opinion on others.[9]

This rule operates at times subtly, at others blatantly, as I hope the following examples demonstrate. During one show, a mother of five birth and five adoptive children spoke against "open adoption" (a type of adoption where "open lines of communication" are maintained between adoptive parents, biological parents, and children). She repeatedly stated her disagreement: "Open adoptions sound so good, but it's very confusing for kids...." She was saying, in effect, "open adoption" should not be an option for *anyone* in our society because it "confuses kinds" and "children should be the top priority." Donahue replied to her: "No one is going to deny you your position, but the question is why do you impose it on others?" Donahue began with the prefatory comment: "No one is going to deny you your position...," which functioned, in part, to affirm the woman's "right" to her *personal* opinion. But notice that her opinion was heard to be an imposition of sorts upon others. She was not saying, as Donahue, and some others would have liked for her to say: "Open adoption is not an option for me." She was saying: it should not be an "option" for anyone. Donahue reacted, therefore, by labeling her opinion as an imposition. Thus, the woman was being called to account by Donahue for "impos[ing]...on others." As such, his question evaluated negatively her more general, and non-personally stated, opinion. Through his prefatory comment and question, he granted the woman her "right" to speak, but evaluated her speaking negatively. To paraphrase Donahue: "Yes, you can say that, but it is wrong." Thus, Donahue affirmed her "right" to speak personal opinions, but denied her opinion legitimacy — as originally stated — on the more social level, despite his prefatory remark.

This framing of communicative acts through "non-impositional" or "negative face" rules is invoked on almost any topic. For example, several guests and audience members were discussing President Reagan's televised endorsement of National Bible Week. An audience member said: "I challenge everybody to name a philosophy that isn't dangerous when it is held by a majority... I don't care what it is, as soon as the majority has the power, it is dangerous." Donahue added: "But it's not about the philosophy; it's about the possibility that the majority will assume the absolute righteousness of that philosophy [and] presume to impose it on other people..." And a gay atheist guest exclaimed: "The president has no right to endorse this [the Bible] as a moral code of the country because other people are being discriminated against because of it!" The only "majority" opinion acceptable to speak, therefore, is that which, in a polity or on a "talk show," enables all individuals to state their own opinions. What is highlighted then in speaking is the individual voice; what is hidden is the collective sayings. So conceived, proper communication enables everyone to speak individually, while disallowing one person's, or "the majority's," opinion to dominate others.

Interlocutors enforce this rule of non-imposition by co-orienting to its violation, often by framing the violation as a "self-righteous" act. This pejorative native frame is invoked to identify and broadcast an improper kind of speaking that "imposes" on other people and, therefore, does not enable them to fully exercise their "rights." Consider the woman audience member who condemned sex outside of marriage, a practice of some guests, by quoting passages from the Bible. Donahue responded to her: "The Bible says it's wrong and you cannot tell that woman [a widowed guest] she's wrong." Another audience member supported Donahue: "There's been other living patterns in the history of the world and what's right for some is not right for others. Maybe it's wrong for her [the audience member], okay. but maybe it's right for other people and we don't have a right to judge others." Donahue responded: "You have a right to your feeling about the Bible but it's wrong for you to use this book and impose your interpretation of its principles on other people. ...While you're entitled to your beliefs, it may not be right for you to impose them on others." Another audience member summed it up: "We don't have a right to be self-righteous. I think that's the worst thing we do to each other." Donahue and the other interlocutors corrected the woman's "self-righteous" speaking by using what they considered to be a superior source of data for their claim, a present widowed guest who had "intimate relations." Their redressive acts condemn the audience member's statement of absolute moral "principles," while praising the importance of personal opinions, thus guaranteeing for each person the "right" to act and speak freely and individually.

This brief "drama of living" demonstrates several of the above rules. First, interlocutors gather in this scene and engage in the preferred activity of "self" presentation, mostly through the giving of personal opinions. Second, all interlocutors co-orient to the "right" to state any and all opinions, regardless of their public evaluation. Third, the conversation displays a general dispreference for statements of absolute judgments, and a preference for statements of personal opinions. This is in part accomplished through the above statement, "Maybe it's wrong for her, okay. But maybe it's right for other people." Conversational reframing such as this functions to identify some statements as impositions, and illustrates how such statements and broad societal and public standards, e.g. "Sex outside of marriage is wrong," are dispreferred, and to become preferred, must be stated in more personal terms, e.g. "extra-marital sex is not for me." Finally, the above demonstrates the negative sanctioning of impositional discourse through the native term, "self-righteous."

There is an implicit paradox here between rule #2 and rule #4, between the "right" to speak opinions freely and the proper stating of them in a non-impositional way. In a sense the paradox involves an interaction of legal and cultural codes: the legal code giving American citizens a relatively unconstrained "right" to free expression; and the cultural code offering moral guidance for expressions deemed most proper within American social life. In the *Donahue* scene, the cultural code constrains the practice of its legal counterpart through the rules of "respect" and non-imposition.

Conversational and Cultural Functions of the Rules

Given the above rules as generative motives in *Donahue* discourse, I now turn to a discussion of some of their functions. My purposes here are to explicate some of the conversational functionings that co-occur with the social use of the rules, and to frame these within their more cultural motives and meanings.

The conversational use of these rules results in three notable accomplishments: 1) the public enactment of free expression; 2) the perpetuation of topical dissensus; and 3) the disinclination for explicitly stating public standards for (non-communication) conduct.

The combination of values in "self-presentation," opinion-giving, "rights" for and "respect" of speaking, combine to make *Donahue* an event supporting free expression. It is here that all individuals may speak, from unrepentant murderers and gay atheists, to absentee mothers (mothers who have abandoned their families), nurses who abuse drugs, children who abuse their parents, etc. *Donahue* offers a soap-box from which virtually any such "self" may address America. And as their voices echo across the land, free expression is witnessed.

However, as noted above, the free expressions occur in a preferred way, i.e. "self" presentation that is properly non-impositional. Thus, each participant tends to speak for his or her "self," and in so doing, conforms to the social rule for doing so. In sum, free expression and "right" to speech are experienced by these interlocutors as "freedom," but they do not entail, in this scene, freedom from all constraints. Rather, they entail freedom to speak for one's "self," as an individual, through a form that preserves for others the similar "right" (cf. Bellah, et al., 1985, pp. 27-51).

A necessary conversational outcome of the social rules is a degree of dissensus on the topics of discussion. The folk logic could be recast as follows: participants are expected to present opinions as constituents of "self"; "self" presentations are expected to reveal unique and distinctive qualities of participants; unique opinions taken severally on any topic, result necessarily in a degree of topical dissensus. No matter what the issue, from herpes to gifted children, as unique participants state their rightful opinions, and those various opinions are "respected," dissensus results. Take for example the discussion about religion and the USA when participants stated: the USA is a religious nation; the USA is not a religious nation; George Washington dealt with Moslems; President Reagan has a right to his religious beliefs as an individual; President Reagan oppresses those who believe differently from him; President Reagan is supporting discrimination by endorsing the Bible; etc. No matter what the topic of discussion, there is always room for varied opinions, and such varied statements are necessary if participants are to feel the requisite latitude for various self-expressions. What results? Dissensus. Topical dissensus.

Yet, while a dissensus on the current topic is created, there is often overlooked the consensual rules that enable the performance. It is through communicative rules such as the ones described above that participants' efforts may be coordinated meaningfully. Thus, while participants tend to display dissensus on the content of concern, *they display consensus for a way of speaking it.* While they have not agreed generally what to say, they have agreed how they should say it.

A third consequence of these rules is a disinclination for stating public standards of (non-communication) conduct. While standards for communication conduct are indeed spoken, generally agreed upon, and used as bases for evaluation, other standards for belief, feeling, and acting are much less intelligible. What people should believe, how they ought to feel, and what is proper for them to do, are all said to be matters of *personal*, as opposed to social, judgment. As a result, given any problem for public address, various opinions are offered as responsive, with the individual person being the crucial variable in the selection of the one deemed most appropriate. Thus, any topic of social concern, from open adoption to sexually permissive senior citizens, is met with a barrage of reactions, with some perhaps more applaudable than others, but each packaged within a rhetoric of "individual choice" and personal judgment that tends to silence *shared* standards for belief, feeling, and action. As a result, participants seem to share a disinclination for the explicit speaking of common standards. What is marked for speech then is individuality more than commonality, diversity more than unity, personal more than social rules. Thus, when communication conduct is the topic of concern, consensus may be realized, but as other concerns arise, dissensus results. These preferences of personal rules for non-communication conduct, and social rules for communication conduct, are both, of course, social constructions that are constituted as interlocutors use common communication rules.

The three conversational phenomena sketched here, free expression, topical dissensus, and personal standards, all suggest cultural features in this communication. By looking at conversations as cultural performances, we may highlight their widely accessible and commonly intelligible features (Scruton 1979; Schneider 1976). I will now show how an analysis of certain cultural features mentioned above helps organize an understanding of communication rules and their conversational consequences.

A long-standing feature in cultural studies of human action is the native conception of personhood (De Laguna, 1954; Gardner, 1966; Geertz, 1976; Kirkpatrick, 1983; Harrison, 1985; Marsella, Devos, and Hsu 1985; Westen, in press). The above rules suggest the question: what, and how, are models of the person conceived and evaluated communicatively? Through the American discourse described above, a model of, and for, the person is constructed through the cultural term, "self." It is as "self" that persons are heard to speak, attempt to speak, and have a "right" to speak. As a "self," persons are asked to become aware of who they are, of the distinctive qualities that make of them a unique individual with important opinions. In the process, persons are treated as individual beings, as separate and separable entities. The "self," at least as these natives speak it, is a rather uniquely bounded thing, conceived through a container metaphor as something that may become "lost" or "found," "scattered" or "together." In short, these conversational enactments create a common sense of the person who is conceived and evaluated through native dimensions of communicativeness, awareness, and independence, respectively (Carbaugh, 1984, pp. 174-225). Such a symbolic "web" motivates persons to speak their own "minds," consciously, without "imposing" on others. Thus, one cultural feature in these conversations is the construction of a model person, in this case the "self," who is compelled to communicate, to be aware of its internal qualities, and to think and act independently.

There are important links here between the model speaker as "self" and the conversational accomplishments of free expression, dissensus, and individuality. In short, this model person is realized through free expression, is responsible for and tolerant of a degree of dissensus, and speaks the virtues of individual "choice" over majority standards. In such communication, a model for the person is displayed. As such, the accepted model for the person is intimately linked to a free, dissensual, and individual mode of public discourse. It is in this sense that conversational functions of discourse, such as free expression, dissensus, and individuality, are intimately linked to models of persons, such as "self." Considered in the abstract, ways of speaking a language are linked intimately to ways of conceiving personhood (cf. Rosaldo 1982).

Such a link can be explored further through the cultural symbols of "rights" and "respect." One's "rights," in this scene, highlight certain moral capacities of *each* participant to be uniquely "who one is," to speak one's own opinions, to separate one's acts from any and all others, and to be unimpeded by others. The exercise of these common premises is most visible in moments of free expression, as when an "absentee mother" who had left her family described her "life-long process in search of [her] self" (cf. Yankelovich, 1981). Through these shared moral premises, participants enact a sense of being a person. Such a person is suggested upon hearing the imperatives to be who one is (as opposed to being what someone else thinks you should be), to speak assertively, independently, and respectfully. To be a fully applaudable person in this scene, is to be more than a private "self," it is to be a public "self" capable of its proper and independent expression. Through the cultural symbols of "rights," and their "respect," a model for the speaker is displayed in a manner of speaking. It is partly through these co-orienting symbols of "self" and "rights" (and analogously through "individual" and "choice") that participants come to construct socially a model for the person that is accessible and acceptable to a vast audience. Such a performance shows participants a model for speaking, a model for rendering their world commonly intelligible. It is this molding and modeling of life in public communication that helps make of *Donahue* a successful cultural performance.

The cultural performance of "self," "rights," and "respect" can be summarized as a personal style of cultural communication (cf. Hymes 1972). That "self" should be displayed, that "rights" of free expression should prevail, that "respect" should be given, that one should not speak "self-righteously," are all prominent social rules constructing a way of speaking and living together. Taken several-ly, these rules create a personal style of communication that depends "upon the continuing response of individuals. The point of communication is to excite interest and bring together persons who will then respond with emotion to whatever event has occurred" (Hymes 1972, pp. 47-48). Thus, this type of sociality, involving as it does conversations of free expression, dissensus, and personal standards, and cultural performances of "self," "rights," and "respect," creates, and is generated from, personal thoughts, feelings, and actions. Through such a cultural performance, interlocutors may at once display a way of speaking and being deemed favorable to them, while witnessing and applauding its collective personal force.

Code and Normative Rules

So far, we have come to understand a way of speaking in a prominent American scene, i.e. the preference for "self" presentation, the obligatory "rights" of interlocutors, a preferred tone of "respect," and a rule of non-imposition, the breaking of which risks accusations of "self-righteousness." We have examined some of the conversational functions of the rules, and the cultural meanings and style that organize their use.

As I was formulating this report of communication rules, I soon realized that I was using two identifiable conceptualizations of communication rules, with each suggested by different communicative enactments, and each directed toward distinctive empirical claims. I will now turn to a discussion of the analytic procedures that lead to identifying two types of rules for communication inquiry.

The two general types of rules that run through the above will be called code rules and normative rules, following similar distinctions drawn by others, e.g. norms of interpretation/norms of interaction (Hymes 1972), alternation/co-occurrence rules (Ervin-Tripp, 1972), constitutive/regulative rules (Searle, 1969; Cronen et al., 1982; Sanders and Martin, 1975), and content/procedural rules (Cushman and Whiting, 1972).[10] It is my basic claim that a distinction in types of rules analyses is necessary for communication study, for each type raises distinctive questions, requires different abstractions, and yields complementary insights. Thus, the present discussion calls into question Gumb's (1972) and Shimanoff's (1980) conflating of the two types.[11]

Both code and normative rules are alike in that they both refer to socially patterned communicative action, capture some consensual imperative for interlocutors, and have practical force in identifiable contexts. It is as such, that they both qualify as rules (cf. Shimanoff 1980; Cushman et al., 1982). Both are alike as well in that they require similar types of evidence for their construction. Specifically, at least one of the following is necessary for constructing a rule, e.g. an observed and recurrent pattern in communication, a native statement of a rule, and/or corrective actions that co-orient actors to a rule.

However, the two types of rules have distinctive qualities. Take for example code rules. It is the nature of code rules to specify patterns of meaning, or mutual intelligibility, spoken through native symbols and symbolic forms. Such rules attempt to capture a system of folk belief by interpreting the hierarchical relations between and among cultural terms and domains. This type of analysis probes the general questions: What does this native act, symbol, or symbolic form commonly mean? What does the unit of concern (act, symbol, or form) count as on another cultural level? For example, through the above rules, we came to understand how opinion-stating counts as a proper act of "self," that is, how a type of communicative act is associated with an accepted model of the person. Likewise, we came to understand how being "self-righteous" is meaningful as an impositional and disrespectful type of speech, i.e. how a cultural symbol is linked to a way of speaking. Thus, it is through code rules that abstractions at one level, e.g. communicative acts and cultural symbols, are linked to abstractions at another, e.g. accepted models of the person and ways of speaking, respectively.

Code rules as these function in conversation to frame actions, to define contexts, to construct a coherent sense. They define the practical nature of the spoken game as it is played by interlocutors, what the game in general is, what it means to play the game, what moves are made within the game, the meanings of each particular move, and so on. The units of analysis in the abstraction of code rules may be any cultural act, symbol, or symbolic form, most generally native terms and tropes. The unit of observation is a system of symbols, a symbolic orientation, terministic screen (Burke, 1966), galaxy, or universe (Schneider, 1976; Berger and Luckman, 1966). By examining native terms, clusters of terms, and clusters of clusters, code rules may be discovered, and their semantic forces unveiled (e.g Seitel, 1976; Kartriel and Philipsen, 1981; Carbaugh, ms).

There is also an interactive process in conversations that code rules help us understand. Consider the cathartic exchange discussed above between the woman audience member and the man who interrupted others, imposed his position upon them, spoke to them disrespectfully, and violated their "rights." Given that he broke these rules, his interlocutors were posed with the question: what common sense is to be made of this person? Given the continuous rule violations, in what cultural frame can he be put? Following his rather untoward acts, he was negatively sanctioned by others who referred to his "negative personality." So, a symbolic resource was used here to summarize a set of instances, to render the individual's specific behaviors widely intelligible. It is in this sense that code rules erupt conversationally as bottoms-up rules; they take several concrete instances of action and place them into broader symbolic frames, in this case by subsuming untoward acts within a "negative" agent, and in others by placing several previously unnamed acts into a frame of "self-righteousness" (cf. Harré, Clark, and De Carlo 1985, pp. 20-21). Through such uses of code rules, puzzling instances are instantly rendered into coherent frames of action. This is the conversational use of code rules.

In sum, then, code rules abstract patterns of common meaning, systems of folk belief, that function to create mutual intelligibly and shared coherence in communicative action; they can be stated in the form: in context C, the unit, X, counts as meaningful on another level as y, y'...; and they often erupt conversationally as a bottoms-up type of sense-making.

Normative rules, on the other hand, are abstractions of patterns for acting (Schneider, 1976). Normative rules involve abstractions of conduct deemed proper in identifiable contexts. Formulating such rules brings into focus sequential organization in talk; it helps delineate what acts properly initiate events, and what acts should follow others (cf. Schegloff, 1972; Philipsen, 1975). Note that normative rules involve explicit standards of appropriateness, and of evaluation, which are central criteria in discovering and specifying such rules. It is what should be done, rather than what is, that sustains a normative analysis of communication rules. Abstracting communication rules this way raises the questions: what behavioral acts are appropriate in this context? what communicative conduct is deemed proper here? Consider two examples. One, as stated above, in the context of the *Donahue* "talk show," persons should state their opinions without imposing on others. Such acts are appropriate and proper in this speech situation. In another context, called Teamsterville, it is not only appropriate but highly preferable for "a man" to punish his child nonverbally (Philipsen, 1975). Failing to comply, brings the male's social status, as "a man," into question. Such normative rules abstract patterns deemed proper in identifiable contexts.

Normative rules function to guide actions in social contexts. They derive from pre-existing templates and provide standards for judging what to do, and for evaluating whether what has been done, has been done properly. The units of analysis in formulating normative rules are the regular sequences of communicative acts deemed proper, with special attention to instances of rule-violations. Note how the "negative personality" above helped demonstrate the normative rules of "rights," "respect," and non-imposition. The unit of observation is generally a speech community whose members interact frequently and share at least one standard for social communication (cf. Enninger, 1984; Ervin-Tripp, 1972). By discovering the communicative acts deemed proper, and the sequences in which they occur, one can specify native appraisals of appropriateness through normative rules.

Where code rules surface conversationally in a bottoms-up fashion, normative rules operate prominently from the top down. Consider the conversation above in which an audience member stated the very unpopular opinion: "A woman's role is a woman's and a man's a man's," to which the audience responded, "Oooohhhh!" To this, Donahue replied, "Class, we will show respect to all of the members." In his act, Donahue is legislating the normative law. He is prescribing a kind of conduct deemed proper, that is in this case a tolerant "respect." His reply functions to instruct his interlocutors in appropriate conduct and to evaluate a particular act as improper. As such, it is prescriptive in force, providing a template for the doing of future acts if they are to be considered appropriate. Stating the normative rule this way provides a pattern for future communicative acts that functions to evaluate and instruct his interlocutors. It is this legislative, top-down use that helps distinguish normative rules from code rules.

In sum, normative rules abstract patterns for acting appropriately, templates for communication, that function to instruct and evaluate social conduct. Normative rules can be stated in the form: In context C, if X one should/not do Y; and are often used conversationally to guide future action from the top down.

The relationships between normative and code rules are summarized in Table 1.

I should stress that one cannot abstract normative rules, e.g. children should address elders with respect, without also abstracting codes, e.g. what counts as an elder? Normative rules always entail the use of some constitutive codes. Likewise, code rules, e.g. in *Donahue* discourse, opinion-giving counts as "self" presentation, can be erroneously construed into normative rules, e.g. if one wants to display "self," one should give opinions. But this construal wrongly translates a constitutive definition of logical relations into an appraisal of social conduct. The two are not the same abstractions, do not point to the same types of analysis, nor to the same types of converational enactments. If we are to unravel an understanding of communication from a rules perspective, such a distinction in types of rules is warranted.

TABLE 1
Code and Normative Rules

	Code Rules	*Normative Rules*
Focus:	system of meaning	pattern for action
Formula:	X counts as Y.	If X, one should/ not do Y.
Unit of Observation:	symbol system	speech community
Unit of Analysis:	acts, symbols, forms	act sequences
Criterion:	coherence	appropriateness
Functions:	unify actions define contexts	instruct actors evaluate actions
Prominent use:	bottom up	top down

Conclusion

The above analysis has demonstrated how a rules perspective can contribute to our understanding of situated communication conduct. More specifically, it has unveiled four rules in the communication of a prominent American media event, examined some of the conversational and cultural functions of the rules, and based on the inquiry, proposed a distinction between two types of rules for communication inquiry.

This ethnographic approach to rules research suggests several avenues for future study. Perhaps most important is the need for theory-driven, empirical studies of situated communication conduct. Such a call was made long ago by Hymes (1962, 1972), and a considerable literature has developed (Philipsen and Carbaugh, 1986). Yet, what seems lacking is theoretical sophistication in our research and parsimony in our theorizing (cf. Sherzer, 1977). Two complementary means to this goal are comparative study of communication patterns, and rigorous conceptual analysis based on previous case studies (cf. Keenan, 1976; Rosaldo, 1982; Scollon and Scollon, 1981; Brietborde, 1983). The present study suggests giving more systematic attention to the construction of model person in communication (Chick, 1985; Scollon and Scollon, 1981), and their relations to cultural and conversational features. The questions are raised: what model(s) for the person is spoken? what premises provide for this performance? what common meanings are socially constructed? through what communicative codes, forms, and styles? By addressing these questions, we may further be able to identify what, in particular communication systems, needs to be understood, and what, in general, this tells us about communication. I hope to have contributed not only to our understanding of "self" presentations, "rights" and "respect" in some American communication, but also to an understanding of communication theory *via* the conversational and cultural functions of code and normative rules.

Notes

1 The following report, as an ethnographic study of communication, meets four defining criteria: 1) it is a descriptive study of communication patterns in the context of their use; 2) it is a cultural study that organizes communication patterns in native terms, or "in terms of its own patterns" (Hymes, 1962, p. 101); 3) it is a theoretical study that uses a specialized vocabulary (Hymes, 1972) to achieve the twin goals of local theories of communication, and a grand theory of human communication, and 4) it is a comparative study that draws from the ethnographic literature (Philipsen and Carbaugh, 1986) for illumination of the particularities of a case, and the generalities across cses (Hymes, 1972). While the following report uses each in varying degrees,

it is this set of attributes in descriptive, cultural, theoretical, and comparative study, that motivates this report, and makes of it an ethnographic study of communication.

2   Of course not all communication rules of concern to analysts fulfil all of these criteria. But the following system of rules does.

3   The fundamental problem addressed here is the nature and function of the rules, rather than the frequency of their use, or their distribution. However, there is considerable evidence to suggest that such a system is widely used in the heart-land of America (Hawkins, Weisberg, and Ray, 1980), across the nation in several social institutions (Coles, 1980), and readily available as a discourse for the "expressive individual" (Bellah et al., 1985). And, if I might add, the following rules have been applied in several academic discussions to legitimate the saying of virtually any opinion, whether or not it was well-grounded. In communication accomplished this way, one can hear the powerful practical force of an "ideology of non-ideology" (Weiler, 1984).

4   In a recent Gallup Poll, Phil Donahue was ranked second only to Walter Cronkite as most recognized media figure (Craig, 1986).

5   All materials quoted below and not referenced to published sources are native sayings.

6   On the other hand, through mere re-statements of others' opinions, or agreeing with others, one lacks full cultural status as "self," for one has replicated the beings of others without displaying an uniqueness of one's own.

7   Donahue preaches as much in his pre-show "pep-rallies" when he tells the audience, "I'm nothing without you," and creates a tone of "dinner table conversation" where "self" revelations are expected and accepted (Donahue wows..., 1982).

8   A similar cultural code of "respect" has been lamented by Erwin (1983).

9   The "positive face" operating in this scene is "self," as summarized with rule # 1 (see Brown and Levinson (1978).

10   Note that the former rules suggest inquiry into the semantic codes of folk logics that are used in a way of speaking; for example, the interpretations of native beliefs as enacted in speaking (Hymes, 1972); the social meanings of selections from among linguistic alternatives, be they e.g. lexical choices or choices of pronunciation, with each entailing social messages interpretable through rules of alternation (what is meant by choosing this feature of that verbal repertoire) and ("vertical") co-occurrence (what social meaning is conveyed through e.g. this act in that tone) (Ervin-Tripp, 1972); the logical links between utterances, acts, episodes, social expectations, and cultural themes (Searle, 1969; Cronen et al., 1982); and the logical links between concepts, their attributes, and their social functions in communication (Cushman and Whiting, 1972). The latter rules suggest inquiry into the norms that govern standards of appropriateness in communication; for example, norms for interaction that regulate when one may or may not interrupt another (Hymes, 1972); rules of ("horizontal") co-occurrence that specify sequential relations among linguistic items in utterances, acts, and episodes (Ervin-Tripp, 1972); and other standards for social conduct that prescribe proper sequences for spoken actions (Searle, 1969; Cronen et al., 1982; Cushman and Whiting, 1972). By following the two paths of inquiry used in the above ethnography, sketched here, and detailed below, analysts of communication rules may understand both the common standards of coherence in and of spoken actions (an organization of mutual intelligibil-

ity through common codes), and the standards for speaking appropriately (an organization of appropriate actions through norms). Both paths may be pursued independently, as in a cultural or normative analysis of communication rules, or each may be considered in relation to the other, as in communication norms from the standpoint of cultural codes, or cultural codes from the standpoint of communication norms. (The distinction introduced here, and developed below, draws upon Schneider's (1976) important discussion of culture and norm, and is analagous to, but distinct from, the paradigmatic and syntagmatic axes long used in sociolinguistics.)

11 The discussion compares rules *as abstractions* from behavior. Thus, code and normative rules result from two distinctive perspectives on communication, as illustrated in Rule # 1, with each complementing the other.

References

Bellah, R., Madsen, R., Sullivan, W., Swidler, A., and Tipton, S. *Habits of the heart: Individualism and commitment in American life.* Berkeley, CA: University of California Press, 1985.

Berger, P. & Luckman, T. *The social construction of reality.* New York: Doubleday & Co., 1966.

Brietborde, L. Levels of Analysis in sociolinguistic explanation: Bilingual code switching, social relations, and domain theory. *International Journal of the Sociology of Language,* 1983, *39,* 5-43.

Brown, P. & Levinson, S. Universals in language usage: Politeness phenomena. In E. Goody (Ed.), *Questions and politeness.* London: Cambridge University Press, 1978.

Burke, K. *Permanence and change.* Indianapolis, IN: Bobbs-Merrill, 1965.

Burke, K. *Language as symbolic action.* Berkeley, CA: University of California Press, 1966.

Burke, K. Dramatism. *International Encyclopedia of the Social Sciences,* 1968, *7,* 445-452.

Carbaugh, D. *On persons, speech, and culture: Codes of "self," "society," and "communication" on Donahue.* Unpublished doctoral dissertation, University of Washington, 1984.

Carbaugh, D. *Deep agony: "Self" vs. "society" in Donahue discourse.* Unpublished manuscript, University of Pittsburgh.

Chick, J. The interactional accomplishment of discrimination in South Africa. *Language in Society,* 1985, *14,* 309-326. [Also ch. 16, this volume.]

Coles, R. Civility and psychology. *Daedalus,* 1980, *109,* 133-141.

Craig, J. What you, the people, think about the media. *Pittsburgh Post-Gazette,* January 18, 1986, p. 7.

Cronen, V., Pearce, B., & Harris, L. The coordinated management of meaning: A communication theory. In F. Dance (Ed.), *Human Communication Theory*. New York: Harper & Row, 1982.

Cronen, V., Pearce, B., & Snavely. A theory of rules-structure and types of episodes, and a study of perceived enmeshment in undesired repetitive patterns (URP's). In B. Ruben (Ed.), *Communication Yearbook III*. New Brunswick, NJ: Transaction Press, 1979.

Cushman, D. & Pearce, B. Generality and necessity in three types of communication theory with special attention to rules theory. *Human Communication Research*, 1977, *3*, 344-353.

Cushman, D., Valentinsen, B., & Dietrich, D. A rule theory of interpersonal relationships. In F. Dance (Ed.), *Human Communication Theory*. New York: Harper & Row, 1982.

Cushman, D. & Whiting, G. An approach to communication theory: Towards consensus on rules. *Journal of Communication*, 1972, *22*, 217-238.

Davis, P. *Hometown*. New York: Simon & Schuster, 1982.

De Laguna, F. Tlingit ideas about the individual. *Southwestern Journal of Anthropology*, 1954, *10*, 172-191.

Delia, J. Alternative perspectives for the study of human communication: Critique and response. *Communication Quarterly*, 1977, *25*, 46-62.

Donahue, P. & Co. *Donahue: My own story*. New York: Fawcett Crest, 1981.

Donahue staff, personal communication, Chicago, IL, 1983.

Donahue wows Seattle: "I'm nothing without you." *Seattle Post-Intelligencer*, July 26, 1982, D1.

Enninger, W. On the role of artifactual signification and communication in the organization of speaking. *Papers in Linguistics: International Journal of Human Communication*, 1984, *17*, 53-88.

Ervin-Tripp, S. On sociolinguistic rules: Alternation and co-occurrence. In J. Gumperz & D. Hymes (Eds.), *Directions in sociolinguistics: The ethnography of communication*. New York: Holt, Rinehart, & Winston, 1972.

Erwin, R. What happened to respectability? *American Scholar*, 1983, *52*, 354-362.

Gardner, P. Symmetric respect and memorate knowledge: The structure and ecology of individualistic culture. *Southwestern Journal of Anthropology*, 1966, 22, 389-415.

Geertz, C. "From the native's point-of-view": On the nature of anthropological understanding. In K. Basso & H. Selby (Eds.), *Meaning in Anthropology*. Albuquerque, NM: University of New Mexico Press, 1976.

Gumb, R. *Rule-governed linguistic behavior*. Paris: Mouton, 1972.

Harré, R., Clarke, D., De Carlo, N. *Motives and Mechanisms: An introduction to the psychology of action*. New York: Methuen, 1985.

Harrison, S. Concepts of the person in Avatip religious thought. *Man*, 1985, *20*, 115-130.

Hawes, L. How writing is used in talk: A study of communicative logic-in-use. *Quarterly Journal of Speech*, 1976, *62*, 350-360.

Hawes, L. Alternative theoretical bases: Toward a presuppositional critique. *Communication Quarterly*, 1977, *25*, 63-68.

Hawkins, J., Weisberg, C., & Ray, D. Spouse differences in communication style: Preference, perception, behavior. *Journal of Marriage and the Family*, 1980, *42*, 585-593.

Heath, S. *Ways with words: Language, life, and work in communities and classrooms.* Cambridge: Cambridge University Press, 1983.

Hopper, R. The taken-for-granted. *Human Communication Research*, 1981, *7*, 195-211.

Hymes, D. The ethnography of speaking. In T. Gladwin & W. Sturtevant (Eds.), *Anthropology and human behavior.* Washington D. C.: Anthropological Society of Washington, 1962.

Hymes, D. Models of the interaction of language and social life. In J. Gumperz & D. Hymes (Eds.), *Directions in Sociolinguistics: The ethnography of communication.* New York: Holt, Rinehart, & Winston, 1972.

Hymes, D. *"In vain I tried to tell you": Essays in Native American ethnopoetics.* Philadelphia: University of Pennsylvania Press, 1981.

Johnson, C. & Johnson, F. The Japanese and Caucasians in Honolulu. *Social Forces*, 1975, *54*, 452-466.

Katriel, T., & Philipsen, G. "What we need is communication": "Communication" as a cultural category in some American speech. *Communication Monographs*, 1976, *5*, 67-80. [Also ch. 7, this volume.]

Kirkpatrick, J. *The Marquesan notion of the person.* Ann Arbor, MI: UMI Research Press, 1983.

Lasch, C. *The culture of narcissism.* New York: W. W. Norton & Co., 1979.

Lehtonen, J. & Sajavaara, K. The silent Finn. In D. Tannen & M. Saville-Troike (Eds.), *Perspectives on Silence.* Norwood, NJ: Ablex, 1985.

Marsella, A., Devos, G., & Hsu, F. *Culture and self.* New York: Tavistock Publications, 1985.

Nofsinger, R. On answering questions indirectly: Some rules in the grammar of doing conversation. *Human Communication Research*, 1976, *2*, 172-181.

Pearce, B., & Conklin, F. A model of hierarchical meaning in coherent conversation and a study of indirect responses. *Communication Monographs*, 1979, *46*, 75-87.

Philipsen, G. Speaking "like a man" in Teamsterville: Culture patterns of role enactment in an urban neighborhood. *Quarterly Journal of Speech,* 1975, *61*, 13–22. [Also ch. 1, this volume.]

Philipsen, G. Places for speaking in Teamsterville. *Quarterly Journal of Speech*, 1976, *62*, 15-25.

Philipsen, G. & Carbaugh, D. A bibliography of fieldwork in the ethnography of communication. *Language in Society,* 1986, *15*, 387–398.

Reisman, K. Contrapuntal conversations in an Antiguan village. In R. Bauman and J. Sherzer (Eds.), *Explorations in the ethnography of speaking.* London: Cambridge University Press, 1974.

Robertson, J. *American myth, American reality.* New York: Hill & Wang, 1980.

Robinson, B. Family experts on television talk shows: Facts, values and half-truths. *Family Relations*, 1982, *31*, 369-378.

Rosaldo, M. The things we do with words: Ilongot speech acts and speech act theory in philosophy. *Language in Society,* 1982, *11,* 203-237. [Also ch. 25, this volume.]

Sanders, R., & Martin, L. Grammatical rules and explanations of behavior. *Inquiry*, 1975, *18*, 65-82.

Schegloff, E. Sequencing in conversational openings. In J. Gumperz & D. Hymes (Eds.), *Directions in sociolinguistics: The ethnography of communication.* New York: Holt, Rinehart, & Winston, 1972.

Schneider, D. Notes toward a theory of culture. In K. Basso & H. Selby (Eds.), *Meaning in Anthropology.* Albuquerque, NM: University of New Mexico Press, 1976.

Scollon, R. & Scollon, S. *Narrative, literacy, and fact in interethnic communication.* Norwood, NJ: Ablex, 1981. [See chs. 18 & 19, this volume.]

Scruton, R. The significance of common culture. *Philosophy*, 1979, *54*, 51-70.

Searle, J. *Speech acts.* Cambridge: Cambridge University Press, 1969. [See ch. 24 & 26, this volume.]

Seitel, P. Haya metaphors for speech. *Language in Society*, 1974, *3*, 51-67.

Sennett, R. *The fall of public man.* New York: Vintage Books, 1978.

Sherzer, J. The ethnography of speaking: A critical appraisal. In M. Saville-Troike (Ed.), *Linguistics and anthropology.* Georgetown University Round Table Series on Language and Linguistics, 1977.

Shimanoff, S. *Communication rules.* Beverly Hills, CA: Sage, 1980.

Sigman, S. On communication rules from a social perspective. *Human Communication Research*, 1980, *7*, 37-51.

Stewart, J. Interpretive listening: An alternative to empathy. *Communication Education*, 1983, *32*, 379-392.

Stokes, R. & Hewitt, J. Aligning actions. *American Sociological Review*, 1976, *41*, 838-849.

Tocqueville, A. *Democracy in America.* New York: Vintage Books, 1945. (Originally published, 1835.)

Varenne, H. *Americans together.* New York: Columbia University Press, 1977.

Veroff, J., Douvan, E. & Kulka, R. *The inner American: A self-portrait from 1957 to 1976.* New York: Basic Books, 1981.

Wieder, L. & Pratt, S. On being a recognizable Indian among Indians. Paper presented at the International Communication Association, Honolulu, Hawaii, 1985.

Weiler, M. The rhetoric of neo-liberalism. *Quarterly Journal of Speech*, 1984, *70*, 362-378.

Westen, D. *Self and society: Narcissism, collectivism, and the development of morals.* Cambridge: Cambridge University Press, in press.

Wittgenstein, L. *Philosophical investigations* (G. Anscombe, trans.). New York: Macmillan, 1958.

Yankelovich, D. *New rules: Searching for self-fulfilment in a world turned upside down.* New York: Bantam Books, 1981.

II
Intercultural Communication

DONAL CARBAUGH

Several of the studies in the first part of this book (those by Philipsen, Daniel and Smitherman-Donaldson, and Wieder and Pratt) describe situations of intercultural contact. Introduced in these studies were some occassions in which one culture contacted another, such as in Teamsterville when upon disciplining children, one community's norms for "being a male" confronted another's; or with regard to initial interactions, when contrastive codes of silence were used by Osage and Whites; or with regard to ritual celebrations especially in secular scenes, when a highly energized form of call/response confronted another less animated and more restrained. Each of these studies thus demonstrates how communication is performed in particular times and places, by those who share—and choose to use—a common pattern of communication, and each demonstrates at least one situation in which the culture pattern is not shared with some interactional partner(s), leading to problems such as asynchrony, misinterpretations, misunderstanding, and discrimination.

The chapters in this second part are based on exactly this kind of communicative situation, situations of intercultural contacts. But this does not make the studies in this part something different from studies of cultural communication. In fact, like those in the first part, the studies here demonstrate again how communication is motivated—at least in part—on the basis of culture patterns; each shows again how some norms, forms, and codes of communication are deeply situated; and, each associates such patterns with the sentiments and performances of a cultural identity; yet, each shows further how situations of intercultural contact can unveil the depth and force of culture patterns, as well as perpetuate deep perplexities between peoples.

Whether, if, and how one can come to coordinate conduct in particular situations of intercultural contact is of course a fundamental practical problem. As is especially pronounced in some courtrooms and classrooms

151

discussed here, cultural preferences for speaking do exist in contexts, where some patterns are valued, others are rendered somehow problematic, with translations from one into another being difficult at best. Resulting issues span from the undermining of some ethnic traditions, to the role of power in intercultural contacts (power being the articulation of desired resources, with what constitutes "desired" in such situations being always problematic), and the equality not only to speak, but also to be heard as having something worthy to say, and so on.

There are serious pragmatic problems in realizing a goal of "diversity" in such situations. To refine our sense of that general goal, and what might be done to achieve it, a theory of practical action is needed that can ably identify the possible loci and sources of intercultural asynchrony in actual situations of intercultural contact, and thus guide its efficacious production. It is toward these practical and theoretical goals that the readings in this unit contribute. With these goals in mind, I preview the studies in the following part, then treat briefly but schematically some of the issues they address with regard to intercultural communication.

Some Common Threads

The studies in this second part (as well as those mentioned previously from part I and some in Part III), all confront and address the practical and theoretical problems of intercultural communication in various and productive ways. Yet, as a group, they share three commitments. First, as do the studies in Part I, these focus on the performance of *communication patterns* that are *situated socially* and give voice to *cultural identities*. But, unlike the main concerns in the studies of Part I, these explore situations in which different culture patterns are communicated simultaneously, situating social relations differently, thus interweaving cultural identities and their distinctive patterns of action and meaning into one performance. The complexities and perplexities explored help uncover — following Chick — the interactional accomplishment of such things as discrimination, negative stereotypes, and misunderstandings, but do so in order to enhance both our knowledge about and competence in such performances. The readings in this part, therefore, reveal a second common thread: They inquire about *loci and sources of intercultural asynchrony* by examining *actual instances of intercultural contacts.* By exploring intercultural encounters, the authors are able to identify patterns characteristically used by those of each participating group, and thus lay bases for understanding — and coping better with — some of the loci and sources of intercultural asynchrony.

A general caveat is in order with regard to the types of claims being made by these authors. Given their focus on group patterns, at times it may sound as if the authors claim, something like, "Whites speak one way, Blacks another." But note that the main concern in the studies is *patterns* in—and of—communication, which are *not linked in any deterministic way to a people.* People can use various patterns, as well as create new ones of their own. A Black may speak a characteristically White pattern, and as Blacks know in some situations—if not to stand out—they must do so, just as any person, on any occassion, may choose to speak her group's patterns, or another's. People, at least on some occassions, and with regard to some features of the patterns, have some choice in the matter. To identify patterns, and to characterize them with regard to one group rather than another, is thus not to draw a deterministic link between people and communication patterns. Any person can choose variously to reaffirm, to create with, to live by, or against, such patterns. Some such selection process is at the heart of culturally critical practice. What the studies identify are some ways, in real situations, some communication has been done, one way by some, another by others, in order to show how such cultural patterns of communication operate. The patterns, although being characteristic of a class of people, need not necessarily be used by any one of them. By identifying patterns at this level, the authors contribute to our understanding of the intercultural process, practically and theoretically. Juxtaposing culture patterns this way, some associated with one people, others with another, enables the authors to develop our understanding of intercultural communication by identifying some possible loci and sources of intercultural asynchrony.

Studying intercultural contacts this way brings some features of cultural patterns to the fore, throwing them—as cultural phenomena—into sharper relief. Resulting is the third common thread, as some *levels of theory are introduced anew,* clarifying what needs attention theoretically and practically in situations of intercultural contact. For example, interactional structures such as what constitutes a turn at talk, patterns of turn exchange, the length of a turn, or the length of pauses between turns, the way content is structured communicatively including the domains elaborated and the ways they are elaborated, communicative processes such as formulas for greeting and departing, nonverbal features such as types and amount of gestural cueing, prosody and intonation, all vary in important cultural ways. We review these sources of cultural variability in some detail here. But for now, note how there is variation in each such phenomenon, with the variation understandable in part on the basis of the cultural system(s) in use. Such an approach yields productive foci for understanding intercultural practices through various levels of communication theory. If we are to develop our practical knowledge about intercultural communication, we would do well to develop the theoretical leads introduced by these authors. Our theory could then help us know generally what levels are potentially involved in intercultural contacts, so we may listen accordingly, coming to know better what is cultural in the sayings and its various uses in intercultural situations.

The readings in this part demonstrate the complexity of cultural features in intercultural communication. Which features vary, and how, from group to group, place to place, and moment to moment, needs studied. And that is just what the readings in this unit do, providing a look at the important and particular forces at work when cultures contact one another in contexts. Let us preview the readings in some more detail, now that we have some sense of common threads.

A Preview

In the first chapter, Kenneth Liberman (chapter 12) begins by examining a rule for speaking among Aboriginal Australians, stated simply, in public discourse, consensus among participants must be preserved. Liberman finds the rule is prominently spoken through a cyclical form, a "serial production of summary accounts," which amounts to a repetition of consensual themes. The discursive rhythm of the performance is rapid and intense, involving at times several participants talking at the same time, yet the form assumes a highly cooperative and unassertive tone. The general purpose in such cyclical discourse is the collective creation and display of a unanimous agreement prior to a formal, public decision. Ruled out of discourses performed in accord with the rule are individual arguments and confrontational sequences, yet these are precisely what is required in some Anglicized contexts such as Australian classrooms and courtrooms. Liberman discusses how Aboriginal discourses that orient to and display the rule of consensus are rendered problematic in these situations, because the situations require individual rather than a collective performance, a defensive rather than cooperative tone. Liberman is able to account for intercultural contacts in these situations, most generally, by unveiling the contrastive rules, forms, rhythms, and tones of discourse involved in the encounters. He relates each to its respective cultural identity, with Aboriginal coding being done prominently on the bases of group mutuality and respect, and "Anglo" on the bases of individual freedom and competition. In his epilogue, Liberman argues for basing (inter)cultural communication studies on such moment-to-moment practices, with special attention to — what could be called — an ethnotheoretical position.

Chapter 14 by Thomas Kochman explores general differences between Blacks and Whites in, what could be called, feeling tone, or mode of verbal expressiveness. Kochman notes how Black identity displays often attend mainly to the speaker's performance abilities (or positive face), with valued performances being emotionally intense, highly demonstrative, and involving vigorous nonverbal action such as boisterous handshakes, loud laughter, and grand smiles. Cultural communication is organized in order to embrace robustness of feeling. White identity displays, on the other hand, according to Kochman, attend mainly to the hearer's sensibilities (or negative face concerns), valuing performances more restrained and subdued. Created is another cultural system organized not to embrace intense emotional expression, but precisely to constrain it. Kochman notes—interestingly—two key differences in these cultural systems, two loci and sources of intercultural asynchrony. One relates to the interval between arousal and response, with the Black interval being generally much shorter than the White, or as in call/response when speaking is aroused quickly on impulse as an emotional and spiritual release, thus culturally embracing moments of overlap and simultaneous performance. Another source of asynchrony relates to the level of expressiveness deemed appropriate, with Blacks able managers of highly expressive modes and forms, and Whites preferring a level more moderate in expressiveness. In his epilogue, Kochman links these contrastive features of mode and level of expressiveness to more general issues of cultural style, arguing toward a goal of cultural diversity in which different styles are heard and understood, with the potential contributions of each to contexts being acknowledged, as such, rather than unknowingly being bebased or devalued.

Chapter 16 by Keith Chick—like the others in this part—raises a seminal question: How does one account for asynchrony of conduct in intercultural encounters? Chick explores a university setting in South Africa with special attention given to review sessions between native speakers of English and Zulu. Note how Chick conducts a fine-grained analysis of specific moments in three review sessions between a teacher and a student. On the basis of such study, Chick identifies cultural differences in discourse conventions that lead to misinterpretations of intent, and when repeated over time, lead to negative cultural stereotypes. Special attention is given to issues of framing, or how speakers signal what is going on, its goals, and ways to achieve them. Chick finds that some speakers share framing conventions, while others do not, leading to contrastive means and goals, as when the teacher intitiates "a review of study habits" with a student who is being guided by "a defense of poor exam performance." Resulting are misinterpretations of meanings, and a lack of coordination of actions. Chick identifies a second source of asynchrony in prosodic cueing, or features such as tone grouping, accent placement, loudness, and rate of speech. These concerns are seen to vary by cultural system, and thus contribute to intercultural asynchrony. Finally, Chick explores "face" concerns finding that those who performed poorly in the class, were motivated partly to improve their face, while another who performed well was concerned less to repair face. But, there is more involved here than classroom performance. Chick shows how the two who performed poorly (who were from different cultural backgrounds—one male Zulu, one male English), initiated face repair on the basis of two different strategies. The English student asserted solidarity (or minimized differences in power and social distance between himself and the teacher), a preference aligned with the teacher's. The Zulu however asserted deference (or maximized social distance), a preference which challenged the teacher's stated desires. Part of the intrigue in Chick's chapter is his finding a person in a subordinate position (student) who asserts deference/respect for the superordinate (teacher), but in doing so challenges the teacher's desires for solidarity with students (for relations appearing more equitable). Thus, the teacher asserts solidarity/equality, whereas the student asserts deference/respect, but in doing so challenges the teacher. By attending to such concerns of face, Chick shows how the use of one's best cultural manners (based in one case on respect of differences or in another on searches for commonalities), can lead rather unknowingly and innocently to intercultural asynchrony, linking cultural differences in discourse conventions to grander patterns of discrimination and negative stereotyping. In his epilogue, Chick highlights the micro–macro relationship in his studies, noting some reactions to them, with special attention given to the relationship between his interactional studies and the current political situation in South Africa.

In chapter 18 Ronald Scollon and Suzanne Wong-Scollon use the theory of face as one way to trace sources of intercultural asynchrony between Athabaskan and (American, Canadian, Anglo) English speakers. They present a rather comprehensive framework for examining cultures in contact. The areas of study they suggest—based on their findings of Athabaskan-English contacts—are: how "self" is displayed, including the amount of talk preferred, in specific relational contexts, and the nature of prohibited actions; how talk is distributed, with regards to who speaks first, controls the topic, the nature of turn exchanges and departure formulas; how information is structured, with special attention to prosody and pausing; and, how content is organized, with regard to which domains are elaborated, and how concepts are organized. Particularly intriguing in their discussion is the fundamental importance attributed to how the exchange of turns is cued, mainly the cultural differences in the length of a pause necessary for cueing the possibility of a turn exchange. They show how differences in such a minute feature of conversation can influence who speaks first, how often they speak, as well as what speakers make of each other, leading eventually—like Chick—to grander patterns of discrimination and negative cultural stereotyping. There is much that hinges on such minutae in discourse, and their cultural variation. In their epilogue, they note how some of the aspects in their general framework apply to Chinese and American-English interaction.

As is shown in these chapters, there are many sources, loci, and consequences of asynchrony in intercultural contacts. Let us now turn to a more schematic look at these with special attention to cultural variations in the coding of cultural identities, forms, and norms, as these are played out in intercultural contacts.

Some Sources and Loci of Intercultural Asynchrony

As is demonstrated in the chapters here, there are many sources of cultural variability in communication. These become especially important in intercultural contacts for they can lead to misinterpretations of intent, misunderstandings generally, a lack of coordination in moment-to-moment interactions, discrimination among classes of people, negative stereotyping and so on. I have been using the term *asynchrony* to capture the interactional dynamics producing this wide range of detrimental outcomes that, in turn, stem — in part — from cultural variations in communication. In what follows, I present a more schematic overview of these sources of asynchrony, looking across the studies just previewed. The issues addressed of course coalesce empirically and are separated here solely for analytic purposes. I organize the issues around three areas: the interactional coding of cultural identity, cultural forms for performance, and structuring norms.

The Interactional Coding of Cultural Identity

Cultural identity is everywhere coded in communication, but nowhere is it coded exactly the same in all contexts. The interactional and moment-by-moment coding of an Osage, Black, Athabaskan, Zulu, Anglo-American, and so on varies. One way to unravel the variation is to ask: what cultural model (s) for the person is being coded in a situation, and how is this coding accomplished interactionally?

The authors of the previewed studies suggest at least four very general aspects of cultural identity that are interactionally coded: a cultural model of personhood, itself consisting of targeted goals, loci of motives, and bases of social relations.

First, *the cultural model for being a person* focuses attention on the senses that constitute personhood, or the concepts and premises for being a cultural agent that are marked for communication performance. That there is variation in such models is hinted by reviewing at least four general types. The Aboriginal who performs public discourse in an intensely cooperative and collective way, orients to an identity, the sense and performance of which, is—or seeks to be—connected and included within consensual themes. The Anglo American on the other hand performs socially as an extricable individual, saying what is "on the mind" and what can be said truthfully, honestly, on one's own. The Teamster, or in some situations the Osage, or the Burundi speak more as holders of positions in a social hierarchy. And, as Kochman suggests, Black Americans model interaction more as performers, making the verbal activity itself a focal interactional concern, presenting "self" with regard to what is good and artful performance. One might summarize the types crudely as—respectively—the collective we, the individual me, the positional us (always among others), and the performative me/we. Possible dimensions underlying and distinguishing the types may be individual/collective, positional/personal, productive/reproductive, with these, regarding the situated communication of cultural identity, to be discovered. Toward such an end, Hymes (1972, pp. 44–52), Hofstede (1980), Hall (1976) and Ting-Toomey (1988) provide useful suggestions.

With regard to the communication of each such dimension and type—granting of course these vary from time to time and place to place within any social group—there are some *targeted goals* toward which cultural communication moves, or in local parlance should move. Respective to the types, we see communal conversations varying with the Aboriginal moving toward consensus, the Anglo toward truth, the Teamster toward social positioning, the Black toward inventive verbal performance. And, for each of course, the other goals may also be relevant. A hierarchy of goals is most likely operating. The point emphasized here is simply that goals are prioritized with one or a small number being culturally coded and associated with the person as a situated cultural actor, in times and places.

One may further identify cultural identity with regard to the *loci of motives,* or the basic moral agencies grounding the communication of the identity. For example, the Aboriginal people share a relational locus, seeing and being motivated by the connections among them, the Anglo an individual one, based on one's own thoughts and feelings, with others, such as some speakers of Hindi, situating actions at base among suborganismic particles and substances rendering the cultural agent more a "dividual"—a divisible entity (Marriott & Inden, 1977)—than a relation or an "individual."

The cultural model person, targeted goals, and loci of motives may co-relate with some *bases of social relations.* Two dimensions used by Chick and the Scollons—and that form a central core of Brown and Levinson's politeness framework—are power (P) and distance (D). With regard to Zulu and Athabaskan speaking, we see discourse strategies based on a minimization of power with an affirmation of distance $(-P, +D)$. Such systems may be called, following the Scollons, a *deference-based system,* a respecting of distance and difference. Conversely, an Anglo system — among others — as seen in the Anglo teacher and other English speakers, is based on a minimization of power and distance $(-P, -D)$. Such systems may be called a *solidarity-based system,* displaying commonalities among persons. Of course a third possibility is asymmetrically based, maximizing power differences $(+P, \pm D)$. Hearing in cultural communication systems, such bases of sociation, along with the cultural person, targeted goals, and loci of motives, enables one to conceptualize the type(s) of identity being brought to intercultural contacts, perhaps pinpointing some sources of asynchrony, especially as these are played out in moment-to-moment interactions.

An example I recently collected, as part of an ongoing project on Soviet-American dialogue, helps demonstrate cultural persons in action. As part of an institutional arrangement, Soviet and American scholars were being brought together — for the first time — to discuss their respective university programs, in this case, to discuss "schools of management." The purpose expressed (to the American audience) for the meetings — a series of informal "gatherings" — was to provide some on-site, detailed information about the American program to the Soviets, so they could learn about it, and adapt it in order to design a similar program of their own. After several such "gatherings," the Americans were frustrated because they could not figure out what the Soviets wanted and needed to know. The Soviets, also frustrated, were not gathering the information they wanted. Why? The interactional dynamics of the encounters give some possible explanation. Throughout the meetings, the Soviets were displaying relentlessly and proudly a corporate identity, through themes of solidarity, by disclosing only what was agreeable publicly to them. In their speech, they displayed a united, and collective, person who did not ask for information and guidance, because such asking perhaps implied a fault with their system, itself risking a sense of disloyalty, which in turn threatened the most proper base of sociation, solidarity. The Soviet person being put forward, then, disallowed explicit disclosures of their program limitations or problems, because both risked discrediting the proper face (or sociopolitical system) being put forward, at least during this early stage of meeting. The Americans, during the process, therefore, did not, and could not know what information was needed by the Soviets, and hearing only the virtues of the Soviet program, unwittingly invoked the reciprocity norm, and began displaying the problems they had confronted in their own program. The American identity — speaking as it did, individually, about "the problems with the system" — thus displayed its characteristic problem-orientation, self-focus, and individual base, at least in this context. The intercultural result, co-created by all — from these initial meetings — was a Soviet pattern unwilling to make known what most needed to be known, and an American pattern eagerly disclosing what needed to be known the least. The resulting confusions and misalignments of actions and meanings were frustrating to both parties.

What is being suggested here is that any system of cultural communication can be rendered generally with regard to a cultural model(s) for the person, what such an identity takes as its targeted goals, its locus of motives, and its bases for sociation. The intent of such an assessment is a general one, not to categorize persons for once and for all, but to identify some dimensions of cultural variation in order to trace their shape and use in particular situations, including those of intercultural contacts. Such an assessment of course may assume the status of a diagnosis, being the culmination of much detailed study, but I introduce it here as one way to characterize the dimensions around which the communication of cultural agents varies. So posed, it suggests movements beyond concepts such as "face," "model person," "individual," or "speaker," to questions of the form: what patterns creatively display cultural identities in the communication systems, and situations, under study? In part, the remainder of the schema provides some specifics for elaborating a response.

Cultural Frames and Forms of Performance

Every people has some sequences for communicating that they can and do identify. In chapter 12, Kenneth Liberman shows how Aboriginal Australians perform public discourse through the frame "all speak with one voice" (*wangka kutjungka*), elaborating themes of consensus, a cooperative tone, and a spiralling form. Also, through a serial production of "summary accounts" the Aboriginal persons display a collective identity, driven by consensus, motivated corporately, and based on relations of deference and respect. Such a frame and form enacts what a person, in public, is and should be. But in other contexts, like the Australian court room, other frames are prescribed, like "a defense." Producing speech efficaciously, in this context, requires displays of an individual identity, themes of dissonance, an antagonistic tone, through a more linear form.

The examples introduced here demonstrate what can be called *cultural frames* and *forms of performance*. The framing often involves a culturally coded term, such as *defense,* which identifies a kind of speaking familiar to, identified, performed, and evaluated by "native" speakers.[1] One might think of these as cultural terms for talk, or a metacommunicative repertoire, which provides a cultural sense of communication performances. Of

---

[1]Note also that the coding may involve culturally salient content, as with "defending *oneself,*" or as in "sharing *feelings*" (Carbaugh, 1988).

course not all peoples have a refined vocabulary about communication, but every people identifies some sequences of action routinely, and this is something that needs to be studied, especially with regard to intercultural contacts. The chapters in this part by Chick, who explores culturally contrasting frames of "reviewing study habits" versus "defending poor performance," and Kochman, who explores the levels of intensity coded in cultural terms like "discussion," "argument," "woofing," and "rapping," provide examples. From Part I, the cultural terms, "communication," "griping," "call/response," and "razzing," provide others. All demonstrate sequences of communication that are coded culturally. For each one can ask: What means of expression does this frame make available? What goals are being targeted? What is the relationship between this kind of talk, so coded, and the cultural identity under study? Is this talk aligned with it? valued? why so or why not?

The studies in this unit, among others, also suggest a concept of *form* as useful for identifying the general shape of the sequences. For example, the "summary account" illustrates a cyclical form, or a "round-the-rally" as Liberman puts it, a repetition of agreeable topics and themes. Similarly, the "griping" ritual discussed in unit one displays a spiralling shape to discourse. Interestingly, both make solidarity one of their targeted goals. The Black "call/response" form seems shaped somewhat similarly. By contrast, note how "communication," and "defense" are more linearly shaped, and target goals of problem solving. The general point is simply that culturally coded sequences assume different forms, target different goals, and are associated with variant cultural identities, thus providing possible sources of difficulty in intercultural encounters.

How cultural identities, frames, and forms are structured interactionally is a question requiring much more detailed treatment. Toward this end, we can think and act in terms of structuring norms.

Structuring Norms

Are there parameters of variation, within intercultural encounters, which may help us understand further the communication of cultural identities, frames, and forms? We now turn to various features of intercultural communication, all of which help structure encounters, but each of which does so in culturally variable ways. I discuss in turn the structuring of interaction, of information, and of content.

It is important to note here that I am extending the concept of "norm" introduced in Part I. There, *norm* referred to the relationship between cultural forms and targeted goals, such as one should reply to insults from friends with a counter-insult, intitiating rather than a fight with fists, a battle of bards. Thus, *norm* was used to describe patterns for proper communication conduct that are used discursively to instruct, regulate, and evaluate routine practices. In this sense, normative patterns are granted moral status within identifiable speech situations as "the right thing to do." The guiding criterion is appropriateness. Here I extend the concept from moral imperatives, to practical actions, from normative considerations of "the right thing to do," to the more practical "thing to do." Exploited here is the equivocal sense of norm as referring both to normative action (moral imperatives for acting), and to standards of normalcy (the conventional things done). With regard to the latter, we see that many interactional structures—such as pause lengths, and intonation—are communally patterned, and are at times out of awareness, becoming matters less of morality, than of conventionality. But even this kind of structuring, we see, although not necessarily granted moral status in and of itself, sometimes grounds such judgments, perhaps unknowingly, especially when generating intercultural asynchrony and its possible cycles of discrimination and misunderstanding.

The Structuring of Interaction.   How is interaction structured step by step, so participants know when to speak, for how long, and so on? In Ron and Suzanne Scollon's study of Athabaskan-English interaction, we see how an Athabaskan generally prefers speaking when among intimates and when topics hold some degree of consensus. Athabaskans thus tend to speak after a relationship is established. The English pattern is often the inverse, preferring speaking among strangers in order to establish a relationship, with intimacy being one context where silence is premissible. Because of these preferences for speaking, we see the English speaker tending to initiate interaction when with an Athabaskan for the first time, thus introducing topics first. The interactional picture is further convoluted as the English speaker uses a shorter pause length to cue the exchange of turns, thus continuing to take the floor before the Athabaskan, according to her structuring norms, is given the chance. The English thus tends to speak first, introducing topics, and controls subsequent interaction. And finally, when it is time to close the conversation, the English pattern suggests referring to future interaction and perhaps the relationship among participants. Athabaskan departures, however, orient to a general norm prohibiting reference to the future, unless one wants to court bad luck.

The picture here is a complex one, but one that suggests several parameters of cultural variation in the structuring of intercultural encounters:

1. Whether to talk? Given a physical setting, a social situation, types of persons, relationships, and topics of discussion, should one speak? For some, such as the Athabaskan and Western Apache when among strangers,

silence is preferred, whereas for others, in the same type of situation, speaking is preferred.

2. If one should talk, who should speak? Should speaking, like for some public forums among the Osage, be performed by one type of person only? Or as on "Donahue," be freely available to all?

3. If one speaks, how much talk should be forthcoming? Are longer monologues permissible and expected as among the Zulu and Osage, or should turns be shorter?

4. What rules for opening are operating? Danielle Godard (1977) has shown how rules for opening a phone call vary between some speakers of French and others of English.

5. Furthermore, what constitutes a conversational move? Some situations for some Black Americans, Antiguans, Aboriginal Australians, Kuna, some Yucatec Mayan storytelling, and so on, permit or require two persons speaking at the same time. Can one person do the move? Is co-production of speech required or preferred?[2]

6. How are turns among speakers exchanged? This is sometimes done by pausing, but as we see in Athabaskan-English encounters, the length of pauses can vary. For others, as Reisman describes the Antiguans, turn exchanges apparently are cued differently, if at all, with interlocutors simply entering into—by speaking on top of—others who are already speaking. Overlap and co-production is not out of place. Philips argues (in chapter 22) that signalling a turn is qualitatively different for Warm Springs Indians than it is for Anglo-Whites.

7. How does one depart from an intercultural encounter? As we have seen, rules for departure formulas vary by culture, particularly in the status of referring to future events and present relationships.

The aforementioned combine in some ways to account for further variations in *rhythm,* or length of interval between stimuli and responses. According to Kochman, Blacks orient to a much shorter interval than Whites. Gumperz (1978) and Erickson and Schultz (1982) addressed conversational rhythms similarly. Also, *pacing* derives from the aforementioned suggesting variations in turn length and density, as well as the length of turn exchange cues, as is evident in the Aboriginal "summary account" being very rapid compared to the Anglo-Australian, with the Zulu and Warm Springs Indian (see Phillips, chapter 22) being somewhat slower than the dominant culture pattern. Both rhythm and pacing are likely related to *volume and intensity,* with quicker conversational rhythms and faster pacing combining with louder volume to create, as Kochman shows, a Black

---

[2]Note the important distinctions between turn, move, and floor discussed in Hymes (1986, pp. 61–64).

style of communication highly demonstrative and intense, or as Liberman shows in some classrooms, Aborigines tend to speak in lower volume and intensity. Kochman contrasts the Black style with the White by reference to cultural configurations of rhythm, pacing, and volume, among other features including gestural displays mentioned here.

The structuring of interactions varies by culture pattern, as these loci of variation suggest, and we need to acknowledge as much if we are to enhance the quality of interaction in intercultural encounters, and understand better some sources of intercultural asynchrony.

Information Structuring.   What are the ways of cueing how information is to be interpreted? One source of some intercultural asynchrony is the simultaneous use of two signalling systems to cue how information is to be interpreted. Ron and Suzanne Scollon describe how Athbaskans typically cue how speech is to be taken through morphemes (such as suffixes or words that inform one how to take a phrase), whereas English speakers rely more on prosodic cues (such as intonation). In their epilogue, they show further how Chinese use, in addition to prosodic cues, a morphemic system of particles (e.g., *ne, bA*) that cues attitudes toward the topic, proper ways of responding, and relations among speakers. Which system is preferred for cueing interpretation, and what can be cued with each system? These are important questions which the Scollons raise and address.

In addition to variation in the use of cueing systems, for example a preferred use of prosodic over morphemic, there is of course cultural variation within systems. Keith Chick shows how prosodic systems vary by culture. He discusses for example how "yes" said with rising intonation can signal for Anglos, "please continue," whereas for Zulus the same intonation signals, "I see." The different interpretations lead of course to different next moves, risking further asynchrony. Gumperz' (1982, p. 173) work is especially relevant here, as he so ably demonstrates how prosodic cues unfold in specific situations (co-occurring with other discourse features) and signal the interpretation of acts differently, because they are based in different ethnic systems.

Systems that signal how to interpret information, whose function is at least partially metacommunicative, are of course of various shapes and guises. And in addition to the prosodic and morphemic, we must also mention some more kinesic. Several levels of analysis are suggested by the following chapters. Note the cultural variations in facial expressions (Kochman contrasts the laughs and smiles of Blacks with Whites), or, gazing and eye movement (with Aboriginal children averting eyes from teachers as a signal of distance and respect; also see Philips, chapter 22). Elsewhere, Loveday (1983, p. 174) has shown how in Japan, gazing away from, rather than at, one's interlocutors signals an opportunity for turn selection. Of course, body positioning in both type and amount varies by culture (see especially Philips), and signals as well how information is to be taken, or is being heard. Taken together, and when uniquely combined in culture patterns, these elements undoubtedly help constitute differences in *affective tone* (for example, the cueing in Black discourse of verbal play, or among Aboriginal Australians of harmonious cooperation, or in other contexts when more serious confrontations prevail) and *mode* (as indirection is preferred when discussing oneself among Athabaskans, which contrasts with a more direct English pattern).

As the studies in this volume, show, signalling systems such as the prosodic, morphemic, and kinesic, are complex and are related intimately to culturally patterned frames and forms of speech. When acting in, and trying to theorize about intercultural encounters, especially with regard to questions of local patterns for cueing information, these systems need to be considered, if sources and loci of intercultural asynchrony are to be understood.

The Structuring of Content.   What cultural domains are elaborated in speaking, and how are they organized and developed? Is "self" a topic of discussion? emotions? communication? religion? science? nature? Which domains are elaborated, in what ways, by whom, and in what contexts, varies of course by culture. Ron and Suzanne Scollon note that Athabaskans, unlike English others, do not make self a key category for discursive elaboration. Also, they organize concepts in twos and fours, rather than the English preference for threes (as Dundes, 1980, discussed in *Interpreting Folklore*). Resulting is the impression, by the English, that the Athabaskan has said too little, or too much, or by the Athabaskan, that the English said too much or too little. As for topic development, Athabaskans, at least in public discourse, prefer a kind of repetitive pattern, Blacks, a more inventive pattern, and Whites, a more scientistic pattern. Which topics are appropriate for elaboration, when, by whom, and in what ways they are introduced, organized, and developed, all vary by culture. In the following chapters, although not given great depth or detailed treatment, we find the organization and development of contents varies culturally as well as the ways for speaking them.

Some recent studies have induced culturally distinct domains, their organization and contextual development, on the basis of symbol systems-in-use, exploring local symbol systems and their meanings, the premises they enable, their placement within larger episodic sequences, and their interpretation within broader codes for conduct and meaning (Carbaugh, 1988; Philipsen, 1986).

Toward a Tentative model for the Theory
and Practice of Intercultural Communication

In a recent review of some programs of intercultural communication research, William Gudykunst (1985) concluded the following: "By recognizing the similarity in the underlying process of all forms of communication, the need for a theory 'of' intercultural communication disappears. Rather, there is a need to develop general theories explaining all forms of communication, or middle range theories explaining particular aspects of communication between people from different cultures or ethnic groups" (p. 24). The following formulation proposes, albeit tentatively, some elements in one such theory, but it seeks not only cross-cultural generalizations, and theories of "aspects" of intercultural encounters, but also—and at base—theories of culture patterns in order to come to grips with the varieties of locally designed and commonly used communicative systems as they help organize, and give coherence to, the conduct of sociocultural lives. Perhaps Hymes (1974) put it best: The intent is to acknowledge the diversity of human creations, and to "encompass and organize, not abstract from, the diversity" (p. 33).

I organize my comments with a series of figures that summarizes the three main elements just discussed (and the subparts of each). The formulation is of course a tentative one, built primarily but not exclusively on the chapters included here, and offered as a heuristic for further inquiry. To begin, Fig. 1 sketches more schematically the basic elements just discussed.

Figure 1 shows the main elements in the cultural communication system. The elements are separated of course for analytic purposes and coalesce in communication performances—as the particular studies in this unit make clear—revealing particular configurations of features. The model is *circular* because each element contributes to the others while itself being influenced by the others. Put another way, each element is both a medium, and outcome, of the communication process. It is this dynamic that makes

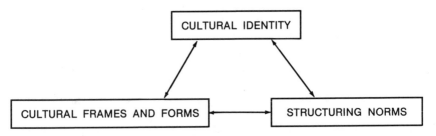

FIG. 1. The circularity of the system.

cultural communication systems more or less stable, and more or less resistant to change, because any element (or subpart) is being continually reinforced by others within the system (cf. Scollon & Scollon, 1981, p. 192).

Any communicative situation is subject, potentially, to basic interactional and social tensions, to *dialectically elastic forces.* One view of such tensions involves the interactional forces of creation and affirmation, and social forces of autonomy and union (Carbaugh, 1988/1989). These were introduced in Part I, and I return to them here to emphasize some dialectical tensions intrinsic to some communicative situations, influencing the communication of cultural identities, forms, and norms. Any such system opens itself at times to creation, change and choice, but the amount and type of change being possible, or desirable, depends on the particular configuration of the system-in-use (i.e., cultural communication system) in a community/situation. Efforts to change, when conceived dialectically, are then subject to an equipoise in the direction of affirmation. Similarly, any social or cultural identity elaborating autonomy subjects the system, potentially, to an equipoise of union. Each such moment suggests movement within a dialectically elastic process, especially evident when counterforces are initiated, with reverberations perhaps being felt throughout the system. For example, the object of change may be located at one place (structuring norms) in order to alter another (a cultural frame) while unintentionally effecting others (cultural identity). Because of the elasticity and circularity of cultural communication systems, changes designed to enhance intercultural encounters — like teaching Aboriginal peoples the art of verbal defense in Anglo courts — are often more fleeting than enduring, with sometimes questionable and unintended results — debasing the cultural identity itself.

The studies in the first two parts also help demonstrate three basic social processes which ground the system diagrammed in Fig. 1. Each such system is *historically grounded,* deriving from roots running into its own past, and as is often the case, tapping into many others (Geertz, 1973, p. 89). Each such system, built of its own historical resources, is also *learned* through particular processes of socialization, providing cultural actors with what they are and should be, what they do and should feel, what should be done, in which situations, at which points in life (Scruton, 1979). But further, especially in intercultural encounters, each such system is *locally and interactionally managed* to meet the contingencies of daily life. As Moerman (1988,) noted in his discussion of ways culture speaks, cultural models of persons and knowing

are produced and problematic. They are problematic in that they are contingent, consequential, defeasible, etc. for the members, speakers, actors themselves; problematic because negotiated by the actual situated agents of society, language, and culture. Formulations of . . . 'person' or 'knowing' as entities that exist outside of and determine what happens can never account for what happens. . . . [Dynamics as these] have an interactive, and in that strong sense, social and occasioned structure. (pp. 46–47)

The historically grounded, socially learned, and interactively produced cultural systems brought to intercultural encounters may thus be conceived as invoking these resources — cultural identity, cultural forms, and structuring norms — with each system operating within these basic social processes.

The communication system can be characterized, summarily, as circular, dialectical, historically grounded, learned, and always locally and interactionally managed.

Figure 2 sketches cultural identity as the central element, varying from culture to culture and scene to scene by bases of sociation, loci of motives, and targeted goals.

Cultural identity is conceived here as a most complex interactional accomplishment, built most immediately upon concerns of sociation, motives, and goals, but also linked — as shown earlier — to structuring norms and forms. The concept of cultural identity is linked to other notions of agents, such as "face" (Brown & Levinson, 1978; Goffman, 1967) and "personhood" (Carbaugh, 1988; Geertz, 1976; McHugh, 1989), and may be further elaborated into finer social categories (man/woman, unemployed/employed, elderly) inquiring about the rights and obligations, dimensions

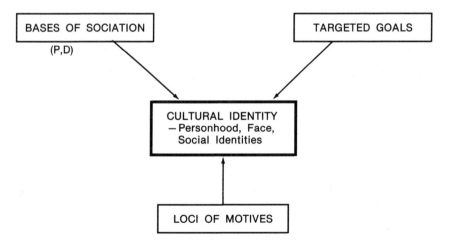

FIG. 2.   The interactional coding of cultural identity.

and types of persons within the social system.[3] The concept *cultural identity* may be used then to raise questions like: What constitutes "face" in cultural systems? What is the actors' sense of the cultural agent? How is it produced interactionally? In what forms? and, How does the cultural communication of it influence intercultural encounters?

Earlier, we examined how several intercultural encounters between Zulu and English, Athabaskan and English, displayed differing bases of sociation for cultural actors, some cueing distance whereas others cued commonality and closeness. Thus, the figure includes the two relational dimensions of power and distance (P, D). Similarly, we noticed that the loci of motives varied, some like the Aboriginal and many South Asians being relationally, rather than individually, motivated, with each targeting distinctive goals, be they consensus, or freedom of expression, respectively. In each intercultural situation, concerns of relational contexting, motivational placing, and targeting may vary (Varonis & Gass, 1985), but within cultural systems the systematic variations are commonly known, leading less to outcomes of asynchrony, and more to those of community.

Figure 2 suggests a framework for describing any cultural identity, suggesting explanations (tracing arrows backwards) both within this main element, and as developed here, between elements, and within the system generally. Other sources of explanation not pictured here, but important are individual variations. Variables such as cognitive complexity, mood, personal taste, psychological traits, skills, physical size, vocal qualities, self-concept and so on undoubtedly influence the moment-to-moment interaction among cultural identities. Such psychological and physical variation is of course operative, and possibly contributes to an overall explanation, but needs to be distinguished analytically, from parameters of cultural variation, the main concerns in the present scheme.

Figure 3 shows culturally coded talk as the central element. Highlighted here are the communicative acts, the forces of acts, and sequences that are identified, evaluated, and performed by actors. Phenomena as these give particular forms to human energy, moving people, when aligned, in similar ways, providing bases for coordinating actions and meanings, but when misaligned, produce asynchrony. As much is evident in the studies in this unit, especially when an Anglo teacher initiates a "review," whereas the students (Zulu and Anglo) conduct a "defense," or when the Aboriginal litigant conducts a cyclical form in an Anglicized context where a linear production is warranted legally.

Culturally coded talk as this can be described by attending to lexical items that identify for actors, during interaction, that which they are saying, and

---

[3]Within each system, such dimensions and types of course need to be discovered and described.

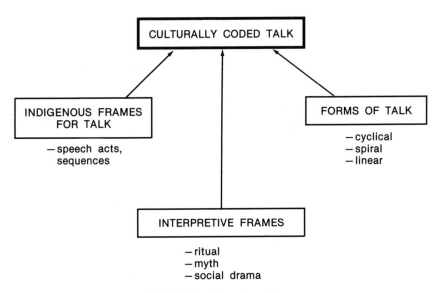

FIG. 3 Cultural frames and forms.

doing.[4] Speech-act theory provides a way of unraveling forces of acts and the cultural features in the sayings (see Part III). Ethnographic and conversation analysis provides complementary ways of formulating sequences (cf. Hymes, 1972; Moerman, 1988; Schegloff, 1972). Of special note with regard to the interpretation of cultural sequences and forms is Philipsen's (1987) formulation of ritual, myth, and social drama as symbolic forms in which to hear cultures in communication. One might come to grips with diversity similarly, by focusing less on sequences and more on the meanings culturally coded in indigenous terms for talk. A recent review of 50 cultural terms for talk found that indigenous terms for talk organized information at three general levels, a literal level about communication itself, a metaphorical level about sociality, and another metaphorical level about personhood, explaining the cultural variation among such terms on the basis of content structuring (Carbaugh, 1989). As is especially apparent in Liberman's study, various shapes of cultural discourses—some more cyclical, others more linear—can also be identified by participants, and analysts (see Carbaugh, 1988, pp. 167–176; Verschueren, 1985, 1987). Of general concern here are the various ways cultural talk is coded by actors, the ways their metacommunicative repertoire is conceived, used, and

---

[4]Introduced here is one domain, terms about talk, the content of which is especially important for understanding cultural forms and frames of talk. Afforded is a view of culturally coded talk from the standpoint of content structuring norms. See Fig. 5.

evaluated. Exploring cultural frames and forms of talk provides one path into the communication of cultural systems, producing media and outcomes complementing those of cultural identity and structuring norms.

Figure 4 presents the central element of structuring norms. Note again the two aspects of communication, normative conduct ("the right thing to do") and practical action ("the thing to do"). Undoubtedly both are operating in communication situations, but the nature, weighting, and value of each may of course vary, from person to person, place to place, culture to culture, and time to time, with each in turn suggesting features of, and intimately related to, cultural forms and identity. The figure helps identify how practical action involves a complex interrelation among the structuring of interaction, information, and content, with these further refined previously.

A recent study helps explore linkages among structuring norms. Anna Wierzbicka (1989) has explored cultural variations in the contents of

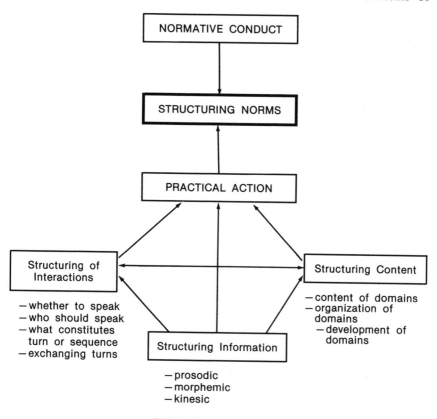

FIG. 4   Structuring norms.

personhood through the categories of "soul" and "mind" in Russian and English. Her interpretations ably show how the English category, "soul" has shifted its meaning from domains more metaphysical and ethical, to those more epistemological. Where "soul" once spoke transcendentally of the good, it now has become a matter more of "mind" and thought. She contrasted the English "soul" with the Russian analogue, *dusa,* revealing the latter's operation within phenomenological and ethical domains. Her detailed discussion is illuminating in many ways, and is particularly relevant to structuring norms, for it identifies in two cultural systems, related terms with each meaningful through distinctive but overlapping domains. She further demonstrates the historical development of the category, "soul," through its general meaning domains in English. She thus, in terms of the present model, ably explores links between content structuring and cultural identities through indigenous terms, but she does not explore particular situations of use or interactional dynamics. She thus suggestes cultural domains, their organization, and development, but does so outside of particular interactional contexts. Wierzbicka acknowledges as much when discussing the Russian *dusa,* "in actual use it is by no means always clear which sense [or domain] is intended" (p. 53). Her study is instructive both because of what it does (suggesting specific domains related to cultural identities, ways they are organized, and developed over time), and what it does not do (linking the structuring of content and its development to interactional structures, cultural frames, and forms of speaking). Without the latter, we are left with a picture of what is communicated, but without a sense of how it is done by people in places. The ways such things are interactionally managed, and how interpretations are cued, are necessary for understanding cultures in communication. Although content and topical domains are too often neglected in cultural studies of communication, little remedy can be found when these are investigated outside of particular social situations, above local patterns of communication. Some specific suggestions for linking these are made by Loveday (1983) where he discusses (following Hymes, 1972, and Van Dijk, 1980,) concepts, respectively, of "scenes" and "archetypical frames."

Considered together, Fig. 4 displays a discursive complex, a particular structuring of interaction, content, and information, suggesting conventional standards for communication practices that, along with normative conduct, helps identify structuring norms in communication, their patterning in cultures, and their use in intercultural encounters.

Figure 5—a bit cumbersome perhaps—attempts to summarize the elements, their subparts, and the interrelations discussed earlier. Hopefully the figure has a degree of utility for three main tasks. First, what do you describe when describing a cultural pattern of communication? The model suggests some elements. It thus seeks a descriptive adequacy, providing a

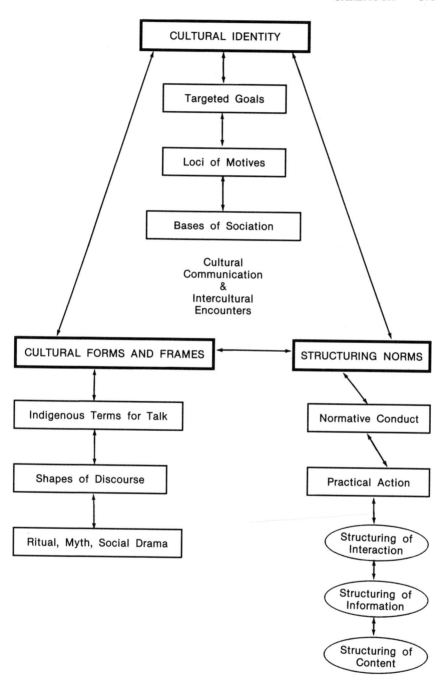

FIG. 5. A tentative heuristic for modeling cultural communication systems.

way to discover and describe particular culture patterns of communication, in social situations, with regard to the display of cultural identity, forms, and norms. Second, how do you explain cultural variations in communication? The model suggests some types of explanation, in terms of cultural communication. By tracing the arrows backwards, explanations are suggested (and one need not stop of course at intermediate places). A variation within one element, for example of a cultural identity, may be explained by variations in its subparts, for example by positing systematic variation in its bases of sociation. Variations between different models of a same element are also suggested. A recent study of politeness and power demonstrates as much when the author accounts, in part, for variations between cultural identities (Japanese and English) by positing variations in the loci of motives for each (relational and individual) (Wetzel, 1988).[5] Explanations are thus suggested within and between elements, and between subparts of elements. With regard to the latter, bases of sociation are undoubtedly related to the ways interaction, information, and content, are structured. The epilogue by Suzanne and Ron Scollon suggests as much for certain Chinese particles. Third, what is suggested for the practice of intercultural communication? Some possible sources and loci of asynchrony in intercultural communication are identified. The figure suggests a framework for monitoring conduct in intercultural encounters, thereby identifying possible sources of problems, which along with education in cultural particulars, suggests ways to proceed.

References

Brown, P., & Levinson, S. (1978). Universals in language usage: Politeness phenomena. In. E. Goody (Ed.), *Questions and politeness: Strategies in social interaction* (pp. 56–310). Cambridge: Cambridge University Press.

Carbaugh, D. (1988). *Talking American: Cultural discourses on "Donahue."* Norwood, NJ: Ablex.

Carbaugh, D. (1988/1989). Deep agony: Self vs. Society in *Donahue* discourse. *Research on Language and Social Interaction, 22,* 179–212.

Carbaugh, D. (1989). Fifty terms for talk: A cross-cultural study. *International and Intercultural Communication Annual, 13,* 93–120.

Dundes, A. (1980). *Interpreting Folklore.* Bloomington, IN: Indiana University Press.

Erickson, F., & Schultz, J. (Eds.). (1982). *The counselor as gatekeeper: Social and cultural organization of communication in counselling interviews.* New York: Academic Press.

Geertz, C. (1973). *The interpretation of cultures.* New York: Basic Books.

Geertz, C. (1976). "From the native's point-of-view": On the nature of anthropological understanding. In K. Basso & H. Selby (Eds.), *Meaning in anthropology* (pp. 221–237). Albuquerque, NM: University of New Mexico Press.

Godard, D. (1977). Same setting, different norms: Phone call beginnings in France and the

---

[5]This same study also explores the communicative structuring of "power," finding its cultural contents so variable that its adoption, as an analytic term, is discouraged.

United States. *Language in Society, 6,* 209-219.

Goffman, E. (1967). *Interaction ritual.* New York: Garden City.

Gudykunst, W. (1985). Intercultural communication: Current status and proposed directions. *Progess in communication sciences, 6,* 1-46.

Gumperz, J. (1978). Dialect and conversational inference in urban communication. *Language in Society, 7,* 393-409.

Gumperz, J. (1982). *Discourse strategies.* Cambridge: Cambridge University Press.

Hall, E. (1976). *Beyond culture.* Nerw York: Doubleday.

Hofstede, G. (1980). *Cultures, consequencces: International differences in work-related values.* Beverly Hills, CA: Sage.

Hymes, D. (1972). Models of the interaction of language and social life. In J. Gumperz & D. Hymes (Eds.), *Directions in sociolinguistics: The ethnography of communication* (pp. 35-71). New York: Holt, Rinehart & Winston.

Hymes, D. (1974). *Foundations in sociolinguistics: An ethnographic approach.* Philadelphia: University of Pennsylvania Press.

Hymes, D. (1986). Discourse: Scope without depth. *International Journal of the Sociology of Language, 57,* 49-89.

Loveday, L. (1983). Rhetoric patterns in conflict: The sociocultural relativity of discourse-organizing processes. *Journal of Pragmatics, 7,* 169-190.

McHugh, E. (1989). Concepts of the person among the gurungs of nepal. *American Ethnologist, 16,* 75-86.

Marriott, M. & Inden, R. (1977). Toward an ethnosociology of South Asian caste systems. In K. David (Ed.), *The new wind: Changing identities in South Asia.* (pp. 227-238). Paris: Mouton.

Moerman, M. (1988). *Talking culture: Ethnography and conversation analysis.* Philadelphia: University of Pennsylvania Press.

Philipsen, G. (1986). Mayor Daley's council speech: A cultural analysis. *Quarterly Journal of Speech, 72,* 247-260.

Philipsen, G. (1987). The prospect for cultural communication. In L. Kincaid (Ed.), *Communication theory: Eastern and western perspectives* (pp. 245-254). New York: Academic Press.

Schegloff, E. (1972). Sequencing in conversational openings. In J. Gumperz & D. Hymes (Eds.), *Directions in sociolinguistics: The ethnography of communication* (pp. 346-380). New York: Holt, Rinehart & Winston.

Scollon, R., & Scollon, S. (1981). *Narrative, literacy, and face in interethnic communication.* Norwood, NJ: Ablex.

Scruton, R. (1979). The significance of common culture. *Philosophy, 54,* 51-70.

Ting-Toomey, S. (1988). Intercultural conflict styles: A face negotiation theory. *International and Intercultural Communication Annual, 12,* 213-235.

Van Dijk, T. (1980). *Textwissenschaft* [The study of discourse]. Munchen: Deutscher Taschenbuch Verlag.

Varonis, E., & Gass, S. (1985). Miscommunication in native/nonnative conversation. *Language in Society, 14,* 327-343.

Verschueren, J. (1985). *What people say they do with words.* Norwood, NJ: Ablex.

Verschueren, J. (1987). *Linguistic action: Some empirical-conceptual studies.* Norwood, NJ: Ablex.

Wetzel, P. (1988). Are "powerless" communication strategies the Japanese norm? *Language in Society, 17,* 555-564.

Wierzbicka, A. (1989). Soul and mind: Linguistic evidence for ethnopsychology and cultural history. *American Anthropologist, 91,* 41-58.

12

Intercultural Communication in Central Australia

KENNETH LIBERMAN

The Aboriginal people of central Australia have evolved a unique form of public discourse. Ordinary public discussion among the Pitjantjatjara, Ngaanyatjarra, Pintupi, and other Western Desert dialect groups proceeds within the constraint that a consensus among discussion participants be preserved. The preservation of this consensus is achieved by the unassertiveness of participants, avoidance of direct argumentation, a deferral of topics that will produce disharmony, and, above all, by an objectification of discourse that is effected by a serial production of summary accounts of the participants' deliberations.

Ordinary Western Desert Aboriginal discourse is characterized by a perpetual monitoring of the progress of a group's discussion, a monitoring that takes the form of a round-the-rally repetition of a candidate summary account for the ongoing talk at hand. These summary accounts, and their repetition, are produced in rapid succession with little regard for who the particular speakers may be, with no respect for proprietary rights to a turn of speaking, without direction from a formal leader or leaders, and generally with the vociferous vocal participation of all present parties.

The serial production of summary accounts constitutes an objective formulation of the talk at hand, displaying (i.e., making publicly available) the developing achievement of the participants in such a way that the parties may move forward in their thinking together — oriented to the objective version of their developing talk — so that when they have secured any substantial conclusion it is already a conclusion that is unanimous. If any dissension is present, the round-the-rally production of accounts is halted and in most instances the gathering will abandon attempts to force a decision. There is a strict refusal to force a way of thinking on others, and so Aboriginal parties will only ratify what is universally supported. Correct Aboriginal discourse is that in which the parties "all speak with one voice" (*wangka kutjungka*).

Throughout Western Desert public discussion, participants try to avoid being exposed personally in public settings, and good interactional style forbids speakers from forcing themselves on fellow participants in a manner that will lead to any such exposure. Embarrassment occurs when public attention becomes focused on a person in a way that individualizes his or her participation. Argument and direct confrontation are avoided, and the success of interaction very much depends on participants being unassertive and remaining open for the collective will of the group. An embarrassed participant has the prerogative of keeping silent, and fellow participants will assist by leading the conversation into other directions. Above all, there is an emphasis on the mutuality of speakers and a devaluation of egoistic presentations of self.

Such a structure of discourse has struck Anglo-Australians with whom Aboriginal people have occasional relations as disorderly, excessively repetitive and as occupying more time than is necessary for making adequate decisions. The first explorers and settlers observed such congenial, collaboratively produced talk and considered it to be evidence of a lack of civilization on the Aboriginals' part. Writing in 1789, Tench observed Aboriginals "talking to each other at the same time with such rapidity and vociferation as I had never before heard" (p. 56). Flinders noted (1814):

> the manners of these people are quick and vehement, and their conversation vociferous like that of most uncivilized people. (p. 66)

And the Frenchman Peron wrote (1809):

> the passions were strongly marked, as they succeeded each other in rapid succession, and their whole figure was changed and modified with their affections. (p. 217)

The vital role of unanimity in Aboriginal experience and the fact that the Aboriginals' capability of proceeding "with one voice" is in fact highly respectful of individual feelings and opinions is something persons of European descent have not appreciated. Accustomed to their own procedures of individualized and dialectical discourse, Europeans have been unable to engage in structures of discourse that are traditional to Aboriginal people.

Representatives from the government, engaging in negotiations with Aboriginal people on a variety of matters, are impatient to reach decisive resolutions. The Aboriginal reluctance to make a decision that fails to meet their consensual standards calls for their taking considerable time before any meaningful decision can occur. Frequently, hesitation by Aboriginal assemblies results in their failure to take advantage of the presence of high-ranking government officials to strike agreements that would be to their benefit. The one day limits that constrain the visits of such officials to remote outback communities almost guarantees such failure. Alternatively, the impatience of Europeans may unintentionally force Aboriginal people to make decisions that have not received the customary validation that can come only from the serial articulation of summary accounts. The inclination of Aboriginal people to preserve congenial relations and their social unassertiveness (both to be distinguished from deference behavior) can lead them to bend under the weight of unintentionally assertive government officials, thereby producing an "agreement" that satisfies the visiting officials but has no real basis.

Throughout Anglo-Australian society traditionally oriented Aboriginal people find themselves confronted by a society whose modes of discursive interaction are contradictory to their own. This is readily apparent in Australian courts of law, where failure to appreciate opposition as a structural feature of English jurisprudence results in Aboriginal people presuming a personal antagonism that in many instances does not exist. Embarrassed by being personally exposed in a public setting and faced with highly assertive courtroom personnel, Aboriginal people find it difficult to articulate a defense, and very frequently concur with any matter that is proposed to them. In this illustration (Liberman, 1981), the Aboriginal defendant agrees with whatever the magistrate suggests:

> Magistrate: Can you read and write?
> Aboriginal Defendant: Yes.
> Sergeant: Can you sign your name?
> A: Yes.
> M: Did you say you cannot read?
> A: Hm.
> M: Can you read or not?!
> A: No.
> M: [Reads statement.] Do you recall making that statement?
> 10 A: Yes.
> M: Is there anything else you want to add to the statement?
> A: [No answer.]
> M: Did you want to say anything else!?
> A: No.
> M: Is there anything in the statement you want to change?
> A: No.
> M: [Reads a second statement.] Do you recall making that statement?
> A: Yes.
> M: Do you wish to add to the statement?
> 20 A: No.

M: Do you want to alter the statement in any way?
A: [Slight nod.]
M: What do you want to alter?
A: [No answer.]
M: Do you want to change the statement?
(1) A: No.

It is doubtful that the Aboriginal understands very much, and it is also questionable whether his "statement," previously tendered to police officers at the station, has any value. He is only guessing what answers will best placate the court, and he generally succeeds in providing the court with what it requires, the exercise of justice notwithstanding. Anglo-Australians miss the overwhelmingly gratuitous character to the Aboriginals' agreement.

A successful defense requires a vigorous ability to argue one's point, but such discourse skills are not common among Aboriginals, whose rhetorical capabilities are more subtle and less confrontational. Unfamiliar with the structure of interaction in Australian courts, Aboriginal people are uncertain even about when they can speak and how much they may say. In the second example (Lester, 1976, pp. 116–119), the Aboriginal Jimmy is doing little more than searching for the place where he may begin to present his side of the story:

Constable: Jimmy, I am going to have to talk to you about something
           that happened yesterday, do you understand that?
Jimmy: Yes.
C: I want you to understand that you do not have to speak to me if you
   don't want to, do you understand that?
J: Yes.
C: What I will do is type on this paper what we say, and it may later be
   shown to the magistrate in court, do you understand that?
J: Yes.
10 C: Do you have to speak to me? (Translator translates.)
J: Yes.
C: Can you tell me what that means?
J: (No answer.)
C: Do you want to tell me anything?
J: Yes.
C: What do you want to talk about?
(2) J: We bin camping we go ask 'im Leo what happened last night. . . .

The Aboriginal person's operating strategy here involves a procedure of sense-assembly locally contingent to the particulars available to him at each turn of speaking. His responses are his best guesses at what will be the least offensive. In a court of law the Aboriginal's natural prerogative to remain silent when talk becomes too individualized is inoperative (even when defendant rights permit silence), and the rules of the court forbid the repetitive discussion with which Aboriginal people are comfortable. During examination, the repetition of questions is not allowed, and this seriously constrains the ability of the prosecutors and Aboriginal witnesses from developing an order for the talk that the Aboriginal witness can recognize and rely on. Even taking oaths is problematic:

> Clerk: The evidence you shall give will be the truth, the whole truth and nothing but the truth, so help me God? Do you understand that?
> Aboriginal Witness: (No answer.)
> C: Please say, "So help me God."
> A: (No answer.)
> C: Say, "So help me God."
> A: (No answer.)
> (Court accepts the Aboriginal's silence.)
> . . .
> 10 Magistrate: He didn't say, "So help me God."
> Clerk: Say, "So help me God."
> (3) Aboriginal Witness: So help me God.

Occasionally the meaning of the oath is translated for Aboriginal witnesses by a court appointed translator, but these translations — *wangka palya* (talk good) and *wangka tjukurala* (talk straight), and the like — create more difficulties than they solve. *Wangka palya* is often used at Aboriginal gatherings, when no Europeans are present, to mean, "Let's keep our talk harmonious," and this translation of the oath will likely be interpreted as something like, "Don't make anyone upset," an instruction damaging to an Aboriginal person's willingness to defend himself in the court. Here again, the more forceful and aggressive style of Europeans is able to overwhelm their Aboriginal partners.

Aboriginal children suffer from similar difficulties when in attendance at Australian schools. Australian researchers (Malcolm, 1979) have found that White teachers complain about Aboriginal children's failure to respond to questions, the inadequate volume of Aboriginal speakers' voices, and failure to look up or to look the teacher "in the eye." These problems result from the Aboriginal child feeling embarrassed when called on to stand up and address the class in the individualized and exposed manner common to European classroom discourse. In Aboriginal society it is impolite to look directly into another person's eyes; looking aside, speaking moderately, and even covering one's face slightly with one's hands are all actions that demonstrate a commendable self-depreciation and respect for others. Silence is not viewed to be insolence; on the contrary, it is evidence of good manners. What is more, any egoistic behavior is out of place.

Australian teachers also complain that Aboriginal answers, when given, are too frequently single-worded responses and are highly repetitive of what has already been said. Single-worded responses are common summary accounts, even preferable ones because Aboriginal interlocutors strive to capsulize their collaboratively produced accounts in the briefest possible objective form (cf. Liberman, 1982). And repetition is the delight of Aboriginal discursive life—it permits all participants to share in the produced agreement and is the vehicle for a celebration of congeniality. Further, teachers complained that requests of the children are more like statements or observations, but this is consistent with their avoidance of personalized talk and their inclination to proceed according to objective statements.

Teachers report that Aboriginal children say too little when called on to speak, yet talk too much when they are not being addressed, and that much of such talk is characterized by a failure to wait for another to finish speaking, a failure to "take turns." Like Tench and Flinders two centuries before, the coherence of the serial order of Aboriginal talk is missed and the network of interlocutors collaborating in a productive effort is unrecognized. For the Aboriginals' part, they are confronted by notions of "proper decorum" that they find not only strange but suspect. Although the Aboriginal children are participating as an ensemble, monitoring their behavior carefully with regard to the other Aboriginal children in the class (Malcolm, 1979), the teacher is perceiving them as a gathering of individual members. In such a fashion teachers miss essentially the mutuality that is the basis of the Aboriginals' participation in the class.

In fact, Australian educators have viewed the secondary socialization of Aboriginal children in Australian schools as a frank effort to individualize their collective modes of self-perception and social interaction:

> School helps the child to move away from collective to individualistic orientation. This is the movement for autonomy. By acquiring knowledge the child begins to acquire a status. Increased internal control helps a child to live as an individual, and as a person. Development of personal autonomy— freedom to choose a life and freedom to live it—is a necessary function of school. However, this may increase competitive orientation in the child. He may have problems of working together with other members. This problem may be a realistic one. (Pareek 1976, p. 106)

Such interactional asymmetries are repeated throughout Australian society, in all the ordinary contacts Aboriginal people have with Anglo-Australians.

Disagreement is viewed by Whites to be a mark of one's individuality and ability to think for oneself; frequently, it is considered an asset to be a "good competitor." The unobtrusive style of Aboriginal people leads to their being easily dismissed as being without substance. When European interaction individualizes the participants, Aboriginal people feel embarrassed, and this limits their effectiveness. The more forceful style of self-presentation of Anglo-Australians is sometimes viewed to be evidence of anger where none exists. What is certain is that the relative assertiveness of most Europeans in ordinary interaction assists their dominance over Aboriginal people.

For the most part, Anglo-Australians are unaware of the constraints that their style of sociability places on Aboriginal people, for they know it only as their natural mode of participation in social life. Regrettably, Aboriginal failures to satisfy European demands of discourse are viewed to be grounds for their reeducation, ad hoc or by way of formal institutions. It may be said that after a century of contact in central Australia, such re-education has met with little success, as Aboriginal people have adhered to their own structures of interaction. Is is unfortunate, however, that so few of these mutually produced obstacles to communication, occurring as structural features of Aboriginal/Anglo-Australian interaction, have been recognized by the parties involved.

References

Flinders, M. (1814). *A voyage to terra Australis.* London: G. & W. Nicol.

Lester, Y. (1976). Courtroom testimony. *Legal Aid Bulletin,* pp. 116–119.

Liberman, K. (1981). Understanding Aborigines in Australian courts of law. *Human Organization, 40* (3), 247–255.

Liberman, K. (1982). The organization of talk in Aboriginal community decision making. *Anthropological Forum, 5* (1), 38–53.

Malcolm, I. (1979). *Classroom communication and the Aboriginal child.* Perth: University of Western Australia.

Pareek, U. (1976). Orientation toward work and school. In G. E. Kearney & D. W. McElwain (Eds.), *Aboriginal cognition* (pp. 98–112). Canberra: Australian Institute of Aboriginal Studies.

Tench, W. (1789). *A narrative of the expedition to Botany Bay.* London: J. Debrett.

13

An Ethnomethodological Agenda in the Study of Intercultural Communication

KENNETH LIBERMAN
University of Oregon

The majority of studies of intercultural communication may be divided into two branches of inquiry: one branch that emphasizes the cultural bases of interactional conflict and missed communication and one branch that examines the linguistic, paralinguistic, or conceptual foundations of communication from a more or less phenomenological perspective. These two agendas in intercultural communication research are not antagonistic, yet they are rarely combined, such as I attempted in the previous chapter.

The former approach to the study of intercultural communication trades in broad, although frequently apt, generalization and pays special attention to the objective political consequences of missed communication. The analyst generates ideal typical explanations of the actions of parties to an interaction, and these explanations are based on observations about the character of discourse or usual interaction in the respective parties' cultures. An illustration of such a research strategy, taken from the foregoing study, is the contrast I drew between the individualized character of Anglo-Australian discourse and the more corporate orientation of Aboriginal discourse, which places "an emphasis upon the mutuality of speakers and a devaluation of egoistic presentations of self" (p. 178). To draw this contrast and then "talk about" the interactional problems in Australian classrooms that occur when teachers call on Aboriginal children to rise and address the class does not provide the reader (or the analyst) with the material detail of the phenomenon itself, in the form of verbatim transcripts of the interaction and an assessment (based on the contingent detail such transcripts provide) of the interactive work in which each party is engaged.

The latter approach, an approach that is ethnomethodological, is concerned with examining the material detail of a conversation, and its interest is to locate the technical problems that parties face in a given attempt to communicate. These analysts investigate how each party is assembling together the sense of a conversation, and the perspective offered is that of the parties themselves, as each is embedded in the contingent details of the conversation. An illustration of this approach can be found in the transcript in chapter 12 (pp. 179–180), in which the Aboriginal defendant is engaged in a strategy of determining which answers will best placate the court and is not working out a strategy for his legal defense. At the point of each reply, the transcript displays the Aboriginal defendant's able search for the "Yes," "No," or "Hm," that will best placate the court's interrogation, although the magistrate is unaware of the facile nature of the testimony. Here the analytic deductions are tied to the material detail of the interaction that the transcript offers.

The Cultural–Political Agenda

The inquiry into the cultural–political bases of missed communication involves a procedure that develops ideal types for cultural behavior and then invokes these ideal types in characterizing generally the nature of the conflicts that occur. This conforms with a requirement that European culture demands of its analysts: phenomena must be rendered as representational versions of themselves that are then amenable to rational manipulation. Martin Heidegger (1973) described succinctly this European representational praxis as "the reinterpretation of Being as objectivity and representedness" (p. 88). Within this praxis the wordly phenomena themselves are lost and their objective representations stand in their stead. Accordingly, an ideal type is developed (e.g., some variety of the observation that Japanese are introverted, whereas Americans are extroverted, or that Aboriginal people are corporate in their social orientation while Anglo-Australians are individualistic) and then the ideal typicalities are put into the heads of the actors whose intercultural communication the analyst is attempting to explain. Under such a procedure, some serious analytic victories may be won (e.g., Aboriginal children do not speak as eloquently when called on as they do when they are speaking together among themselves, which explains the "teachers' complaint" discussed on pp. 181–182), but detailed explications of embedded conversational detail is usually foregone.

The difficulty with such a mode of analysis is that the corporate nature of Aboriginal discourse, for example, does not achieve its character or its efficacy from how the analyst might generalize about it. It is not what the analyst can say about it that matters, but what in the end it amounts to, as the only thing an ideal type could be about — interactional phenomena in the world. There is no "corporate character," there is only the actual discourse and interaction of Aboriginal people. Put another way, *corporate character* has no "essence;" similarly, *individualism* is only what it is as the social practices of which it is composed, and these practices need to be identified in their specificity. Giving ontological priority to the ideal type is a form of mystification, a relic of the Platonic essence extant in modern civilization.

The Ethnomethodological Agenda

The ethnomethodological inquiry is oriented to what is taking place in the understanding of interacting parties. One can think of it as an ethnoher-meneutic concern, in that the objects of investigation are the strategies of "interpretation" that are employed by the parties concerned. To be sure, all interactants are engaged in understanding their interaction, regardless of whether they are in an intercultural context or not, but this does not mitigate the fact that the interpretative efforts of parties are critical to any intercultural communication.

It is the first requirement of an ethnomethodological study to find just where any ideal typical features of culture are located, in and as the practices they are. These practices are not necessarily deliberate or rational, but they are there in the interaction, as the conversation itself carries along its participants to places and possibilities none of them may have charted. Participants are met frequently with a swarm of communicative possibilities, and they are very skillful at coping with them. The Aboriginal defendant in chapter 12 (p. 179) is brilliant at determining when the appropriate gratuitous reply is a "No," instead of a "Yes,"; and his "Hm" is no less capable. The court misses entirely the purport of his replies and turns them into legally competent interaction, inscribed into the court record that stands as written evidence for this competence. But many sociolinguists are no different. Frequently, an interpretation is derived from analytic achievements, which preexist the conversation; a written transcript may even be invoked along with its analytic interpretation as evidence of the accuracy of the explanation. What is not invoked is the horizon of possible sense to which the participants to a conversation are addressed, each in his or her own way. Although it frequently seems as if participants were single-minded in their interests and motivations, in most instances they remain open to avenues of possible sense, for which only the solution retrospectively institutes any convergence. This open horizon is a critical feature of the never resting understanding of the parties. Sans the open horizon, the parties are made over into marionettes, with the analyst "minding" the strings.

Phenomenology

Phenomenologists treat linguistic signs as objects, available to all persons for interpretation, although not necessarily in the same way. As Husserl

(1969) wrote in the fourth Cartesian meditation, "Objects exist for me, and are for me what they are only as objects of actual and possible consciousness" (p. 65). That is to say, linguistic signs are not merely what they are in themselves, they are what consciousness makes out of them. But this, too, is an overly rationalistic reduction of what is occurring, for it views consciousness as some sort of calculating machine that controls its field of operations.[1] Consciousness does not "produce" anything; rather, it is caught up in and carried along by the field of signification-pregnant activities that compose the conversation. As Wittgenstein (1972) observed, "Understanding is not a mental process" (p. 61). Understanding is a social activity and is embedded in the various systems of articulation of signs, and rearticulation, that provide parties to a conversation with a developing, never completed structure of opportunities for communication. And we are involved in that field of practical activities in ways that are not reflective. These ways need to be investigated, but the rationalistic prejudice of much sociolinguistic analysis militates against this.

If the ways of our practical understanding are in some part unreflective, then the task of securing analytic access to the work of that understanding is all the more problematic. Although the tools of classical phenomenology have opened the way to such an inquiry, they are not fully adequate to carry out the investigation. We need to locate social phenomena in which the practical work of understanding can be made observable, and so available for analysis. In taking up the study of intercultural communication, ethnomethodology provides us with a perspicuous instance of observable understanding, observable there because communication is so frequently breaking down.

The Horizontal Character of Understanding

We retain from phenomenology, however, its interest in the horizontal character of understanding; that is, the "open horizon" across which parties to an intercultural conversation are searching for practical solutions to the communicative problems that face them is retained in the analysis. This open horizon is never lost sight of. It is that which stands "ahead of" the participants: "The germ of universality . . . is to be found ahead of us in the dialogue into which our experience of other people throws us by means of a movement not all of whose sources are known to us" (Merleau-Ponty, 1964, p. xv).

Because the horizon is open, it is not settled. All the solutions are never

---

[1]Such "control" is symptomatic of the moral individualism of logocentric European rationality.

in hand. Indeed, the indeterminate character of understanding is critical to the interaction. Indeterminacy is the vague yet progenerative medium that "points ahead to possible perceptual multiplicities" (Husserl, 1982, p. 94). Meanings are rarely clear and distinct, fully determined. Meanings are fluid:

> the meaning of meaning . . . is infinite implication, the indefinite referral of signifier to signifier . . . its force is a certain pure and infinite equivocality which gives signified meaning no respite, no rest, but engages in its own *economy* so that it always signifies again and differs (Derrida, 1978, p. 25)

Garfinkel taught us that the meaning of every utterance in a conversation bears an etcetera that offers to one's conversational partners the observation that what is meant cannot be reduced to just so many words, but that its sense is apparent nevertheless and includes even what cannot be foreseen at present but what will come to seem reasonable as the interaction progresses. In intercultural communication, this etcetera is license for permitting an indeterminacy to persist that is perhaps greater than that found in monocultural interaction, or at least it seems so. As Garfinkel (1979) commented in another context:

> There is an etcetera. But it is not an etcetera that is left over, it is an etcetera that is the inhabitant of the house. And it is not even a mysterious inhabitant. It is not something wistfully waving around in the air—it is the most cogent, practical thing. It is the activity we engage in, the open horizon which inhabits the world.

Thus, the indeterminacy "is not something wistfully waving around in the air" as some vague generality. It is a "determined indeterminacy" (Husserl, 1962, p. 125). It exists specifically as possible lines of signification to be taken up, roads to be travelled, or what William James termed *fringe meanings*. But it turns out these indeterminate meanings are not quite so "fringe"; or if they are marginal, then all signification is marginalized. It is impossible to understand interaction between Aboriginal people and Anglo-Australians without a deep appreciation of the material consequences of this indeterminacy, and this appreciation is available only when one has captured the open horizon of the progressively developing sense to which the parties—as their own enterprise and expertise—are addressed.

In intercultural communication, neither the analyst nor the participants can demand that everything be made explicit, that meanings be definite. The meaning of words depends on their use, not on being interrogated. As participants, we must "play along," letting the others presume we are full participants, so that we may be able to witness the realm of signification in which some incomprehensible talk will come to find its sense. Capturing the looks of this horizon of possible signification "ahead" of parties is an important task of the discourse analyst.

Post-Phenomenology

If meanings were fully determinate in intercultural communication, then, as analysts, we should preserve this determinacy. But if meanings have an indeterminate character—if participants are capable of talking with each other incomprehensibly—then as analysts we need to capture and preserve this indeterminacy and not make up tidy stories for the telling. In this way the work of understanding in its postmodern sense can be made observable. Here ethnomethodology can make an original and much needed contribution to postmodern thought.

Talk of *sense-assembly* was useful in studies of intercultural communication during the phenomenological phase of analysis; however, the term is flawed because it lays far too much emphasis upon rational, fully deliberative conceptualization. A more accurate portrayal of what is occurring in intercultural communication may be provided by recognizing that neither participant is in full control of the work of signification of even her own utterances. Rather, the utterances find their possible signification according to what they achieve in the interaction, and gradually a field of signification is articulated that is open and yet provides the participants with what communicative possibilities are materially at hand. The participants are tied to the equipmental detail of this emerging field. The potential meanings that accompany this field of local detail established by utterances is more than participants can account for, yet it is within this field that parties to intercultural communication engage in their skillful work of communicating. In a figure, persons are not the masters of their speech, as in the classical (individualist) phenomenological model, according to which one party speaks and the second interprets:

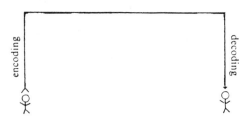

Instead, both parties are addressed to a practical field of emerging local detail (material, equipmental detail: actual signs in their syntagmatic organization) that offers a plenum of possible meanings and associations:

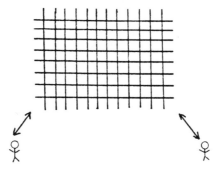

This field of signification is constantly shifting. As soon as the meaning of one sign changes, the rest of them slip, as they are each held in place by their relations with all the others. This very slippage of meanings is a fertile arena of investigation for intercultural communication studies. Further, one can have an idea about what one's partner means, yet not know explicitly.

"I know what this is all about." But what is it all about? I should not want to say. (Wittgenstein, 1972, p. 143)

Even an experience is not, and never is, perceived in its completeness, it cannot be grasped adequately in its full unity. It is essentially something that flows, and starting from the present moment we can swim after it, our gaze reflectively turned towards it, whilst the stretches we leave in our wake are lost to our perception. (Husserl, 1962, p. 127)

This refers us to a peculiar phenomenon well known to students of intercultural communication: parties are capable of speaking without being sure of what the other is meaning; that is to say, parties are capable of speaking incomprehensibly. But they are not speaking in a vacuum, they are oriented to the collaboratively generated field of signification that is constantly shifting. As Geertz (1973) has observed, "Thinking is a public activity" (p. 360). The field carries the participants, who muster what inscriptions they can. But here observe something important: Geertz' statement is only a proclamation; he never specified in detail just how thinking is public. As Moerman (1988) wrote in a similar context, " 'Person-definition' is connected to the 'symbolic order' solely by stipulation . . . Geertz' studies of the person in Bali explicates words without recourse to the social organization that gives them meaning" (pp. 88–89, 99). Here we seek a more precise display of the public character of thinking. My study of the competent system of Australian Aboriginal discourse (Liberman 1985, cf. chapter 2) can serve as a concrete illustration of an ethnomethodological approach to the question.

What is going on in people's heads? Well, it is not so much in their heads as between them, let us say in the developing structures or practices of communication, in that very field of equipmental detail. Garfinkel (n.d.) wrote "Accountable thinking and knowing must be put back into the world . . . into the very places where thinking and knowing are first encountered as the most obvious facts of life, namely in the looks of ordinary things". Analysts of intercultural communication need to pay more attention to the looks of things for parties to the interaction.

As the multicultural character of social interaction increases, investigations of intercultural communication with this ethnomethodological agenda are required. Such studies need not be carried out at the expense of the cultural–political agenda, for both perspectives refer to modalities of communication that operate, with no time off. Cultural–political studies should incorporate the orientation to the contingent material details of communication that ethnomethodological analysis provides, and ethnomethodological analysts should apply their discoveries to the vital cultural–political issues that are always at stake. Although I have been arguing for closer attention to be paid to the ethnomethodological agenda, what I am really arguing for is a convergence of perspectives.

References

Derrida, J. (1978). *Writing and difference*. London: Routledge.

Garfinkel, H. (1979). University lectures, UCLA, Los Angeles, CA.

Garfinkel, H. (1987). *Ethnomethodological studies of work*. London: Routledge.

Geertz, C. (1973). *Interpretation of cultures*. New York: Basic Books.

Heidegger, M. (1973). *The end of philosophy*. New York: Harper & Row.

Husserl, E. (1962). Husserl, E. (1969). *Cartesian meditations*. The Hague: Martinus Nijhoff. *Ideas: General introduction to pure phenomenology*. (W.R.B. Gibson, Trans.). London: Collier-Macmillan.

Husserl, E. (1982). *Ideas pertaining to a pure phenomenology*. (F. Kersten, Trans.). The Hague: Martinus Nijhoff.

Liberman, K. (1982). The economy of central Australian aboriginal expression: An inspection from the vantage of Merleau-Ponty and Derrida. *Semiotica 40*, (3/4), 267–346.

Liberman, K. (1985). *Understanding interaction in central Australia: An ethnomethodology of Australian aboriginal people*. London: Routledge.

Merleau-Ponty, M. (1964). *Sense and non-sense*. Evanston, IL: North-western University Press.

Moerman, M. (1988). *Talking culture: Ethnography and conversational analysis*. Philadelphia: University of Pennsylvania Press.

Wittgenstein, L. (1972). *Philosophical investigations*. Oxford: Basil Blackwell.

14
Force Fields in Black and White Communication

THOMAS KOCHMAN

The differing potencies of black and white public presentations are a regular cause of communicative conflict. Black presentations are emotionally intense, dynamic, and demonstrative; white presentations are more modest and emotionally restrained. Where whites use the relatively detached and unemotional *discussion* mode to engage an issue, blacks use the more emotionally intense and involving mode of *argument*. Where whites tend to *understate* their exceptional talents and abilities, blacks tend to *boast* about theirs. Where white men— meeting women for the first time—*defuse* the potency of their sexual messages by disguising their sexual content, black men make their sexual interest explicit and hope to *infuse* their presentations with sexual potency through artful, bold, and audacious sexual proposals.

In essence, the black speech acts and events—argument, woofing, cursing, sounding, boasting, rapping, load-talking—have animation and vitality as their key attributes. As Paul Carter Harrison has noted, "The word MUTHAFUKA, however profane, owns more force than the tentative invective of GOSH DAMN! when trying to harmonize the vitiating effects of a depressed mode" (1972, p. xix). One even might consider animation and vitality *necessary* attributes for these speeach acts and events to qualify *as* black.

Blacks and whites also have conflicting attitudes on the appropriateness of more or less potent forms of expressive behavior. Blacks favor forceful outputs. Beth Day, a white anthropologist who worked among blacks in the South, reported that the friendships that she had been able to establish with some blacks were in part attributable to her vigorously expressive nonverbal behavior. Blacks told her, "You don't hold back from a handshake," "When you laugh you are not afraid to make a big noise," "Your smile is open, like a child's" (Day 1974, p. 186). Consistent with this view, blacks regard more subdued or restrained expressive outputs as "cold," "dead," or not "for real." Thus one black woman whose expressive behavior tends to be low-keyed said that she occasionally finds herself criticized by other blacks for "acting white," blacks typically associating unemotional and undemonstrative behavior with whites. As Kenneth Johnson notes, the black pejorative racial label "gray" characterizes the lifelessness that blacks see in whites' unimpassioned behavior (Johnson 1972, pp. 144–45). Whites, for their part, favor more modest and subdued outputs, regarding more forceful expressive behavior as "irresponsible" or in "bad taste." As a result, in contexts where white standards and prescriptions prevail, blacks often find their more intensely expressive behavior criticized as a result. Joan McCarty reported receiving such criticism some years ago while watching *Lysistrata* for the first time at the university theater. As she described it, she was laughing heartily, thoroughly enjoying the play's bawdiness and humor, when a white woman turned to her and said, "You are really outrageous!" McCarty, hurt by the remark, asked what was wrong. The white woman replied, "You are laughing *so* loud. I mean, come on! It's funny, but . . . ." McCarty said, "Daag. It's a comedy. Ain't you supposed to laugh?" But as she reflected in her report of the incident, "that was just seen as inappropriate, rude behavior. I guess I was supposed to feel the laughter, but not express it, at least not in the way that I felt it."

Emotional Force

The animation and vitality of black expressive behavior is in part owing to the emotional force or spiritual energy that blacks habitually invest in their public presentations and the functional role that emotions play in realizing the goals of black interactions, activities, and events.

For example, a common goal of black cultural activities and events is the revitalization of energy through emotional and spiritual release. To achieve this, three elements are necessary: (1) a sufficiently powerful agent-stimulus to activate the emotional (spiritual) forces that the body has imprisoned, (2) a structure like song, dance, or drum that allows for the unrestricted expression of those forces that the agent-stimulus has aroused, and (3) a manner of participation that gives full value to the power of the agent-stimulus and to the individual's ability to receive and manipulate it. This manner of participation entails a mind/body involvement of considerable depth, what blacks call *getting down into* the mode through which emotional release and spiritual rejuvenation are effected. Harrison speaks of the "gut-rending song of the blues singer who virtually *gets down* into the mode of sadness, happy to be blue, so as to purge the soul of sorrow by dealing directly with the onus of his wretchedness" (1972, p. xx). Linda Wharton and Jack Daniel describe getting down at a black social gathering in which a lead couple—through the dance structure known as *solo and circle*—is called upon to improvise a basic dance step. This couple is then encouraged by others, who start clapping and yelling, " 'Git down, baby! throw down! Oh, Lawd,' thus spurring the soloists on to unimagined spontaneous creativity." As Wharton and Daniel describe the event,

Aunt Pewee, pushed further by the people and possibly the liquor too, has thrown off her shoes—ready to sho nuff git down!

James Brown is hitting loose boodie, and Pewee is gone, doing her thang. Now Aunt Bertha, who is dancing along with Pewee just lifted up her skirt slightly over her right knee exposing half of the left thigh. At this point she is ready to burn Pewee. Uncle John yells, "Look out now, move on over Pewee. Make room for Big Bert!" Suddenly just as Aunt Bertha hit her best lick, Pewee goes off, off into a frenzie, doing movements she didn't know she could do. Pewee went down to the floor, did her split, rolled over twice, and in one twirl spun around and stood straight on her toes. Aunt Bertha, as you would expect, sat down and everybody continued to party the night away. [1977, pp. 78–79]

The black cultural pattern of *call and response* is basic to black expressive behavior because it integrates all three elements of stimulus, structure, and manner of participation (response) into a working relationship with one another. Like solo and circle in dance, call and response embodies an interlocking and synergistic dimension, in which members of the group participate by adding their own voice to those of others, to serve both as counterpoint and counterforce, alternating stimulating others and receiving the stimulus of others until collective spiritual release and regeneration is achieved.

Within the more formal call and response structure, as in a black Baptist church service, the preacher is generally identified with the call, that is, the one who supplies the initial activating stimulus. But, as Geneva Smitherman has pointed out, the word force of the preacher that functions as the call in the church service is itself a *response* to an earlier call to preach (1977, p. 110). And it is from this spiritual connection to his own calling that the preacher derives a good measure of his word power to invoke (call) the spirit in others. The spiritual connection of the audience to the preacher and his call is shown by the emotional intensity of their response, which in turn spiritually binds the preacher to his audience and, in the energy that it transmits to the preacher, functions also as a further call to preach (Holt 1972b, p. 192). Within the reciprocal and interlocking call and response structure, each call is itself a response and each response a further activating call.

In secular performances, call and response also underlies *doing your thing*, which in black culture does not mean, as it has come to be translated in white culture, acting independently of the group. Rather, as Roger Abrahams has noted and as the dance example offered by Wharton and Daniel illustrates, doing your thing means asserting yourself *within* the group, such as entering into a performance by adding your voice to the ensemble, by playing off against others—competitively and cooperatively at the same time—as each instrument does in jazz (Abrahams 1976, p. 83). It is, as Harrison states, "an invitation to bring YOUR OWN THING into a complementary relationship with the mode, so that . . . all might benefit from its power" (1972, p. 73).

Blacks also incorporate call and response into their more casual, everyday expressive routines. Thus the rhythmic style of walking that blacks call *bopping* represents a feeling action response to impulses coming from within. Yet bopping also sets a tempo for others to play with, on, off of, or against: a *beat* to ignite their sensibilities and actions. When activated, these also serve in reciprocal fashion, to revitalize the initial rhythmic step that sets off the exchange. Likewise, the hand-to-hand exchange that blacks call *giving skin* is invigorated by its connection to inner impulses and feelings and one's spiritual connection with others in the group. The genuineness and strength of both connections act as a catalyst to ignite the sensibilities and actions of others who respond by giving skin in return (Cooke 1972, p. 42). The integrated structuring of elements within call and response means that giving is getting and getting giving, in a rhythmic, interlocking, escalating, synergistic go-round.

The development of blacks' capacity for intense and spontaneous emotional behavior occurs within the framework of patterns—like song, dance, drum, call and response, or simply the speech channel—that allow for or can be manipulated to accommodate, free and uninhibited emotional expressions. For example, the structure of call and response places the intervals for calls and responses very close together, thereby enabling feelings to be expressed at or near the moment they are being felt. One can even say that if the audience and performer are spiritually locked into the cadence of the call and response pattern, the impulses and their release will occur almost simultaneously. Nonetheless, one cannot just come in *any* time. One must "drop in" or "drop out," as Grace Holt has said, in such a way that will not interrupt the rhythmic interactive flow. The same is true of black musical performances. As Charles Keil puts it, feeling is engendered to the extent that the rhythms conflict with or exhibit the pulse without destroying it altogether. Consequently, entering any ongoing black performance and being considered *on* time, whether it be music, conversation, or argument, requires that individuals coming in keep "careful track of the pulse" (Holt 1972a, p. 67; Keil 1966a, p. 345).

Emotionally intense black responses also occur because there are no restrictions on how forceful emotions can be expressed. The only requirement here, perhaps, is that the level of expression of feelings genuinely reflects the intensity with which they are felt. An obviously exaggerated response would therefore probably be considered inappropriate. Understated or muted responses would, since they not only belie the potency of the spiritual invocation (call); they are also dysfunctional in working toward generating the kind of intense emotional drive and energy necessary to achieve spiritual release.

Responses are obligatory within the call and response pattern. Thus, while there is considerable variation in the *kinds* of responses that individuals may give, some response is nevertheless called for when the slot within the structure designates that it should occur. As Smitherman notes, about the only *incorrect* thing you can do is not to respond at all (1977, p. 108). The main function of responses is to sustain the spiritual connection between performers and their audience. But the nature of the response also communicates to performers how they are *getting over* (Daniel and Smitherman 1976, p. 47). When no response is forthcoming, blacks are doubly chagrined; they are denied the feedback which they habitually use and upon which they rely to assess and sustain their ongoing performance. Black performers have been known to criticize an audience for their non-participation, or the indifferent manner of their participation, as I saw one black singer comment upon to a black high school audience she was entertaining, for making her work up there on the stage "all by herself."

The habitual use of the call and response pattern in black everyday presentations has led to communicative conflict with whites, who do not use the pattern. As Smitherman points out, black speakers tend to infer from the absence of a response that the whites to whom they are speaking are not listening. White speakers tend to infer from various responses like "Dig it!" or "I hear you!" which blacks consider necessary and appropriate interpolations to an ongoing performance—like saying "uh-huh" periodically on the telephone to let the speaker on the other end know that you are still listening—that blacks are constantly *interrupting* them (Smitherman 1977, p. 118).

Emotional expressiveness has considerably less force and effect in white cultural activities and events, because white norms for proper participation require that individuals exercise greater emotional self-restraint. For example, even where whites are given some latitude for emotional expression, as is the case when they are members of an audience at concerts or plays, the intervals between times when emotions are aroused and when they can appropriately be expressed are much further apart than with black call and response. Far from enabling feelings to be expressed at or near the moment they are being felt, white protocol here obliges audience members to check their impulses and contain aroused feelings until the appropriate moment.

Furthermore, even when the authorized moment for the release of feelings comes, the level at which these may be expressed is to be determined principally not by the force of the feelings themselves—as at black performances—but by the norms that are embodied in the white concept of *good taste*, which have set ceilings on how intense expressive behavior may appropriately become (Slater 1976, pp. 114–15).

The protocol pertinent at such white performances as concerts or plays allows for some emotional display, however contained. But the norms governing proper participation in other white cultural activities and events hardly allow any, let alone emotional display of any intensity. For example, the engagement of individuals in public discussion of an issue, without having their rationality or emotional maturity called into question requires that they also keep their emotions contained and relatively subdued. To engage in "polite conversation" requires that individuals keep emotions in check and avoid issues about which poeple are likely to have strong feelings. Like Trevor Patemen's "idle discourse," polite conversation is static rather than dynamic: "Once begun it aims only to stay where it is" (Pateman 1975, p. 40).

Other everyday public presentations are expected to be governed by the standards for "proper demeanor," which, as Erving Goffman notes, in white culture includes such attributes as modesty in claims regarding self and self-control over emotions (1967, p. 77). Note that "self-control" here should be understood as the ability of individuals to check impulses and contain feelings rather than, for example, to be able to manage them at more intense levels of expression or, as Philip Slater has observed, to be able to call upon a particular emotion when you want it (Slater 1976, p. 33).

Whites rely heavily upon the ability of individuals to exercise self-restraint in realizing the norms for proper social conduct in public contexts. But as a safeguard, they also invest individuals acting as *others* with the social right to intervene to restore a more subdued public tone should people, following their emotions, produce behavior that is too potently expressive. Note that this special right of others to intervene directly is restricted to containing or suppressing what white cultural norms have determined is unduly forceful assertive or expressive behavior. However, others are given no special social rights to *induce* more active or forceful behavior, as when muted participation or nonparticipation is dysfunctional, even to levels that white norms would consider appropriate. That is why it is easier to suppress irresponsible self-assertion in the classroom than to overcome irresponsible nonassertion. White students will yield to intervention by others to produce the first result—conceding that others have a role as custodians of public order—but will not yield to intervention by other (black students or the instructor) to produce the second result, viewing the right to muted or nonparticipation to belong entirely to individuals themselves.

White culture also grants individuals acting as "others" an indirect role in working against more forceful expressive or assertive behavior. It does this by presuming the sensibilities of "others" to be susceptible and by the interactional rule that says that individuals should moderate the forcefulness of their behavior to the level that others can tolerate. Both the presumption and the rule are manifest in the caution that whites often express about not doing or saying anything that might "hurt other people's feelings."

Capacities

Whites' capacity for exercising emotional self-restraint is developed by the standards set for proper participation in white cultural activities and events in which emotional expression is seen as having little or no functional role. But this capacity for exercising emotional self-restraint operates effectively only when other people are also exercising emotional self-restraint, which is to say, when everyone cooperates in keeping the expressive intensity of public interaction low. It is a gentleman's agreement within white social circles that self-control over emotions should not be made more of an exercise than it already is. And to keep self-restraint from becoming too much of a strain, whites also choose outputs and environments that have low stimulus value, thereby minimizing their capacity to arouse and excite. As Slater notes, clothes should be drab and inconspicuous, colors of low intensity, sounds quiet, smells nonexistent, words emotionless (1976, p. 115). But these concerns and precautions also indicate that self-restraint can become too much of an exercise for whites when the level of interaction becomes expressively intense. This is because white culture develops controls to contain emotions, but few or no controls to manage them at more intense levels of expression. Rather, whites typically consider self-control over emotions to have broken down when such emotionally intense interaction occurs. And for them it has, which is one reason why others intervene when individuals begin to behave in a loud and emotional fashion.

This lack of control over emotions at more expressively intense levels also affects the capacity and willingness of whites to engage in spontaneous and intense emotional behavior. A lifetime of practicing emotional self-restraint enhances a capacity for such self-restraint, but it does not develop a reciprocal ability to *let go* emotionally, or confidence in one's ability to control the impact of intense emotions once they are expressed. This "incapacity" affects the way white actors project emotions on the stage. For example, Harrison notes that actors in the American theater operate under the concept of *affective memory*, which tries to recall emotional events in order to approximate the tensions that they had experienced and thereby produce a similar response. "However, as exercised, only the cerebral acquisition of the emotion is desired, rather than the full visceral response . . . . The exercise is designed merely to allow the actor to repeat the same emotion night after night." In the black theater one finds an *effective memory* working, one that produces "the truest emotional response in order that one might galvanize the collective consciousness." But this requires an ability to produce "real, spontaneously conceived emotions" that, Harrison notes, white actors avoid, "for fear of not being able to control the impact of them."

Blacks have lifelong experience engaging in cultural events in which their emotions have become aroused. This has developed in them the freedom to abandon themselves to the force of their feelings without fear of being unable to control their impact. Whites often consider such an abandonment to signify that the emotions are *out of control*. But they are not—at least not within the framework of ritualized expression. Rather, here blacks have transferred a measure of control from themselves to the feeling mode (sorrow, exultation, spirit possession) and to the cultural form (song, dance, greeting exchange, call and response) through which the emotions are released and within which they are also contained. As Harrison says, "an emotion is never out of control when it fits the modality it is released in," to which he adds, "Only when it is outside the mode, however benign or malignant, does the emotion seem peculiarly threatening or unintelligible" (Harrison 1972, p. 157).

Because whites do not have such an acquired sense—either from their own culture or from their knowledge of black or other cultures—that intensely expressed emotions can be contained by the mode through which they are released (such as those which blacks express in *argument*), they regard *all* emotional behavior as outside the mode and therefore "peculiarly threatening and unintelligible."

Interactional Roles and Responsibilities

The responsibility for realizing the appropriate emotional level in public interaction is one to be shared by individuals acting in response to their own feelings and individuals acting as "others." The nature of one's role and responsibility in this regard is determined by how intense emotional and expressive behavior can appropriately become in the two cultures.

For example, the desired emotional level in white social interaction is generally lower than an uninhibited expression of feelings would make it. Thus individuals acting in response to their own feelings are expected to exercise emotional self-restraint, and those individuals acting as "others" are given a preemptive role in seeing to it that expressed feelings do not exceed the level of intensity that the culture has designated as appropriate. On the other hand, the level of emotional intensity in black social interaction is at least equal to what an uninhibited expression of feelings would produce and frequently *greater* than what individuals happen to be generating at the time. Consequently, blacks acting as others often try to get some action going by spurring individuals acting in response to their own feelings to greater activity— *agitatin'*, Harrison calls it—thereby increasing the levels of emotional intensity being displayed and so satisfying the need of others for power, emotional excitement, and revitalization of energy (Harrison 1972, pp. 36–37). James Maryland's examples of signifying between Sweet Red and Black Power at a shoe-shine stand and between black teenagers at the "outpost" illustrates well the agitating (signifying) role of others in this process.

Reciprocities

The relationship between the freedom (or capacity) of individuals to produce intense emotional behavior and their ability to receive and manipulate it is a reciprocal one. This is because the level of emotional intensity that individuals show is regulated in part by what they know or presume others are capable of withstanding. Conversely, the level of susceptibility of individual sensibilities is developed culturally by the intensity of the feelings they are accustomed to receiving.

Whites keep a lid on their more emotionally intense outputs in part because they presume that the capacity of other whites to receive and manipulate them is relatively low. Of course this also ensures that the capacity of whites to receive and manipulate more intense emotional outputs will *remain* low, precisely because more intense outputs are being withheld that would give whites the opportunity to become more acquainted with them—to give whites the sense that strong emotions *can* be contained by the mode through which they are released. Such release would help whites become more interpersonally effective in receiving and manipulating intense outputs.

Blacks' capacity to deal with intense emotional outputs is relatively greater than that of whites because blacks have greater experience of being confronted with them. Reciprocally, this capacity also gives blacks acting in response to their own feelings greater freedom to express them intensely, knowing that others have developed the capacity to receive them without becoming overwhelmed.

The actual level of tolerance that blacks and whites develop toward emotionally or expressively intense behavior is determined by the different cultural norms of how intense emotional and expressive behavior may become. Through the kinds of outputs they are respectively accustomed to receiving, black and white individual sensibilities internalize a sense of appropriateness which they then work to maintain. These cultural norms also define the respective patterns of accommodation. Whites want social interaction to operate at an emotionally subdued level. To realize this goal, they first establish the rule that expressive behavior shall be subdued, which develops sensibilities capable of tolerating only relatively subdued outputs. The white rule then establishes that individuals should let their more emotionally intense behavior be governed by what other people's sensibilities are capable of withstanding. Since others are only capable of receiving and manipulating comfortably outputs that are emotionally subdued, the rule hopes to ensure that outputs will remain subdued. Thus white sensibilities become adjunct regulatory agencies assisting the dominant social group in keeping social interaction low-keyed and public contexts relatively cool.

Black cultural norms desire levels of public interaction that are more emotionally intense. Consequently they allow individuals to express themselves at the level at which feelings are felt and accordingly oblige others to accommodate such outputs at the same level. In this way black sensibilities also function as adjunct regulatory agencies working to keep the level of social interaction vigorous and animated and public contexts relatively hot.

Tact
Doing unto Others

The white interaction rule that individuals should adjust the potency of their assertions and expressions to the level that others can withstand is incorporated in their general notion of showing consideration for other people's feelings. Yet it is also clear that individuals do not automatically qualify for consideration as "others." Rather, individuals win or forfeit consideration for their feelings in accordance with their behavior. Thus whites who do not moderate the potency of their self-assertions or expressions to the level that cultural norms have determined to be appropriate or that others can withstand are judged to have considered the feelings of others improperly. Consequently these individuals have forfeited consideration for themselves as "others." The social punishment for that is withdrawal by other people of consideration for their feelings.

We saw this in an earlier example in this chapter. The white woman considered herself entitled to tell McCarty that the latter's behavior during *Lysistrata* was "outrageous" because the white woman identified herself and other members of the audience as the "others" whose feelings McCarty had not considered with her loud laughter. The white woman considered that McCarty had thereby disqualified herself as an "other" and forfeited consideration by others of her own feelings. The white woman did not consider herself rude in criticizing McCarty as she did since, conventionally, one cannot be rude to people whose behavior has just disqualified them from consideration as "others."

However, it is also clear that the feelings of others for which whites generally show consideration are not active or expressive feelings. Rather, they are passive and consequently should more properly be regarded as *sensibilities* than *feelings*. This distinction is important, because active feelings—which is simply to say *feelings*—have no claim on other people's consideration in white social interaction. Quite the contrary: individuals whose feelings become active risk forfeiting consideration for themselves as "others," especially if these feelings become expressively intense or threaten to override established order and procedure.

The distinction between feelings and sensibilities also enables us to be more accurate in characterizing what happened in the cited incident during the play. The white woman did not regard McCarty's *feelings,* expressed by her loud laughter, as qualifying her for consideration as an "other." Rather, she saw the latter's behavior as a forfeit of consideration for herself as an "other" and therefore a forfeit as well of protection for her sensibilities which the white woman then considered herself entitled—even obligated—to punish as custodian of the public order and, perhaps, also as someone whose own sensibilities had been offended.

Of course McCarty did not consider her laughter inconsiderate of other people's sensibilities, since in black culture, feelings and emotions are seen as primary and independent forces. They are primary in that they are seen principally to motivate and guide black action and to serve as a reference to explain why individuals behave in the way that they do. They are independent in that blacks relinquish to feelings the freedom to exert their *own* will on their behavior, and, consequently, on whatever proceedings they happen to be engaging in at the time. Thus McCarty saw herself as behaving appropriately in giving full value to the force of her inner feelings by expressing them as they were felt, thereby also acknowledging their primary and independent status. Moreover, as already noted, other blacks regard the manifestation of the primary and independent force and effect of feelings *positively*–whether at the level of expression or motivation. When during his fieldwork in Antigua Karl Reisman asked Afro-Antiguans why people can fall asleep or shift subjects in the middle of sentences, the answers he received were usually given in terms of the person's feelings. "That's what he feels to do," which denoted for Reisman the strong value Afro-Antiguans "put on not constraining one's feelings by artificial structures." He concludes, "A very beautiful and subtle attention to the feelings of others is a marked feature of West Indian tact" (Reisman 1974b, p. 67). When blacks express their feelings or act otherwise in accordance with their feelings, not only do they not consider themselves doing something for which they might *risk* disqualification as others. They believe that they are acting in ways that have a *preemptive* claim on others' consideration and respect. McCarty saw not herself but the white woman in the theater as being "inconsiderate" of other people's feelings. As evidence she would offer not only her own sensibilities, which the white woman offended with her gratuitous remark, but also her own exuberant laughter, which others within her culture would respond to favorably and appreciatively.

White students in my classes do not usually understand how Afro-Antiguans are being *tactful* in their consideration of other people's feelings, from Reisman's description of their behavior. This is because they identify the "others" in Reisman's statement ("a very beautiful and subtle attention to the feelings of others") to be the people who were *listening* to those individuals who fell asleep and who were left hanging in mid-air as a result. They do not consider that the individuals who fell asleep might qualify as the "others" here, because whites show consideration for sensibilities, not feelings. Thus the feelings that prompted the individual Antiguans to fall asleep do not qualify, within the white conception of tact, for consideration from others; moreover, to the extent that they overrode established order and procedure, they would cause those individuals who acted in accordance with them also to forfeit consideration from others for themselves. Finally, because whites see feelings as sensibilities, they do not conceive that the feelings of others to which Afro-Antiguans were giving subtle attention were the sensibilities of those individuals who fell asleep. Again, according to the white cultural conception, these individuals forfeited consideration for their sensibilities because of their own lack of consideration for the sensibilities of those other individuals who were listening.

But of course the feelings of others which Afro-Antiguans were attending to were precisely those that prompted the individuals who shifted subject in the middle of a sentence to do so. Within the Afro-Antiguan and larger black conception of tact, individuals who express their feelings or act in accordance with their feelings continue to qualify as "others" in people's consideration: even preemptively so, given the primary status accorded to feelings within the culture. These feelings, as already noted, are also those whose determinative force—at the level of expression or motivation—white cultural patterns and norms work to preclude.

The white social interaction rule that grants individuals the right to claim consideration from others for their sensibilities, but not for their feelings, extends to interpersonal contexts. Here, whites have been taught that to act on behalf of their own feelings is unjustified if someone else's sensibilities might become offended as a result. So strongly ingrained is this rule that it has the force of a moral injunction. Rather than violate it and feel guilty or, as a further embarrassment, have to engage in repair work (apologies, expiation), whites will hold back what they truly feel, even if this will result in an injustice to their feelings or create for themselves an unwanted social situation. This often happens to whites, especially white women who have been socialized to be more acquiescent and less assertive than white men. This may create interpersonal difficulties for white women when confronted with the assertive raps of black men.

Whites are not simply being altruistic in placing the sensibilities of others before their own feelings. Whites, after all, are "others" in other people's consideration just as other people are "others" in theirs. The same rule that protects the sensibilities of others at the expense of one's own feelings also protects one's sensibilities at the expense of the feelings of others. Furthermore, because the rule has the force of a moral injunction, those who violate it not only risk incurring feelings of guilt but in effect grant others the opportunity to assault their sensibilities, since they will have forfeited consideration for themselves as an "other" as a result of not having properly considered (protected) the sensibilities of others. Moreover, others can now assault their sensibilities self-righteously, since such an assault is also considered proper social punishment for the rule being violated. Thus there are strong practical reasons also for whites to follow their rule. The weight given to protecting the sensibilities of others in white culture leaves individuals with little or no moral justification for acting in accordance with their own feelings.

The black social interaction rule that grants individuals the right to claim consideration from others for their feelings also extends to interpersonal contexts. And while sensibilities also have a moral claim on other people's consideration, feelings are seen to have a preemptive claim. The primary and independent status accorded feelings within the culture means that individuals must place their own feelings first—indeed are seen to have no other choice than to do so if they are to respond as a *total* person—even if other people's sensibilities might become offended in the process (Harrison 1972, p. 155). Of course this also means that blacks must come to grips with others also placing their own feelings first at the expense of *their* sensibilities.

The different relative weight that blacks and whites give to protecting feelings and sensibilities was brought into focus some years ago in my graduate course on interpersonal communication. As their final assignment, the students, eight black and fourteen white, were asked to confront other members of the class individually and comment on the projected image or communicative style that each had showed in class during the past term. Such an assignment meant that, if done candidly, student sensibilities might well become offended. As a result, several students expressed concern over how it should be carried out or even whether it should be done at all. In discussing these questions, their negotiation ultimately centered upon the issue of whether feelings or sensibilities should receive preemptive consideration: specifically, the rights of those students who had something to say and wanted to say it (whether others wanted to hear it or not) versus the rights of students not to hear what others might want to say about them, irrespective of how much others might want to tell them. The way the class divided on this issue was culturally revealing. Twelve of the fourteen white students argued for the rights of students *not* to hear what others might want to say to them—thus giving priority to the protection of individual sensibilities, those of others as well as their own, even if this might result in forfeiting their own chance to say what they felt. This group decided that they would comment on others only if other students gave them permission to do so. The eight black students and remaining two white students, on the other hand, argued for the rights of those students to express what they had to say about others even if the protection of all individual sensibilities would be forfeited in the process. On this last point, one black woman said, "I don't know about others, but if someone has something to say to me, I want to hear it."

Many other examples documenting this difference have subsequently occurred. One took place in a restaurant at lunch time. A black friend of mine had his pocket radio on at a moderately low volume when the white manager asked him to turn it off, as it bothered some of the other customers. My own white cultural orientation then was to see the sensibilities of others as deserving preemptive consideration, even if it should be at the expense of feelings—my own or those of others. My black friend, however, gave the feelings stimulated by the music greater value than I did. He lowered the radio's volume a bit to show consideration for other people's sensibilities, but he refused to turn it off altogether in consideration of his *own* feelings—as well as those of mine and several others who were also enjoying the music—much to the chagrin of the white manager.

From a white standpoint, the black cultural pattern that would withdraw protection for sensibilities to save feelings is insensitive and even cruel. But of course the white view is based on the assumption that individual sensibilities are quite fragile—thus others need to be vigilant in giving them special social protection. Also, the special social rights that white culture gives to others to protect individual self-esteem makes any violation of other sensibilities especially potent and sinful. Finally, whites see the black emotional response as too intense. This is true even if blacks have been provoked and are *reacting* to individuals who have just offended them and who, according to both black and white norms, would have forfeited their right to receive polite consideration for *their* sensibilities. Whites would still consider the black response an overreaction. They would wonder what horrendous offense the other person could have committed to deserve such an emotionally powerful retaliatory response. White sympathies will typically be with the person on the receiving end of such an exchange—almost without regard to provocation—rather than with the person asserting himself in such an intense manner.

From a black standpoint, individuals asserting themselves in accordance with their feelings are seen not as violating the sacred rights of others but, rather, as preserving the sacred rights of self, especially the sanctity of individual feelings and the primary and independent status that feelings have within the culture. With the shift in focus from *doing unto others* to *doing for oneself,* blacks can also act as their feelings direct without subsequent guilt. Of course they also do not consider the rights of others to be especially violable here, because they do not consider the sensibilities of others to be so fragile that they will be overwhelmed by individuals expressing their feelings intensely. Nor do blacks see sensibilities as so weak that they cannot withstand a forthright expression of opinion. Hence the comment "If someone has something to say about me, I want to hear it" from the black cultural standpoint is not especially brave, since blacks regularly confront each other in a direct manner as a matter of course. Moreover, they consider it cowardly and devious that information about themselves should come from anyone other than the source in any other way than direct and forthright. This is especially true when what someone has said has already been said to others and is slanderous. This is called "talking behind someone's back" or, as one black woman called it, "bitchin' behind the barn"; and it is a social offense. The response in such a case is to confront the one alleged to have committed the offense. Marjorie Goodwin shows in some detail the structure of this interactional pattern and how it functions for young black females as a way to deal with and prevent slanderous gossip (1980, p. 681). Finally, blacks do not share the white view that the black emotionally intense response to an offense is an overreaction; it is seen as simply the customary way blacks would react when their sensibilities have been offended and their beelings activiated and aroused. As Harrison put it,

> blacks are not known . . . to ever be totally desensitized, defused, or repressed in their emotions when dealing with definable antagonisms. A black person would not pussyfoot with an insult from a white—or a black—if rendered with the slightest edge of an acerbity that might threaten one's security: the response would be fully acted out, regardless of the name of the game which deems it necessary to be *sensitive* to the other feller. [1972, p. 150]

Consequently blacks find distressing as well as prejudicial the fact that whites regard a black emotional reaction to an offense major but its provocation minor. One black woman fired from a Chicago bank gave as an example a situation in which the white employees with whom she had been working occasionally made racial slurs. For a while she let these pass, but when she was convinced that her fellow workers had also been tampering with her purse when she was away from her station, she reacted emotionally and vociferously. The white bank managers involved were barely concerned with the racial slurs and prejudicial acts that provoked her response. Rather, their behavior indicated that they believed the *real* problem to be the emotional intensity of her reaction, which to whites in that context suggested not merely lack of self-control but more general psychological instability.

Blacks, on the other hand, do not see emotional reactions to "definable antagonisms" as the problem, since responding to such feelings is for them simply being "for real." As Harrison put it, "It is behavior which gives affirmation to an inner essence which seeks when the organism is under duress, to achieve the necessary harmony required to be a complete man" (1972, p. 155). What is of greater concern to blacks, and what they regard as a more serious violation of the rights of others—but what whites consider hardly a violation at all—is to be in a situation where for compelling social reasons (such as keeping a job at a bank) they are not free to act in accordance with the force of their feelings. Blacks call this constraining mode of behavior fronting, and they generally regard negatively situations in which it is necessary to front. Whites do not typically notice when blacks front, since the mode—emotionally subdued—is one that whites consider normal, achieved as a matter of course in their cultural development through the habitual exercise of emotional self-restraint and repression. Consequently they are not aware of the conscious effort that blacks must make on a day-to-day basis to contain their emotions when working in what they regard as a racially hostile environment. All blacks consider fronting to be a strain. Some consider it downright painful, especially since black culture gives them the freedom to express their anger. This culture serves blacks in their effort to restore and maintain spiritual harmony, while white culture compels individuals to internalize and repress anger. Harrison considers fronting ("those anxious mental adjustments that are made in deference to the mode of oppression'') precisely the kind of social behavior that creates apparent conflicts in the black psyche. He considers those blacks who try desperately to hold the lid on and thus appear calm and collected by white standards the ones who should be watched. "As Frantz Fanon observed, most black people play out the 'racial drama' down front because they have 'no time' to 'make it unconscious'" (Harrison 1972, p. 120, quoting Fanon 1967, p. 150).

Whites would consider this paradoxical, but blacks will regard a white context that allows them to express their feelings—even negative ones—as less alien than one in which they do not feel free to express feelings or act in accordance with their feelings at all. For whites an expression of negative feelings (such as anger) would signify that individuals have reached the stage where they are totally fed up with a situation, one in which their emotions can no longer be contained. Conversely, they would consider the absence of negative feelings a sign of contentment or at least acquiescence. Because of this difference, I regard nonassertion or nonexpression of feelings by black and white students quite differently. When blacks are behaving nonassertively or nonexpressively, I think that they have not as yet become comfortable enough to begin opening up. But I consider the same behavior by white students their basic cultural mode and thus not one that has any special significance.

The greater capacity of blacks to express themselves forcefully and to receive and manipulate the forceful assertions of others gives them greater leverage in interracial encounters at more intense levels of interaction. It applies not only to classroom debate but to *argument* generally. One black woman remarked that she was always surprised at the difficulty her white college roommate had in contending with her when they had a difference of opinion. This observation has often been made by blacks, who consider whites as a result interpersonally weak as well as seeming to be "forever demanding an apology over nothing." The basis for the last remark has already been established: whites consider an assault on the sensibilites of others a social offense. However, blacks do not consider the simple expression of opinions at a high degree of emotional intensity in the same way, especially since they regard the force of feelings as something that the sensibilities of other should be readily capable of withstanding.

But blacks also consider the demand of whites for an apology to be unjustified, because it suggests that the responsibility for the feelings and reactions of individuals belongs primarily to others, whereas blacks themselves consider individuals primarily responsible for their own feelings. Blacks will commonly say to those who have become angry, "*Others* did not make you angry"; rather, "You *let yourself* become angry." This view is that blacks stand accused only when individuals acknowledge the truth of the accusation by the way that they respond to it. "if the shoe fits, wear it" and "Only the truth hurts." But whites stand accused when *others* make an accusation: whites consider the social responsibility for protecting individual sensibilities—self-esteem—to belong primarily to others. Consequently, they can also call others to account when their sensibilities become offended. Blacks consider the responsibility for protecting individual sensibilities to fall primarily on individuals themselves. Perhaps for this reason, among others, blacks work hard to strengthen their individual capacity to withstand and manipulate the various forces with which individuals need to contend to maintain spiritual harmony—what blacks call "getting themselves together." Individuals develop and demonstrate their degree of togetherness by respectively developing and demonstrating their ability to contend. Black performers do so when they heat up the environment while, as Abrahams says, proclaiming their own cool (Abrahams 1976, p. 82). Black professional athletes do so when they execute extremely difficult feats without showing any visible strain (Greenfield 1975, p. 170). This cultural notion of togetherness is perhaps the central spiritual element within the larger conception of being *cool,* and constitutes a forceful ally for blacks in their continuing struggle to manage and manipulate the high-energy feelings within.

Feeling in Doing

Misunderstandings and conflicts also arise between blacks and whites because of their different views on the functional relevance of feelings in what Goffman has termed "guided doings," especially guided doings that are expressive (Goffman 1974, pp. 22–26). Blacks consider feelings here of fundamental importance, but whites consider them at best incidental, and at times even irrelevant. For example, a black and a white jazz musician on a Studs Terkel radio program in Chicago (aired July 17, 1979) were discussing the relative importance of technique and feeling with respect to both the historical development of jazz and playing jazz. The white musician considered only the importance of the development of technique. His black counterpart, however, said that he knew "lots of jazz musicians who got all the technique in the world but can't play worth a lick because they don't have the feeling." He added that that was why he could not play the blues. The white musician asked him incredulously, "You can't play the blues?" He answered, "Not really, because I'm too much concerned with technique. You got to have the *feeling* if you *really* want to play the blues."

The same difference in perspective was shown in a disco place. Allen Harris commented, on some music that was being played, "I can't dance to that." A white woman in the group said, "Oh, it's easy," and she proceeded to demonstrate the movements that corresponded to the dance being played. Therein she also demonstrated that for her, "knowing how" meant simply remedying a lack of information or technique, as the white jazz musician viewed playing the blues. But what Harris meant was that the music was not capable of activating the kind of feeling he needed in order to dance. Thereby he indicated that his expressive movements were directly responsive to his feelings. Notwithstanding his technical knowledge of the intricacies of the steps involved, without the right kind of music to activate the right kind of feeling, *he could not* dance.

In summary, the different consideration that blacks and whites give to feelings shows itself in many different situations. The one that occurs most frequently and is probably most troublesome socially for both blacks and whites comes about when activated black feelings threaten to override white established order and procedure. This situation can be illustrated with regard to turn-taking in the classroom when debate on an issue becomes heated. Here whites feel that blacks should be giving principal attention to

white-imposed constraints against feelings becoming determinative. In just *coming in,* blacks ignore these constraints, following
instead their own rules for entering into an ongoing presentation,
giving greater consideration to the determinative and occasionally
overriding force that activated feelings can have. When this
happens, whites become indignant, viewing blacks as inconsiderate
of the sensibilities of other who are showing proper emotional
self-restraint in awaiting their authorized turn. They also view
blacks as "socially immature" here, in not showing emotional
self-restraint in awaiting their *own* proper turn.

Whites also become resentful, for example, when blacks, as
audience members, respond verbally to some action that is taking
place on the stage—following their call and response pattern—in
a way that is out of place with respect to white structures and
norms that have determined the proper intervals and kinds of
audience response. Finally, whites are distressed when blacks
let their feelings become too expressively intense, in disregard of
established white norms and the sensitiveness of white sensibilities.

From their standpoint, blacks see whites as especially inconsiderate in not properly granting feelings the freedom to exert
their own independent effect on proceedings. Blacks get upset
when whites "hog the floor" in debate by not allowing them to
come in with something immediately relevant. This prevents
blacks from transferring the emotional energy of an impulse to the
pulse of the proceedings, which they consider essential if the
contentiousness of debate is to remain vigorous, animated, and
individually involving. Nor do blacks like it when whites come
down hard on them afterward because the expressive force of
their feelings has overwhelmed individual sensibilities or violated
white established norms. Blacks especially resent this last white
reaction, because they regard structures inhospitable to
feelings—like those of white culture—as constraining and artificial. Instead of being chastised for investing spiritual energy in
white proceedings, blacks feel that they should be credited with
having given what would otherwise be a lifeless process the kind
of vitality it needs to generate and sustain human interest and
involvement.

References

Abrahams, Roger, D. 1976. *Talking Black*. Rowley, Mass.: Newbury.
Cooke, Benjamin G. 1972. "Non-verbal Communication among Afro-Americans: An Initial Classification." In *Rappin' and Stylin' Out,* edited by Thomas Kochman, Urbana: University of Illinois Press.
Daniel, Jack L., and Smitherman, Geneva. 1976. "How I Got Over: Communication Dynamics in the Black Community." *Quarterly Journal of Speech,* 62:26–39. [also ch. 3, this volume]
Day, Beth. 1974. *Sexual Life Between Blacks and Whites*. London: Collins.
Fanon, Frantz. 1967. *Black Skin, White Masks*. New York: Grove.
Goffman, Erving. 1967. *International Ritual*. New York: Doubleday, Anchor.
——— . 1974. *Frame Analysis. New York: Harper & Row*.
Goodwin, Marjorie H. 1980. "He-Said-She-Said: Formal Cultural Procedures for the Construction of a Gossip Dispute Activity." *American Ethnologist,* 7(4): 674–94.
Greenfield, Jeff. 1975. "The Black and White Truth about Basketball.", *Esquire,* (October), p. 170.
Harrison, Paul C. 1972. *The Drama of Nommo*. New York: Grove.
Holt, Grace Sims. 1972a "Communication in Black Culture: The Other Side of Silence." *Language Research Reports, 6:51–84.*
——— . 1972b. "Stylin' outta the Black Pulpit." In *Rappin' and Stylin' Out,* edited by Thomas Kochman. Urbana: University of Illinois Press.
Johnson, Kenneth R. 1972. "The Vocabulary of Race." In *Rappin' and Stylin' Out,* edited by Thomas Kochman, Urbana: University of Illinois Press.
Keil, Charles, 1966. "Motion and Feeling in Music." *Journal of Aesthetics and Art Criticism* 24(3): 337–49.
Pateman, Trevor, 1975. *Language, Truth and Politics*. Nottingham: Stroud and Pateman.
Reisman, Karl. 1974. "Noise and Order." In *Language in its Social Setting,* edited by William W. Gage. Washington, D.C.: Antropological Society of Washington.
Slater, Philip. 1976. The Pursuit of Loneliness. Rev. ed. Boston: Beacon.
Smitherman, Geneva. 1977. *Talkin and Testifyin: The Language of Black America*. Boston: Houghton Mifflin.
Wharton, Linda F., and Daniel, Jack L. 1977. "Black Dance: Its African Origins and Continuity." *Minority Voices* 1(2): 73–80.

15
Cultural Pluralism: Black and White Styles

THOMAS KOCHMAN

American society is presently in a period of social transition from a
structurally pluralistic society to a culturally pluralistic one. The differences
between the two kinds of pluralism is in the political arrangement of its
culturally heterogeneous parts. Within *structural* pluralism the socially
subordinate cultural person or group unilaterally accomodates the dominant (Anglo-American male) cultural group on the latter's terms. The
dominant metaphor within *cultural* pluralism is the "salad bowl," not the
"melting pot," in which the identity and integrity of the culturally distinctive
units remain intact while contributing to the overall quality, effect, and
purpose of the whole. Within cultural pluralism, A *plus* B is a better choice
than A *or* B, both for the individual and for society as a whole, especially
when the climate is set for culturally different people to become cultural
resources for each other.

Insofar as present mainstream American attitudes toward cultural diversity by and large have been those generated by structural pluralism,
differences in Black and White mainstream linguistic and cultural patterns,
perspectives, and values are likely to be seen through a mindset that attaches
greater social respectability, if not conceptual validity, to the White
mainstream cultural style. The ubiquity of such a mindset becomes obvious
when we realize that Black and White cultural and linguistic differences are
manifested in approaches to assessing others and being assessed oneself in
terms of ability and performance in school, college, and the workplace.
Indeed, through its school system and other social agencies, the dominant
social group still insists on "linguistic and cultural assimilation as a
prerequisite to social incorporation" thereby instituting a policy and
program whereby pressures are brought to bear upon Blacks and members
of other minority groups to accommodate the dominant social group
exclusively on the latter's terms. And in fact, when interest has been shown
in American minority languages and cultures in the past it has generally

been geared to understanding them *for the purpose of easing their social and cultural transition into the American mainstream* (Aarons, Gordon, & Stewart, 1969; Cazden, John, & Hymes, 1972; Zintz, 1963), an attitudinal stance consistent with the "melting pot" concept within structural pluralism.

What disturbs me about this accomodation process is its unidirectional and nonreciprocal character. Those members of minority cultures who wish to become socially incorporated into the American mainstream do need to learn about mainstream American linguistic and cultural patterns. In some instances, it might even benefit them to use and embrace such patterns as necessity or desire might dictate.

But what about the needs of the American mainstream? The nonreciprocal nature of the process of cultural assimilation of minorities does not permit the mainstream American culture to learn about minority cultural traditions nor benefit from their official social incorporation. It also suggests an unwarranted social arrogance: that mainstream American society has already reached a state of perfection and cannot benefit from being exposed to and learning from other (minority) cultural traditions. I reject that assumption, and I demonstrate that in the stance I take here by promoting a view of the culturally different patterns and perspectives of Blacks and mainstream Whites from a social standpoint that regards them as equally respectable and valid (of course, therefore, also equally accountable to criticism (as on functional grounds) when such may be warranted (Kochman, 1981, pp. 34–35, 151).

Stylistic Self-Expression

Stylistic self-expression within White mainstream culture is minimalist in character: "a style of no style" (Abrahams, personal communication, but see also Abrahams, 1976, pp. 8–9, 90–91); thus, characterized by economy and efficiency ("the shortest distance between two points," "no wasted moves"), and modest (self-effacing) understatement and restraint ("If you've got it, you don't need to flaunt it").

Stylistic self-expression within Black culture is characterized by dramatic self-conscious flair. A nice descriptive example comes from Milhomme's (1986) portrait of Felix Toya, Ghana's dancing traffic policeman.

> Dubbed "Toyota" or "Life Boy" by the city's taxi drivers, Constable Toya attracts as much pedestrian traffic as he directs vehicles. Lookers applaud and cheer, drivers toot their horns, and sometimes take an extra turn on the roundabout as Felix oscillates and gyrates, lifts, bends and pirouettes, making an art form out of his assigned task, never missing a step or a signal-change. Few Ghanians own Walkmans, but in the privacy of his own mind, Constable

Toya creates a symphony of sounds and rhythms to which he moves with grace and precision. He is the ultimate street performer, taking cues from his environment and entertaining a diverse audience of fleeting yet appreciative fans. (pp. X–37)

Black stylistic self-expression is also characterized by inventive (humorously ironic) exaggeration as in the self-promotion of demonstrably capable aspects of self ("If you've got it, flaunt it;") or even by less demonstrably positive capabilities ("If you don't have it, flaunt it, anyway"), which is all part of Afro-American boasting: the "making of one's noise" (Kochman, 1981, p. 65; Reisman, 1974, p. 60). As "Hollywood" Henderson said, "I put a lot of pressure on myself to see if I can play up to my mouth" (Atkin, 1979, p. 16). But exaggeration also serves to characterize (and neutralize the impact of) negative situations, such as poverty ("The soles on my shoes are so thin, I can step on a dime and tell you whether it's heads or tails").

Conflict and Confluence: Individuality/Functionality

The functional rule for getting things done follows the norms for appropriate stylistic self-presentation and expression within the two cultures. The White mainstream cultural rule is governed by the principles of economy and efficiency, which serve to promote the uniform, impersonal, minimalist and instrumental (role-oriented) style considered standard within mainstream White organized work and play. Thus, the rule here is "make only moves that are necessary to getting the job done."

The Black cultural rule serves to promote the standards within the Black performance tradition, which is, as Abrahams has said (1976, p. 9) for individual performers to bring about an experience in which their creative energies and the vitality of others may find expression. Blacks accomplish this by executing tasks with bold originality and dramatic flair. Insofar as it is in "how" things get done that the energetic involvement of others and stylistic self-expression occur, rather than in "what" gets done, Blacks say (to protect the individual right of original self-expression), "Tell me what to do but not how to do it." Consonant with this purpose, the functional rule for Blacks is "so long as the moves that are made do not interfere with getting the job done, they should be allowed."

These two different cultural rules clash in the workplace and in the playground with great regularity (see Kochman, 1981, pp. 145–52). One example of this clash is in the restrictions set forth in the rules in professional football governing "spiking" the football (throwing it forcefully to the ground): a self-celebrating expression of personal accomplishment (resembling an exclamation point [!]) by which Black players punctuate their achievement. Were a player to "spike" the football after scoring an important first down he would be penalized. The official reason given for assessing the penalty is "delay of game." In actuality there is no real "delay of game" because after a team scores a first down the line markers have to be moved, and a new football is thrown in from the sidelines; there may even be a TV commercial. At issue is the different aesthetic standards governing stylistic self-expression within Black and White mainstream culture. "Spiking" the football is permitted in the endzone after a touchdown, but only by the player who actually scores the touchdown. So when the White quarterback of the Chicago Bears, Jim McMahon, scored a touchdown and gave it to one of the lineman to spike (in recognition of their cooperative and instrumental role in his success) the officials assessed a penalty on the ensuing kickoff. As a measure of the acceptance of the Black cultural view on such matters in professional sports, it is significant that the reaction by both White announcers at the time of its occurrence, and of Bear quarterback Jim McMahon, when interviewed afterward, was to regard the penalty assessment as "stupid."

Other aspects of cultural conflict center around the issue of individual entitlement for stylistic self-expression and authorization for making changes in how a task is to be done. In White mainstream organizational culture, stylistic self-expression, when it occurs at all, tends to be a function of rank. Consequently, it is the chief executive male officer in the organization who is often the one who, in manner or dress, "shows-off," or otherwise demonstrates a more individually expressive (non-instrumental?!) style (e.g., Lee Iacocca, Ray Kroc, Douglas MacArthur, and so on).

In Black culture, however, stylistic self-expression is an individual entitlement. Consequently, one does not have to be the president of the company to drive an expensive top-of-the-line car or wear fashionable clothes. However, this cultural pattern often gets Blacks into trouble in White mainstream organizations because the latter interpret such individual stylistic self-expression as a presumption: a laying claim to a greater rank or title in the organization than the Black person actually holds.

As to authorization for how a task is to be accomplished, the Black dictum "Tell me what to do, but not how to do it," although establishing a protection for the individual right to self-expression, also asserts that the final authority for the implementation of a task rests with the doer/ performer. However, White mainstream organizational culture, through the framework of "mental set," sees the authorization of a standard protocol or procedure to rest with the designer of the plan: the manager/ composer. This difference also gets Blacks into trouble in the organization insofar as they get accused here once again of either arrogating to themselves authority that their rank or role in the organization does not entitle them to, or of being insubordinate or uncooperative, even when they do the task differently in the interests of getting the job done, when doing it in the way it was officially prescribed would have failed.

In American mainstream culture, Whites (especially males) are taught to see themselves as individuals rather than as members of a group. Yet when they become members of an organization or team they are frequently called on to subordinate their individuality to fit the hierarchy and role requirements established by the group. The nature of the subordination process takes the form of seeing the group as more important than oneself ("There is no letter 'I' in the word 'team' "). This process often leads to a fused self or identity (organized around what mainstream individuals do professionally) such as when White males talk about themselves in terms of a corporate "we" rather than as an individual "I."

Black individuality is realized within the framework of strong interpersonal connectedness, but, as Young (1970, p. 255) stated "not with absorption or acceptance of group identity as higher than individual identity" (see also Lewis, 1975, p. 225). Moreover, although there is also emphasis on instrumental forms of doing, focus is also on individual character and style ("doing one's *own* thing"), leading to more personalized and idiosyncratic expressions of doing (as opposed to the more routine, uniform and impersonal (role-oriented) forms of doing characteristic of self-presentation within White mainstream organizational culture).

TABLE 15.1
Styles of Work and Play

"Black"		"White"
	Patterns	
Mental "Reflex"		Mental "Set"
Spontaneous		Methodical
Improvisational		*Systematic*
Exaggerated		Understated
Expressive		Restrained
Personalized		Role-oriented

References

Aarons, A. A., Gordon, B Y., & Stewart, W. A. (Eds.). (1969). *Linguistic-cultural differences and American education. Florida FL Reporter, 7* (1).

Abrahams, R. D. (1976). *Talking black.* Rowley, MA: Newbury.

Atkin, R. (1979). Hollywood Henderson' at Super Bowl. *Christian Science Monitor, 18,* p. 16.

Cazden, C. B., John, V. P., & Hymes, D. (Eds.). (1972). *Functions of language in the classroom.* New York: Teachers College Press.

Kochman, T. (1981). *Black and white styles in conflict.* Chicago: The University of Chicago Press.

Lewis, D. K. (1975). The black family: Socialization and sex roles. *Phylon, 36* (3), 221-237.

Milhomme,   . (1986). Brake dancing in Accra. *LA Extra,* 16-22 May, p. X-37.

Reisman, K. (1974). Noise and order. In W. W. Gage (Ed.), *Language in its social setting* (pp. 56-73). Washington, DC: Anthropological Society of Washington.

Young, V. H. (1970). Family and childhood in a southern negro community. *American Anthropologist, 72,* 269-288.

Zintz, M. V. (1963). *Education across cultures.* Des Moines, IA: Wm. C. Brown.

16

The Interactional Accomplishment of Discrimination in South Africa

J. KEITH CHICK

INTRODUCTION

It is not difficult to document discrimination on grounds of race in South Africa. More problematic, however, is the task of specifying the causes. In attempting to do so, most researchers have adopted a macro or structural approach and usually made use of quantitative methods. In other words, they have attempted to explain discrimination in terms of historically given, structural features of the wider society (e.g., social stratification, distribution of power, economic system, belief system, etc.) and have usually drawn their conclusions from quantitative analyses of data from official statistics and, frequently, large-scale surveys.

A case in point is Schlemmer's (1977) paper entitled "Racial attitudes in Southern Africa: The contribution of culture, economic interests, and history." In it, he attempts to identify the various factors which have contributed to the formation of race attitudes in Southern Africa, past and present. He presents a historical review of the origins of discrimination and the results of a survey of present-day race attitudes based on acceptance or rejection responses of ninety carefully worded statements in an interview situation. He concludes that the results "mirror the consequences of South Africa's historical development in which ethnicity, nationalism, material interests and status concern have been articulated into a complex and self-reinforcing process, which in turn has produced a general 'culture of racism' in which the original parameters of the constituent factors have become obscured'' (80).

An alternative, a micro approach, which I present here, uses a fine-grained sociolinguistic analysis and comparison of intra- and intercultural encounters to discover the mechanisms or processes that generate and reinforce the negative racial stereotypes which lead to prejudice and discrimination.[1]

These two approaches are often presented in the social science literature as irreconcilable, and much energy has been expended by the advocates of each in pointing out the limitations of the other. However, increasingly, scholars (e.g., Collins 1975; McDermott & Roth 1978; Akinnaso 1981) have begun to argue that neither approach on its own is likely to give an adequate explanation of such social phenomena as stereotyping and discrimination on the basis of race, and that while it may be heuristic to use one approach or the other, ultimately it would be more productive to articulate the two.

In terms of this argument, macro studies provide the summaries of long-term, large-scale interactions necessary for deciding which of an infinite number of possible micro studies would be productive. The role of micro studies is to verify (or not) the findings of the macro studies, by identifying the interactional mechanisms in terms of which the variables in the macro studies can be said to work. Since scholars using the micro approach use circumscribed settings, few subjects, and limited data, they are often accused of spending an absurd amount of time documenting what is so context-specific as not to be generalizable to other situations. Thus, an additional advantage of the articulation of the two approaches for scholars using the micro approach is that they are able, with some degree of confidence, to make claims for the generalizability of their findings when these prove to be consistent with the findings of macro studies (though any strong claims must wait for the confirmation of the findings of micro studies in a wider range of situations). This productive cooperation is explained by Collins (1975:14): ''micro does not precede macro; progress goes along both fronts, with each setting problems for the other and suggesting where the solutions lie.''

In this paper, I present analyses of comparable intra- and intercultural encounters involving native speakers of English and Zulu and focus on how negative stereotypes of cultural and racial groups are generated or, when already existing, confirmed. These analyses further suggest what sorts of differences in sociocultural background and communication conventions contribute to the miscommunication. Finally, I sketch how the larger, structural, historically given forces (which are the concern of macro studies) combine with the results of intercultural encounters to achieve a negative cycle of socially created discrimination. In this way I provide some flesh to the bare bones of the notion of a ''complex and internally self-reinforcing process'' which Schlemmer writes of.

WHAT INTERACTIONAL SOCIOLINGUISTICS HAS REVEALED ABOUT INTRA- AND INTERCULTURAL COMMUNICATION

It is only in the last couple of decades that technological advances in sound and visual recording have enabled scholars to catch spoken interaction in flight, as it were, and subject it to fine-grained analysis. The results of such analyses have been surprising to most people, who have tended to think of conversational behaviour as spontaneous, unpredictable, and lacking in organization.

Examining conversational interaction within a single culture and focusing principally on verbal behaviour, ethnomethodologists (e.g., Sacks 1972; Schegloff 1973; Schegloff and Sacks 1973; Sacks, Schegloff, & Jefferson 1978) have established that such behaviour is, in fact, highly organized, and have identified some of the rules and strategies (the mechanisms or, as they express it, the methods) by which participants (members), for example, may distribute turns to speak and arrange smooth turn change with minimum overlap or interruption, and develop coherent topics or themes.

Again working within a single culture, but focusing chiefly on nonverbal behaviour, context analysts (Scheflen 1973; Condon 1977; Kendon 1973, 1979; McDermott, Gospodinoff, & Aaron 1978) have shown how participants organize their nonverbal behaviour (postures, patterns of looking, proxemic configurations, gestures) in cooperative, reciprocal, rhythmically coordinated ways to inform one another what the context is, in terms of which they can know what they are doing with one another, for example, chatting socially, solving a problem, negotiating agreement, and so on.

The fine-grained analysis of successful intracultural communication, then, reveals a synchrony of conversational behaviour which is somewhat like ballroom dancing partners of long standing, confident in the mutual knowledge of the basic sequence of dance steps and of the signals by which they inform one another of changes in direction or tempo, moving in smooth harmony.

By contrast, as Erickson (1975, 1976, 1978), Erickson and Schultz (1981), and Gumperz (1982a, 1982b) have shown, interactions between persons from different cultures may be marked by a series of uncomfortable, asynchronous moments. Because of differences in sociocultural background and communicative conventions, participants find it difficult to establish and maintain conversational cooperation. Like ballroom dancers who are strangers to one another, they misinterpret one another's signals, struggle to develop a sequence or theme, or establish a rhythm, quarrel over rights to lead, and, metaphorically speaking, trample one another's toes.

Since they tend to be only subconsciously aware of the sociocultural knowledge and the communicative conventions that contribute to their interpretations, participants, while aware that certain intercultural encounters have been stressful, seldom identify the·cause accurately. They account for what has happened in psychological rather than sociological or cultural terms, perceiving the other person as uncooperative, aggressive, callous, stupid, incompetent, or having some other undesirable personal traits. Repeated intercultural encounters between the same persons can generate biographies of the other as an uncooperative, aggressive, incompetent person. Intercultural communication involving different persons but having similar results can, over time, generate negative cultural stereotypes.

DIFFERENCES IN BACKGROUNDS AND COMMUNICATION CONVENTIONS AS SOURCES OF ASYNCHRONY

There is much anecdotal evidence that intercultural communication in South Africa, particularly between whites and blacks, tends to be relatively unsuccessful. For example, compensatory education programmes for blacks in tertiary education or in business and industry invariably include a communication component. In order to gather data which would allow me to investigate what differences in background, sociocultural information, and communication conventions contribute to the relative asynchrony of encounters between native English-speaking South African whites (S. A. English speakers) and Zulus using English (Zulu-English speakers), I made sound recordings of postexamination interviews involving a S. A. English academic and twelve postgraduate students, including S. A. English, Asian English, and Zulu-English speakers.

The students, who are all mature, experienced English-language teachers (either teaching English as L_1 or L_2), had recently completed two three-hour papers at the end of the first year of a two-year, part-time honours course in applied linguistics for language teaching. A month prior to the examination, they had been informed in general terms what topics would be examined, though they did not see the final wording of the questions until they were in the examination room. After the papers had been marked, the students were informed by post whether they had passed or failed. At the first class meeting of the year, they were invited to make appointments to discuss their papers with the course coordinator. They were told that the examiners felt that many students did not do well, not because they did not have the ability or had not prepared well, but because they were unsure of the examiners' expectations. They were told further that the discussion, when they met, would focus on the extent to which expectations were shared.

Other relevant background information is that most of the teaching in the course was through seminar presentation and discussion, and that the people responsible for teaching the course felt dissatisfied with the quality of discussion. As they expressed it, they felt that they were being constantly pressured by the group to adopt less egalitarian leadership roles. The Zulus and the Asians found it difficult to use the leader's first names though they were frequently invited to do so, and differences in the use of address terms in different languages and cultures were discussed openly in the sociolinguistics component of the course. Moreover, the Zulu-English students seldom offered unsolicited contributions, and invitations by name to contribute were sometimes followed by what the S. A. English speakers felt were embarrassing pauses. The Zulu-English speakers seldom developed an extended line of argument partly because, so it seemed to the leaders, the white students took over at the first opportunity.

Since a possible alternative explanation for what took place in the intercultural encounters is that the coordinator was prejudiced against students of different backgrounds than his own, it is important to note that the enrollment by blacks in this course was highly valued by the staff responsible for teaching it. Quite apart from the staff's conviction that universities should have the right to admit whoever has matriculated, irrespective of colour, race, or creed, they are motivated by the recognition that such participation gives them access to information necessary for research such as that reported on here.[2]

Initially two of the recorded interviews were chosen for closer analysis: one with female S. A. English-speaking student (referred to in the transcript as C), which the male course coordinator (A) (also a S. A. speaker) felt intuitively was the most successful interaction, and the other with a male Zulu-English speaker (B), which the coordinator felt was probably the least successful. The object of the analysis was to establish: i) whether there was greater evidence of asynchrony in A–B than A–C (which could account for the feelings of A about the relative success of each) and, if so, ii) whether the relative asynchrony of the interviews could be accounted for in terms of differences or similarity in sociocultural backgrounds and communicative conventions.

However, since it was apparent that in the interviews there was not a one-to-one relationship between degree of difference in cultural background and relative success of the interview, a third interview (A–D) was chosen for close analysis after the analysis of A–B and A–C had been completed. A found the interview with D (a male S. A. English-speaking student) to be very stressful and judged it almost as unsuccessful as the A–B interview. The object of this analysis was again to account for asynchrony, but, this time, in a situation where differences in sociocultural background and communicative conventions could not be hypothesised as the causes. As will be explained more fully below, what emerged from the analysis is that it was problems relating to strategies employed by the participants in trying to save face that contributed greatly to the asynchrony of the A–D interview. This prompted a further examination of the A–B and A–C interviews to see whether face considerations needed also to be brought into the explanation of the very different outcomes of these two interviews.

In the case of the initial analysis of the A-B and A–C interviews, the methods of analysis are modelled on those outlined by Gumperz (1982a:136–37): In an attempt to recover the interpretative or inferential processes of the participants from recordings of interactions, Gumperz and his associates play the recordings to independent listeners, some of whom share and some of whom do not share the sociocultural backgrounds of the participants. They first try to elicit from the listeners an interpretation of what is going on generally, for example, what was ultimately intended, what went right or wrong, and so on. Thereafter, the analysts test their hypotheses about the participants' communicative intent, the illocutionary force of particular utterances, and the interpretation of the participants by asking questions which oblige the listeners to relate their judgments to the details of what they have heard. Listeners' answers are followed up with elicitation techniques designed to yield hypotheses about what features of the message form (or as Gumperz expresses it, what "contextualization cues") are actually processed by the participants and what, in each case, the paradigmatic range of alternatives is, in terms of which the participants' interpretations are made. These elicitation techniques include questions such as, "What is there about the way A speaks that makes you think . . . ?" "Can you repeat it in the way he said it?" "What is another way of saying it?" "Is it possible that he merely wanted to ask a question?" "How would he have said it if he . . . ?" "How did the answerer interpret what A said?" "How can you tell that he interpreted it in that way?" Contextualization cues are marked usages at multiple levels (lexical; syntactic; paralinguistic; prosodic; formulaic expressions; conversational openings and closings; sequencing strategies; style, register, dialect, and code switches) which channel or guide interpretation by allowing the participants to signal to one another what they are doing together (whether chatting about the weather, lecturing about communication, telling a story, flirting), how the semantic content of the message is to be interpreted, and how what is being uttered relates to the developing topic or theme.

Interpretation obtained by means of these methods is used in this study to test hypotheses about

1. the interpretative schemata or frames (Fillmore 1975, 1976, 1977; Chafe 1977a, 1977b; Tannen 1979) or structures of expectations (Ross 1975) the participants relied on in determining what was meant at any point in the interviews. Schemata, which are based on participants' experience of similar situations in their culture or subculture, constrain their interpretations. They do this by causing the participants to predict the likely manner in which the interaction will unfold, and selectively perceive which permutations of behaviours at particular stages in the interaction constitute contextualization cues.

2. what features of the message form were perceived as salient and what are possible *systematic* differences in the contextualization cues S. A. English and Zulu-English speakers rely on in making sense of what is going on in conversations.

All the listeners (who were comprised of both male and female; staff and students; Zulu-English and S. A. English-speaking) were in agreement that the interview between A and C was more successful than that between A and B. They felt that there were no uncomfortable moments in the A–C interview, that A and C understood one another and probably ended the interview with an enhanced opinion of one another and with a sense that their goals (agendas) had been achieved. By contrast, the A–B interview was described as very stressful, with the participants frequently misinterpreting one another, with little progress being made with the agenda of either party, and with both parties probably arriving at the end of the interview with a poorer opinion of one another. For example, when asked what B thought of A by the end of the interview, one Zulu informant responded, "Son of a bitch!"[3]

Part of the differences among the interviews can be accounted for in terms of culture-specific schemata or frames. A and C apparently have access to a schema in which participants review the preparation of examinations retrospectively, analytically, and evaluatively. C signals that she shares A's assumptions and expectations about what activity (see Gumperz 1982a:131, 166) they are engaged in, what its goals are, and how they are to be accomplished, by engaging in the targeted (or expected) behaviour without preamble or prompt.

```
31. A:                        . . . look⌈ er
32.                        C:⌊one  thing
33. A: ya
34.    C:⌈one thing I really did want to ask you was um . . . just
35.    thinking gauging my own reactions to both papers
36.                        A:⌈aa
37.                        C:⌊I felt
38.    very strongly that I'd done much better I'd performed much better
39.    on the second pap⌈er than I had on the first
40.              A:⌊ya           A:⌈right
```

In a remarkably short time, A and C achieve conversational cooperation, fitting their individual contributions into an overall theme which fits the activity that they have implicitly agreed upon. Further evidence of the matching of expectations and the high degree of conversational synchrony is A's observation (lines 58–60):

no well I'm glad you're approaching it from that point of view because that's more or less the situation I wanted to put you in

and the way in lines 79 and 80 A and C "duet" (Falk 1979) in completing A's utterance.

By contrast, B does not appear to have access to this schema. Evidence of his assumptions and expectations about the activity appears only in lines 149–53.

```
149. A :                              . . . sorry to
150. be firing ⌈ you these questions I don't know if you expected me to
151.     B: ⌊ ya I see           yes
152. say this is where you went wrong ⌈ I'm trying to yes what I'm trying
153.                        B: ⌊ ya I expected that
```

More important, since even in intracultural encounters common themes have to be negotiated and expectations adjusted, A and B make little progress in achieving conversational cooperation. They fail to conform to one another's expectations, to build on one another's signals, and to develop a consistent, coherent theme to such an extent that A feels constrained to renegotiate what they are doing together as late as lines 149–64. Continuing from line 153 above, the interaction proceeds as follows:

```
154. A:  to find out is really how you set about doing it because I think if
155.     we can find out I'm not trying to blame you
156.                                    B: ⌐ye
157.                                    A: ⌐in any way I'm
158.     trying to find out where your preparation was not enough so I can
159.     tell you
160.     B: ⌐ye
161.         A: ⌐how you can learn
162.                         B: ⌐ ya
163.                             A: ⌐ er next time to do it
164.     properly
```

This lack of progress can be partly accounted for in terms of systematic differences in contextualization conventions between the S. A. English speaker and the Zulu-English speaker, in the "constellations of surface features of message form" which are "the means by which speakers signal and listeners interpret what the activity is, how semantic content is to be understood and how each sentence relates to what precedes or follows" (Gumperz 1982a:131).

Though B's responses in lines 7–27 (see Appendix) are not very informative, they are apparently synchronous and appropriate enough to assure A that agreement has been reached as to what they are doing together, for A proceeds to signal (line 44) the first discourse task (see Gumperz 1982a:208) consistent with that activity, namely that of comparing B's assessment of his performance on specific questions with the examiners' assessment.

```
44. A:  alright now perhaps you can tell me which of those er you
45. thought . . . you did best in . . . which you were happiest about
46. B:  I I'm not sure but
47.         A: ⌐yes
48.             B: ⌐I think it number 5
49.                             A: ⌐number 5
50. B:  (not clear)
51.             A: ⌐ alright . . . that that's right that that was the
52. question that we thought was your best question
53.                                         B: ⌐m
54.                                             A: ⌐alright . . . erm
```

55. and then which of the two there
56.   B: ⌐I . . . I think one and two are
57. which was equally difficult
58.   A: ⌐equally difficult
59.   B: ⌐yah
60.   A: ⌐and
61. B: and not actually difficult but I think er not prepared

There is considerable evidence in this extract that B is uncertain of what A wants them to do together. For example, there is B's hedged, tentative response in line 46. Then, too, there is the way he interprets "happiest," which A uses to signal again the culture-specific interpretative schema (described earlier), as "least difficult." Perhaps most interesting is his interpretation of A's utterance in line 58. Possibly because B has responded tentatively (lines 56–57), A asks him to reconsider his judgment of which question was more difficult. B however interprets this as a request to reconsider whether both questions were difficult or not.

An important contributing factor to B's interpretations is his apparent failure to "read" the implicit cue provided by the accentuation of "equally" (line 58). A's utterance here is marked as a single tone group or information unit with the nucleus placement – a rise fall pitch movement – on "equally":

ēqually difficult

In terms of the contextualization conventions of S. A. English, by accentuating "equally," A signals that it is this part of his message that he would like B to build on. After listening carefully to the sequence 54–58 and then being asked whether, in 58, A was querying the information that B found the questions difficult to answer, or that B found the questions *equally* difficult, S. A. English informants, without exception, opted for the latter interpretation.

As Gumperz (1982a) and Gumperz, Aulakh, and Kaltman (1982) have shown, the ability of interlocutors to effect smooth turn change or build on one another's contributions in developing an argument or theme depends crucially on shared assumptions or expectations about how prosodic cues such as tone grouping, accent placement, and paralinguistic choices (e.g., loudness and rate of speech) interact with lexical and syntactic choices to signal, for example, speaker transition points and relationships among different parts of the interaction. Smooth interactions also depend on participants' assumptions/expectations about the balance of the signalling load carried by these cues and choices. B's response to A's utterance in line 58 is but one of a number of instances that suggest that A and B do not share these expectations. Given that the prosody of Zulu, a tone language, is very different than that of English, and that few people master the prosody of a second language, it should not be surprising to find that there are systematic differences between S. A. English and Zulu-English in this respect. Pending further investigation, I hypothesize that

1. the signalling load marked prosodically is less in Zulu-English than in S. A. English;

2. Zulu-English speakers rely on prosodic cues to signal information different than that outlined above for S. A. English.

To continue with the analysis, the failure to build upon one another's signals is evident in the sequence from lines 66–76.

```
66.        A: alright . . . now well let me let me give this information
67. er your question 1 was a very bad answer in our terms whereas
68. your question 2
69.            B:⌐ yah
70.            A:⌊was a pass you passed question 5
71.                              .                          B:⌐ yah
72. A: you passed question 2 but you failed question 1 rather badly
73. B: oh I I see the reason now with question 1 I think I said something
74. about performance . . . although (B continues to speak – unclear)
75.            A:        do you yah you know you spoke about . . . sorry
76. can I cut in there
```

B apparently interprets the information supplied by A as an indirect, implicit request to explain his poor performance in question one rather than to consider why his assessment of his performance did not match that of the examiner.

Of course, poor progress in achieving conversational cooperation and negotiating a common theme is as much a failure of A to conform to the expectations of B and build on his signals as the reverse. It could well be that B is more voluble in 73, because A seems to be conforming to his (B's) expectations of the activity, namely for A to provide details of the strengths and weaknesses of particular answers. A, however, instead of building on this contribution, breaks into it, thus preventing B from developing this new theme or topic further.

Taking the view that participants' sense of interruption derives not directly from observed structural regularities (see Bennet 1981), such as speech overlapping at what is not a possible completion point, but from their interpretations in terms of assumptions and expectations which they bring to the interaction and which evolve in the course of it, it is likely that A and B will have perceived what happens here quite differently. B will probably have felt A's behaviour to be face threatening (see Brown & Levinson [1978]; R. Lakoff [1973, 1979]; and the discussion below), denying him, as it does, an equal role or at least a share in negotiating the direction of talk. A shows that he is aware that breaking in is potentially face threatening by using the politeness strategies of apologising and then asking permission, thereby lessening the sense of imposition. A does this, however, only when B struggles to hold onto the floor, which suggests that A did not perceive his first attempt to break in as an interruption. Because B's contribution is irrelevant to the theme that, as A sees it, B has implicitly agreed to develop, breaking in is not a denial of B's rights. Moreover, the pause which follows "performance" is sufficient, in terms of S. A. English norms, to function as a contextualization cue which, interacting with other cues, takes on the value of a signal that B has possibly completed his turn.

This again points to the possibility of systematic differences between Zulu and English and S. A. English in the signalling load carried via prosodic cues and in the sort of information signalled prosodically. There is anecdotal evidence that Zulu-English speakers, on average, speak more slowly than S. A. English speakers (or are perceived by both groups to do so), that pauses of relatively short duration do not function as turn exchange signals in Zulu English, and that Zulu-English speakers are generally more tolerant of extended monologue than S. A. English speakers. Such characteristics of Zulu English may be related to the survival of a strong oral tradition, since Zulus have a relatively short history of literacy, and to targeted behaviour within that culture.[4] As one Zulu informant explained, *what is highly valued within his culture is behaviour which proceeds at a steady, measured, dignified pace.* A person who speaks fast or without greeting is perceived by Zulus as rude. By contrast, targeted discourse behaviour within S. A. English culture is that which is consistent with Gricean maxims (see Grice 1975), that is, brief and to the point.

Such differences could account for the limited contributions of Zulu-English speakers in the honours seminar meetings described above and for the more general perceptions by Zulu-English speakers that they are often interrupted by S. A. English speakers, and by S. A. English speakers that Zulu-English speakers are poor contributors. The results on two items of a questionnaire that I conducted with S. A. English and Bantu-English undergraduates (most of whom were Zulus) are very revealing.[5] Asked to choose from four different generalizations about turn exchange behaviour when interacting with the other group, 50 percent of S. A. English speakers chose the generalization that Zulu-English speakers fail to take the opportunity to speak when given a turn, while 39 percent chose the generalization that Bantu-English speakers fail to produce a whole coherent idea. By contrast, 69 percent of Bantu-English speakers chose the generalization that S. A. English speakers interrupt them before they have completed their point. Asked to choose from three descriptions of the behaviour of members of their own group when meeting for the first time at a social gathering, 60 percent of the S. A. English speakers chose the description that they would be uncomfortable with even short silences, while only 15 percent of Bantu-English speakers chose this option.

Returning to the analysis once more, it is significant to note that B seems unsure as to how to interpret A's request (lines 84–86) and then gives a reply which is consistent with the theme he tried unsuccessfully to develop in lines 72–73, namely the explanation of his poor performance.

81.   A: can I ask you you remember
82. we gave you the outline here
83.   B:| yes
84.   A:| can I ask you how set about . . .
85. preparing that question
86.   B:| I . . . I . . . ⌈(unclear) my problem was
87.   A:| what did you do   B:|er
88. reading material to cover the topic

A apparently considers this reply sufficiently related to his own theme/agenda to build on it, which he does by signalling that B should continue by using, in conjunction with other cues, a fall rise intonation cue:

89. A: yĕs

Once again it is evident that A and B's expectations in respect of prosodic cues are not shared, for B apparently interprets A's "yes" not as meaning "continue," but as a sort of preclosure, meaning "I see."

A similar problem arises when A, in line 91, attempts to continue with the development of a theme which B has apparently attempted to close.

89.   A: yes
90.   B:| yes
91.   A:| you mean you . . . you
92. didn't have the reading ⌈ . . . or you didn't know what the reading was
                            B:⌊ (starts to speak)
93. B: yes sir

Partly because he is beginning to reply subsequent to "reading," (line 92) and partly because he does not share A's prosodic conventions, B sees A as recycling his interpretation of what B said in lines 86-88, rather than querying which of two alternative interpretations is correct. This demonstrates the unfortunate consequences of asynchrony in intercultural communication. Because the second alternative comes "at the wrong time" (cf. Erickson 1978), namely when he has already started to speak himself, and because he has apparently some other means of signalling, B misses the significance of the accentuation of "know."

A decides (probably incorrectly) that B's reply relates to the second alternative but has so little success in pursuing this subtheme that he feels obliged once again (line 110) to recycle his task initiation of line 84 [A: Can I ask you how you set about preparing that question].

110. A: I'm interested in knowing how you set about your preparation

B's response (line 117) suggests that he is just as unsure of what A is trying to get them to do together as he was at the beginning, while A (line 149) is still guessing about B's assumption and expectations (. . . sorry to be firing you these questions I don't know if you expected me to . . .)

Thus far, I have presented evidence which suggests that the relative asynchrony of the A–B encounter in comparison with the A–C encounter can be accounted for in terms of differences in culture-specific interpretative schemata and contextualization conventions. As I explained earlier, I had hypothesized before starting to analyse that no further explanation would be required, but was obliged to reconsider this after analysing the A–D encounter, to which I now turn.

DIFFERENT FACE VALUES AS SOURCES OF ASYNCHRONY

Since mismatch of schemata or contextualization conventions cannot be posited in the case of A–D, I was initially at a loss as to what was responsible for the asynchrony. A clue was provided by a Zulu informant who commented that B seemed to be devious. Further questioning revealed that what he meant was that B was trying, at any cost, to save face. Looking at all three encounters in terms of potential face loss, I recognized, for the first time, that the A–B and A–D situations were potentially more face threatening than A–C because, whereas C had fared very well in the examination, B and D had fared poorly. When persons have just experienced loss of face, acts which in other circumstances are not particularly risky become, for them, face-threatening acts.

Close examination of A–D reveals that the asynchrony is a function not of different contextualization conventions and/or mismatch of culture-specific schemata, but of different "readings" by A and D of how face threatening the accomplishment of the activity A signals he wants them to engage in together, really is. What has not been emphasized so far in this paper is that the participants signal to one another, not merely *what* is happening (the activity), but also *who* each is at each moment in the unfolding of the interaction, for example, what their relative status is and hence what their communicative rights and obligations, including rights to the floor and deference to face, are. When D, lines 57–59, attempts to short-circuit the process of retrospectively reviewing the preparation of the examination in which he fared poorly, which he senses is fraught with great risk of face loss, he appears to A to challenge A's view of their relationship and respective rights and obligations.

To understand what happens here in terms of face, we can draw on Brown and Levinson's (1978) model of politeness strategies. They argue that people, universally, have the need on the one hand to have freedom of action and freedom from imposition (negative face) and on the other hand to be approved of by others (a positive self image or positive face). Such needs are often difficult to reconcile since people who are overly concerned to preserve their freedom of action may impose their wills on others (i.e., threaten others' negative face) at the expense of their popularity (i.e., by losing positive face). Similarly, people who are over concerned with their popularity (with saving their positive face) may find themselves imposed upon (i.e., their negative face threatened).

It is the balancing of the desire to maintain face oneself against the need to preserve the face of others which provides the motivation for the choice of different strategies for minimising threat to face. These are listed by Brown and Levinson as follows:

1. Baldly on record without redressive action (e.g., "Give me a hand").
2. Positive politeness (e.g., "Give me a hand pal").
3. Negative politeness (e.g., "Look I'm terribly sorry to bother you but . . ."").
4. Off record, where the act is phrased in such a way that, if necessary, it can be interpreted as not implying an imposition at all (e.g., "This task is really more than one person can reasonably handle").
5. Not done, where a person feeling that the act is too risky does not say or do anything.

Scollon and Scollon (1982) helpfully refer to the low-numbered strategies (1 & 2) as "solidarity politeness," this highlighting the fact that they can be strategies for emphasising the closeness of the relationship between the participants, that is, little distance ($-D$) and power differences ($-P$) between them. The other strategies they refer to as "deference politeness," thus emphasising the social distance ($+D$) between the participants.

According to Brown and Levinson, three factors determine which of these strategies will be chosen: power (P), distance (D), and the extent or "weightiness" (W) of the threat. Brown and Levinson express the relationship among these factors in terms of the following formula:

$$Wx = D (S, H) + P (H, S) + Rx$$

Wx, the weightiness of a face-threatening act, is determined by adding D, a value for the social distance between speaker (S) and hearer (H), P, a measure of the power the hearer has over the speaker; and Rx, a value that measures the degree to which the act is rated as an imposition in the culture of the participants.

Brown and Levinson suggest that different global politeness systems are created as a consequence of the different ways groups typically treat these factors (D, P, & W). If a group typically maintains distance ($-P$, $+D$), this will create an overall deference politeness system, and, if it typically emphasises the closeness of the relationships among its members ($-P$, $-D$), this will create an overall solidarity politeness system. Both deference and solidarity politeness systems are symmetrical, in the sense that both speaker and hearer use the same strategies in their interaction. In both cases, this reflects the small difference in power between the participants. Where there is a great difference in power ($+P$), an overall asymmetrical system is created in which the powerful participant uses solidarity politeness, as it were, "downwards," and the less powerful participant uses deference politeness "upwards."

In the A–D encounter, as in A–B and A–C, A consistently uses bald, on record strategies, apparently to signal the operation of a symmetrical solidarity politeness system ($-P$, $-D$) which reflects the democratic style of teaching used in the course, which is discussed above. However, in lines 57–67, D threatens A's face by denying him the floor by means of the strategy of increasing volume and speed (line 57) and of putting words in A's mouth.

57. the application (increasing volume and speed) now I don't think I did
58. this in this essay um answered that question entirely in that frame
59. of reference
60.   A:⌊ya
61.   D:⌊_I think that is what you're going to say
62.   A:⌊ well
63. well I'm I'm ⌈ wanting to see
64.   D: ⌊ you're you're going to say I didn't actually um answer
65. the essay in relation to what he can do to his pupils as to develop
66. his pupils' awareness of situation that's what the position is ⌈ (con-
67. tinues)
68.
                                                          A:⌊   well I

That A sees D's behaviour as face threatening is evident from his metacomment in lines 68–70:

A: well I no I'm what I want to know is um you know don't don't make me more Machiavellian than I am

What D is apparently doing is challenging the assumptions of A about distance (i.e., −D), thereby implying that A is not sympathetic. Significantly, he does not challenge A's assumptions about the power differential (i.e., −P). This is evident from the fact that he, the less powerful participant, does not produce deference politeness, which would be the appropriate way of signalling an asymmetrical relationship.

In the light of what I had observed in A–D, I reexamined the A–B encounter and discovered that face considerations played an important role in that interaction as well. However, *in response to similar behaviour by A, B and D choose different strategies, which lead to quite different outcomes.*

Whereas D consistently uses low-numbered strategies (solidarity politeness), going on-record usually without any redressive action, B tends to use high-numbered strategies (deference politeness). B thus challenges the value assigned by A to both P and D. The clearest example is his use of the address term "sir" (line 93), a deferential, high-numbered strategy which contrasts with the absence of any address term earlier in the interaction, and which represents an attempt to deal with what is becoming an ever more stressful encounter by signifying that he does not wish to challenge A in any way. More difficult to substantiate is the possibility that one of the reasons B fails to claim the floor, and to resist attempts by A to take it from him, is that he constantly goes off-record or decides that the act is too risky to attempt at all (strategies 4 & 5).

There are probably many reasons why B consistently chooses deference strategies. An important reason could be that B's behaviour is consistent with what is viewed as desirable target behaviour within his culture and, therefore, behaviour that he has been socialized into adopting. Lakoff (1979) has argued that differences in the targeted behaviour of male and female subcultures in the United States are reflected in the tendency for women to choose strategies that make them appear, to people outside their cultures, as deferential and insecure, and in the tendency for men to appear confident and competitive. Similar differences seem to exist between S. A. English and Zulu-English speakers. The high-numbered, deference strategies appear to be survival strategies adopted consistently by members of dominated groups in their interactions with members of dominant groups. The findings of research carried out by O'Barr and Atkins on the language of men and women in the American trial courtroom appears to substantiate this generalization. They found that features of women's language identified by Lakoff (1975) correlated less with sex than with social status. Based on this evidence, they suggest that the tendency for more women to speak what they call "powerless language" is due, at least in part, to the fact that they tend to hold relatively powerless positions in society. Similarly, the tendency for men to use "powerful language" is related to the tendency for them to hold powerful positions.

An explanation of the tendency for dominated groups to use "powerless language" is to be found in Brown and Levinson's observation, noted above, that different global politeness systems are created as a consequence of the different ways groups typically treat the factors D, P, and W. When the lowly status of a group persists over a long period of time, deferential behaviour associated with the less powerful participant in an asymmetrical politeness system can become a conventionalized, targeted communication style.

A communication style which assumes a relationship of +P, +D between speakers no doubt serves the Zulu-English speakers well, in that it helps ensure that they do not seem to be challenging the authority of the more powerful persons they are interacting with nor to be too familiar. It creates problems in intercultural communication when members of the dominant group, whites, fail to realize that the deference is conventional or customary rather than what is really felt. When Zulus refuse to be "treated as doormats," as their deferential behaviour appears to invite, or submit resentfully to it, they are perceived as unreliable, fickele, inconsistent, or even illogical. It creates problems also, as we have seen, when, in a particular situation, participants assume the operation of different politeness systems. In the A–B encounter, it appears that whereas A is assuming the operation of a symmetrical solidarity system (−P, −D), B is assuming the operation of an asymmetrical deference system (+P, +D).

Deference could have become targeted conventional behaviour for Zulu-English speakers for another reason: For them, the set of persons they want to be similar to and liked by, as opposed to the set by whom Zulu-English speakers want a special trait or ability they possess, admired but nothing more, is larger than it is for S. A. English speakers (see Brown & Levinson 1978:249). The first set for S. A. English speakers usually includes only immediate family, close friends, and a select group of colleagues, whereas for Zulu-English speakers, it usually includes kinship or peer group. This means that competitive, baldly on-record, solidarity strategies are more risky for Zulu-English speakers than for whites, which could account for stereotypes of Zulu-English speakers as unwilling to innovate or to take risks and responsibilities. Significantly, on the questionnaire, 29 percent of S. A. English speakers described Zulu-English speakers' behaviour as "modest and respectful" whenever the latter were asked by someone in authority about their (the Zulu-English speakers') knowledge, abilities, or achievements; 28 percent described them as "rather unsure of themselves." Only 4 percent chose the response that the Zulu-English speakers were "rather boastful or cocky," and only 3 percent that they were "confident and purposeful."

Another reason for deference becoming targeted behaviour could be the heavy weighting in terms of potential face loss given to certain activities by Zulu speakers (see Brown & Levinson 1978:249). For example, Gowlett (1979:7) has pointed out that, rather than risk the potential face loss of a confrontation with an employer, many blacks leave without notice, thus sacrificing their jobs. The querying of superiors' instructions, according to Gowlett, is similarly face threatening, which could account for the tendency for blacks to interpret as best they can instructions they do not fully understand, rather than ask for clarification. Seventy-nine percent of S. A. English speakers who completed the questionnaire referred to above chose the option that Bantu speakers "give the impression that they understand when they don't," in preference to the option that they tend "to be so concerned with the facts that they often fail to sense what you mean" or the option that they "say so if they don't understand what you mean or want." Misunderstanding of intentions and motives from this source may underlie stereotypes of black employees as irresponsible and as lacking in initiative, self confidence, and openness.

The adoption of deference strategies by B brings him certain short-term benefits. Despite the fact that A and B share far fewer assumptions and expectations than A and D, the A–B encounter is no less synchronous than the A–D encounter. However, the long-term effects are unfortunate. Not only does he not have his agenda attended to and thus get the help he feels he needs to perform better, but he is probably perceived by A as a student with few ideas of his own who is unlikely to take initiative for his own progress.

To sum up, the above analysis reveals how differences in the culture-specific interpretative schemata, contextualization conventions, and strategies for preserving face of S. A. English and Zulu-English speakers can lead to misinterpretation of motives and attitudes and negative evaluations of the abilities of members of the other group. It remains to show briefly how the results of such encounters combine with larger, structural, historically given forces to achieve a negative cycle of socially created discrimination.

NEGATIVE CYCLE OF SOCIALLY CREATED DISCRIMINATION IN SOUTH AFRICA

Macro studies reveal that historical, structural forces in South Africa have led to the majority of the dominant white group's development and adoption of an ideology of separation, to legally enforced segregation among the various race groups, and to considerable social barriers and disparity among the power, status, and material resources of the white and black groups. This means that few people have the opportunity to establish long-lasting personal relationships with members of other groups which, according to Gumperz (1982a:209), are necessary if they are to learn enough about one another's communication conventions and backgrounds to communicate efficiently interculturally and/or be willing to take time out to negotiate the meaning of what their background knowledge (sociocultural and linguistic) does not permit them to understand initially (see Figure 1).

Since cultural knowledge at this level is unconscious, participants, while conscious that certain intercultural encounters have been stressful, seldom identify the cause accurately. Instead, they perceive the other person as uncooperative, aggressive, callous, stupid, incompetent, or having some other undesirable personal traits.

Miscommunication in intercultural encounters can have serious consequences for persons from groups that do not enjoy power in South Africa (e.g., blacks, women, immigrants). Their ability to improve their socioeconomic positions depends vitally on successful communication with persons belonging to the dominant group (white male), who occupy most "gatekeeping" (see Erickson & Schultz 1981) positions (e.g., social welfare officers, job interviewers, examiners, educational and career counsellors, bureaucrats, etc.). Such people have the power to decide who is to get opportunities and a greater share of help, goods, and services a society has to offer. Where their abilities are misjudged as a consequence of miscommunication, persons from disadvantaged groups fare badly in attempts to secure housing, gain access to educational institutions, or get a job, an educational loan, promotion, and so on. In this way, miscommunication can lead directly to discrimination and the reinforcement of the inequity in the socioeconomic system.

Moreover, over time, repeated miscommunication of this kind generates negative cultural stereotypes. Examples of such stereotypes were given above, particularly in the discussion of face considerations. These stereotypes further reduce the effectiveness of intercultural communication because, even where cultural and linguistic differences do not cause problems, they predispose people to

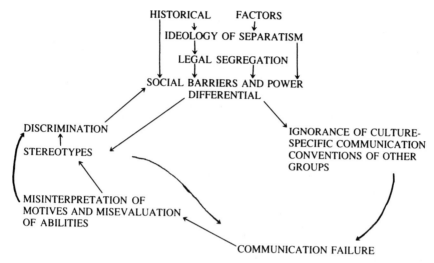

FIGURE I: Negative cycle of socially created discrimination.

selectively perceive whatever reinforces the stereotypes and ignore whatever does not.

Their negative role does not end there, for, once generated, stereotypes are passed on from generation to generation without the need for the reinforcement of repeated communication failure. Moreover, by providing a justification or rationalization for discrimination, they contribute to forces which maintain the social barriers and power differential among the different groups which made it difficult in the first place for people to learn the communication conventions and backgrounds of the other groups. This completes the negative cycle of socially created discrimination (illustrated in Figure I), which is difficult to arrest and in which even people who feel goodwill towards other groups find themselves admitting, reluctantly, that the negative stereotypes are apparently confirmed within their experience.

CONCLUSION

In this paper, I have attempted to demonstrate the potential contribution of interactional sociolinguistic analyses of intercultural encounters to the explication of discrimination in South Africa. I have also attempted to show how the findings of such analysis can be articulated with the findings of macro studies.

Though an examination of what can be done to break into the vicious, negative cycle of socially created discrimination outlined above is the subject of another paper, it is appropriate to note, in conclusion, that analyses such as the above demonstrate the naivete of proposals for eliminating discrimination by structural reform alone. In other words, the results of such analyses suggest that the scrapping of such measures as job reservation, the equalization of the per capita expenditure on the education of the various racial groups, or even integration at all levels of the education system, are unlikely to result in equality of educational and economic opportunity unless, simultaneously, people responsible for the evaluation of individuals (teachers, testers, employment officers, managers, and others in gatekeeping roles) are made aware of the potentiality of misinterpretation and make allowances for this. Indeed it may well be that the structural changes which are not accompanied by attention to the microprocesses are likely to prove counterproductive, because the failure of the former to produce anticipated results can be used as an argument against further reform.

NOTES

1.   The author wishes to acknowledge the helpful criticisms of John Gumperz, Doug Campbell, Cheryl Crawley, Ralph Adendorff, and Roy Dace. Research for this paper was supported by a grant from the Human Sciences Research Council.
2.   It is worth noting that at that time, as a consequence of the Universities Extension Act of 1955, the University was permitted to admit only blacks who had obtained the necessary approval. This requirement has since fallen away, although, by law, the government still has the power to determine the racial composition of the student intake to universities, should it decide to do so.
3.   The reader would find it useful at this stage to read the transcripts of these interviews in the Appendix in order to make his/her own interpretation of what is going on in each and to make greater sense of the analyses which follow.
4.   What I mean by targeted behaviour here is behaviour which is consistent with the implicit notion shared by members of a cultural group of how a "good" person should conduct him- or herself.
5.   By Bantu-English I mean one of the Bantu languages of Southern Africa (e.g., Zulu, Xhosa, Sotho, Tswana, Tsonga, Venda) is the mother tongue.

REFERENCES

Akinnaso, F. N. (1981). Research on minority languages and educational achievement: A synthesis and an interpretation. Paper presented at symposium on Urban Communication and Social Inequality at the 80th Annual Meeting of the American Anthropological Association, Los Angeles, California.
Bennet, A. (1981). Interruption and the Interpretation of conversation. *Discourse Processes* 4:171–88.
Brown, P., & Levinson, S. (1978). Universals in language usage: Politeness phenomena. In E. N. Goody (ed.), *Questions and politeness*. (Cambridge Papers in Socilal Anthropology 8.) Cambridge University Press. 56–289.
Chafe, W. (1977a). The recall and verbalization of past experience. In R. W. Cole (ed.), *Current issues in linguistic theory*. Bloomington: Indiana University Press. 215–45.
———— (1977b). Creativity in verbalization and its implications for the nature of stored knowledge. In R. D. Freedle (ed.), *Discourse production and comprehension*. Vol. 1. Norwood, N.J.: Ablex. 41–55.
Collins, R. (1975). *Conflict sociology: Towards an explanatory science*. New York: Academic.
Condon, W. (1977). The relation of interactional synchrony to cognitive and emotional processes. In M. Key (ed.)., *The relationship of verbal and nonverbal communication*. The Hague: Mouton. 50–65.
Erickson, F. (1975). Gatekeeping and the melting pot: Interaction in counselling encounters. *Harvard Educational Review* 45(1):44–70.

———— (1976). Gatekeeping encounters: A social selection process. In P. Sanday (ed.), *Anthropology and public interest*. New York: Academic. 111–145.

———— (1978). Timing and context in everyday discourse: Implications for the study of referential and social meaning. Paper delivered at the Conference on Children's Oral Communication Skills. University of Wisconsin.

Erickson, F., & Schultz, J. (1981). When is a context? Some issues and methods in the analysis of social competence. In J. L. Green & C. Wallat (eds.), *Ethnography and language in educational settings*. (Advances in Discourse Processes V.) Norwood, N.J.: Ablex,. 147–60.

Falk, J. (1979). The duet as a conversational process. Ph.D. dissertation, Princeton University.

Fillmore, C. J. (1975). An alternative to checklist theories of meaning. In *Proceedings of the First Annual Meeting of the Berkeley Linguistic Society*. University of California, Berkeley. 123–31.

———— (1976). Frame semantics and the nature of language. In S. R. Harnad et al. (eds.), *Origins and evolution of language and speech*. New York: Academy of Science. 20–32.

———— (1977). Scenes-and-frames semantics. In Zampoli (ed.), *Linguistic structures processing*. North Holland. 55–81.

Gowlett, D. F. (1979). Towards black-white understanding in South Africa. *I.S.M.A. Paper No. 36.* Johannesburg.

Grice, H. P. (1975). Logic and conversation. In P. Cole & J. Morgan (eds.), *Syntax and semantics, vol. 3: Speech acts*. New York: Academic. 41–58.

Gumperz, J. (1982a). *Discourse strategies*. (Studies in Interactional Sociolinguistics 1.) Cambridge University Press.

———— (ed.) (1982b). *Language and social identity*. (Studies in Interactional Scociolinguistics 2.) Cambridge University Press.

Gumperz, J., Aulakh, G. E., & Kaltman, A. (1982). Thematic structures and progression in discourse. In J. Gumperz (ed.), *Language and social identity*. Cambridge University Press. 22–56.

Kendon, A. (1973). The role of visible behaviour in the organization of social interaction. In M. Von Cranach (ed.), *Social communication and movement*. New York: Academic. 30–74.

———— (1979). Some theoretical and methodological aspects of the use of film in the study of social interaction. In G. Ginsberg (ed.), *Emerging strategies in social psychological research*. New York: John Wiley. 67–91.

Lakoff, R. (1973). The logic of politeness: Or minding your p's and q's. In C. Corum, T. C. Smith-Stark, A. Weiser (eds.), *Papers from the Eighth Regional Meeting of the Chicago Linguistics Society*. 292–305.

———— (1975). *Language and woman's place*. New York: Harper & Row.

————. (1979). Stylistic strategies with a grammar of style. In J. Oraisainn, M. Slater, & L. Loeb Adler (eds.), *Annals of the New York Academy of Sciences*, 327. New York: Academy of Sciences. 53–78.

McDermott, R., Gospodinoff, K., & Aron, J. (1978). Criteria for an ethnographically adequate description of concerted activities and their contexts. *Semiotica* 24(3,4):245–75.

McDermott, R. P., & Roth, D. R. (1978). The social organization of behaviour: Interactional approaches. In B. Siegel, et al. (eds.), *Annual Review of Anthropology*. Palo Alto: Annual Review. 321–345.

O'Barr, W. M., & Atkins, B. K. (1980). "Women's language" or "powerless language"? In S. McConnell-Ginet, R. Barker, & N. Furman (eds.), *Women and language – Literature and society*. New York: Praeger. 93–110.

Ross, R. (1975). Ellipsis and the structure of expectation. *San Jose State Occasional Papers in Linguistics*. Vol 1. 183–91.

Sacks, H. (1972). On the analysability of stories by children. In J. Gumperz & D. Hymes (eds.), *Direction in sociolinguistics*. New York: Holt, Rinehart and Winston. 329–45.

Sacks, H., Schegloff, E., & Jefferson, G. (1978). A simplest systematics for the organization of turn taking for conversation. In J. Schenkein (ed.), *Studies in the organization of conversational interaction*. New York: Academic. 7–55.

Scheflen, A. E. (1973). *Communicating structures: Analysis of a psychotherapy transaction*. Bloomington: Indiana University Press.

Schegloff, E. A. (1973). Recycled turn beginnings: A precise repair mechanism in conversations' turn-taking organization. Paper presented at the Summer Institute of Linguistics sponsored by the L.S.A., University of Michigan.

Schegloff, E. A., & Sacks, H. (1973). Opening up closings. *Semiotica* 8(4):289–327.

Schlemmer, L. (1977). Racial attitudes in southern Africa: The contributions of culture, economic interests, and history. In T. M. Shaw & K. A. Heard (eds.), *Cooperation and conflict in southern Africa: Papers in a regional subsystem*. Washington, D.C.: University Press of America. 161–83.

Scollon, R., & Scollon, S. (1982). *Narrative, literacy, and face in interethnic communication*. Norwood, N.J.: Ablex. [Also ch. 18, this volume.]

———— (1983). Face in interethnic communication. In J. C. Richards & R. W. Schmidt (eds.), *Language and communication*. London and New York: Longman. 156–88.

Tannen, D. (1979). What's in a frame? Surface evidence for underlying expectations. In R. Freedle (ed.), *New directions in discourse processing*. (Advances in Discourse Processes II.) Norwood, N.J.: Ablex. 137–181.

APPENDIX

A–B ENCOUNTER

Conventions used

conversation overlap ⌐⌐   turn change . . . speech pause

7. A: the best way of doing this . . . I can't show you the
8.   paper . . . right
9.   B: ⌐ ye
10.   A: ⌐ um . . . because that's um would be
11.   against university regulations
12.   B: ⌐ yes
13.   A: ⌐ but what I
14. thought I would do
15.   B: ⌐ ye
16.   A: ⌐ is to try and find out what
17. You thought were your good and your bad papers and then
18. see how it ties up with what we think . . . cos I think what's
19. important is that
20.   B: ⌐ yah
21.   A: ⌐ you . . . what your expectations
22. are are the same as our expectations
23.   B: ⌐ I see
24.   A: ⌐ so this
25. will help you where you thought you'd prepared well say . . .
26. and and knew what you were doing and we didn't agree you'll
27. be able to see
28.   B: ⌐ yah
29.   A: ⌐ alright . . . er can we turn to paper two
30. do you ⌐ have a copy of paper two here
31.   B: ⌐ ye   ye   ye   paper two (unclear)
32.   A: ⌐ alright let's um let me
33. try and make use of er of . . . my . . . question paper . . . there's
34. paper . . . paper one rather okay . . . let's put it there then we both
35. can have a look at it . . . um . . . you answered questions 2 . . . um
36. that's Halliday erm question 3 . . . I'm sorry no I'm wrong (not clear)
37. question 1 the Chomsky question
38.   B: ⌐ yes
39.   A: ⌐ question 2 the Halliday
40. question
41.   B: ⌐ mmm
42.   A: ⌐ and question 5 which was the tense question
43. B: yes
44.   A: ⌐ alright now perhaps you can tell me which of those er you
45.   thought . . . you did best in . . . which you were happiest about

46. B: I I'm not sure but
47.   A:⌊ yes
48.   B: ⌊I think it number 5
49.   A:⌊ number 5
50. B: (not clear)
51.   A: ⌊ alright . . . that that's right that that was the
52. question that we thought was your best question.
53.   B: ⌊ m
54.   A: ⌊alright . . . erm
55. and then which of the two there
56.   B: ⌊I . . . I think one and two are
57. which was equally difficult
58.   A:⌊ equally difficult
59.   B: ⌊yah
60.   A: ⌊ and
61. B: and not actually difficult but I think er not prepared
62.   thoroughly or my approach in answering was not quite . . . according to
63.   expected standard
64.   A:⌊ er in the case of which one both of them
65. B: I think both
66.   A: ⌊ alright . . . now well let me let me give this information
67.   er your question 1 was a very bad answer in our terms whereas
68.   your question 2
69.   B: ⌊ yah
70.   A:⌊ was a pass you passed question 5
71.   B:⌊ yah
72. A: you passed question 2 but failed question 1 rather badly
73. B: oh I I see the reason now with question 1 I think I said something
74.   about a performance . . . ⌈ although (B continues to speak – unclear)
75.   A⌊ do you yah you know you spoke about . . . sorry
76. can I cut in there
77.   B: ⌊ yes
78.   A:⌊erm you know you spoke about er your
79. preparation
80.   B: ⌊ ye
81.   A: ⌊ can I ask you you remember
82. we gave you the outline here
83.   B: yes
84.   A: can I ask you how set about . . .
85. preparing that question
86.   B:⌊ I . . . I . . . ⌈ (unclear) my problem was
87.   A: ⌊ what did you do   B:⌊ er
88. reading material to cover the topic
89.   A:⌊ yes
90.   B: ⌊ yes
91.   A: ⌊you mean you . . . you
92.   didn't have the reading ⌈ . . . or you didn't know what the reading was
                              B: ⌊ (starts to speak)
93. B: yes sir
94.   A: ⌊ what what reading did you use in fact . . . in in preparing
95.   for that one
96.   B: ⌊ `. . . I I think I found some portion in the notes
97.   and one ⌈ of the
98.   A: ⌊ from the seminar
99.   B: ⌊ ya ya from the seminars sir
100.   A: ⌊ yes

101. B: ya
102.   ⌐and
103.   B: ⌊I I thought it was not enough for the question
104. A: why why did you choose that question then rather than the other
105.   question . . . did you how many of the questions did you actually
106.   prepare
107.   B: ⌊I I prepared those three
108.   A: ⌊those three . . . yes
109. B: but a (slight pause)
110.   A: ⌊ I'm interested in knowing how you set about
111.   your preparation
112.   B: ⌊ ya
113.   A: ⌊what what you felt you needed to do
114.   because I think this is the important thing to sort out what did
115.   B: ⌊ye
116. A: you feel you needed to do in order to prepare for that question . . . say
117. B: (unclear) yaa (softly)
118.   A: ⌊do you did you feel that um you should
119.   rely on what you had got from seminars . . . .
120.   B: ⌊ . . y ye yes er some part
121.   of the question but I I thought I should have used the Chomsky
122. A: yes
123.   B: ⌊ but a
124.   A: ⌊which Chomsky did you think you would use
125.   B: ⌊th the
126.   the precise book
127.   A: ⌈ which one . . . the the one by Lyons
128.   B: ⌊(unclear)
129.   B: ⌊oh yes yes
130. A: the one by Lyons
131.   B: ⌊ yes
132.   A: ⌊ yes and did you feel that that would be
133.   enough for the whole question
134.   B: ⌊ . . . . I think I discovered later that
135.   it was not enough
136.   A: ⌊when
137.   B: ⌊ when wh wh
138.   A: ⌊ how late I mean ⌈ (laugh)
139.   B: ⌊ I mm mean
140. A: in the exam
141.   B: ⌊in the exam yes
142.   A: ⌊ ye
143.   B ⌊yaa
144.   A: ⌊ which
145.   B: ⌊because
146.   this er
147.   A: ⌊in other words did you feel that the topic we
148.   actually gave you was too different from what we had said here . . .
149.   which part of the question er worried you in the exam . . . sorry to
150.   be firing ⌈ you these questions I don't know if you expected me to
151.   B: ⌊ ya I see   yes
152.   say this is where you went wrong ⌈ I'm trying to yes what I'm trying
153.   B: ⌊ ya I expected that
154.   to find out is really how you set about doing it because I think if
155.   we can find out I'm not trying to blame you
156.   B: ⌊ ye
157.   A: ⌊in any way I'm

158.   trying to find out where your preparation was not enough so I can
159.   tell you___
160.   B:⌊ ye
161.   A:⌊how can you learn
162.   B:⌊ ya
163.   A:⌊ er next time to do it
164.   properly___
165.   B:⌊ (reading aloud) to what extent subsequent developments
166.   within generative theory (unclear)
167.   A:⌊yes which is the part of the
168.   question that you felt you couldn't⌈ deal with
169.   B:⌊ er . . . the last part

A—C ENCOUNTER

7.   (tape starts) the *Articulate mammal* oh no they didn't have the
8.   *Articulate mammal*
9.   A:⌊ ya
10.   C:⌊they ordered (unclear) they didn't seem to
11.   know very much about anything at all and this lot here have got
12.   virtually nothing___
13.   A:⌊ yes
14.   C:⌊very little . . .
15.   A:⌈ so have they got it I mean
16.   C:⌊   what
17. A: are___
18.   C:⌊ no no copies available at either Logans or Adams
19.   A:⌊ ya
20. C: which is very typical I suppose two months to order three months
21.   after (unclear)
22.   A:⌊well we're having trouble with our undergraduate
23.   course where er we you know we asked them to we said we're going to
24.   have over 300 students in Durban and anything up to 100 students in
25.   Pietermaritzburg
26.   C:⌊and they just haven't accommodated ⌈you at all
27.   A:⌊ and you know there
28.   are a whole lot of students who haven't got copies . . . it's just so so
29.   frustrating___
30.   C:⌊mm and then they overcater when one doesn't need
31. A: ya well I've not yet had the overcater yet . . . look⌈ er
32.   C:⌊ one thing
33. A: ya
34.   C:⌊one thing I really did want to ask you was um . . . just
35.   thinking gauging my own reactions to both papers___
36.   A:⌊ aa
37.   C:⌊I felt
38.   very strongly that I'd done much better I'd performed much better
39.   on the second pap⌈ er than I had on the first___
40.   A:⌊ ya   A:⌊ right
41.   C:⌊which made me
42.   decide very definitely that you are obviously looking for different
43.   things because I felt desperate in the first one I couldn't I had
44.   no facts at immediate recall.
45.   A:⌊ ya ya
46.   C:⌊I couldn't sit down and say
47.   right I've got a broad overview pe⌈ rspective
48.   A:⌊ ya

49.   C: ⌐I got sort of vaguely
50.   panic stricken at the fact that I didn't have facts at immediate
51.   recall⌐
52.   A: ⌊yes
53.   C: ⌊I couldn't just say fine I've got a reasonably
54.   structured approach and so on I was very much feeling for things
55.   and articulating things that I hadn't formulated before
56.   A: right⌐
57.   C: ⌊and left it feeling immensely dissatisfied⌐
58.   A: ⌊no well I'm
59.   glad you're approaching it from that point of view because that's
60.   more or less the situation I wanted to put you in⌐
61.   C: ⌊mm
62.   what I've done with the other people is to say to them well you tell
63.   me what things you think⌐
64.   C: ⌊ya⌐
65.   A: ⌊you did best in and worst in so that you
66.   can find out if our your expectations are ⌈ (unclear) are matching ours
67.   C: ⌊ matching yours

A–D ENCOUNTER

3. A: what I thought we might do . . . is to sort of . . . explore assump-
4.   tions . . . about what what are the requirements of a of an essay topic
5.   say in other words um you tell me what you think the demands of a
6.   particular topic are of a particular question . . . and then I tell you
7.   what I think they are⌐
8.   D: ⌊m⌐
9.   A: ⌊and because I think this is more or less
10.   what's what what shall we say goes wrong where people don't get um
11.   the marks that they think they ought to have got or ⌈ their
12.   D: ⌊ (unclear)
13.   A: ⌊amount
14.   of work is not necessarily translatable into the marks it's often
15.   that they're straining at what is not required (laughter in voice)
16.   than what is required⌐
17.   D: ⌊ya ya⌐
18.   A: ⌊and some in some cases you'll find
19.   that what you assume is the right thing is what we assume is the
20.   right thing in other occasions it will be quite different⌐
21.   D: ⌊ya⌐
22.   A: ⌊so I
23.   think this is what I see as as the value of of a chat like this
24.   alright um let's put a this register thing away and have a look at a
25.   the essay . . . do you remember the topic was um ⌈ ⌈ reading ⌉ being appro-
26.   D: ⌊ ⌊ together ⌋
27.   priate to the situation is not some optional extra in language it is
28.   an essential element in the ability to mean⌐
29.   D: ⌊ya⌐
30.   A: ⌊alright (continuing
31.   to read) how can language teacher develop his pupils' awareness
32.   of this and their ability to respond appropriate to the different
33.   situations um which⌐
34.   D: ⌊to different situations⌐
35.   A: ⌊to different
36.   situations which of these two parts of the topic would you say um

37.   tells you what you actually have to do in the essay
38.   D: ⌊well well it's
39.   the second part ⌈ (continues)
40.   A:⌊ the second the second part
41.   D:⌊ ya
42.   A: ⌊now what would you
43.   say the function of a (speeding up) because you often get a sort of
44.   rubric like this don't you
45.   D: ⌊ya ya
46.   A: ⌊ in a in a examination or some-
47.   thing they give you a quotation ⌈ and
48.   D: ⌊ um the function of the first part of
49.   the essay is obviously is to is to is to point to the um the area of
50.   linguistic study un which has um contributed to a
51.   A: ⌊to what
52.   D: ⌊to to
53.   perhaps people making applications of a situation in relation to
54.   language teaching um the function of this is just to to highlight the
55.   area of a of the a of the theoreticians who (unclear, low volume)
56.   relationship of language to situation I think this would lead towards
57.   the application (increasing volume and speed) now I don't think I did
58.   this in this essay um answered that question entirely in that frame
59.   of reference
60.   A:⌊ ya
61.   D: ⌊I think that is what you're going to say
62.   A: ⌊ well
63.   well I'm I'm ⌈ wanting to see
                  D: ⌊ you're you're going to say I didn't actually um answer
65.   the essay in relation to a what he can do to his pupils as to develop
66.   his pupils' awareness of situation that's what the position is ⌈(con-
67.   tinues)
68.   A:⌊ well I
69.   no I'm what I want to know is um you know don't don't make me more
70.   Machiavellian than I ⌈ am (continues)
71.   D:⌊ no no I I am awa ⌈ re of what you (continues)
72.   A: ⌊ no what I'm interested in
73.   is really in is to see as um as the function of different
74.   parts of the essay a in other words what constraints does it
75.   put upon you
76.   D: ⌊well you have to answer the the question in relation
77.   to the pupils' awareness I mean of of how the teacher can develop his
78.   pupils' awareness um
79.   A:⌊ alright so what which part of this are you are
80.   focusing on . . . ⌈ (starts to say something)
                      D: ⌊ um the . . . I would say I would say my my essay was
82.   based on the relationship of situation to the teacher and um
83.   A:⌊ yes
84.   what I was quite interested in in your discussion here is that you're
85.   saying how can the language teacher develop his pupils' awareness and
86.   you're saying a this essay should have been more about how the language
87.   teacher can develop his pupils' awareness
88.   D:⌊ no . . . a . . .
89.   A: ⌊um
90.   D: ⌊ya I
91.   a um I had some difficulty with the essay I was going to say you
92.   anticipated me when you said that you said you'd been Machiavellian

93.   but um the thing is that um what I said was that I had some difficulty
94.   with the essay in tension between these two things
95.   A: ⌐ yes
96. D: a for a start teacher cannot develop his pupils' awareness until he
97.   realises the relationship between language and situation himself
98.   A: ⌐_ya
99. D: so therefore
100.   A: ⌐ did you say that
101.   D: ⌐_um ya I did say that well I
102.   A: ⌐_was
103.   that the point of your essay
104.   D: ⌐ I quoted Bloomfield
105.   A: ⌐_yes but I ⌐ mean
106.   D: ⌐   I
107. (A)   a you see   if you had said that if you'd made that
108. (D)   quoted Brumfit and Johnson yes
109. (A)   your key point
110.   D: ⌐ it was a key point in the essay
111.   A: ⌐ ya but in other
112.   words if you had said um that first of all the teacher needs to
113.   know . . . THIS if you like
114.   D: ⌐ ya . . . I mean essentially that that
115.   A: ⌐_well
116.   that that was your your major essay I mean that was your major point
117.   which you developed ⌐ that would be that would be dealing with
118.   D: ⌐ ya ya that was part of my essay
119. (A)   that point
120.   D: ⌐ ya⌐ (continues unclear)
121.   A: ⌐ now if you'd done that would you say that you had
122.   met the constraints that were um that were put on you by the topic
123. D: . . . not tha alone no

17
Reflections on Language, Interaction, and Context: Micro and Macro Issues

J. KEITH CHICK

The paper re-printed here as chapter 16 is part of a larger research program in which I am investigating what the emerging field of interactional sociolinguistics has to contribute to the better understanding of the relationship between language and context. I am concerned, in the first place, with the relationship between language and context in the sense of small scale (micro-cosmic) conversational settings: with how participants' interpretations of intent and evaluation of attitude and ability, at any stage of the conversation, depend on the speech setting, the meanings of other parts of the conversation and on the backgrounds of the participants. I am concerned, also, with the relationship between language and context in the sense of large-scale (macro-cosmic) social structure: with how what takes place at the micro-level of social life affects such features of the macro-level of social life as prejudice, discrimination, and the distribution of power.

As I explain more fully elsewhere (Chick, 1984, 1987), the work of interactional sociolinguists, and particularly their investigations of intercultural miscommunication, has important theoretical implications for linguistics. Tannen (1984), for example, argued that intercultural communication contributes to linguistic theory by providing a discourse analog to the starred (ungrammatical) sentence in linguistic argumentation. In such argumentation, ungrammatical rather than the grammatical sequences generated by linguists' syntactic rules are taken as grounds for modifying these rules. Similarly, the examination of asynchronous discourse — assembled by participants whose expectations about how to show what is meant do not match — reveals semantic processes that go unnoticed in successful communication.

The focus of the research of which this paper represents a part, however, is more applied than theoretical in purpose. Accordingly, in this epilogue, I focus on what for me have been the two areas of major applied interest. One of these areas is addressed in chapter 16, and I point to those aspects of the account given in it which I believe need to be revised. In the case of the second area of interest, I merely confine myself to outlining two important insights that have emerged from this area of the research. I also refer to some of the criticisms leveled against the research, and my responses to these. I conclude by highlighting what I see as the major limitation of the research to date. In so doing, I point to avenues for further research.

First, as is evident in the previous chapter, I am using interactional sociolinguistic methods to investigate the sources and consequences of asynchrony in interethnic encounters in South Africa. To date, I have focused exclusively on interactions through the medium of English. Analyses of interactions between South African English and Zulu English speakers (see, e.g., chapter 16) and between South African English and Afrikaans English speakers (reported in Chick, 1987, in press) have revealed some of the sources of asynchrony in such encounters. The consequences of such asynchrony in terms of misinterpretation, misevaluation, prejudice, and stereotyping, and the reinforcement of a negative cycle of socially created discrimination are outlined in this paper. What, on reflection, I believe is missing from this account, is some reference to prejudice that has its source in the needs and anxieties of individuals. Not all intercultural encounters are equally asynchronous, and presumably one of the factors contributing to the levels of synchrony or asynchrony is the personalities of the participants. For example, a particularly prejudiced individual might contribute to asynchrony in an intercultural encounter by being insensitive to the face needs of the other participants. This acknowledgment that the personalities of individuals may be sources of asynchrony does not, of course, represent a shift in the view expressed in chapter 16 that instances of asynchrony that have sociocultural sources are often erroneously accounted for in psychological terms.

However, even if this account were elaborated along these lines, it would still be partial. It focuses on the features of the macro-social structure that have a negative effect on the quality of intercultural communication, and on how asynchrony in such communication reinforces the negative features of the macro-structure. It does not acknowledge the existence of positive features of the wider society, or the beneficial consequences of synchrony in intercultural communication. A more comprehensive account would be one showing the vicious negative cycle as operating in the context of a larger pattern that includes a positive system opposed to discrimination, and with which it interacts. I see such a positive system as involving—like the negative cycle of discrimination—structural, interactional, and individual elements. Simpson and Yinger (1985) explained that, on the individual level, people are not only dominated by competitive aggressive impulses but also by co-operative, altruistic impulses, and that powerful religious and political ideologies consolidate the latter into norms and values that stress co-operativeness and helpfulness and that become embodied in institutions. Thus, in contemporary South Africa, we have alongside structural supports for apartheid, structural supports for an alternative democratic society in the form of a wide range of organizations, some operating with relatively little interference from the state, and others, perforce, underground. These organizations are concerned with improving group relations and reducing discrimination in such areas as education, housing, job opportunities, labor relations, and justice. Crucial to the maintenance of this positive system, I argue, is the quality of intercultural communication. Just as in the context of countless asynchronous intercultural encounters negative cultural stereotypes are generated, so, in synchronous encounters, negative stereotypes are either not generated, or where already present are eroded. Then too, just as the negative effects of asynchronous intercultural encounters feed into structural supports for apartheid, so synchronous encounters feed into structural supports for an alternative, integrated, just society.

A second applied interest is the investigation of what can be done to improve the quality of intercultural communication. This is too large a subject to attempt to summarize here. It is addressed in papers by Gumperz and Roberts (1980), Erickson (1985), and Chick (1986). One of the most important insights provided in these papers is that the competencies that ensure effective intercultural communication are so complex, covert, and context bound that they cannot be taught as a body of knowledge in any straightforward way. These scholars argued, however, that effective inter-cultural communication can be learned. Awareness of the potential sources of asynchrony, and of the possible negative consequences of it is seen as a prerequisite for such learning. Erickson (1985) suggested that, armed with such awareness, participants can develop further the natural process of retrospectively scanning discourse as it is unfolding. Where, through this process, they detect asynchrony, they can affect appropriate repair strate-gies. Another important insight that emerges directly from interactional sociolinguistic research is that interactional miscommunication is mutually accomplished by all participants, rather than unilaterally by one. Erickson suggested that this insight is a liberating one for those who wish to improve the quality of intercultural communication, enabling them to avoid un-helpful repair strategies that arise from blaming the other person.

Predictably, criticism of this research has come principally from local sources. In South Africa there is an understandable suspicion of the attaching of cultural labels to the behaviors of people and, in particular, of the focusing on the differences between people from different racial groups. Too often in the past the culture of indigenous people has been labeled as primitive, and the cultural and other differences between peoples exagger-ated and used as a rationale for segregation and discrimination. Accordingly, many opponents of apartheid would like to see more research that focuses on what is universal, rather than on what is culture-specific, and are concerned that the findings of my research may be misused to justify segregation. Presumably those who would misuse it would argue that, if communication between people from different cultural groups is so problematic, it is in the interests of all to reduce the need for it by keeping people apart.

My response to this criticism, is that misuse would involve a deliberate or unintentional misinterpretation of the findings. Although, to date there have been no attempts to deliberately misinterpret my findings, I do recognize that there is this danger. I am not convinced, however, that the potential for such misinterpretation is sufficiently strong grounds for not engaging in such research. This is particularly so because the potential for correct interpretation, and for the use of the findings for such positive purposes as helping people to interpret and evaluate members of other groups more accurately, is, surely, equally great. The best defense against unintentional misinterpretation is to clarify ones meaning. I am, therefore, at pains to stress that I see culture, in the sense in which I use it, as continually being confirmed and changed by the members of the relevant cultural group as they interact with one another, and with members of other groups. This is in keeping with the interactional sociolinguistic notion that cultural expectations and assumptions, and even communication conventions are interactionally constituted. In other words, culture is dynamic rather than static. Perhaps most important, I remind critics that, although I do focus on differences in communication conventions, I do not assume that the communication conventions of subordinate groups (even where they are not native speakers of the language medium) are deficits. As noted earlier, my analyses show that asynchrony in intercultural encounters is, more often than not, mutually accomplished by all participants. Ironically, critics have not focused on where the research is most vulnerable to criticism, namely the narrowness of the empirical base. This is a limitation it shares with other interactional sociolinguistic studies. In order to achieve the rigour associated with an adequately fine-grained analysis of interactions, the researcher has to give quality of analysis priority over quantity. Consequently, interactional sociolinguists usually end up knowing a considerable amount about a limited body of data, but being uncertain as how generalizable their findings are to other situations. To discover whether the characteristics of the culture-specific communicative conventions of the various groups presented is accurate, there is the need not only for data collection and analyses of encounters between Zulu English – S.A. English and between Afrikaans English – S.A. English speakers in a far wider range of situations, but also of encounters between these groups and other English speaking groups. In asynchronous intercultural encounters, culturally specific characteristics of group-interactional styles that usually go unnoticed in intracultural communication, become visible. Accordingly, a productive way of investigating these styles is to look for mismatches in the characteristics of styles in intercultural encounters in English that involve as wide a range of different groups as possible. Potentially as revealing would be the analyses of similar encounters, but where, for example, Afrikaans or Zulu rather than English were the medium. Such research could, additionally, help establish the extent to which interactional styles remain constant across language boundaries.

To summarize, I have attempted to contextualize the research reported on in this paper by showing how it is related to the larger program of which it is a part. I have highlighted two areas of applied interest in this program, and attempted to show how my thinking has changed since I wrote the paper. I have, also, outlined some of the reactions to my findings. Although I remain convinced that the program is a worthwhile one, I am very conscious of how tentative my findings are, and how much more empirical work is required.

References

Chick, J. K. (1984). Interactional sociolinguistics: Insights and applications. *Proceedings of the 20th National Conference of the Linguistic Society of Southern Africa* (pp. 144–156). Pretoria, South Africa: University of Pretoria.

Chick, J. K. (1986). Interactional perspectives on communicative needs of Zulu work seekers. *Journal of Multilingual and Multicultural Development, 7* (6), 479–491.

Chick, J. K. (1987). Linguistics, language and power. In D. Young (Ed.), *Festschrift in honor of Len Lanham* (pp. 115–131). Cape Town, South Africa: Maskew Miller-Longman.

Chick, J. K. (in press). Sources of conflict in Afrikaans-English-S.A. English encounters. In J. Cheshire (Ed.), *English around the world.* Cambridge: Cambridge University Press.

Erickson, F (1985). Listening and speaking. In D. Tannen & J. Alatis (Eds.), *Languages and linguistics: the interdependence of theory, data, and application.* (pp. 294–319). Washington, DC: Georgetown University Press.

Gumperz, J., & Roberts, C. (1980). *Developing awareness skills for interethnic communication.* Singapore: SEAMED Regional Language Centre.

Simpson, J., & Yinger, J. Mn. (1985). *Racial and cultural minorities: An analysis of prejudice and discrimination* (5th ed.). New York: Plenum.

Tannen, D. (1984). The pragmatics of cross-cultural communication. *Applied Linguistcs, 5* (3), 189–195.

18

Athabaskan-English Interethnic Communication

RONALD SCOLLON
SUZANNE WONG-SCOLLON

INTERETHNIC COMMUNICATION

Communication between members of different ethnic groups in Alaska and northern Canada, as elsewhere, frequently results in confusion, misunderstanding and conflict. This situation is not new, but in recent years is becoming aggravated by the increased amount of intrusion into every aspect of life of the bureaucratic and technological systems of modern western society. Legal and economic pressures have made many individuals feel that it is necessary in pursuit of their own best interests for them to engage in communication with members of other ethnic groups. This interethnic communication is between members of the dominant, English-speaking, western American and Canadian society and members of native groups in most cases. The confusion and misunderstanding that often results from this interethnic communication is a source of frustration for native people who feel that their legitimate and urgent needs are being ignored or misunderstood. This miscommunication is also a source of frustration for members of the dominant English-speaking society who feel they are unable to make their own points of view clear as well as being unable to understand native points of view. As miscommunication increases, racial and ethnic stereotyping begin to develop and impede further communication.

Recently we have begun to see that the main problem in inter-ethnic communication is not caused by grammar (Gumperz 1977a, 1977b, Gumperz & Roberts 1978). Although languages use grammar as the system of expressing ideas, in interethnic communication it is the discourse system which produces the greatest difficulty. It is the way ideas are put together into an argument, the way some ideas are selected for special emphasis, or the way emotional information about the ideas is presented that causes miscommunication. The grammatical system gives the message while the discourse system tells how to interpret the message. The greatest cause of interethnic problems lies in the area of understanding not *what* someone says but *why* he is saying it. This information about *why* people are speaking is not signaled in the same way in all ethnic groups, and so some misunderstandings can result even where the grammatical systems are nearly identical. By the same token, even where grammatical systems are quite different, communication can succeed if there is agreement about the discourse system.

We will be looking at some of the linguistic sources of inter-ethnic conflict in this chapter. First of all, the discourse system a speaker uses is learned very early in life (Scollon 1976, Halliday 1976a,b,c); probably much of it is learned before the child speaks any words. This system is learned through a long and highly involved process of socialization and communication with caregivers. It is unconscious and affects all communication in language. This discourse system is closely tied to an individual's concept of identity. Any change in the discourse system is likely to be felt as a change in personality and culture. We will describe in this chapter how inter-ethnic communication works in order to provide a basis for our later discussion of face and the interpersonal grounds on which facework is founded.

Athabaskan-English

We will only talk about communication between Athabaskans and speakers of English in this chapter. There are no good terms to refer to the two groups of which we are speaking. By "Athabaskan" we mean anyone who has been socialized to a set of communicative patterns which have their roots in the Athabaskan languages. These people are ethnically Athabaskan on the whole but may not speak any Athabaskan language. We mean by "speakers of English" anyone whose communicative patterns are those of the dominant, mainstream American and Canadian English-speaking population. We know this is awkward since most of the communication we are looking at takes place in English. It seems better than using a term such as Standard English, which seems to suggest that one variety of English is to be preferred over another. Although we realize that there are many individual differences among people, we still feel that the patterns we are describing here hold true in a general way and are the patterns on which people have developed ethnic stereotypes. Because of the consistency of these ethnic stereotypes we feel there is a consistent pattern of discourse underlying this stereotyping.

FOUR AREAS OF DISCOURSE STUDY

This chapter is organized around four topics: the presentation of self, the distribution of talk, information structure, and content organization. Talking is one of the main ways in which we present ourselves to other people in the world. It is our chance to give our side of the story, to show ourselves in a particular light, to put in certain details and leave out others so that others will take our view of things. Goffman (1974) has called this aspect of communication the presentation of self. Here we will look at how differently Athabaskans and English speakers view the presentation of self and how this leads to misinterpretation.

When people talk, they have to agree on who gets to speak first, how they exchange turns and how they interrupt. One of the main areas in which interethnic communication runs into problems is when people have different ways of beginning and ending a conversation or when people have different ways of getting the floor. We call these problems the distribution of talk.

The third area we will look at is how talk makes sense. When someone is speaking and we understand the system, we can tell when he is going to go on or when he is going to quit. We can tell when he has made a statement or asked a question. We can tell what parts of his ideas he is emphasizing and what parts he is excited about. The information structuring system is what tells us these things. One reason there is difficulty in communication is that in some discourse systems information structuring is done with prosody, while in others prosody is less important. That is, in some cases it is the pitch or loudness or tone of voice that indicates information structure, while in other cases this is done with words or morphemes and with little or no change of prosody. In interethnic communication where these systems are different there is often confusion in the information structure.

Finally, we will look at what is actually said. Even here there are often disagreements about how much you should actually say and how much your listener should be able to figure out. If too much is said the listener may feel it is rude. If too little is said the listener may feel the speaker is vague or doesn't understand what he or she is talking about. The organization of the contents of talk is the fourth area we will look at.

THE PRESENTATION OF SELF

Even though we talk for many reasons, one of the main things we do when we talk is to present a view of ourselves to the listener, and of course when the listener takes a turn at speaking he either confirms or questions our view at the same time as he presents a view of himself. This presentation of self is done in many ways. It is reflected in our choice of words, in our tone of voice, in the attitudes we display and in the topics about which we talk. In talking, each participant presents a particular view of the world and the self, and as the conversation progresses these views become altered and affected by the views of the other participants. Goffman (1974, 1976) calls this changing of views the negotiation of intersubjective reality. That is, the subjective reality of each participant in a conversation is checked out against the reality of each other participant as an ongoing negotiation through which we create a social world.

Taciturnity and Volubility

One of the first observations people make about Athabaskan–English conversations, especially when these conversations are between strangers, is that Athabaskans do not talk as much as English speakers. From the Athabaskan point of view what is usually experienced is that English speakers talk all the time, or talk too much. From the English point of view Athabaskans are said not to like to talk, or to be silent. Basso (1970) has said that Apaches (southern Athabaskans) are silent in situations where the participants are unsure of how they stand with each other. That is, it is probably not right to say that Athabaskans do or do not speak less than English speakers. It seems better to focus on situations in which one group has a preference for not speaking or being taciturn.

In our own work (Scollon & Scollon 1979) we have suggested that there is a real difference between Athabaskans and English speakers in how much they choose to speak, and that this difference has to do with the negotiation of intersubjective reality. Athabaskans have a very high degree of respect for the individuality of others and a careful guarding of one's own individuality. As a result, any conversation can be threatening because of the possibility of a negotiated change of point of view. Athabaskans avoid conversation except when the point of view of all participants is well known.

On the other hand, English speakers feel that the main way to get to know the point of view of people is through conversation with them. Cocktail parties among strangers or near strangers are probably the best example of the use of conversation by English speakers to seek out acquaintance and agreement.

These ideas lead us to see that if two people who are not well known to each other meet, the English speaker will want to talk so that they can get to know each other, but the Athabaskan will want to wait until they get to know each other before feeling it would be very easy to talk. These are the situations in which the English speaker feels the Athabaskan is unusually taciturn or reserved in speaking and the Athabaskan feels that the English speaker is too talkative.

Taking the other extreme, where the participants are well known to each other, we can find Athabaskans to be very talkative. At the same time, for English speakers, the situations of longstanding personal knowledge are among the few in which it is appropriate not to talk. It is in a way a sign of intimacy for an English speaker that talk is not needed.

We can see that a very basic difference between Athabaskans and English speakers has to do with taciturnity and volubility, and this relates to the presentation of self. For English speakers, volubility is related to social distance and taciturnity to intimacy. For Athabaskans the relationship is the reverse, with volubility possible only in contexts of intimacy where there is no threat to the speaker's view of himself or the world. Since by far the greatest number of contacts between Athabaskans and English speakers happen in semi-formal business, medical, legal, or educational contexts, it is not surprising that the English preference is for a lot of talking and the Athabaskan preference is for a reserved amount of talking. This can lead to the ethnic stereotyping mentioned above. English speakers come away from the situation saying that Athabaskans do not want to talk. Athabaskans come away feeling that English speakers talk all the time. The disagreement is a very fundamental one about the presentation of self. Athabaskans prefer to show a deep respect for the individuality of others, even if this produces a difficulty in getting to know them. English speakers prefer developing contacts widely with strangers and non-intimates, even if this produces a constant state of change in the concept of self. Interethnic communication threatens a shift in these basic premises, not for the English speaker, but for the Athabaskan. Thus we can begin to see that interethnic communication in and of itself constitutes a danger to the Athabaskan. Taciturnity in the face of this danger is a viable response.

Social Relations of Dominance

Another issue in the presentation of self has to do with the power relationships between speakers. We present a different "face" to our children, to our husbands and wives, and to our parents. If the relationship between two people is one of dominance and submission, that is, if one is in a more powerful position than the other, the way one speaks will depend very much on which position he is in. The difficulty that we want to look at here is that there are several dimensions to power relationships, and Athabaskans and English speakers do not agree on how they are related.

The three relationships we want to look at are dominance, display, and dependence. Each of these has two possibilities— superordinate and subordinate for dominance, spectatorship and exhibitionism for display, and caregiving and petitioning for dependence. Bateson (1972) and Mead (1977) have said that these are different for British and Americans. Canadians appear to share many of the properties of British English speakers, and in doing so contrast with Americans. English-speaking Canadians may be said to find interethnic communication with Athabaskans somewhat less problematical in this respect. To highlight areas of potential difficulty we will talk primarily about Americans here as the extreme case when we speak of English speakers.

For American English speakers, the person in the superordinate or dominant position is the spectator and the subordinate person is the exhibitionist. What that means is that the parent as a spectator expects to watch what a child does. The child should show off his abilitities to the parents and is often expected to be entertaining. In school English speakers expect children to display their abilities as exhibitionists to the teacher as spectator. There is no doubt at the same time that the teacher is in the dominant or superordinate position. To use Bateson and Mead's term, for English speakers (in America) the superordinate role is "linked" with spectatorship and the subordinate role is "linked" with exhibitionism.

This is different for Athabaskans. Children are not expected to show off for adults. Adults as either parents or teachers are supposed to display abilities and qualities for the child to learn. The adult or superordinate is in the exhibitionist role while the child is in the spectator role.

It is not difficult to see how this different linkage of dominance and display can cause confusion in any interethnic communication between nonequals. If the English speaker is the teacher and the Athabaskan is the child, then the teacher expects to be in charge, to be in the dominant role, but at the same time expects the child to display his abilities. The child, on the other hand, either expects the teacher to be the exhibitionist while he is the spectator, or if the child becomes the exhibitionist, he expects to be treated as the dominant member of the pair.

For the English-speaking teacher an Athabaskan child will either seem unduly reserved because he is spectating, or unduly aggressive if the child has assumed the superordinate role that he feels is consistent with display or exhibitionism. For the Athabaskan child the teacher will seem either incompetent because he is not exhibiting his abilities, or unduly bossy because in spite of not exhibiting he is taking the superordinate role.

These same relationships exist in other situations as well. Wherever the two participants are of unequal status this problem with the difference in linkage between dominance and display will show up. If we look back at what we said about taciturnity and volubility we can see that taciturnity is related to spectatorship and volubility to exhibitionism. What this means is that from the English speaker's point of view the person in the subordinate role, the exhibitionist, should do a lot of speaking, especially in presentting the self. The Athabaskan point of view is that the person in the superordinate role should do most of the speaking, again as the exhibitionist. So if the English speaker does most of the speaking in interethnic communication with the Athabaskan, he must interpret the Athabaskan taciturnity as displaying superiority. It is not surprising to see conflict in a situation where each speaker believes the other to be displaying a superior attitude, but this is a natural reaction to this difference in the linkage of dominance and display in nonequal social relations. As each speaker tries to take a position of subordination to the other, he unknowingly is communicating just the opposite in the other speaker's system.

The third dimension is that of dependence. In the Athabaskan system, the person in the superordinate role is assumed to have the responsibility for taking care of the one in the subordinate role. In fact, traditionally it was this dimension that gave one a position of dominance. The person who provided for others was given the dominant position as well as the right to direct others' behavior. Others were in a position of dependence and could expect the dominant person to take care of them. Basically all that was required was to make the need known for support to be given.

In the English system there is no very strong relation between dominance and dependence except between parents and children. There is little expectation that a wealthy or powerful person should distribute his wealth or power to others with less. There is even less expectation that the way to achieve power or dominance is by taking care of other people by distributing one's wealth or goods.

The result of this difference in conversation is that for Athabaskans, being in the superordinate role is related to being in the position to grant assistance to the one in the subordinate role. This produces very different assumptions about what should happen in such petitioning situations as counseling, job interviews, or welfare interviews, where the petitioner is in a dependent role. The Athabaskan point of view is that the counselor or interviewer is in the position of dominance and therefore should do most of the speaking as the exhibitionist and grant the good or service as the caregiver. The English speaker's point of view is that in the same situation, the person being interviewed should be the exhibitionist and display a full view of himself for evaluation through significant amounts of talking.

As a result of this difference in the linkage of dependence, dominance, and display, Athabaskans often feel that their clear rights as dependents of the American bureaucratic system have not been granted, even though they have taken the proper subordinate, petitioning position by not speaking and carefully observing the English speaker. English speakers, on the other hand, feel that Athabaskans being interviewed do not display enough of themselves for the interviewer to evaluate their need, that they have become sullen and withdrawn or perhaps even acted superior, as if they needed no help.

Prohibited Actions

The English idea of "putting your best foot forward" conflicts directly with an Athabaskan taboo. It is normal in situations of unequal status relations for English speakers in Canada as well as in America to display oneself in the best light possible. In job interviews, in school, in meeting strangers, or in getting arrested for speeding it is expected that one will display only one's best qualities, abilities, and accomplishments. One will speak highly of the future, as well. It is normal to present a career or life trajectory of success and planning.

In conversations where this presentation of self is done in face-to-face contact this display of one's accomplishments is played down only by what Pawley and Syder (n.d.) have called the "reduction principle." By this they mean that instead of showing your qualities, abilities, or opinions in the strongest light you reduce them somewhat, just by the right amount, so that the other speaker can boast for you. This is a kind of lure that is cast out in order to make your conversational partner do some of the work of displaying your abilities. You understate your case and your partner then builds it up.

One must be careful in this system neither to overstate nor to understate the view one presents of oneself. This view must be good but not so good that there will be nothing left for your partner to say on your behalf. On the other hand, too much reduction, too much playing down of your own position is heard as too big a lure. Your partner must either take your position too strongly, and thereby endanger his own position, or take your position at face value.

This English system is very different from the Athabaskan system in which it is considered inappropriate and bad luck to anticipate good luck, to display oneself in a good light, to predict the future, or to speak badly of another's luck. The concept of *injíh* as it is expressed in Tanacross Athabaskan means that if you intended to go out hunting moose you would never say so directly. The most you might say is that you are going out and you hope you will not be hungry. To speak too directly of the future prospect of a good hunt would be to court bad luck.

It would be quite inappropriate to speak of one's plans for some time later in life or in any way to indicate some expectation that one's future life will be good. Since it might be taken as suggesting having had such plans, even good references to one's past experiences are often uncomfortable for Athabaskan speakers.

It is not surprising, then, that much Athabaskan–English interethnic communication gets confused by a misinterpretation on this dimension. Especially in interviews and other gatekeeping situations the English speaker expects the Athabaskan to present himself in the best possible light. He must display his achievements of the past and his ambitions for the future if he wants the job. At the same time the Athabaskan will feel that any good presentation of himself will court bad luck and work against his prospects of getting the job. Because this self-deprecation is so strong for Athabaskans, the English speaker cannot take it as simple reduction and so takes it as the simple truth instead. Again, we have a case in which the more the Athabaskan seeks to succeed the stronger it works against him in communications with English speakers. The more the English speaker wishes to "draw out" the Athabaskan, the more embarrassing it becomes for both; these situations often end in failure.

In the reverse situation, where the Athabaskan is in the dominant position and the English speaker is in the subordinate position, the English speaker seems too boastful or too careless with his luck because of his predictions of his future and the open display of his past. Again, the result is that these communicative difficulties turn into ethnic stereotypes. The Athabaskan thinks of the English speaker as boastful or careless with luck and the future, while the

English speaker thinks of the Athabaskan as unsure of himself, withdrawn, and aimless.

The Dilemma in the Presentation of Self

The problems encountered by Athabaskans and English speakers in interethnic communication begin with the presentation of self. The English speaker seeks to display his own abilities, the best side of himself, through talking. The Athabaskan, on the other hand, avoids these self-displays. The result is a feeling that English speakers prefer to speak a lot more than Athabaskans.

Where the relationship is one of dominance and submission this problem is accentuated by a different linkage of dominance, display, and dependence. The English speaker expects the dominant person to be the quiet one, the spectator, and expects that aid will only be given where the need is clearly displayed, and, we might add, where there is a legal or strong social requirement. The Athabaskan expects the dominant person to be the main speaker, the exhibitionist, and to maintain his dominance by giving help to the ones he dominates.

The difficulties produced by these different linkages of dominance, display, and dependence are further compounded by the English speaker's assumption that one will put his best foot forward and the Athabaskan assumption that one will not speak very well of himself.

The result of these communication problems is that each group then ethnically stereotypes the other. The English speaker comes to believe that the Athabaskan is unsure, aimless, incompetent, and withdrawn. The Athabaskan comes to believe that the English speaker is boastful of his own abilities, sure he can predict the future, careless with luck, and far too talkative.

These ethnic stereotypes are widely believed to be true because each encounter, especially under stressful conditions, tends to replicate the last and produces more deeply entrenched attitudes. It is important to see that from the Athabaskan point of view, the English speaker is not really as sure of himself and as cocky about the future as he seems. From the English point of view, the Athabaskan is not as aimless and unsure as he appears to be. These stereotyped views are the result of very predictable factors relating to the cultural expectations of the two groups. The two groups have very different views of the purpose of talking and how their goals should be accomplished through talk. These different views are closely related to structural features of the discourse. These features are the means by which we display the attitudes and expectations we have discussed here as the presentation of self. As we will begin to show in the following three sections, these structural factors can be isolated and analyzed. We feel that by undertaking this analytical study of the discourse factors governing interethnic communication we can move toward loosening some of the stereotyped ethnic attitudes that we have discussed.

THE DISTRIBUTION OF TALK

When two or more people talk together, it takes a lot of coordination to keep things going smoothly. Although it does not seem like it, in ordinary conversation the various speakers are careful not to talk all at once or to interrupt or to fail to answer if there is a question. This cooperation takes a good bit of work and common understanding. In interethnic communication there are often differences in the systems of the speakers, so that mistakes happen that lead to further misunderstandings. We will look in this section at how conversationalists decide who speaks first, how topics are controlled, how turns at talking are exchanged, and how conversations are ended.

Who Speaks First

When an Athabaskan and a speaker of English talk to each other, it is very likely that the English speaker will speak first. Many people have observed this. It is not hard to see why the English speaker will speak first if we consider what was said about the presentation of self. The Athabaskan will feel it is important to know the relationship between the two speakers before speaking. The English speaker will feel talking is the best way to establish a relationship. While the Athabaskan is waiting to see what will happen between them, the English speaker will begin speaking, usually asking questions in fact, to find out what will happen. Only where there is a longstanding relationship and a deep understanding between the two speakers is it likely that the Athabaskan will initiate the conversation.

Control of Topic

It might not seem very important at first glance who speaks first in a conversation. Studies of conversation have shown, however, that the person who speaks first also controls the topic of conversation. Schegloff (1972) found that the person who spoke first took the role of the summoner. His speech in effect asks the other speaker for the right to talk. The second speaker answers but in a very open way. The answer of the second speaker gives the first speaker the right to go ahead and talk. The first speaker then introduces the topic of the conversation to which the second must then reply. If the second speaker wants to introduce his own topic he must wait for a chance to introduce it later, after they have talked about the first speaker's topic.

These general rules seem so obvious and trivial that it is hard to believe how strictly we hold to them. It is easy to see how strong these rules are, though, by trying to break them. If someone calls on the phone (the phone ring is the first speaker), and if you answer by talking about what you want to talk about, both you and the caller will feel something very strange has happened. During their study, one of Schegloff's colleagues was being troubled by obscene phone calls. She found that if she picked up the phone but did not say anything, the caller would not go on to say any obscenities. He was following the conversational rules that would only allow him to speak after the second speaker answered. He followed conversational rules even though he was violating the moral rules of the same society.

In another study Scollon (1976) found that a one year old child learned these conversational rules before she was two years old. A one year old has very little she can say easily. The child in that study, Brenda, found that if she was the first speaker she could talk about what she wanted to talk about. She used one word, "here," as a summons. She would give a piece of paper or trash or almost anything to someone else and say "here." The other person would take it and say "thank you." Then Brenda would say whatever she wanted to say.

Sometimes an adult would try to speak to Brenda first. She would refuse to answer. If the adult persisted she would say "here" and hand him something. That would make her the first speaker and ultimately give her the right to introduce her topic. Brenda had learned how to use speaking first to keep control of the topic of conversation by the time she was two years old.

We have said that in Athabaskan–English conversations the English speaker almost always speaks first. This has the consequence of allowing him to introduce his own topic and of making it very difficult for the Athabaskan to introduce any other topic. The general result of these two facts is that in interethnic communications between Athabaskans and English speakers the topic of conversation is almost always the English speaker's topic, not the Athabaskan's.

Another complication is introduced by the fact that at least some Athabaskans use a conversational greeting that gives the answerer the right to introduce the topic. At Fort Chipewyan, Alberta, it is common to greet people with ʔɛdlánɪ̨ðen "what are you thinking?" The appropriate response is an open-ended introduction of the answerer's topic if he should choose to say something.

Here as before these discourse problems lead to stereotyping. The Athabaskan starts to feel that his ideas are always being ignored. At the same time he feels that the English speaker is either egocentric or ethnocentric. He feels that the English speaker only wants to talk about his own ideas. From the English speaker's point of view it seems either that the Athabaskan does not have any ideas of his own or that when they are introduced these ideas are off the topic. By putting together the assumptions about the presentation of self that Athabaskans and English speakers hold and a quite mechanical rule of conversational interchange, we get a situation in which one speaker is always in control of what the participants talk about.

The Exchange of Speaking Turns

We have said that at least in English conversation one speaker begins, a second answers, the first introduces the topic, and the second continues on that topic. Of course, conversations can be more complicated than that. There may be more than two speakers, for one thing. But to keep this discussion from getting too complex, we will just talk about two-person conversation.

As the conversation goes on the speakers continue to take turns in speaking. They do not normally both speak at the same time. In fact, simultaneous speech is usually a good sign that something has gone wrong. When the timing goes off so far that both speakers start speaking together it usually takes some time to smooth things out again. Usually after one speaker finishes the other can take a turn. If the other one does not say anything, then the first speaker can take another turn if he wishes. If the other comes in too soon it feels as if he is interrupting.

Problems start to come up when two speakers have different systems for pausing between turns. Generally speaking, Athabaskans allow a slightly longer pause between sentences than do English speakers. The difference is probably not more than half a second in length, but it has an important effect on interethnic communication. When an English speaker pauses he waits for the regular length of time (around one second or less), that is, *his* regular length of time, and if the Athabaskan does not say anything, the English speaker feels he is free to go on and say anything else he likes. At the same time the Athabaskan has been waiting his regular length of time before coming in. He does not want to interrupt the English speaker. This length of time we think is around one and one-half seconds. It is just enough longer that by the time the Athabaskan is ready to speak the English speaker is already speaking again. So the Athabaskan waits again for the next pause. Again, the English speaker begins just enough before the Athabaskan was going to speak. The net result is that the Athabaskan can never get a word in edgewise (an apt metaphor in this case), while the English speaker goes on and on.

The Athabaskan point of view is that it is difficult to make one's whole point. The length of pause that the Athabaskan takes while expecting to continue is just about the length of pause the English speaker takes in exchanging turns. If an Athabaskan has in mind a series of sentences to say, it is most likely that at the end of the first one the English speaker will think that he has finished because of the length of the pause and will begin speaking. The Athabaskan feels he has been interrupted and the English speaker feels the Athabaskan never makes sense, never says a whole coherent idea. Much of this misunderstanding is the result of something like a one-half second difference in the timing of conversational pauses, but it can result in strong stereotypical responses to the opposite ethnic group.

A second factor in the exchange of speaking turns that only increases the difficulty we are looking at here is that there are different expectations about how long a speaker should be allowed to speak at one turn. Generally Athabaskans expect that a speaker will take as long as necessary to develop an idea. The ideal situation is that of an older speaker, a person in a clear superordinate position, narrating a traditional story. Although this ideal may not often be practiced, there is nevertheless an expectation that something like a monologue is the normal speaking turn. The role of other speakers is that of an audience that by frequent traffic signal responses indicates that it is following. English speakers, on the other hand, treat monologues as exceptions, with the norm being the dialogue in which speakers exchange more or less equal turns.

In Athabaskan–English interethnic communication, the expectation that English speakers have is rarely fulfilled. True dialogue rarely occurs. The reason for this has been given. The exchange of turns works toward the English speaker's continually regaining the floor and against the Athabaskan's being able to hold the floor for more than brief speaking turn. Where an Athabaskan may expect to get his turn after a long English monologue he rarely gets more than a brief statement before another English monologue begins. The result is again stereotyping of the English speaker as egocentric and the Athabaskan as having no ideas of his own.

Departure Formulas

It is safe to say that an Athabaskan–English conversation will usually begin with the English speaker speaking first. It is almost as certain that it will end with the Athabaskan making no formal close. On the surface the explanation seems simple enough. Most of the formulas for ending conversation refer to the future. As we have said, Athabaskans feel it is bad luck to make predictions about the future. This applies even to such routine statements as "I'll see you later" or "I'll see you tomorrow." Where the English speakers feel these are simple closing statements, ways of saying "Now our talk is ended," they carry an overtone of bad luck for the Athabaskan and thus are avoided.

The impression of these closing formulas from the Athabaskan point of view again confirms the English speaker's bravado regarding his good luck and future. From the English speaker's point of view, the lack of closings gives a feeling that something has gone wrong in the communication. As we have reason to believe now, that is very likely to be true; but it may be misleading. The conversation may have been very compatible and yet leave the English speaker feeling that something went wrong because of the lack of a close.

We need to look a bit closer at departures to understand this problem. As Goffman (1974) has said, departures do much more than bring a conversation to a close. They set up the conditions for future conversations. English speakers feel it is essential at the end of each encounter to be clear just where you stand with the other speaker. The closing formula is the way this is done. Something as simple as "It's been nice talking to you" suggests that you expect to do more of it in the future. As we depart we prepare the future, and it is this aspect of the formula that for the English speaker fits in well with the general negotiation of intersubjective reality. The departure is the final check on where you have gotten to in the negotiation that has taken place. It cements this into place so that the negotiation can be resumed at the next opportunity.

This preparation of the future through the departure formula is directly contrary to the Athabaskan prohibition on speaking strongly of the future. If one enjoyed a conversation, it would be bad luck indeed to say so and that you hoped it would happen again. So in closing a conversation as in beginning it, the Athabaskan is careful not to display carelessness or to present himself in too favorable a light. The English speaker who has begun the conversation as a way of getting to know the other closes the conversation with an indirect but important summary of how things have gone. Perhaps the worst outcome from the English point of view is a complete rupture of the relationship. This would be shown by a violation of discourse conventions, including the convention of a formulated departure. The Athabaskan, being careful of courting bad luck, may quite unknowingly signal to the English speaker the worst possibility, that there is no hope of getting together again to speak.

The Importance of Discourse and Cultural Factors

In interethnic communication between English speakers and Athabaskans, talk is distributed so that the English speaker is favored as first speaker, as controller of topic, as principal speaker, and yet in the end he may not have any conclusive idea of what went on. For the Athabaskan speaker it is difficult to get the floor, to bring the conversation around to his own topic, and in the end to feel he has had much effect on the outcome. This situation is prepared by cultural expectations about the presentation of self. It works through the mechanics of a slight difference in pausing systems and the general mechanics of turn taking in human communication. The result is a considerable potential for difficulty in interethnic communication. It is important to point out now that we have not yet mentioned any factors that have to do with the grammatical or lexical structure of language directly. The potential difficulties and misunderstandings that we have discussed are the same whether the communication is carried on in English, Athabaskan, so-called Village English, or any combination of these. As long as the discourse patterns and the presentation of self are clearly Athabaskan in origin on the one hand and English in origin on the other these possibilities of problems will arise.

At first it will seem ironic that the situation in which there is the greatest potential for problems is where the language being used by the two speakers is the most similar. We are so accustomed to thinking that communication is a matter of grammar and vocabulary that if the grammar and vocabulary are the same or similar for two speakers it is difficult to believe that there might be trouble. Yet, as we have said earlier, these discourse patterns and cultural expectations are learned very early in life and change slowly. Even where someone learns to speak a new language later in life, it is very likely that he will speak it using the discourse patterns of his early language training. In present-day Alaska and Canada, many people who do not speak any Athabaskan language have nevertheless learned Athabaskan discourse patterns which are essential for effective communication within the village, even though the language used may be English. We want to be careful then not to think that understanding will be automatic just because two speakers do not differ greatly in grammar or vocabulary. Assumptions about the presentation of self and the distribution of talk in interethnic communication lie at the bottom of many communicative conflicts.

INFORMATION STRUCTURE

We now want to look at some of the ways information is signaled in Athabaskan and English. When we say information we do not mean the basic idea being expressed. What we mean is information about how the listener is supposed to interpret that idea. The basic idea in spoken English on the whole is expressed by the words and the grammar and the information structure is expressed by the intonation and stress. We will use the word *prosody* to cover intonation, stress, tone of voice, and other non-grammatical elements of the message.

As an example of information structure, if I say, "I saw a moose standing there," it means one thing. If I say "I saw a *moose* standing there," and stress the word "moose," it means something else. When I stress "moose" by saying it a little louder and higher in pitch, the sentence means that I saw a moose but I expected to see something else, or nothing at all. The stress means I not only saw the moose, but I was surprised by it. There are two messages here. The primary one is about seeing the moose and it is expressed by the sentence in its plain form. The secondary message is that I was surprised. That message is expressed by prosody, in this case with stress. When we say "information structure," then, we mean the messages about the message that are expressed by such things as the prosody in English.

Prosody and Morphemes

In English the information structure is normally shown by the prosody. You can tell how to interpret the main message by paying attention to the stress, intonation, or tone of voice. In Athabaskan, though, the information structure is often expressed by morphemes rather than by prosody. These are normally suffixes or words at the beginning or the end of a phrase that tell you how to interpret the whole phrase. As an example, a man was telling a story in Chipewyan about a beaver hunt. On his way home he came across a bear in the trail. Of course he was surprised by it, and in Chipewyan he said sas náðer k'ɛ́. sas means "bear", náðer means "it was standing there," and k'ɛ́ does not really have any meaning of its own. It means the same thing as the stress on *moose* when I said, "I saw a *moose* standing there." The morpheme k'ɛ́ means he was surprised. The meaning of this morpheme is that the phrase is to be emphasized. It tells you something about the information structure, not the basic idea of seeing the bear.

We have used this example to show how Athabaskan uses a morpheme with no change in the stress to show the information structure, but English uses stress without any additional morphemes. This can cause confusion in two ways. When someone who speaks English tries to learn Athabaskan, he has a tendency to try to use stress to mark information structure instead of emphatic morphemes and the like. On the other hand, when an Athabaskan learns English, he has a tendency to make mistakes with stress and other prosodic marking of information structure. The result is the same in both directions. It is difficult for listeners to follow what is being said. You can understand *what* a person says but not *why* he said it or what his attitude toward it was. These *why*'s are absolutely essential for making sense in conversation.

Another morpheme that is very important in Chipewyan is the morpheme ʔɛkú· or kú· (Scollon 1977, Scollon & Scollon 1979). If it is translated it means "and then" but more often than not it does not literally mean "and then." It is used much more as a way of signaling information structure. The main function we found in stories was to set off main sections of the story. It is much like the indentation we use for paragraphs in written English. Athabaskan languages all have some morpheme that functions like kú·, and as a result when Athabaskans learn English they often feel a need for a morpheme to signal the episodic structure of a story. Most often the choice is *and* or *and then*. These sound like hesitations or indicators of insecurity to an English speaker. When we have analyzed stories told by Athabaskans in English, however, we have found that *and* (or *and um*) is used as a very formal marker of the plot and episodic structure.

This can of course cause difficulty in interethnic communication. Where the Athabaskan is careful in speaking English to show the formal structure of the story, the English speaker hears it as halting and unsure. At the same time the English use of prosody to mark episodic structure may not be perceived at all by the Athabaskan who is expecting morphemes as formal markers. The English narrative may sound unorganized to the Athabaskan listener.

In conversational uses similar problems arise. When the morpheme kú· in Chipewyan comes between two clauses, if the first one is a subordinate clause kú· is reduced to –ú or sometimes just a high tone on the last syllable of the subordinate clause. When a Chipewyan speaker speaks in English he may raise the last syllable to show grammatical subordination. The English speaker would hear this rise in pitch as a question, and would answer. The result is that the English speaker has taken over the floor right between a subordinate clause and a main clause because of a misinterpretation of the marker of subordination. To the Athabaskan it seems like a rude interruption in the middle of a sentence. To the English speaker it sounds as if the Athabaskan does not finish his sentences.

Here we can see how the distribution of talk can become confused because of a difference in information structure. Basically the same structures are marked, but in English it is done prosodically and in Athabaskan morphologically. Attempts by English speakers and Athabaskans directly to transfer their prosodic systems or their morphological systems into the other language produce misinterpretation of the information structure which results in further problems with the general distribution of talk.

Pausing

We have mentioned pausing several times, especially in connection with the distribution of talk. The role of pausing in oral narratives is extremely important. As a general statement we can say that pausing figures more importantly in Athabaskan information structure than in English. Pauses in Athabaskan speech are more frequent and longer than in English speech. Pauses are essential in indicating the difference between backgrounded and foregrounded information. Emphasis is largely determined by pausing. For now it is important to note that the pause is a vulnerable point in the discourse because of the problems with the distribution of talk we have discussed here. Just as the Athabaskan is emphasizing a point, the English speaker interrupts because he feels the Athabaskan is not going to go on. The result is the failure of communication and the ethnic stereotyping that follows.

On the Border of Grammar

We have suggested several ways that differences between Athabaskan and English information structuring affect interethnic communication between the groups in this section on information structure. As we have seen, the information structure relates much more closely to the grammatical structure of the English and Athabaskan languages than the presentation of self and distribution of talk that we discussed above. We are at the border of the grammar.

Earlier in this paper we said that the main problems in interethnic communication were not caused by grammar. Now we can expand that statement a bit and say that we do not see any clear connection between grammar and interethnic communication except for the obvious connection that people have to speak in the same language or at least understand each other's languages for interethnic communication to happen at all.

Athabaskan is very different from English in grammatical structure. The Athabaskan verb is complex with many prefixes, suffixes, and stem variants all contributing to quite subtle semantic distinctions. In English these distinctions, when they are made, are indicated by either the choice of the word or by the order of the words, with fairly uncomplicated prefixes and suffixes. We do not see at the time of writing this that there is any clear connection between these major differences between English and Athabaskan grammar and any problems in interethnic communication.

Village English is more often talked about in discussions of interethnic communication in Alaska and Canada. We would say the same thing about grammar in that case. In spite of differences in grammar and vocabulary between Village English and other varieties of English, we have little evidence that these differences are very important in causing problems in interethnic communication. The problems caused by differences in discourse structure certainly loom much larger in any total picture of Athabaskan–English interethnic communication. We would like to suggest a deemphasis on grammatical and vocabulary issues in understanding interethnic communication. In our research these have largely been beside the point in trying to understand communicative conflict.

CONTENT ORGANIZATION

The last problem we want to look at has to do with what is actually said and how it is conceptually organized. We have already talked about some of this under the presentation of self and can begin with the problem of explicitness.

Explicitness

We have observed that both Athabaskans and English speakers sometimes feel that the others do not "come right out and say" things. We do not want to say that either group is more explicit but that they are explicit in different ways or at different times. This is what causes the confusion.

We have already looked at one example. Athabaskans feel uncomfortable about presenting themselves in too favorable a light. This often results in not being very explicit about one's own accomplishments, abilities, or plans. The English speaker on the other hand is likely to be very explicit about such things. If we think about this we can see then why direct questions can be felt by Athabaskans to be rude. A direct question asks the answerer to be quite explicit about something. If that person has been avoiding a delicate area the question may sound like a request to boast or in general to court bad luck, and it will be evaded.

In another case we can see both explicitness and inexplicitness working. English speakers use people's names to refer to them and generally do not show respect for elders by avoiding their names. An aunt would be referred to as "Aunt Jessie" without any feeling of disrespect, and it would be clear to which aunt the speaker was referring. An Athabaskan in the same situation would prefer not to mention the aunt by name but would rather use the Athabaskan term meaning perhaps "my father's sister" or an English translation. This would be fully explicit in most cases and identify the right person without showing disrespect by using a personal name. Yet this explicit reference is heard by the English speaker as evasive or unnecessarily inexplicit.

Conceptual Organization, Threes and Fours

For some time folklorists have known that European folktales are organized around themes of three parts. We have "Goldilocks and the Three Bears;" if a character has to go through ordeals there are usually three of them; if a king has daughters he has three, and they marry three brothers; and so on. We have only really noticed recently that this organization around threes is more than just folklore. The September 1978 (Vol. 80, no. 3) issue of *American An-*

thropologist is a good example of "three bears" organization. On the cover the key papers are listed as follows:

> The Veil of Objectivity: Prophecy, Divination, and Social Inquiry
>
> Sex, Status, and Authority in Egalitarian Society
>
> Structures, Realities, and Blind Spots

There are three papers. Each has three subsections in its title. We are not sure yet just how significant this sort of patterning is in organizing human thinking, but it is likely to be quite important.

Some time ago Toelken (1969) said that Navajo stories were organized around themes of four, not three. This would mean a potential source for confusion in interethnic communication if English speakers were organizing around threes and Athabaskans around fours.

We found in our work at Fort Chipewyan (Scollon & Scollon 1979) that when a storyteller told a story in Athabaskan it was organized around twos and fours. This organization was carefully and formally marked and regular throughout. The story had two main episodes, plus an initial and a final making four sections. Each of the main two episodes was subdivided again in units of two and four. When the same person told the same story to us in English the story was organized in groups of threes. At first we thought that it was because he had conceptually reorganized the story for the second telling. We found out, however, that this reorganization was because of our responses. We had not been able to follow the Athabaskan version and so had not interfered with his telling. We did understand the English version and all the way through said "uh huh" where we thought it was appropriate. His reorganization into different units reflects *our* responses more than his own organization. Or maybe it is better to say that in the English version the storyteller and the listeners cooperated to create a situational reorganization of the story.

We can see then how this difference in organization could produce disorganization in the discourse with the listener often responding at the wrong time from the speaker's point of view. This organization by regular units or "chunks" of three or four is probably even more important in terms of memory and cognitive processing. Kintsch (1977, Kintsch & Green 1978) has found that if you ask English-speaking college students to remember Athabaskan stories (in English) they only remember three of the four parts. Either one part is left out completely or two are combined to produce a total of three parts. The same students have no difficulty with European folktales organized around themes of threes.

Differences in Organization

This suggests that some of the conflict in Athabaskan–English interethnic communication may come from a very basic difference in themes of conceptual organization. These differences would affect ongoing communication by causing speakers always to be out of synchrony with each other. Each would often feel the other was responding at the wrong time. In longer units of talk such as stories it would give the English speaker the feeling that an Athabaskan story was always a little bit too long or had an irrelevant section. It would give the Athabaskan a feeling that an English story always left something out—the fourth part.

This difference would also affect longstanding communication patterns by producing different memory structures of communicative events. An Athabaskan and an English speaker may well remember very different things to have happened in a conversation because of different themes of organization. The result in all cases would be a feeling that the other did not make sense in some profound way, that one could just never figure out what interethnic communication had been about.

ETHNIC STEREOTYPES

We have now outlined what we see as the main issues involved in Athabaskan-English interethnic communication. Now we would like to summarize the problems in a fairly schematic way by rephrasing them from the point of view of both sides. We will defer until later our recommendations for how these patterns might be brought into better synchrony. For now we only wish to register a caution about the tentativeness of our understanding and the deep personal and social significance of change in discourse patterns.

What's Confusing

We list, in the following table, in a brief way the things that English speakers and Athabaskans find confusing in interethnic communication.

Table 1

What's confusing to English speakers about Athabaskans	What's confusing to Athabaskans about English speakers
They do not speak	They talk too much
They keep silent	They always talk first
They avoid situations of talking	They talk to strangers or people they don't know
They only want to talk to close acquaintances	They think they can predict the future
They play down their own abilities	They brag about themselves
They act as if they expect things to be given to them	They don't help people even when they can
They deny planning	They always talk about what's going to happen later
They avoid direct questions	They ask too many questions
They never start a conversation	They always interrupt
They talk off the topic	They only talk about what they are interested in
They never say anything about themselves	They don't give others a chance to talk
They are slow to take a turn in talking	They are always getting excited when they talk
They ask questions in unusual places	They aren't careful when they talk about things or people
They talk with a flat tone of voice	
They are too indirect, inexplicit	
They don't make sense	
They just leave without saying anything	

We hope that this chapter will help the reader to see why each group says and feels these things about the other group. Of course there are other things that might be added to this list. We think that the things in this list are all related to discourse processes. People feel this way because of what happens when they talk together. If there is any hope of improving interethnic communication we feel it will have to be based on understanding discourse processes.

A CAUTION ABOUT CHANGE

We have spent almost all of our space in this chapter talking about differences in discourse systems and how they may produce conflict and confusion in interethnic communication. It is because of these confusions that much ethnic stereotyping develops. While we would hope for an improvement in interethnic relations through an understanding of discourse processes we want to point out that stereotyping works in two directions. A speaker not only decides what another person is like on the basis of how he carries on in discourse; he also makes important decisions about what he himself is like from the same discourse. We believe that discourse patterns are among the strongest expressions of personal and cultural identity. To a great extent a person feels he is what he is because of the way he talks with others. Discourse patterns are very closely tied up with a person's personality and culture.

If we suggest change we have to be very aware that we are not only suggesting change in discourse patterns. We are suggesting change in a person's identity. If someone says that an English speaker should be less talkative, less self-assertive, less interested in the future, he is saying at the same time that he should become a different person. He is saying that he should identify less with his own culture and more with another. If someone says an Athabaskan should talk more about plans, should speak out more on his own opinions, or not be so indirect, he is saying that he should stop being so Athabaskan. He is saying he should change in personal identity and cultural identity.

As we write this it is impossible and undesirable for us to say what decision any person or groups should want to make about their own discourse patterns. Change is both slow and serious. That is exactly why the confusions and conflicts continue to exist. We believe it is important for all of us to know and understand just how we are communicating the stereotypes that others hold about us. We feel it is also very important for anyone engaged in language work whether teaching or research to fully understand what it means to propose changes in people's use of language. We believe that the understanding of discourse in interethnic communication is a matter of deep human importance.

References

Basso, Keith. 1970. To give up on words: Silence in the Western Apache culture. *Southwestern Journal of Anthropology* 26(3): 213–230. [also ch. 20, this volume]

Bateson, Gregory. 1972. Steps to an ecology of mond. New York: Ballantine Books.

Goffman, Erving. 1974. Frame analysis. New York: Harper and Row.

———. 1976. Replies and Responses. *Language in Society 5(3): 257–313.*

Gumperz, John. 1977a. The conversational analysis of interethnic communication. In: E. Lamar Ross (ed.), *Interethnic communication Proceedings of the Southern Anthropological Society,* University of Georgia. University of Georgia Press.

———. 1977b. Sociocultural knowledge in conversational inference. 28th Annual Roundtable Monogrpah Series on Languages and Linguistics. Washington, D.C.: Georgetown University.

Gumperz, John and Celia Roberts. 1978. Developing awareness skills for interethnic communication. Middlesex, England: National Centre for Industrial Language Training.

Halliday, M. A. K. 1976a. Meaning and the construction of reality in early childhood. In: H. L. Pick, Jr., and E. Saltzman (eds.)–, *Modes of perceiving and processing information.* Hillsdale, N.J.: Lawrence Erlbaum Associates.

———. 1976b. How children learn language. In: R. D. Eagleson and K. Watson (eds.), *English in secondary schools: Today and Tomorrow.* Syndney: English Teachers' Association.

———. 1976c. On the development of texture in child language. In: T. Myers (ed.), *Proceedings of the First Edinburgh Speech Communication Seminar.* Edinburgh: Edinburgh University Press.

Kintsch, W. 1977. On comprehending stories. In: J. Just and P. A. Carpenter (eds.), *Cognitive processes in comprehension.* Hillsdale, N.J.: Lawrence Erlbaum Associates.

Kintsh, W., and E. Greene. 1978. The role of culture-specific schemata in the comprehension and recall of stories. Discourse Process 1(1): 1–13.

Mead, Margaret. 1977. End linkage: A tool for cross-culture analysis. John Brockman (ed.), *About Bateson.* New York: E. P. Dutton.

Pawley, Andrew and Frances Syder. n.d. Sentence formulation in spontaneous speech: The one-clause-at-a-time hypothesis. Ms.

Schegloff, Emanual. 1972. Sequencing in conversational openings. John Gumperz and Dell Hymes (eds.), *Directions in sociolinguistics.* New York: Holt, Rinehart and Winston.

Scollon, Ronald. 1976. *Conversations with a one-year-old: A case study of the developmental foundation of syntax.* Honolulu: University Press of Hawaii.

Scollon, Ronald. 1977. Two discourse markers in Chipewyan narratives.International Journal of American Linguistics 43(1): 60–64

Scollon, Ronald and Suzanne B. K. Scollon. 1979. *Linguistic covergence: An ethnography of speaking at Fort Chipewyan,* Alberta, New York: Academic Press.

Toelken, Barre. 1969. The "pretty language" of Yellowman: Genre, mode and texture in Navaho Coyote narratives. Genre 2(3): 211–235.

19
Epilogue to "Athabaskan-English Interethnic Communication"

SUZANNE WONG-SCOLLON
RONALD SCOLLON

In the decade since we first wrote the paper that appears as chapter 18, we have found that the discourse patterns we describe for interethnic communication between Athabaskans and speakers of English are more general than we at first believed. Many people, academic researchers as well as native Americans, have told us that what we say about Athabaskan people is true of other native Americans. Moreover, differences in pausing also occur in any interethnic communication and between individuals from different areas of the country. For example, Tannen (1984, 1986) described differences in conversational style between New Yorkers and Californians. In fact, between any two individuals, rhythmic differences can result in miscommunication and stereotyping.

Not only the specific findings but the framework of discourse analysis has been helpful to us in thinking about interethnic communication. We have most recently returned to a comparative study of Chinese and English discourse that we began for quite personal reasons well before our research in Athabaskan-English discourse. In the following we limit our discussion to the interaction of differences between Chinese and English speakers in the presentation of self, the distribution of talk, and the sequencing of topics that often result in miscommunication in intercultural contacts.

By "Chinese" we mean primarily people of an older generation who speak Chinese and seek to uphold traditional Chinese values. These people can be found on both sides of the Taiwan Strait and in overseas Chinese communities all over the world. Where individuals or social groups have sought to change traditional values the patterns we discuss may be less marked, but anyone who has learned to speak Chinese to any extent will have internalized some of these patterns. Most of the people we describe as "Chinese" are bilingual in Chinese and English, although the patterns may persist even among members of overseas communities who do not speak

Chinese. By "English speakers" we include primarily North Americans, although other English speakers may also fit the description.

Presentation of self for a Chinese person is a matter of casting one's family, profession, or other group affiliation in a favorable light. One's individual identity is tied up in one's identity with various groups. Chinese people will seldom introduce themselves without also mentioning other family members, whereas English speakers usually find such information irrelevant. Chinese gain face by speaking reverently of the ancient sages and national heroes. Chinese people can hardly begin to speak unless they know where they stand vis-à-vis the other persons present. They have to first establish their relative social rank within the society in which the interaction takes place. In intercultural communication they will often want to know the attitude of their interlocutor toward their country and their culture.

Chinese people are ordinarily quite voluble and are constantly maintaining their social world through talk. Silence is noticeable, however, in situations where Chinese are concerned with showing respect. People prefer to think in terms of showing respect rather than dominance and subordination. Patterns of distribution of talk, including conversational traffic signals and topic control as well as the sequencing of topics all follow from relations of respect (Scollon & Wong-Scollon, 1990). We first discuss how Chinese people decide who speaks first, how topics are controlled, how turns are exchanged, and how conversations are ended.

Although in many situations people maintain social distance through silence, in other situations people show respect by speaking. For example, Chinese children are taught to greet their elders as soon as they wake up in the morning or return home. Students greet their teachers in chorus at the beginning of classes. Although they may generally avoid their teachers, when they need to speak with them they will initiate the conversation, if the teachers signal their availability.

As in American conversation, the person who speaks first also introduces the topic. Where the speakers are of equal status, the introduction of topic may not differ markedly from the American pattern. However, it is more typical for the person who initiates a conversation to show respect by doing some preliminary face work before introducing the main topic. The greater the seriousness of the topic, the more its introduction will be delayed.

The flow of talk and exchanges of turns are regulated by a different system of conversational traffic signals for Chinese speakers than for English speakers. Although Chinese and English both make use of intonation and tag questions, Chinese also has a variety of particles such as *a, ba, ma,* and *ne*) that are used both within sentences to raise attention to the subject or topic and at the end of sentences (Chao, 1968). These particles indicate the speakers' attitude toward what they are saying and the ways in which they expect their listeners to respond, whether by action, agreement, explanation, proposal, or contrition. The particles chosen will depend to a great extent on the relative position of the speakers.

Chinese speakers constantly monitor the response of their audience through the use of particles. As a result, they can make a fairly accurate assessment of the reaction of the listener to what they are saying. They can thus decide which topics it is necessary to introduce and the extent to which they need to elaborate them. If they want to make a request, they will first do a considerable amount of work to establish the felicity conditions for their request. They will try to find out through casual talk whether the person is able and willing to grant their request. Then, at the end of the conversation, they will present it as an afterthought. It is customary to summarize what has been said before departing.

Intercultural communication between Chinese and English speakers may be complicated by different assumptions about the presentation of self and different systems of conversational traffic signals that result in different expectations for the sequencing of topics. In speaking English, Chinese people may feel handicapped not only by their own lack of fluency, but also by what they feel is an inadequacy of English in monitoring audience response. Unless they have a very good command of English, they will not be able to express all the ways in which they feel they require a response in order to proceed. They will not receive the conversational traffic signal responses that they are accustomed to. Because social rank in North American society is far from being as clearly defined as it is in Chinese society, the inadequacy of English in obtaining feedback may be complicated by ambiguity in social relations of dominance.

When Chinese approach English speakers, then, they may proceed to establish some common ground for the interaction by testing which of their presuppositions are shared by their listeners. This may feel to English speakers like a sequence of riddles. They may respond to the surface content of the Chinese person's statements and questions, not realizing there is a purpose behind them. Because the expectation among English speakers is that one will state one's purpose at the beginning of an interaction, they will be trying to guess at the Chinese person's intention while the Chinese is trying to feel them out with what seems like small talk. By the time the Chinese get around to stating their purpose the English speaker may have already decided they had no serious business. The Chinese may feel like they never were able to get their listener's attention. When they try to summarize the conversation before departing, the English speaker may respond to the summary as though the Chinese speaker were introducing a new topic.

We have described what often happens in interactions between Chinese and English speakers. We are researching in more detail the ways in which Chinese speakers call for a particular response from their listeners through the use of particles and intonation and the ways in which English speakers signal an equivalent intention through intonation, lexical choice, and syntactic devices. A comparative analysis of the information structure of Chinese and English will be required for this task. Although Chinese and English both use word order to signal information structure, Chinese uses particles to convey attitudes and information that in English are signaled with prosody. The role of pausing is important in relation to the topic–comment structure of Chinese discourse both in conveying information and in calling for feedback in connection with the distribution of talk. The pause between topic and comment may be misinterpreted by English speakers as a pause for exchanging turns.

We are also looking into ways in which different assumptions about the presentation of self are displayed when Chinese people write, both in Chinese and in English. We hope that these studies will make a contribution both to understanding the nature of literacy and to understanding the nature of intercultural communication.

References

Chao, Y. R. (1968). *A grammar of spoken Chinese.* Berkeley, CA: University of California Press.

Scollon, R., & Wong-Scollon, S. (1990). Some cultural aspects of teaching English to Asian adults. Seoul, Korea: Sogang Institute for English as an International Language.

Tannen, D. (1984). *Conversational style.* Norwood, NJ: Ablex.

Tannen, D. (1986). *That's not what I meant!* New York: Ballantine.

III
Cross-cultural Comparisons of Communication Phenomena

DONAL CARBAUGH

The chapters in Part III examine specific communicative phenomena as they are used in different cultural systems. In so doing, they display some common threads. First, note that the chapters here are focused on a particular phenomenon of communication, such as the uses and interpretations of silence, the regulation of talk, and the performing of speech acts, with the thrust of the chapters focused primarily on the nature and uses of such a phenomenon. They are thus focused on a specific phenomenon that serves to anchor the study conceptually and empirically. Second, they, together, show how theories of specific phenomena of communication can be developed through cross-cultural or comparative study. Each phenomenon discussed in this part is, at some point, subjected to comparative analysis in order to determine which features of it are specific to particular cultures and which hold generally across cultures. Each phenomena is thus subjected to analysis in distinctive and different cultural systems in order to assess cultural specificities and cross-cultural generalities. Third, studies of each phenomenon display movement through three moments of research. The movement could be characterized very crudely — following Kenneth Pike — as follows, from etic-1 to emic to etic-2. Each phenomenon is studied by moving through these three rather distinct phases. The first such phase presents a general etic framework of the phenomenon, which grounds the study conceptually, providing an initial orienting definition of the phenomenon (e.g., speech act theory). In the second phase, the studies apply the etic framework heuristically, in particular situations and communities, in order to discover the nature of such phenomena, and rules for its use, in local systems. The application thus yields local knowledge, a theory of a particular communicative field, or the emics of the phenomenon (e.g., Ilongot speech acts). Finally, the chapters ask — in the course of such study — what the local systems (the emic orders) suggest generally about the phenomenon under study, a movement from emics back to the etic (what does the study of Ilongot speech acts suggest about speech act theory?). Put differently, each phenomenon addresses twin concerns: what is generally of interest (etic order); and, what is particularly interesting about it in specific interactional moments, situations and communities (the emic orders)?

Note, then, how this distinguishes studies of cross-cultural communication from those in Part II, of intercultural communication. The generic question of this part is, how does one account for a particular communicative phenomenon within and across cultures? The generic question of Part II was, how does one account for sources of asynchrony in intercultural encounters? The former explores a particular feature of communication in and across cultures; the latter inquires about various features of two cultural systems as they are used in particular intercultural encounters. The former holds a phenomenon constant and searches cultural variability in order to understand its general forces and particular features. The latter holds the intercultural context relatively constant and searches the various sources of cultural variability in communication conduct.

The distinction drawn here is of course not definitive but suggestive, and it points to approaches which are not exclusive but complementary. The point of the distinction is to note general differences between cross-cultural and intercultural research, with one concerned mainly with a communication phenomenon and its use in different cultural systems, whereas the other is anchored in contexts of intercultural encounters bringing various features into play.[1]

The chapters and epilogues in part III explore cross-cultural communication by introducing particular phenomena for study, describing their use in particular systems, comparatively analyzing these, and discussing the issues raised by such study, all the while working toward the twin goals of cultural particularity and cross-cultural generality. The specific phenomena addressed here are the communicative uses and interpretations of silence, the regulation of talk, and the performance of speech acts.

A Preview

Silence

When one has a choice to speak, or not to speak, and one chooses to remain silent, what message(s) is being conveyed by the silence?

In chapter 20, Keith Basso presents a cultural patterning of silence in Western Apache culture. He describes six scenes in Western Apache culture

---

[1]One could argue, of course, that the quality of intercultural accounts rests ultimately on the cultural and cross-cultural adequacy of communication theory.

where silence is used communicatively. The scenes are "meeting strangers," "courting," "children coming home," "getting cussed out," "being with people who are sad," and "being with someone for whom they sing." Within each such scene, there are important variations in structuring norms including the length of silences, and in social identities including the social attributes of persons. For example, when "children come home," silence from children may last up to 15 minutes, or from parents up to 2 to 3 days. Also, there are important differences in interpretation if one is not silent. For example, if one speaks upon "meeting strangers," then one symbolizes, to Apache, perhaps condescension, or being too forward. Similarly, for a girl to speak too much when "courting" symbolizes prior "experience" with men. In evidence is an Apache patterning of silence, displaying a cultural identity, through cultural frames and structuring norms.

Based on these particularities of communicative scenes, Basso asks more generally: Are there commonalities across these Apache scenes that enable a cultural understanding of silence? By exploring the role of silence in—and across—these scenes, Basso is able to explain its cultural use: to address a focal participant when social relations are ambiguous and/or unpredictable. Exploring silence across scenes within this community, Basso develops a general understanding of the cultural and social bases of silence in the Western Apache community of Cibecue.

Note that Basso's chapter investigates how one resource of communication is linked to particular scenes, given Western Apache premises for communicating. Basso thus identifies, respectively, how one structuring norm, uses of silence, occurs within six cultural frames, and displays a cultural identity. The identity may be further elaborated, with regard to silence, as it targets the goal of "acknowledging distance" when in social situations of ambiguity or unpredictability. Thus, counter to some more "mainstream American culture patterns," talk is dispreferred in social contexts of uncertainty, and is apparently not the main channel for reducing uncertainty. It is reserved for contexts more familiar and predictable.

But Basso goes further. He wonders if his hypothesis about silence, as associated with ambiguous social relations, can be generalized beyond the Apache case. Through a brief comparative analysis, he finds convergent evidence from the Navajo, and thus suggests tentatively that there is some cross-cultural data in support of his hypothesis.

A decade later, Braithwaite (chapter 21) conducted a follow-up study of Basso's hypothesis in order to subject it to more extensive comparative study. In the intervening decade, 18 ethnographic studies of communication had been conducted, each with data relevant to Basso's hypothesis. By juxtaposing these studies, Braithwaite finds support for Basso's earlier statement, but also finds that it needs extended. On the basis of his cross-cultural analysis, he claims that silence is associated not only with social relations of ambiguity, but also with unambigous relations in which a great difference in power and/or status is evident. This leads him to speculate about possible general premises for the use of silence (as signalling a lack of interrelatedness or mutual influence) as distinct from those for speaking (signalling the existence or possibility of interrelatedness and mutual influence).

With regard to the common threads outlined here, the readings by Basso and Braithwaite (a) explore one communicative phenomenon, silence, (b) develop hypotheses about its use and interpretation cross-culturally, based on data from 20 or so ethnographic studies, and (c) demonstrate movement from emic features to etic forces for silence (in Basso's study), and from this to emics and back again (in Braithwaite) in order to understand both the particular shaping of silence in local communities, and its general forces in communicative action.

Regulation of Talk

In the course of conversation, how do participants regulate talk?

Susan U. Philips (chapter 22) explores sources of cultural variability in the regulation of talk. More specifically, she examines the role of turns, nonverbal cues, and interactional sequences as they contribute to the regulation of talk. Note how Philips does so through what might be called a controlled comparison, juxtaposing two cultural patterns with a focus on this one general phenomenon.

Philips finds that Anglicized patterns for regulating talk vary from those of the Warm Springs Indian (WSI). With regard to turns, she notes how WSI are paced more slowly, include longer pauses for turn exchange cues, with turn lengths varying less, thus creating a more even distribution of talk — each speaker getting roughly the same allocation of time for a turn — across participants. Concerning nonverbal configurations of the head, face, and body, she finds WSI use less body motion and less direct gazing generally, but make greater use of eye and brow movement. Relative to Anglicized patterns, WSI find important nonverbal regulators around the eyes, creating a qualitatively different regulation system, in both type and amount of nonverbal cueing. Finally, Philips explores cultural practices of "tieing" utterances one to another. She notes that sequences, such as question/answer, are culturally variable, one being more elastic than the other. WSI patterns — in this regard — may include answers to questions that were asked a week earlier, whereas Anglicized "tieing" sequences seem more constrained temporally.

Because of the cultural differences in turns, nonverbal cueings, and "tieing" sequences, Philips concludes that the WSI system maximizes the speaker's ability to regulate turns while minimizing other's influences; with the Anglicized system supporting a pattern of symmetrical influence. As noted earlier, the nonverbal systems are apparently qualitatively different (but see her epilogue in chapter 23). And with regard to sequences, she notes the relatively more tightly constrained pattern of responding in the Anglicized system, "tieing" acts such as answers more closely to their precipitative questions. This comparative analysis leads Philips to conclude, yes, talk is regulated in culturally variable ways, but it varies in general ways, with the structuring of turns, nonverbal cues, and tieing sequences identifying some general and important parameters of such variation.

Note that Philips, unlike the studies in Part II, explores two cultural communication systems, *and* comparatively analyzes them with regard to one general phenomenon, the regulation of talk. She is not focused primarily on an intercultural context, like a schoolroom or classroom, although particular contexts are identified in her report. She is focused on this one phenomenon, a system of structuring norms, and its patterns of variation within and across cultural systems. She shows how systems of structuring norms, more particularly the structuring of interaction and information, is intimately linked to cultural identities, with their attendant premises about goals, motives, and social relations.

Some special features of Philips' chapter deserve some further comment. Note that she uses some reports in the scholarly literature — reported as if cross-culturally general — and treats them as data about an Anglicized culture pattern. This effort to evaluate extant — and purportedly general — theory, whatever its vintage, with ethnographic data, is worth noticing, and emulating. Our theoretical frameworks, if they are to be particularly interesting, and generally worthwhile, must withstand tests of particular practices. Second, note Philips' focus on regulation as a socially negotiated process, including the co-participation of speakers and listeners. Of special interest to her are ways listeners regulate conversations. Too often, theory becomes prey to a speaker-focus. In order to advance a "listener sensitive" theory of conversation regulation, and to hold it accountable to specific practices, she proposes in her epilogue, following Matsuki (1989), adoption of the concept "floor-holding" (rather than turn) as a way to address joint foci of interactional attention between participants.

Philips' chapter, thus, covers much ground: It (a) explores one general and complex phenomenon, the regulation of talk, (b) juxtaposes through a kind of controlled comparison two cultural systems, and (c) moves from general etic frameworks, to a viewing of (them as emic) cultural data, including the Warm Springs communication system, in order to understand the cultural particulars of conversational regulation, as well as the general forces, parameters, or etics, at work.

Speech Acts

The study of speech acts presumes a basic distinction between the propositional content of an utterance (reference and predication) and the force of the utterance (illocutionary force).[2] Consider the following utterances: (a) Montana is beautiful; (b) Is Montana beautiful?; and, (c) Montana is BEAUTIFUL! In uttering each, the speaker expresses propositional content (p) which is common to the three examples: Each refers, or designates an object, Montana; each also predicates the same about the object, is beautiful. But each utterance also has a distinctive force. In saying the first, the speaker could be making a simple declaration of truth, or could be trying to get someone to go to Montana. In saying the second, the speaker is asking a question, inviting a hearer to respond. With the third, a speaker is exclaiming. So, the propositional content is common across these utterances, with their reference to Montana and their predication that it is beautiful. However, the forces of the utterances are variable (e.g. declaring, asking, exclaiming). In the following readings about speech acts, it is the kinds of things people do with their propositions, their illocutionary forces, that is the main concern.

By presuming that the illocutionary force is fundamental to human communication, and thus by focusing on the forces of speech acts, the basic question—according to Searle—becomes: How many ways of using language are there?, with its more specific forms: What is the force, or purpose, of an utterance? and, How many types—or points, or purposes—of illocutionary acts are there? How many forces like declaring, asking, and exclaiming are there?

In the first chapter on this topic, we are introduced to the highly influential taxonomy of illocutionary acts proposed by John Searle (chapter 24). Searle responds to the previous questions by suggesting 12 basic criteria, continua, or dimensions (see Hymes, 1986), which underly the different forces in illocutionary acts. These vary widely by considering such things as the basic purpose of the utterance, the state of the speaker, and the direction of fit between words and the world. Searle then argues for the adequacy of his formulation (over the earlier taxonomy proposed by Austin) because it more ably classifies speech acts on the basis of consistent principles, distinguishes illocutionary verbs from illocutionary acts, and so on. Searle then develops, on the basis of three of his continua (point, expressed psychological state, and direction of fit), his five basic types of illocutionary acts. He thus argues that there are five basic types of speech acts, with his continua defining and differentiating the five types.

---

[2]Every illocutionary act (e.g. "ouch!") need not have a propositional content (Searle, 1969, p. 30), nor only one illocutionary force.

Searle's taxonomy has been widely used in the social sciences and the humanities, producing insights into communication patterns in educational and legal settings, as well as in oral and written channels. But the taxonomy has not gone without its challengers. In chapter 25, Rosaldo uses and critically evaluates Searle's taxonomy in her study of Ilongot speech acts.

Note that Rosaldo is taking Searle's philosophical framework and using it to unravel the Ilongot's communication system. What she finds generally—as she puts it—is this: "ways of thinking about language and about human agency and personhood are inextricably linked." She demonstrates her point by showing how Ilongot uses of speech acts, such as directives (commands and requests), vary by two cultural continua. The most important is related to "urgency" and the desired speed of response—a concern for the efficaciousness of speech as a situated agency. The other is a concern for persons, having more to do with lines of social rank, in this case especially age and gender. On this basis, Rosaldo argues that the force of speech acts is inextricably tied to cultural models of agency and personhood.

Rosaldo argues that Searle's speech act philosophy is skewed in the direction of Western culture. Why? Because, she says, it is based on Western premises of agency and personhood. This leads, she claims, to a model of speech acts based on norms of self-presentation and individuation, to thinking of speech as things *individuals* do with their words. Within such a model, utterances issue forth from a kind of person; the Westernized notion of person-as-self is a given. Acts of Ilongot speech, Rosaldo argues, are something else. They issue forth from persons as relational bonds, and in an agency that is a contextual and constant achievement. In the presumed Western case, she argues, cultural identity is based on loci of motives more individual and intentional; speech activates conditions of psychological states, sincerity, and the like. For the Ilongot, the loci of motives are more communal and relational; speech activates "social bonds and interactive meanings." Imposing a Westernized (Searlian speech act) view of speech on Ilongot communicative acts skews, Rosaldo argues, our understanding of Ilongot speech acts, agency and personhood.

Rosaldo helps us see how the forces of speech are media and products of sociocultural worlds. She argues that the three continua emphasized by Searle—although not the sole basis of his taxonomy—like "expressed psychological state" and "individualized purpose," are not those emphasized by the Ilongot. In their place are concerns with interruption/movement, hierarchy/cooperation, and constant achievement of social bonds. Rosaldo eventually shows how the latter Ilongot continua can articulate with the "terms of categories proposed by Searle" (see his seventh, fifth, and eighth continua, respectively), even if they are not emphasized by him. Her main criticism then, is less about Searle's taxonomy, than it is with its premises.[3] Because Rosaldo is concerned with socially performed communication, cultural models of agency and personhood, their interactional realization and meanings through episodic sequences—all things outside the specific focal concern of speech act theory, the illocutionary act—she helps identify several concerns relevant to the conduct of speech acts, but not highlighted by the speech act framework.

In the next reading, Searle restates his basic claim, suggests how his taxonomy is to be evaluated through further empirical study and "transcendental deduction," grounds his framework in human biology, and then goes on to respond to several criticisms made by Rosaldo.

In the final chapter of the book (chapter 30), Dell Hymes distinguishes questions about philosophical possibilities of speech acts, such as the basic dimensions and types in existence, from those of cultural communication systems, such as what gets done locally by a people. Knowledge of what it is possible to do with words, is distinct from, but can complement, what is actually done in cultural contexts. With regard to the latter, Hymes discusses how Rosaldo uses Searle's framework heuristically in order to discover a local system of communication. The application yields both a system of communicative means in a sociocultural world, and a system of meanings powerfully evoked with it. Rosaldo thus shows how speech act theory can be a useful component of ethnography, a component embraced and praised by Hymes. Hymes goes on however to question the taxonomy itself. He wonders how conversational moves such as remarks and comments relate to the taxonomy. If they seem to be something other than illocutionary acts, as Searle suggests (p.417), then that implies a broader taxonomy of discourse of which Searle's is a part. The broader taxonomy, if developed, Hymes argues, would inevitably lead to considering how illocutionary acts relate to broader interactional sequences, as well as social relations. Note in his discussion how Hymes praises Searle's taxonomy, and proposes its empirical use. As it suggests dimensions and types of speech acts that *may* be present, so it also needs used to discover what is actually *there,* in cultural communication contexts. It is these uses of Searle's framework that Hymes encourages in particular: the discovery of local systems; the use of such knowledge—of local systems—to reflect on, and develop, the theory of acts of speech; and the extension of such knowledge to include larger communicative sequences and social life. Searle's framework helps move us in these directions, with Hymes suggesting ways it can be developed through further ethnographic and cross-cultural work.

The exchange between Searle, Rosaldo, and Hymes foregrounds several issues that are discussed momentarily. For now, notice how the debate takes one phenomenon, speech acts, works with it in two cultural systems, and

---

[3]See the complementary argument sketched by Frentz and Farrell (1976, pp. 340–342).

does so by moving from the etic framework (Searle's dimensions and types), to emic cases, and back again. The debate demonstrates these bases of cross-cultural study. In so doing, it also raises several fundamental issues. One concerns what is considered basic as a unit of human communication, a focus on illocutionary force at a moment in time, or its interactional management within episodes or larger sequences. A second concerns the kinds of claims being made, on the one hand of philosophical possibilities of linguistic meaning, on the other of cultural meanings. A third concerns what is foundational to spoken interaction, human biology, psychology, and/or sociocultural patterns. And so on. The debate on speech acts helps highlight central problematics in the study of human communication, suggesting places for cross-cultural study, with each such place responding to these issues as well as providing important ways to proceed.

A Brief Summary of Issues

The issues raised in the following chapters are involving and complex. At this point, I cannot detail any one, but I briefly sketch four, then suggest other phenomena for comparative study. The four issues could be put in the form of questions: which level of theory is priveleged? What types of claims are being made? What criteria are proposed for evaluating the claims? and, What are the ultimate foundations of the theory?

Which Level of Theory is Privileged?   The chapters in Part III vary with regard to what might be called a field dependent–independent dimension. Note how the major part of Basso's chapter on silence develops a field dependent theory, the uses and interpretations of silence in six cultural scenes of Western Apache life. Basso thus grounds his theory of silence in a particular sociocultural field. Note on the other end, how Searle presents his theory of speech acts as independent of any sociocultural field. His claim is of a cross-cultural and universal system of dimensions and types of illocutionary acts. Note further how Philips and Rosaldo, along with Basso and Braithwaite, work in the middle range, developing theories adequate to particular phenomena and fields, but also asking what these suggest generally. Hopefully the readings, taken together, demonstrate how theory interpenetrates these levels and functions in distinctive, and complementary, ways.

What Types of Claims are Being Made?   Perhaps it is useful to distinguish three general types of claims in the following readings. First is a claim of *cultural validity*. The author presents various data from a cultural field, demonstrates how they are related systematically, and argues the patterns represent a "native view." Basso provides an instructive exemplar here, as does Rosaldo. Second is a claim of *cross-cultural generality*. The author presents data from various cultural fields, demonstrating how some pattern holds at least in some cases, and thus argues the pattern—to a degree—is general. Effort is taken to develop general hypotheses that are sensitive to cultural particularities. The hypothesis eventually proposed by Basso, and Braithwaite's development of it provide two examples, as does Philips general framework. Third is a claim of *philosphical possibility*. The author collects or creates data with regard to some problem, demonstrating the necessary and sufficient elements of an objective conceptual apparatus that accounts for such data, and thus argues for the adequacy of the apparatus. Searle presents such an argument.

In the following chapters, each author priveleges one type of claim over others, but does so in order to advance an understanding of a communication phenomenon. Ideally, each could be brought into focus in order to generate claims sensitive to situated communication practices (being culturally valid), which are generalizable beyond a given case (cross-culturally general), so as to embrace, understand, and state with precision the possibilities in communication phenomena.

What Criteria are Proposed for Evaluating the Claims? Most scholars of communication would agree that there are such things as communicative silence, regulation of talk, and illocutionary acts. Many also would accept Basso's, Philips', and Rosaldo's ethnographies as adequate descriptions of sociocultural worlds. In so many words, these phenomena and the ethnographic accounts of them would be regarded as adequate, or *true*. However, future investigators may find evidence of inaccuracies in these accounts and thus could question their validity, perhaps finding with the passage of time that the claims are no longer true, or somehow just short of the whole truth. Of course, evidence of stability and continuance of a pattern is equally valuable. Of any such phenomenon and report, one can ask: is there such a thing, and is this description of it (still) accurate, or true.

There is a second general criterion. With regard to it, rather than asking about truth value, perhaps even granting a degree of truth to a claim, one might ask, is this the right way to go about understanding communication? Does this perspective hold some *utility*? One thus might ask of any phenomenon, is attending to this in this way a productive way to proceed? Responses to questions of utility ultimately reveal personal and professional interests and goals, which differently prioritize phenomena and intellectual problems. For some, questions about local patterns of silence and so on, will be enough. For others, there are other questions.

With regard to the debate on illocutionary acts, it seems there is general agreement on the truth value of such a thing, that is, we do perform acts when we make utterances. But, there is some disagreement with regard to its utility, especially in seeing it—as Searle does—as the basic unit of human communication. It is this premise of Searle's argument that Rosaldo finds most troubling, leading her to question the utility of the speech act framework—its ability to capture the cultural communication of agency and personhood—more than its truth. But in so doing, she leads eventually back to the criterion of truthfulness, granting Searle's apparatus truth value, but questioning two of its premises, both its placement of illocutionary force as the basic unit of communication and its status as culturally neutral.

A final issue in the following chapters could be posed: *What are the ultimate foundations of the communication theory?* Is the theory grounded ultimately in human biology, or psychology? If so, one writes of communication as "manifesting" or "revealing" some other more basic order, usually one grounded in organisms and individuals. Or, is the theory grounded in social and cultural patterns? If so, one writes of communication as it "creates" and constitutes, as medium and outcome, of sociocultural life. Of course, both foundations can ground communication theory, as is evidenced in the following chapters, with appeal made to whichever is appropriate given the phenomenon of concern, or preferable given the author.

These are a complex set of issues that are of course no more than sketched here. But hopefully they help the reader anticipate some of the issues in the following readings. Cross-cultural studies of communication as these, perhaps in the form of meta-ethnographies, need to be done. Further evidence of movement in that direction—demonstrating further its possibilities—can be found in studies of politeness (Brown & Levinson, 1978; Katriel, 1986), conversational maxims (Keenan, 1976), conversational sequences (Hopper & Doany, 1989), person reference (Moerman, 1988), the communal function of talk (Philipsen, 1989), and cultural terms for talk (Carbaugh, 1989; Griefat & Katriel, 1989). If we are to understand communication across cultures, as well as cultures in communication, cross-cultural study of this kind is warranted.

References

Brown, P., & Levinson, S. (1978). Universals in language usage: Politeness phenomena. In E. Goody (Ed.), *Questions and politeness* (pp. 56–310). Cambridge: Cambridge: University Press.

Carbaugh, D. (1989). Fifty terms for talk: A cross-cultural study. *International and Intercultural Communication Annual, 13,* 93–120.

Frentz, T., Farrell, T. (1976). Language action: A paradigm for communication. *Quarterly Journal of Speech, 62,* 333–349.

Griefat, Y. & Katriel, T. (1989). Life demands *Muusayra:* Communication and culture among

Arabs in Israel. *International and Intercultural Communication Annual, 13,* 121–138.

Hopper, R. & Doany, N. (1989). Telephone openings and conversational universals. *International and Intercultural Communication Annual, 13,* 157–179.

Hymes, D. (1986). Discourse: Scope without depth. *International Journal of the Sociology of Language, 57,* 49–89.

Katriel, T. (1986). *Talking straight.* Cambridge: Cambridge University Press.

Keenan, E. (1976). The universality of conversational postulates. *Language in Society, 5,* 67–80.

Matsuki, K. (1989). *Floor phenomena in Japanese conversational discourse: Talk among relatives.* Unpublished masters thesis, Department of Anthropology, University of Arizona, Tucson, AZ.

Moerman, M. (1988). *Talking culture.* Pennsylvania: University of Pennsylvania Press.

Philipsen, G. (1989). Speech and the communal function in four cultures. *International and Intercultural Communication Annual, 13,* 79–92.

Searle, J. (1969). *Speech acts.* Cambridge: Cambridge University Press.

20

"To Give up on Words": Silence in Western Apache Culture[1]

KEITH H. BASSO

Combining methods from ethnoscience and sociolinguistics, this paper presents an hypothesis to account for why, in certain types of situations, members of Western Apache society refrain from speech. Though cross-cultural data on silence behavior are almost wholly lacking, some evidence has been collected which suggests that this hypothesis may have relevance to other societies as well.

It is not the case that a man who is silent says nothing.
  Anonymous

I

ANYONE WHO HAS READ ABOUT AMERICAN INDIANS has probably encountered statements which impute to them a strong predilection for keeping silent or, as one writer has put it, "a fierce reluctance to speak except when absolutely necessary." In the popular literature, where this characterization is particularly widespread, it is commonly portrayed as

1 At different times during the period extending from 1964-1969 the research on which this paper is based was supported by U. S. P. H. S. Grant MH-12691-01, a grant from the American Philosophical Society, and funds from the Doris Duke Oral History Project at the Arizona State Museum. I am pleased to acknowledge this support. I would also like to express my gratitude to the following scholars for commenting upon an earlier draft: Y. R. Chao, Harold C. Conklin, Roy G. D'Andrade, Charles O. Frake, Paul Friedrich, John Gumperz, Kenneth Hale, Harry Hoijer, Dell Hymes, Stanley Newman, David M. Schneider, Joel Sherzer, and Paul Turner. Although the final version gained much from their criticisms and suggestions, responsibility for its present form and content rests solely with the author. A preliminary version of this paper was presented to the Annual Meeting of the American Anthropological Association in New Orleans, Lousiana, November 1969. A modified version of this paper is scheduled to appear in *Studies in Apachean Culture and Ethnology* (ed. by Keith H. Basso and Morris Opler), Tucson: University of Arizona Press, 1970.

the outgrowth of such dubious causes as "instinctive dignity," "an impoverished language," or, perhaps worst of all, the Indians' "lack of personal warmth." Although statements of this sort are plainly erroneous and dangerously misleading, it is noteworthy that professional anthropologists have made few attempts to correct them. Traditionally, ethnographers and linguists have paid little attention to cultural interpretations given to silence or, equally important, to the types of social contexts in which it regularly occurs.

This study investigates certain aspects of silence in the culture of the Western Apache of east-central Arizona. After considering some of the theoretical issues involved, I will briefly describe a number of situations—recurrent in Western Apache society—in which one or more of the participants typically refrain from speech for lengthy periods of time.[2] This is accompanied by a discussion of how such acts of silence are interpreted and why they are encouraged and deemed appropriate. I conclude by advancing an hypothesis that accounts for the reasons that the Western Apache refrain from speaking when they do, and I suggest that, with proper testing, this hypothesis may be shown to have relevance to silence behavior in other cultures.

II

A basic finding of sociolinguistics is that, although both language and language usage are structured, it is the latter which responds most sensitively to extra-linguistic influences (Hymes 1962, 1964; Ervin-Tripp 1964, 1967; Gumperz 1964; Slobin 1967). Accordingly, a number of recent studies have addressed themselves to the problem of how factors in the social environment of speech events delimit the range and condition the selection of message forms (cf. Brown and Gilman 1960; Conklin 1959; Ervin-Tripp 1964, 1967; Frake 1964; Friedrich 1966; Gumperz 1961, 1964; Martin 1964). These studies may be viewed as taking the now familiar position that verbal communication is fundamentally a decision-making process in which, initially, a speaker, having elected to speak, selects from among a repertoire of available codes that which is most appropriately suited to the situation at hand. Once a code has been selected, the speaker picks a suitable channel of transmission and then, finally, makes a choice from a set of referentially equivalent expressions within the code. The intelligibility of the expression

---

2 The situations described in this paper are not the only ones in which the Western Apache refrain from speech. There is a second set—not considered here because my data are incomplete—in which silence appears to occur as a gesture of respect, usually to persons in positions of authority. A third set, very poorly understood, involves ritual specialists who claim they must keep silent at certain points during the preparation of ceremonial paraphernalia.

he chooses will, of course, be subject to grammatical constraints. But its acceptability will not. Rules for the selection of linguistic alternates operate on features of the social environment and are commensurate with rules governing the conduct of face-to-face interaction. As such, they are properly conceptualized as lying outside the structure of language itself.

It follows from this that for a stranger to communicate appropriately with the members of an unfamiliar society it is not enough that he learn to formulate messages intelligibly. Something else is needed: a knowledge of what kinds of codes, channels, and expressions to use in what kinds of situations and to what kinds of people—as Hymes (1964) has termed it, an "ethnography of communication."

There is considerable evidence to suggest that extra-linguistic factors influence not only the use of speech but its actual occurrence as well. In our own culture, for example, remarks such as "Don't you know when to keep quiet?" "Don't talk until you're introduced," and "Remember now, no talking in church" all point to the fact that an individual's decision to speak may be directly contingent upon the character of his surroundings. Few of us would maintain that "silence is golden" for all people at all times. But we feel that silence is a virtue for some people some of the time, and we encourage children on the road to cultural competence to act accordingly.

Although the form of silence is always the same, the function of a specific act of silence—that is, its interpretation by and effect upon other people—will vary according to the social context in which it occurs. For example, if I choose to keep silent in the chambers of a Justice of the Supreme Court, my action is likely to be interpreted as a sign of politeness or respect. On the other hand, if I refrain from speaking to an established friend or colleague, I am apt to be accused of rudeness or harboring a grudge. In one instance, my behavior is judged by others to be "correct" or "fitting"; in the other, it is criticized as being "out of line."

The point, I think, is fairly obvious. For a stranger entering an alien society, a knowledge of when *not* to speak may be as basic to the production of culturally acceptable behavior as a knowledge of what to say. It stands to reason, then, that an adequate ethnography of communication should not confine itself exclusively to the analysis of choice within verbal repertoires. It should also, as Hymes (1962, 1964) has suggested, specify those conditions under which the members of the society regularly decide to refrain from verbal behavior altogether.

III

The research on which this paper is based was conducted over a period of sixteen months (1964-1969) in the Western Apache settlement of Cibecue, which is located near the center of the Fort Apache Indian Reservation in east-central Arizona. Cibecue's 800 residents participate in an unstable economy that combines subsistence agriculture, cattle-raising, sporadic wage-earning, and Government subsidies in the form of welfare checks and social security benefits. Unemployment is a serious problem, and substandard living conditions are widespread.

Although Reservation life has precipitated far-reaching changes in the composition and geographical distribution of Western Apache social groups, consanguineal kinship—real and imputed—remains the single most powerful force in the establishment and regulation of interpersonal relationships (Kaut 1957; Basso 1970). The focus of domestic activity is the individual "camp," or gowąą. This term labels both the occupants and the location of a single dwelling or, as is more apt to be the case, several dwellings built within a few feet of each other. The majority of gowąą in Cibecue are occupied by nuclear families. The next largest residential unit is the gotáá (camp cluster), which is a group of spatially localized gowąą, each having at least one adult member who is related by ties of matrilineal kinship to persons living in all the others. An intricate system of exogamous clans serves to extend kinship relationships beyond the gowąą and gotáá and facilitates concerted action in projects, most notably the presentation of ceremonials, requiring large amounts of manpower. Despite the presence in Cibecue of a variety of Anglo missionaries and a dwindling number of medicine men, diagnostic and curing rituals, as well as the girls' puberty ceremonial, continue to be performed with regularity (Basso 1966, 1970). Witchcraft persists in undiluted form (Basso 1969).

IV

Of the many broad categories of events, or scenes, that comprise the daily round of Western Apache life, I shall deal here only with those that are coterminous with what Goffman (1961, 1964) has termed "focused gatherings" or "encounters." The concept situation, in keeping with established usage, will refer inclusively to the location of such a gathering, its physical setting, its point in time, the standing behavior patterns that accompany it, and the social attributes of the persons involved (Hymes 1962, 1964; Ervin-Tripp 1964, 1967).

In what follows, however, I will be mainly concerned with the roles and statuses of participants. The reason for this is that the critical factor in the Apache's decision to speak or keep silent seems always to be the nature of his relationships to other people. To be sure, other features of the situation are significant, but apparently only to the extent that they influence the perception of status and role.[3] What this implies, of course, is that roles and statuses are not fixed attributes. Although they may be depicted as such in a static model (and often with good reason), they are appraised and acted upon in particular social contexts and, as a result, subject to redefinition and variation.[4] With this in mind, let us now turn our attention to the Western Apache and the types of situations in which, as one of my informants put it, "it is right to give up on words."

V

1. "Meeting strangers" (*nda dòhwáá'iłtsééda*). The term, *nda,* labels categories at two levels of contrast. At the most general level, it designates any person—Apache or non-Apache—who, prior to an initial meeting, has never been seen and therefore cannot be identified. In addition, the term is used to refer to Apaches who, though previously seen and known by some external criteria such as clan affiliation or personal name, have never been engaged in face-to-face interaction. The latter category, which is more restricted than the first, typically includes individuals who live on the adjacent San Carlos Reservation, in Fort Apache settlements geographically removed from Cibecue, and those who fall into the category *kii dòhandáágo* (non-kinsmen). In all cases, "strangers" are separated by social distance. And in all cases it is considered appropriate, when encountering them for the first time, to refrain from speaking.

The type of situation described as "meeting strangers" (*nda dòhwáá'iłtsééda*) can take place in any number of different physical settings. However, it occurs most frequently in the context of events such as fairs and rodeos, which, owing to the large number of people in attendance, offer unusual opportunities for chance encounters. In large gatherings, the lack of verbal communication between strangers is apt to go unnoticed, but in smaller groups it becomes quite conspicuous. The following incident, involving two strangers who found themselves part of a four-man round-up crew,

---

3 Recent work in the sociology of interaction, most notably by Goffman (1963) and Garfinkel (1967), has led to the suggestion that social relationships are everywhere the major determinants of verbal behavior. In this case, as Gumperz (1967) makes clear, it becomes methodologically unsound to treat the various components of communicative events as independent variables. Gumperz (1967) has presented a hierarchical model, sensitive to dependency, in which components are seen as stages in the communication process. Each stage serves as the input for the next. The basic stage, i.e., the initial input, is "social identities or statuses." For further details see Slobin 1967:131-134.

4 I would like to stress that the emphasis placed on social relations is fully in keeping with the Western Apache interpretation of their own behavior. When my informants were asked to explain why they or someone else was silent on a particular occasion, they invariably did so in terms of *who* was present at the time.

serves as a good example. My informant, who was also a member of the crew, recalled the following episode:

> One time, I was with A, B, and X down at Gleason Flat, working cattle. That man, X, was from East Fork [a community nearly 40 miles from Cibecue] where B's wife was from. But he didn't know A, never knew him before, I guess. First day, I worked with X. At night, when we camped, we talked with B, but X and A didn't say anything to each other. Same way, second day. Same way, third. Then, at night on fourth day, we were sitting by the fire. Still, X and A didn't talk. Then A said, "Well, I know there is a stranger to me here, but I've been watching him and I know he is all right." After that, X and A talked a lot. . . . Those two men didn't know each other, so they took it easy at first.

As this incident suggests, the Western Apache do not feel compelled to "introduce" persons who are unknown to each other. Eventually, it is assumed, strangers will begin to speak. However, this is a decision that is properly left to the individuals involved, and no attempt is made to hasten it. Outside help in the form of introductions or other verbal routines is viewed as presumptuous and unnecessary.

Strangers who are quick to launch into conversation are frequently eyed with undisguised suspicion. A typical reaction to such individuals is that they "want something," that is, their willingness to violate convention is attributed to some urgent need which is likely to result in requests for money, labor, or transportation. Another common reaction to talkative strangers is that they are drunk.

If the stranger is an Anglo, it is usually assumed that he "wants to teach us something" (i.e., give orders or instructions) or that he "wants to make friends in a hurry." The latter response is especially revealing, since Western Apaches are extremely reluctant to be hurried into friendships—with Anglos or each other. Their verbal reticence with strangers is directly related to the conviction that the establishment of social relationships is a serious matter that calls for caution, careful judgment, and plenty of time.

2. "Courting" (*liigoláá*). During the initial stages of courtship, young men and women go without speaking for conspicuous lengths of time. Courting may occur in a wide variety of settings—practically anywhere, in fact—and at virtually any time of the day or night, but it is most readily observable at large public gatherings such as ceremonials, wakes, and rodeos. At these events, "sweethearts" (*zééde*) may stand or sit (sometimes holding hands) for as long as an hour without exchanging a word. I am told by adult informants that the young people's reluctance to speak may become even more pronounced in situations where they find themselves alone.

Apaches who have just begun to court attribute their silence to "intense shyness" (*'isté'*) and a feeling of acute "self-consciousness" (*dàyéézi'*) which, they claim, stems from their lack of familiarity with one another. More specifically, they complain of "not knowing what to do" in each other's presence and of the fear that whatever they say, no matter how well thought out in advance, will sound "dumb" or "stupid."[5]

One informant, a youth 17 years old, commented as follows:

> It's hard to talk with your sweetheart at first. She doesn't know you and won't know what to say. It's the same way towards her. You don't know how to talk yet . . . so you get very bashful. That makes it sometimes so you don't say anything. So you just go around together and don't talk. At first, it's better that way. Then, after a while, when you know each other, you aren't shy anymore and can talk good.

The Western Apache draw an equation between the ease and frequency with which a young couple talks and how well they know each other. Thus, it is expected that after several months of steady companionship sweethearts will start to have lengthy conversations. Earlier in their relationship, however, protracted discussions may be openly discouraged. This is especially true for girls, who are informed by their mothers and older sisters that silence in courtship is a sign of modesty and that an eagerness to speak betrays previous experience with men. In extreme cases, they add, it may be interpreted as a willingness to engage in sexual relations. Said one woman, aged 32:

> This way I have talked to my daughter. "Take it easy when boys come around this camp and want you to go somewhere with them. When they talk to you, just listen at first. Maybe you won't know what to say. So don't talk about just anything. If you talk with those boys right away, then they will know you know all about them. They will think you've been with many boys before, and they will start talking about that."

3. "Children, coming home" (*čəgəƷe nakáii*). The Western Apache lexeme *iltá'inatsáá* (reunion) is used to describe encounters between an individual who has returned home after a long absence from his relatives and friends. The most common type of reunion, *čəgəƷe nakáii* (children, coming home),

---

5 Among the Western Apache, rules of exogamy discourage courtship between members of the same clan (*kii àlhánigo*) and so-called "related" clans (*kii*), with the result that sweethearts are almost always "non-matrilineal kinsmen" (*dòhwàkíida*). Compared to "matrilineal kinsmen" (*kii*), such individuals have fewer opportunities during childhood to establish close personal relationships and thus, when courtship begins, have relatively little knowledge of each other. It is not surprising, therefore, that their behavior is similar to that accorded strangers.

involves boarding school students and their parents. It occurs in late May or early in June, and its setting is usually a trading post or school, where parents congregate to await the arrival of buses bringing the children home. As the latter disembark and locate their parents in the crowd, one anticipates a flurry of verbal greetings. Typically, however, there are few or none at all. Indeed, it is not unusual for parents and child to go without speaking for as long as 15 minutes.

When the silence is broken, it is almost always the child who breaks it. His parents listen attentively to everything he says but speak hardly at all themselves. This pattern persists even after the family has reached the privacy of its camp, and two or three days may pass before the child's parents seek to engage him in sustained conversation.

According to my informants, the silence of Western Apache parents at (and after) reunions with their children is ultimately predicated on the possibility that the latter have been adversely affected by their experiences away from home. Uppermost is the fear that, as a result of protracted exposure to Anglo attitudes and values, the children have come to view their parents as ignorant, old-fashioned, and no longer deserving of respect. One of my most thoughtful and articulate informants commented on the problem as follows:

> You just can't tell about those children after they've been with White men for a long time. They get their minds turned around sometimes . . . they forget where they come from and get ashamed when they come home because their parents and relatives are poor. They forget how to act with these Apaches and get mad easy. They walk around all night and get into fights. They don't stay at home.
>
> At school, some of them learn to want to be White men, so they come back and try to act that way. But we are still Apaches! So we don't know them anymore, and it is like we never knew them. It is hard to talk to them when they are like that.

Apache parents openly admit that, initially, children who have been away to school seem distant and unfamiliar. They have grown older, of course, and their physical appearance may have changed. But more fundamental is the concern that they have acquired new ideas and expectations which will alter their behavior in unpredictable ways. No matter how pressing this concern may be, however, it is considered inappropriate to directly interrogate a child after his arrival home. Instead, parents anticipate that within a short time he will begin to divulge information about himself that will enable them to determine in what ways, if any, his views and attitudes have changed. This, the Apache say, is why children do practically all the talking in the hours following a reunion, and their parents remain unusually silent.

Said one man, the father of two children who had recently returned from boarding school in Utah:

Yes, it's right that we didn't talk much to them when they came back, my wife and me. They were away for a long time, and we didn't know how they would like it, being home. So we waited. Right away, they started to tell stories about what they did. Pretty soon we could tell they liked it, being back. That made us feel good. So it was easy to talk to them again. It was like they were before they went away.

4. "Getting cussed out" (*šiłditéé*). This lexeme is used to describe any situation in which one individual, angered and enraged, shouts insults and criticisms at another. Although the object of such invective is in most cases the person or persons who provoked it, this is not always the case, because an Apache who is truly beside himself with rage is likely to vent his feelings on anyone whom he sees or who happens to be within range of his voice. Consequently, "getting cussed out" may involve large numbers of people who are totally innocent of the charges being hurled against them. But whether they are innocent or not, their response to the situation is the same. They refrain from speech.

Like the types of situations we have discussed thus far, "getting cussed out" can occur in a wide variety of physical settings: at ceremonial dance-grounds and trading posts, inside and outside wickiups and houses, on food-gathering expeditions and shopping trips—in short, wherever and whenever individuals lose control of their tempers and lash out verbally at persons nearby.

Although "getting cussed out" is basically free of setting-imposed restrictions, the Western Apache fear it most at gatherings where alcohol is being consumed. My informants observed that especially at "drinking parties" (*dá'idlą́ą́*), where there is much rough joking and ostensibly mock criticism, it is easy for well-intentioned remarks to be misconstrued as insults. Provoked in this way, persons who are intoxicated may become hostile and launch into explosive tirades, often with no warning at all.

The silence of Apaches who are "getting cussed out" is consistently explained in reference to the belief that individuals who are "enraged" (*haškéé*) are also irrational or "crazy" (*biné'idíí*). In this condition, it is said, they "forget who they are" and become oblivious to what they say or do. Concomitantly, they lose all concern for the consequences of their actions on other people. In a word, they are dangerous. Said one informant:

When people get mad they get crazy. Then they start yelling and saying bad things. Some say they are going to kill somebody for what he has done. Some keep it up that way for a long time, maybe walk from camp to camp, real angry, yelling, crazy like that. They keep it up for a long time, some do.

People like that don't know what they are saying, so you can't tell about them. When you see someone like that, just walk away. If he yells at you, let him say whatever he wants to. Let him say anything. Maybe he doesn't mean it. But he doesn't know that. He will be crazy, and he could try to kill you.

Another Apache said:

When someone gets mad at you and starts yelling, then just don't do anything to make him get worse. Don't try to quiet him down because he won't know why you're doing it. If you try to do that, he may just get worse and try to hurt you.

As the last of these statements implies, the Western Apache operate on the assumption that enraged persons—because they are temporarily "crazy" —are difficult to reason with. Indeed, there is a widely held belief that attempts at mollification will serve to intensify anger, thus increasing the chances of physical violence. The appropriate strategy when "getting cussed out" is to do nothing, to avoid any action that will attract attention to oneself. Since speaking accomplishes just the opposite, the use of silence is strongly advised.

5. "Being with people who are sad" (nde dòbiłgòzóóda bigą́ą́). Although the Western Apache phrase that labels this situation has no precise equivalent in English, it refers quite specifically to gatherings in which an individual finds himself in the company of someone whose spouse or kinsman has recently died. Distinct from wakes and burials, which follow immediately after a death, "being with people who are sad" is most likely to occur several weeks later. At this time, close relatives of the deceased emerge from a period of intense mourning (during which they rarely venture beyond the limits of their camps) and start to resume their normal activities within the community. To persons anxious to convey their sympathies, this is interpreted as a sign that visitors will be welcomed and, if possible, provided with food and drink. To those less solicitous, it means that unplanned encounters with the bereaved must be anticipated and prepared for.

"Being with people who are sad" can occur on a foot-path, in a camp, at church, or in a trading post; but whatever the setting—and regardless of whether it is the result of a planned visit or an accidental meeting—the situation is marked by a minimum of speech. Queried about this, my informants volunteered three types of explanations. The first is that persons "who are sad" are so burdened with "intense grief" (dółgozóóda) that speaking requires of them an unusual amount of physical effort. It is courteous and considerate, therefore, not to attempt to engage them in conversation.

A second native explanation is that in situations of this sort verbal communication is basically unnecessary. Everyone is familiar with what has happened, and talking about it, even for the purpose of conveying solace and sympathy, would only reinforce and augment the sadness felt by those who were close to the deceased. Again, for reasons of courtesy, this is something to be avoided.

The third explanation is rooted in the belief that "intense grief," like intense rage, produces changes in the personality of the individual who experiences it. As evidence for this, the Western Apache cite numerous instances in which the emotional strain of dealing with death, coupled with an overwhelming sense of irrevocable personal loss, has caused persons who were formerly mild and even-tempered to become abusive, hostile, and physically violent.

That old woman, X, who lives across Cibecue Creek, one time her first husband died. After that she cried all the time, for a long time. Then, I guess she got mean because everyone said she drank a lot and got into fights. Even with her close relatives, she did like that for a long time. She was too sad for her husband. That's what made her like that; it made her lose her mind.

My father was like that when his wife died. He just stayed home all the time and wouldn't go anywhere. He didn't talk to any of his relatives or children. He just said, "I'm hungry. Cook for me." That's all. He stayed that way for a long time. His mind was not with us. He was still with his wife.

My uncle died in 1941. His wife sure went crazy right away after that. Two days after they buried the body, we went over there and stayed with those people who had been left alone. My aunt got mad at us. She said, "Why do you come over here? You can't bring my husband back. I can take care of myself and those others in my camp, so why don't you go home." She sure was mad that time, too sad for someone who died. She didn't know what she was saying because in about one week she came to our camp and said, "My relatives, I'm all right now. When you came to help me, I had too much sadness and my mind was no good. I said bad words to you. But now I am all right and I know what I am doing."

As these statements indicate, the Western Apache assume that a person suffering from "intense grief" is likely to be disturbed and unstable. Even though he may appear outwardly composed, they say, there is always the possibility that he is emotionally upset and therefore unusually prone to volatile outbursts. Apaches acknowledge that such an individual might welcome conversation in the context of "being with people who are sad," but, on the other hand, they fear it might prove incendiary. Under these conditions, which resemble those in Situation No. 4, it is considered both expedient and appropriate to keep silent.

6. "Being with someone for whom they sing" (*nde bìdádistááha bigą́ą́*). The last type of situation to be described is restricted to a small number of physical locations and is more directly influenced by temporal factors than any of the situations we have discussed so far. "Being with someone for whom they sing" takes place only in the context of "curing ceremonials" (*gòjitáł; èdotáł*). These events begin early at night and come to a close shortly before dawn the following day. In the late fall and throughout the winter, curing ceremonials are held inside the patient's wickiup or house. In the spring and summer, they are located outside, at some open place near the patient's camp or at specially designated dance grounds where group rituals of all kinds are regularly performed.

Prior to the start of a curing ceremonial, all persons in attendance may feel free to talk with the patient; indeed, because he is so much a focus of concern, it is expected that friends and relatives will seek him out to offer encouragement and support. Conversation breaks off, however, when the patient is informed that the ceremonial is about to begin, and it ceases entirely when the presiding medicine man commences to chant. From this point on, until the completion of the final chant next morning, it is inappropriate for anyone except the medicine man (and, if he has them, his aides) to speak to the patient.[6]

In order to appreciate the explanation Apaches give for this prescription, we must briefly discuss the concept of "supernatural power" (*diyi'*) and describe some of the effects it is believed to have on persons at whom it is directed. Elsewhere (Basso 1969:30) I have defined "power" as follows:

> The term *diyi'* refers to one or all of a set of abstract and invisible forces which are said to derive from certain classes of animals, plants, minerals, meteorological phenomena, and mythological figures within the Western Apache universe. Any of the various powers may be acquired by man and, if properly handled, used for a variety of purposes.

A power that has been antagonized by disrespectful behavior towards its source may retaliate by causing the offender to become sick. "Power-caused illnesses" (*kásitį diyi' bił*) are properly treated with curing ceremonials in which one or more medicine men, using chants and various items of ritual paraphernalia, attempt to neutralize the sickness-causing power with powers of their own.

---

6 I have witnessed over 75 curing ceremonials since 1961 and have seen this rule violated only 6 times. On 4 occasions, drunks were at fault. In the other 2 cases, the patient fell asleep and had to be awakened.

Roughly two-thirds of my informants assert that a medicine man's power actually enters the body of the patient; others maintain that it simply closes in and envelops him. In any case, all agree that the patient is brought into intimate contact with a potent supernatural force which elevates him to a condition labeled *gòdiyó'* (sacred, holy).

The term *gòdiyó'* may also be translated as "potentially harmful" and, in this sense, is regularly used to describe classes of objects (including all sources of power) that are surrounded with taboos. In keeping with the semantics of *gòdiyó'*, the Western Apache explain that, besides making patients holy, power makes them potentially harmful. And it is this transformation, they explain, that is basically responsible for the cessation of verbal communication during curing ceremonials.

Said one informant:

When they start singing for someone like that, he sort of goes away with what the medicine man is working with (i.e., power). Sometimes people they sing for don't know you, even after it (the curing ceremonial) is over. They get holy, and you shouldn't try to talk to them when they are like that . . . it's best to leave them alone.

Another informant made similar comments:

When they sing for someone, what happens is like this: that man they sing for doesn't know why he is sick or which way to go. So the medicine man has to show him and work on him. That is when he gets holy, and that makes him go off somewhere in his mind, so you should stay away from him.

Because Apaches undergoing ceremonial treatment are perceived as having been changed by power into something different from their normal selves, they are regarded with caution and apprehension. Their newly acquired status places them in close proximity to the supernatural and, as such, carries with it a very real element of danger and uncertainty. These conditions combine to make "being with someone for whom they sing" a situation in which speech is considered disrespectful and, if not exactly harmful, at least potentially hazardous.

VI

Although the types of situations described above differ from one another in obvious ways, I will argue in what follows that the underlying determinants of silence are in each case basically the same. Specifically, I will attempt to defend the hypothesis that keeping silent in Western Apache culture is associated with social situations in which participants perceive their relationships *vis-à-vis* one another to be ambiguous and/or unpredictable.

Let us begin with the observation that, in all the situations we have described, *silence is defined as appropriate with respect to a specific individual or individuals.* In other words, the use of speech is not directly curtailed by the setting of a situation nor by the physical activities that accompany it but, rather, by the perceived social and psychological attributes of at least one focal participant.

It may also be observed that, in each type of situation, *the status of the focal participant is marked by ambiguity*—either because he is unfamiliar to other participants in the situation or because, owing to some recent event, a status he formerly held has been changed or is in a process of transition.

Thus, in Situation No. 1, persons who earlier considered themselves "strangers" move towards some other relationship, perhaps "friend" (*šìdikéé*), perhaps "enemy" (*šìkédndìí*). In Situation No. 2, young people who have had relatively limited exposure to one another attempt to adjust to the new and intimate status of "sweetheart." These two situations are similar in that the focal participants have little or no prior knowledge of each other. Their social identities are not as yet clearly defined, and their expectations, lacking the foundation of previous experience, are poorly developed.

Situation No. 3 is somewhat different. Although the participants—parents and their children—are well known to each other, their relationship has been seriously interrupted by the latter's prolonged absence from home. This, combined with the possibility that recent experiences at school have altered the children's attitudes, introduces a definite element of unfamiliarity and doubt. Situation No. 3 is not characterized by the absence of role expectations but by the participants' perception that those already in existence may be outmoded and in need of revision.

Status ambiguity is present in Situation No. 4 because a focal participant is enraged and, as a result, considered "crazy." Until he returns to a more rational condition, others in the situation have no way of predicting how he will behave. Situation No. 5 is similar in that the personality of a focal participant is seen to have undergone a marked shift which makes his actions more difficult to anticipate. In both situations, the status of focal participants is uncertain because of real or imagined changes in their psychological makeup.

In Situation No. 6, a focal participant is ritually transformed from an essentially neutral state to one which is contextually defined as "potentially harmful." Ambiguity and apprehension accompany this transition, and, as in Situations No. 4 and 5, established patterns of interaction must be waived until the focal participant reverts to a less threatening condition.

This discussion points up a third feature characteristic of all situations: *the ambiguous status of focal participants is accompanied either by the absence or suspension of established role expectations.* In every instance, non-focal participants (i.e., those who refrain from speech) are either uncertain of how the focal participant will behave towards them or, conversely, how they should behave towards him. Stated in the simplest way possible, their roles become blurred with the result that established expectations—if they exist—lose their relevance as guidelines for social action and must be temporarily discarded or abruptly modified.

We are now in a position to expand upon our initial hypothesis and make it more explicit.

1. In Western Apache culture, the absence of verbal communication is associated with social situations in which the status of focal participants is ambiguous.

2. Under these conditions, fixed role expectations lose their applicability and the illusion of predictability in social interaction is lost.

3. To sum up and reiterate: keeping silent among the Western Apache is a response to uncertainty and unpredictability in social relations.

VII

The question remains to what extent the foregoing hypothesis helps to account for silence behavior in other cultures. Unfortunately, it is impossible at the present time to provide anything approaching a conclusive answer. Standard ethnographies contain very little information about the circumstances under which verbal communication is discouraged, and it is only within the past few years that problems of this sort have engaged the attention of sociolinguists. The result is that adequate cross-cultural data are almost completely lacking.

As a first step towards the elimination of this deficiency, an attempt is now being made to investigate the occurrence and interpretation of silence in other Indian societies of the American Southwest. Our findings at this early stage, though neither fully representative nor sufficiently comprehensive, are extremely suggestive. By way of illustration, I quote below from portions of a preliminary report prepared by Priscilla Mowrer (1970), herself a Navajo, who inquired into the situational features of Navajo silence behavior in the vicinity of Tuba City on the Navajo Reservation in east-central Arizona.

I. *Silence and Courting:* Navajo youngsters of opposite sexes just getting to know one another say nothing, except to sit close together and maybe hold hands. . . . In public, they may try not to let on that they are interested in each other, but in private it is another matter. If the girl is at a gathering where the boy is also present, she may go off by herself. Falling in step, the boy will generally follow. They may just walk around or find some place to sit down. But, at first, they will not say anything to each other.

II. *Silence and Long Absent Relatives:* When a male or female relative returns home after being gone for six months or more, he (or she) is first greeted with a handshake. If the returnee is male, the female greeter may embrace him and cry—the male, meanwhile, will remain dry-eyed and silent.

III. *Silence and Anger:* The Navajo tend to remain silent when being shouted at by a drunk or angered individual because that particular individual is considered temporarily insane. To speak to such an individual, the Navajo believe, just tends to make the situation worse. . . . People remain silent because they believe that the individual is not himself, that he may have been witched, and is not responsible for the change in his behavior.

IV. *Silent Mourning:* Navajos speak very little when mourning the death of a relative. . . . The Navajo mourn and cry together in pairs. Men will embrace one another and cry together. Women, however, will hold one another's hands and cry together.

V. *Silence and the Ceremonial Patient:* The Navajo consider it wrong to talk to a person being sung over. The only people who talk to the patient are the medicine man and a female relative (or male relative if the patient is male) who is in charge of food preparation. The only time the patient speaks openly is when the medicine man asks her (or him) to pray along with him.

These observations suggest that striking similarities may exist between the types of social contexts in which Navajos and Western Apaches refrain from speech. If this impression is confirmed by further research, it will lend obvious cross-cultural support to the hypothesis advanced above. But regardless of the final outcome, the situational determinants of silence seem eminently deserving of further study. For as we become better informed about the types of contextual variables that mitigate against the use of verbal codes, we should also learn more about those variables that encourage and promote them.

BIBLIOGRAPHY

BASSO, KEITH H.
    1966   *The Gift of Changing Woman.* Bureau of American Ethnology, bulletin 196.
    1969   *Western Apache Witchcraft.* Anthropological Papers of the University of Arizona, no. 15.
    1970   *The Cibecue Apache.* New York: Holt, Rinehart and Winston, Inc.
BROWN, R. W., AND ALBERT GILMAN
    1960   "The Pronouns of Power and Solidarity," in *Style in Language* (ed. by T. Sebeok), pp. 253-276. Cambridge: The Technology Press of Massachusetts Institute of Technology.

CONKLIN, HAROLD C.
  1959 Linguistic Play in Its Cultural Context. *Language* 35:631-636.

ERVIN-TRIPP, SUSAN
  1964 "An Analysis of the Interaction of Language, Topic and Listener," in
        The Ethnography of Communication (ed. by J. J. Gumperz and D.
        Hymes), pp. 86-102. *American Anthropologist,* Special Publication, vol.
        66, no. 6, part 2.
  1967 *Sociolinguistics.* Language-Behavior Research Laboratory, Working Paper
        no. 3. Berkeley: University of California.

FRAKE, CHARLES O.
  1964 "How to Ask for a Drink in Subanun," in *The Ethnography of Com-
        munication* (ed. by J. J. Gumperz and D. Hymes), pp. 127-132. *American
        Anthropologist,* Special Publication, vol. 66, no. 6, part 2.

FRIEDRICH, P.
  1966 "Structural Implications of Russian Pronominal Usage," in *Sociolinguis-
        tics* (ed. by W. Bright), pp. 214-253. The Hague: Mouton.

GARFINKEL, H.
  1967 *Studies in Ethnomethodology.* Englewood Cliffs, N. J.: Prentice-Hall, Inc.

GOFFMAN, E.
  1961 *Encounters: Two Studies in the Sociology of Interaction.* Indianapolis:
        The Bobbs-Merrill Co., Inc.
  1963 *Behavior in Public Places.* Glencoe, Ill.: Free Press.
  1964 "The Neglected Situation," in *The Ethnography of Communication*
        (ed. by J. J. Gumperz and D. Hymes), pp. 133-136. *American Anthro-
        pologist,* Special Publication, vol. 66, no. 6, part 2.

GUMPERZ, JOHN J.
  1961 Speech Variation and the Study of Indian Civilization. *American Anthro-
        pologist* 63: 976-988.
  1964 "Linguistic and Social Interaction in Two Communities," in *The Eth-
        nography of Communication* (ed. by J. J. Gumperz and D. Hymes), pp.
        137-153. *American Anthropologist,* Special Publication, vol. 66, no. 6,
        part 2.
  1967 "The Social Setting of Linguistic Behavior," in *A Field Manual for
        Cross-Cultural Study of the Acquisition of Communicative Competence
        (Second Draft)* (ed. by D. I. Slobin), pp. 129-134. Berkeley: University
        of California.

HYMES, DELL
  1962 "The Ethnography of Speaking," in *Anthropology and Human Behavior*
        (ed. by T. Gladwin and W. C. Sturtevant), pp. 13-53. Washington,
        D. C.: The Anthropological Society of Washington.
  1964 "Introduction: Toward Ethnographies of Communication," in *The Eth-
        nography of Communication* (ed. by J. J. Gumperz and D. Hymes), pp.

1-34. *American Anthropologist*, Special Publication, vol. 66, no. 6, part 2.

KAUT, CHARLES R.

1957   *The Western Apache Clan System: Its Origins and Development.* University of New Mexico Publications in Anthropology, no. 9.

MARTIN, SAMUEL

1964   "Speech Levels in Japan and Korea," in *Language in Culture and Society* (ed. by D. Hymes), pp. 407-415. New York: Harper and Row.

MOWRER, PRISCILLA

1970   Notes on Navajo Silence Behavior. MS, University of Arizona.

SLOBIN, DAN I. (ED.)

1967   *A Field Manual for Cross-Cultural Study of the Acquisition of Communicative Competence (Second Draft).* Berkeley: University of California.

21
Communicative Silence: A Cross-Cultural Study of Basso's Hypothesis

CHARLES A. BRAITHWAITE

One function of an ethnography of communication is to develop a descriptive theory of speech in a particular community. But to formulate a descriptive theory of *orality* is not enough. A clearer understanding of the interaction between language and social life requires additional information on a community's rules for *not speaking*. According to Basso (ch. 20, this volume), "an adequate ethnography of communication should not confine itself exclusively to the analysis of choice within verbal repertoires. It should also . . . specify those conditions under which members of the society regularly decide to refrain from verbal behavior altogether" (p. 305). In other words, we must study when people speak *and* when they do not.

The study of *silence* in a community is important for at least three reasons. First, the use of silence can be seen as one among a range of strategies or options that can itself be part of, or constitute, a "way of speaking." Silence can be viewed in much the same way talk is viewed. It is another important symbolic resource that can be used by any member of a community. Therefore, silence is interesting to study in its own right. In any ethnography of communication, silence is potentially something of importance.

Second, the use and interpretation of silence can also be a central part of the "foundations" of communication in community. Because silence is a significant communicative resource, and because it, like talk, is patterned in culturally significant ways, the detailing of the patterning of silence, in use and in cultural evaluation, can implicate a larger pattern in human communication. According to Hymes (1972), "The distribution of required and preferred silence, indeed perhaps most immediately reveals in outline form a community's structure of speaking" (p. 40). One of the basic building blocks of competence, both linguistic and cultural, is knowing when not to speak in a particular community. Therefore, to understand where, when, and how to be silent, and the meanings attached to silence, is to gain a keen insight into the fundamental structure of communication in that world. Silence is not just the absence of behavior. As Samarin (1965) noted, "Silence can have meaning. Like the zero in mathematics, it is an absence with a function" (p. 115).

A third and a most compelling reason for examining silence in a community is that it has been posited that some communicative functions of silence may be general. That is, the way silence is used as a strategy and the meaning attached to that particular use might not vary cross-culturally. Basso's (ch. 20) study of the Western Cibecue Apache and some early data on the Navajo led him to hypothesize that "the absence of verbal communication is associated with social situations in which the status of focal participants is ambiguous" (p. 317). In other words, in some situations when social relationships are characterized by uncertainty and unpredictability, silence will be the appropriate behavior. But Basso saw, in 1970, that ethnographic descriptions were insufficient either to support or refute his general, cross-cultural hypothesis.

Given that silence is such an important feature of communicative behavior, a fundamental question for comparative analysis should be: What are the interactive and cultural uses and meanings of silence? And, more specifically: Can Basso's hypothesis of silence account for behavior across cultures?

"Since one human group's theories of speaking can best be isolated by contrast with those of another, the comparative approach to field work is probably the most useful at this stage" (Hymes, 1972, p. 36). For Hymes, the primary concern for the ethnographer is to focus on descriptive, comparative analysis from a variety of communities. Therefore, to approach the research question concerning the uses and meanings of silence across cultures, ethnographic reports from 13 speech communities were accumulated and examined, each containing findings relevant to Basso's hypothesis[1] (Abrahams, 1974, 1975; Basso, 1970; Bauman, 1970, 1972, 1983; Fisher & Yoshida, 1968; Irvine, 1974; Johnson & Johnson, 1975; Keenan, 1975; Messenger, 1960; Mitchell-Kernan, 1972; Philips, 1970, 1976; Philipsen, 1975, 1976; Rushforth, 1981; Salmond, 1975). These 18

---

[1]Accounts were selected from a review of the following journals: *Journal of American Folklore, Journal of Anthropological Research, Journal of Communication, Language in Society, Practical Anthropology, Quarterly Journal of Speech, Semiotica, Social Forces, Southwestern Journal of Anthropology,* and *Urban Life.* These particular journals were selected because they have been the primary publishers of ethnographies of communication over the last 20 years. Accounts were also selected from the following anthologies of ethnographies of speaking: *Directions in Sociolinguistics: The Ethnography of Communication* (Ed. J. Gumperz & D. Hymes, 1972); and *Political Language and Oratory in Traditional Society* (Ed. M. Bloch, 1975). These anthologies were selected because they are the most comprehensive collections of ethnographies of communication published to date.

ethnographic accounts were studied with the intent of juxtaposing their descriptions of the uses and interpretations of silence, the goal being to discern where they were similar, where they were different, and where they *systematically* related.

In each ethnographic study the when, where, and how of silence, and the meanings attached to it, were explored. There is special significance to these accounts in that all used a similar descriptive framework for the study of a community's pattern of speaking.[2] Each was concerned, to varying degrees, with those elements identified by Hymes (1962, 1972). Those included an examination of setting or *scenes* for communication, the *participants,* their roles and relationships, the ends or *purposes* of communication, the *act sequences* of communication, the keys or *tones* that accompany communication, the various instrumentalities or *linguistic varieties* in a community, the *norms* for interpretation of communication, and the various *genres* or "types" of communication (e.g., jokes, curses, greetings, etc.).

A basis for comparative analysis exists in that a similar descriptive framework was used in the various studies. In short, the investigators had similar starting points. A comparative analysis of these particular studies makes possible the study of many diverse groups and to compare their communicative behavior in a way that could suggest very general features of silence. Such a comparative analysis would permit a test of Basso's hypothesis about the patterning of silence.

The examination of each ethnographic study revealed two warrants that account for the use and interpretation of silence. The term *warrant* is used because each statement is a generalization based on particular features in particular speech communities associated with the uses and interpretations of silence.

> **Warrant 1.** Silence as a communicative action is associated with social situations in which the relationship of the focal participants is uncertain, unpredictable, or ambiguous.

Basso's hypothesis was found to apply to the use and interpretation of silence in five of the studies examined: Western Apache (Basso, 1970), Warm Springs Indians (Philips, 1970, 1976, ch. 22, this volume), Japanese-Hawaiians (Johnson & Johnson, 1975), and Japanese (Fisher & Yoshida, 1968). In each of these studies, the presence of uncertainty,

---

[2]Each of these studies refers to Hymes' theory and method for the study of communication. Other studies of silence were examined (e.g., Tannen & Saville-Troike, 1985), however they were not used for comparison if the particular ethnographies did not make use of the components of the ethnography of speaking descriptive framework.

unpredictability, or ambiguity in role relationships co-occurred with silence. In each of the cultures examined, the primary warrant for the appropriate   use and interpretation of the absence of talk centered on the participants perception that the role relationships present were lacking in clarity or were unknown.

However, this link between silence and uncertainty in role relationships was not the only account discovered in the ethnographies. Other explanations were posited for the use and interpretation of silence in various cultures that did not center on uncertainty, ambiguity, or unpredictability among focal participants. Instead, it was the perception of an unequal distribution of power that was the key to understanding the communicative use of silence.

Warrant 2. Silence as a communicative action is associated with social situations in which there is a known and unequal distribution of power among focal participants.

Warrant 1 concerning the use and interpretation of silence was not found to account for the rules described in the ethnographies concerning 13 other studies. Basso's hypothesis did not explain silence as described in accounts of the Anang of South Western Nigeria (Messenger, 1960); the Wolof of Senegal (Irvine, 1974); the Maori in New Zealand (Salmond, 1975); the Malagasy in Madagascar (Keenan, 1975); some Urban American Black Women (Abrahams, 1974, 1975; Mitchell-Kernan, 1972) the La Have Islanders (Bauman, 1972); Bear Lake Athapaskan (Rushforth, 1981); 17th-century Quakers (Bauman, 1970, 1983); and some American White Working Class (Philipsen, 1975, 1976). However, a second warrant for the use and interpretation of communicative silence should account for their behavior. Warrant 2 states — as Basso speculated in his second footnote (ch. 20, p. 304) — that it is not ambiguity in their perceived status or relationship of the other that will influence a participant's use of silence, but, rather, it is the perception that the other is of a *recognizably* different status. Knowledge that there is a discrepancy in the relative power of participants or in degrees of social control creates — at times — social scenes where silence is appropriate. In each of these 13 speech communities, the presence of perceived differentiation in power (e.g., adult vs. child, friend vs. enemy, king vs. subject, etc.) provided a condition under which silence was performed.

A significant implication of the findings of this comparative study concerns the very nature of talk itself. Speaking has a peculiar place in human relations in that the use of talk provides the "power" people respond to, and may presume a degree of membership in a social world. Arnold

(1968) discussed this function of talk in "Oral Rhetoric, Rhetoric, andLiterature." In treating speaking as action, Arnold stated, "the fact of orality means some degree of interdependence prevails or is going to prevail between speaker and others, for mutually influential interaction or the expectations of it is inescapable in speaking and being spoken to" (p. 196). His point is that membership in human groups is presumed and instigated through orality. When one chooses to speak, one acknowledges there exists a "mutual, working relationship of considerable intellectual and psychological interdependence" (p. 103).

If orality may entail some degree of membership and mutual influence, then when one chooses to speak in an interaction, one may implicitly signal, on some level, a claim of membership and a potential for influencing the other interlocutors. Just the act of speaking can be a way of acknowledging these "unique human relationships that constitute the conditions of orality" (p. 217).

This particular attribute of talk may help explain the significance of silence in human communication. For if speaking presumes a degree of membership and influence, then silence may signal social ambiguity and/or distance. Silence can be viewed as a way of dissolving, breaking, rejecting, or refusing to recognize social bonds among participants, or as a way of displaying nonreciprocal influence. The warrants regarding role ambiguity and differentiation in power among participants when silence is used indicates that this is the case. Silence apparently is a response to, or a momentary signal of, social ambiguity and/or important differences in social control.

It should be noted that the suggestion that silence signals—at times—ambiguity and/or power difference among focal participants, is not of course to suggest that silence is in some way harmful or dysfunctional. The ethnographic data indicate that speech communities find silence necessary for the protection of physical and social integrity. Silence is functional in providing the necessary protection against uncertain "outsiders," as well as in providing a powerful communicative code to signal the presence of differentiation in power. Both warrants suggest a special role for silence as an identifier of social boundaries, both in scenes where social roles are ambiguous, expectations being unclear, and/or in scenes where focal participants are importantly different with regard to the means of social control.

This comparative study has thus identified how silence as a rule-governed activity is used and interpreted in a variety of cultures. The "rules" have been found to be similar across many cultures, and two warrants for the use and interpretation of silence have been posited. Brown and Levinson (1978) stated that "interactional systematics are based largely on universal principle. But the application of the principles differs systematically across cultures, and within cultures, across subcultures and groups" (p. 288). The warrants posited here concerning social relations, influences, and the relationship of these to the uses and interpretations of silence, seem to suggest such "universal" principles. In short, silence is associated with social situations of ambiguity and/or unequal distribution of power. Therefore, the hypotheses set forth by Basso concerning the general features of silence—such as its association with ambiguity in relationships—is supported, yet needs extended. Basso's hypothesis provides a fundamental relational basis for silence that crosses some cultural boundaries, but must be extended to include recognizable differences in power and status in addition to the presence of uncertainty, ambiguity and unpredictability.

Acknowledgment

This chapter is based on the author's master's thesis completed at the University of Washington under the direction of Gerry Philipsen (Braithwaite, 1981).

References

Arnold, C. C. (1968). Oral rhetoric, rhetoric, and literature. *Philosophy and Rhetoric, 33,* 191–210.

Abrahams, R. D. (1974). Black talking on the streets. In R. Bauman & J. Sherzer (Eds.), *Explorations in the ethnography of speaking* (pp. 240–262). London: Cambridge University Press.

Abrahams, R. D. (1975). Negotiating respect: Patterns of presentations among black women. *Journal of American Folklore, 88,* 58–80.

Basso, K. (1970). 'To give up on words': Silence in western Apache culture. *Southwestern Journal of Anthropology, 26,* 213–230. [also ch. 20, this volume]

Bauman, R. (1970). Aspects of 17th century Quaker rhetoric. *Quarterly Journal of Speech, 63,* 67–74.

Bauman, R. (1972). The La Have Island general store. *Journal of American Folklore, 85,* 330–343.

Bauman, R. (1983). *Let your words be few: Symbolism and silence among seventeenth-century Quakers.* Cambridge: Cambridge University Press.

Bloch, M. (Ed.). (1975). *Political language and oratory in traditional society.* London: Academic Press.

Braithwaite, C. (1981) *Cultural uses and interpretations of silence.* Unpublished master's thesis, University of Washington, Seattle, WA.

Brown, P., & Levinson, S. (1978). Universals in language usage: Politeness phenomena. In E. Goody (Ed.), *Questions and politeness* (pp. 56–289). Cambridge: Cambridge University Press.

Fisher, J., & Yoshida, T. (1968). The nature of speech according to Japanese proverbs. *Journal of American Folklore, 81,* 34–43.

Frake, C. (1972). How to ask for a drink in Subanun. In P. Giglioli (Ed.), *Language and social context* (pp. 127–132). Middlesex: Penguin

Gumperz, J., & Hymes, D. (Eds.). (1972). *Directions in sociolinguistics: The ethnography of communication.* New York: Holt, Rinehart & Winston.

Hymes, D. (1962). The ethnography of speaking. In. T. Gladwin & W. Sturtevant (Eds.), *Anthropology and human behavior* (pp. 13-53). Washington, DC: Anthropological Society of Washington.

Hymes, D. (1972). Models of interaction of language and social life. In J. Gumperz & D. Hymes (Eds.), *Directions in sociolinguistics: The ethnography of communication* (pp. 35-71). New York: Holt, Rinehart & Winston.

Irvine, J. T. (1974). Strategies of status manipulation in the Wolof greeting. In R. Bauman & J. Sherzer (Eds.), *Explorations in the ethnography of speaking* (pp. 167-191). London: Cambridge University Press.

Johnson, C. L., & Johnson, F. A. (1975). The Japanese and caucasians in Honolulu. *Social Forces, 54,* 452-466.

Keenan, E. (1975). A sliding sense of obligatoriness: The polystructure of Malagasy oratory. In M. Bloch (Ed.), *Political language and oratory in traditional society* (pp. 93-112). London: Academic Press.

Messenger, J. (1960). Anang proverb-riddles. *Journal of American folklore, 73,* 225-235.

Mitchell-Kernan, C. (1972). Signifying and marking: Two Afro-American speech acts. In J. Gumperz & D. Hymes (Eds.), *Directions in sociolinguistics: The ethnography of communication* (pp. 161-179). New York: Holt, Rinehart & Winston.

Philips, S. (1970). Acquisition of rules for appropriate speech usage. In J. Alatis (Ed.), *Reports of the 21st Roundtable Meeting* (Monograph Series in Language and Linguistics, 23). Washington, DC: Georgetown University Press.

Philips, S. (1976). Some sources of cultural variability in the regulation of talk. *Language in Society, 5,* 81-95. [also ch. 22, this volume]

Philipsen, G. (1975). 'Speaking like a man' in Teamsterville: Culture patterns of role enactment in an urban neighborhood. *Quarterly Journal of Speech, 61,* 13-22.

Philipsen, G. (1976). Places for speaking in teamsterville. *Quarterly Journal of Speech, 62,* 15-25.

Rushforth, S. (1981). Speaking to "relatives-through-marriage": Aspects of communication among Bear Lake Athapaskan. *Journal of Anthropological Research, 37,* 28-45.

Salmond, A. (1975). Mana makes the man: A look at Maori oratory and politics. In M. Bloch (Ed.), *Political language and oratory in traditional society* (pp. 45-63). London: Cambridge University Press.

Samarin, W. (1965). The language of silence. *Practical Anthropology, 12,* 115-119.

22

Some sources of cultural variability in the regulation of talk[1]

SUSAN URMSTON PHILIPS

Recent efforts to analyze the structure of talk have focused primarily on the conversation of persons from a white middle-class background. This paper compares the way in which talk is regulated, both verbally and non-verbally, in Anglo interaction with the regulation of talk among Indians of the Warm Springs Reservation, in central Oregon. The purpose of this comparison is to begin to assess the sources and nature of cultural variability in this one aspect of language use.

I

This paper has three purposes. First, I want to consider the role of the listener in regulating face-to-face interaction in which a single focus of attention is sustained chiefly through talk. How does a hearer and potential speaker exert control over other speakers' turns at talk, and how does he or she influence the sequential structuring of talk? Some answers to these questions will be suggested.

A second purpose is to show some of the ways in which verbal and nonverbal modes of regulating talk are integrated into a single system for the regulation of interaction.

My third purpose is to explore what is culturally diverse or variable in these regards. Many properties have been suggested, either implicitly or explicitly, as 'universal'. It should be useful to consider what features are actually shared by two groups of culturally different backgrounds. (This

---

[1] I wish to express my appreciation to Dell Hymes, Erving Goffman, and Ward Good-enough, members of my dissertation committee who have all commented on earlier drafts covering this same material. I am also grateful to the students in my graduate seminar on sociolinguistics for their contributions to discussions on topics covered here: Carolyn Dirksen, Bill Hobson, Lydia McConnell, Byron Olson, Susan Seligson, and Fran Stier.

approach to interaction has been characterized as ethnographic, as in Hymes' (1974) advocacy of the ethnography of communication.)

The two groups whose systems for the regulation of talk will be compared are the Indians of the Warm Springs Indian Reservation, in central Oregon, and Anglos of Anglo-American heritage. In using the term 'Anglos', I refer to those persons, usually of the white middle class, who have participated in the taped interactions and experiments that are used as a data base by students of conversation in the United States and England. Telephone conversations, group therapy sessions, formalized experimental structurings of interaction that draw their subjects from British and American college student populations, medical interviews, and grade school classrooms have been some of our main sources of data. The classroom is the setting of some of my own work in this area (Philips 1972, 1974). All of these sources involve activities familiar to persons of Anglo or white middle-class background, although clearly we need, where possible, to become more specific about just who is involved. In my own case, the white children and adults I have closely observed and recorded live in the town of Madras, Oregon, fifteen miles from the Warm Springs Indian Reservation.

The Indians of the Warm Springs Indian Reservation are easier than Anglos to identify closely. Present-day members of the Warm Springs Confederated Tribes number around 1800. Most are descended from Sahaptin- and Chinookan-speaking groups that lived on or near the Columbia River just east of the Cascade mountain range. A few tribal members are descended from a small number of Paiutes who moved up toward the Columbia River during the second half of the nineteenth century from what is now southern Oregon. Today most tribal members speak English, although many of the adults over forty are bilingual; most of these speak Sahaptin, only a few speak Chinookan. The aboriginal economy of these groups included the hunting of small game animals and the gathering of roots and berries. Salmon was an important source of food for the Chinookan speakers, known today as 'Wascos', but also for the Sahaptin speakers who are now often referred to as 'Warm Springs'. Today the strongest traditional influence comes from the Sahaptin 'Warm Springs' Indians, who are also the most numerous of the three groups on the reservation. The Wascos are prominent in the management of tribal industries, primarily logging and sawmill operations, but also a growing tourist industry. As a result of the success of these industries, the tribal members of the Warm Springs Confederated Tribes are economically much better off than residents of other reservations in Washington and Oregon. Although the cultural influence of the surrounding white populations has been considerable, many domains of Indian life continue to show traditional influences. Those domains include many aspects of the way in which language is used, including the way it is used to structure communication in face-to-face interaction.

II

I will begin the comparison of the Indian and Anglo systems for the regulation of talk with a discussion of what is known about Anglo spoken interaction. Recently Sacks, Jefferson & Schegloff (1973) have proposed a number of 'facts' they believe to hold true for 'conversation'. From their point of view conversation is just one of many 'talk exchange systems'. While they do not state clearly how conversation differs from such other systems of talk exchange, they do clearly state some features of conversation. Among those features, I would note the following (Sacks, Jefferson & Schegloff, 1973: 6):

(1) Speaker change recurs, or, at least, occurs.
(2) Overwhelmingly, one party talks at a time.
(3) Occurrences of more than one speaker at a time are common, but brief.
(4) Transitions from one turn to a next with no gap and no overlap between them are common. Together with transitions characterized by slight gap or slight overlap, they make up the vast majority of transitions . . .
(12) Turn allocation techniques are obviously used. A current speaker may select a next speaker (as when a current speaker addresses a question to another party); parties may self-select, in starting to talk.
(13) Various turn-constructional units are employed for the production of the talk that occupies a turn. Turns can be projectedly 'one word long' obviously, or, for example, they can be sentential in length . . .

No explicit claim of universality has been made for these features. At the same time, no effort has been made to identify the specific social groups or situations for which they might hold true. Sacks, Jefferson and Schegloff deal exclusively with data on the verbal structuring of interaction in the form of transcriptions of tape recordings. The information they offer is presented in terms of what one speaker after another does verbally that contributes to the regulation of talk. But of course for every speaker at a given point in time, there is also assumed to be at least one listener. Tape recordings do not capture the listener's contribution to the regulation of interaction; and a speaker-by-speaker sequence analysis does not allow room, analytically, for consideration of the listener.

For models of interaction that consider both speaker and listener, one must turn to the students of nonverbal communication who closely scrutinize films and videotapes of talk.

The body movement of both speakers and hearers is considerable during Anglo talk. There are shifts in 'alignment', or the direction in which the front of the body is facing in relationship to the fronts of the bodies of others (Scheflen 1964). Similarly, in the course of interaction, there will be shifts in head/face alignment in relationship to others; and while the head often moves with the body, sometimes it moves alone.

Both speakers and hearers also engage in shifting of body position that may or may not be related to changes in body and head alignment. They lean backward and forward, fold and unfold arms and legs, and shift their weight.

In addition, both speakers and hearers move the mobile portions of their faces: the eyebrows, the muscles around the eyes, the irises and pupils of the eye (or actually the eyeball), and all of the muscles in the lower part of the face that allow for smiling, grimacing, lip-biting, and the like.

Speakers and hearers are most obviously *differentiated* in their behavior by virtue of the fact that a speaker is communicating both verbally and nonverbally, while a listener is communicating nonverbally only. Condon & Ogston (1967, 1968) have described an 'interactional synchrony' between speaker and hearer (1968: I):

> . . . the body change pattern of a speaker moves synchronously with his speech. A listener, in turn, also moves synchronously with a speaker, primarily up to and including the word level.

Speakers also use *types* of nonverbal behavior directly related to speech that are not apparent in hearers (Birdwhistell 1970). Their heads bob slightly in rhythm to their speech; they gesture with their hands and arms in a manner that qualifies and punctuates speech. Duncan (1972, 1974) suggests it is partly the cessation of such speaker-distinctive nonverbal movements that signal a speaker is giving up the floor. For the auditor to begin to speak without any signal that the current speaker is finished would constitute an inappropriate claim to the floor. The speaker 'turn signals' include the termination of speaker hand gesticulations, as well as distinctive paralinguistic cues. As Duncan notes (1974:165):

> The display of any single cue was sufficient to constitute a display of the signal. However, the probability of an auditor turn claiming response to a signal was found to be a linear function ($r = 0.96$) of the number of cues displayed, without regard to the specific cues comprising the display.

At the same time, a speaker gesticulation signal negates any turn signal.

A number of studies suggest that Anglo speakers and hearers also differ in their patterns of gaze direction (Nielsen 1964; Exline 1963; Kendon 1967). While individuals vary greatly in the amount of time they spend looking at their co-interactants rather than away from them (Kendon 1967), listeners spend more time looking at speakers than speakers spend looking at listeners (Nielsen 1964; Exline 1963; Kendon 1967). And speaker glances tend to be of shorter duration than hearer glances (Kendon 1967: 37).

Kendon also found a relationship between frequency of gaze direction toward co-participants and the beginnings and endings of turns at talk (1967: 33):

> . . . P (the speaker) tends to look away as he begins a long utterance, and in many cases somewhat in advance of it; . . . he looks up at his interlocutor as the end of the long utterance approaches, usually during the last phrase, and he continues to look thereafter.

In interpreting this behavior, Kendon suggests that in looking away as he or she begins to talk, the speaker forestalls a response from his auditor. In looking toward his auditor as he finishes talking, the speaker indicates his expectation of a response. This interpretation was corroborated by Kendon's finding that when the speaker does *not* direct his gaze at the listener as he finishes speaking, the frequency of delayed response and no response is much greater (Kendon 1967: 37). In Kendon's work, and in Duncan's, we begin to see how nonverbal signaling contributes to the regulation of interaction.

Thus far I have only discussed the differences between speaker and hearer in the use of nonverbal signaling, particularly gaze direction. Studies done in this area typically make use of two-person conversations, so no further distinctions can be made. However, in many Anglo interactions involving more than two persons, there is a further distinction made between hearers who are being directly addressed by a speaker, and hearers who are not being directly addressed and are, if only for a brief time, audience to the interaction of others. Following Goffman (1974: 565), listeners who are parties to an interaction, but are not at a given moment being addressed by a speaker will be referred to as 'unaddressed recipients', while those who *are* being directly addressed will be referred to as 'addressed recipients'. Address will be termed 'general' when the speaker is addressing all parties to an interaction, and 'focused' where specific individuals are being addressed.

Speaker identification of addressed recipients is accomplished nonverbally in part. In grade-school classroom discussions where teachers often distinguish between addressed and unaddressed recipients among students, the teacher's head and body typically directly face the person she is addressing, and her alignment shifts as she shifts the focus of her address.

Addressed recipients are also identified by the speaker's gaze. Teachers, for example, gaze more frequently and for longer periods at their addressed recipients than at unaddressed recipients. The student thus addressed as the teacher finishes speaking is more likely to be the next speaker than are unaddressed recipients.[2]

This differentiation between addressed and unaddressed recipients is also accomplished verbally by the speaker. In many cases addressed recipients are identified through the kind of 'tieing' that occurs between the utterances of adjacent speakers. Thus what we recognize as an answer to a question is construed as addressed to the person who asked the question.

Addressed recipients are also identified through speakers' specific selection of 'membership categorization devices' (Sacks 1972) and 'locational formulations' (Schegloff 1972a). Schegloff suggests that when a speaker verbally identifies 'places' — e.g. 'my house', 'Sam's bar', 'the school' — he or she must have done a 'membership analysis' of the person for whom the identification is being done. For example, a speaker may choose between 'a bar on the other side of town' and 'Sam's bar' on the basis of his addressed recipient's familiarity with the bar (Schegloff 1972a). One can immediately see how an addressed recipient will be identified by the choice the speaker makes, when there is more than one recipient, one of whom is personally familiar with the bar and one of whom is not. Similarly, when in the presence of both a secretary and a colleague, a professor first refers to 'Dr Peters' and then to 'Jack', where the referent is Dr Jack Peters, we are likely to infer that the first identification is directed to the secretary and the second to the colleague.

Finally, addressed recipients are also often identified by name.

Speakers, then, can and do identify addressed recipients in a way that enables those addressed to comprehend their addressors in a different fashion than those who are not so selected. Since such word selection affects the hearer's comprehension of the utterance, it also affects the hearer's ability to produce a response that will demonstrate comprehension of what has been said. The probability that the person addressed will be the next person to speak is in this way increased, suggesting the kind of control Anglo speakers exert over who will speak next.

Listeners' behavior suggests a similar differentiation between addressed and unaddressed recipients. Students being directly addressed by a teacher look at her more often and for longer periods than do unaddressed listeners. The individual being addressed also displays more facial movement or expression, providing what Yngve (1970) refers to as 'back channel' work, conveying to the teacher that she is being attended.

Kendon (1970) has described behavior similar to that of students, in the

---

[2]Similar findings have been reported by Weisbrod (1965).

informal talk of a group of seven persons. Pursuing Condon and Ogsten's interest in interactional synchrony in this same study, Kendon found that the movements of persons being directly addressed were more closely synchronized with the speech and body movement of the speaker more of the time than were the movements of other listeners.

In classroom interaction, as elsewhere, some students who are not being directly addressed by the teacher will also sometimes behave in the same way as those being addressed. These students are in a sense encouraging the teacher to select them as addressed recipients. In other contexts, such persons would be termed 'good listeners': for when an addressed recipient suddenly withdraws his or her attention, leaving the speaker in the sometimes embarrassing position of talking 'to the air', the speaker can quickly shift his or her attention to sympathetic unaddressed recipients who are already behaving as if they were being addressed.

If the relationship between speaker and addressed recipient is examined for its contribution to the regulation of talk, a structure can be seen. An addressed recipient controls interaction through his decisions to attend or disattend those who designate him as an addressed recipient. His influence may be greatest when two people begin to verbally importune him at the same time, and he must choose between them. A speaker contributes to the regulation of talk through his selection of addressed recipients; he determines who will exert control over his turn at talk by choosing to attend or disattend him. A speaker also influences who will speak next, because the person who is his addressed recipient as he finishes speaking is more likely to be the next speaker. In addition, a speaker may or may not respond to what a former speaker has said, and in this way determine whether a former speaker's utterance will be incorporated in the sequencing of interaction.

Through the cooperation of particular speakers and addressed recipients, some persons may speak more often than others by virtue of their ability to attract the attention of selected addressed recipients; and some persons may be selected more often as addressed recipients through their ability to attract the attention of speakers. This interdependence of speaker and addressed recipient has other consequences. Because an addressed recipient sometimes neither attends to nor responds to a speaker who has designated him as addressed recipient, the number of times a person speaks will not necessarily be equivalent to the number of times his speaking is ratified or legitimated by others.[3]

Thus far I have discussed some 'facts' about adjacent turns at talk, described some nonverbal behaviors that differentiate speaker and hearer in

---

[3]It is this feature of the regulation of talk that causes me to question Sacks, Jefferson & Schegloff's (1973) notion of a 'turn at talk'. It appears that their approach does not allow for a distinction between speaking and speaking that is ratified or legitimated.

ways that contribute to the regulation of talk, and outlined the verbal and nonverbal means used by both speakers and hearers in distinguishing addressed and unaddressed recipients in Anglo interaction.

One other aspect of Anglo interaction that has received some attention is the way in which different speakers' utterances are sequentially related. Sacks (1967) argues that Anglo utterances are 'tied' to one another so that one person's talk can often only be made sense of if the talk of the person who spoke before him was heard. Thus if A says 'Thank you', and B says 'You're welcome', B's talk is heard as a 'response' to A's. Unlike 'Hello' or 'Good-bye', 'You're welcome' can only be made sense of as a second position utterance. 'Yes' can usually be made sense of only if one has perceived something to which 'Yes' is a reply.

Other more specific types of relatedness among utterances that follow one another in a temporal linear sequence have been described. Schegloff (1972b) discusses the order of utterances that occur at the 'openings' of conversations, and Schegloff & Sacks (1974) point out sequential restrictions in the 'closings' of conversion. Jefferson (1972) identifies the phenomenon of 'side sequences'—exchanges that are clearly marked off from the main sequence of a conversation. Schegloff (1972b) directs attention to the activity of 'repairing' sequences that are not carried out in an appropriate manner, as when the party who answers the phone does not speak first, or says something inappropriate for a first-person telephone greeting slot. Often an utterance that is responded to in a manner indicating non-comprehension or non-hearing on the part of the respondent will be gone back over by the first speaker, as in: A: 'Hello'. B: 'What?' A: 'Hello'. In this way there is a cycling back through of a segment that accomplishes a repair of that segment and the sequence then continues.

Most of the sequential relatedness with which Sacks, Schegloff and Jefferson deal is between utterances that are either 'adjacent' or quite close to one another so that only several speaker changes are being dealt with at any given time. Sacks (1967, 1971) takes the position that conversation is a 'locally managed' system of speech exchange. In other words, the sequential structure of conversation is by and large created as people go along in their talk. There is little significant predetermination of who will talk, in what order people will speak, or what they will say. Thus what structure or relatedness one finds in conversation will be among utterances that are adjacent to or very near one another.

III

The system for regulation of interaction on the Warm Springs Indian reservation contrasts with this Anglo system in several interrelated ways that are apparent in both informal conversations and more formally structured interactions such as meetings.

First, Indian exchanges proceed at a slower pace than those of Anglos. Quite possibly the number of syllables per minute is less, particularly when there are more than three or four parties to an encounter. The pauses between two different speakers' turns at talk are frequently longer than is the case in Anglo interactions. There is a tolerance for silences—silences that Anglos often rush into and fill. Indian speakers rarely, if ever, begin to speak at the same time, and rarely interrupt one another. Their turns at talk vary less in length of time, as does the number of turns by each person during the course of interaction than is true of Anglos. Talk is thus more evenly distributed than among Anglos.

When we again turn to a model of interaction that considers the contribution to the regulation of talk of Warm Springs listeners as well as speakers, other differences emerge.

Body motion is apparent in the behavior of both speakers and hearers in Warm Springs Indian interaction that is structured through talk, just as it is in Anglo interaction. However, the total amount of body motion is less. To the Anglo observer, an impression of calmness, stillness, and control on the part of Warm Springs interactants is conveyed. Such impressions are supported by close examination of videotaped interaction involving both Anglos and Warm Springs tribal members, in which the behavioral contrast is heightened.

Warm Springs Indians engage in less shifting of body and head alignment. There is also less shifting of body position—less leaning forward and backward, less folding and unfolding of the arms and legs.

There are also differences in facial movement and expression. To this point, the available evidence suggests that movement in the area around the eyes is greater than that found in Anglos. 'Widening' of eyes and eyebrow movement occurs with greater frequency. There also appears to be more eye movement. Both speakers' and hearers' gazes rest on their individual co-interactants for shorter periods of time, about which more will be said below.

It appears that there is less motion, generally in the lower portion of the face. This does not mean there is less 'smiling', although smiling does occur at different points in interaction. The lips move less during speaking, and there is less of the teeth-to-lips and tongue-to-lips play so much in evidence in Anglo facial movement.

This behavioral difference is matched by an apparent greater attention on the part of Indian interactants to the quality of movement in the area around the eyes: in verbal characterizations of the behavior of others, Warm Springs Indians make much more frequent reference to this area of the face to convey the emotional quality of expression—e.g. 'They were snapping eyes' (darting glances exchanged in anger).

Because of these differences, there is an overall impression (to the Anglo observer) of less nonverbal differentiation between speaker and hearer. Although Indian speakers display more motion than hearers, there is less body movement accompanying the speaker's talk than is true with Anglos, and what movement there is is qualitatively different. The head does not visibly bob up and down in rhythm with the speech. And although the head is sometimes turned from side to side as listeners are scanned, the turns are not as sharp or abrupt in initiation and termination, nor as sweeping in the axis of the turn. More of this scanning is done by the movement of the eyes alone. There is also a rhythmic relationship between eye movement and speech that is different from that of Anglos in a manner it is not as yet possible to characterize in detail.

There is less arm and hand gesturing accompanying speech in most conversation, and the gestures themselves are qualitatively different.[4] The fingers are rarely splayed and open as they often are with Anglos. The arms are kept closer to the body, and most movement is from the wrists or elbows. Even in the highly stylized gesturing that accompanies the telling of myths, the arms move up more than they move out. Thus the impression that Warm Springs speakers take up less physical space than their Anglo counterparts is conveyed.

As was suggested earlier, the gaze direction of speakers and hearers in Warm Springs interactions also differs from that of Anglos. Both speakers and hearers spend more time looking away from their co-interactants. Speakers gaze directly at hearers less of the time and hearers gaze directly at speakers less of the time. In encounters of more than a few persons, older Indian listeners will sometimes spend periods of over several minutes gazing downward with lids lowered as the talk flows on.[5]

Because there is less body movement and gesturing among Warm Springs Indian speakers, the cessation of such movement is not as conspicuous a part of the speaker's signaling that he is ending his turn, as it is among Anglos. And the Indian speaker's movement that is ceasing is different in locus, shape and size. Thus far, it does not appear that gaze direction is usually directed toward a hearer as a speaker finishes speaking, or away from the hearer as he begins to speak, as described for Anglos (for reasons that should become clearer further on). Thus the function of nonverbal signaling in the regulation of Indian talk is qualitatively different.

One of the most notable features of Warm Springs Indian regulation of

---

[4]To the degree that Warm Springs Indians use hand gestures less than Anglos to punctuate and qualify their talk, they differ from some of the Plains Indians who use gestures of a form related to that of the sign language a great deal, and complain that when Anglos talk, all one can see is the mouth moving.

[5]Warm Springs Indians in my company often complained of being stared at by Anglos where I perceived only glances. It is quite possible, however, that some Anglos *do* stare at Indians in a way they would not stare at other Anglos.

interaction is the rarity of occurrence of the distinction between addressed and unaddressed recipients so commonly sustained in Anglo interaction. When it does occur, and it will be found more in the interactions involving younger Indians, it is accomplished through means similar to those used by Anglos — e.g. the speaker will gaze more frequently in the direction of one or some of the hearers, and the structure of his utterance may identify a specific individual as his addressee. However, address is much more frequently general or undifferentiated in Indian interactions, in both informal conversation and more formally structured interactions such as meetings.

Indian speakers maintain general address both nonverbally and verbally. As noted above, there is generally less shifting in body position and alignment on the part of Indian speakers. Here it is appropriate to add that the alignment of Indian speakers is less frequently sustained directly toward a specific hearer. Similarly, the gaze direction of the speaker does not focus more on some hearers than others as often. Gaze direction of the speaker shifts continuously and more often than not appears to be directed in the general vicinity of hearers rather than toward their faces, or more specifically their eyes.

Verbal address is also typically generalized in a variety of ways. The structure of utterances is such that addressed recipients cannot readily be identified, in a manner that will be illustrated farther on.

In keeping with the absence of speaker designation of addressed recipients, there is an absence of differentiated hearer roles. One does not perceive some persons in greater interactional synchrony with the speaker than others. Nor is the gaze direction of some hearers more frequently oriented to the speaker, especially not in the direction of his eyes.

All of this suggests that: (1) Indian speakers do not typically exercise influence over who will speak next through identification of addressed recipients (who tend to be next speakers), as in Anglo interaction; and (2) Individual Indian listeners do not typically exercise control over who speaks as a result of being selected by speakers as addressed recipients, or by selecting themselves as addressed recipients through extra-attentive nonverbal behavior.

The Warm Springs system for 'tieing' different utterances together in the sequence of talk also differs from the Anglo system. Much more 'tieing' is done in Warm Springs sequencing between utterances that are not within the range of several different speakers' turns.

This wider range for the tieing of utterances is most evident in the Warm Springs Indian handling of questions. For Anglos, answers to questions are close to obligatory, even if they take the form of 'I can't answer that right now', or a brief shake of the head. Robin Lakoff (1972) has stated that in 'normal conversation', speakers make assumptions about the discourse, including: '. . . Rule IV. With questions, the speaker assumes that he will get a reply' (Lakoff, 1972: 916). That this is not the case with Warm Springs Indians was pointed out to me by an Indian from another reservation who had married into the Warm Springs reservation. He observed wryly that it is often difficult to get an answer out of 'these old people' (and I should add that the phrase 'old people' has the connotation of respect). And he told an anecdote about posing a question that got answered a week after it was asked.

In other words, answers to questions are not obligatory. Absence of an answer merely means the floor is open, or continues to belong to the questioner. This does not mean, however, that the question will not be answered later. Nor does it mean that it ought not be raised again, since the questioner may reasonably assume his audience has had time to think about it.

This absence of a requirement for immediate response is also apparent in the handling of invitations. Anglos on the reservation sometimes complain that they are never invited to Indian homes. Some Indians tell them they are welcome anytime, and mean it, but this is not treated as sufficient by the Anglos. Some Indians will tell Anglos that if they are visiting an Indian home, they should not wait to be invited to eat when a meal is served. They should assume there is a place for them and may join the others as they move to the table, if they choose to.

When a family or larger group event is to take place on the reservation, people inform one another of it; to the degree that this informing is selective, it is invitational. But invitations are not posed in the form of a 'Would you like to come?' that requires a yes or no answer. The person who is informed of an activity that is to take place at a later time need not immediately indicate whether he will or won't come, or must think about it. Absence of a response indicates that it will be given later, if only through the absence or presence at the event of the person invited. Undoubtedly not all invitations can be handled in this way, but the majority are. Such handling of interaction is again more apparent among the old people.

Both 'general address' and this wider-ranging tieing of utterances can best be illustrated through an extended example of Warm Springs Indian interaction, drawn from a public General Council meeting, although they are typical of more private informal encounters as well.

General Council meetings typically occur at least once a month, and are usually called by a member of the Tribal Council, the elected governing body for the Warm Springs Reservation. Often these evening meetings are requested by tribal members. They are open to the entire reservation and usually announced at least a week in advance on signs posted in places frequented by many tribal members. Such meetings often begin with the presentation of information by one or several persons. These persons may be council members or tribal administration personnel reporting on tribal business. Sometimes they are outsiders, like tribally hired architects or lawyers, or school personnel, providing information about their work that is relevant to tribal members.

Later the floor is opened to tribal members, who then make comments and ask questions. Sometimes the subjects raised during this second phase of the meeting will have nothing to do with topics on which information was earlier provided. And some meetings are almost entirely given over to the period when the floor is open to all.

At one such General Council Meeting, where the topic announced on signs for the meetings was 'Forest Product Industries', a report on the earnings and prospective earnings of the saw mill was given by the men who manage the mill. After several questions about the timber industries, an old woman spoke, in English. She said that (1) tribal members never get anything back from their investments; (2) a certain person (whom she named) took a trip to Washington, D.C.; (3) the interpreter doesn't interpret her correctly (when she speaks in Sahaptin and her talk is interpreted in English); (4) certain persons (whom she named) go to Washington to make laws. And she concluded with the question: 'Why can't the people sell fish from Sherar's Bridge?' There was then a one-second pause. Then a man spoke. He said, 'I don't have any questions, but I heard a statement I want to speak on. Someone said we have to move ahead.' Then he went on to make a general statement supporting the mill operation and urging that more young men from the tribe seek jobs there.

Fifteen minutes later, after eight other persons had spoken, in the context of discussion of a report given during that fifteen minutes from a member of the Fish and Wildlife Committee on the laws regulating commercial fishing, the first person named by the first speaker said; 'I've taken a lot of trips to Washington and I can account for every one of them.'

Half an hour later, after further discussion of both timber and fishing, a woman spoke. She asked whether tags are supposed to be attached to the fish nets, a question that was answered. Then she said that the older people think they are supposed to get first access to fish caught on a certain day, and to be given the fish, and she didn't know where they got that idea. She said, 'I would like to be related to all of them, would like to be related to_____ (the first speaker who had posed a question forty-five minutes earlier), but we have to think of our own family first.'

In this way, two and possibly three of the first woman's concerns were responded to: the first man's generally supportive statement *can* be interpreted as a response to the old woman's claim that tribal members do not get anything back on their investments. The trips to Washington and the fishing problems were also eventually dealt with much later, as I have noted, however obscure the responses may seem to the reader. The criticism of the interpreter (who was present) was never taken up.

Note then that (1) in all of this, neither the first woman nor those who responded to her ever spoke directly to one another, although they did refer to one another by name; (2) the first woman never called for a response to her statements; and (3) the 'responses' that were forthcoming were widely separated from speech to which they were a response, and no effort was made to connect them to one another beyond what I have reported here. It may be worth noting that with this approach to sequencing, conflict between persons can be muted and obscured.

Both 'general address' and the availability of wider-ranging tieing allow subsequent speakers much more choice in or determination of the point or juncture in the interaction where they will speak than is available to Anglos.

These various features of the structuring of interaction, when combined, yield a system for the regulation of Warm Springs Indian interaction that is qualitatively different from that of Anglos. In most general terms, the Anglo system allows for both speakers and addressed recipients to exert a good deal of influence over past and future speakers' turns at talk. By comparison, the Indian system maximizes the control a speaker has over his own turn, and minimizes the control he has over the turns of others.

Indian speakers control the lengths of their own turns. They are not interrupted. They are rarely cut off by the sudden inattention of selected addressees, primarily because address is so often general. Because Indian speakers less often select and identify addressed receivers, it is less often the case that some hearers have more control over the floor than others.

Indian speakers also have more control over *when* they will speak (especially about specific topics) because immediate response is not obligatory to the degree that it is with Anglos. Speakers, then, do not set up or determine who will speak next in the way that Anglos do.

These features of Indian regulation of talk, when taken together, result in a different approach to the incorporation of utterances into the sequence of interaction. For an Anglo speaker, being attended to is problematic, since more than one person often speaks at the same time, and individual addressed recipients may choose between speakers. Consequently, for Anglo speakers, a 'response' (i.e. a next utterance that cannot be made sense of without the understanding of the previous speaker's utterance) is more crucial in the validation and incorporation of a turn at talk. In Anglo interaction the presence or absence of a response is taken as the key indicator of whether or not a speaker has been heard. In Indian interaction, the speaker may be certain of attention from hearers. Response consequently functions in a different fashion. Since a response need not immediately follow that to which it is a reply, its immediate absence can neither confirm nor disconfirm that the speaker was heard and his utterance incorporated into the sequencing of the interaction. Thus in general, in Anglo regulation of talk, the presence or absence of immediate response carries more weight than among Warm Springs Indians in indicating to those present that a particular utterance is being recognized, received as a message, and incorporated into the sequence of talk.

IV

From this comparison of Anglo and Warm Springs Indian interaction, it should be apparent that there is cultural variability in the ways that verbal and nonverbal modes of communication function together in the regulation of talk. And the contribution of the listener to such regulation will vary in keeping with differences in the overall system.

At the same time, some similarities may be noted. First, even though the systems differ in the ways in which tieing between the utterances of different speakers is accomplished, tieing contributes to the sequential structuring of interaction in both systems. Second, while body alignment, body positioning, and body movement (including gesture, facial expression and gaze direction) are different in form and amount for Anglo and Indian interactions, and are not synchronized with speech in the same way, they are nevertheless made use of in the regulation of talk in both systems.

Thus, as Sapir pointed out many years ago in discussing language (Sapir 1925), and Hall (1969) and Birdwhistell (1968) have shown for nonverbal realms of behavior, we find the same communicative resources or means, but organized in qualitatively different ways. This suggests a continuing contribution for the ethnographic approach in determining what is universal and what is culturally variable in the regulation of face-to-face interaction.

References

Birdwhistell, R. (1968). Kinesics. In David L. Sills (ed.), *International encyclopedia of the social sciences*. New York: Macmillan and The Free Press. Vol. 8, p. 379.

_____ (1970). Kinesic stress in American English. In R. Birdwhistell, *Kinesics and context*. Philadelphia: University of Pennsylvania Press. 110–27.

Condon, W. S. & Ogsten, W. D. (1967). A segmentation of behavior. *Journal of Psychiatric Research* 5. 221–35.

_____ & _____ (1968). Speech and body motion of the speaker-hearer. Manuscript.

Duncan, S. (1972). Some signals and rules for taking speaking turns in conversations. *Journal of Personality and Social Psychology* 23. 283–92.

_____ (1974). On the structure of speaker-auditor interaction. *LinS* 3. 161–80.

Exline, R. (1963). Exploration in the process of person perception: Visual interaction in relation to competition, sex and need for affiliation. *Journal of Personality and Social Psychology* 31. 1–20.

Goffman, E. (1974). *Frame analysis.* New York: Harper & Row.

Hall, E. (1969). *The hidden dimension.* Garden City: Doubleday.

Hymes, D. (1974). *Foundations in sociolinguistics: an ethnographic approach.* Philadelphia: University of Pennsylvania Press.

Jefferson, G. (1972). Side sequences. In D. Sudnow (ed.), *Studies in Social Interaction.* New York: Collier-Macmillan. 294–338.

Kendon, A. (1967). Some functions of gaze-direction in social interaction. *Acta Psychologica* 26. 22–63.

———— (1970). Movement coordination in social interaction: some examples described. *Acta Psychologica* **32.** 100–25.

Lakoff, R. (1972). Language in context. *Language* **48.** 907–27.

Nielsen, G. (1964). *Studies in Self-Confrontation.* Copenhagen: Munksgaard.

Philips, S. (1972). Participant structures and communicative competence. In C. Cazden, V. John & D. Hymes (eds.), *The function of language in the classroom.* New York: Teachers College Press. 370–94.

———— (1974). *The invisible culture: communication in classroom and community on the Warm Springs Indian Reservation.* Unpublished Ph.D. Dissertation, Department of Anthropology, University of Pennsylvania.

Sacks, H. (1967). Lecture notes.

———— (1972). On the analyzability of stories by children. In J. Gumperz & D. Hymes (eds.), *Directions in sociolinguistics.* New York: Holt, Rinehart & Winston. 325–45.

———— (1974). An analysis of the course of a joke's telling in conversation. In R. Bauman & J. Sherzer (eds.), *Explorations in the ethnography of speaking.* New York: Cambridge University Press. 337–53.

———— , G. Jefferson & E. Schegloff (1973). A simplest systematics for the organization of turn-taking for conversation. Manuscript.

Sapir, E. (1925). Sound patterns in language. *Language* I. 37–51.

Scheflen, A. (1964). The significance of posture in communication systems. *Psychiatry* **27.** 316–21.

Schegloff, E. (1972a). Notes on a conversational practice: Formulating place. In P. Giglioli (ed.), *Language and Social Context.* Baltimore: Penguin. 95–135.

———— (1972b). Sequencing in conversational openings. In J. Gumperz & D. Hymes (eds.), *Directions in sociolinguistics.* New York: Holt. 346–80.

———— & Sacks, H. (1974). Opening up closings. In R. Turner (ed.), *Ethnomethodology.* Baltimore: Penguin.

Weisbrod, R. (1965). Looking behavior in a discussion group. Term paper submitted for Psychology 546 under the direction of Prof. Longabaugh. Ithaca: Cornell University Press.

Yngve, V. H. (1970). On getting a word in edgewise. *Papers from the sixth regional meeting Chicago Linguistic Society.* Chicago: Chicago Linguistic Society. 567–77.

23

Epilogue to "Some Sources of Cultural Variability in the Regulation of Talk"

SUSAN U. PHILIPS

It has been about 15 years since I originally wrote the paper reprinted here as chapter 22. And it is easier to see now than it was then certain lines of thinking about human communication within anthropology and other disciplines that this paper is a part of and to which it hopefully contributes. In this epilogue I trace some of those developments, in part to provide a present-day context for this paper, but also to suggest that we are in fact getting somewhere in the social scientific study of communication (i.e., there is such a thing as progress and development in this area).

During the last two decades, cultural and linguistic anthropology have been significantly influenced by several waves of European phenomenology. In linguistic anthropology the first wave was introduced through the ethnography of communication by Dell Hymes and John Gumperz and the use of the sociological work of ethnomethodologists Garfinkel (1967); Cicourel (1973); and Sacks, Schegloff, and Jefferson (1974). Their work offered a concept of meaning as socially negotiated rather than individual, and as located or situated in the human communication process of face-to-face interaction rather than in the head of the individual speaker of a language. Such a focus on interaction was also very compatible with George Herbert Mead's familiar concept of the self as essentially developing out of the process of human interaction, and with Goffman's (1959) more semiotic analysis of the manipulation of symbolic systems to enhance the self.

Since Garfinkel's ethnomethodology was introduced into anthropology, cultural anthropologists have eagerly responded to other phenomenological theories of cultural meaning as interactionally constructed, as for example in the work of Berger and Luckman (1967), Ricoeur (1983), and Foucault (1972), so that at present there is considerable awareness in anthropology of the reflexive nature of interpretive processes and of the interactive nature of the creation of knowledge. But a number of anthropological linguists

345

writing in the early 1970s and influenced by the ethnography of communication were responding to ethnomethodological rather than to other more
recent phenomenological strains coming into anthropology.

During that period, the important point was made that aspects of
behavior that had been presented in anthropology as fixed and static were
actually quite dynamic and creative. For example, in Irvine's (1974)
treatment of Wolof greeting behavior, she revealed the constant negotiations of relative status in greetings, which we typically stereotype as
routinized.

There was also concern to reveal the extent to which forms of speech
thought of as individual acts were actually cooperatively or jointly done.
Watson-Gegeo's demonstration of part Hawaiian children's storytelling as
joint, as dialogic rather than monologic (Watson, 1972) was an early
important example of this development.

Given this heightened awareness of the interactional production of
meaning, information, and knowledge, eventual attention to the role of the
listener, as in chapter 22, seems almost inevitable. Other scholars similarly
following out the logic of ethnomethodological phenomenology to focus on
the hearer, include Goodwin (1981) and Erickson (1979). Goodwin's
evidence of the ways in which listener behavior influences the ongoing
construction of a speaker's turn at talk is particularly compelling as an
argument for the impact of listeners in the emergence of shared and
individual meaning in human interaction.

Possibly the most important development to come out of a focus on the
listener is the concept of "floor holding" as an alternative to the concept of
the "turn at talk" (Matsuki, 1989). Both concepts identify basic units of
interaction out of which jointly constructed meaning emerges. They differ
in that turns at talk are done by speakers in sequence, whereas floor
holdings, which are also sequenced, are jointly and contemporaneously
sustained shared foci of attention between speakers and addressed recipients. The concept of floor holding is an analytically useful alternative to the
concept of turn at talk because, by encorporating the hearer, it more fully
represents how meaning actually is jointly created in face-to-face interaction.

What distinguishes anthropological contributions to our understanding
of human communication is a salient concern with what is universal and
what is variable, and with explaining both. In the paper reprinted here, I
specifically address cultural differences in listening behavior, and therefore
in the nature of the contribution listeners make to the joint construction of
meaning.

As should be evident from comparing this paper with the papers in this
volume by Basso (ch.20) and by the Scollons (ch. 18), there are important

and interesting areal similarities, as well as differences, among North American Indians in the regulation of interaction (Philips, 1988). Analogous regional similarities are also found in other parts of the world. Recently I have been doing research on the language of dispute management in Tonga, a small Polynesian nation in the South Pacific. My experience there makes me wonder whether there might not also be general differences between the New World and the Old World in many aspects of nonverbal behavior, because of the thousands of years during which the New World was cut off from processes of cultural transmission in the rest of the world.

Today, I generally stress what is universal in nonverbal behavior and in the regulation of interaction more than I did when I wrote this paper. There is a sharedness in form-meaning relations in nonverbal communication that we rely on to get us by when we engage in cross-cultural encounters until we can learn the language. But in general I think whether the anthropologist is focussing on variability within a comparative framework of similarity, as I did in this paper, or more generally on where and why similarities across cultures are found in communicative behavior, behind those strategies is a continuous concern with the dynamic relation between variability and universality in human behavior.

References

Berger, P., & Luckman, T. (1967). *The social construction of reality*. London: Allen Lane.

Cicourel, A. (1973). *Cognitive sociology: Language and meaning in social interaction*. Harmondsworth: Penguin.

Erickson, F. (1979). Talking down: Some cultural sources of miscommunication in interracial interviews. In A. Wolfgang (Ed.), *Nonverbal behavior: Applications and cultural implications* (pp. 99–126). New York: Academic Press.

Foucault, M. (1972). *The archaeology of knowledge*. New York: Pantheon Books.

Garfinkel, H. (1967). *Studies in ethnomethodology*. Englewood Cliffs, NJ: Prentice-Hall.

Goffman, E. (1959). *The presentation of self in everyday life*. Garden City, NY: Doubleday.

Goodwin, C. (1981). *Conversation organization: Interaction between speakers and hearers*. New York: Academic Press.

Irvine, J. T. (1974). Strategies of status manipulation in the Wolof greeting. In R. Bauman & J. Sherzer (Eds.), *Explorations in the ethnography of speaking* (pp. 167–191). Cambridge: Cambridge University Press.

Matsuki, K. (1989). *Floor phenomena in Japanese conversational discourse: Talk among relatives*. Unpublished master's paper, Department of Anthropology, University of Arizona, Tuscon, AZ.

Philips, S. (1988). Similarities in North American Indian groups' nonverbal behavior and their relation to early childhood development. In R. Darnell & M. Foster (Eds.), *Native North American interaction patterns* (pp. 150–167). Hull, Quebec: Canadian Museum of Civilization.

Ricoeur, P. (1983). *Hermeneutics and the human sciences.* New York: Cambridge University Press.

Sacks, H. Schegloff, E., & Jefferson, G. (1974). A simplest systematics for the organization of turntaking for conversation, *Language, 50,* (4), 696–735.

Watson, K. A. (1972). The rhetoric of narrative structure: A sociolinguistic analysis of stories told by part-Hawaiian children. Unpublished doctoral dissertation, University of Hawaii, Manoa, HI.

24

A classification of illocutionary acts[1]

JOHN R. SEARLE

There are at least a dozen linguistically significant dimensions of differences between illocutionary acts. Of these, the most important are illocutionary point, direction of fit, and expressed psychological state. These three form the basis of a taxonomy of the fundamental classes of illocutionary acts. The five basic kinds of illocutionary acts are: representatives (or assertives), directives, commissives, expressives, and declarations. Each of these notions is defined. An earlier attempt at constructing a taxonomy by Austin is defective for several reasons, especially in its lack of clear criteria for distinguishing one kind of illocutionary force from another. Paradigm performative verbs in each of the five categories exhibit different syntactical properties. These are explained.

I. Introduction

One of the crucial questions in studying language in society is, 'How many ways of using language are there?' Most of the attempts to answer that question suffer from an unclarity about what constitutes a use of language in the first place. If you believe, as I do, that the basic unit of human linguistic communication is the illocutionary act, then the most important form of the original question will be, 'How many categories of illocutionary acts are there?' This article attempts to answer that question.

The primary purpose of this paper, then, is to develop a reasoned classification of illocutionary acts into certain basic categories or types. Since any such attempt to develop a taxonomy must take into account Austin's classification of illocutionary acts into his five basic categories of

---

[1]This article was originally written for an audience of philosophers and linguists (it was first presented as a lecture at the Summer Linguistics Institute in Buffalo in 1971). It is published here in the belief that it may be of use to others interested in the special roles that language plays in human social behavior.

verdictive, expositive, exercitive, behabitive, and commissive, a second purpose of this paper is to assess Austin's classification to show in what respects it is adequate and in what respects inadequate. Furthermore, since basic semantic differences are likely to have syntactical consequences, a third purpose of this paper is to show how these different basic illocutionary types are realized in the syntax of a natural language such as English.

In what follows, I shall presuppose a familiarity with the general pattern of analysis of illocutionary acts offered in such works as Austin, *How to Do Things with Words,* Searle, *Speech Acts,* and Searle, 'Austin on Locutionary and Illocutionary Acts'. In particular, I shall presuppose a distinction between the illocutionary force of an utterance and its propositional content as symbolized F(p).

The aim of this paper then is to classify the different types of F.

II. Different Types of Differences Between Different Types of Illocutionary Acts

Any taxonomical effort of this sort presupposes criteria for distinguishing one (kind of) illocutionary act from another. What are the criteria by which we can tell that of three actual utterances one is a report, one a prediction and one a promise? In order to develop higher order genera, we must first know how the species *promise, prediction, report,* etc., differ one from another. When one attempts to answer that question one discovers that there are several quite different principles of distinction; that is, there are different kinds of differences that enable us to say that the force of this utterance is different from the force of that utterance. For this reason the metaphor of force in the expression 'illocutionary force' is misleading since it suggests that different illocutionary forces occupy different positions on a single continuum of force. What is actually the case is that there are several distinct criss-crossing continua.

A related source of confusion is that we are inclined to confuse illocutionary verbs with types of illocutionary acts. We are inclined, for example, to think that where we have two nonsynonymous illocutionary verbs they must necessarily mark two different kinds of illocutionary acts. In what follows, I shall try to keep a clear distinction between illocutionary verbs and illocutionary acts. Illocutions are a part of language as opposed to particular languages. Illocutionary verbs are always part of a particular language: French, German, English, or whatnot. Differences in illocutionary verbs are a good guide but by no means a sure guide to differences in illocutionary acts.

It seems to me there are (at least) twelve significant dimensions of variation in which illocutionary acts differ one from another and I shall— all too briskly—list them:

(1) *Differences in the Point (or Purpose) of the (Type of) Act*

The point or purpose of an order can be specified by saying that it is an attempt to get the hearer to do something. The point or purpose of a description is that it is a representation (true or false, accurate or inaccurate) of how something is. The point or purpose of a promise is that it is an undertaking of an obligation by the speaker to do something. These differences correspond to the essential conditions in my analysis of illocutionary acts in *Speech Acts* (Searle 1969: Ch. 3). Ultimately, I believe, essential conditions form the best basis for a taxonomy, as I shall attempt to show. It is important to notice that the terminology of 'point' or 'purpose' is not meant to imply, nor is based on the view, that every illocutionary act has a definitionally associated perlocutionary intent. For many, perhaps most, of the most important illocutionary acts, there is no essential perlocutionary intent associated by definition with the corresponding verb, e.g. statements and promises are not by definition attempts to produce perlocutionary effects in hearers.

The point or purpose of a type of illocution I shall call its *illocutionary point*. Illocutionary point is part of but not the same as illocutionary force. Thus, e.g., the illocutionary point of request is the same as that of commands: both are attempts to get hearers to do something. But the illocutionary forces are clearly different. In general, one can say that the notion of illocutionary force is the resultant of several elements of which illocutionary point is only one, though, I believe, the most important one.

(2) *Differences in the Direction of Fit Between Words and the World*

Some illocutions have as part of their illocutionary point to get the words (more strictly—their propositional content) to match the world, others to get the world to match the words. Assertions are in the former category, promises and requests are in the latter. The best illustration of this distinction I know of is provided by Miss Anscombe (1957). Suppose a man goes to the supermarket with a shopping list given him by his wife on which are written the words 'beans, butter, bacon, and bread'. Suppose as he goes around with his shopping cart selecting these items, he is followed by a detective who writes down everything he takes. As they emerge from the store both shopper and detective will have identical lists. But the function of the two lists will be quite different. In the case of the shopper's list, the purpose of the list is, so to speak, to get the world to match the words; the man is supposed to make his actions fit the list. In the case of the detective, the purpose of the list is to make the words match the world; the man is supposed to make the list fit the actions of the shopper. This can be further demonstrated by observing the role of 'mistake' in the two cases. If the detective gets home and suddenly realizes that the man bought pork chops instead of bacon, he can simply erase the word 'bacon' and write 'pork chops'. But if the shopper gets home and his wife points out he has bought pork chops when he should have bought bacon he cannot correct the mistake by erasing 'bacon' from the list and writing 'pork chops'.

In these examples the list provides the propositional content of the illocution and the illocutionary force determines how that content is supposed to relate to the world. I propose to call this difference a difference in *direction of fit*. The detective's list has the *word-to-world* direction of fit (as do statements, descriptions, assertions, and explanations); the shopper's list has the *world-to-word* direction of fit (as do requests, commands, vows, promises). I represent the word-to-world direction of fit with a downward arrow thus ↓ and the word-to-word direction of fit with an upward arrow thus ↑. Direction of fit is always a consequence of illocutionary point. It would be very elegant if we could build our taxonomy entirely around this distinction in direction of fit, but though it will figure largely in our taxonomy, I am unable to make it the entire basis of the distinctions.

(3) *Differences in Expressed Psychological States*

A man who states, explains, asserts or claims that p *expresses the belief that p;* a man who promises, vows, threatens or pledges to do a *expresses an intention to do a;* a man who orders, commands, requests H to do A *expresses a desire (want, wish) that H do A;* a man who apologizes for doing A *expresses regret at having done A;* etc. In general, in the performance of any illocutionary act with a propositional content, the speaker expresses some attitude, state, etc., to that propositional content. Notice that this holds even if he is insincere, even if he does not have the belief, desire, intention, regret or pleasure which he expresses, he none the less expresses a belief, desire, intention, regret or pleasure in the performance of the speech act. This fact is marked linguistically by the fact that it is linguistically unacceptable (though not self-contradictory) to conjoin the explicit performative verb with the denial of the expressed psychological state. Thus one cannot say 'I state that p but do not believe that p', 'I promise that p but I do not intend that p', etc. Notice that this only holds in the first person performative use. One can say, 'He stated that p but didn't really believe that p', 'I promised that p but did not really intend to do it', etc. The psychological state expressed in the performance of the illocutionary act is the *sincerity condition* of the act, as analyzed in *Speech Acts,* Ch. 3.

If one tries to do a classification of illocutionary acts based entirely on differently expressed psychological states (differences in the sincerity condition) one can get quite a long way. Thus, *belief* collects not only statements, assertions, remarks and explanations, but also postulations, declarations, deductions and arguments. *Intention* will collect promises, vows, threats and pledges. *Desire* or *want* will collect requests, orders, commands, askings, prayers, pleadings, beggings and entreaties. *Pleasure* doesn't collect quite so many — congratulations, felicitations, welcomes and a few others.

In what follows, I shall symbolize the expressed psychological state with the capitalized initial letters of the corresponding verb, the B for believe, W for want, I for intend, etc.

These three dimensions — illocutionary point, direction of fit, and sincerity condition — seem to me the most important, and I will build most of my taxonomy around them, but there are several others that need remarking.

(4) *Differences in the Force or Strength with Which the Illocutionary Point is Presented*

Both, 'I suggest we go to the movies' and 'I insist that we go to the movies' have the same illocutionary point, but it is presented with different strengths. Analogously with 'I solemnly swear that Bill stole the money' and 'I guess Bill stole the money'. Along the same dimension of illocutionary point or purpose there may be varying degrees of strength or commitment.

(5) *Differences in the Status or Position of the Speaker and Hearer as These Bear on the Illocutionary Force of the Utterance*

If the general asks the private to clean up the room, that is in all likelihood a command or an order. If the private asks the general to clean up the room, that is likely to be a suggestion or proposal or request but not an order or command. This feature corresponds to one of the preparatory conditions in my analysis in *Speech Acts,* Ch. 3.

(6) *Differences in the Way the Utterance Relates to the Interests of the Speaker and the Hearer*

Consider, for example, the differences between boasts and laments, between congratulations and condolences. In these two pairs, one hears the difference as being between what is or is not in the interests of the speaker and hearer respectively. This feature is another type of preparatory condition according to the analysis in *Speech Acts.*

(7) *Differences in Relations to the Rest of the Discourse*

Some performative expressions serve to relate the utterance to the rest of the discourse (and also to the surrounding context). Consider, for example 'I reply', 'I deduce', 'I conclude', and 'I object'. These expressions serve to relate utterances to other utterances and to the surrounding context. The features they mark seem mostly to involve utterances within the class of statements. In addition to simply stating a proposition, one may state it by way of objecting to what someone else has said, by way of replying to an earlier point, by way of deducing it from certain evidentiary premises, etc. 'However', 'moreover' and 'therefore' also perform these discourse-relating functions.

(8) *Differences in Propositional Content that are Determined by Illocutionary Force-Indicating Devices*

The differences, for example, between a report and a prediction involve the fact that a prediction must be about the future whereas a report can be about the past or present. These differences correspond to differences in propositional content conditions as explained in *Speech Acts.*

(9) *Differences Between Those Acts That Must Always Be Speech Acts, and Those That Can Be, But Need Not Be Performed As Speech Acts*

For example, one may classify things by saying 'I classify this as an A and this as a B'. But one need not say anything at all in order to be classifying; one may simply throw all the A's in the A box and all the B's in the B box. Similarly with estimate, diagnose and conclude. I may make estimates, give diagnoses and draw conclusions in saying 'I estimate', 'I diagnose', and 'I conclude' but in order to estimate, diagnose or conclude it is not necessary to say anything at all. I may simply stand before a building and estimate its height, silently diagnose you as a marginal schizophrenic, or conclude that the man sitting next to me is quite drunk. In these cases, no speech acts not even an internal speech act, is necessary.

(10) *Differences Between Those Acts That Require Extra-Linguistic Institutions for Their Performance and Those That Do Not*

There are a large number of illocutionary acts that require an extra-linguistic institution, and generally a special position by the speaker and the hearer within that institution in order for the act to be performed. Thus, in order to bless, excommunicate, christen, pronounce guilty, call the base runner out, bid three no-trump, or declare war, it is not sufficient for any old speaker to say to any old hearer 'I bless', 'I excommunicate', etc. One must have a position within an extra-linguistic institution. Austin sometimes talks as if he thought all illocutionary acts were like this, but plainly they are not. In order to make a statement that it is raining or promise to come and see you, I need only obey the rules of language. No extra-linguistic institutions are required. This feature of certain speech acts, that they require extra-linguistic institutions, needs to be distinguished from feature (5), the requirement of certain illocutionary acts that the speaker and possibly the hearer as well have a certain status. Extra-linguistic institutions often confer status in a way relevant to illocutionary force, but not all differences of status derive from institutions. Thus, an armed robber in virtue of his possession of a gun may *order* as opposed to, e.g., request, entreat, or implore victims to raise their hands. But his status here does not derive from a position within an institution but from his possession of a weapon.

(11) *Differences Between Those Acts Where the Corresponding Illocutionary Verb Has a Performative Use and Those Where It Does Not*

Most illocutionary verbs have performative uses — e.g., 'state', 'promise', 'order', 'conclude'. But one cannot perform acts of, e.g., boasting or threatening, by saying 'I hereby boast', or 'I hereby threaten'. Not all illocutionary verbs are performative verbs.

(12) *Differences in the Style of Performance of the Illocutionary Act*

Some illocutionary verbs serve to mark what we might call the special *style* in which an illocutionary act is performed. Thus, the difference between, for example, announcing and confiding need not involve any difference in illocutionary point or propositional content but only in the *style* of performance of the illocutionary act.

III. Weaknesses In Austin's Taxonomy

Austin advances his five categories very tentatively, more as a basis for discussion than as a set of established results. 'I am not', he says (1962: 151), 'putting any of this forward as in the very least definitive.' I think they form an excellent basis for discussion but I also think that the taxonomy needs to be seriously revised because it contains several weaknesses. Here are Austin's five categories:

Verdictives. These 'consist in the delivering of a finding, official or unofficial, upon evidence or reasons as to value or fact so far as these are distinguishable'. Examples of verbs in this class are: acquit, hold, calculate, describe, analyze, estimate, date, rank, assess, and characterize.

Exercitives. One of these 'is the giving of a decision in favor of or against a certain course of action or advocacy of it . . .', 'a decision that something is to be so, as distinct from a judgment that it is so'. Some examples are: order, command, direct, plead, beg, recommend, entreat and advise. Request is also an obvious example, but Austin does not list it. As well as the above, Austin also lists: appoint, dismiss, nominate, veto, declare closed, declare open, as well as announce, warn, proclaim, and give.

Commissives. 'The whole point of a commissive', Austin tells us, 'is to commit the speaker to a certain course of action.' Some of the obvious examples are: promise, vow, pledge, covenant, contract, guarantee, embrace, and swear.

Expositives are used in acts of exposition involving the expounding of views, the conducting of arguments and the clarifying of usages and reference'. Austin gives many examples of these, among them are: affirm, deny, emphasize, illustrate, answer, report, accept, object to, concede, describe, class, identify and call.

Behabitives. This class, with which Austin was very dissatisfied ('a shocker', he called it) 'includes the notion of reaction to other people's behavior and fortunes and of attitudes and expressions of attitudes to someone else's past conduct or imminent conduct'.
Among the examples Austin lists are: apologize, thank, deplore, commiserate, congratulate, felicitate, welcome, applaud, criticize, bless, curse, toast and drink. But also, curiously: dare, defy, protest, and challenge.

The first thing to notice about these lists is that they are not classifications of illocutionary acts but of English illocutionary verbs. Austin seems to assume that a classification of different verbs is *eo ipso* a classification of kinds of illocutionary acts, that any two non-synonymous verbs must mark different illocutionary acts. But there is no reason to suppose that this is the case. As we shall see, some verbs, for example, mark the manner in which an illocutionary act is performed, for example 'announce'. One may announce orders, promises and reports, but announcing is not on all fours with ordering, promising and reporting. Announcing, to anticipate a bit, is not the name of a type of illocutionary act, but of the way in which some illocutionary act is performed. An announcement is never just an announcement. It must also be a statement, order, etc.
Even granting that the lists are of illocutionary verbs and not necessarily of different illocutionary acts, it seems to me, one can level the following criticisms against it.
(a) First, a minor cavil, but one worth noting. Not all of the verbs listed are even illocutionary verbs. For example, 'sympathize', 'regard as', 'mean to', 'intend', and 'shall'. Take 'intend': it is clearly not performative. Saying 'I intend' is not intending; nor in the third person does it name an illocutionary act: 'He intended . . .' does not report a speech act. Of course there is an illocutionary act of *expressing an intention,* but the illocutionary

verb phrase is: 'express an intention', not 'intend'. Intending is never a speech act; expressing an intention usually, but not always, is.

(b) The most important weakness of the taxonomy is simply this. There is no clear or consistent principle or set of principles on the basis of which the taxonomy is constructed. Only in the case of Commissives has Austin clearly and unambiguously used illocutionary point as the basis of the definition of a category. Expositives, in so far as the characterization is clear, seem to be defined in terms of discourse relations (my feature (7)). Exercitives seem to be at least partly defined in terms of the exercise of authority. Both considerations of status (my feature (5) above) as well as institutional considerations (my feature (10)) are lurking in it. Behabitives do not seem to me at all well defined (as Austin, I am sure, would have agreed) but it seems to involve notions of what is good or bad for the speaker and hearer (my feature (6)) as well as expressions of attitudes (my feature (3)).

(c) Because there is no clear principle of classification and because there is a persistent confusion between illocutionary acts and illocutionary verbs, there is a great deal of overlap from one category to another and a great deal of heterogeneity within some of the categories. The problem is not that there are borderline cases — any taxonomy that deals with the real world is likely to come up with borderline cases — nor is it merely that a few unusual cases will have the defining characteristics of more than one category; rather, a very large number of verbs find themselves smack in the middle of two competing categories because the principles of classification are unsystematic. Consider, for example, the verb 'describe', a very important verb in anybody's theory of speech acts. Austin lists it as both a verdictive and an expositive. Given his definitions, it is easy to see why: describing can be both the delivering of a finding and an act of exposition. But then any 'act of exposition involving the expounding of views' could also in his rather special sense be 'the delivering of a finding, official or unofficial, upon evidence or reasons'. And indeed, a look at his list of expositives (pp. 161–2) is sufficient to show that most of his verbs fit his definition of verdictives as well as does describe. Consider 'affirm', 'deny', 'state', 'class', 'identify', 'conclude', and 'deduce'. All of these are listed as expositives, but they could just as easily have been listed as verdictives. The few cases which are clearly not verdictives are cases where the meaning of the verb has purely to do with discourse relations, e.g. 'begin by', 'turn to', or where there is no question of evidence or reasons, e.g. 'postulate', 'neglect', 'call', and 'define'. But then that is really not sufficient to warrant a separate category, especially since many of these — 'begin by', 'turn to', 'neglect' — are not names of illocutionary acts at all.

(d) Not only is there too much overlap from one category to the next, but within some of the categories there are quite distinct kinds of verbs. Thus

Austin lists 'dare', 'defy' and 'challenge', alongside 'thank', 'apologize', 'deplore' and 'welcome' as behabitives. But 'dare', 'defy' and 'challenge' have to do with the hearer's subsequent actions, they belong with 'order', 'command' and 'forbid' both on syntactical and semantic grounds, as I shall argue later. But when we look for the family that includes 'order', 'command' and 'urge', we find these are listed as exercitives alongside 'veto', 'hire' and 'demote'. But these, again as I shall argue later, are in two quite distinct categories.

(e) Related to these objections is the further difficulty that not all of the verbs listed within the classes really satisfy the definitions given, even if we take the definitions in the rather loose and suggestive manner that Austin clearly intends. Thus 'nominate', 'appoint' and 'excommunicate' are not 'giving of a decision in favor of or against a certain course of action', much less are they 'advocating' it. Rather they are, as Austin himself might have said, *performances* of these actions, not *advocacies* of anything. That is, in the sense in which we might agree that ordering, commanding and urging someone to do something are all cases of *advocating* that he do it, we can not also agree that nominating or appointing is also advocating. When I appoint you chairman, I don't advocate that you be or become chairman; I *make* you chairman.

In sum, there are (at least) six related difficulties with Austin's taxonomy; in ascending order of importance: there is a persistent confusion between verbs and acts, not all the verbs are illocutionary verbs, there is too much overlap of the categories, too much heterogeneity within the categories, many of the verbs listed in the categories don't satisfy the definition given for the category and, most important, there is no consistent principle of classification.

I don't believe I have fully substantiated all six of these charges and I will not attempt to do so within the confines of this paper, which has other aims. I believe, however, that my doubts about Austin's taxonomy will have greater clarity and force after I have presented an alternative. What I propose to do is take illocutionary point, and its corollaries, direction of fit and expressed sincerity conditions, as the basis for constructing a classification. In such a classification, other features—the role of authority, discourse relations, etc.—will fall into their appropriate places.

IV. Alternative Taxonomy

In this section, I shall present a list of what I regard as the basic categories of illocutionary acts. In so doing, I shall discuss briefly how my classification relates to Austin's.

Representatives. The point or purpose of the members of the representative class is to commit the speaker (in varying degrees) to something's being the case, to the truth of the expressed proposition. All of the members of the representative class are assessable on the dimension of assessment which includes *true* and *false*. Using Frege's assertion sign to mark the illocutionary point common to all and the symbols introduced above, we may symbolize this class as follows:

⊢ ↓ B(p).

The direction of fit is words to the world; the psychological state expressed is Belief (that p). It is important to emphasize that words such as 'belief' and 'commitment' are here intended to mark dimensions; they are so to speak determinable rather than determinates. Thus, there is a difference between *suggesting* that p or *putting it forward as a hypothesis* that p on the one hand and *insisting* that p or solemnly *swearing* that p on the other. The degree of belief and commitment may approach or even reach zero, but it is clear or will become clear, that *hypothesizing that p* and *flatly stating that p* are in the same line of business in a way that neither is like requesting.

Once we recognize the existence of *representatives* as a quite separate class, based on the notion of illocutionary point, than the existence of a large number of performative verbs that denote illocutions that seem to be assessable in the True–False dimension and yet are not just 'statements' will be easily explicable in terms of the fact that they mark features of illocutionary force which are in addition to illocutionary point. Thus, for example, consider: 'boast' and 'complain'. They both denote representatives with the added feature that they have something to do with the interest of the speaker (condition (6) above). 'Conclude' and 'deduce' are also representatives with the added feature that they mark certain relations between the representative illocutionary act and the rest of the discourse or the context of utterance (condition (7) above). This class will contain most of Austin's expositives and many of his verdictives as well for the, by now I hope obvious, reason that they all have the same illocutionary point and differ only in other features of illocutionary force.

The simplest test of a representative is this: can you literally characterize it (*inter alia*) as true or false. I hasten to add that this will give neither necessary nor sufficient conditions, as we shall see when we get to my fifth class.

These points about representatives will, I hope, be clearer when I discuss my second class which, with some reluctance, I will call

Directives. The illocutionary point of these consists in the fact that they are attempts (of varying degrees, and hence, more precisely, they are determinates of the determinable which includes attempting) by the speaker to get the hearer to do something. They may be very modest 'attempts' as when I invite you to do it or suggest that you do it, or they may be very fierce attempts as when I insist that you do it. Using the shriek mark for the illocutionary point indicating device for the members of this class generally, we have the following symbolism:

$$! \uparrow W \text{ (H does A)}$$

The direction of fit is world-to-words and the sincerity condition is want (or wish or desire). The propositional content is always that the hearer H does some future action A. Verbs denoting members of this class are ask,[2] order, command, request, beg, plead, pray, entreat, and also invite, permit, and advise. I think also that it is clear that dare, defy and challenge, which Austin lists as behabitives, are in this class. Many of Austin's exercitives are also in this class.

Commissives. Austin's definition of commissives seems to me unexceptionable, and I will simply appropriate it as it stands with the cavil that several of the verbs he lists as commissive verbs do not belong in this class at all, such as 'shall', 'intend', 'favor', and others. Commissives then are those illocutionary acts whose point is to commit the speaker (again in varying degrees) to some future course of action. Using C for the members of this class, generally we have the following symbolism:

$$C \uparrow I \text{ (S does A)}$$

The direction of fit is world-to-words and the sincerity condition is Intention. The propositional content is always that the speaker S does some future action A. Since the direction of fit is the same for commissives and directives, it would give us a simpler taxonomy if we could show that they are really members of the same category. I am unable to do this because, whereas the point of a promise is to commit the speaker to doing something (and not necessarily to try to get himself to do it), the point of a request is to try to get the hearer to do something (and not necessarily to commit or obligate him to do it). In order to assimilate the two categories, one would have to show that promises are really a species of requests to oneself (this had been suggested to me by Julian Boyd), or alternatively one would have to show that requests placed the hearer under an obligation (this has been suggested to me by William Alston and John Kearns). I have been unable to make either of these analyses work and am left with the inelegant solution of two separate categories with the same direction of fit.

Expressives. The illocutionary point of this class is to express the psychological state specified in the sincerity condition about a state of affairs specified in the propositional content. The paradigms of Expressive

---

[2]Questions are a species of directives since they are attempts by S to get H to answer—i.e. to perform a speech act.

verbs are 'thank', 'congratulate', 'apologize', 'condole', 'deplore', and 'welcome'. Notice that in expressives there is no direction of fit. In performing an expressive, the speaker is neither trying to get the world to match the words nor the words to match the world, rather the truth of the expressed proposition is presupposed. Thus, for example, when I apologize for having stepped on your toe, it is not my purpose either to claim that your toe was stepped on or to get it stepped on. This fact is neatly reflected in the syntax (of English) by the fact that the paradigm-expressive verbs in their performative occurrence will not take *that* clauses but require a gerundive nominalization transformation (or some other nominal). One cannot say:

* I apologize that I stepped on your toe; rather the correct English is,
  I apologize for stepping on your toe.
  Similarly, one cannot have:
* I congratulate you that you won the race nor
* I thank you that you paid me the money.

One must have: I congratulate you on winning the race (congratulations on winning the race).

I thank you for paying me the money (thanks for paying me the money).

These syntactical facts, I suggest, are consequences of the fact that there is no direction of fit in expressives. The truth of the proposition expressed in an expressive is presupposed. The symbolization therefore of this class must proceed as follows:

$$E \emptyset (P) (S/H + \text{property})$$

Where E indicates the illocutionary point common to all expressives, $\emptyset$ is the null symbol indicating no direction of fit, P is a variable ranging over the different possible psychological states expressed in the performance of the illocutionary acts in this class, and the propositional content ascribes some property (not necessarily an action) to either S or H. I can congratulate you not only on your winning the race, but also on your good looks. The property specified in the propositional content of an expressive must, however, be related to S or H. I cannot without some very special assumptions congratulate you on Newton's first law of motion.

It would be economical if we could include all illocutionary acts in these four classes, and to do so would lend some further support to the general pattern of analysis adopted in *Speech Acts,* but it seems to me the classification is still not complete. There is still left an important class of cases, where the state of affairs represented in the proposition expressed is realized or brought into existence by the illocutionary force-indicating device, cases where one brings a state of affairs into existence by declaring it to exist, cases where, so to speak, 'saying makes it so'. Examples of these cases are 'I resign', 'You're fired', 'I excommunicate you', 'I christen this ship, the battleship Missouri', 'I appoint you chairman', and 'War is hereby declared'. These cases were presented as paradigms in the very earliest discussions of performatives, but it seems to me they are still not adequately described in the literature and their relation to other kinds of illocutionary acts is usually misunderstood. Let us call this class.

Declarations. It is the defining characteristic of this class that the successful performance of one of its members brings about the correspondence between the propositional content and reality, successful performance guarantees that the propositional content corresponds to the world: if I successfully perform the act of appointing you chairman, then you are chairman; if I successfully perform the act of nominating you as candidate, then you are a candidate; if I successfully perform the act of declaring a state of war, then war is on; if I successfully perform the act of marrying you, then you are married.

The surface syntactical structure of many sentences used to perform declarations conceals this point from us because in them there is no surface syntactical distinction between propositional content and illocutionary force. Thus, 'You're fired' and 'I resign' do not seem to permit a distinction between illocutionary force and propositional content, but I think in fact that in their use to perform declarations their semantic structure is:

I declare: your employment is (hereby) terminated.
I declare: my position is (hereby) terminated.

Declarations bring about some alternation in the status or condition of the referred-to object or objects solely in virtue of the fact that the declaration has been successfully performed. This feature of declarations distinguishes them from the other categories. In the history of the discussion of these topics since Austin's first introduction of his distinction between performatives and constatives, this feature of declarations has not been properly understood. The original distinction between constatives and performatives was supposed to be a distinction between utterances which are sayings (constatives, statements, assertions, etc.) and utterances which are doings (promises, bets, warnings, etc.). What I am calling declarations were included in the class of performatives. The main theme of Austin's mature work, *How to Do Things with Words,* is that this distinction collapses. Just as saying certain things constitutes getting married (a 'performative') and saying certain things constitutes making a promise (another 'performative'), so saying certain things constitutes making a statement (supposedly a 'constative'). As Austin saw but as many philosophers still fail to see, the parallel is exact. Making a statement is as much performing an illocutionary act as making a promise, a bet, a warning or what have you. Any utterance will consist in performing one or more illocutionary acts.

The illocutionary force-indicating device in the sentence operates on the propositional content to indicate among other things the direction of fit between the propositional content and reality. In the case of representatives, the direction of fit is words-to-world, in the case of directives and commissives, it is world-to-words; in the case of expressives there is no direction of fit carried by the illocutionary force because the existence of fit is presupposed. The utterance can't get off the ground unless there already is a fit. But now with the declarations we discover a very peculiar relation. The performance of a declaration brings about a fit by the very fact of its successful performance. How is such a thing possible?

Notice that all of the examples we have considered so far involve an extra-linguistic institution, a system of constitutive rules in addition to the constitutive rules of language, in order that the declaration may be successfully performed. The mastery of those rules which constitutes linguistic competence by the speaker and hearer is not in general sufficient for the performance of a declaration. In addition, there must exist an extra-linguistic institution and the speaker and hearer must occupy special places within this institution. It is only given such institutions as the Church, the law, private property, the state and a special position of the speaker and hearer within these institutions that one can ex-communicate, appoint, give and bequeath one's possessions or declare war. The only exceptions to the principle that every declaration requires an extra-linguistic institution are those declarations that concern language itself, as for example, when one says, 'I define, abbreviate, name, call or dub'.[3] Austin sometimes talks as if all performatives (and in the general theory, all illocutionary acts) required an extra-linguistic institution, but this is plainly not the case. Declarations are a very special category of speech acts. We shall symbolize their structure as follows:

$$D \; \updownarrow \; \emptyset(p)$$

Where D indicates the declarational illocutionary point; the direction of fit is both words-to-world and world-to-words because of the peculiar character of declarations; there is no sincerity condition, hence we have the null symbol in the sincerity condition slot; and we use the usual propositional variable p.

The reason there has to be a relation of fit arrow here at all is that declarations do attempt to get language to match the world. But they do not attempt to do it either by describing an existing state of affairs (as do representatives) nor by trying to get someone to bring about a future state of affairs (as do directives and commissives).

---

[3]Another class of exceptions are supernatural. When God says "Let there be light" that is a declaration.

Some members of the class of declarations overlap with members of the class of representatives. This is because in certain institutional situations we not only ascertain the facts but we need an authority to lay down a decision as to what the facts are after the fact-finding procedure has been gone through. The argument must eventually come to an end and issue in a decision, and it is for this reason that we have judges and umpires. Both, the judge and the umpire, make factual claims; 'you are out', 'you are guilty'. Such claims are clearly assessable in the dimension of word-world fit. Was he really tagged off base? Did he really commit the crime? They are assessable in the word-to-world dimension. But, at the same time, both have the force of declarations. If the umpire calls you out (and is upheld on appeal), then for baseball purposes you are out regardless of the facts in the case, and if the judge declares you guilty (on appeal), then for legal purposes you are guilty. There is nothing mysterious about these cases. Institutions characteristically require illocutionary acts to be issued by authorities of various kinds which have the force of declarations. Some institutions require representative claims to be issued with the force of declarations in order that the argument over the truth of the claim can come to an end somewhere and the next institutional steps which wait on the settling of the factual issue can proceed: the prisoner is released or sent to jail, the side is retired, a touchdown is scored. The existence of this class we may dub 'Representative declarations'. Unlike the other declarations, they share with representatives a sincerity condition. The judge, jury and umpire can, logically speaking, lie, but the man who declares war or nominates you cannot lie in the performance of his illocutionary act. The symbolism for the class of representative declarations, then, is this:

$$D_r \downarrow \updownarrow B(p)$$

Where D_r indicates the illocutionary point of issuing a representative with the force of a declaration, the first arrow indicates the representative direction of fit, the second indicates the declarational direction of fit, the sincerity condition is belief and the p represents the propositional content.

V. Some Syntactical Aspects of the Classification

So far I have been classifying illocutionary acts and have used facts about verbs for evidence and illustration. In this section I want to discuss explicitly some points about English syntax. If the distinctions marked in section IV are of any real significance they are likely to have various syntactical consequences and I now propose to examine the deep structure of explicit performative sentences in each of the five categories; that is I want to examine the syntactical structure of sentences containing the performative occurrence of appropriate illocutionary verbs appropriate to each of the five categories. Since all of the sentences we will be considering will contain a performative verb in the main clause, and a subordinate clause, I will abbreviate the usual tree structures in the following fashion: The sentence, e.g., 'I predict John will hit Bill', has the deep structure shown in Figure 1. I will simply abbreviate this as: I predict + John will hit Bill. Parentheses will be used to mark optional elements or elements that are obligatory only for restricted class of the verbs in question. Where there is a choice of one of two elements, I will put a stroke between the elements, e.g. I/you.

Representatives. The deep structure of such paradigm representative sentences as 'I state that it is raining' and 'I predict he will come' is simply, I verb (that)+S. This class, as a class, provides no further constraints; though particular verbs may provide further constraints on the lower node S. For example, 'predict' requires that an Aux in the lower S must be future or, at any rate, cannot be past. Such representative verbs as 'describe', 'call', 'classify', and 'identify' take a different syntactical structure, similar to many verbs of declaration, and I shall discuss them later.

Directives. Such sentences as 'I order you to leave' and 'I command you to stand at attention' have the following deep structure:

I verb you + you Fut Vol Verb (NP) (Adv)

'I order you to leave' is thus the surface structure realization of 'I order you + you will leave' with equi NP deletion of the repeated 'you'. Notice that an additional syntactical argument for my including 'dare', 'defy', and 'challenge', in my list of directive verbs and objecting to Austin's including

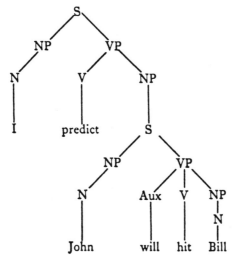

FIGURE 1

them with 'apologize', 'thank', 'congratulate', etc., is that they have the same syntactical form as do the paradigm directive verbs 'order', 'command', and 'request'. Similarly, 'invite', and 'advise' (in one of its senses) have the directive syntax. 'Permit' also has the syntax of directives, though giving permission is not strictly speaking trying to get someone to do something, rather it consists in removing antecedently existing restrictions on his doing it.

Commissives. Such sentences as 'I promise to pay you the money', and 'I pledge allegiance to the flag', and 'I vow to get revenge', have the deep structure

I verb (you) + I Fut Vol Verb (NP) (Adv).

Thus, 'I promise to pay you the money' is the surface structure realization of I promise you + I will pay you the money, with equi NP deletion of the repeated I. We hear the difference in syntax between 'I promise you to come on Wednesday' and 'I order you to come on Wednesday' as being that 'I' is the deep structure subject of 'come' in the first and 'you' is the deep structure subject of 'come' in the second, as required by the verbs 'promise' and 'order' respectively. Notice that not all of the paradigm commissives have 'you' as an indirect object of the performative verb. In the sentence 'I pledge allegiance to the flag' the deep structure is not 'I pledge to you flag + I will be allegiant'. It is

I pledge + I will be allegiant to the flag.

Whereas there are purely syntactical arguments that such paradigm directive verbs as 'order', and 'command', as well as the imperative mood require 'you' as the deep structure subject of the lower node S, I do not know of any purely syntactical argument to show that commissives require 'I' as the deep structure subject on their lower node S. Semantically, indeed, we must interpret such sentences as 'I promise that Henry will be here on Wednesday' as meaning

I promise that *I will see to it* that Henry will be here next Wednesday, in so far as we interpret the utterance as a genuine promise, but I know of no purely syntactical arguments to show that the deep structure of the former sentence contains the italicized elements in the latter.

Expressives. As I mentioned earlier, expressives characteristically require a gerundive transformation of the verb in the lower node S. We say:

I apologize for stepping on your toe,
I congratulate you on winning the race,
I thank you for giving me the money,

The deep structure of such sentences is:

I verb you + I/you VP $\Longrightarrow$ Gerundive Nom.

And, to repeat, the explanation of the obligatory gerundive is that there is no direction of fit. The forms that standardly admit of questions concerning direction of fit, that clauses and infinitives, are impermissible. Hence, the impossibility of

* I congratulate you that you won the race,
* I apologize to step on your toe.

However, not all of the permissible nominalization transformations are gerundive; the point is only that they must not produce *that* clauses or infinitive phrases, thus, we can have either

I apologize for behaving badly,
or
I apologize for my bad behavior,
but not,

* I apologize that I behaved badly,
* I apologize to behave badly.

Before considering Declarations, I want now to resume discussion of those representative verbs which have a different syntax from the paradigms above. I have said that the paradigm representatives have the syntactical form

I verb (that) + S.

But, if we consider such representative verbs as 'diagnose', 'call' and 'describe', as well as 'class', 'classify' and 'identify', we find that they do not fit this pattern at all. Consider 'call', 'describe' and 'diagnose', in such sentences as

I call him a liar,
I diagnose his case as appendicitis

and

I describe John as a Fascist.

and in general the form of this is

I verb NP_1 + NP_1 be pred.

One cannot say

- * I call that he is a liar,
- * I diagnose that his case is appendicitis (perversely, some of my students find this form acceptable.),
- * I describe that John is a Fascist.

There, therefore, seems to be a very severe set of restrictions on an important class of representative verbs which is not shared by the other paradigms. Would this justify us in concluding that these verbs were wrongly classed as representatives along with 'state', 'assert', 'claim' and 'predict' and that we need a separate class for them? It might be argued that the existence of these verbs substantiates Austin's claim that we require a separate class of verdictives distinct from expositives, but that would surely be a very curious conclusion to draw since Austin lists most of the verbs we mentioned above as expositives. He includes 'describe', 'class', 'identify' and 'call' as expositives and 'diagnose' and 'describe' as verdictives. A common syntax of many verdictives and expositives would hardly warrant the need for verdictives as a separate class. But leaving aside Austin's taxonomy, the question still arises, do we require a separate semantic category to account for these syntactical facts? I think not. I think there is a much simpler explanation of the distribution of these verbs. Often, in representative discourse, we focus our attention on some topic of discussion. The question is not just what is the propositional content we are asserting, but what do we say about the *object*(s) referred to in the propositional content: not just what do we state, claim, characterize, or assert, but how do we describe, call, diagnose or identify *it,* some previously referred to topic of discussion. When, for example, there is a question of diagnosing or describing it is always a question of diagnosing a person or his case, of describing a landscape or a party or a person, etc. These Representative illocutionary verbs give us a device for isolating topics from what is said about topics. But this very genuine syntactical difference does not mark a semantic difference big enough to justify the formation of a separate category. Notice in support of my argument here that the actual sentences in which the describing, diagnosing, etc., is done are seldom of the explicit performative type, but rather are usually in the standard indicative forms which are so characteristic of the representative class.

Utterances of

He is a liar,
He has appendicitis,
He is a Fascist,

are all characteristically *statements,* in the making of which we call, diagnose and describe, as well as accuse, identify and characterize. I conclude then that there are typically two syntactical forms for representative illocutionary verbs; one of which focusses on propositional content, the other on the object(s) referred to in the propositional content, but both of which are semantically representatives.

Declarations. I mention the syntactical form

I verb NP_1 + NP_1 be pred

both to forestall an argument for erecting a separate semantic category for them and because many verbs of declaration have this form. Indeed, there appear to be several different syntactical forms for explicit performatives of declaration. I believe the following three classes are the most important.

(1) I find you guilty as charged.
   I now pronounce you man and wife.
   I appoint you chairman.
(2) War is hereby declared.
   I declare the meeting adjourned.
(3) You're fired.
   I resign.
   I excommunicate you.

The deep syntactical structure of these three, respectively, is as follows:

(1) I verb NP_1 + NP_1 be pred.

Thus, in our examples, we have

   I find you + you be guilty as charged.
   I pronounce you + you be man and wife.
   I appoint you + you be chairman.

(2) I declare + S.

Thus, in our examples we have

   I/we (hereby) declare + a state of war exists.
   I declare + the meeting be adjourned.

This form is the purest form of the declaration: the speaker in authority brings about a state of affairs specified in the propositional content by saying in effect, I declare the state of affairs to exist. Semantically, all declarations are of this character, though in class (1) the focussing on the topic produces an alteration in the syntax which is exactly the same syntax as we saw in such representative verbs as 'describe', 'characterize', 'call' and 'diagnose', and in class (3) the syntax conceals the semantic structure even more.

(3) The syntax of these is the most misleading. It is simply I verb (NP)

as in our examples,

I fire you.
I resign.
I excommunicate you.

The semantic structure of these, however, seems to me the same as class (2). 'You're fired', if uttered as performance of the act of firing.someone and not as a report means

I declare + Your job is terminated.

Similarly, 'I hereby resign' means

I hereby declare + My job is terminated.

'I excommunicate you' means

I declare + Your membership in the church is terminated.

The explanation for the bemusingly simple syntactical structure of the three sentences seems to me to be that we have some verbs which in their performative occurrence encapsulate both the declarative force and the propositional content.

VI. Conclusion

We are now in a position to draw certain general conclusions.

(1) Many of the verbs we call illocutionary verbs are not markers of illocutionary point but of some other feature of the illocutionary act. Consider 'insist' and 'suggest'. I can insist that we go to the movies or I can suggest that we go to the movies; but I can also insist that the answer is found on p. 16 or I can suggest that it is found on p. 16. The first pair are directives, the second, representatives. Does this show that insisting and suggesting are different illocutionary acts altogether from representatives

and directives, or perhaps that they are both representatives and directives? I think the answer to both questions is no. Both 'insist' and 'suggest' are used to mark the degree of intensity with which the illocutionary point is presented. They do not mark a separate illocutionary point at all. Similarly, 'announce', 'present' and 'confide' do not mark separate illocutionary points but rather the style or manner of performance of an illocutionary act. Paradoxically as it may sound, such verbs are illocutionary verbs, but not names of kinds of illocutionary acts. It is for this reason, among others, that we must carefully distinguish a taxonomy of illocutionary acts from one of illocutionary verbs.

(2) In section IV I tried to classify illocutionary acts, and in section V I tried to explore some of the syntactical features of the verbs denoting members of each of the categories. But I have not attempted to classify illocutionary verbs. If one did so, I believe the following would emerge.

(a) First, as just noted some verbs do not mark illocutionary point at all, but some other feature, e.g. insist, suggest, announce, confide, reply, answer, interject, remark, ejaculate and interpose.

(b) Many verbs mark illocutionary point plus some other feature, e.g. 'boast', 'lament', 'threaten', 'criticize', 'accuse' and 'warn' all add the feature of goodness or badness to their primary illocutionary point.

(c) Some few verbs mark more than one illocutionary point, e.g. a *protest* involves both an expression of disapproval and a petition for change.

Promulgating a law has both a declaration status (the propositional content becomes law) and a directive status (the law is directive in intent). The verbs of representative declaration fall into this class.

(d) Some few verbs can take more than one illocutionary point. Consider 'warn' and 'advise'. Notice that both of these take either the directive syntax or the representative syntax. Thus,

I warn you to stay away from my wife!	(directive)
I warn you that the bull is about to charge.	(representative)
I advise you to leave.	(directive)
Passengers are hereby advised that the train will be late.	(representative)

Correspondingly, it seems to me, that warning and advising may be either telling you *that* something is the case (with relevance to what is or is not in your interest) or telling you *to* do something about it (because it is or is not in your interest). They can be, but need not be, both at once.

(3) The most important conclusion to be drawn from this discussion is this. There are not, as Wittgenstein (on one possible interpretation) and many others have claimed, an infinite or indefinite number of language games or uses of language. Rather, the illusion of limitless uses of language

is engendered by an enormous unclarity about what constitutes the criteria for delimiting one language game or use of language from another. If we adopt illocutionary point as the basic notion on which to classify uses of language, then there are a rather limited number of basic things we do with language: we tell people how things are, we try to get them to do things, we commit ourselves to do things, we express our feelings and attitudes and we bring about changes through our utterances. Often, we do more than one of these at once in the same utterance.

References

Anscombe, G. E. M. (1957). *Intention.* Oxford: Basil Blackwell.

Austin, J. L. (1962). *How to do things with words.* Harvard and Oxford.

Searle, J. R. (1968). Austin on locutionary and illocutionary acts. *Philosophical Review* **LXXVII.** 405–424.

_____ (1969). *Speech acts: an essay in the philosophy of language.* Cambridge.

25

The Things We Do With Words: Ilongot Speech Acts and Speech Act Theory in Philosophy*

MICHELLE Z. ROSALDO

I begin by introducing the Ilongots and some of their attitudes toward speech. Whereas most modern theorists think of language as a tool designed primarily to "express" or to "refer," Ilongots think of language first in terms of action. They see commands as the exemplary act of speech, displaying less concern for the subjective meanings that an utterance conveys than for the social contexts in which utterances are heard. An ethnographic sketch thus outlines how Ilongots think of words and how their thought relates to aspects of their practice – providing an external foil for theorists found closer to home. Speech Act Theory is discussed and questioned first on internal grounds, as an approach that recognizes but slights important situational and cultural constraints on forms of language use. A consideration of the application of Searle's taxonomy of acts of speech to Ilongot categories of language use then leads to a clarification of the individualistic and relatively asocial biases of his essentially intra-cultural account. Last, I return to Ilongot directives. A partial analysis of Ilongot acts of speech provides the basis for a statement of the ways in which indigenous categories are related to the forms that actions take, as both of these, in turn, reflect the sociocultural ordering of local worlds. [1]

Through analyses that show the mutual bearing of activities and thoughts in cultures other than our own, anthropologists can make clear the ways in which accounts of human action are dependent on an understanding of the actors' sociocultural milieu. [2] More narrowly, I want to argue here that ways of thinking about language and about human agency and personhood are intimately linked: [3] our theoretical attempts to understand how language works are like the far less explicated linguistic thoughts of people elsewhere in the world, in that both inevitably tend to reflect locally prevalent views about the given nature of those human persons by whom language is used.

Speech Act Theory[4] is at once my inspiration and my butt. The work of Austin, Searle, and others commands my interest as an attempt to show the mutual relevance of technically linguistic and more loosely social and contextual concerns. Speech act theorists seek to comprehend the fact that to talk about the world "out there" will of necessity involve not only propositions to be judged for truth, but something more: communicative intentions. The meanings carried by our words must thus depend not just on what we say, but who we are and what we hope our interlocutors to know. Yet in focusing on the ways "intentions" are embodied in all acts of speech, speech act theorists have failed to grapple with some of the more exciting implications of their work. They think of "doing things with words" as the achievement of autonomous selves, whose deeds are not significantly constrained by the relationships and expectations that define their local world. In the end, I claim, the theory fails because it does not comprehend the sociality of individuals who use its "rules" and "resources" to act. Stated otherwise, it fails because it construes action independent of its reflexive status both as consequence and cause of human social forms.

These limitations are clarified, I suggest, through a consideration of the ways in which it does, and does not, prove adequate in grappling with speech among a people who think about and use their words in ways that differ from our own.

THE ILONGOTS

One striking feature of the Ilongot households where my husband and I lived, for close to two years in 1967–69 and again for nine months in 1974, was the salience, in daily life, of brief and undisguised directives. Although a sense of balance and reciprocity obtained in what appeared to be quite egalitarian relations among both children and adults, demands for services were so common that one quickly learned to turn to others rather than obtain desired objects by oneself.

So, for example, Bayaw, who finished eating moments before his wife was heard to issue this directive:[6]

  ta dēnum Sawad ya, 'aika 'egkang   "That (implying, 'over there, unconnected to you') water, Sawad c'mon, come and get up now."

And 'Insan, wanting a bit of lime in preparation for his betel chew, remained seated while he told his wife to move:

  tu tangtangmu Duman, rawmu   "This (implying, 'it is yours, is not far, alien from you') your lime container, Duman, go get it."

Duman, already occupied, did not challenge his command, but instead responded by communicating the father's words to a young daughter:

  rawmud tu 'umel   "Go get it over here, little girl."

Again, Tepeg, a middle-aged man, desired to share a roasted sweet potato with his senior companion; thus, his wife became the object of this brief command:

Midalya 'irawim si kabu nima 'ula ya   "Midalya, go get my friend here a
   sweet potato, c'mon.''

But then Midalya, much like Duman, found a child to do the job:

'irawim nu sit nima 'ula Delali   "Go get one of those sweet potatoes for them,
   Delali.''

What is involved here? Lacking such institutions as the office, church, or
court, most Ilongot social life took place within large one room houses. Each
family in these simple homes was apt to store its goods and concentrate for sleep
and eating in the vicinity of a single sunken hearth – the number of hearths per
household (between one and three) serving as a reasonable index of its component family units. Hearth and family space were located on the "edges" –
usually raised platforms – that surrounded larger, undivided "centers," where
young children talked and played, and adults cooked and then apportioned food
for regular household meals where individualized plates of rice and viand would
be distributed equally to all. Characteristically, life at an "edge" was calm and
quiet. When positioned comfortably on a platform, the whittling muser could
ignore much of the bustling life around him, and enjoy the silent pleasures of a
window that might serve to ease and "open out" his burdened heart.

Within the house, no single space was delegated to a single category of
persons. But it was not long before I found it all too clear that adult men alone
were regularly privileged to enjoy the "lazy" ease of platforms. These men
would pass requests for betel, water, and supplies to youths, and, in particular, to
women. And women, when themselves at rest or else engaged in their routine
domestic chores, would either move or else command, in turn, their "children,"
to "get up" and "fetch" things in quick and relatively unordered movement
across the common floor.

Although it is not difficult to find exceptions to the rule – men ask children
directly; juniors make demands of seniors; women call on men to help with their
domestic tasks, to join in garden work or hunt – one can, in general, say that in
the household men enjoy a relatively silent space and are rarely the objects of
directives. Women, engaged more frequently than men in daily household tasks,
are both more likely to receive commands and to command their children. And
children, following hierarchies of age, receive and then pass on directives from
their seniors – unwittingly disrupting things and so confirming their subordinate
place through tired pleas of laziness and lack of skill, or else through abrupt
movements that contribute to an ever-present sense of chaos on the central floor.
Adults, by contrast, rarely challenge a request, unless to state that they are
occupied (and so, cannot conceivably comply) or question a subordinate's sheer
shamelessness in voicing inappropriate demands.

These Ilongots, who in many ways appeared more flexible and egalitarian than
any people I have known, recognized and apparently enjoyed in their domestic

life a hierarchy of commands blatant and (to me) unjust. In laughter, they remarked on how my husband often ''moved'' for me and typically joined with me at the river to wash clothing. I, in turn, would argue that all husbands should respect and try to ease their wives' incessant work. They would answer, ''so they do, we all must eat,'' but then again that women should ''respect'' and be reluctant to command more ''angry'' men because the latter have, in travels, hunts, and taking heads,[7] displayed superior energy and poise. Contrasting men and women, Ilongots would say that female hearts were ''vague'' and lacking ''focus.'' Of children, they declared that all youth ''knew'' was ''how to play,'' and so, that youngsters were dependent on adults to channel wild energies toward work. Unlike adults (and in particular, of course, men) who stooped to cross the room in their infrequent errands, children moved too frequently and all too often, ''without purpose.'' And unlike men – both men and women would recount – most women often failed to ''know'' what was demanded by the social situation presently at hand.

Thus, at much the same time that they recognized that commanded parties need not (and do not) necessarily comply – that children must be coaxed to heed a parent's wish and women often answer men's commands with an unhearing silence – Ilongots also seemed convinced that through commands they both articulated and shaped ongoing forms of social order. Women would, for instance, readily explain that they rarely urged domestic chores upon a spouse because they knew that men were ''lazy'' and could not be moved when in the home – and even more, because they felt ''respect'' and ''fear'' towards an accomplished husband's ''angry'' force. The goaded husband would, Ilongots claimed, occasionally beat his taunting wife; although men, recognizing their dependence on a good wife's work and care, declared as well that they were ''fearful'' to estrange a spouse through violence. And yet more generally, Ilongots suggested that true *tuydek,* or ''commands'' – unlike *bēge,* ''requests'' (see below) – were rare from young to old or women to men, because ''respect'' and the display of ''care'' and ''reticence'' or ''shame'' appropriate in asymmetric bonds, were typified by a readiness to rise and a reluctance to stir others to unneeded tasks.

But if commands typically move in lines associated with age- and sex-linked social rank, Ilongots insist as well that children may direct their parents to provide them with snacks, mend clothing or supplies, prepare their things for travel. And men, who issue *tuydek* to their wives within the home, may be commanded by their wives in turn when a discussion concerns the need for forest foods. *Commands, in short, involve particular and limited ideas of social rank.* They are constrained by everyday concerns for orderly cooperation and expectations that decide what different persons ought to know and do.

Thus, while *tuydek* vary considerably in linguistic form, it would appear that differences – in such things as manner, mode, aspect, and focus of the verb – have more to do with what Ilongots see as reasonable expectations and accounts of their objective needs than with desires to accommodate those whose relative status differs from one's own.[8] A command in (what I tentatively gloss as) incompletive aspect, brief, imperative form, such as:

> *'ekarka* "get going";
> *mambēyuka* "start pounding rice";
> *pilisim* "squeeze it (e.g., vegetables, to see if they are cooked)";
> *nangasim* "pour it out (for them, into containers, to be distributed)";

although most common in directives to the young, is used primarily, Ilongots say, as an efficient tool that wins immediate and limited responses. No rule of etiquette would lead the busy woman to attempt to qualify these simple verbs should she desire a man to look and see if vegetables are cooked, or pour out water for a thirsty child. Again, commands in the subjunctive:

> *'engraw'uka 'enakdu 'enginumak* "if only (i.e., hurry and) you'd fetch water, I want to drink";
> *'enakduw'uka ma dēnum* "(while you're there), would you fetch water at the river";
> *tunur'u muy tan* "if only you would (would you please) light this."

can be used either to plead or to complain. They are most likely in interactions with such mature persons as can claim competing goals and needs; but the form appears much more concerned with the "impersonal" fact that some desired act has yet to be performed than with assumptions about status. And finally, it is significant that Ilongots, in reflecting on the difference between straightforward:

> *rawka manakdu* "go and fetch water,"

and

> *'engraw'uka enakdu* "if only (subjunctive) you would go fetch water";
> *'irawim 'itakduwi* "go fetch water (for him)";
> *mangkerawka manakdu* "just (make a little effort to) go and fetch water";
> *durutmu dēken 'itakduwi* "just quickly, go fetch water for me",

or any of a variety of ways of issuing what are often seen as "softer," "slower" *tuydek* forms, point out again that choice is shaped, primarily not by differential rank, but rather by the sense of speed and likelihood with which the speaker seeks compliance.[9]

What this suggests, of course, is that for Ilongots the social expectations realized in how they use commands do not in any simple sense defy their notion that all people, ultimately, are "equal" or, as they put it, *'anurut* "the same." Commands to men or children may be equally "abrupt" (*'u'awet* "quick") or "soft" (*'uyamek*). It all depends on what is wanted; what commanded parties may reasonably be asked to do; and what sorts of helpers are available. And yet, to speak of flexibility does not deny a sense of rule. Rather, it is to argue that the hierarchies associated with Ilongot commands are social facts that must themselves be understood within the context of folk views about the nature of their local social world. In particular, it would appear that Ilongot hierarchies of prerogative and respect must be seen ultimately as matters not of power, deference, or control, but rather of particular persons' needs and skills and of the reciprocities (and inequities) that grow through regular performance of sex/age appropriate chores.

This point needs stressing. Attention to universal "features" such as "power," "dominance," and the like will be misleading if the social relationships so described go unexplored. Inequities exist for Ilongots; they are articulated and negotiated in the social uses of commands. But an understanding of what Ilongot directives mean requires an account not just of rank but of ideas defining social roles and bonds. [10] Thus, Ilongots will sometimes claim that male adults rarely need be the objects of commands because men tend to "know" (bēya, see M. Rosaldo 1980) what chores are reasonably theirs, and realize these (such things as hunting, killing, joining oratorical debate) in relatively independent actions that remove them from domestic contexts. Similarly, they say that women typically receive commands within the household because the place where people concentrate is the place where women work. But then, they claim that women – who are thought to have less differentiated or "focused" hearts and thoughts than men – are apt to need direction in order to best compensate for social "knowledge" that they lack.

Those who in general give commands, are said to have a "knowledge" that their objects need, and to deserve "respect," because, in giving food (or joy, through taking heads), they have provided their consociates with life. Furthermore, Ilongots say that those who most receive commands are "lightest" and "most quick" to stir and stand: the woman who "knows" little of the world and yet takes pride in her agility around the home; the child who, still lacking "shame," appears inclined to constant movement. Not simply do unmarried youngsters have an energy and readiness lacked by more constrained adults; as evidenced by their disruptive taste for noise and play, most children need formal directives in order to prevent their causing stress.

When asked why they want offspring of their own, Ilongots often say that children are desired so that adults can have young hands to work – or, as they put it, "be commanded." But Ilongots believe as well that tuydek serve to guarantee that children learn to recognize and respect the "mothers" and "fathers" who gave them life; to follow them, and thus achieve an active consciousness regarding work; and from this, to attain the sort of "heart" that can direct and focus speech and action on its own. The child needs commands, Ilongots say, because its heart lacks "knowledge" of the world. And it is through tuydek, or commands, that adults first shape the movements of young hearts, thus teaching youths to think of things that should be done, and speak in knowing words. [11]

Commands, in short, are significant not only in organizing the energy and labor of the powerless or immature. They form critical moments in the child's education. For Ilongots, the tuydek, "fetch me that" is what instructs young children both in their relationships to adults, and in their knowledge of what language is and how it should be used. Where we incline, I think, to regard linguistic learning as a matter of acquiring phrases that identify and describe, Ilongots would often claim that children learn to speak by learning *tuydek*. In fact, my own desires, when in the field, to help by fetching things that my companions sought were seen as testimony to linguistic youth – explicable with reference not to inner generosity or grace but my quite sensible attempts to learn to use their words.

Tuydek, then, were seen as the exemplary act of speech. As significant in ordering domestic life as in the socialization of the young, directive utterances were, for my Ilongot friends, the very stuff of language: knowing how to speak itself was virtually identical to knowing how and when to act. Language was, in the Ilongot view, a paradigm of thought. Thoughts were seen as utterances of the heart. And human choice and effort were themselves construed as a response to silent *tuydek* through which the knowing heart could give directions to unknowing hands.

Thus, when Ilongots told stories, a brief imperative: "So I said to my sister/wife/mother, 'pound me rice for I am going off'," emerged in almost every text as an introduction to core protagonists and their actions. In the same way that Ilongots think children require *tuydek* if they are to learn to act, commands through which the heart informs the hand: "And I said in my heart, 'Draw the bow', and I drew it," appear recurrently in recollections and reports as a description of human activity itself. Similarly, when Ilongots were asked to illustrate through sample sentences the use of words that I had written on vocabulary cards, close to 50% were cast in utterance frames associated with directives.[12] And finally, in magical spells, a pairing of evocative imagery and directive speech:

"Here is a plant called 'meeting', hand, meet the game, hand . . .";
"Here is a plant that springs up after floods; so may this body spring up in health . . .";
"Make my body like a spinning bug, dizzy with the thickness of this harvest . . .";

appeared to link desired outcomes to such words and images as were able both to name, and change, human activity in the world. Magical spells could be successful if practitioners managed to "hit upon" appropriate commands.

In short, for Ilongots, domestic scenes elaborating hierarchies of command are not embarrassments to universal equalizing rules. If anything, Ilongot uses of commands are rooted in their views of human action and of human social order. Ilongots value "sameness" and yet assign to differences a necessary place. If adults failed to use their "knowledge" to direct the "energy" of the young, or if adults among themselves were not concerned to "reach" and equal the achievements of their peers, then human life itself would fail for lack of energy and cooperation. Ideas of "sameness" for the Ilongots are not like legal notions that describe what people "are," but images that speak to their desires. Young men, for instance, strive to be "the same" as more achieved adults; lacking sameness, they are "envious" and try to prove themselves through shows of "energy" and "anger." Lack of sameness – or its threat – is what encourages adults in daily work. Conflict resolution is a matter of acknowledging and discarding lack of "sameness" among persons who are either "similar" to or "angry" at their fellows. And yet, the irony, from our point of view, is that the ordering of mundane life requires a recognition of difference, of hierachy, and complementarity. For Ilongots, such order is achieved when people recognize themselves as kin, and thus as persons who cooperate and share in daily life and labor. Yet, given the ability of autonomous human beings to insist on sameness and deny the claims of kin, it is precisely in the proferring and acknowledgment of commands that Ilongots are able to display commitment to ongoing kinship bonds. For enemies to turn kinsmen they must prove themselves to be "the same." But then, for kin to act as kin they must acknowledge difference, show "respect," using not "envy" but the "knowledge" of adults to organize the "energy" in young hearts.

Stated otherwise, Ilongot social life – like that of many peoples in the world – is organized in terms of norms of sex, age, and relation, wherein kinship is what permits people to make age/sex appropriate claims. But equally, kinship itself depends not on a set of jural fictions binding futures to the past, but on repeated shows of care, cooperation, and respect in everyday affairs. Thus, kin *are* those people who arrange sex/age appropriate divisions of labor. And similarly, they are the people who articulate their relations in mundane services and commands.

Thus, if most Western linguists have been primarily impressed with language as a "resource" that can represent the world (and that the individual can then "use" as a tool to argue, promise, criticize, or lie),[13] the Ilongot case points toward a rather different view of speech and meaning. For them, words are not made to "represent" objective truth, because all truth is relative to the relationships and experiences of those who claim to "know."[14] We may well recognize the context-boundedness of speech – and yet tend ultimately to think that meaning grows from what the individual "intends" to say. For Ilongots, I think, it is relations, not intentions, that come first.

SPEECH ACT THEORY

J. L. Austin was, of course, an heir to Wittgenstein, who stressed connections between forms of social life and forms of meaning. Like Ilongots, whose view of language-as-command links speech to socially expected modes of knowledge, energy, and skill, his writings argue that we would do well to think of language first as an activity, conventionally defined, and subject to norms operative in the various situations where we speak. And yet, the very fact that Austin's notions had their roots in language bound to relatively limited and ritualized domains permitted later thinkers to begin to question his concerns, abandoning his interest in the institutional constraints on talk in favor of more universalizing views of what it means to say that utterances are acts at all.[15]

Thus, most recent writers have come to concentrate on how our deeds – or utterances – are shaped by what the individual "intends" or "means," without attention to the social and cultural contexts in which meanings are born.[16] Linguistic action is construed much less in terms of "where" and "how" than of just "what" is said and "why" – as if it were, in fact, the case that only in the courtroom or in church is subjectivity constrained or shaped by situationally bound norms. Unlike Austin then, such recent writers as the philosopher, John Searle[17] tend overwhelmingly to view familiar acts of speech not primarily as social facts, but as the embodiments of universal goals, beliefs, and needs possessed by individuated speakers. And whereas Austin discovered illocutionary force in speech by concentrating on conventional acts that have the power to change the world, Searle uses "promising" – in place of Austin's oath of marriage or the Ilongot command – to serve as paradigmatic of our ways of "doing things with words."

I argue later that the act of "promising" is alien to the Ilongot repertory of kinds of speech. More immediately relevant, however, is the question as to why, and with what consequences, the act of promising has been used as a paradigm in theories presently available.[18] To think of promising is, I would claim, to focus on the sincerity and integrity of the one who speaks. Unlike such things as greetings that we often speak because, it seems, "one must," a promise would appear to come, authentically, from inside out. It is a public testimony to commitments we sincerely undertake, born of a genuine human need to "contract" social bonds, an altruism that makes us want to publicize our plans. Thus the promise leads us to think of meaning as a thing derived from inner life. A world of promises appears as one where privacy, not community, is what gives rise to talk.

Not surprisingly, then, when Searle (1965; 1969) describes how speech acts work, his "constitutive rules" – when the promise is defined as a sincere undertaking, by the speaker (S), of a commitment to do A, where A is something S would not ordinarily undertake, and something, furthermore, that S believes that hearer (H) desires – do not reveal that there is more than a commitment and sincere intent to please involved in issuing a promise. What Searle forgets, and yet to me seems clear, is that the good intentions that a promise brings are things we only offer certain kinds of people, and at certain times. Introspection suggests, for example, that promises to one's child are typically didactic and tendentious. A promise to, or from, a candidate for public office is apt to prove neither sincere nor insincere but in equal measure suspicious, significant, and grand. Sincere promises to my colleagues are typically no more than that: sincere commitments. To a high administrator, my promises may seem peculiar. And I cannot escape a sense of awkwardness in imagining a promise to my spouse.[19]

There are, in short, quite complex social "rules" that circumscribe the happy "promise" – although our ideology of promising leads one to focus not on these but on the "inner" orientations and commitments of the speaking self. Moreover, it would appear that Searle, by focusing on the promise as a paradigmatic act of speech, himself falls victim to folk views that locate social meaning first in private persons – and slight the sense of situational constraint (who promises to whom, and where, and how) that operates in subtle but important ways in promising, and in yet more salient ways in the case of a directive, like "commanding," or such apparently expressive acts as "congratulating," "greeting," and "bidding farewell." The centrality of promising supports a theory where conditions on the happiness of a speech act look primarily not to context, but to beliefs and attitudes pertaining to the speaker's private self.

Searle argues that we recognize the significance of psychological constraints on acts of speech in observing, for example, that it makes odd sense to say, "I tell you X, but don't believe it" or similarly, "I send condolences with joy." We cannot conjure a linguistic world where utterances bear no relation to assumptions about truth; just as we fear that "thank-you's" become empty without "gratitude," and yet more generally, that conversation is untenable if speakers prove entirely insincere. Through negative arguments such as these, Searle clearly shows that the acknowledgment of certain contrary psychological states may undermine an act of speech. But what he fails to see is that such observations do not prove the positive claim that if performatives are to work, then the presumption of a given psychological orientation is required. "Sincerity," and such related terms as "feeling," "intention," and "belief," may well be things whose absence is impossible to conceive. But to the analyst sensitive to the cultural peculiarity of such words, more than a negative argument would seem necessary to define them.[20]

In brief, by generalizing culturally particular views of human acts, intentions, and beliefs, Searle fails to recognize the ways that local practices give shape at once to human actions and their meanings. Ignoring context, he discovers that linguistic action can be classified in universal (and essentially subjective) terms, but in so doing he projects misleading patterns on our categories of speech.

SEARLE'S BIASES AND ILONGOT NAMES FOR ACTS OF SPEECH

I now compare Ilongot notions about acts of speech to the five categories (assertives, directives, commissives, expressives, declarations) proposed by Searle (e.g., 1976, 1979f) as the foundations for a cross-cultural typology of linguistic action.[21] While Searle's categories provide a reasonable heuristic for introducing speech act verbs, the *rationale* that he details proves unsuccessful as a gloss on Ilongot materials. Some of Searle's limitations are methodological: One imagines that a comparable investigation of cultural ordering among English acts of speech would present comparable points of challenge. But most important, the

Ilongot data show that accounts of verbal action cannot reasonably proceed without attention to the relations between social order, folk ideas about the world, and styles of speaking.[22]

Assertives.[23] Searle's first category grants "propositions" the status of an act, one of *asserting* something true or false about the world. Assertive acts, to Searle, may range from "boasts" to "answers," "explanations," "statements," "arguments," and "claims." Their names are such familiar "referential" verbs that form the stock-in-trade of politicians, legal witnesses, and academics who are professionally concerned with certainty and proof. And I imagine that this fact itself may be related to their philosophical salience.[24] Surely, the many comparable Ilongot names for acts of speech – *'upu* "word, to talk"; *petpek* "to explain"; *sibēr* "to answer"; *reteb* "to guess"; *ta'en* "to think, to say, to resemble"; *tudtud* "story, to tell a story"; *tadēk* "story, to tell a story"; *bēita* "gossip, to gossip, to report"; *purung* "oratory, to orate"; *'aked* "to give (words), to speak, to advise" – are associated with quite different institutions and conventional concerns.[25]

Thus, much as in English, Ilongot assertive verbs are sometimes used as true performatives, that can announce assertive acts:

'eg ki pa 'entudtudēk "don't speak, I'm going to tell a story";

'upuluwengku diyu petpeki tuy ma 'en'ara'anden "I'll tell you in full, explaining all, what they are doing";

rawengku diyu 'akedi tuy ma 'u'likin bēyak nun . . . "I'm going to give you my little bit of knowledge, to the effect that . . ."

And yet, far from addressing a concern for truth, my understanding is that words like these are used with different purposes and in different sorts of contexts. Heard most frequently at the beginnings of encounters, or in oratorical debate, Ilongot verbs describing statements and accounts clearly have less to do with ascertaining truths than with ongoing formulations of relationship and claims, through a discussion that alludes repeatedly to the character of discourse:[26]

'away bērita'engku say bi'ala legem "I have no news to tell, it's just that the old lady . . .";

ten tum a'enakay nawengku diyu 'upuwi nu nagiata "don't think I am going to speak bad, aggressive, words to you . . ."

'awana purung, legema 'entudtudēk "this isn't oratory, I'm just going to tell a story."

Ilongots will, of course, make clear at times that some of what they say is hearsay, some experienced truth. But they will rarely dwell on arguments designed to ferret out an undetermined fact, or clarify the accuracy of an assertion. Rather than pursuing truths, Ilongot speakers seem inclined to grant each other privileged claims to things that all, as individuals, may claim to "know." And so – much less concerned with factual detail than with the question as to who withholds, and who reveals, a knowledge of well-bruited fact – Ilongots use denial and assertion in discourse as a device for the establishment of interactional roles. [27]

Thus, for example, I have known Ilongots to deny that they had taken heads of kin of interlocutors who in fact *had* been their victims in the past, and then, when challenged, to pronounce a readiness to undergo dangerous ordeals and oaths in order to test the mettle of accusers who appeared less certain, or more fearful, than they thought themselves. Clearly, at times like these, my secretive friends were not concerned with telling lies or telling truths. As always, what they claimed was "true" depended less on "what took place" than on the quality of an interaction where what mattered most was who spoke out and claimed the privilege to reveal or hide a public secret hitherto clothed in silence.

To "be the one to tell you that," "let out a secret hidden in my heart," "go at you with my words," "share knowledge," or "tell stories" are, then, in most Ilongot speech, a matter less of representing facts about the world in words, than of articulating relationships and claims within the context of a history that is already known. Or stated otherwise, assertives used in a performative mode – especially in formal speech – appear equivalent to a variety of devices used to talk about alliance and opposition in particular social groups by talking about the character of spoken words. Thus, artful oratory is replete with cautious qualifying verbs:

bukud ma sa'usa'ulengku dimu 'upuwa   "well, what I will just, uncertainly, say to you";

'ebtarengku saws as away . . .   "I guess, wildly (what you want to hear)";

verbs marking boundaries and relations in discourse:

nu 'alagam 'iman   "if you are finished there";

'etu'etuydengengku duduwala maman   "I'll extend that (idea) with just two words";

'awana rawengku ma rawenmu 'engara'i 'empupurunga   "I will not go for (address) the things you are going to get at in your oratory";

and metaphors designed to qualify the speaker's actions:

siya'ak ta 'umuri bumugkut ten betar nima lapura   "I'll be the one to run ahead again (and speak out) since it's the way with young dogs";

pebtuwenta 'ipani'ungip'ungiptan 'upu   "(let's talk until) we are filled up, contented, from hand feeding one another words";

aligsi nud ma ke'ewengtu 'away tulanitu legema renērekbuta   "(my heart is something) we can compare to a new plant (*'eweng*?), without roots or thorns, and so easy to pull up (i.e., I hold nothing back)."

And what these share has less to do with ways certain words can represent the world than with the fact that speakers' naming and describing their assertive acts itself becomes the stuff of verbal duels – becomes a medium for the construction and manipulation of social bonds. Assertive verbs appear, in short, as counters in confrontations with one's "same" or equal men. As such, they help to shape discourse. Their power seems much closer to the force that Searle assigns to our "declaratives" than to assertive acts like "arguing" and "stating facts."

Directives.   Unlike assertives, Ilongot names for their *directive* acts are rare in oratory or in speakers' own accounts of their ongoing speech. Where they emerge, instead, is in the conduct and the criticism of everyday social interaction:

ngaden 'itu 'ed metuydeka 'anaka   "what kind of children are these, who won't be commanded";

nii ta sinengtengku dimu   "now (don't forget) what I ordered you to do";

'enngadenanmuwak bēt   "are you naming, ordering, accusing me?"

Along with *tudyek,* or "commands," directive acts include as well: *bēge* "to ask, request"; *tengteng* "to order, warn, instruct"; and *tukbur* "to forbid." In addition, there are a set of verbs more limited in directive sense: *'ungi'ungi* "to coax, plead"; *tawaw* "to call, summon"; *maiw* "to ask to stay, stall"; and compounds like *pekamu* "to cause, tell to hurry," formed by linking the causative prefix *pe-* to the root *kamu* "hurry, to be fast."

All directive acts have multiple possible realizations in everyday Ilongot speech, although (much as in English) few actually appear as first person incompletive aspect performatives, of the form, "I order you . . ." or "I command . . ." But while overt performatives are rarely heard in Ilongot discourse, the "force" intended by particular directive acts is characteristically made clear through use of recognized and stereotyped linguistic formulae. Thus, the typical *tuydek,* or "command," makes use of modal verbs like *raw* "go and," *geptay* "cut off an activity and," *durut* "hurry and," *legem* "just":

rawmu ma dēnum   "go for the water";

'irawi itakduwi   "go and fetch water for me";

legemka raw 'engriyak   "just go get some rice from the granary";

geptaymu pa dēken 'iya'den   "interrupt yourself a moment to go up the hill for me (and see if . . .)."

Stereotyped *tukbur* ("prohibitions") – heard both in daily speech and in the formulaic lines of magic – employ imperative negation (*'ed/'eg mu/ka Vb.*):

'eg kin 'anak 'en'upu'upu   "don't keep talking, you children";

'ed musu dēdengēra   "don't listen to him";

'eg kan pagi mendēdēsi dēsi pagi   "don't, rice, act foolish (lose your fertility), rice."

And *tengteng* ("orders, warnings") – found in magical spells, in daily salutations and goodbyes, as well as oratorical encounters – typically use *ten,* "because," plus an incompletive verb to issue words of warning:

ten mita'engka   "don't let yourself fall";

ten tuma 'engkay' amunga dimayu kami   "don't think we have become lazy, silent, unwilling to talk";

ten rawenmu 'ipeka'kanamkanama'i   "don't go making a lot of this, speaking more than is necessary."

A general reluctance to assert unequal bonds in words may well explain the fact that while one hears, "I ask you to . . . ," performative use of most directive verbs seems odd. Ilongots in general understood, but tended to correct my efforts to perform directives that began, "I forbid . . . ," "I summon . . . ," or "I warn . . . ."

In Ilongot, as in English, one can formulate directive acts with reference to a speaker's wants. But while one can say, for example:

kermakangku ma dēnum   "I want the water";

say ramakku ma 'u'ursige 'upu   "I want (you to speak in) straight, noncontentious words";

kermakangku nem 'enakduka   "I would like for you to fetch water,"

with a recognized directive sense, it seems to me that utterances like these, much like overt performatives, were rarely heard, and that in general, they implied much less sincere desire than an unwarranted claim to precedence on the directing speaker's part.[28]

Again, Ilongot speakers questioning if hearers could or would perform as asked ("can you take out the garbage") did not use the verb *giwar* "can, with reference to ability or skill," but *medarum* "can," implying "is it possible, would it be appropriate to act," as in *medaruma rawenmy dēken ma panak* "could you go and get my arrow," (although here too, my data indicate that even this directive form was seen as awkward). Certainly, only children spoke in terms of *giwar,* and they did this not in issuing commands but in attempting to evade unwanted tasks: *'awana giwarengku* "I can't do it (i.e., I will not perform as asked)."

What these and the facts discussed above suggest is that, while Searle's category of *directives* may hold in Ilongot as much as in English speech, the rules and the significances associated with Ilongot directive acts are, in most important ways, quite different from the ones that Searle proposes. Like us, Ilongots vary their directives by speaking of the mode or manner of an act; describing things that should be done; questioning the appropriateness of tasks; or otherwise, appealing to the expectations that decide prerogatives and claims in everyday communication. But where Ilongots may differ most significantly from ourselves[29] is that, for them, *overt directive formulae are not construed as harsh or impolite.* And this, I would suggest, is true because directive use is seen as having less to do with actor-based prerogatives and wants than with relationships affirmed and challenged in their ongoing social life.[30]

Reflections on Ilongot may thus highlight an apparently universal fact that Searle is blind to. Directive acts, unlike assertives, tend to be characterized by uptake-demanding verbs.[31] Or, stated otherwise, directive acts are vacuous unless acknowledged. To "ask," of course, demands an "answer," and to "command," insofar as one is "heard," is to require "compliance." Ilongot directive verbs thus form a class with such Ilongot acts as *'amit* "to demean, belittle", *bēngen* "to insult," *maduran* "to voice disappointment," *pakiw* "to criticize, find fault," in that they typically initiate what Sacks (1973a) has called "adjacency pairs" – routines wherein the utterances that follow them are necessarily heard as "answers" (*sibēr*), "agreements" (*tebēr*); "acknowledgments, acceptances" (*telu*), or else "counters, denials" (*sima'lad*).

As Searle would argue, then, directive utterances may generally be seen as an attempt to match the world to spoken words. But their power to do this depends upon their placement in socially organized conversational contexts. Not only is their happiness dependent on the relationships and expectations particular interactants claim; their social significance itself is indissociable from their vulnerability to disregard.

Commissives, Expressives. Not surprisingly, given my remarks above, Searle's categories of *commissive* and *expressive* acts differ from the assertives and directives previously discussed in that they lack substantial Ilongot exemplars. One can communicate a firm intent to act by adding an intensifying (/-Vl-/) affix to first person incompletive verbs:

upuluwengku ma 'eg kusu kē'weri   "I say (and mean) that I won't forget (to do) it";

'arale'engku tuy ma 'embēge'enmu   "I'll really do what you are asking."

But utterances such as these could also mean, "I say it over and over . . . ," or "I am intent on, exerting myself in doing . . . ," where no element of "commitment" is involved. Similarly, numerous enclitics can be used in something like "expressive" acts of speech, wherein, for example, *'anin* "oh dear," may signal acts of *dimet* "pity," and *ngu'dek* "unfortunately," communicates a feeling of *kidē'ri* "sympathy, desire to help." But overwhelmingly, expressive acts like these appear concerned with only fleeting recognition of such things as limitation, longing, misfortune, and distress. Rather than communicate a feeling one might then expect to find sustained in subsequent shows of empathy and regard, their meaning seems the relatively "phatic" one of indicating awareness of, perhaps connection to, disturbing facts at once associated with and distanced from, oneself.

To Westerners, taught to think of social life as constituted by so many individuated cells, prosocial impulses and drives may seem a necessary prerequisite to social bonds, and so the notion of a world where no one "promises," "apologizes,'' ''congratulates,'' ''establishes commitments,'' or ''gives thanks,'' may seem either untenable or anomic. Certainly, when in the field, I was consistently distressed to find that Ilongots did not appear to share in my responses to such things as disappointment or success, and that they lacked expressive forms with which to signal feelings of appreciation, obligation, salutation, and regret, like our ''I'm sorry'' or ''good morning.'' Repeatedly, I was outraged to find that friends who had arranged to meet and work with me did not appear at the decided time – especially as they would then speak not of commitments broken, or of excuses and regrets, but of devices (such as gifts) that might assuage the generally unexpected and disturbing anger in my heart. To them, it mattered that I was annoyed (a dangerous and explosive state), but not that someone else, in carelessness, had hurt and angered me by failing to fulfill commitments I had understood as tantamount to promises.

My point is not, of course, to claim that Ilongots in daily life do not coordinate their plans or that they fail to recognize varying degrees of reliability of people with whom they live and share. But what Ilongots lack from a perspective such as ours is something like our notion of an inner self continuous through time, a self whose actions can be *judged* in terms of the sincerity, integrity, and commitment actually involved in his or her bygone pronouncements. Because Ilongots do not see their inmost ''hearts'' as constant causes, independent of their acts, they have no reasons to ''commit'' themselves to future deeds, or feel somehow guilt-stricken or in need of an account when subsequent actions prove their earlier expressions false. [32]

In linguistic terms, what seem to be the Ilongot equivalents closest to our ''expressive'' and ''commissive'' acts will most often function more like the members of Searle's ''declarative'' class, wherein what matters is the act itself and not the personal statement it purportedly involves. Thus, apparently ''expressive'' acts include, as we have seen, *dimet* ''pity,'' *dē'ri, kidē'ri* ''to express sympathy, to help,'' as well perhaps as *takit* ''love,'' *'imanu* ''greet formally'' and *turun* ''bid farewell.'' As with directives these acts tend to be associated with stereotyped expressive forms. And further, as with all Ilongot acts of speech, it is clear that words of ''pity,'' ''sympathy,'' and the like are apt to have much more to do with social roles and bonds than with the inner feelings they apparently signify.

''Love,'' for example, is characteristically expressed by ''naming'' one's desired object in a dream. And such expressions, in and of themselves, can serve to ''call'' the other's heart, so that it will begin to ''love'' – by interacting with – oneself. Expressions of ''sympathy'' may similarly assert, and thus create, new social ties. One does not begin by ''feeling'' sympathy and then decide to act; instead, it is through shows of care and help that ''sympathy'' is known. In fact, it is because ''expressive'' acts in word or deed can, in and of themselves, give rise to social bonds, that the Ilongot fear of ''pity'' from the dead makes sense: only death can come of sustained links with the departed.

Thus, for dead ancestors to say *'anin* "oh dear," in pity for still living kin, as for adults to voice a sense of "pity/longing" for once youthful bodies, or then again, for killers to pronounce their "pity" towards the victims of headhunting raids – involve, in every case, the forging of new kinds of ties through recognition of their lack. And just as headhunters can hope to be envigorated through the establishment of mystic bonds to their poor victims' lives, so the old may feel enlivened by their reminiscences of youth – and living people ordinarily will fear increased involvement with beloved departed. Finally, we can begin to understand why "farewell" (*turun*) songs from women to young headhunters when the latter leave on raids appear to make a very special claim upon the would-be killers' hearts: accomplished headhunters recount that they were "shameful" to return without successful boasts to answer women's words, and further, that before attacking, they required special rituals to expunge the weighty thoughts and feelings born of their connection to the female dirge.

Apparently expressive acts do not, of course, in every case, have social and affective implications of such weight. But while at times statements of feeling seem no more than revelations of affective truths, it seems in general that as Ilongots give voice to aspects of their inner hearts, they are likely to be engaged in something we would see as a "declarative" and creative act, which holds immediate consequences for the character and quality of social life itself. Feelings are not the sorts of things one nurtures and then, necessarily, reveals. If silenced, they will typically have no effect. But if evoked in an expressive act, they can well change the world. I can think of only one "expressive" – the *'imanu* "formal greeting" – for which this characterization does not hold. And since *'imanu*s are, like taunts and insults, devices used primarily to announce a stalwart presence and then call for a response, they should probably be distinguished from "farewells" and sounds of "pity," as "expressives" that resemble not "declaratives" but "directives" in their force.

A similar argument can, I think, be made for the two Ilongot verbs with an apparently *commissive* function.[33] The closest Ilongot equivalent to our "promise" is called *sigem,* a formulaic oath by salt, wherein participants declare that if their words prove false, their lives, like salt, will be "dissolved." But Ilongot oaths are different from our "promises" in the central fact that *sigem* speaks not to commitments personally assumed (and for which subsequent violators might, as individuals, be held in fault) but to constraints based on external, "supernatural" sorts of law.

Some years ago, for instance, an old man accidentally dropped his load of game upon a gun (not his own) that fired and killed him. Because of circumstance, his death was construed as punishment for the breaking of an oath of peace by a young nephew who, in killing enemies sworn as friends, provided supernatural cause for the loss of the unfortunate old man. And yet, to my surprise, immediate kin of the deceased did not seek recompense from the young man whose violent actions had apparently "caused" the accident in the first place. Whereas I thought that blame belonged to the young man who violated the oath, my friends declared that "angry" vengeance would have turned upon the innocent owner of the accidentally triggered gun, had he not subsequently died.

Thus, where our "promises" assume that things like blame, intention, and responsibility are all intimately linked, Ilongots in a case like that described above ignore the very issues we find necessary in deciding obligation, wrong, and right. They fixed their "anger" on the man whose gun occasioned harm, and sought, not an acknowledgment of "doing wrong," but a repayment, on the one hand, from the man who owned the gun, and on the other, from the one-time enemies who had been party to the now disastrous "promise."

In subsequent years, the Ilongots concerned made known a sense of wariness and distrust toward the oath-breaking younger man. But only when their one-time enemies asked that gifts be given in exchange for kin of theirs whom the unruly youth had killed, was he made answerable, not to the "broken" oath, but to the *enemy* death he caused. In short, within a world in which "intentions" are not understood as "cause," no agreement is quite like the "promise" we know because the involved parties need not ask who is "responsible" for subsequent events as long as all can recognize the objects and the perpetrators of loss.

Of course, most peoples' actions bear some resemblance to their words. But in those rare cases where a violation does in fact occur, appeal is made, not to the obligations particular persons have assumed, but to dynamics in which damaged parties either damage others or demand some recompense for hurt. "Blame" is thus dissociated from one's "disappointment" with another's failure to perform as hoped. Violations have much less to do with breach than with the suffering occasioned by one's (innocent or guilty) deeds. And friendly dealings are established through declarative "oaths by salt," that provide a context wherein enemies can hope to forge a sense of kin-like bonds.

As a last and related example, I would remark that regular appeal to an external (although not "supernatural") constraint is used by Ilongots to secure agreements that they forge by tying knots in strings to count the days until encounters (*getur*). When such arrangements fail, blame will most likely fall, not on the individuals involved, but on the string itself. As with the *sigem* promise, then, *getur*-agreements forged in knots are not properly "commissive" acts, because a string – external to the actors' selves – is seen as bearer of the expectations, plans, and bonds that it evokes.

Declarations.   These speech acts are, for Searle, all cases where mere "saying so" can really change the world, by virtue of the fact that, given interactants' roles, some one of them is privileged to declare the others "married," "guilty," "innocent," "cursed," or "fired." Utterances where the supernatural is evoked may, similarly, have this sort of "strong" illocutionary force because transforming action is (at least potentially) performed in the mere uttering of the appropriate words themselves. [34] And in a somewhat different way, declarative force belongs as well to numerous metalinguistic acts, like "I define" and "I conclude," which in and of themselves decide the nature of ongoing talk.

Of course, traditional Ilongots do not enjoy such things as churches, court-rooms, offices, and schools, all institutional forms, wherein the power of words as acts is indissociable from positions of recognized authority. For Ilongots, there are no roles or contexts wherein individual speakers can expect, definitively, to change their world, at least in part because their lives are far too fluid to assure that any utterance is certain to be "heard." Thus, it is hardly surprising that the Ilongot speech acts most obviously related to Searle's "declarative" class are those whose power depends not on a human interlocutor's ear, but the attentions of diffuse, yet ever present, supernatural forces. And though in every case, effectiveness de-pends upon one's luck in "hitting" the "right words" in speech, a variety of "invocations" (*nawnaw*) – including "magical spells" (*nawnaw, 'aimet*), "curses" (*'ayu*) and "boasts" (*'eyap,* which are, at times, capable of causing harm to less accomplished fellows) – provide clear instances of "declarative" acts wherein formulaic expressions, if uttered in the appropriate tones, may lead directly to more joy or suffering in one's immediate environment.

Considering strictly "supernatural" or "invocational" verbs alone, the set of Ilongot declarative acts appears quite small – a fact one might associate with their relatively low level of institutional differentiation. But such a characteriza-tion would, I think, prove far from adequate in light of facts discussed above, where all but Ilongot "directive" verbs were characterized as "declarative" in their force. Thus, I suggested that apparently "assertive" verbs, used most frequently in oratorical debates, are like "declaratives" in that they operate as "metalinguistic" glosses on political relationships that are forged in a discussion where the speakers are concerned not just with "what took place," but with the way the past will be described and used in present talk. In naming verbal actions, assertive verbs are thus in fact employed much less to clarify, than to impose, the terms through which debate proceeds; they help create/define a social world by stressing its unfolding form in ongoing political discourse. The same, of course, is true of much English assertive speech: in saying what the world is like, authoritative figures manage to impose their versions of reality. But whereas it is common practice for English speakers. to confront an assertive statement with a discourse honed to test its claims to truth, Ilongots seem much less concerned with what is said than who it is who gets to name which point of fact, and how, given relationships immediately at stake, the statement of that point of fact is to be relationally construed.

Again, although for rather different reasons, I have argued that most of the possible members of Ilongot "commissive" and "assertive" groups should actually be seen as "declarations." Although in English, too, it seems that the expression of emotions can be a way of making claims, Ilongots differ from us in a tendency to focus less on *feelings* harbored deep within the self, than on the way that feelings *spoken* may – like tears that bring disaster in their wake –

themselves shape human worlds. In fact, it makes but little sense to speak of Ilongot "expressive" acts because Ilongots do not think in terms of inner "feelings" needing to emerge, but rather of social contexts in which people do or do not take for granted previously asserted claims and bonds.

OF CULTURE AND CLASSIFICATIONS

My review of Ilongot categories of acts of speech might lead modern philosophers to conclude that Ilongots, unfortunately, have not evolved the subtleties enjoyed by us – perhaps because of "supernatural" orientations (or "under-differentiated" social forms) that preclude our psychological grasp of human persons.[35] And yet my point has been a very different one of challenging our common sense, so as to better think about relationships that link a set of categories of forms of action to the sociocultural world where they are used. Although one can, in Ilongot, discriminate verbal actions in terms of categories like those proposed by Searle—and demonstrate, in English, that discriminations such as his may be misleading for the analyst concerned with interactive functions—the *cultural* limitations of Searle's categories and his assumptions about individuated human selves appear precisely in the fact that Ilongots do not appear to find in one another's speech appropriate circumstance to talk about or query Searle's concerns. Ilongots lack "out" interest in considerations like sincerity and truth; their lives lead them to concentrate, instead, on social bonds and interactive meanings. And so, where Searle proposes speech act categories that correspond to speakers' states, for Ilongots I suggest instead that verbal actions be divided into *those which roughly correspond to social situations wherein norms of "sameness" and autonomy prevail,* and *those belonging to relationships be defined by continuity and hierarchy.*

The division is a crude one. Interactants mix their modes. But what I am proposing is that, just as *sameness* and *hierarchy* can be seen as interdependent moments in Ilongot social life, so Ilongot speech acts may be grouped, roughly, into two categories. The first – including Searle's apparently "expressive," "commissive," "assertive," and "declarative" sets – may be distinguished by the fact that they can "act" upon the world without demanding interlocutor response. The second – clearly recognized as a category in Ilongot folk reflections upon speech – involve "directive" speech acts wherein relation, even hierarchy, is characteristically presupposed and utterances include demand for uptake from one's fellows. The clearest case of acts belonging to the first, "declarative" set, are those in which mere saying so creates a challenge, mere longing makes one's fellows ill – those cases where, in short, the act of speech itself creates a bond defining the relations of potentially autonomous and unconnected selves. By contrast, verbal actions like directives that require a response depend upon, as they articulate, ongoing daily patterns of cooperation, care and talk. The *tuydek,* or command, is thus, as we have seen, at least in part a paradigmatic act of speech because Ilongots use directives to articulate and display ongoing kinship bonds.

In separating *tuydek* as a category from all other acts of speech, I may be motivated, in part, by the universal presence of imperative and interrogative (i.e., "directive") verbal modes in human language. But I would argue that for Ilongots the special status of directives makes good social sense as well. Ilongot interest in directives is derived, I would suggest, first from a sense that speech is of necessity embedded in and so dependent on a pattern of (often asymmetrical) relational bonds; and secondly, from an awareness that the hierarchies that define their everyday cooperative affairs are also daily undermined, so that the order in their world is not a thing accomplished for all time, but an achievement needing constant recreation.

In general, the analytical distinction I have drawn, between "declaratives" and "directives" among Ilongot acts of speech appears consistent with their ways of organizing – and understanding – social action. And categories of speech acts that they recognize with distinctive verbal names reflect indigenous concerns with order in their social world.

In order to illustrate this point I focus again on directives. Dimensions necessary to a grasp of how Ilongots differentiate directive acts at once confirm my previous observations concerning Ilongot sociality, and help me demonstrate the sense in which varieties of action are themselves the products of the ways relationships are organized and understood by native speakers.

In general, Ilongots claim, "commands" or *tuydek* should be distinguished from related acts of speech – like "prohibitions" (*tukbur*), "orders, warnings" (*tengteng*), "requests" (*bēge*), "appeals" (*'ungi'ungi*) and a variety of unclassified directives that include such things as "awakening" (*pabēngun*) and "hurrying up" (*pekamu*). And even though they were aware of ambiguity and difficulty in discriminating among such acts as these, informants found it reasonable to assign directive utterances different directive names – and in so doing, to reflect on meanings implicated in their names for verbal deeds.

How then were various directive acts distinguished? Neither grammar nor a concern for things like deference and "face" emerged consistently in Ilongot talk about directives. "Is there some water here" and "give me water" were not distinguished as a "soft" request versus a "hard" command form. Nor did employment of grammatically distinct imperatives correlate in any simple way with the varieties of directive use.[36] Certain formulae, illustrated above, proved unambiguous markers of such things as "warnings," "supplications," and "prohibitions." But, as will be seen in discussion of directive categories below, the issues that consistently emerged as most salient in indigenous discussions of varieties of directives used had less to do with our concern for things like proper form and indirection, deference and politeness, than with Ilongot views of the cooperative activities that a directive act evoked.[37]

ILONGOT DIRECTIVE ACTS

1. *Tuydek* "Commands." As already indicated, *raw* "go and," as well as certain other modal verbs, appear to mark the prototypical *tuydek*. Further, and not surprisingly, Ilongots asked to give examples of *tuydek* characteristically use *raw*-forms in conjunction with verbs that name routine domestic tasks. In addition (and again as seen above) the use of different modal verbs, subjunctive forms, and verbal foci, may serve to "soften" a command's intended force, but they do not themselves suffice to turn instances of *tuydek* into unambiguous cases of "appealing/pleading" or "requesting." Instead, commands are singled out from other directive forms in terms of the kind and character of action they call forth.

What seems distinctive about *tuydek* are, thus, three things: (a) the call for an activity marked by interruption/movement; (b) appeal to social hierarchies and expectations of unequally distributed knowledge, energy and skill; and (c) concern for finite, easily realized, sorts of tasks.

(a) First – as is suggested by the cultural fact that *tuydek* typically are received by those most likely to "get up" and move (and similarly, by those thought generally to be least "focused" in their "concentration") – "commands," unlike "requests," require motion. Imperatives are not in general seen as *tuydek* if they do not require addressees to interrupt themselves and move. In fact, the modal verbs used characteristically in *tuydek* – not only *raw* "go for/and", but others like *durut* "hurry and," *legem* "just (go ahead) and," as well as *ra'mut* "unhesitatingly go and," *lipalipa* "cautiously, slowly do it," *'ai* "come, orient toward me and" – all seem concerned with qualifying motion, and so either "softening" or specifying the quality of the activity in which the addressee is to engage. By contrast, a directive that begins, "ask/tell him . . ." is seen in general as an "order, instruction"; and "give me . . . (something near you, or something you already have)" is usually construed as a "request." Directives seen as *tuydek* thus require public manifestation of a quality – mobility – that signifies both the energy and the lack of knowledge that together figure prominently in Ilongot justifications of hierarchicalized directive use.

(b) Second (and as again makes sense given my earlier remarks on how chains of command figure in age/sex hierarchies) the typical *tuydek* calls for services in which one person "moves" out of "respect" or deference towards some other. Thus, not only:

nangatka   "pour it out (into a container)";
'edēm ta   "take, carry this";

but also:

nangasi   "pour me some";
nangasim   "pour some (for someone other than speaker)";
'i'dē'imuwak   "carry it for me, bring it to me";

are all instances of *tuydek*. But interestingly, cooperative actions:

'aika dēken 'emēmekmek   "come with me to chop shrubs in the field";
pemen'ara kisi   "let's work together (in one another's fields)";
'edēm dēken ta   "carry this for me (with implication that I have already been carrying it for a while)";

are seen as instances of "requesting," as are imperatives like "eat" or "drink" in which the beneficiary is not the giver, but the recipient of the command.

(c) Third, *tuydek* are concerned with finite, easily realized sorts of labor. Characteristically, one fulfills *tuydek* not by "promising" or "assuming obligations," but by engaging in required actions in immediate response to the directive utterance itself. Thus, imperatives demanding no particular task or action – like "hurry up," "be cautious," and "wake up" – are seen in general as unclassified directives. Imperatives which specify the time, or place, or persons likely to be implicated in an action (e.g., "fetch me water over there"; "ask him to come") are usually "orders, instructions," as are imperatives that make use of incompletive verbs. And, as already indicated, imperatives in which the addressee is not expected to work for an inactive party are not "commands," or *tuydek,* but *bēge* "requests."

2. *Bēge* "Requests." The class "request," or *bēge,* is easily specified given these comments. In contrast to the English speaker's sense of the "request" as a more indirect, less hierarchical, variety of "command," Ilongots typically assume that what distinguishes "requests" is, first of all, the quality of movement they evoke, and secondly, the sorts of social relationships and claims that they imply. Thus, unlike "commands," Ilongot *bēge,* or "requests," will only rarely involve a major movement from or interruption in the addressee's ongoing action. To ask a woman to prepare a meal: *panganmut X* "feed, prepare a meal, for X"; or fix a betel chew: *pakibi'enmuwak* "fix me a betel chew," are actions recognized as "commands," or *tuydek.* But people saw the following as instances of "requests": *pakanmut X* "feed, give (some of the prepared) food to X"; *pabi'enmuwak* "give me some betel, supplies"; *panabakum* "give (someone) some tobacco." Commonly recognized as "requests," again, are such imperatives as employ the verb *'aa* "to give, to hand" – suggesting that most acts of "giving" do not require the addressee to move: *nara'im ta sabitmu 'embi' enak* "give me your betel pouch, I want to chew"; *nu waden man ta dēnum mad kudilya 'inara'i* "if there is water in the cup, give it to me"; *'aam pa ngu dēken ta* "come on and hand that to me." In fact, one woman told me that "respect" due to an affine keeps her from either "naming" or "commanding" her husband's sister. "All I ever say," she told me, "is so-and-so, now give me that." Significantly, however, when "giving" requires "going for," the directive is classified as a "command": *nara'im 'irawi ta dēnum* "go and get some water to give me."

A second characteristic of requests is that – to the extent that they in fact call for some kind of interrupted action – the goal is either one of securing the addressee's welfare (as is the case in "eat this," "come in," "watch out") or else of winning his or her cooperation with a person who seeks help. Thus,

Ilongots often use a superficially expressive verb in the imperative form, *kadē'-dē'rika* "have pity, please," in uttering request directives; and at still other times, verbal affixes (*meki-, pemen-*) and pronouns (*kita* "the two of us," *kisi* "all of us") implying collective or reciprocal forms of action may be used to turn "commands" into acts recognized as "requests for cooperative aid":

> *'aika dēken mekitakdu*   "come and help me fetch water";
> *'entalabaku kisi ngu*   "let's get to work."

3. *Tengteng* "order, warning." While those imperatives marked unambiguously with a completive verbal aspect are characteristically seen as *tuydek* or "commands," directives classed as *tengteng* are associated either with notions of futurity or with incompletive verbs. Thus, "warnings" may, as we have seen, use *ten* + incompletive verb to warn against an undesired future action:

> *ten tuma'engki . . .*   "don't think . . ." (*-um-* marks incompletive aspect);
> *ten rawenyu dēken . . .*   "don't think . . ." (*-en* here indicates continuity, in marked contrast, e.g., to the *rawmu,* "go and," of commands).

And – almost surprisingly like "warnings"[38] – most "orders" also appear to differ from "command" directives in terms of the (implicit or explicit) verbal aspect they evoke:

> *manakduka mad denum*   "go fetch water at the river" (*mang-* prefix + *takdu,* "to fetch water" may mark incompletive aspect, or else, the sense of incompleteness may belong to the fact that locative information is stressed);
> *(when I leave) mampēpedegkid tu*   "when I leave, you stay here" (*mang-* prefix plus reduplicated *pe-* together suggest continuity);
> *(when you are in the lowlands)'itaiwmu dēken ta . . ."*   (when you are in the lowlands) buy me . . ." (here incompletive aspect seems a function of the introductory clause).

In addition, those imperatives which tell the addressee to "ask" or "speak with" some third party are more likely to be understood as "orders" than "commands":

> *'ibēgēm nud X 'ungkitur nu mawa'wa*   "tell X to come downstream tomorrow";
> *mēkibēgē'im puy nitu bēitatu*   "ask her, for me, what is new";
> *mambēgēka nud ta'u nima lapit*   "ask uncle for a pencil."

Quite possibly, what makes "orders" of directions of this sort is something like the open-endedness of the actions that they call for. To ask someone to ask someone, is, I would suggest, to focus less on finite tasks to be performed within a circumscribed social context than to chart a course of future action with still undetermined limits. By projecting their desires on a yet untested person, place, or context, *tengteng*-givers necessarily extend their view beyond the confines of immediate relations and look instead toward situations wherein present projects lose their relevance and the present speaker is unlikely to retain an instrumental role.

In this respect, pairings of *tengteng*-utterance plus response may well appear, in fact, to have a force resembling that of Searle's commissives. And just as Ilongots may confirm their dates and plans by tying knots in strings to count the days until projected meetings, so it makes sense that many acts of "order/ warning" are accompanied by the tying of a string onto the ordered party's hand. Clearly, the use of such external marks designed to guarantee the force of speakers' words upon another's actions is far from necessary in the case of the more certain, and situationally constrained, "commands."

In summary then, three culturally situated concerns emerge as necessary to a characterization of differences between directives. First, because divisions of labor in terms of sex and age are (as we have seen) conceived by Ilongots in terms of differences in "knowledge" and capacities to "move," directives are distinguished in terms of their concern with interruption/movement. Second, because directives concern coordination of tasks and services in a world where hierarchy is balanced by parity, and autonomy by cooperative work, directives are distinguished in terms of hierarchical as against more mutual or reciprocal chains of service and command. And third, because directives figure centrally in the articulation of a kinship order that is experienced, most of the time, as given, and yet in fact requires repeated realization in concrete cooperative displays, directives differ with reference to the action context that a directive act evokes. In short, indigenous views of human actions and interactions – concerns for movement; for social hierarchy and cooperation; and for the temporal fragility of social bonds – prove necessary to an understanding of conventions that discriminate among directive categories that Ilongots recognize as such.

CONCLUSIONS

It is a social science commonplace that the ways the natives talk about behavior must be recognized as different from the analysts' accounts of how and why they act the way they do.[39] Thus, it seems that analysts more astute than I might well dismiss the bulk of what has been said above as evidence of the confusions that are born from an undeserved love of Oxford. We need not dwell on men like Searle and Austin if what we really want to know is how real people, not philosophers, manage to "do their thing" with words. But my difficulties with a set of categories like those proposed by Searle are not simply those of a behaviorist who claims Searle's data is limited as an account of how real people really act, but those of an anthropologist who insists that action is something constituted by social beings who, in acting, implicate their understanding of the world in which they live.

Surely, Searle's categories are versatile enough to be applied to other peoples' acts of speech. But at the same time, they can be criticized for undue emphasis upon the speaker's psychological state, and corresponding inattention to the social sphere.[40] The fact that "we" stress propositions whereas Ilongots see directives as a paradigmatic act of speech reflects, I think, our relatively individualistic (and sociologically, problematic) view of human sociality and communication. If social relationships are to be recognized in analytical accounts of verbal acts, it will prove necessary to grasp the different ways that social worlds shape things that one can do or say with words by shaping notions about personhood, society, and speech. Thus, the difficulty with such categories as "assertion" and "expression" when applied to Ilongot acts of speech is that they do not help us comprehend the common Ilongot understandings of the designated acts – as these, in turn, are documented both in Ilongot names for verbal acts and in the ways they use these names and understand and answer to each other's speech. Ilongot notions lead, instead, to my proposal that Ilongot speech acts be distinguished as "declaratives" and "directives." And furthermore, Ilongot marking and differentiation of the category of directive acts is something which, we see, makes sense with reference to the ways they think about and order their ongoing social bonds and deeds.

One reason to attend some of the ways in which Ilongot notions of linguistic action differ from the select Western notions documented by Searle is thus to show that certain of our culturally shaped ideas about how human beings act have limited our grasp of speech behavior, leading us to celebrate the individual who acts without attending to contextual constraints on meaning. Ilongot views of language – and, in particular, their emphasis on commands – suggest alternatives to the philosopher's account of referential, individually deployed, systems of speech. They help display the problems that inhere in all attempts to construe action in universal and subjective terms, without regard for how societies and cultures shape our selves, our motives, and our activities. Searle uses English performative verbs as guides to something like a universal law. I think his efforts might better be understood as an ethnography – however partial – of contemporary views of human personhood and action as these are linked to culturally particular modes of speaking.

In sum, there is no question in my mind but that Ilongots conduct social life in ways quite similar to and yet quite different from ourselves – and that these differences are revealed, at once, in how they think about and categorize each other's acts, and in the forms through which their interactions actually proceed. The differences between Ilongot *tuydek* and comparable English directive acts are indissociable from our respective ways of thinking about labor, language, human skill, and human action, and such social facts as "sameness," hierarchy, cooperation, and prestige. And I would argue that these differences, in turn, prove consequential on the one hand, for an analysis of our distinctive socioeconomic forms, and on the other, for a technical understanding of the ways we use our words in speech.

Reflections on Ilongot notions concerning acts of speech should serve, then, as a reminder that the understanding of linguistic action always, and necessarily, demands much more than an account of what it is that individuals intend to say: because, as Ilongots themselves are well aware, the "force" of acts of speech depends on things participants expect; and then again, because, as our comparison makes clear, such expectations are themselves the products of particular forms of sociocultural being.

NOTES

*One of a series of papers commemorating a decade of *Language in Society*.

1.   This paper was written while the author was a Fellow at the Center for Advanced Study in the Behavioral Sciences, partially supported by a grant from the National Endowment for the Humanities. Gregory Accaioli, A. Becker, Eve Clark, Jane Collier, Jean Comaroff, Paul Friedrich, Ian Hacking, Dell Hymes, Beatriz Lavandera, Fred Myers, Carol Pateman, Mary Pratt, Renato Rosaldo, Gillian Sankoff, Michael Silverstein, and Elizabeth Traugott are all to be thanked for their helpful conversations and comments.

2.   This goal – essentially, of characterizing the necessary interaction between action and structure, instrumentality and meaning – is more or less explicitly recognized as a central problematic in much modern social theory. See, e.g., Giddens (1976), Bourdieu (1977), or the recent polemic by Thompson (1978) against Althusser (1971).

3.   The claim, of course, is not a new one. It has been developed in a variety of ways in the literature associated with the Ethnography of Speaking (e.g., Gumperz & Hymes 1972; Bauman & Sherzer 1974). Recently, M. Silverstein (1979) has made a suggestive, and relevant, argument concerning the relationship between cultural tradition, linguistic form, and dominant theories about language, insisting that our representational view of linguistic phenomena is at once the product of our ways of speaking and the cause of a certain conservatism in our conceptions of how language works. For an earlier and still important formulation of the interdependence of conceptions of action, personhood, moral order, and modes of speech, see K. Burke (e.g., 1950).

4.   Although reference to "speech acts" is found in the work of quite diverse authors (e.g., Voloshinov 1973; Hymes 1972), and was not, to my knowledge, used by Austin – the notion of "speech act theory" tends to refer to developments initiated by Austin's discussions of the "performative/constative" distinction and of "illocutionary force" (1962, 1963), receiving their fullest formulation in the writings of the Berkeley philosopher, John Searle (1965, 1969, 1976, 1979a). The 1970s saw the adoption of speech-act-theoretic concepts by linguists (see, Cole & Morgan 1975; Saddock 1974), literary critics (e.g., Fish 1979; Pratt 1978; Searle 1979d) and anthropologists (e.g., Ahern 1979; Tambiah 1973), as well as numerous philosophers – largely, I think, because of their promise to relate the formal study of language to questions of the use and effectiveness of speech. It is because of the wide-ranging appeal of the theory that I think it worthwhile to try to clarify – from a sympathetic, and yet empirically oriented perspective – one critical (and largely unnoted) area where it goes wrong.

5.   Research among the Ilongots of Northern Luzon, Philippines, was conducted by Renato Rosaldo and myself over a period of nearly two years in the late 1960s and again in 1974 (under the sponsorship of a National Institute of Health Predoctoral Fellowship and a National Institute of Health Research Grant, 5 FI MH-33, 243-02, BEH-A, and a National Science Foundation Research Grant No. GS-40788). For additional sources on Ilongot language and culture, see M. Rosaldo 1972; 1973; 1975; 1980; and R. Rosaldo 1980.

6.   For a detailed sketch of Ilongot phonology (and aspects of Ilongot grammar), see M. Rosaldo 1980. In reading the examples to follow, the following conventions should be noted: /e/ is a low mid vowel; /ē/ is a lengthened, high mid vowel; /r/ is a voiced velar fricative; /'/ is a glottal stop; /i/ and /u/ are front and back vowels respectively, with high and low allophones determined, in large part, by the preceding consonant.

7.   The interrelations between headhunting, violence, gender concepts, and notions of obedience and respect in everyday affairs are developed in M. Rosaldo (1980; n.d.b). Collier & Rosaldo (in press), provide a model for interpreting these and other aspects of Ilongot society and culture.

8.   Recently, some extremely suggestive work has been done on the relationship between syntactic alternates and politeness phenomena cross-linguistically, wherein it is suggested, e.g., that "indirection," the use of passives, and of qualifications as to name, modality, and so on, may all figure in complex attempts by speakers to appear at once effective and polite (for different, but not unrelated

inquiries, see Ervin-Tripp 1976; Brown & Levinson 1978; Searle 1975, 1979b). Part of my purpose here and in what follows is to point to some of the limitations of our (implicitly, I think, universalizing) ideas of politeness – by suggesting that concerns for "politeness" themselves are dependent on local forms of social inequality and hierarchy, forms which differ considerably between such relatively "egalitarian" peoples as the Ilongots and ourselves. Consequently, I would argue, Ilongots use and elaborate linguistic resources in ways that do not correspond with our categories; the semantics of their linguistic varieties is not random, but it cannot be understood without some appreciation of the distinctive conceptual and relational shape of Ilongot society.

9.   That variation in directive forms may be concerned not just with etiquette but urgency and speed is indicated in Lavandera's (1977) discussion of Argentine Spanish, suggesting that some of the considerations raised by my Ilongot analysis may well have cross-linguistic analogues. In fact, it may turn out that emphasis on simple notions of "power" and "solidarity" in much sociolinguistic analysis reflects the poverty of our analytical grasp of human social life.

10.   Stated otherwise, it seems to me that we cannot understand Ilongot acts of *tuydek* without some grasp of the ways that Ilongots themselves construe their social context; our understandings of speech acts cannot be linked directly to our views of universal human nature without some attempt to reconstitute their immediate "world." In a related vein, see P. Ricoeur (1971) who argues that "inscribed" human behavior (i.e., social science data) is like a literary text lacking an ordinary communicative context, and so requiring some sort of situating in a world or context if the things it "says" are to be "understood."

11.   A more detailed study of children's linguistic-learning-of-relationships would include an account of "learning to plead" (*kidē'ri*), which is almost simultaneous with "learning to obey commands." These reflections were occasioned, in part, by consideration of Ilongot similarities and contrasts to the Kaluli described by Schieffelin (n.d.). Kaluli children learn about (by learning to perform within) a special sort of sibling bond in which one party's "pleading" guarantees that the other will obey.

12.   Michael Silverstein points out (personal communication) that, as directive verb forms are often unmarked, this result may be an accident. I think not. When asked, for example, for a gloss on "to cross a river," one schoolboy wrote, "the game I killed is across the river, go across and get it''; for a gloss on "to belittle", I received, "I am your equal, do not belittle me." Most instances resemble these in having a clearly intended directive sense.

13.   "Most" here refers to dominant themes in "generative" (or structural) linguistics. Surely, there have been other – and more sociological – schools of linguistic thinking, from Wittgenstein to Whorf, Sapir, Malinowski, Hymes, and Halliday. At the same time, it seems to me fair to say that "functional" linguistics has not enjoyed the centrality of more "structural" schools, and that many would-be sociological or cultural linguistic thinkers tend in fact to see issues of "use" and "function" as things "added on" to a proposition-making core. Surely, this characterization is appropriate to all theorists who are concerned to differentiate, e.g., "utterance/sentence meaning" from "speaker's meaning" or "statement meaning" (e.g., Searle 1969; Graham 1977), in a manner that construes the relative stability of the former as a condition for the latter. Although his formulation is somewhat different, Grice's work is based on rather similar views. Thus, Grice argues that our conversational maxims are formed with reference to "the particular purposes . . . that talk is adapted to serve . . . . I have stated my maxims as if this purpose were a maximally effective exchange of information; this specification is, of course, too narrow and the scheme needs to be generalized to allow for such general purposes as influencing or directing the actions of others" (1975: 47). Whatever the difficulties with his argument (see, e.g., Sapir 1979), M. Silverstein's work (1976) is significant for its suggestion that analyses that begin in a Gricean fashion will never achieve the sort of generalization that Grice himself finds desirable.

14.   Here as elsewhere, constraints of space require that I make general ethnographic statements without elaborating their ethnographic basis. To demonstrate, for instance, the "relativity" built into Ilongot views of truth, I would cite their readiness to acknowledge differences in, e.g., botanical naming practices among adults who "grew up in different houses"; their lack of interest in ascertaining "the facts" when engaged in legal argument; their use of the word *bēya*, or "knowledge" in contexts where what seems to matter is knowing *how* rather than knowing *that*.

15.   With the exception of a few anthropologists (e.g., Finnegan 1969; Foster 1974), interested in highlighting ritual and oratory contexts where speech takes on a special sort of force, none of the recent commentators on Austin (e.g., Graham 1977; Holdcroft 1978) seem to pick up on the

sociological perspective implicit in his account. Part of the problem here, as Paul Friedrich (1979, and personal communication) points out, is that the transformationalist's stress on freedom and creativity has led to a distrust of convention and a systematic discounting of regularized linguistic and social expectations concerning speech. The significance of routines for our grasp of memory and meaning (e.g., Tyler 1978: 229–48) or for an understanding of communication generally is, of course, a central insight among ethnographers of communication (e.g., Hymes 1972: 57). And it seems ironic that those theorists most wedded to freedom and invention seem willing to accept a very narrow view of the sorts of "intentions" likely to be realized in speech. In fact, I would suggest that a good deal of what people like Searle see as inconsistency in Austin's speech act classification derives from the latter's attempt to retain a sense of interactional relevance in his categories; the casual character of Austin's typology is, in part, a testimony to his own scepticism of ever realizing a definitive classification of all forms of action, or all ways of doing things with words. If my reading is correct, Austin remains in spirit a good deal closer than his followers to the (more or less) Marxist claim that forms of action cannot be classified absolutely, but must be analyzed with reference to socioeconomic contexts in which activities are performed (e.g., Giddens 1979; Asad 1979; Voloshinov 1973). It also seems to me that Austin's explorations are much closer to Derridian inquiry (e.g., Derrida 1977) than Searle (1977) allows.

16.   See Anthony Giddens (1976, 1979) for a particularly illuminating discussion of the consequences of an unfortunate division of labor between social scientists, concerned to understand human "behavior" as the product of unintended "forces," and philosophers of "action" who tend to stress agency at the expense of any grasp of social and cultural factors shaping what we do and mean.

17.   A progression can be traced in Searle's published work, from a concern with delimiting the notion of "speech act" and "illocutionary force" by offering illustrative sets of "rules" (1965, 1969), to one with speech act typology or taxonomy (1976, 1979a, 1979f). The two converge, of course, in that many of the "rules" constituting a successful speech act in Searle (essential conditions, propositional content rules, preparatory conditions) are paralleled by the dimensions of his taxonomy (essential, words/world, psychological state). Furthermore, I believe that it is this convergence that gives him confidence in his anti-Wittgensteinian claim that there are, in fact, limited kinds of actions that human beings do, or can, perform with words (1979a: vii). Graham's critique of Austin is also, implicitly, at odds with Searle in this regard (1977: 107–08). Of course, Searle's formulations continue to be modified, expanded, and criticized, both in his own work (1979; Searle & Vanderveken, n.d.) and that of writers who are more or less disturbed than he about the kinds of lines he draws between, for example, semantics and pragmatics (e.g., Katz 1977; Morgan 1975; Labov & Fanshel 1977). Some theorists have tried to prove the relevance of Austin's claims by putting speech acts "under," "over," or "behind" conventional propositional forms in speaker's minds and/or in depths of grammar (Ross 1970; Gordon & Lakoff 1971; Grimes 1975; Saddock 1974; Searle 1975, 1979e). And work by Grice (1975), Strawson (1971), and others concerned with comprehending the very *flexible* rule-governedness of talk has developed in lines essentially compatible with Searle's own. But it remains, unfortunately, the case that the empirical and largely antagonistic voice of ethnomethodologists (e.g., Sacks 1973b; and others, e.g., Ervin-Tripp 1976; Gumperz in press; Rosaldo 1974) interested in how real speakers both interpret and respond to one another's words has not yet managed to enrich the rather abstract and idealized view of conversation characteristic of this dominant philosophical account of talk. In fact, for Habermas (1979), it is just the way in which Searle's theory at once refers to and apparently transcends constraints of actual (and "distorted") forms of talk that makes it useful to philosophers who are concerned to claim that people can communicate in ways more moral, searching, and humane than we do now.

18.   See C. Pateman (1979) for a complementary discussion of the use – and misuse – of concepts of promising in philosophical discussions of political obligation. Although Pateman sees the promise as a crucial concept, mediating an overly "socialized" view of human beings and an "individualizing" stress on free action (which leads to "contracts"), she realizes that promises have, in general, been evoked in essentially individualistic analyses which assume that people accept obligations and make promises without prior obligations and constraints.

19.   I haven't made HIM a promise "since the big one," as my friend, John Haugeland once pointed out. But the example is telling. If we were to consider "oaths of marriage" as meta-promises that hold across all future interactions, we might as well assume that our very entry into (THE, or any) "social contract" constitutes such a "promise," thus mitigating the need to voice commitments in our day-to-day affairs. And yet – to look ahead to my discussion of the Ilongots – the very notion of a "contract" suggests that a particular sort of contingency is built into our social relationships. Social relations elsewhere need not be utterly stable or non-contingent, but if people do not see themselves as bearers of inevitably divisive interests, it may be that such connections as do take hold have less the quality of "contracts" than of inherently incontestable (for Ilongots, "kinship" dissolves when people cease to cooperate or when they argue about their relations) bonds. Furthermore, it may well be that in a world in which people do not assume themselves to be divided, there is no reason to voice "promises" – acts that presuppose division, in order then to make commitments clear.

20.   For critiques in a similar spirit, see the papers by Philips (1976) and Keenan (1976) in *Language in Society*. What both suggest is that terms we use as analytical tokens of necessity are, in fact, culturally "loaded." Thus, for example, while on some level it makes sense to claim that a spoken language only randomly related to beliefs about what is true would not be intelligible, it is also clear that the particular ways in which utterance and "truth" may be related are diverse enough, across contexts and cultures, to make some of Grice's conversational maxims a good deal less powerful than one might think.

21.   As I understand it, Searle would pose two objections before I started. First, he would argue that the fact that not all languages have "evolved" syntactic means for performing, e.g., "commissives," does not undermine the logical status of his categories (1979a: viii) – a point that I would answer by referring to critiques of "evolutionary" biases in Austin (e.g., Graham 1977: 46) and furthermore, insisting that a set of analytical categories that work better for some languages, or cultures, than for others *are* to be suspected on those grounds alone. Second, Searle might argue (as, e.g., do Brown & Levinson 1978), that his appeal to, e.g., indirect speech acts (1975, 1979b), to confirm aspects of his analysis, requires simply that predicted alternates be recognized as intelligible and not that they be idiomatic – a point that I can answer only by suggesting (a) that since contemporary analyses are built upon the idiomatic possibilities of English, we might learn something new from looking elsewhere; and (b) that it seems possible that what emerges, historically, as idiomatic in any language may well reflect culture-specific dynamics, wherein certain speech forms come to be associated with particular (desirable or undesirable) institutions and social contexts. Thus while accepting, e.g., with Vendler (1967: 26), the argument that "the only way of arriving at conclusions that are necessarily true is to explore the necessary truths in some language . . ." and that this limitation does not mean that we are "trapped in the conceptual network of our language ´. . .´", I would insist that philosophers have yet to grapple seriously with the question of the *kinds* of biases that are likely to be built into *our* cultural/linguistic tradition, or of the kinds of things that they might learn through serious investigation of traditions elsewhere in the world.

22.   Although philosophers are unlikely to make use of data of this sort, it is worth noting that English language data *is* used – for the most part, unquestioningly – in philosophical arguments. Thus, to note that, for example, our performative vocabulary seems evenly distributed across the categories designed by Searle; to comment on semantic and grammatical affinities between our names for actions (e.g., "I assert . . .") and their corresponding psychological states ("I believe . . ."); or then again, to recognize the availability (in English) of "indirect speech acts" that appear to work by questioning or asserting, rules that govern more "straightforward" acts of speech – so that, e.g., "I want you to take the garbage out," "the garbage should be taken out," and "can you take the garbage out," may all be roughly similar to a straightforward imperative command – are all rhetorical techniques employed in demonstration that the analyses set forth are philosophically and (of course) empirically well-founded.

23.   In the paragraphs that follow, I may be accused of confusing evidence on "illocutions" (the conventional force, that *constitutes* a kind of action) with evidence on "perlocution" (the actual force, or effect, realized by a particular act of speech). Stated otherwise, I may seem to be lumping rules and behaviors. My response is that ethnographers have no alternative. Searle and Austin both seem to assume that the primary use of performative verbs is one of clarifying the performative force of utterances (in fact, Searle's categories of speech acts all derive from performative verbs). I question this assumption and insist, furthermore, that in lieu of rule-formulating natives (full of "native intuitions"), we can only figure out what people are up to and what their words mean through a dialectic that moves back and forth, from tentative translation to an examination of actual practices. In fact, Searle's analytical technique is similar. Searle learns what constitutes, e.g., an assertion, by considering conventional markings of violations, "you said X but did not believe it . . ." Many of my arguments concerning Ilongot have to do with the fact that, while one is unlikely to hear protests of *this* sort, there is a good bit of "are you trying to answer me . . . ," "I am not orating, just telling news . . ."

24.   Mary Pratt (personal communication) points out that the very salience of "assertions" in recent speech act theory has had the ironic consequence of inhibiting analysis of this class of "acts." Thus, Searle writes on issues concerning "reference" and "predication," but never explores in depth conventional rules which "constitute" varieties of assertive acts.

25.   For more data on these and other Ilongot names for acts of speech see M. Rosaldo (1973, 1980).

26.   See M. Rosaldo (1973, 1980, and n.d.a) for a discussion of the nature of political/legal debate in Ilongot oratory, the lack of concern for "finding out the facts" or "passing judgment" and the ways that "talk about talk" is used to manipulate interactional roles. My work on Ilongot oratory suggests some interesting parallels with the fact that Austin's interest in performatives grew initially from a concern with legal discourse. Surely, it seems no accident that we and the Ilongots use performative verbs in somewhat comparable settings, or that a recognition of language as action would emerge from considerations of contexts – like legal ones – where talk, in fact, can shape the world.

27.   Lavandera (1978) makes a similar claim for the use of the subjunctive in Argentine Spanish, suggesting that analyses that highlight "certainty" may often say more about the concerns of linguists than with the actual salience of particular meanings in informal speech.

28.   The one instance I have recorded comes from an oratorical encounter in which a young, government appointed "captain" tried to direct a bridewealth meeting by telling participants what kind of speech he wanted to hear. As far as I could tell, his self-oriented directives were seen as "the kind of thing that captains (i.e., non-Ilongot leaders) do" and had no influence on the way the debate proceeded.

29.   Gillian Sankoff (personal communication) suggests that bald directives may be more common in American English speech than many of us believe to be the case – an instance of practice deviating from folk expectations. The appropriate conclusion to be drawn, however, is not that evidence of this sort proves Searle wrong about English or shows Ilongots to be identical to ourselves, but instead that we need to learn more about what the American folk rule, "don't be rude or imposing; say please," *means* by asking when it *does* (and when it does not) dictate practice – and why.

30.   Issues of relationship are, of course, at issue in English directive use as well, e.g., "your request is my command." I would guess, however, that the relational concerns at stake in English have largely to do with issues of imposition, i.e., can I impose my will on your activity? For Ilongots, by contrast, the key issues have to do with social relationships and roles, i.e., are you my "child"? What is at stake in English discourse seems to have more to do with a conception of a private and privileged self, leery of imposition; whereas, what matters for Ilongots is the nature of social bonds.

31.   Several analysts (e.g., Sacks 1972; Goody 1978a, 1978b) have noted that an important interactional fact about questions is that they "demand" responses, a fact that makes them particularly relevant to the study of politeness, status manipulation in discourse, and the interaction between individual intentions and contextual facts of power and solidarity as both are realized in speech. My point here is that in Ilongot (and probably universally) "demand for uptake," or for "recognition" may be a general property of "directive," as opposed, e.g., to "assertives": one can "state" although no one hears you, but it seems difficult to "promise" without an audience, and impossible to "command" with no hope of response. It is significant – and disappointing – that this sort of interactional fact has no place in the analysis developed by Searle.

32.   See my discussions of Ilongot notions of exchange, anger, and wrongdoing (M. Rosaldo 1980, n.d.a, n.d.b).

33.   Here I am speaking of the verbs, *sigem* "to swear an oath by salt," and *getur* "to make a date by tying knots in string," both discussed below. One feature of *sigem* is that it is used only in making negative statements of commitment: one swears by salt in promising *not* to kill; more casually, one says, *nansigem.* "I swear by salt," when, e.g., *denying* that one has any betel nuts to share. What then of positive commitment? Two words, *tebēr* "to say yes, agree," and *telu* "to obey," might be considered names for commissive actions – although they can equally describe an action like getting up and fetching water when performed in immediate compliance with a command. I do not treat these here, however, because they, like *sibēr* "to answer," have the property of occurring only as second-pair-part members to directives, and the sense in which they may in fact entail "commitments" binding in the future has more to do with the direction than the response. To me, then, more important than their possible function as "commissives" are the ways they are embedded in discursive interaction, and their affinities with and dependence on directives – properties far from evident in our English "commissive" acts.

34.   The phrase, "strong" illocutionary force, comes from an important and incisive article by Ahern (1979) in which it is argued that even supernaturally oriented "declarations" need not always be assumed to have the same sort of illocutionary power, and that one must attend to native views and institutional contexts in order to determine the particular kind of force speakers intend.

35.   Austin, adopting an evolutionary view, suggested that in "primitive" languages, performative verb forms might not have been available to mark illocutionary force – a view I was appalled to learn that one contemporary critic still finds "plausible" (Holdcroft 1978: 34). Searle seems to agree, although he also writes as though all languages must, of necessity, have performatives or performative-like devices to unambiguously distinguish between such acts as "threatening" and "warning" (1969: 16). My point, of course, is not that performative verbs have nothing to do with (the evolution of) social institutions (quite the contrary!), but rather than an evolutionary view is unacceptable insofar as it does no more than offer theoretical support to the universalistic pretensions of Western ideologies.

36.   Ideally, I would offer at this point a full grammatical account of Ilongot imperatives, but unfortunately, my grasp of Ilongot root classes, affixes, and verbal aspects is still imperfect. For the following discussion, these remarks, however, should suffice:

a) "simple" imperatives are not marked for aspect, although they may at times have an incompletive sense.

i) these verbs typically have the form, *Vb-ka* (actor focus) or *Vb-(i)m* (object focus) as in: *'ekarka di dēnum* "go to the water"; *tawawim si X* "call X."

ii) some "simple" imperatives use the prefix, *mang-*, again, I believe, not marked for aspect: *mangangka* "eat" (root *kan*); *mambēyuka* "pound rice" (root *bēyu*).

iii) again, not marked for aspect are varieties of modal + verb: *rawka manakdu* "go and fetch water"; *rawkasu 'etakduwi* "go over to his place to fetch water."

iv) finally, aspect unmarked imperatives can take a benefactive verbal focus: *'irawi 'itakduwi* "go fetch water for me"; *'irawim si kabu nima 'ula* "go get Kabu a sweet potato."

b) "subjunctive" imperatives use affix *'u: 'engraw'uka 'enakdu* "if only you would go fetch water"; *tunur'umuy tan* "if only you would (would you please) light that."

c) perfective (completive) imperatives use affixes *-im, -in, nang-*: *kimitaka di denum* "go to the water"; *'ingrawmu tuy ma ganagana mad . . .* "put the goods in . . ."; *nangasi* "pour out the water (for me)."

d) imperfective (incompletive) imperatives may use affix *-um-*, or reduplication: *(ten) kumitaka* "(don't) go"; *mangangangka* "eat, eat up, keep eating"; *'eg kin 'en'epu'upu* "don't keep talking."

37.   As E. Traugott (personal communication) pointed out to me, my method in what follows is closer in spirit to that of field, or componential, semantics than to the propositional semantics used by Searle. The choice probably reflects the kind of holistic and relational thinking I find appropriate to a cultural problematic, wherein indigenous ideas and practices are defined through their relations. I would point out, however, that unlike many anthropologists who base analyses on semantic contrasts, I concentrate on the ways in which not only *categories* but *dimensions* must be understood with reference to a cultural field. Ilongot categories of action overlap with our own, but they differ not just in scope but quality. As will be seen in what follows, dimensions that discriminate among these categories are rooted in the Ilongot sociocultural milieu.

38.   Interestingly, Searle (1976: 22) notes a similar ambiguity in the English performative, "I warn you . . ." which can be used either to "warn/forbid" (a directive) or to "warn/advise" (representative, assertive). But where his analysis highlights the disjunction in our uses of "warning," mine suggests that both kinds of Ilongot *tengteng* ("orders" and statements of "warning/advise") are best seen as directives that share an "open-ended" aspectual quality.

39.   For a particularly clear statement of this position, see Ervin-Tripp (1966: 28): "Terms like 'promise', 'tell', 'request' . . . are derived from the vocabulary of indirect speech, in which speech events are reported as categories. . . . But the English verbs used in reporting are not necessarily the best analytical categories for classifying speech events. . . . There is no reason to believe that

English has a good metalanguage for itself. . . ." The difficulty with Ervin-Tripp's position is that it provides no alternative *theoretical* account for discriminating kinds of acts, or functions, and makes the relationship between linguistic "structure" and linguistic "function" a wholly arbitrary one (in radical contrast, e.g., to the sort of intimate linkage scholars like Halliday (1975) propose.) John Dore's (1979) work on conversational acts, wherein conversationally realized typifications of linguistic actions provide the basis for speech act classification seems to meet Ervin-Tripp's behavioral concern and yet give theoretical space to the sorts of cultural and institutional issues considered here.

40. An interesting point about several of the writers who attempt to modify, without rejecting, Searlian speech act classification, is that their modifications move in the direction of adding sociological and interactional dimensions to his taxonomy. Thus, e.g., Labov & Fanshel (1977: 60–61) propose the categories Meta-linguistic, Representation, Request, and Challenge as sufficient to a speech act analysis of therapeutic discourse; Longacre suggests that it is profitable to think about performative verbs "in terms of the various discourse genre with which they are associated" (1976: 251) and in terms of the "resolving utterances" they "solicit" (ibid); Dore (1979) proposes *conversational* as against *speech* (implying sentence-unit?) acts as units of analysis; and Hancher (1979) argues that Searle's taxonomy must be expanded to include what he calls "cooperative" speech acts, like betting. I am in sympathy with these revisions, but wish that the theorists concerned had recognized the ways in which their emendations tend to undermine the "intentional" (and noninteractional) bias built into Searle's analysis itself. Bach & Harnish (1979) make what is perhaps the most significant attempt in this direction, by speaking of speech acts in the context of a theory concerned with communication and interpretation. For them, "rules" governing performance and interpretation are distinguished from conventions and constitutive meanings, so that, e.g., "sincerity" bears no necessary relation to the use of a conventional token, like "thanks." Their scheme, however, leads to a radical dissociation of "convention" from linguistic action, and thus fails to grapple with the social and interactional character of meaning-produced-in-speech.

REFERENCES

Ahern, E. M. (1979). The problem of efficacy: Strong and weak illocutionary acts. *Man* **14**(1). 1–17.

Althusser, L. (1971). *Lenin and philosophy*. New York: Monthly Review.

Asad, T. (1979). Anthropology and the analysis of ideology. *Man* **14**(4).

Austin, J. L. (1962). *How to do things with words*. J. O. Urmson (ed.). Oxford: Clarendon Press.

——— (1963). Performative-constative. In C. Caton (ed.), *Philosophy and ordinary language*. Urbana: University of Illinois Press. Reprinted in J. R. Searle (ed.), *The philosophy of language*. Oxford: Oxford University Press.

Bach, K., & Harnish, R. (1979). *Linguistic communication and speech acts*. Cambridge, Mass.: MIT Press.

Bauman, R., & Sherzer, J. (1974). *Explorations in the ethnography of speaking*. Cambridge University Press.

Bourdieu, P. (1977). *Outline of a theory of practice*. Cambridge University Press.

Brown, P., & Levinson, S. (1978). Universals in language usage: Politeness phenomena. In E. Goody (ed.), *Questions and politeness*. Cambridge University Press.

Burke, K. (1950). *A rhetoric of motives*. New York: Prentice-Hall.

Cole, P., & Morgan, J. (eds.) (1975). *Syntax and semantics, vol. III: Speech acts*. New York: Academic Press.

Collier, J., & Rosaldo, M. (in press). Sex & politics in simple societies. In S. Ortner & H. Whitehead (eds.), *Sexual meanings*. Cambridge University Press.

Derrida, J. (1977). Signature, event, context. *Glyph* I. 172–97.

Dore, J. (1979). Conversational acts and the acquisition of language. In E. Keenan & B. Schieffelin (eds.), *Developmental pragmatics*. New York: Academic Press. 339–62.

Ervin-Tripp, S. (1976). Is Sybil there? The structure of American English directives. *Language in Society* **5**(1). 25–66.

Finnegan, R. (1969). How to do things with words: Performative utterances among the Limba of Sierra Leone. *Man* **4.**

Fish, S. (1979). Normal circumstance, literal language, direct speech acts, the ordinary, the every-day, the obvious, what goes without saying and other special cases. In P. Rabinow & W. Sullivan (eds.), *Interpretive social science: A reader*. Berkeley: University of California Press.

Foster, M. (1974). When words become deeds: An analysis of three Iroquois Longhouse speech events. In Bauman & Sherzer. 345–67.

Fraser, B. (1975). Hedged performatives. In Cole & Morgan. 187–210.

Friedrich, P. (1979). *Language, context and the imagination*. Stanford: Stanford University Press.

Giddens, A. (1976). *New rules of sociological method*. London: Hutchinson.

———— (1979). *Central problems in social theory*. Berkeley: University of California Press.

Goody, E. (1978a). Introduction. In E. Goody (ed.). *Questions and politeness*. Cambridge University Press.

———— (1978b). Towards a theory of questions. In E. Goody (ed), *Questions and politeness*. Cambridge University Press.

Gordon, D., & Lakoff, G. (1971). Conversational postulates. *Papers of the Chicago Linguistic Society*. Chicago: Department of Linguistics, University of Chicago. 63–84.

Graham, K. (1977). *J. L. Austin: A critique of ordinary language philosophy*. Atlantic Highlands, N.J.: Humanities Press.

Grice, H. P. (1975). Logic and conversation. In Cole & Morgan. 41–58.

Grimes, J. E. (1975). *The thread of discourse*. The Hague: Mouton.

Gumperz, J. (in press). The sociolinguistic basis of speech act theory. In J. Boyd & S. Ferrara (eds.), *Speech act ten years after*. Milan: Versus.

Gumperz, J., & Hymes, D. (1972). *Directions in sociolinguistics: The ethnography of communication*. New York: Holt, Rinehart & Winston.

Habermas, J. (1979). *Communication and the evolution of society*. (Originally published in Germany 1976.) Boston: Beacon Press.

Halliday, M. (1975). *Learning how to mean*. London: Edward Arnold.

Hancher, M. (1979). The classification of cooperative illocutionary acts. *Language in Society* 8(1). 1–14.

Holdcroft, D. (1978). *Words and deeds*. Oxford: Clarendon Press.

Hymes, D. (1964). Introduction: Toward ethnographies of communication. *American Anthropologist* 66(6), part 2. 1–34.

———— (1972). Models of the interaction of language and social life. In J. Gumperz & D. Hymes (eds.), *Directions in sociolinguistics*. New York: Holt, Rinehart & Winston. Revised from *Journal of Social Issues* 23(2): 8–28, 1967.

Katz, J. (1977). *Propositional structure and illocutionary force: A study of the contribution of sentence meaning to speech acts*. New York: Crowell.

Keenan, E. O. (1976). On the universality of conversational implicatures. *Language in Society* 5(1). 67–80.

Labov, W., & Fanshel, D. (1977). *Therapeutic discourse: Psychotherapy as conversation*. New York: Academic Press.

Lavandera, B. (1977). Inferencia y referencia en la teoria del lenguaje. *UICUS Cuadernos. Lingüística* 1. 117–38.

———— (1978). Analysis of semantic variation: The Spanish moods. *NWAVE VII* Georgetown University.

Longacre, R. E. (1976). *An anatomy of speech notions*. Lisse: Peter de Ridder Press.

Morgan, J. (1975). Some interactions of syntax and pragmatics. In Cole & Morgan. 289–304.

Pateman, C. (1979). *The problem of political obligation*. New York: John Wiley & Sons.

Philips, S. U. (1976). Some sources of cultural variability in the regulation of talk. *Language in Society* 5(1). 81–95. [also ch. 22, this volume]

Pratt, M. (1978). *Towards a speech act theory of literature*. Bloomington: Indiana University Press.

Ricoeur, P. (1971). The model of the text: Meaningful action considered as text. *Social Research* 38 (3).

Rosaldo, M. (1972). Metaphor and folk classification. *Southwestern Journal of Anthropology* 28(1).

———— (1973). I have nothing to hide: The language of Ilongot oratory. *Language in Society* 2(2). 193–223.

———— (1974). Review of J. Searle, *Speech acts*. *American Anthropologist* 76(1).

_____ (1975). It's all uphill: The creative metaphors of Ilongot magical spells. In M. Sanches & B. Blount (eds.), *Sociocultural dimensions of language use*. New York: Seminar Press.

_____ (1980). *Knowledge and passion: Ilongot notions of self and social life*. Cambridge University Press.

_____ (n.d.a) Words that are moving. Paper presented Spring 1978, SSRC conference on Southeast Asian Aesthetics.

_____ (n.d.b). The shame of headhunters and the autonomy of the self. Paper presented December 1980, Meetings of the American Anthropological Association.

Rosaldo, M., & Atkinson, J. (1975). Man the hunter and woman. In R. Willis (ed.), *The interpretation of symbolism*. London: Dent.

Rosaldo, R. (1980). *Ilongot headhunting, 1883–1974: A study in history and society*. Stanford: Stanford University Press.

Ross, J. R. (1970). On declarative sentences. In R. A. Jacobs & P. S. Rosenbaum (eds.), *Readings in English transformational grammar*. Waltham, Mass.: Ginn. 222–72.

Sacks, H. (1972) On the analyzability of stories by children. In J. Gumperz & D. Hymes (eds.), *Directions in sociolinguistics*. New York: Holt, Rinehart & Winston.

_____ (1973a). Lectures at Summer Linguistic Institute. Ann Arbor, Michigan.

_____ (1973b). Tout le monde doit mentir. *Communications* **20**.

Saddock, J. (1974). *Toward a linguistic theory of speech acts*. New York: Academic Press.

Sapir, D. (1979). Review of K. Basso & H. Selby (eds.), *Meaning in anthropology. Language in Society* **8**(2). 245–70.

Schieffelin, B. B. (n.d.). A sociolinguistic analysis of a relationship. Paper presented November 1978, Meetings of the American Anthropological Association.

Searle, J. (1965). "What is a speech act?" In M. Black (ed.), *Philosophy in America*. London: Allen and Unwin. Reprinted in J. Searle (ed.), *The philosophy of language*. Oxford: Oxford University Press, 1971.

_____ (1969). *Speech acts*. Cambridge University Press.

_____ (1975). Indirect speech acts. In Cole & Morgan. 58–82.

_____ (1976). The classification of illocutionary acts. *Language in Society* **5**(1). 1–23. [also ch. 24, this volume]

_____ (1977). Reiterating the differences: A reply to Derrida. *Glyph* **I**. 198–208.

_____ (1979a). *Expression and meaning*. Cambridge University Press.

_____ (1979b). Indirect speech acts. In J. Searle, *Expression and meaning*.

_____ (1979c). Literal meaning. In J. Searle, *Expression and meaning*.

_____ (1979d). The logical status of fictional discourse. In J. Searle, *Expression and meaning*.

_____ (1979e). Speech acts and recent linguistics. In J. Searle, *Expression and meaning*.

_____ (1979f). A taxonomy of illocutionary acts. In J. Searle, *Expression and meaning*.

Searle, J. R., & Vanderveken, D. (n.d.). Foundations of illocutionary logic. Ms.

Silverstein, M. (1976). Shifter, linguistic categories, and cultural description. In K. Basso & H. Selby (eds.), *Meaning in anthropology*. Albuquerque: University of New Mexico Press.

_____ (1979). Language structure and linguistic ideology. In P. Clyne, W. F. Hanks, & C. L. Hofbauer (eds.), *The elements: A parasession on linguistic units and levels*. Chicago: Chicago Linguistic Society.

Stampe, D. W. (1975). Meaning and truth in the theory of speech acts. In Cole & Morgan. 1–40.

Strawson, P. (ed.). (1971). *Philosophical logic*. Oxford: Oxford University Press.

Tambiah, S. J. (1973). Form and meaning in magical acts: A point of view. In R. Horton & R. Finnegan (eds.), *Modes of thought: Essays on thinking in Western and non-Western societies*. London: Faber & Faber.

Thompson, E. P. (1978). *The poverty of theory and other essays*. New York: Monthly Review.

Tyler, S. A. (1978). *The said and the unsaid*. New York: Academic Press.

Vendler, Z. (1967). *Linguistics in philosophy*. Ithaca, N. Y.: Cornell University Press.

Voloshinov, V. N. (1973). *Marxism and the philosophy of language*. Translated by Ladislav Matejka & I. R. Titunik. New York: Seminar Press. Originally published in Russia, 1930.

26

Epilogue to the Taxonomy of Illocutionary Acts

JOHN R. SEARLE

The Original Claim

I wrote the paper reprinted here as chapter 24 while I was teaching a course in Speech Acts at the Linguistic Society of America Summer Institute in Buffalo New York in the Summer of 1971. I presented it as a forum lecture at the Institute, and later also at conferences at the University of Minnesota and the University of Texas at Austin. The publication was delayed several years because it was promised to the University of Minnesota series in the Philosophy of Science and the editor took a great deal of time to publish the volume. The original article (Searle, 1975) has since been reprinted on a number of occasions,[1] and the ideas in the taxonomy later formed the basis of a formal logic of speech acts that I wrote with Daniel Vanderveken (1985).

Looking it over, after a period of nearly two decades, I believe that the

---

[1] Originally published as "A Taxonomy of Illocutionary Acts," in *Language, Mind and Knowledge,* Minnesota Studies in the Philosophy of Science, Vol. XI, Keith Gunderson (ed.), University of Minnesota Press, 1975a. Reprinted as: "A Classification of Illocutionary Acts," in *Language in Society,* Vol. 5, 1975b. Reprinted in: *Proceedings of the Texas Conference on Performatives, Presuppositions, and Implicatures,* Andy Rogers, John P. Murphy, Bob Wall (eds.), Center for Applied Linguistics, 1977. Translated into Spanish as: "Una Taxonomia de los actos Illocucionarios," *Teorema,* Vol. VI/I, 1976. Translated into Italian as: "Per una tassonomia degli atti illocutori," in *Gli Atti Linguistici,* M. Sbisa (ed.), Feltrinelli, 1978. Translated into German as: "Eine Klassifikation der Illokutionsakte" in *Sprechakt Theorie,* P. Kussmaul (ed.), Athenaion, 1980. Translated into Dutch as: "Den Taxonomie van illocutionaire handelingen," in *Studies over Taalhandelingen,* F. H. van Emeren and W. K. B. Koning (eds.), Boom, 1981. Reprinted in Searle, J. R., *Expression and Meaning: Studies in the Theory of Speech Acts,* Cambridge University Press, 1979. Translated into French as: *Sens et espression; etudes de theorie des actes du language,* Les Editions de Minuit, 1982a. Translated into German as: *Ausdruck und Bedeutung; Untersuchungen zur Sprechakttheorie,* Suhrkamp, 1982b. Translation into Chinese, 1989. Pirated edition published in South Korea.

piece has stood the test of time remarkably well. In this epilogue, I want to try to explain how the taxonomy works and what general philosophical issues are at stake.

The basic unit of human communication is the illocutionary act, and the general form of the illocutionary act is $F(p)$, where the "F" marks illocutionary force and the "p" marks propositional content. Now, since the number of possible ps is presumably infinite, the question naturally arises: what about the Fs? Are they infinite too? How many things can you do with propositions anyhow? Well, of course, trivially we can generate an indefinite number of new Fs by iterating adverbial modifiers or logical operators. This is most obvious with performative verbs (e.g. I urge that p, I strongly urge that p, I very strongly urge that p, etc.). But are there some kernel elements in illocutionary force on which these various operations are performed, and is there a finite list of these elements? I give an affirmative answer to both questions, and in the course of giving that answer I make a strong claim: In the illocutionary line of business there are five and only five basic things we can do with propositions: We tell people how things are (assertives), We try to get them to do things (directives), We commit ourselves to doing things (commissives), We express our feelings and attitudes (expressives), and We bring about changes in the world so that the world matches the proposition just in virtue of the utterance (declarations). This is a strong claim, in the sense that it is not just an empirical sociolinguistic claim about this or that speech community, but is intended to delimit the possibilities of human communication in speech acts. And it is subject to strong refutation in this sense: To refute, or at least revise, the taxonomy you need only to find or invent illocutionary points that it cannot account for.

How would one justify such a claim? A well-motivated taxonomy must spring from essential features of the domain being taxonomized. In this case there are two ways to go about such a justification, one in terms of the structure of speech acts, (this is the one I used in the article in chapter 24), and one in terms of the nature of meaning itself. The first is "empirical" in the sense that it proceeds from features exhibited by natural languages; the second is "transcendental" in the sense that it proceeds from the conditions of possibility of there being speech acts at all. I consider each in turn.

The Basic Criteria

Our initial question was: How many types of illocutionary acts are there? But of course, in that form the question does not admit of a unitary answer. One can always select arbitrarily any number of different criteria for classifying illocutionary acts. To take an extreme case, if Bill is in love with Sally, Bill may be interested only in the distinction between two different kinds of illocutionary acts, those that are about Sally, and those that are not about Sally. That is a possible taxonomy of illocutionary acts; but it is not one that the rest of us would find interesting or useful. So, we need to make the question more precise. The question is not: How many types of illocutionary acts are there? Rather it is: How many types of illocutionary points are there? But what is an illocutionary point?

It is characteristic of human actions that they have a point or purpose. An illocutionary act may be performed for any number of different points or purposes. A man may make a promise or give an order, in order to keep the conversation going, in order to have something to say, in order to try to appear intelligent or stupid, and so on. But, and this is the crucial feature, *for each type of illocutionary act there is a point or purpose built into instances of the type in virtue of their being acts of that type.* Thus, for example, although a man may make a promise for any number of reasons, in virtue of its being a promise it is an undertaking of a commitment or obligation to do something, normally for the benefit of the hearer. A man may issue a command for any number of reasons, but in virtue of its being a command, it is an attempt by the speaker to get the hearer to do something. So, now we have narrowed the question down a little more by shifting it from, "How many types of illocutionary acts are there?" to "How many types of illocutionary points are there?"

To this it can be objected that the notion of illocutionary point is still rather vague, and I agree that it is. But now notice another feature, namely, illocutionary point, as I have intuitively characterized it, is systematically related to the notions of direction of fit and expressed psychological state. Those notions are not vague or unclear, they seem to me reasonably precise; and indeed they have the additional merit that they are not peculiar to this or that theory of speech acts; rather they are essential to any account of language and mind. In the case of direction of fit, for example, the existence of the phenomenon is linguistically manifested in the existence of a large number of terms that are used to appraise success or failure in achieving a direction of fit: terms like *true, false, exaggerated, obeyed, disobeyed, kept, broken, fulfilled,* and so forth. By embedding the notion of illocutionary point into the notions of expressed psychological state and direction of fit we now have a reasonably well-defined criterion for posing the question. The basic ideas that underlie the taxonomy, the ideas of illocutionary point, direction of fit of propositional content, and psychological state, are all independently motivated; so the taxonomy is based on an apparatus that we need anyway and that we can justify on grounds that have nothing to do with the taxonomy. The notion of illocutionary point, together with the

notions of direction of fit and expressed psychological state, yields assertives, directives, commissives, expressives, and declarations as the basic
categories.

But the discovery is so far so-to-speak still too "empirical." It looks like
we are just claiming that natural languages can contain these five or some
subset of them. But of course, even if our investigation is empirical in some
of its methods, it should not be just empirical in its results, and the actual
facts of existing human languages are philosophically interesting to us in so
far as they reveal fundamental features of the nature of linguistic representation in general. If our claim is really valid, there must be a justification for
the taxonomy in addition to the fact that we can actually locate no more
than these five in human languages. That is where the "transcendental
deduction" comes in.

The Transcendental Deduction of the Categories

A taxonomy like the one that I proposed cannot simply be a matter of
accident. It cannot just happen that these are the five types of illocutionary
points. If I am right, there must be some deeper explanation of these facts.
And I believe there is one. I devoted a chapter of *Intentionality* (Searle,
1983) to motivating the taxonomy in terms of a theory of the mind. I do not
repeat the argument here, but the basic idea is this: There are only so many
ways in which mental states can relate their propositional contents to
reality. There are those like beliefs, that have the mind-to-world direction of
fit, those like desires, and intentions that have the world-to-mind direction
of fit, and those like sorrow and gladness that have the null direction of fit.
Language also creates the possibility of another direction of fit, the double
direction of fit, characteristic of declarations. If one does an analysis of the
intentionality of meaning and distinguishes, within the theory of meaning,
between representation and communication, it emerges that the essence of
meaning is in the double level of intentionality expressed in the speaker's
utterance. In making an utterance with a certain meaning, a speaker
intentionally imposes conditions of satisfaction on conditions of satisfaction. But conditions of satisfaction are always determined by propositional
content and there are only so many forms that the direction of fit of
propositional content can take. The basic types of direction of fit are uphill,
downhill, null, and both ways. In communication between speaker and
hearer, the uphill direction of fit admits of two basic variants, one hearer
directed, and the other speaker directed. The hearer directed variant is
characteristic of directives, the speaker directed variant is characteristic of
commissives. So, we get five basic types, one for each direction of fit, with
the exception of the world-to-utterance direction of fit that yields two.

I have left out all the details of the argument, but at bottom the grounding of the taxonomy is really as simple as that. What we are talking about here is something that transcends sociological or anthropological considerations. We are talking about how fundamental features of human mental representation, themselves grounded in biology, can be manifested in language.

Some Common Misunderstandings

Although I thought I presented it in a rather simple fashion, the taxonomy has been misunderstood in a variety of ways. Perhaps the most striking misunderstandings are in Rosaldo's article "The Things We Do With Words: Ilongot Speech Acts And Speech Act Theory in Philosophy" (chapter 25), and because that article is included in this volume, I correct here some misapprehensions.[2] I became convinced that Rosaldo must be in the grip of a misconception when I noticed that she thinks the absence of promises among the Ilongot and the scant importance they attach to commissives generally is somehow counterevidence to the taxonomy. This would be like supposing that the absence of tigers at the South Pole and the general scarcity of felines in the Antarctic is an objection to standard classifications of animals. She must have a skewed conception of the enterprise if she thinks that is an objection.

In any investigation, but in philosophy especially, it is important to know exactly what question we are trying to answer, and exactly what answer we are giving. Rosaldo's misunderstandings of the taxonomy derive from her failure to see which question is being asked and what answer is being given. She thinks I am doing what she calls a "cross-cultural" study of uses of language; that is, she really seems to think that I am doing an "ethnography" of which the "data is limited." But I am doing nothing of the sort. I am doing an investigation into the possibilities of linguistic representation in illocutionary acts. The question I am asking, to repeat, is: How many types of illocutionary points are there? That question when fully expanded amounts to the question how many ways are there of relating propositional content to an independently existing reality by way of the manifestation of intentionality in utterances. It is not a simple question, although the answer that I propose is a simple one. Her misunderstandings of me derive from her supposition that the question I am trying to answer is something like this: What sorts of cross-cultural or linguistic universals can we find by applying

---

[2]Rosaldo's tragic death cut short her career before we could continue this discussion. In this chapter I continue to speak of her in the present tense as though she were still a participant in the discussion.

our notion, our western rationalistic notion, of illocutionary acts across different cultures.

Her discussion of the Ilongots seems to me fascinating and perceptive; but it consists in large part of an application of the taxonomy. She is, perhaps inadvertently, answering the question: How much of the possible resources of the taxonomy do the Ilongot use and in what ways do they use them? How are their uses of speech acts shaped by other features of their culture? She finds, for example, that Ilongot utterances can only be fully understood given an extreme sensitivity to their social contexts and social nuance, that the Ilongots have a different sense of the self than we do, that they do not place much store by commissives and expressives, that they attach a lot of importance to the directives, and that they do not take their psychological states as expressed in utterances nearly as seriously as we take ours. I find all of these points interesting as items of anthropology (I assume that she is correct about all of this), but they are an application of the taxonomy of the illocutionary acts not an objection to it. Even if it turned out that the Ilongots make no promises or other sorts of commissives whatever, that the notions of promising and related speech acts were totally unintelligible to them, that would not affect the taxonomy. The taxonomy, to repeat, is not an anthropological, empirical claim about existing forms of speech acts in every language. It is rather an attempt to analyze the possibilities of linguistic representation. To find a counterexample she would have had to find speech acts among the Ilongot that could not be accomodated in the taxonomy at all. I said earlier that the absence of promises in the Ilongot is like the absence of tigers at the South Pole, but a better analogy might be the following: It follows from Peano's axioms that there is an infinite sequence of natural numbers. Now, suppose an anthropologist objected to this claim on the grounds that some tribes do not have a system of counting that enables to count beyond ten.

There are several other misunderstandings in her criticisms of the taxonomy, but for the sake of brevity I confine myself to five of the most salient of these.

First, I do not think she has fully grasped the notion of propositional content as it applies to the structure of the illocutionary act. This is shown by the fact that she contrasts directives with propositions. But every directive must contain a proposition, implicitly or explicitly, because every directive must contain a representation of what the hearer is directed to do. This follows from the definition of directives. All of her many examples are cases in which the directives contain a propositional content.

Second, she is impressed by the fact that the Ilongots are not as obsessively concerned about keeping their commissives as are North Americans. But the fact that many people are relaxed about keeping their commissives is not an exclusive feature of Ilongots, it is very common in our culture and in many others.

Third, I do not think that she understands what a declaration is. When she says that the Ilongot assertives, commissives and expressives would be more appropriately thought of as declarations (she sometimes uses the term *declaratives* for declarations), it seems to me clear that she does not understand the definition of a declaration. A declaration is a speech act that brings about a change in the world so that the world matches the propositional content of the speech act solely in virtue of the declaration. She seems to think that a declaration is any speech act that brings about a change in the world and that is aimed at bringing a change in the world. But of course, every speech act brings about a change in the world; the world is changed, among other things, by the fact that the speech act has been performed. But not every speech act is thereby a declaration. Only those speech acts that satisfy the definition are declarations.

Fourth, she is struck by the fact that the Ilongots in their speech do not manifest the same sense of inner self and of the importance attaching to notions such as personhood and of the stability of intentional states that we have in Western societies. This is possibly so, but the main point is that the Ilongots like other human beings have to have something corresponding to cognition and volition; they have to be able to perceive and act, to believe, desire, and intend. This is a basic fact about human biology; it has nothing to do with this or that culture. The fact that we in English taxonomize our mental states conveniently with words like "believe," "desire," and "intend," for example, is not even essential to the analytic apparatus that I use. The important thing is to see that organisms relate to reality by way of intentionality through a variety of forms, most notably cognition and volition, and I exploit these as the basis of the taxonomy. Anthropological variations in the role of intentionality in social life can be pointed out as further contributions to the discussion, but they are not counter-examples to the taxonomy, because the biological basis of intentionality is the same in all human societies.

Finally, she complains that I neglect the "social" dimension of speech acts. Actually, I think, if anything she underestimates the importance of the social component in the production and comprehension of speech acts in a society such as ours. I believe, in fact, that only an extreme subtlety in the awareness of social practices and social situations enables us to communicate at all. It is quite likely that the more complex the society the more this will be so. I have discussed some of these issues in *Intentionality* (Searle, 1983). However, I was not addressing myself to this question in "A Taxonomy of Illocutionary Acts" (Searle, 1975). The question in that article was "How do speakers relate propositional contents to the world by way of making utterances with illocutionary points in the performance of intentional actions?" I discussed the role of social contexts only in so far as it was relevant to that question. Her rival taxonomy for the Ilongot, of "directives" and "declaratives," frankly does not seem to me to get off the ground.

Her notion of a directive is essentially the same as the one I use, (although, of course, she has many perceptive things to say about how directives play a special role in the Ilongot social life and social relations). The notion of a declarative, as she uses it, just seems to me ill-defined. She does not bring to bear an analytic apparatus sufficient to give us a well-defined category. It may be that she thinks my apparatus of propositional content, direction of fit, conditions of satisfaction, and so on, is inadequate; but if so, she does not tell us how and she does not propose an alternative.

To summarize my objections to Rosaldo: There is always a danger that one's own limitations of history, culture, psychology, and social background will impede one's investigations. I am as much subject to these limitations as any other investigator. However, even assuming that I now know everything that she has to tell me about the Ilongot, and assuming that I knew all of this information at the time I wrote the original article, it would not have affected the taxonomy in the least. Her remarks are addressed to a different set of questions.[3]

Some Other Objections

I said earlier that one way to refute the taxonomy would be to find illocutionary forces that it could not accommodate. And some authors have tried, in fact, to present such examples. I believe one of the most interesting and revealing of these is the case of *permit*. Wunderlich (1980) pointed out, correctly in my view, that permitting someone (e.g., to walk across my property) is not a case of "trying to get someone to do something." But notice that logical operations can be performed on illocutionary points, and in fact permitting someone to do something is precisely the negation of the illocutionary point of directing them not to do it. That is, permission consists in the removal of an antecedently existing prohibition. Logically speaking, the distinctions here are between ordering, forbidding and permitting as revealed by the following trio:

$!(p) =$ order p

$!(\text{not } p) =$ forbid p

$\text{not}! (\text{not } p) =$ permit p

---

[3]A minor historical point is worth making. Rosaldo says "J. L. Austin was, of course, an heir to Wittgenstein. . . ." As a matter of historical fact, Austin learned next to nothing from Wittgenstein. Indeed, Austin found Wittgenstein's whole mode of sensibility profoundly antipathetic. About the *Philosophical Investigations,* he once said to me, "It's all in Moore." Austin was an heir to Moore and Prichard, but not to Wittgenstein.

Another objection that was commonly made to the theory of speech acts can now be obviated by the taxonomy. It was frequently objected that the sort of analysis that I proposed for orders, commands, promises, statements, and so forth, would not work for cases of, for example, remarks or comments. But what the taxonomy reveals is that "remark" and "comment" are not, in fact, names of types of illocutionary acts. They are illocutionary verbs, and every comment or remark is, indeed, an illocutionary act, but these verbs do not contain the specification of an illocutionary point as part of their meaning, and therefore, they do not name types of illocutionary acts. Roughly speaking, to say of something that it was a comment or remark is to specify how it fits into the discourse. But such verbs, like many other illocutionary verbs, do not specify an illocutionary point.

In a sense, then, some of the deeper claims generated by the taxonomy are circular, but they have the right kind of circularity. Remarks and comments do not fit the taxonomy under these descriptions, because these expressions do not name types of illocutionary acts. But the reason they are not types of illocutionary acts is that they do not fit the taxonomy.

Conclusion

The main point I have been trying to make in this chapter is that a taxonomy, such as I have proposed, is not just an arbitrary division of a territory, like drawing county lines in Arkansas, but it is a theoretical claim about the nature of a domain. Taxonomy and theory stand or fall together. I tried to revise Austin's taxonomy using the resources of a richer theory. If this taxonomy is in turn revised, it will be because we have achieved deeper understanding of speech acts.

References

Searle, J. R. (1975). A taxonomy of illocutionary acts. In K. Gunderson (Ed.), *Language, mind and knowledge. Minnesota studies in the philosophy of science* (Vol. 11, pp. 344–369). Minneapolis, MN: University of Minnesota Press.

Searle, J. R. (1983) *Intentionality,* Cambridge: Cambridge University Press

Searle, J. R., & Vanderveken, D. (1985). *Foundations of illocutionary logic.* Cambridge: Cambridge University Press.

Wunderlich, D. (1980). Methodological remarks on speech act theory. In J. R. Searle, F. Kiefer, & M. Bierwisch (Eds.), *Speech Act theory and pragmatics* (pp. 291–312). Reidel: Dordrecht.

27

Epilogue to "The Things We Do With Words"

DELL HYMES

I do not know what Shelly Rosaldo would have wanted to say about Ilongot speech acts now some years after her article first appeared. I am sure she would have had something to say. She would have reflected further, and have had further insight to share with us, just as she reflected further about Ilongot oratory, the subject of an earlier paper in *Language in Society* (Rosaldo, 1973), and deepened her interpretation of it in a later book, *Knowledge and Passion* (1980).

It is difficult to try to take her place. Difficult for the reason just given, and because it brings back the memory of standing reading a postcard from her about this article, already knowing she was dead. Yet, having published both the article by Searle that she addresses, and her article, which Searle now addresses at length in his own epilogue, I can try to take her place while trying to be fair to both.

Erving Goffman and I had known John Searle at Berkeley, in the early 1960s when John Gumperz especially was bringing together several of us in different departments with a concern for the serious investigation of speech, and John was developing the analysis of "to promise" that entered into his first book (1969). Erving urged that we publish John's article in *Language in Society* (Searle, 1975), where it would reach people working in sociolinguistics and the ethnography of communication, and I was delighted to do so. It seemed to me then, and does now, uniquely penetrating, a brilliant gift one could not have guessed. I questioned the absence of a cross-cultural dimension, of course, and John was generous enough not to fuss about the "Editor's note" that I appended. I would stand by the note now.

The editor believes, as stated in his correspondence with the author, that this article will be of use to linguistic ethnographers. The work of identifying locally valid systems of illocutionary acts will be stimulated and aided by the clarity of focus attained here by Searle. In turn, ethnographic discoveries will

419

test the universality of the criteria and kinds of illocutionary acts, and enable us to begin to understand typologically differences in hierarchy and markedness among local systems. [The supernatural exceptions, noted in n. 3, p. 363, are likely to prove particularly important.] (p. 23)

The statement is in keeping with my belief that Austin's initial presentation of speech acts as a focus of attention was a contribution to the same goal as that of the ethnography of speaking (Hymes, 1965). And with my belief that Searle provided ethnographers a clear, concise, reasoned starting point, such as had hitherto been lacking.

Let me now take up the debate between Rosaldo and Searle. And let me apologize to both, to Shelly inasmuch as what I say may not be what she would have said, and to John for not being able to entirely agree with him. In excuse, I can note that my general view is not presented here for the first time, but is already in print, although apparently it has escaped his notice (Hymes, 1986).

Searle is right that the discussion of the Ilongots "consists in large part of an application of the taxonomy." Indeed, Rosaldo says as much (pp. 203–204, 212 of her original publication, see also pp. 373–374, 382, this volume). Searle takes Rosaldo's account, however interesting, not to be a refutation. His taxonomy attempts to analyze possibilities: How many types of illocutionary points are there? If something it allows for is not present, or of little importance, that is not a counterexample. A counterexample would have to find a type of illocutionary point, and speech act, that could not be accommodated in the taxonomy at all. Searle is right that Rosaldo has not done that. Yet I think that she points to limitations of the taxonomy that do matter. How can that be so?

The answer has to do with what it means to engage in "an application of the taxonomy." In this regard, Searle and Rosaldo do indeed ask different questions. He asks, what basic categories are present. She asks, what is the system of which the categories are part.

I do not think Rosaldo thought that Searle himself was trying to answer the question, 'What sorts of cross-cultural or linguistic universals can we find. . . . across different cultures?', although no doubt she would have thought that the question should be asked. I think her main concern was with meaning.

Speech acts are means of speech. That is one leg of an adequately ambulatory ethnography of speaking. The other is the meaning of means of speech to those who use them (Hymes, 1972). Rosaldo thought that the arguments and assumptions accompanying and justifying the taxonomy in part expressed a way of understanding action through speech that is part of one culture, but not of all; that the Ilongot have a different way; and, by implication, that there no doubt are yet others. By implication she was saying that it would not be enough to discover that the taxonomy's five types of illocutionary point are exhaustive and in that sense universal. That would not tell us what *systems* of speech act there are in the world, how many and what types of system, systems in the sense both of organization and of its meanings.

For a linguist or anthropologist or theorist who grasps the methodological starting point of modern linguistics, the *sine qua non* of its development, Sapir's (1925) "Sound patterns in language" is the explicit key. There he set forth the "thought experiment" (for which there are in fact many empirical examples) of two languages that agree in the presence of certain sounds. When the function of the sounds in the system of the language is investigated, however, the languages differ. Again, he considered the case of two languages that differ as to the presence of certain sounds, but which, when function is investigated, prove to be alike.

Rosaldo is saying something like this when she says that there is a common 'declarative' character to Ilongot acts other than directives. This is not to say that the difference of elementary illocutionary point established by Searle, and adopted by Rosaldo, disappears. It is rather to say that there is a further level, a level of interaction and speech events, a level at which the distribution of speech acts, their weighting and hierarchy, their relations to each other, are patterned.

Phonology is not an exact parallel, although those of us concerned with phonetic reality as part of the expressive character of speech in performance insist that distinctions not relevant at a phonological level may remain so at their own. Relations of grammar may be more exact. To say that such-and-such are the possible types of illocutionary point is like saying that such-and-such are the possible types of case relation. To know this is to know something essential. Yet one does not describe the grammar of a language by saying what types of case relation are present. One also says how they work.

Let me step back for a minute and say in my own behalf that I do not want to concede that nothing more is to be learned about types of illocutionary point, that no additions will occur. Studies of the history of my disciplines, and my own experience of research have constantly confirmed a dialectic in which theoretical frameworks are employed to describe and discover systems, and such discoveries in turn change the frameworks. Those three moments (the etic-1, emic, and etic-2 of Pike, 1954) are fundamental to linguistics and anthropology insofar as they are more than imposition or avocation. In this regard, I would not be surprised if at some point cross-cultural work were to require an addition to the five-point taxonomy (even though I am a student of a culture that privileges five-point patterns, and partial to them), or if the news had to do with cultural limitations on what seems evident to transcendental thinking, even at the level of Kant or Searle. New work to this effect continues to appear (e.g., Duranti, 1988; Matsumoto, 1988).

I have thought indeed that observations in my earlier article (1986) amount to required additions, at least from the standpoint of being able to describe systems, Still, Searle might find that most of these points are refinements, not refutations, so far as the five points are concerned. There is one observation, however, that I think he would not find a refinement, but an addition, for it has to do with the development of discourse. It is in keeping with his own response to certain objections (not by Rosaldo), namely, that his taxonomy does not account for such things as remarks or comments. Such things are illocutionary acts, Searle says, but not *types* of illocutionary act (the passage in his epilogue appears to make this distinction), because they do not specify an illocutionary point as part of their meaning. Rather, they specify fit into discourse.

Two things do trouble me about this argument. First, it is not clear to me that remarks and comments do not involve a relation between words and the world, and thereby, some illocutionary point. Second, remarks and comments are discussed in terms of verbs, and I do not believe that a language is a perfect metalanguage for the acts of its users. Rather, I believe that a language is a *selective* metalanguage, and that much of the interest in study of its relation to action is to discover which verbal acts of its users it names and which it does not. (This principle might obviate criticism of Searle's taxonomy, if someone said that an important kind of illocutionary point was lacking in a community, the reason being that the community language had no name for it. Perhaps the kind of point exists, even though not explicitly named. The principle might make suspect validations of Searle's taxonomy, if someone reported only kinds of illocutionary point for which the language did have names. Perhaps a kind of point outside the taxonomy exists, even though not encoded with a name.)

But set that aside. On the one hand, Searle himself has elsewhere distinguished clearly between names and categories (1979, p. ix; cf. Wierzbicka, 1987, p. 9), and on the other, careful investigation of verbs that name speech acts is of course essential. Let us accept what Searle says, and consider the implication. There are such things as remarks and comments, and such things are not a part of a taxonomy of illocutionary point. There exists, therefore, a taxonomy of larger scope. There exists a taxonomy that comprises both illocutionary point and fit into discourse. Someone concerned to understand the speech acts of a community would be well advised to employ this larger taxonomy, of which illocutionary point is but a part.

Those who analyze recorded interaction, indeed, being faced with the question of assigning each and every bit of interaction to some category, have devised classification schemes that allow for fit with discourse, its monitoring, repair, control, acknowledgment, and the like (cf. e.g., Dore,

1979). It is a general question for the study of language, indeed, as it engages discourse, as to whether or not there is a concept, like those of syllable, morpheme, word, phrase, that answers at the level of action to what Hockett once called "total accountability." All of an utterance, or sequence of verbal interaction, can be given an account in terms of a sequence of syllables, a sequence of morphemes, a sequence of words, a sequence of phrases. Is "speech act" such a concept? Is everything that happens in a sequence of verbal action referrable to one or another of a sequence of speech acts? Or instead, to one or another of a sequence of turns and moves?

I believe that firm foundations for the study of speaking require a descriptive theory, adjacent to a descriptive theory of language in its usual sense, in which such questions have answers. If we cannot think of speech as a sequence of speech acts, then again there would appear to be some more inclusive concept and taxonomy, of which a taxonomy of speech acts in the sense of acts with illocutionary point is a part.

This would be to parallel the role of Brown and Levinson's (1978, 1987) analysis of styles and strategies of politeness. An initial model has been both used and criticized. Brown and Levinson share Searle's concern for a universal framework, and are prepared to doubt the ultimate force of ethnographic challenges (pp. 9–10). Yet with regard to Rosaldo's paper, they observe (1987):

> But it is not clear that our folk notion of tact is relevant in all societies. It perhaps reflects the bias of a culture obsessed with individual rights and wants, and so with tact (as e.g., Wierzbicka, 1985b, claims). Rosaldo (1982), in a critique of speech act theory based on ethnography among the Philippine Ilongot, argues that the Ilongot do not interpret each other's speech in terms of the expression of sincere feelings and intentions, but stress the expectations due to group membership, role structures, and situational constraints; her description suggests to us that Ilongot notions of politeness would minimize a component of tact. Such cultural differences doubtless exist and work down into the linguistic details of the particular face-redressive strategies preferred in a given society or group. Nevertheless, for the purposes of cross-cultural comparison developed here, *we consider that our framework provides a primary descriptive format within which, or in contrast to which, such differences can be described.* (pp. 14–15; italics added)

The work of Brown and Levinson, and others, such as Leech (1983), on politeness and pragmatics, points to the lively general context in which work on speech acts now finds itself. No one can expect to see all that is now published, or even a representative part, but the work that I do see seldom concerns the classification of speech acts. Any usable account of speech as act must ask how verbal means are organized in relation to interaction and social relations, and that is predominantly what one finds.

Much of the ongoing work can be located in relation to the three dimensions of language articulated by M. A. K. Halliday (1970) two decades ago, when he took the important step of going beyond the usual limitation of formal grammar implicitly to a single function. Halliday distinguished three functions, *ideational, interpersonal, textual.* (To say this is not to say that Halliday's initial way of connecting each function with networks elements in English structure was necessarily successful. A helpful assessment is given by Butler, 1988.)

Speech acts of course imply action, but the question of an adequate taxonomy of illocutionary points, in terms of kinds of fit between words and world, centered around relations to propositional meaning, suggests the sphere that Halliday dubbed "ideational." An alternative mode of work in this sphere contrasts with Searle's by being lexicographic in scope. An example is Ballmer and Brennenstuhl (1981; cf. Randall, 1982, 1985). A growing and productive line of work is that of Wierzbicka (1985a, 1987), who has introduced an original technique for formulating the point and meaning of speech acts. Wierzbicka doubts the cultural independence of formulations such as those of Searle, and at the same time believes that culture-specific formulations and comparisons require a succinct meta-language formulation, which she seeks to provide. So far as I know, no one has undertaken to analyze her extensive body of work to determine whether or not its statements of point and condition can be accomodated within Searle's taxonomy.

Much of the work that deals with speech acts does not concern itself with sets or systems of speech acts. It focuses on a single class of act as observed in interaction (Halliday's "interpersonal" function). Such is the work on compliments and on apologies. It seeks empirical patterns of form, of occurrence, and of similarity and difference across genders, situations, groups. Some surprising regularities emerge, such as Wolfson's (1985) concept of the "bulge," namely, that the great variation in verbal interaction occurs in the zone between people who are neither strangers nor intimates.

A second type of work is that kind concerned with interaction that has taken on the label, "politeness," as given definition in terms of implicature (Grice, 1975) and face (Goffman, 1967) by Brown and Levinson. Specific predictions are made as to what to expect, and a framework for placing prevalent device such as "hedges." More and more work appears to make use of their framework as a starting point. Criticism of the original scheme is joined with testimony to its heuristic value.

A third type of work focuses on interaction in terms of the sequential organization of conversation, small genres that such a focus brings to light (e.g., repair, telling troubles, unpackaging a gloss; Jefferson, 1985; Pomerantz, 1984), and possible general principles of interpretation (as to preference in interpretation, etc.). Such work does not assume that what happens in acts of speech can be analyzed in terms of the preexisting intentions of a speaker, but must be analyzed as emergent in the course of interaction and interpretive work on the part of participants, including often enough the speaker (Bilmes, 1988). A usable taxonomy of speech acts and illocutionary point, however, can and should be independent of particular psychological and social assumptions. It should survive across cases and cultures, whether an act and point in question is accomplished through the realization, or the imputation, or the subsequent recognition of an intention.

There are of course many approaches to connected discourse in the form of texts. Much of the interactional work of conversational analysts can be considered in terms of the very foundation of Halliday's textual function, namely, what makes a verbal sequence coherent, rather than a disjointed series? There are many other approaches, especially to narrative and analogous genres, including "ethnopoetics" (Hymes, 1981; Tedlock, 1983).

What these lines of investigation have in common is an active attention to empirical discovery of the patterns, meanings and purposes that inform sustained verbal sequences. The term "strategies" has become common-place. It is not, to be sure, a term that I like, for two related reasons. It seems odd to speak of "strategy" when one observes a single, seemingly automatic apology, something that seems a product more of one's mother's efforts in childhood than of consulting Clausewitz or Mao. And to use "strategy" in this way (instead of "tactic" or "device") seems to leave no larger term for intentions that are indeed reflected on and intended to be overall (as in the formulation by Burke quoted here). The prevalence of the term nonetheless speaks to the widely shared concern to deal directly with interaction. All this is to bring the study of language more and more into the sphere envisioned a half-century ago by Kenneth Burke (1941), when he wrote in a way that can sum up all sustained use of language:

> Critical and imaginative works are answer to questions posed by the situation in which they arose. They are not merely answers, they are *strategic answers,* stylized answers . . . think of . . . any work of critical or imaginative cast . . . as the adopting of various strategies for the encompassing of situations. These strategies size up the situations, name their structure and outstanding ingredients, and name them in a way that contains an attitude towards them. (p. 3)

A future for speech act theory as a part of the study of speech depends on integration of attention to types of single act into this larger context, the context of speaking (and writing) itself. In such a context, any taxonomy, any framework, cannot be a set of pigeonholes, of categories in which to file observations. In the climate established by Chomsky's turn to introspection as a source of data, and the prominence of an a-cultural cognitive psychology, there is a great danger of reading ourselves into the world. What seems plausibly and universally out there may be a projection of unexamined cultural assumptions about conversation, interaction, politeness and the like (let me mention again my study of 1982 and paper of 1986). Especially those who think of their work as contributing to the liberation of mankind must ask if the seemingly evident categories, principles, and processes are not like the seemingly self-evident aspects of human nature and society that Marx a century ago showed to be specific to European history. We could do today with *a critique of linguistic economy.* But the equivalent does emerge, insofar as there is an open dialectic, and interaction between framework (model) and empirical work. What are proposed as universals, whether as maxims of conversation, or strategies of politeness, or types of illocutionary point, are best understood as *dimensions.* Their universality does not consist of ready-made explanation of another context, purpose, way of life, but consists of aspects of verbal interaction with which others can be expected to deal. The universality is in the fact that they do something about the dimension, not in what they do about it.

Having said all this, let me end by advocating sustained attention to taxonomies of speech acts. It remains that one can expect every person, community, and culture to have some classification of speech acts, and that one can expect such systems both to vary and to have some universal grounding. It is worth noting what Brown and Levinson (1987) have said. In their initial formulation of a model of politeness strategies, they took speech acts to provide a basis for a mode of discourse analysis. In the second edition of their work they go on to say (Brown & Levinson 1987, p. 10):

> For many reasons, we now think this not so promising . . . ; speech act theory forces a sentence-based, speaker-oriented mode of analysis, requiring attribution of speech act categories where our own thesis requires that utterances are often equivocal in force. The alternative is to avoid taking such categories as the basis of discourse analysis, choosing other more directly demonstrable categories as done in conversation analysis, and then to give a derivative account of the intuitions underlying speech act theory' . . . we must know acknowledge that the speech act categories that we employed were an underanalyzed shorthand, but one which, were we to try again today, would still be hard to avoid. (p. 10)

It seems to me that any model of discourse will find it hard, indeed impossible, to avoid the question of a taxonomy of speech acts, and that ethnography is not an opponent of what Searle has accomplished, but the place to look for its further development and continuation.

For decades anthropology has been the home of sustained concern with folk classification, whether it be of kin terms, color terms, life forms, space, time, or things done with words.

Criticism of some kinds of cognitive anthropology for the absence of social life, social theory, social criticism (Keesing, 1987) is parallel to criticism (quite muted and respectfully noted, to be sure) of the same absence in Searle's foundations (Cicourel, 1987). Of course I agree that work that excludes social life can never be adequate. That is what I have been saying in terms of ethnography of speaking, sociolinguistics, and communicative competence, for many years (e.g., Hymes, 1977). Yet it is necessary to be precise about components. Consider the study of oral narrative. Types of line and relations among line are a component of oral narrative, not the whole. Yet interpretations of wholes miss essential details of meaning if that component is ignored, and the nature of the universality of such relations has its own interest as part of a theory of language. So for types of illocutionary point, and, more generally, of illocutionary act. By themselves they do not explain interaction and meaning, any more than do kinship terms or color terms. One needs to know about speech events of which they are part, relationships among participants, genres, and so forth. Yet such categories evolve in relation to ways of life, and in turn condition what can be meant and done within them. Differences and similarities among them alike call for explanation. Changes in them can be revealing.

Very little is know about such things. There are few descriptions, and not much of a literature concerned with providing and refining descriptions. There was no section on "speech acts" in Conklin (1980), and it is not certain that there could be a large one now. The explosion of literature about speech acts a decade or so ago seems to have left behind little in the way of cumulative work. (The work of Ervin-Tripp, 1976, 1982, 1984 is a notable exception; see also the valuable work of Anita Puckett, 1988a, 1988b.) Whether or not there is yet an ultimate etics of illocutionary point, we do not have one for all kinds of speech act, and we know very little about kinds of system and their dimensions. The task should become an elementary one, analogous to asking what the phonemes and word orders of a language are, what the kinship terms are. Are there more than a handful of communities of which one can say, even approximately, these are the kinds of speech act, these are the dimensions on which they are based, this is the focus or configuration of the system? That in Papua New Guinea one can expect to find this, but in the northeastern Amazon that?

To Searle it will probably not seem important, but nonetheless I should like to exhort ethnographers to make his findings a standard input to their own. Take his findings as a provisional framework. Ask of a community, do people do these things, do they do other such things, and, what do they do about them? In other words, use his findings in discovering the means and the meanings of speech.

References

Ballmer, T., & Brennenstuhl, W. (1981). *Speech act classification: A study in the lexical analysis of English speech activity verbs.* Berlin: Springer-Verlag.

Bilmes, J. (1988). Category and rule in conversation analysis. *Papers in pragmatics, 2*(1/2), 25–59.

Brown, P., & Levinson, S. C. (1987). *Politeness. Some universals in language usage* (rev. ed.). (Studies in interactional sociolinguistics 4). Cambridge: Cambridge University Press. (Originally published, 1978)

Burke, K. (1941). *Philosophy of literary form.* Baton Rouge: Louisiana State University Press (3rd ed., Berkeley & Los Angeles: University of California Press, 1973).

Butler, C. S. (1988). Pragmatics and systemic linguistics. *Journal of Pragmatics, 12,* 83–102.

Cicourel, A. V. (1987) Review of Searle, *Intentionality. Journal of Pragmatics, 11*(5), 641–660.

Conklin, H. C. (1980). *Folk classification. A topically arranged bibliography of contemporary and background references through 1971.* New Haven CT: Department of Anthropology, Yale University.

Dore, J. (1979). Conversational acts and the acquisition of language. In E. Ochs & B. Schieffelin (Eds.), *Language socialization across cultures* (pp. 235–261). New York: Academic Press.

Duranti, A. (1988). Intentions, language, and social action in a Samoan context. *Journal of Pragmatics, 12*(1), 13–33.

Ervin-Tripp, S. (1976). Is Sybil there? The structure of some American-English directives. *Language in Society, 5,* 25–66.

Ervin-Tripp, S. (1982). Ask and it shall be given unto you. In H. Byrnes (Ed.), *Contemporary perceptions of language* (pp. 235–243). Washington, DC: Georgetown University Press.

Ervin-Tripp, S., O'Connor, M., & Rosenberg, J. (1984). Language and power in the family. In C. Kramarae, M. Schultz, & W. O'Barr (Eds.), *Language and power* (pp. 116–135). Los Angeles: Sage.

Halliday, M. A. K. (1970). Functional diversity in language as seen from a consideration of modality and mood in English. *Foundations of Language 6,* 322–366.

Hymes, D. (1965). Review of J. L. Austin, How to do things with words. *American Anthropologist, 67,* 587–588.

Hymes, D. (1972). Editorial introduction. *Language in Society 1*(1), 1–14.

Hymes, D. (1977). *Foundations in sociolinguistics.* London: Tavistock Press. (Originally published, Philadelphia: University of Pennsylvania Press, 1974)

Hymes, D. (1981). *"In vain I tried to tell you."* Philadelphia: University of Pennsylvania Press.

Hymes, D. (1982). *Ethnolinguistic study of classroom discourse* (Final report to the National Institute of Education). Philadelphia: University of Pennsylvania, Graduate School of Education.

Hymes, D. (1986). Discourse: Scope without depth. *International Journal of the Sociology of Language, 57,* 48–89. (Extract from 1982)

Jefferson, G. (1985). On the interactional unpacking of a "gloss." *Language in Society 14*(4), 435–66.

Keesing, R. M. (1987). 'Models, "folk" and "cultural": Paradigms regained? In D. Holland & N. Quinn (Eds.), *Cultural models in language and thought* (pp. 369-393). Cambridge, New York: Cambridge University Press.

Leech, G. N. (1983). *Principles of pragmatics.* London & New York: Longman.

Matsumoto, Y. (1988). Reexamination of the universality of face: Politeness phenomena in Japanese. *Journal of Pragmatics, 12*(4), 403-26.

Pike, K. L. (1967). *Language in relation to a unified theory of the structure of human behavior* (2nd rev. ed.). The Hague: Mouton. (First published, Glendale: Summer Institute of Linguistics, 1954, 1955, 1957)

Pomerantz, A. (1984). Pursuing a response. In J. M. Atkinson & J. Heritage (Eds.), *Structure of social action. Studies in conversation analysis* (pp. 152-163). Cambridge: Cambridge University Press.

Puckett, A. (1988a). *Ask, don't tell: Speech acts and economic relationships in rural Appalachia.* Paper presented at 87th annual meeting, American Anthropological Association, Phoenix, AZ.

Puckett, A. (1988b) *Seldom ask, never tell: Directives and the division of labor in a rural Appalachian community.* Austin, TX: University of Texas, Department of Anthropology.

Randall, R. (1982). Review of Ballmer & Brennenstuhl. *Language in Society, 11*(2), 285-291.

Randall, R. (1985) Steps toward an ethnosemantics of verbs: Complex fishing technique scripts and the problem of listener identification. In J. Dougherty (Ed.), *New directions in cognitive anthropology* (pp. 249-268). Urbana: University of Illinois Press.

Rosaldo, M. (1973). I have nothing to hide: The language of Ilongot oratory. *Language in Society, 2*(2), 193-223.

Rosaldo, M. (1980). *Knowledge and passion: Ilongot notions of self and social life.* New York: Cambridge University Press.

Rosaldo, M. (1982). The things we do with words: Ilongot speech acts and speech act theory in philosophy. *Language in Society 11,* 203-37. [also ch. 25, this volume]

Sapir, E. (1925). Sound patterns in language. *Language,* 1, 37-51. (Reprinted in D. Mandelbaum (Ed.), *Selected writings of Edward Sapir.* Berkeley & Los Angeles: University of California Press, 1949, 1985)

Searle, J. R. (1969). *Speech acts.* Cambridge & New York: Cambridge University Press.

Searle, J. R. (1975). A classification of illocutionary acts. *Language in Society 5,* 1-24. [also ch. 24, this volume]

Searle, J. R. (1979). *Expression and meaning: Studies in the theory of speech acts.* Cambridge & New York: Cambridge University Press.

Searle, J. R. (1985). *Foundations of illocutionary logic.* Cambridge & New York: Cambridge University Press.

Tedlock, D. (1983). *The spoken word and the work of interpretation.* Philadelphia: University of Pennsylvania Press.

Wierzbicka, A. (1985a) A semantic metalanguage for a crosscultural comparison of speech acts and speech genres. *Language in Society, 14*(4), 491-514.

Wierzbicka, A. (1985b). Different cultures, different languages, different speech acts: Polish vs. English. *Journal of Pragmatics, 9*(2/3), 145-178.

Wierzbicka, A. (1987). *English speech act verbs. A semantic dictionary.* Sydney & New York: Academic Press.

Wolfson, N. (1985). The bulge: A theory of social distance and sociolinguistic interaction. In J. Fine (Ed.), *Discourse approaches to second language* (pp. 21-38). Norwood, NJ: Ablex.

Author Index

Subject Index